SONJA DÜNNWALD

Bilateral and Multilateral Investment Treaties and Their Relationship with Environmental Norms and Measures

Schriften zum Internationalen Recht

Band 202

Bilateral and Multilateral Investment Treaties and Their Relationship with Environmental Norms and Measures

By

Sonja Dünnwald

Duncker & Humblot · Berlin

The Faculty of Law
of the Johann Wolfgang Goethe-Universität Frankfurt am Main
accepted this work as thesis in the year 2014.

Bibliographic information of the German national library

The German national library registers this publication in
the German national bibliography; specified bibliographic data
are retrievable on the Internet about http://dnb.d-nb.de.

Typesetting: L101 Mediengestaltung, Berlin
Printing: buchbücher.de gmbh, Birkach
Printed in Germany

ISSN 0720-7646
ISBN 978-3-428-14506-5 (Print)
ISBN 978-3-428-54506-3 (E-Book)
ISBN 978-3-428-84506-4 (Print & E-Book)

Printed on no aging resistant (non-acid) paper
according to ISO 9706 ♾

Internet: http://www.duncker-humblot.de

Speak well of the law.
Take care of your chest and voice, my good friend,
and leave the law to take care of itself.

Charles Dickens, A Tale of Two Cities

Preface

This study was submitted for the degree of Doctor of Law at the Johann Wolfgang Goethe University Frankfurt (Germany) in January 2013. The text has been updated for this publication to reflect subsequent decisions of investment tribunals until June 2014.

I would like to express my sincere thanks to my supervisor Prof. Dr Dr Rainer Hofmann for his guidance and encouragement. I have greatly benefited from his advice and the freedom to approach the subject in the way I felt most rewarding. I would also like to thank Prof. Dr Isabel Feichtner, LL.M., for her rapid preparation of the second opinion.

Since such a book is the result of a prolonged personal and legal formation, many people have contributed to my foundations for writing it. Accordingly, I am deeply indebted to all those dedicated and inspiring teachers and practitioners of international law that I have had the privilege to encounter and to learn from throughout my legal education. Likewise, I am obliged to my family and friends for partaking in passionate discussions on environmental and societal issues throughout the years – instilling in me the desire to pursue this study.

My greatest thanks go to my parents for enabling and encouraging my academic endeavours and for their continuous, loving support. A special acknowledgment goes to my mother for her assistance in proofreading. This study is dedicated to them.

Frankfurt, July 2014 *Sonja Dünnwald*

Table of Contents

Chapter 2

The Influence of Environmental Concepts on the Interpretation of Investment Provisions 95

Chapter 3

Standards of Non-Discriminatory Treatment 164

Chapter 4

Chapter 5

Expropriation 300

Introduction

The law locks up the man or woman
Who steals the goose from off the common
But leaves the greater villain loose
Who steals the common from off the goose.
Anonymous, 17th century

An investment in economic undertakings is likely to have political, social and environmental effects in addition to its economic results.[1] Economic activity regularly changes aspects of the natural environment and it risks having adverse effects: It depletes resources, causes pollution or consumes soil and water in fragile ecological systems. Significant economic projects are frequently driven by foreign investment, so that the desire to preserve the environment consequently has the potential to conflict with the obligation to protect foreign investment activity. Foreign entrepreneurs seek investment opportunities in any profitable business sector. The reasons for the decision to invest abroad are manifold. Particularly relevant motives are more favourable conditions to produce – such as lower wages and less regulation which is considered as 'red tape' – or a high demand for a particular service in the host state.[2]

Foreign direct investment can play an important role in providing financial resources to all sectors of the economy of the host state. One sector that often involves foreign investment is the exploration of natural resources, especially in developing countries, because those countries often do not have sufficient financial means and expertise for the exploration. The potential for tension is obvious with regard to such exploration: Activities such as deep-sea drilling for oil or mining invariably have an adverse impact on the natural environment and there is the inherent risk of significant destruction if things go wrong. The environmental implications resulting from

1 See the detailed portrayal of the development implications of investment, relying on the example of extractive industries, in *United Nations Conference on Trade and Development* (UNCTAD), 'World Investment Report 2007, Transnational Corporations, Extractive Industries and Development' (2007) pp. 130, 145–154. The Report is available at: http://unctad.org/en/docs/wir2007_en.pdf.

2 See, generally, *Giese*, Alenka S. et al., 'Foreign Direct Investment: Motivating Factors and Economic Impact', 20 Journal of Regional Analysis and Policy 1990, 105–127.

excavation processes may differ, but consequences of the extraction of crude oil, coal, bauxite, or rare earth elements are well-documented and understood.[3]

Another sector frequently relying on foreign investment encompasses relevant infrastructure projects – such as the building of a highway, the construction and operation of a sewage system, or the engineering of power plants to provide electric energy. Investments linked to the construction and operation of a large energy generation plant or a hazardous waste facility are intertwined with environmental issues and they fuel the fear of environmental degradation. More generally, the occupation of territory by a factory in an area relevant for biological diversity and the emissions stemming from the productive process can be problematic.

At the same time, the international community and individuals around the globe increasingly become aware of environmental risks.[4] Consequently, some foreign investment projects are likely to raise genuine concern about their environmental impact. There will be legitimate opposition to projects, which stems from fear that an undertaking is not sustainable and will result in environmental degradation. It may take time to scientifically establish evidence on the environmental dangers of certain activities and substances, but the overall volume of recognised environmental dangers is ever-increasing. New scientific evidence and resulting international agreements to restrict detrimental activities often causes the host state to adopt new regulation, which can restrict the investment activity or induce additional costs for the alien investor.

However, host states may also have other reasons to restrict foreign investment activity. An economically profitable investment project is at risk of becoming the target of less legitimate economic desires. The host state may want to take over or participate in the project or may prefer its nationals, and not the foreign investor, to reap the profits. Accordingly, the state may want to assist and favour national competitors to the detriment of the foreign investor. To cover its protectionist intent, the host state may use environmental concerns as a smoke screen. Accordingly, referring to an alleged environmental purpose cannot be enough to consider a measure as legitimate. Investors in a foreign country are particularly vulnerable, because they have given up a substantial part of control, once capital has been invested and rooted in the host state. It is the task of international law to

[3] *UNCTAD*, 'World Investment Report 2007, Transnational Corporations, Extractive Industries and Development' (2007) pp. 145–148.

[4] See portrayal in 'Chapter 1 – Environmental Norms and Principles', p. 30 *et seq*.

divorce legitimate from illegitimate regulation for both subject areas to exist in harmony.

The question whether international investment law exists in harmony with environmental norms and standards has been discussed for nearly two decades, most intensely in connection with the investment provisions of the 1994 North American Free Trade Agreement. The debate, which remains ongoing, is largely characterised by two opposing groups of scholars and practitioners:[5] One group, rooted in investment and trade law, argues that there is no risk of international investment law impeding legitimate environmental regulation. According to this group, respective concerns misrepresent the protective scope of investment law. The opposing group insists that the robust protection offered to foreign investment contravenes necessary efforts by host states to protect the environment. The perception is that investment protection is used as a sword by the investor against environmental protection to "wreak havoc on [...] environmental laws"[6].

This study aims to evaluate the merit of the opposing positions by determining how investment decisions deal with environmental measures, norms and standards. Tensions between international investment law and environmental law will most certainly be dealt with in a forum of investment law – in the light of the ease with which individuals can trigger such proceedings. There are no comparable mechanisms in international environmental law, which lacks specified courts or similar institutions judging on individual claims.[7] In international state-to-state procedures outside the investment arena, environmental conflicts are generally confined to the role of a

---

[5] There are no absolute, distinct categories of professionals working in this segment of law. However, it is more than accidental that the most active professionals appear to divide into either being pro liberalisation – thereby supporting strong investment protection – or being pro state – accordingly favouring the capacity of the state to regulate. In addition, the frequent affiliation of lawyers pro free trade and investment with international law firms has been commented upon.

In contrast, proponents of the role of the state in this context tend to have a background in the traditional areas of public international law and be less connected to major law firms. While there is a very recent trend towards reconciliation of both approaches and lawyers, the 'world' of academic commentary so far remains rather divided.

[6] In these terms, *Lindo*, Victoria R., 'Hydroelectric Power Production in Costa Rica and the Threat of Environmental Disaster through CAFTA', 29 Boston College International and Comparative Law Review 2006, 297 (309). Several commentators appear to share this view, but use less direct language.

[7] It appears as if individuals desiring an enforceable remedy relating to the protection of the environment deriving from an international treaty have to rely on a human rights approach. The most far-reaching instrument in terms of rights of the individual is the 1998 Aarhus Convention on Access to Information, Public Participation in Decision Making and Access to Justic in Environmental Matters. It is a

side issue.[8] Accordingly, potential conflicts between both areas of law are best analysed against the findings in investment decisions. The legitimacy of restrictive environmental regulation is at the core of the issue. The ultimate question is whether a measure that the host state has adopted for purportedly environmental reasons is in conflict with the guaranteed rights of the foreign investor. The answer is influenced by two predominant features – namely the protective scope of foreign investment law on the one hand and the legitimacy of the environmental measure on the other hand. In discussing the respective scopes and their inter-relationship, this study aims to paint a balanced picture of potential conflicts between norms securing the interests of foreign investors and environmental norms and measures.

I. Contemporary Investment Law

The international law of foreign investment is characterised by rules that protect a foreign investor throughout its economic ventures in a host state. The term 'investment' is defined in investment treaties and it constitutes a vast concept. In general terms, it encompasses the entirety of tangible and intangible assets that its owner transfers to another country to generate wealth under his or her total or partial control.[9] Even though the exact understanding of which tangible and intangible assets qualify as investment may differ, assets such as an enterprise, a loan to an enterprise, shares in an enterprise, real estate or other property fall within the scope of the concept.[10] The broadness of the concept and the range of activities and assets consequently captured have potential environmental implications. At the same time, the concept of 'investment' triggers the protective standards

treaty aiming to enhance environmental justice by giving individuals rights to information, but no concrete procedural claims.

[8] See, for example, the decision of the ICJ in *Gabčíkovo-Nagymaros* or the *Case Concerning Pulp Mills on the River Uruguay*. The specific Chamber of the International Court of Justice for Environmental Issues, established in 1993, so far has never been used.

[9] The exact definition of 'investment' depends on the respective investment treaty. Treaties often contain illustrative or exhaustive lists of what is to be considered as investment. An investment tribunal is tasked with identifying whether the relevant asset of the investor qualifies as investment. See, *Sornarajah*, M., The International Law on Foreign Investment (2010) pp. 309–312.

[10] See, for example, enumeration in Article 1139 NAFTA. See also for portrayal of the concept of investment, *Kriebaum*, Ursula, Eigentumsschutz im Völkerrecht (2008) pp. 51–55; *Sornarajah*, M., The International Law on Foreign Investment (2010) pp. 309–312.

In contrast to these assets, pure claims to money are generally excluded from the scope of the definition of investment.

contained in investment agreements, as well as the jurisdiction of investment tribunals.[11]

By obliging the host state to conform to certain protective standards, international investment law restricts the sovereignty of the host state in dealing with the alien investing in its territory. The investor is the beneficiary of a set of procedural and substantive treatment standards obliging the host state to respect notions like non-discrimination, fairness and stability. The alien investor, however, has to respect the laws and regulations in force in the host state.[12] Its investment activity is influenced and affected by the legislation and regulation that the host state has adopted. The applicable rules can have an important impact on the profitability of the entrepreneurial undertaking.

Investments are usually long-term undertakings, which require a significant amount of time to amortise. They need a certain amount of stability in political and economic terms to be successful. An investor decides on and plans its investment on the basis of the regulation in place – and accordingly has an interest in the stability of the regulation. However, the corpus of national regulation typically is not static: It is bound to be altered and amended to better serve the interests of the state and its citizens. Every state has a duty and a legitimate interest in progressively ameliorating its regulatory framework to better protect its citizens or further their well-being and progress. Accordingly, the host state has an interest to introduce effective environmental regulation for the sake of protecting its natural environment and the health and security of its citizens. In certain scenarios, the state may even have an obligation under international environmental law to adjust its national legal framework, by restricting certain activities or the use of substances, to honour its international commitments. The investor, however, will not welcome the tightening of restrictions on its investment activity,

---

[11] See, for example, Article 25 1965 Convention on the Settlement of Investment Disputes Between States and Nationals of Other States (ICSID Convention) and the illustrative decision in Salini Costruttori S.p.A. and Italstrade S.p.A. v. Kingdom of Morocco, ICSID Case No. ARB/00/4, Decision on Jurisdiction of 31 July 2001, paras 50–58; Joy Mining Machinery Limited v. Arab Republic of Egypt, ICSID Case No. ARB/03/11, Decision on Jurisdiction of 6 August 2004, paras 48–63.

The different approaches to determining the scope of the 'investment' are outside of the ambit of this study. This study is based on the premise that the investment activity of the investor falls within the scope of application of both investment agreements and the ICSID Convention. The breadth of the concept of investment has a two-fold relevance for the investor's protection in any case: In the procedural context, it resolves whether the investor can trigger arbitral proceedings against the host state and at a substantive level, it determines whether the investment is eligible for protection under the investment treaty.

[12] *Sornarajah*, M., The International Law on Foreign Investment (2010) p. 88.

which may reduce the economic viability of the investment. Nevertheless, a polluting investor – especially if taking advantage of loosely enforced regulation in a country lacking in functional governmental structures – cannot expect to continue to pollute forever, thereby placing the financial burden of its activity upon the whole society.

Contemporary international investment law strongly reflects the interest of capital exporting states in protecting the position of their citizens that are engaged in economic ventures in other jurisdictions. With ever decreasing costs of communication and transport, economic opportunities in other countries had already become attractive several centuries ago. The cradle of international investment law can be traced back to 17th century Europe, when the progressive development of national economies raised the interest of states to protect foreign commerce. This resulted in agreements which granted basic standards of treatment of foreign capital on a reciprocal, equal basis – most notably the conditioning of expropriation to certain requirements, such as the payment of compensation – which were well accepted among European states in the middle of the 19th century.[13]

The extension around the rest of the globe of these standards and the European concept of property[14], however, involved less reciprocity and more coercion: Colonialism secured the protection of foreign investment by the colonial powers through annexation of territories, capitulation, the system of 'extraterritoriality'[15], and ad hoc diplomatic intervention, which was occasionally infamously backed up by gunboats.[16] This background under-

13 *Lipson*, Charles, Standing Guard, Protecting Foreign Capital in the Nineteenth and Twentieth Centuries (1985) pp. 8–9, 11–12.

14 *Lipson*, Charles, Standing Guard, Protecting Foreign Capital in the Nineteenth and Twentieth Centuries (1985) p. 20, points to the relevance of the European concept of individual ownership for those involved in international commerce in the 19th century. Securing these standards in differing social and cultural contexts sometimes brought with it "a radical revision of local property rights", such as forms of collective ownership and shared use-rights.

15 The system of 'extraterritoriality' ensured that the law of the home state applied to the foreign investor in the host state. See generally, *Sornarajah*, M., The International Law on Foreign Investment (2010) pp. 19–20.

16 One commentator argues that the alleged neglect of environmental concerns in the international law of foreign investment reproduces the patterns of its colonial origins, which considered the resources and the environment of host states as commodities ripe for exploitation, see *Miles*, Kate, 'International Investment Law: Origins, Imperialism and Conceptualizing the Environment', 21 Colorado Journal of International Environmental Law and Policy 2010, 1 (20–21, 24, 30, 45–46).

The author gives an interesting overview of the historical development of the international law of foreign investment as a tool of imperialist and colonial domination. She specifically points to the connection with repression and the use of force in promoting Western economic interests, the influence of trading companies on the

lines the clear connection of the investor's position to the position of its home state. Within the regime of 'diplomatic protection', the protection of the foreign investor effectively depended on the willingness of the home state to confront the potentially violating host state. Working the diplomatic channels or bringing claims and the – more martial – reliance on 'gun-boat diplomacy' conditioned the efficacious protection of the foreign investor on factors unrelated to the strength of its legal case. In reality, not necessarily the investor that was treated the least fairly had the best chance of receiving compensation, but the investor with the best connections to a powerful home government.

Before the beginning of the 20th century, the protective notions developed in the European context began to crystallise as customary international law. However, the precise contours of a host state's obligations were not always clear but differed substantially. In particular, Latin American states focused on the principle of non-discrimination of foreign investment, but renounced the idea of absolute standards of investment protection.[17] Following the struggle against colonialism, the relationship between those states typically in the role of capital exporters – the former colonial powers – and the newly independent states traditionally in the role of capital importers appeared to change. Capital importing states aimed to change the stakes by nationalising key industries to the detriment of foreign companies. These states also emphasised their sovereignty over their natural resources and questioned the traditional outlook on the payment of compensation for expropriation.

At the same time, however, developing states perceived the economic need to become attractive to foreign investment. Despite diametrically opposed rhetoric in the international arena, capital exporting and capital importing states came together to create the central pillar of modern investment law: an ever-increasing net of investment treaties. The past decades have seen the proliferation of – primarily – bilateral investment treaties,

---

creation of rules of international law, the connection of the interests of the investor with those of its home state and their mutual dependence, and the conceptualisation of the environment of the host state as a commodity.

It appears, however, that Miles' explanation for the alleged disregard of foreign investors for the environment of the host state is a bit limited. As a simplified rule, corporations see no intrinsic value in a healthy environment, neither in a host state nor in their home country. Their raison d'être is to make money, so that they generally consider the environment to be a commodity. One might say that this is the essence of a capitalist system. In this sense, environmental measures and rules in Western states face the same risk of being subjected to investment arbitration proceedings.

17 See below, in 'Chapter 3 – Standards of Non-Discriminatory Treatment', p. 166.

which were developed to facilitate the flow of foreign direct investment in response to existing uncertainty and inadequacies. Since the conclusion of the first bilateral investment treaty in 1959,[18] the legal sphere has been complemented by more than 2,700 bilateral investment treaties.[19] In addition, there is an increasing number of free-trade agreements containing equivalent provisions on investment protection. Investment treaties prescribe a continuously consolidating set of substantive and procedural guarantees, with which the state in the role of the host state is obliged to conform.

This new era of investment law is not only characterised by the emergence of a core set of protective standards; it opened the procedural centre stage to the individual investor. As a distinct move away from the regime of diplomatic protection, investment agreements open the way for investors to individually commence arbitral proceedings against the host state. International conventions – most notably the 1965 Convention on the Settlement of Investment Disputes Between States and Nationals of Other States (ICSID Convention) – provide a procedural framework.[20] Accordingly, an investment treaty in force between two states that signed up to the relevant convention can form the substantive basis for a review of the host state's measures in investor-state arbitration. The capacity to legally challenge a measure introduced by a host state is placed directly in the hands of the investor, without its home state acting as intermediary.

Thus, the contemporary regime of international investment law is best described by focusing on two crucial aspects: First, the substantive content is shaped by a myriad of investment treaties. These treaties are much more significant for current investment law than customary international law is. The relevance of investment treaties means that the level of protection owed to one investor depends on the exact content of the applicable investment treaty. Nevertheless, investment treaties frequently contain near-identical

---

[18] Treaty between the Federal Republic of Germany and Pakistan for the Promotion and Protection of Investments, signed at Bonn on 25 November 1959.

[19] *UNCTAD*, 'World Investment Report 2010, Investing in a Low Carbon Economy' (2010), available at: http://unctad.org/en/docs/wir2010_en.pdf. The report found a total of 2,750 BITs and 295 other international investment agreements.

[20] Both the home state of the investor and the host state have to be parties to the ICSID Convention for it to open the road for investor-state arbitration. The ICSID Convention is currently in force in 150 states (http://icsid.worldbank.org/ICSID/FrontServlet?requestType=ICSIDDocRH&actionVal=ShowDocument&language=English, last visited 30 June 2014), meaning that it is a widely accepted legal instrument. The jurisdiction of the ICSID for claims of investors against a host state is set forth in Article 25 ICSID Convention (see above footnote 10). However, investment arbitration can also be conducted outside of the institutional framework of the framework of the ICSID Convention. Relevant is that the investment treaty contains provisions allowing the investor to start investor-state arbitration.

language, which translates into a virtually universal core set of investment standards that are considered to have one and the same protective scope.

A second very influential factor is the possibility for investors to commence arbitral proceedings. Investors no longer have to convince their home state government to act to ascertain the protection of their investment rights, which has boosted the relevance of the legal discipline. The relative ease in bringing proceedings is undoubtedly the reason for the increase in arbitral proceedings and decisions throughout the last two decades – and, consequently, for the extension of the body of jurisprudence. The surge in available arbitral awards is further strengthening the understanding of the protective scope of investment standards. At the same time, however, there is a fear that enabling the investor to trigger arbitral proceedings has negative impacts on the freedom of host states to regulate for the greater good: The catch phrase 'regulatory chill' signifies that the fear of becoming a respondent in expensive arbitral proceedings may deter host states from introducing legislation and regulatory measures.[21] These two characteristic features of modern investment law – the relevance of investment treaties and the impact of arbitral decisions on the subject area – are central to this study and inform the methodological approach to be applied.

II. Outline of Methodological Approach

These observations influence the methodological approach to the subject. The core of international investment law, as it stands today, is the myriad of existing investment treaties. Conventions – like investment treaties – are a primary source of public international law. Accordingly, at a first stage, this study analyses how treaty provisions determine the relationship. However, it would misrepresent the realities of foreign investment law not to accredit investment tribunals with a significant role in the progression of investment law. The decisions and interpretations of investment tribunals significantly shape the development of this area of international law. Investment tribunals have to work within the borders established by investment treaties, but the wording of the protective standards contained in the treaties leave them considerable latitude in determining the respective level of protection.

---

21 The concept 'regulatory chill' is frequently mentioned by commentators critical of the impact of foreign investment. See, for example, *Tienhaara*, Kyla, Expropriation of Environmental Governance: Protecting Foreign Investors at the Expense of Public Policy (2009) pp. 25 *et seq.*; *Jenkins*, Benjamin W., 'The Next Generation of Chilling Uncertainty: Indirect Expropriation under CAFTA and Its Potential Impact on Environmental Protection', 12 Ocean and Coastal Law Journal 2007, 269 (285). See also in 'Chapter 2 – The Influence of Environmental Concepts on the Interpretation of Investment Provisions', pp. 121 *et seq.*

Even though public international law traditionally does not consider judicial decisions as one of the primary sources of law,[22] the relevance of arbitral decisions in investment law cannot be overstated. The arbitral awards of investment tribunals are the "driving force" of investment law, because they have "elaborated the bare bones guarantees" contained in international investment treaties.[23] Arbitral decisions are the means through which the treaties become effective. Accordingly, my approach to foreign investment law is closely tied to the understanding tribunals have manifested in interpreting the substantive guarantees given to foreign investors: The protective scope of investment provisions is determined through a thorough review of investment decisions that are publicly available. Academic commentators and their writings, in contrast, will be used as an additional and additive source of insight into the scope of the protection owed to foreign investors.

Focusing on arbitral decisions to grapple with the scope of the protection afforded by investment law, however, brings with it methodological problems that have to be highlighted. First, arbitral tribunals in international investment law are ad-hoc tribunals, not bound by a formal rule of precedent and lacking a system of hierarchy. In theory, no investment decision has implications for scenarios outside the facts of the individual case, on which the tribunal decided. While this lack of legally enforced consistency is one of the major points of criticism voiced in connection with the procedural aspects of international investment law – and one that will need addressing in the future –[24], case law demonstrates that investment tribunals make an effort to place their findings into the context of earlier decisions. Even

22 Article 38 Statute of the International Court of Justice categorises judicial decisions "as subsidiary means for the determination of rules of law".

23 *Alvarez*, José E., 'The Return of the State', 20 Minnesota Journal of International Law 2011, 23 (233). Similarly, *Commission*, Jeffrey P., 'Precedent in Investment Treaties, A Citation Analysis of Developing Jurisprudence', 24 Journal of International Arbitration 2007, 129 (132).

24 *Stern*, Brigitte, 'The Future of International Investment Law: A Balance Between the Protection of Investors and the State's Capacity to Regulate' in: The Evolving International Investment Regime: Expectations, Realities, Opinions (Alvarez, José/Sauvant, Karl P. (Eds.) 2011) 174 (181–186). The author expresses the view that contradictory trends within the system will finally be resolved by the stakeholders, who will eventually reach compromise policy solutions that are acceptable to all. She also argues – borrowing a term coined by Anthony Sinclair – that the system will be guided by a "hierarchy of reason", rather than a hierarchy of precedent, because a strong and convincing award will have more acceptability than a "bad" one. See, for further reference, *Weidemaier*, W. Mark C., 'Toward a Theory of Precedent in Arbitration', 51 William and Mary Law Review 2010, 1895–1958; *Sureda*, Andrés Rigo, 'Precedent in Investment Treaty Arbitration', in: International Investment Law for the 21st Century: Essays in Honour of Christoph Schreuer (Binder, Christina et al. (Eds.) 2009) 830–842.

though each investment treaty is by definition *lex specialis*, the work of investment tribunals can be understood as leading to the emergence of a sort of *lex generalis* of international investment law.[25] Because of the continuous reference to interpretations adopted and solutions found by other tribunals, which were not necessarily based on identical language in the underlying treaties, the differences existing between all treaties become less and less relevant in the interpretation of the core concepts. This does obviously not mean that identified concepts are always understood in the same manner; however, there is a slowly, but steadily growing understanding of how the most fundamental standards of investment treaties have to be interpreted. This more informal take on the corpus of existing case-law does not erase all problems of uncertainty in the investment arbitration process, but it points to the emergence of uniform protective concepts.

The second and closely connected problem of relying on investment decisions is that the set of decisions that touches upon the relationship of investment rules with environmental protection is still rather limited. Accordingly, there is a danger of over-emphasising the findings of one particular decision. Nevertheless, the approaches taken are crucial to determine existing or potential conflicts between the legal regimes – if only in a relatively restricted number of decisions. Being aware of the potential danger, I intend to develop my findings on the significance of the environmental relevance of the respective protective notion from as many arbitral decisions as available in the public domain. Even though the limitation persists, I aim to reduce its impact by being aware of it.

---

[25] *Subedi*, Surya P., 'The Challenge of Reconciling the Competing Principles within the Law of Foreign Investment with Special Reference to the Recent Trend in the Interpretation of the Term "Expropriation"', 40 International Lawyer 2006, 121 (128). See also *Joubin-Bret*, Anna/*Rey*, Estelle-Marie/*Weber*, Jörg, 'International Investment Law and Development' in: Sustainable Development in World Investment Law (Cordonier Segger, Marie-Claire et al. (Eds.) 2011) 15 (18) who acknowledge a "universal system" of international investment agreements with "a considerable degree of homogeneity".

This understanding is expressly endorsed by the tribunal in Bayindir Insaat Turizm Ticaret Ve Sanayi A.S. v. Islamic Republic of Pakistan, ICSID Case No. ARB/03/29, Award of 27 August 2009, para 145, which stated that a tribunal should follow solutions established in a series of consistent cases, "unless there are compelling reasons to the contrary", "but subject of course to the specifics of a given treaty and of the circumstances of the actual case." Similairly, Bosh International, Inc and B&P Ltd Foreign Investments Enterprise v. Ukraine, ICSID Case No. ARB/08/11, Award of 25 October 2012, para 211. See also the tribunal in Railroad Development Corporation v. Republic of Guatemala, ICSID Case No. ARB/07/23, Award of 29 June 2012, para 217, considering the referencing to former decisions by the state party as statement what states consider to be the law.

The study addresses the tension between different substantive provisions of law. It does not focus on aspects of arbitral proceedings. The following outline guides the presentation of the subject: The first chapter portrays tensions between environmental law and investment activity by introducing concepts and subject areas of international environmental law. To this end, after briefly defining the 'environment', it describes four core principles of environmental regulation in the economic context. Further, it portrays relevant international regulation in three distinct subject areas of environmental interest. Subsequently, the first chapter develops four scenarios of conflicts between investment protection provisions and environmental protection. The chapter is to function both as an introduction to the realm of environmental law and as a portrayal of scenarios of conflict. These scenarios are to guide the discussion in further chapters.

The second chapter focuses on the way environmental issues are addressed in investment treaties. The interpretative scope and influence of the environmental provisions and references contained in investment treaties are at the heart of this theoretical approach. The chapter sets forth references that are found in investment treaties and analyses their relevance by applying the rules of treaty interpretation. The mandate of each investment tribunal is defined by the underlying treaty, but investment treaties do not set this mandate in a uniform manner. They accord the tribunal latitude in defining the scope of the relevant material protections – and environmental references can be one way to shape the mandate. Further, the second chapter addresses the issue of conflicts between both sets of international rules in an abstract manner.

The subsequent chapters three to five analyse the relationship of standards of investment protection with environmental measures and standards. The third chapter portrays the concept of non-discrimination. The forth chapter depicts the protection deriving from standards of fair treatment and the fifth chapter presents the protection against expropriation. Each chapter starts with an overview of the protection granted by the respective treatment standard. Common features acknowledged in a multitude of investment decisions are used to ascertain a common understanding.[26] At the next stage, those investment decisions that concern environmental issues and relate to the standard under review are portrayed in more detail. The reason-

[26] There is no homogenous understanding of the substantive standards of protection in foreign investment law. Differences stem from formulations in the respective treaties and from the different accentuation of elements due to the specific circumstances of each case. Accordingly, the description of the protective standard that I develop throughout the study is an idealisation of each concept. It is derived from the examination of as large a number of investment decisions as was publicly available at the time of writing.

ing adopted by the respective tribunal in dealing with the environmental context is assessed. As a further stage, I evaluate these investment decisions to formulate a hypothesis on the influence the respective standard has in the environmental context. The assessment discusses if and to what extent the concepts of investment protection conflict with environmental standards and states' capacity to regulate for environmental concerns. To this end, the scenarios for a potential collision of standards of investment protection with the environmental measures developed in the first chapter are applied and evaluated.

Chapter 1

Environmental Norms and Principles

The environment is not an abstraction but represents the living space, the quality of life and the very health of human beings, including generations unborn.

International Court of Justice in the Advisory Opinion on the Legality of the Threat or Use of Nuclear Weapons, 1986

'Environment' is a vast concept which lacks a precise definition. What characterises the environmental concept in most perceptions is its natural component: The natural environment can be understood to cover the seas, the atmosphere, climate, forests and other plant cover, fauna, flora as well as other biological elements.[1] In this sense, it has been described as the environment of the human race and of its development – encompassing areas of preservation.[2]

Such a focus on the relationship of humans with nature is central to the understanding of the environmental concept.[3] This is not surprising. Since the beginning of times, human beings have experienced their own existence as part of their natural environment. Nature provided the means for survival as well as evoking risks and dangers. Later, humans started to shape their natural environment and have increasingly become creators. The realisation that, despite significant changes to the underlying parameters, the dependence of the human race on their natural environment persists and that actions affecting it can ultimately impact on humans is at the heart of the conceptualisation of the environment.[4]

---

1 *International Law Commission*, Report of the International Law Commission on the Work of Its Forty-Third Session, 29 April to 19 July 1991 (A/46/10), p. 275.

2 *International Law Commission*, Report of the International Law Commission on the Work of Its Forty-Third Session, 29 April to 19 July 1991 (A/46/10), p. 275. Similarly, Article 2 para 10 Directive 79/117/EEC of 21 December 1978 defining environment as "the relationship of human beings with water, air, land and all biological forms."

3 Similarly, *Bodansky*, Daniel, Art and Craft of International Environmental Law (2010) p. 10.

This chapter establishes an overview of relevant environmental norms and principles. To this end, it first abstractly determines the notion of 'environmental law' and secondly outlines the development of legal standards at the national and international level. Third, the chapter gives an insight into three subject areas of environmental law, focusing on the respective international conventions. With a view to potential conflicts with the interests of foreign investors the chapter, fourthly, portrays three fundamental principles of international environmental law. The fifth and final section of the chapter develops scenarios in which provisions on investment protection contained in international investment treaties could collide with environmental norms and principles. These hypothetic situations are supported by concrete examples relating to the subject matters of environmental law previously portrayed. These scenarios will be intensely discussed in the following chapters of this study in connection with the substantive standards of investment protection. The scenarios serve as tests to establish whether conflicts exist between investment and environmental protection and how arbitral tribunals are likely to perceive them.

A. 'Environment' as a Concept

It is against this background of human development that 'environment' is frequently understood broadly, namely as including the natural environment as well as man-made objects and surroundings. The term can be understood to encompass "both the features and products of the natural world and those of human civilisation".[5] This wider understanding is reflected in international environmental agreements, even if those documents refrain from de-

---

4 Preambular clauses 1, 2, 3, 6 Declaration of the United Nations Conference on the Human Environment of 16 June 1972. The general perception of the importance of environmental protection increases with knowledge about negative impacts of environmental degradation. It increases when environmental disasters or new scientific evidence highlight risks for humans or potential impacts on humans' ability to use certain environmental resources or services. Contemporary examples are changes in the Japanese attitude towards nuclear energy in the aftermaths of the 2011 Fukushima incident and the increase in scepticism towards deep-sea oil drilling following the 2010 oil spill in the Gulf of Mexico.

See also the largely anecdotal portrayal by *MacDonald*, Gordon J., 'Environment: Evolution of a Concept', 12 Journal of Environment & Development 2003, 151–176.

5 *Sands*, Philippe/*Peel*, Jacequeline, Principles of International Environmental Law (2012) p. 13. A similar understanding is expressed in the Declaration of the United Nations Conference on the Human Environment of 16 June 1972, preambular clause 1, which focuses in relevant part on "both the natural and the man-made aspects of man's environment [being] essential to his well-being and to the enjoyment of basic human rights the right to life itself".

fining the term.[6] The close connection between man-made cultural heritage and natural heritage is furthermore underlined by the combining notion of world heritage.[7] From a policy perspective, the incorporation of features of human civilisation into the environmental conception deserves support: A definitional restriction of the environment to the natural environment, so as to only relate to environmental spheres and areas not altered by human activity would discard large parts of the cover of the earth from the scope of the definition. Such a restriction would counter the protective intention of environmental law.[8]

The anthropogenic perspective of the environment can be traced through the development of environmental law and remains at its heart:[9] The impetus to protect the environment is closely connected to the desire to maintain attractive natural surroundings and to retain its resources and services for further human enjoyment.[10] While perceptions of the environment as a system of more intrinsic value have attracted some support,[11] conflicts in all areas of environmental law show that the value attached to environmental protection is balanced against other human needs and interests. In this

---

[6] Directive 85/337/EEC of 27 June 1985 mentions the following factors: human beings, fauna and flora, soil, water, air, climate and the landscape, the interaction between the factors afore-mentioned, as well as material assets and cultural heritage. International conventions defining environmental impacts, effects, or damages – like Article 1 para 2 1992 Convention on the Protection and Use of Transboundary Watercourses and International Lakes and Article 1 lit c 1992 UNECE Convention on the Transboundary Effects of Industrial Accidents and Article 2 para 7 1993 Lugano Convention on Civil Liability for Damage Resulting from Activities Dangerous to the Environment – also refer to these factors. They also include some other factors, like historical monuments and socio-economic conditions resulting from the alterations to the factors.

[7] Article 2 1972 Paris UNESCO Convention Concerning the Protection of the World Cultural and Natural Heritage (UNESCO Convention).

[8] Similarly, *Kloepfer*, Michael, Umweltschutzrecht (2008) p. 11.

[9] Similarly, *Birnie*, Patricia/*Boyle*, Alan/*Redgwell*, Catherine, International Law and the Environment (2009), pp. 8–9, 585; *Meyerholt*, Ulrich, Umweltrecht (2010) p. 25. See also *MacDonald*, Gordon J., 'Environment: Evolution of a Concept', 12 Journal of Environment & Development 2003, 151 (175), who argues that 'environment' embraces science, aesthetics and ethics. The latter two are inherently connected to an anthropogenic perspective.

[10] Preambular clause 2 Declaration of the United Nations Conference on the Human Environment of 16 June 1972; Principle 1 (Report of the United Nations Conference on Environment and Development, UN Doc. A/CONF.151/26 (Vol. I), Annex 1 (Rio Declaration).

[11] Preambular clauses 1, 2 1992 Convention on Biological Diversity, mentioning the "intrinsic value of biological diversity"; Article 20a German Basic Law (*Grundgesetz*), referencing the need to protect animals distinct from safeguarding the ecological foundations of existence.

light, it has been argued that successfully addressing the root-causes of certain environmental problems requires further expansion of the environmental concept – one that encompasses economic, social, and trade policies.[12] Although the interconnectedness of environmental, development, and social issues cannot be denied, this does not necessitate a further blurring of the conceptual borders of the 'environment'.[13] For the sake of precision, the natural environment in the way that it has been modified by human interaction has to remain the core of the environmental concept.

This understanding of the environment will be applied throughout the survey. The 'environment' is the aggregate of human beings (inclusive of their material assets and cultural heritage), fauna and flora, soil, water, air, climate, and landscape and the respective interaction of all parts. Accordingly, the concept encompasses 'nature', understood to be the natural environment as outlined above – which is concerned with the physical and biological features of the world itself. Further embraced by the environmental concept is the notion of 'natural resources'. This term captures both living and non-living resources:[14] Non-living resources, such as coal, oil, gas, minerals and metals are non-renewable, so that exploitation will inevitably lead to their depletion. More relevant from a conservationist perspective are living resources, i.e. species of fauna and flora, which are reproducing themselves, so that sustainable exploitation should not lead to their depletion.

The interactive aspect of the definition of the environment is also reflected in the concept of 'ecosystem', which it encloses. An ecosystem is "a dynamic complex of plant, animal and micro-organism communities and their non-living environment interacting as a functional unit."[15] The final notion to be defined is that of "ecosystem services", which underscores the anthropogenic connotation of the environmental concept: Ecosystem services are the conditions and processes through which ecosystems and their components aid sustain human life – i.e. the benefits that humans derive from natural ecosystems.[16] These services stretch from provisioning services, like water and food, over regulating services, such as the regulation

---

12 *Bodansky*, Daniel, Art and Craft of International Environmental Law (2010) pp. 10–11.

13 These interactions between environmental, economic, and social aspects are encapsulated in the concept of sustainable development, which is portrayed below at pp. 63 *et seq*.

14 See *Birnie*, Patricia/*Boyle*, Alan/*Redgwell*, Catherine, International Law and the Environment (2009) p. 586.

15 Article 2 1992 Convention on Biological Diversity.

16 *Hirokawa*, Keith H., Disasters and Ecosystem Services Deprivation: From Cuyahoga to the Deepwater Horizon, Albany Law Review 2010–2011, 74 Alb. L.

of floods, wastes, or water filtering in wetlands, and supporting services, like soil formation, photosynthesis, and carbon sequestering in vegetation, to cultural services such as recreation and aesthetic enjoyment.[17]

B. Development of Environmental Regulation

Environmental regulation is created when a society agrees that the non-regulation of a specific environmental common leads to its destruction or substantial degradation and that this loss of the common is not acceptable.[18] Broadly speaking, the commons can be affected by excessive taking of resources or by excessive input.[19] Accordingly, the anthropogenic fear of future incapacity to use a natural resource or an ecosystem service is a main driver for such a societal agreement. If – or when – an agreement to regulate is reached differs from society to society and is influenced by a multitude of different factors, with the economic development of the nation being a major factor.

The scientific identification of environmental problems and of the interconnectedness of their elements constitutes a predominant factor for the increasing regulation of environmental matters. Scientific and ecological understanding have raised the general awareness about environmental issues and enabled lawmakers to create increasingly effective environmental regulation. Due to the vastness of the environmental concept and to the innumerable human activities that potentially affect it, it is, however, not easy

---

Rev. 543–561 (543); *Millennium Ecosystem Assessment*, Ecosystems and Human Well-Being, Biodiversity Synthesis (2005) p. 1.

17 *Millennium Ecosystem Assessment*, Ecosystems and Human Well-Being, Biodiversity Synthesis (2005) pp. 1–2; *Hirokawa*, Keith H., 'Disasters and Ecosystem Services Deprivation: From Cuyahoga to the Deepwater Horizon', 74 Albany Law Review 2011, 543 (543).

18 Albeit not expressly coined for the environmental context, the understanding of the 'tragedy of the commons' is helpful: The concept of the commons is based on the historic, psychological, and sociological realisation that the availability of freely available resources will be overused by each individual, which will ultimately lead to the destruction of the common good. The founder of the concept *Hardin*, Garrett, 'The Tragedy of the Commons', 162 Science 1968, 1243 coined the drastic phrase that "freedom in a common brings ruin to all" (1244).

19 *Hardin*, Garrett, 'The Tragedy of the Commons', 162 Science 1968, 1243–1248, provides the examples of classical free pastures, national parks, and living marine resources endangered by excessive consumption. Waste and pollution are examples of harmful input into the commons.

These two aspects, excessive taking and excessive input, – albeit in recognition of the complex interaction of these and other factors – appear to this day to be the main concerns of environmental protection.

to categorise environmental law as a distinct field of law.[20] Considering this, it will be assumed for the purpose of this survey, that 'environmental regulation' encompasses regulation that relates to human-induced impacts on elements of the natural environment, to the interaction of these natural elements, as well as to the interaction of such elements with human beings, their material assets, and cultural heritage. The term 'regulation' is a broad concept, including both international and national legal instruments, which incorporate binding rules.

Regulation thus encompasses 'environmental legislation', which refers to rules adopted by a sovereign state for application in its own sovereign territory.[21] The awareness of the need to legally protect the environment has grown steadily since the 1960s[22] – at the national and at the international level. These two spheres of law, the national one and the international one, cross-fertilise each other. States are the primary subjects of international law, which determine the content of international agreements. It follows that environmental obligations are only adopted when a significant number of states considers the respective issue as worthy of regulation. Prior to such agreements, the participating states will normally have identified the issue to be an environmental problem and will have undertaken some sort of regulative effort at the national level. If a state does not acknowledge the necessity of regulating certain behaviour in its domestic legislation, it is unlikely to commit to regulation at the international level. This cross-fertilisation also works the other direction: When a state has committed to environmental measures at the international level, it is obliged to properly im-

[20] *Aagaard*, Todd S., 'Environmental Law as a Legal Field: An Inquiry in Legal Taxonomy', 95 Cornell Law Review 2009, 221 (262–263), proposes that environmental law should be understood to encompass "laws that reflect a consideration of human impacts on the natural environment". Although this definition appears to be slightly too narrow in the light of the broader definition of the environment above, that author's warning against under-inclusiveness and over-inclusiveness (correctly stating that almost every human activity affects some aspect of the environment) will be borne in mind.

That author further concludes (282) that the "dominant characteristic of environmental lawmaking has been ad-hoc muddling through, and this characteristic is reflected in the complexity and diversity of environmental-law doctrine".

[21] A categorisation of the legal nature of regulation passed by a supranational organisation of states, most notably the European Union, is outside of the scope of this study: In so far as a regulation is directly applicable within the national state, it will be considered as a national regulation. If it requires the state to legally implement it, it will be considered as an international regulation.

[22] Despite the existence of national and international environmental regulation prior to the 1960s, *Birnie*, Patricia/*Boyle*, Alan/*Redgwell*, Catherine, International Law and the Environment (2009) p. 1 consider this decade the starting point of international environmental law.

plement the resulting obligations in its national legislation.[23] Accordingly, international conventions have relevant influence on the environmental regulation enacted in a national state and increase the conformity of environmental rules among all states.

International environmental law is particularly relevant in regulating human activity, which has transboundary effects. Given the vastness of the environmental concept and the interconnectedness of all its elements, most aspects requiring environmental regulation have a transboundary impact. In the international arena, environmental regulation is most frequently incorporated in international conventions.[24] However, there is academic discussion whether some of the more widely accepted principles of international environmental law have acquired the status of customary international law[25] or can be considered general principles of international law[26]. An environmental concept falling into the two latter categories requires states to respect and apply it, even though they never accepted to be bound by it in a treaty. In environmental matters, some state courts have accepted certain concepts as customary international law and therefore as applicable part of their domestic law.[27] Distinct from these categories are expressions at the international sphere that are not law-making and binding. Notable examples are

---

23 See for an overview *Redgwell*, Catherine, 'National Implementation', in: The Oxford Handbook of International Environmental Law (Bodansky, Daniel et al. (Eds.) 2007) 922–946; United Nations Environment Programme (UNEP) Governing Council Decision SS.VII/4 of February 2002, 'Compliance with and Enforcement of Multilateral Environmental Agreements', UNEP(DEPI)/MEAs/WBG.1/3, Annex 2.

24 Article 38 para 1 lit a Statute of the International Court of Justice. International conventions or treaties are "international agreement[s] concluded between States in written form and governed by international law", see Article 2 para 1 lit a VCLT.

25 Article 38 para 1 lit b Statute of the International Court of Justice enumerates "international custom, as evidence of a general practice accepted as law" as one of the sources of international law. The consistency and generality of a specific practice grounded in a sense of legal obligation are the relevant criteria of international custom. See *Brownlie*, Ian, Principles of Public International Law (2008) pp. 6–12; *Ipsen*, Knut, Völkerrecht (2004) § 16 (Heintschel von Heinegg, Wolff).

26 Article 38 para 1 lit c Statute of the International Court of Justice refers to the "general principles of law recognised by civilised nations" as a third source of international law. General principles are those fundamental legal notions that are at the heart of most significant national legal systems, *Ipsen*, Knut, Völkerrecht (2004) § 17 (Heintschel von Heinegg, Wolff).

In practise, this means that international tribunals have "employed elements of legal reasoning and private law analogies", *Brownlie*, Ian, Principles of Public International Law (2008) pp. 16–18 (16).

27 A prominent example is India. See Indian Supreme Court, Vellore Citizens' Welfare Forum v. Union of India (1996), AIR1996SC2715, for the concept of sustainable development, the precautionary principle and the polluter-pays principle.

declarations by conferences of the United Nations or resolutions by the General Assembly of the United Nations. The ideas or principles contained in such instruments, however, give an indication of widely accepted views. Accordingly, they are sometimes referred to as 'soft law'.[28]

Public international law generally only empowers and obliges its subjects – first and foremost states – but not individuals.[29] Therefore, international environmental agreements will not directly oblige a foreign investor when the host state becomes party to them. Nor will obligations undertaken by the investor's home state directly oblige the foreign investor. Furthermore, obligations undertaken at the international level do not generally require or prohibit precise activities. These provisions often give the state parties leeway as to a certain goal that is to be attained or they contain qualifiers that open up margins of appreciation.[30] Accordingly, states have an obligation to nationally implement international conventions to which they are a party: The national measure that derives from the implementation contains the obligations or prohibitions directed at individuals operating within the respective jurisdiction.[31]

For the polluter-pays principle, similarly, Indian Supreme Court, Indian Council For Enviro-Legal-Action v. Union of India and Ors. Etc (1996), 1996 AIR 1446.

[28] 'Soft law' is no source of international law. It refers to expressions of international bodies, conferences or states which lack the binding force of rules of law. It may characterise law in its nascent status – but whether it reaches the status of 'hard law' can only be determined retrospectively. See *Ipsen*, Knut, Völkerrecht (2004) § 19 V (Heintschel von Heinegg, Wolff). See also, *Hillgenberg*, Hartmut, 'A Fresh Look at Soft Law', 10 European Journal of International Law 1999, 499–515, who argues that non-treaty agreements constitute "a self-contained regime subject to legal thinking" constituting a factor, but not a source of law.

[29] See in more detail, *Brownlie*, Ian, Principles of Public International Law (2008) pp. 57–65. The most important exception is human rights law, which directly empowers the individual, *Brownlie*, Ian, Principles of Public International Law (2008) pp. 562–563.

[30] One example is the qualifying language contained in the 1992 Convention on Biological Diversity, which imposes obligations "as far as possible" or "as appropriate". Another example is reflected in the ban on whaling, which allows taking for scientific purposes. Such an exception has to be clearly defined to not render the overall ban meaningless. Further, the systems established under the 1989 Basel Convention on the Control of Transboundary Movements of Hazardous Wastes and Their Disposal (Basel Convention) or the 1973 Washington Convention on International Trade in Endangered Species of Wild Fauna and Flora (CITES Convention) require the establishment of national authorities competent for the issuance of the permits and for giving the required consent. See *Redgwell*, Catherine, 'National Implementation', in: The Oxford Handbook of International Environmental Law (Bodansky, Daniel et al. (Eds.) 2007) 922 (929–930).

[31] See *Redgwell*, Catherine, 'National Implementation', in: The Oxford Handbook of International Environmental Law (Bodansky, Daniel et al. (Eds.) 2007) 922–946

As the obligation of states to 'enact effective environmental legislation' is generally recognised and accepted,[32] all states have a body of national environmental legislation. Due to their sovereignty, states are at liberty to determine which legal forms their environmental framework takes: laws, administrative regulation, judicial interpretations, policies, and other measures and initiatives.[33] The preferences vary according to the respective constitutional requirements and different legal systems of each state.[34] Furthermore, it is accepted – while the national environmental legislation has to be effective[35] – that every state is at liberty to apply the standards which

---

(929), stating that "legislative implementation of a state's international obligations performs a 'delegated normativity' function, conditioning not only state but also non-state actor's behaviour."

[32] Principle 11 Rio Declaration. The Principle reads as follows: "States shall enact effective environmental legislation. Environmental standards, management objectives and priorities should reflect the environmental and development context to which they apply. Standards applied by some countries may be inappropriate and of unwarranted economic and social cost to other countries, in particular developing countries."

[33] See for the context of national implementation of international obligations: *Redgwell*, Catherine, 'National Implementation', in: The Oxford Handbook of International Environmental Law (Bodansky, Daniel et al. (Eds.) 2007) 922–946; UNEP Governing Council Decision SS.VII/4 of February 2002, 'Compliance with and Enforcement of Multilateral Environmental Agreements', UNEP(DEPI)/MEAs/WBG.1/3, Annex 2, para 9.

It is most likely that environmental legislation in one jurisdiction contains elements of all of the above. It is possible for states to regulate precise thresholds for emissions in an administrative instrument, or they can incorporate a general clause into a law, which will be interpreted by judges. Less formal instruments are voluntary agreements, for example, with polluting industries.

[34] For the context of implementation: UNEP Governing Council Decision SS. VII/4 of February 2002, 'Compliance with and Enforcement of Multilateral Environmental Agreements', UNEP(DEPI)/MEAs/WBG.1/3, Annex 2, paras 20, 39.

An important point relating to the constitutional requirement is the internal competence for environmental matters. This is particularly relevant in connection with federal states. The competence for certain environmental considerations of federal sub-entities has been an important issue in some investment treaty disputes. An example is *Metalclad Corporation v. United Mexican States*, see in 'Chapter 4 – Standards of Fair Treatment', p. 265. The division of competences within a federal state, albeit at the outset not a problem of international law, can practically prove to be difficult for the application of environmental legislation.

[35] For the context of implementation: UNEP Governing Council Decision SS. VII/4 of February 2002, 'Compliance with and Enforcement of Multilateral Environmental Agreements', UNEP(DEPI)/MEAs/WBG.1/3, Annex 2 para 40 suggests that laws and regulations should be, inter alia, "clearly stated with well-defined objectives", "technically, economically and socially feasible to implement, monitor and enforce effectively", and "comprehensive with appropriate and proportionate penalties for environmental law violations".

it perceives to be suitable for its own context.[36] Accordingly, national environmental frameworks contain binding obligations as well as measures lacking such a forcing character. Relevant measures that fall short of the imposition of prohibitions or actions are, for example, economic instruments facilitating the efficient implementation of environmental standards.[37] Therefore, the binding character of a measure at the national level has to be determined concretely for every measure potentially conflicting with the protection of foreign investors.

Accordingly, environmental prohibitions and obligations existing for individuals within a specific jurisdiction differ from state to state. What is more, the level of their practical implementation and enforcement furthers such differences.[38] Nevertheless, several thematic areas of environmental law can be detected, which are globally considered to constitute areas of concern worth of regulation. Because of the cross-fertilisation of national and international law, as described above, and the differences arising at the national level, relevant environmental subject areas will be abstractly portrayed through their reflection in international environmental law. Similarly, certain relevant principles of environmental law, which also permeate na-

---

36 Principle 11 Rio Declaration. Similarly for the context of implementation, UNEP Governing Council Decision SS.VII/4 of February 2002, 'Compliance with and Enforcement of Multilateral Environmental Agreements', UNEP(DEPI)/MEAs/WBG.1/3, Annex 2, para 39.

37 See for the context of implementation of international agreements, UNEP Governing Council Decision SS.VII/4 of February 2002, 'Compliance with and Enforcement of Multilateral Environmental Agreements', UNEP(DEPI)/MEAs/WBG.1/3, Annex 2, para 23.

38 Significant differences exist despite international regulation aiming to foster similarities between the existing institutional frameworks. See for the context of implementation, UNEP Governing Council Decision SS.VII/4 of February 2002, 'Compliance with and Enforcement of Multilateral Environmental Agreements', UNEP(DEPI)/MEAs/WBG.1/3, Annex 2, para 41, asking states to consider an institutional framework that promotes (a) the designation of responsibilities to agencies for the enforcement of laws and regulations, the monitoring and evaluation of implementation, collecting and reporting of data, awareness-raising as well as assistance to courts and agencies; (b) control of the import and export of substances and endangered species; (c) clear authority for those involved in enforcement activities to obtain relevant information, monitor and verify compliance, coordinate with other agencies as well as impose sanctions and penalties; (d) procedures that ensure fair and consistent enforcement and imposition of penalties, including courts competent to impose penalties for violations of environmental laws; (e) establishing or strengthening of national environmental crime units to complement civil and administrative enforcement programmes; (f) use of economic instruments promoting economically efficient compliance as well as certification systems; (g) public access to environmental information and procedures.

tional environmental laws, will be described as they are perceived in international environmental law.

An environmental provision or measure can only collide with the protection the host state owes to a foreign investor, if two conditions are fulfilled: First, the provision has to deploy legal effect in relation to the individual, namely the foreign investor. This is generally not the case with obligations stemming from the international legal order, since these obligations exclusively oblige states.[39] Second, the provision has to constitute a binding obligation to act or to refrain from acting in a certain way. Such effect is missing in provisions proclaiming aims or goals without mandating concrete steps to be taken. Voluntary commitments undertaken by an investor, which are not coupled with enforcement mechanisms, also lack binding effect. This characteristic is also doubtful when a regulation imposes on the administration the capacity to allocate rights and restriction according to certain criteria, thus allowing for a margin of appreciation. Rules that fulfil these two conditions qualify as 'environmental norms' for the purpose of this study.

C. Subject Areas of Environmental Law

This section portrays three domains of international environmental law. Even though these domains relate to distinct areas of concern, their interconnectedness is obvious. The first domain regards the concept of conservation and biological diversity. The portrayal introduces some of the natural foundations of the environment, highlighting the importance of the protection of species and their habitats. Their relevance is closely connected to the second domain, which portrays international regulation of toxic substances, waste disposal and hazardous activities. Whereas it is apparent that environmental resources, ecosystems and services function best when they are free of toxins, industrial activity and the modern way of human life are inseparably interconnected with such discharges. The third domain provides an overview over conventions relating to the atmosphere and to the challenge of climate change – which is a very vibrant area of law. The portrayal specifically focuses on mechanisms intended to curb the emission of greenhouse gases.

---

39 *Brownlie*, Ian, Principles of Public International Law (2008) pp. 57–65.

I. Conservation and Biological Diversity

A central component of environmental protection relates to the protection and conservation of elements of the environment. Its core was originally driven by the anthropogenic exploitation of natural resources in the light of their finite nature in the case of over-exploitation: The fear of the extinction of a species – due to the resulting impossibility of its further exploitation – was the driving force behind early conservation agreements, which generally aimed to regulate the exploitation of one specific set of species at a time.[40] Against this background, conservation has rather an anthropogenic impetus: species should be conserved to secure further exploitation. Such use of natural resources[41] remains central to environmental protection. The right of each state to exploit its own natural resources is a key element of contemporary environmental self-conception.[42]

Science has made states more aware of the existence of inter-connections between individual species. In this sense, international environmental law is increasingly characterised by international agreements which embrace a more holistic approach than the protection of certain individual species – especially of 'charismatic mega-fauna'. This comprehensive approach is incorporated in the concept of biological diversity. In the words of the 1992 Convention on Biological Diversity, biological diversity means "the variability among living organisms from all sources including, inter alia, terrestrial, marine and other aquatic ecosystems and the ecological complexes of which they are part; this includes diversity within species, between species and of ecosystems".[43] Accordingly, the focus of biodiversity is on the conglomerate of species and their interaction with each other and the non-living environment, not on individual parts of the whole. It is in this sense that a commentator stated that "biodiversity is valuable precisely because it

---

40 1911 Convention between the United States of America, the United Kingdom of Great Britain and Northern Ireland, and Russia, for the Preservation and Protection of Fur Seals; 1916 Convention between the United States and Great Britain for the Protection of Migratory Birds in the United States and Canada. Also, 1902 Convention to Protect Birds Useful to Agriculture; 1900 Convention Destinée à Assurer la Conservation des Diverses Espèces Animales vivant à l'Etat Sauvage en Afrique qui sont Utiles à l'homme ou Inoffensive.

41 See *Birnie*, Patricia/*Boyle*, Alan/*Redgwell*, Catherine, International Law and the Environment (2009) p. 586. For a more detailed portrayal of the notion of biological resources, *Rayfuse*, Rosemary, 'Biological Resources', in: The Oxford Handbook of International Environmental Law (Bodansky, Daniel et al. (Eds.) 2007) 362 (365–370).

42 Principle 2 Rio Declaration; Article 193 1982 United Nations Convention on the Law of the Sea (UNCLOS).

43 Article 2 1992 Convention on Biological Diversity.

is the output of th[e] four-billion-year-old evolutionary process, not for the sake of the variety itself".[44]

For a multitude of species – most notably fish and other marine species – over-exploitation still constitutes an important threat to their survival.[45] Nevertheless, it is nowadays acknowledged that other factors are equally relevant threats to biological diversity:[46] A very severe threat to the survival of species is presented by the destruction of natural habitat. Habitat loss is an inevitable consequence of an increasingly industrialised lifestyle which requires, inter alia, the cultivation or development of more and more surface areas.[47] Such processes are accompanied by pollution and nutrient loading, which are other factors threatening biological diversity.[48] A further factor having a destructive impact is the intentional or unintentional introduction of invasive alien species.[49] Such species threaten ecosystems, habitats, and other species in areas where they are not native through processes usually spanning several decades.[50] Furthermore, anthropogenic climate change is a factor.[51]

---

44 *Swanson*, Timothy, Global Action for Biodiversity (1997) p. 9.

45 *Millennium Ecosystem Assessment*, Ecosystems and Human Well-Being, Biodiversity Synthesis (2005) p. 8, stating that "the biomass of fish targeted in fisheries (including that of both the target species and those caught incidentally) has been reduced by 90% relative to levels prior to the onset of industrial fishing" and that "about three quarters of the world's commercial marine fisheries are either fully exploited or overexploited". Giving a detailed description of the impact of overfishing on biodiversity, *Kunich*, John Charles, 'Losing Nemo: The Mass Extinction Now Threatening the World's Ocean Hotspots', 30 Columbia Journal of Environmental Law 2005, 1 (22–27).

46 *Adam*, Rachelle, 'Missing the 2010 Biodiversity Target: A Wake-Up Call for the Convention on Biodiversity?' 21 Colorado Journal of International Environmental Law and Policy 2010, 123 (129–130, 134), states that the loss of biodiversity is rooted in "the proliferation of diverse activities that constitute modern daily living" and states that its drivers are, for example, "high population growth, even greater economic growth together with the misuse of fossil fuels as a primary energy source, over-consumption, growing food demand, and overwhelming poverty".

47 *Millennium Ecosystem Assessment*, Ecosystems and Human Well-Being, Biodiversity Synthesis (2005) p. 8.

48 *Millennium Ecosystem Assessment*, Ecosystems and Human Well-Being, Biodiversity Synthesis (2005) pp. 8–9.

49 *Riley*, Sophie, 'A Weed by Any Other Name: Would the Rose Smell As Sweet if It Were a Threat to Biodiversity?', 22 Georgetown International Environmental Law Review 2009, 157 (159–162, 164–165); *Millennium Ecosystem Assessment*, Ecosystems and Human Well-Being, Biodiversity Synthesis (2005) p. 8.

50 *Riley*, Sophie, 'A Weed by Any Other Name: Would the Rose Smell As Sweet if It Were a Threat to Biodiversity?', 22 Georgetown International Environmental Law Review 2009, 157 (164–165, 177).

The aim of protecting specific species as well as biological diversity as a whole is the subject of a multitude of international environmental agreements. These agreements differ in their thematic target (covering different threats to specific species or biological diversity) as well as in their geographic scope (global or more regional agreements). Generally, international agreements play an important role with regard to migratory species, since these are by definition not exclusively subject to one single jurisdiction. There are innumerable possibilities of tensions between such international environmental agreements, namely the preservationist concepts they promote, and the potential interests of foreign investors. For a better understanding of both the regulatory impetus of such environmental agreements and the resulting potential conflicts, some of their provisions will be portrayed in more detail below.[52] On a comprehensive level, three protective concepts of such environmental agreements can be identified, which mirror the threats to biological diversity enumerated above: namely (1) regulation relating to the protection of species from direct interference, (2) regulation of habitat preservation and (3) regulation of conduct indirectly impacting on species.

1. Protection of Species from Direct Interference

One central element of treaties aiming to protect a group of species is – not surprisingly – the reduction in killing or taking of said species. These provisions ban or restrict the taking, reduce possible harvesting to specific seasons, or prohibit certain methods of killing.[53] Such a protective stance is

---

51 *Millennium Ecosystem Assessment*, Ecosystems and Human Well-Being, Biodiversity Synthesis (2005) p. 10; *Pimm*, Stuart L., 'Biodiversity: Climate Change or Habitat Loss – Which Will Kill More Species?' 18 Current Biology 2008, R 117–R 119.

52 See for a critical assessment of the potential of international environmental agreements to effectively stop the loss of biodiversity and mass extinction of species: *Adam*, Rachelle, 'Missing the 2010 Biodiversity Target: A Wake-Up Call for the Convention on Biodiversity?' 21 Colorado Journal of International Environmental Law and Policy 2010, 123 (134–135) argues that the Convention on Biological Diversity is an example of a "myth of action", because it addresses the indicators of biodiversity loss, but not the underlying drivers. See also *Kunich*, John Charles, 'Losing Nemo: The Mass Extinction Now Threatening the World's Ocean Hotspots', 30 Columbia Journal of Environmental Law 2005, 1 (2–4), extensively arguing that international environmental conventions create "a dangerous placebo effect" that will not halt mass-extinction.

53 Prohibition of taking: Article IV para 2 lit a 1996 Inter-American Convention for the Protection and Conservation of Sea Turtles; Articles 1, 3 1973 Agreement on the Conservation of Polar Bears; Article 3 para 5 in connection with Appendix 1,

more difficult to implement with regard to heavily harvested species, like marine species. For these natural resources, international protection is regularly limited to an agreement on a management regime for the respective species. Such management regimes aim to implement the sustainable and optimum use of the resources;[54] albeit, the relevant data to establish the borders of sustainability are difficult to determine with regard to marine resources.[55]

The potential for collision of protective provisions concerning the intentional taking or harvesting of protected species with investment protection obligations appears rather limited. A direct prohibition of the harvesting of specific flora and fauna necessary for the investment activity would constitute a fundamental impact. However, such a scenario appears to be rather improbable. Although it is imaginable that an investment activity directly relates to the use of certain species thus requiring their harvesting, or that it relates to methods for harvesting certain fauna or flora, the probability of a conflict increases when a host state adopts regulation to reduce the unintentional killing of certain species.[56] From the point of view of the investor

---

Article 5 para 4 lit f 1979 Bonn Convention on Conservation of Migratory Species of Wild Animals; Article 6 in connection with Appendix II 1979 Berne Convention on the Conservation of European Wildlife; Articles 2, 1 1972 Convention for the Conservation of Antarctic Seals. See also Article 10 paras 2, 3 1990 Protocol Concerning Specially Protected Areas and Wildlife to the Convention for the Protection and Development of the Marine Environment of the Wider Caribbean Region; 1946 International Convention for the Regulation of Whaling, Schedule 10 lit e.

Harvesting seasons and prohibition of means of taking: Article 4 1973 Agreement on the Conservation of Polar Bears; Articles 7, 8 in connection with Appendix III 1979 Berne Convention on the Conservation of European Wildlife; Article IX para 3 2003 African Convention on the Conservation of Nature and Natural Resources.

54 Article 61 para 3 UNCLOS referring to the maximum sustainable yield; Articles 2, 5 1995 Agreement for the Implementation of the Provisions of the United Nations Convention on the Law of the Sea of 10 December 1982 Relating to the Conservation and Management of Straddling Fish Stocks and Highly Migratory Fish Stocks; Articles 2, 5 2000 Convention on the Conservation of Highly Migratory Fish Stocks in the Western and Central Pacific.

55 *Birnie*, Patricia/*Boyle*, Alan/*Redgwell*, Catherine, International Law and the Environment (2009) pp. 590–592. See for a critical assessment of the effectiveness of regulating of harvest of species, *Rayfuse*, Rosemary, 'Biological Resources', in: The Oxford Handbook of International Environmental Law (Bodansky, Daniel et al. (Eds.) Oxford: Oxford University Press, 2007) 362 (374–378).

56 The killing of animals as bycatch is a fundamental problem in marine fishing. States can adopt regulation requiring the observation of certain standards. A practical example is the obligation for certain methods of fishing to use turtle excluder devices, which allow sea turtles to escape from fishing nets, as it applies in the U.S. See also the obligation for states to regulate, to the extent possible, the inci-

regulation relating to the protection of species from unintentional killing does not differ from other restrictions on the manner in which the investment is conducted.

2. Habitat Preservation

What is far more important is potential interference with an investor's interests by rules aiming at habitat preservation. The natural habitats of species and the integrity of ecosystems often directly concur with industrial or other development projects. Territory is one factor in this concurrence. Another factor relates to the regulation of industrial and development activity: The investor has an interest in facing as little restriction as possible, whereas the integrity of the habitat generally requires strict regulation of potentially destructive activity.

An essential tool for habitat preservation contained in environmental agreements is the establishment of national reserves and protected areas.[57] The provisions aim to stimulate regulation which designates areas for preservation, in which the natural occurrence is protected from interference. The triggering factor for the designation is generally connected either to a specific type of ecosystem or land or to specific species deserving protection. Other concepts relating to habitat protection impose restrictions on the use of territory or on the installations allowed in certain territories. The implementation of rules severely restricting or prohibiting development and industrial activity is likely to clash with the interests of a foreign investor owning the land in question. Such clashes are featured in some

---

dental killing of relevant species in Article 10 para 3 1990 Protocol Concerning Specially Protected Areas and Wildlife to the Convention for the Protection and Development of the Marine Environment of the Wider Caribbean Region.

[57] Article 2 1940 Convention on Nature Protection and Wild Life Preservation in the Western Hemisphere; Article IV para 2 lit d, Annex 2 1996 Inter-American Convention for the Protection and Conservation of Sea Turtles; Article 10 1983 Convention for the Protection and Development of the Marine Environment of the Wider Caribbean Region; Articles 4, 6 1990 Protocol Concerning Specially Protected Areas and Wildlife to the Convention for the Protection and Development of the Marine Environment of the Wider Caribbean Region; Article XII 2003 African Convention on the Conservation of Nature and Natural Resources; Articles 2, 4 1971 Ramsar Convention on Wetlands of International Importance especially as Waterfowl Habitat; Articles 2, 3, 5 1972 Paris UNESCO Convention Concerning the Protection of the World Cultural and Natural Heritage. See also *Rayfuse*, Rosemary, 'Biological Resources', in: The Oxford Handbook of International Environmental Law (Bodansky, Daniel et al. (Eds.) Oxford: Oxford University Press, 2007) 362 (380–383).

investment arbitrations in the past.[58] Similar issues have influenced a recent investment decision.[59]

3. Indirect Impacts on Species

In addition to regulating direct impacts on certain species and their habitat, international conventions also address other factors indirectly influencing the preservation of species and biodiversity. The pollution of habitats

---

[58] Compañiá del Desarrollo de Santa Elena, S.A. v. Costa Rica, ICSID Case No. ARB/96/1, Final Award of 17 February 2000. The dispute concerned the amount of compensation to be paid to the investor that had bought land in an area which was subsequently expropriated to be part of a national park. See in more detail, 'Chapter 5 – Expropriation' at pp. 374 *et seq*., and Industria Nacional de Alimentos, S.A. and Indalsa Perú, S.A. (formerly Empresas Lucchetti, S.A. and Lucchetti Perú, S.A.) v. Republic of Peru, ICSID Case No. ARB/03/4, Award of 7 February 2005. The dispute concerned the withdrawal of the investor's licence to construct a pasta factory, because the plant infringed environmental rules and posed an imminent environmental threat to a nearby natural protected area. The dispute did not proceed to the merit stage for lack of jurisdiction.

See also the facts allegedly underlying the dispute *Harken Costa Rica Holdings v. Costa Rica*. Information about the case and the underlying facts is scarce in the public domain. According to *Juhasz*, 'Antonia, Democracy vs. Corporate Rule: How the Central American Free Trade Agreement (CAFTA) Allows Investor Rights to Trump the Public Interest', Statement of May 2004, available at: http://www.ifg.org/news/CaftaPress.html, the dispute was based on the following facts: The investor had obtained an agreement to drill for crude oil off the Costa Rican coast, subject to the outcome of an environmental impact assessment. The area intended for the drilling was in a region constituting reserves for three indigenous communities, a world heritage site, a national park, and a designated wetlands site. The impact assessment determined the incompatibility of the project with the environmental legislation, so that the drilling could not begin. The investor threatened to bring an investment dispute, demanding an amount equalling three times the annual GDP of Costa Rica. In the absence of a treaty allowing the investor to proceed to arbitration, the case never proceeded. See also the discussion of the impacts of this scenario by *Lindo*, Victoria R., 'Hydroelectric Power Production in Costa Rica and the Threat of Environmental Disaster through CAFTA', 29 Boston College International and Comparative Law Review 2006, 297 (311–312); *Jenkins*, Benjamin W., 'The Next Generation of Chilling Uncertainty: Indirect Expropriation under CAFTA and Its Potential Impact on Environmental Protection', 12 Ocean and Coastal Law Journal 2007, 269 (299–300). See also the analysis of the impact of the threat of arbitration in *Tienhaara*, Kyla, Expropriation of Environmental Governance: Protecting Foreign Investors at the Expense of Public Policy (2009) pp. 240–249.

[59] The decision in Marion Unglaube and Reinhard Unglaube v. Republic of Costa Rica, ICSID Case No. ARB/08/1, ICSID Case No. ARB/09/20, Award of 16 May 2012 concerned regulation prohibiting the development of land owned by foreign investors as part of a hotel complex for eco-tourism. The respondent state introduced legislation to expropriate land to protect the nearly-extinct leatherback turtle. See in more detail below in 'Chapter 5 – Expropriation' at pp. 336 *et seq.*

and of ecosystems is recognised as a fundamental issue.[60] The potential for collision between environmental and investment protection appears to be particularly relevant with regard to prohibitions on pollution. Industrial activity, land development projects, or undertakings relating to the extraction of resources all have the tendency to pollute and thereby destroy prior pristine land and ecosystems. Generally speaking, the lower the level of allowed pollution, the higher are the costs of the activity. International rules relating to the regulation of pollution are portrayed in the next section.

A further important aspect relates to trade in endangered species or their products. This issue is addressed by the 1973 Washington Convention on International Trade in Endangered Species of Wild Fauna and Flora.[61] The Convention classifies species – animals and plants – into three appendices according to the degree to which they are threatened with extinction and accordingly restricts trade by way of a permit system.[62] Albeit practical difficulties relating to the listing and de-listing of species – which is at least as political a decision as it is a scientific one –, the Convention is considered to be a successful instrument in furthering biological diversity within its limited ambit of application.[63] Restrictions on trade in endangered species are also incorporated in several regional agreements.[64] In comparison, the international conventions restricting the trade in certain species are far more relevant in the context of trade law than in connection with the rules

[60] See, for example, Article VI 2003 African Convention on the Conservation of Nature and Natural Resources.

[61] 1973 Washington Convention on International Trade in Endangered Species of Wild Fauna and Flora (CITES).

[62] Article 2 CITES: Trade in species listed in Appendix I, which are threatened with extinction, is prohibited. Species listed in Appendix II are not yet threatened with extinction, but could become so if trade is not monitored or controlled. Thus, trade in them is permitted, but subject to control. Specimen listed in Appendix III are subject to regulation in a national jurisdiction to prevent and restrict their exploitation for which co-operation of the parties is required. The procedure applying to trade with species in the respective categories are set forth in Articles 3–5.

[63] The Convention has a rather large number of parties, namely 180 (homepage of the Convention http://www.cites.org/eng/disc/parties/index.php, last visited 30 June 2014). Similarly and in more detail, *Birnie*, Patricia/*Boyle*, Alan/*Redgwell*, Catherine, International Law and the Environment (2009) pp. 685–692.

[64] Articles 2, 3 1979 Convenio para la Conservación y Manejo de la Vicuña; Articles 10, 11 1990 Protocol Concerning Specially Protected Areas and Wildlife to the Convention for the Protection and Development of the Marine Environment of the Wider Caribbean Region; Article XI 2003 African Convention on the Conservation of Nature and Natural Resources; Article IV para 2 lit a, b 1996 Inter-American Convention for the Protection and Conservation of Sea Turtles.

on foreign investment. Nevertheless, trade and investment implications are not mutually exclusive.[65]

The threat to biodiversity through the introduction of invasive species, albeit being addressed in some international conventions,[66] does not appear to belong to the core of international regulation. The introduction of invasive species might be commercially interesting, so that restrictions could clash with the intentions of foreign investors.[67]

II. Toxic Substances, Waste Disposal, and Hazardous Activities

Another thematic area of environmental law relates to toxic substances and their disposal and to hazardous activities. There are approximately 100,000 chemical substances in commerce, many of which appear as pollutants and contaminants in commercial products, food, and the various environmental media – even though data for risk assessment are often lacking.[68] Among these substances, pesticides constitute a significant subgroup due to their widespread application in high quantities.[69] In the light of increasing scientific acknowledgment as to their negative impacts on human health and the environment as well as to their relevant transboundary effects, toxic chemical substances are especially well-suited for international regulation.

For a long time, however, international efforts in this subject area were mainly characterised by non-binding instruments functioning as standards of

---

65 See as an illustration, S.D. Myers Inc. v. Canada, Partial Award on the Merits, 13 November 2000, para 247. See the detailed portrayal in 'Chapter 3 – Standards of Non-Discriminatory Treatment', footnote 55.

66 Article 8 lit h 1992 Convention on Biological Diversity; Article 196 UNCLOS; Article VIII lit b 2003 African Convention on the Conservation of Nature and Natural Resources.

67 See *Riley*, Sophie, 'A Weed by Any Other Name: Would the Rose Smell As Sweet if It Were a Threat to Biodiversity?', 22 Georgetown International Environmental Law Review 2009, 157–184, portraying the example of the introduction of certain alien species for use in biofuels. Given the economic potential of the production of biofuels, it is a possible scenario that such an activity attracts foreign investors.

68 Agenda 21 (UN Doc. A/CONF.151/26 (Vol. I), Annex 2), para 19.11.

69 See for an overview of the multiple fields of application of and the problems connected with the use of pesticides in developing countries, *Ross*, Jenifer, 'Legally Binding Prior Informed Consent', 10 Colorado Journal of International Environmental Law and Policy 1999, 499 (501–508).

good practice.[70] More recently, existing international conventions focus on two aspects: first, on regulation restricting or banning the production or release of certain toxic substances and second, on regulation relating to the trade in, and export of, toxic substances. The most important example of regulation of the first aspect is the 2001 Stockholm Convention on Persistent Organic Pollutants[71]. Persistent organic pollutants are chemical substances that possess toxic properties, resist degradation, and are prone to long-range transport to accumulate in terrestrial and aquatic ecosystems, predominantly in colder climates.[72] They bioaccumulate, hence, concentrate at higher levels in the food chain and are linked to the disruption of endocrine systems, cancer, birth-defects and immune-system deficiencies.[73] In applying a precautionary approach,[74] the convention reduces or bans the production or the release of the targeted chemicals at the domestic level.[75] It thus constitutes a harmonisation of national policies on the conditions of their use.[76] Furthermore, the convention articulates practices relating to existing stockpiles of the targeted substances.[77] The limitation of releases of persistent organic pollutants with an emphasis on the prevention of air pol-

---

70 See for an overview of diverse regional and global non-binding approaches, *Wirth*, David A., 'Hazardous Substances and Activities', in: The Oxford Handbook of International Environmental Law (Bodansky, Daniel et al. (Eds.) 2007) 394 (397–402, 404–405, 410–411).

71 2001 Stockholm Convention on Persistent Organic Pollutants entered into force in 2004 and currently has 179 parties (homepage of the Convention, http://chm.pops.int/Countries/StatusofRatifications/tabid/252/language/en-US/Default.aspx, last visited 30 June 2014).

See for a detailed portrayal of the regulation contained in the Convention, *Lallas*, Peter L., 'The Stockholm Convention on Persistent Organic Pollutants', 95 American Journal of International Law 2001, 692–708.

72 Preambular clause 1 2001 Stockholm Convention on Persistent Organic Pollutants; *Lallas*, Peter L., 'The Stockholm Convention on Persistent Organic Pollutants', 95 American Journal of International Law 2001, 692 (692, 694).

73 *Yoder*, Andrew J., 'Lessons From Stockholm: Evaluating the Global Convention on Persistent Organic Pollutants', 10 Indiana Journal of Global Legal Studies 2003, 113 (117–121); *Lallas*, Peter L., 'The Stockholm Convention on Persistent Organic Pollutants', 95 American Journal of International Law 2001, 692 (694).

74 Article 1 2001 Stockholm Convention on Persistent Organic Pollutants.

75 The Convention currently targets 21 persistent organic pollutants, falling into the categories pesticides (like DDT and lindane), industrial chemicals (like PCBs) and by-products. The production and use of these substances is either to be eliminated or restricted, or measures to reduce their unintentional production are to be taken (see Annexes A-C to the Convention).

76 *Wirth*, David A., 'Hazardous Substances and Activities', in: The Oxford Handbook of International Environmental Law (Bodansky, Daniel et al. (Eds.) 2007) 394 (403).

77 Article 6 2001 Stockholm Convention on Persistent Organic Pollutants.

lution is in a similar and complementary manner mandated by the regional 1998 Protocol on Persistent Organic Pollutants to the 1979 UNECE Convention on Long-Range Transboundary Air Pollution.[78]

The second focus of international regulation regarding toxics, which relates to trade and export, differentiates between substances exported for use as such and toxics contained in waste. This first group is regulated by the 1998 Rotterdam Convention.[79] The convention applies to a specific set of banned or severely restricted chemicals or pesticides.[80] Regarding the trade in these substances, the convention creates a procedure of prior informed consent. This obliges the importing state to indicate whether it wishes to ban or limit the import of specific chemicals and it obliges the exporting state – while complying with the criteria set by the importing state – to give prior notification of any export, provide required information, and await the consent of the importing state.[81] Although practical details of this regime are subject to criticism – especially because the system predominantly burdens the implementation of the system onto the importing, often developing, state –[82] the procedure of prior informed consent has relevant effects on the possibility to produce, use and trade in hazardous chemicals.

The second group regards the trade in hazardous waste. One problem addressed by international regulation relates to the concern that developed countries may choose to export their waste to developing countries, where hazardous waste will not be handled proficiently enough to prevent toxic impacts on the environment and on the health of inhabitants.[83] Regulating

78 1998 Aarhus Protocol to the 1979 UNECE Convention on Long-Range Transboundary Air Pollution on Persistent Organic Pollutants. The Protocol targets 16 substances and applies the same categories as the Stockholm Convention.

79 1998 Rotterdam Convention on the Prior Informed Consent Procedure for Certain Hazardous Chemicals and Pesticides in International Trade. The Convention entered into force in 2004 and currently has 154 parties (http://www.pic.int/Countries/Statusofratifications/tabid/1072/language/en-US/Default.aspx, last visited 30 June 2014).

80 Articles 2, 3, Annex III 1998 Rotterdam Convention on the Prior Informed Consent Procedure for Certain Hazardous Chemicals and Pesticides in International Trade.

81 Articles 10–12 1998 Rotterdam Convention on the Prior Informed Consent Procedure for Certain Hazardous Chemicals and Pesticides in International Trade.

82 *Emroy Jr.*, Richard W., 'Probing the Protections in the Rotterdam Convention on Prior Informed Consent', 2000 Colorado Journal of International Environmental Law and Policy 2000, 47 (52). See this article for further criticism of the provisions of the Convention. See also *Birnie*, Patricia/*Boyle*, Alan/*Redgwell*, Catherine, International Law and the Environment (2009) pp. 446–448 for critical assessment of the practical difficulties relating to the possibility to amend the listing in Annex III.

83 See paras 20.1, 20.3 Agenda 21. See also relevant Principle 14 Rio Declaration, stating the following: "States should effectively cooperate to discourage or

such trade in waste is the purpose of the 1989 Basel Convention,[84] which applies to hazardous waste and household waste.[85] The Convention focuses on the minimisation of generation and transboundary movements of hazardous waste,[86] for which it prescribes relevant restrictions[87] and sets forth a procedure of prior informed consent[88]. The Convention was amended by the 1995 Basel Ban, which prohibits the export of hazardous wastes intended for final disposal or recycling from developed to developing countries – however, this amendment has not yet entered into force.[89] In addition to the globally applicable 1989 Basel Convention there are several regional treaties relating to trade in hazardous waste.[90] In other contexts, waste disposal

---

prevent the relocation and transfer to other States of any activities and substances that cause severe environmental degradation or are found to be harmful to human health." See also *Kummer*, Katharina, 'The International Regulation of Transboundary Traffic in Hazardous Wastes: The 1989 Basel Convention', 41 The International and Comparative Law Quarterly 1992, 530 (535–536), stating that this North-South issue was the main focus of public attention in the negotiating process of the Basel Convention, despite the fact that the vast majority of transboundary waste movements takes place between industrialised nations.

84 1989 Basel Convention on the Control of Transboundary Movements of Hazardous Wastes and Their Disposal (Basel Convention). The Convention entered into force in 1992 and currently has 176 parties (homepage of the Convention, http://www.basel.int/ratif/convention.htm, last visited 30 June 2014).

85 Article 1 paras 1–2 1989 Basel Convention.

86 Article 4 1989 Basel Convention. These general obligations, inter alia, require the environmentally sound management of hazardous wastes, irrespective of their place of disposal (Article 4 para 8).

87 The Convention gives each state the sovereign right to decide on an import ban of such wastes, which has to be respected by the other parties (Article 4 paras 1–2). It prohibits the export of hazardous waste to non-parties unless the exporting and the importing states are party to an agreement setting forth standards of management of the wastes not less environmentally sound than those of the Basel Convention (Articles 4 para 5, 11).

88 Article 4 paras 1, 2, Articles 6, 7 1989 Basel Convention. The procedure of prior informed consent is strengthened by Articles 8 and 9, which stipulate the obligation to take waste back to the exporting country in cases of illegal traffic or in other situations in which the procedure cannot be completed.

See for a detailed overview of the procedure of prior informed consent, *Kummer*, Katharina, 'The International Regulation of Transboundary Traffic in Hazardous Wastes: The 1989 Basel Convention', 41 The International and Comparative Law Quarterly 1992, 530 (547–551).

89 1995 Basel Convention Ban Amendment (see http://www.basel.int/Countries/StatusofRatifications/BanAmendment/tabid/1344/Default.aspx, last visited 30 June 2014). *Sands*, Philippe/*Peel*, Jacqueline, Principles of International Environmental Law (2012) p. 571.

90 1991 Bamako Convention on the Ban of the Import into African and the Control of Transboundary Movement and Management of Hazardous Wastes Within Africa, which, inter alia, stipulates an import ban of hazardous waste (Article 4

is also subject to international agreements. Important regulation specifically relates to prohibitions of the disposing and dumping of wastes at sea, as well as to the pollution of the sea from land-based sources of pollution.[91]

A further connected aspect refers to international regulatory approaches to hazardous activities. International awareness in this subject area is connected to industrial activity and accidents.[92] Existing national regulation is complemented by international agreements seeking to set certain standards, which may lead to an adjustment of the former. Especially ultra-hazardous activities, like those connected to nuclear technology,[93] will have to be

---

para 1); 1985 Agreement of Cooperation between the United States of America and the United Mexican States Regarding the Transboundary Shipments of Hazardous Waste and Hazardous Substances, which, inter alia, stipulates a notification procedure (Article III) and an obligation of readmission of exports (Article IV); 1986 Agreement Between the Government of Canada and the Government of the United States of America Concerning the Transboundary Movement of Hazardous Waste, which, inter alia, sets forth a notification procedure (Article 3) and an obligation of readmission of exports (Article 6).

91 The major global convention relating to the dumping of wastes at sea is the 1972 London Convention on the Prevention of Marine Pollution by Dumping of Wastes and Other Matter. The convention applies a listing approach, according to which certain identified substances are prevented from dumping altogether, whereas the dumping of other substances requires an advance permit. The 1996 London Protocol to the London Convention prohibits dumping altogether, but contains a list of wastes acceptable for dumping. See also Articles 210, 216 UNCLOS.

Dumping and incineration at sea as well as pollution from land-based sources are also regulated by regional agreements like the 1995 Barcelona Protocol for the Prevention and Elimination of Pollution of the Mediterranean Sea by Dumping from Ships and Aircraft or Incineration at Sea; 1992 Convention for the Protection of the Marine Environment of the North-East Atlantic; 1992 Helsinki Convention on the Protection of the Marine Environment of the Baltic Sea Area; 1992 Convention on the Protection of the Black Sea Against Pollution. See also 1983 Convention for the Protection and Development of the Marine Environment of the Wider Caribbean Region; 1981 Abidjan Convention for Co-Operation in the Protection and Development of the Marine and Coastal Environment of the West and Central African Region; 1982 Jeddah Convention for the Conservation of the Red Sea and Gulf of Aden Environment. See also Articles 207, 213 UNCLOS. See for a comprehensive overview, *Birnie*, Patricia/*Boyle*, Alan/*Redgwell*, Catherine, International Law and the Environment (2009) pp. 451–472.

92 International regulation for accident prevention, preparedness and response was inspired by industrial accidents like the Bhopal/India and the Seveso/Italy incident, see the Directive 96/82/EC of 9 December 1996 (EC Seveso Directive) and the 1992 UNECE Convention on the Transboundary Effects of Industrial Accidents. Similarly, the Chernobyl emergency triggered a regulative response, *Sands*, Philippe/*Peel*, Jacqueline, Principles of International Environmental Law (2012) pp. 542–543.

93 See for a portrayal of the international regime relating to the radioactive substances, *Sands*, Philippe/*Peel*, Jacqueline, Principles of International Environmental Law (2012) pp. 536–546.

identified as such and heavily regulated. However, also new activities can be identified as having relevant hazardous implications. An important example is biotechnology. Threats to health and the environment posed by living genetically modified organisms are addressed by the 2000 Cartagena Protocol on Biosafety.[94] In applying a precautionary approach,[95] the Protocol sets up a system of advanced informed agreement,[96] differentiates between those living modified organisms intended for direct use as food or feed, or for processing,[97] and sets forth provisions relating to unintentional transboundary movements[98]. The threats and potentials of biotechnology are evaluated differently around the world,[99] so that changes to the relevant legal framework of a host state are likely.

The international regulation of toxic substances and waste disposal exemplifies the potential impact of multilateral environmental agreements on a foreign investor. The foreign investor has to accord with the obligations undertaken by the host state if these are properly implemented into national legislation. The overview of the above-mentioned conventions also illustrates the continuous raising of environmental standards and the increasing prohibitions of damaging conduct. Accordingly, an investment activity that did not counter international environmental standards at the time it started can be in conflict at a later point in time. Adjustments may also become necessary for the regulation of a hazardous activity.

It is not unusual for foreign investors to invest in activities which are connected to hazardous substances. This is the reason why some of the international conventions portrayed above have already featured in investment arbitration proceedings. One arbitral tribunal had to consider the impact of the 1989 Basel Convention on a host state's prohibition on the export

---

94 2000 Cartagena Protocol on Biosafety to the Convention on Biological Diversity (Cartagena Protocol). See Article 1 on the objective of the Protocol. According to its Article 4, the Protocol "shall apply to the transboundary movement, transit, handling and use of all living modified organisms that may have adverse effects on the conservation and sustainable use of biological diversity, taking also into account risks to human health."

95 Preambular clause 4, Article 1, Article 10 para 6, Article 11 para 8 Cartagena Protocol.

96 The advanced informed agreement procedure is very similar to the procedure of prior informed content. See Articles 7–10 Cartagena Protocol.

97 Article 11 Cartagena Protocol.

98 Article 17 Cartagena Protocol.

99 See, for example, the rather restrictive Euroepan approach expressed in Directive 2001/18/EC of 12 March 2001.

of PCB waste for disposal to another state.[100] Another investment tribunal had to deal with a host state's restrictions on the handling of the pesticide lindane, which is now – but was not at the time when the dispute arose – listed as a pesticide for elimination in the 2001 Stockholm Convention.[101] The tribunal took into account the continuing international discussion relating to the harmfulness of the substance.[102] Furthermore, national regulations relating to the construction and operation of waste disposal facilities have featured in investment disputes.[103]

III. Atmosphere and Climate Change

The last area of environmental concern to be briefly portrayed relates to the protection of the atmosphere and to the curbing of climate change. This subject area deserves special attention, first, because – despite the fact that public international law links sovereignty over the atmosphere to the territory underlying it –[104] activities impacting on the atmosphere or the climate have the same detrimental effect wherever they occur. A meaningful response to occurring problems thus necessitates the participation of all or most states. Accordingly, global climate change is considered to constitute 'the common concern of mankind'.[105] The consequential second reason for further elaboration lies in the on-going debate as to how the challenges posed by climate change can effectively be addressed. Furthermore, the

---

[100] S.D. Myers Inc. v. Canada, Partial Award on the Merits, 13 November 2000. See the detailed portrayal in 'Chapter 3 – Standards of Non-Discriminatory Treatment', pp. 176 *et seq.*

[101] Chemtura Corporation v. Government of Canada, Award of 2 August 2010. See the portrayal in 'Chapter 3 – Standards of Non-Discriminatory Treatment', pp. 255 *et seq.*

[102] Chemtura Corporation v. Government of Canada, Award of 2 August 2010, paras 135–136.

[103] Metalclad Corporation v. United Mexican States, ICSID Case No. ARB(AF)/97/1, Award of 30 August 2000; Técnicas Medioambientales Tecmed, S.A. v. United Mexican States, ICSID Case No. ARB (AF)/00/2, Award of 29 May 2003 (see 'Chapter 3 – Standards of Non-Discriminatory Treatment', pp. 261 *et seq.*, 271 *et seq.*).

[104] *Ipsen*, Knut, Völkerrecht (2004) § 23 II (Epping, Volker/Gloria, Christian); *Brownlie*, Ian, Principles of Public International Law (2008) p. 105.

[105] General Assembly Resolution, 'Protection of Global Climate for Present and Future Generations of Mankind', UN Doc. A/RES/43/53, 6 December 1988, para 1; Preambular Clause 1 1992 United Nations Framework Convention on Climate Change. Commentators have observed the difference between this terminology and the expression 'common heritage', which is used in conventions relating to the deep seabed and outer space; see *Birnie*, Patricia/*Boyle*, Alan/*Redgwell*, Catherine, International Law and the Environment (2009) pp. 338–339.

market-mechanisms introduced in this context can be relevant in connection with foreign investment.

The first international conventions charged with problems 'in the sky' concerned to the issue of transboundary air pollution. Their object was the reduction of pollutants released through industrial activity or accidents and of resulting deleterious impacts, which frequently occurred outside the territory of the polluting state. Tangible consequences of such emissions were phenomena like acid rain, increased acidity of soil and surface waters, and increased corrosion of surfaces.[106] Despite the understanding that public international law prohibits the causing of pollution in territories of other states,[107] international agreements were necessary to make states reduce such emissions.[108]

The global character of the atmosphere became more apparent in the challenge posed by the use of ozone-depleting substances and the resulting impact on the stratospheric ozone layer. Since the destructive effect of ozone-depleting substances occurred irrespective of where they were used and – albeit to different extents – all states were to be affected by the

---

106 *Kerr*, Richard A., 'There Is More to "Acid Rain" Than Rain', 211 Science 1981, 692–693; *Lee*, S.G./*Kang*, S.G., 'The Effects of Sulphur Dioxide on Atmospheric Corrosion of Galvanized Steel', 16 Journal of Materials Science Letters 1997, 902–905.

107 Trail Smelter Arbitration (U.S.A./Canada) Award of 16 April 1938 and 11 March 1941, 3 UN Reports of International Arbitral Awards 1905 (1965) holding that "under the principles of international law [...] no State has the right to use or permit the use of its territory in such a manner as to cause injury by fumes in or to the territory of another or the properties or persons therein, when the case is of serious consequence and the injury is established by clear and convincing evidence". This statement of the arbitral tribunal has been frequently relied on in subsequent decisions.

See also Principle 2 Rio Declaration, which provides in relevant part that "[s]tates have, in accordance with the Charter of the United Nations and the principles of international law [...] the responsibility to ensure that activities within their jurisdiction or control do not cause damage to the environment of other States or of areas beyond the limits of national jurisdiction."

108 An important regional agreement was the already above-mentioned 1979 Geneva Convention on Long-range Transboundary Air Pollution, which constitutes a framework agreement for co-operation and development of further measures of pollution control. This convention was complemented by two Protocols relating to the reduction of sulphur emissions, more importantly by the 1994 Protocol on Further Reduction of Sulphur Emissions, as well as by the 1988 Protocol Concerning the Control of Emissions of Nitrogen Oxides or Their Transboundary Fluxes. More recent protocols relate to heavy metals, persistent organic pollutants, ground-level ozone, and volatile organic compounds. See for a descriptive overview, *Sands*, Philippe/*Peel*, Jacqueline, Principles of International Environmental Law (2012), pp. 247–257; *Birnie*, Patricia/*Boyle*, Alan/*Redgwell*, Catherine, International Law and the Environment (2009) pp. 344–349.

depletion,[109] a legal regime could not work unless it was applied globally. The first step was undertaken by the 1985 Vienna Convention for the Protection of the Ozone Layer, which in itself constituted little more than an "empty framework"[110]. However, with the 1987 Montreal Protocol to the Convention the participating states undertook commitments regarding restrictions on the production and the use of relevant substances; they regulated trade and introduced a mechanism for financial assistance for developing countries.[111] The Montreal Protocol is generally considered to be a particularly successful international environmental agreement, which had an essential influence on the significant decrease in the world-wide use of ozone-depleting substances and the resulting estimated recovery of stratospheric ozone levels by 2050.[112]

The most challenging task of the international community in relation to the environment and the atmosphere to date is doubtlessly tackling global climate change. As the emission of greenhouse gases – stemming primarily from the combustion of fossil fuels – is intrinsically connected with economic development, the implementation of an international regime is confronted with severe difficulties. The process commenced with the entry into force of the 1992 United Nations Framework Convention on Climate Change (UNFCCC), which established the aim of a "stabili[s]ation of greenhouse gas concentrations […] that would prevent dangerous anthropogenic interference with the climate system"[113]. While this framework convention sets forth certain principles and obligations for its parties,[114] the

---

109 See for a comprehensive assessment of the causes and effects of the depletion of the stratospheric ozone layer, *Dameris*, Martin/*Peter*, Thomas/*Schmidt*, Ulrich/*Zellner*, Reinhard, 'Das Ozonloch und seine Ursachen', 41 Chemie in unserer Zeit 2007, 152–168.

110 *Birnie*, Patricia/*Boyle*, Alan/*Redgwell*, Catherine, International Law and the Environment (2009) p. 350.

111 Articles 2–2 H 1987 Montreal Protocol on Substances that Deplete the Ozone Layer relating to the restrictions on use and production of CFCs, Halons, Hydrochlorofluorocarbons, and other substances; Articles 4-4 B of the Protocol regulating trade with non-parties and parties; Articles 5, 10 relating to the financial assistance to developing countries. In addition, Article 8 of the Protocol, together with Decision II/5 of the Second Meeting of the Parties to the Protocol, UNEP/OzL.Pro.2/3, 29 June 1990), Decision IV/5 and Annexes IV, V of the Fourth Meeting of the Parties to the Protocol, UNEP/OzL.Pro.4/15, 25 November 1992 set up a non-compliance procedure.

112 See the assessment in *Birnie*, Patricia/*Boyle*, Alan/*Redgwell*, Catherine, International Law and the Environment (2009) p. 355. The Montreal Protocol is currently ratified by 197 states (http://ozone.unep.org/new_site/en/treaty_ratification_status.php, last visited 30 June 2014).

113 Article 2 1992 United Nations Framework Convention on Climate Change (UNFCCC).

more relevant rules are contained in its 1997 Kyoto Protocol. The Protocol identifies six targeted greenhouse gases and their relevant sources.[115] It further emphasises the importance of removal of greenhouse gases by sinks. Most importantly, industrialised economies committed to specific quantitative reductions of their emissions of greenhouse gases,[116] while developing countries do not have a comparable obligation[117]. Furthermore, the Protocol introduced the so-called flexibility mechanisms, which enable the committing states to meet their commitments in a cost-effective manner through the application of market-based instruments.[118]

These market-based mechanisms effectively created what is known as the carbon market. One important element of potential relevance to foreign investors is the procedure and functioning of the Clean Development Mechanism.[119] The Mechanism is a procedure through which entities –

---

114 The UNFCCC sets forth the principle of common but differentiated responsibilities (Article 3, 4), the notion of precaution (Article 3), emphasises the importance of sustainability (Articles 2, 3) and of flexibility in the undertaking commitments (Article 4). Article 4, entitled Commitments, further imposes certain obligations on the state parties.

115 Annex A 1997 Kyoto Protocol. The targeted greenhouse gases are carbon dioxide, methane, nitrous oxide, hydrofluorocarbons, perfluorocarbons, and sulphur hexafluoride. The sources identified stem from the following sectors: energy, industrial processes, solvent and product use, agriculture, and waste. The Kyoto Protocol is currently ratified by 192 parties (http://unfccc.int/kyoto_protocol/status_of_ratifi cation/items/2613.php, last visited 30 June 2014).

116 Article 3 1997 Kyoto Protocol in connection with its Annex B. For the commitment period 2008 to 2012, the overall aim is to reduce the emission of greenhouse gases by at least 5 per cent below their 1990 levels.

Parties that committed to such emission reductions are effectively 'Annex B parties'. However, the Kyoto Protocol itself uses the terminology of the Framework Convention and refers to 'Annex I parties'. Even though this terminology lacks precision – most notably the U.S. is an Annex I party, but in the absence of a ratification of the Protocol not an Annex B party – it will mainly be used in the following to reflect the terminology of the Protocol.

117 Article 10 1997 Kyoto Protocol.

118 The Kyoto Protocol introduces three flexibility mechanisms: one is Joint Implementation (Article 6), which allows entities of Annex I parties to participate in low-carbon projects located in other Annex I countries (i. e. industrialised countries) to receive Emission Reduction Units. The second mechanism is the Clean Development Mechanism (Article 12), which allows entities from Annex I Parties to participate in low-carbon projects in non-Annex I parties (i. e. developing countries) to obtain Certified Emissions Reductions. The third flexibility mechanism is Emissions Trading (Article 17), which allows those parties that have committed to a specific reduction to sell spare emission units to other Annex B countries, which have exceeded their emission targets.

119 The portrayal does not feature the Joint Implementation mechanism, because questions arising in connection with the legal position of a foreign investor do not

state, non-governmental organisations, or private companies and investors –[120] of Annex I parties, i.e. industrialised states, can register a project that reduces the emissions of greenhouse gases in a non-Annex I country, i.e. in a developing country,[121] to earn Emission Reduction Credits for its execution.[122] The Credits are valuable because they can be used by Annex B parties, i.e. states that committed to emission reduction, to partly offset their domestic emissions.[123] The implementation of a low-carbon project to earn Emission Reduction Credits is referred to as the primary carbon market. There is also a secondary carbon market, which relates to the trading in existing Credits, which are sold and bought by states or private entities obliged by national regulation to limit their emissions.[124]

---

differ substantially. Neither are there relevant legal differences relating to the resulting carbon credits, here called Emission Reduction Units. The Clean Development Mechanism was chosen because it is by far the more frequently used mechanism of the two.

120 The range of possible project developers is vast: governmental bodies, municipalities, foundations, financial institutions, private sector companies, and non-governmental organisations. See *United Nations Development Programme* (UNDP), 'Clean Development Mechanism: A User's Guide' (2003) at http://content.undp.org/go/newsroom/publications/environment-energy/www-ee-library/climate-change/undp-cdm-manual.en p. 20.

121 The participation in the Clean Development Mechanism is voluntary. A state wishing to participate designates a competent national authority. This designated national authority declares its approval prior to the registration of a project and the national authority of the host state declares that the project contributes to sustainable development. Proposed Clean Development Mechanism activities are validated by designated operational entities. These legal entities are independent and accountable to the treaty bodies of the Protocol through the Kyoto executive board. The executive board registers a proposed low-emission project. The designated operational entity validates and monitors the implementation of projects and verifies their emission reductions. It is important that the project activity is 'additional', meaning that anthropogenic emissions of greenhouse gases are reduced below those that would have occurred in the absence of the registered project activity. See in detail, 2001 Marrakech Accords, especially J, number 3, Modalities and procedures for a clean development mechanism as defined in Article 12 of the Kyoto Protocol (Decision 7/CP.4, FCCC/CP/1998/16/Add.1, 14 November 1998 and Decision 14/CP.5, FCCC/CP/1999/6/Add.1, 4 November 1999) and the respective Annex.

122 Prior to the issuance of Certified Emission Credits, the project and its emission reductions are verified and certified by the designated operational entity. The possibility for a review in cases of fraud, malfeasance, or incompetence of the designated operational exists. On the basis of the verification report, the Credits are issued under the authority of the executive body. See in detail, 2001 Marrakech Accords, especially J, number 3, Modalities and procedures for a clean development mechanism as defined in Article 12 of the Kyoto Protocol (Decisions 7/CP.4 and 14/CP.5) and the respective Annex, paras 61–66.

123 Article 12 para 3 Kyoto Protocol.

Closely connected to the regulations of the Kyoto Protocol is the European Emissions Trading Scheme. To comply with its arising emission reduction obligations,[125] the European Union introduced a cap-and-trade scheme, according to which the greenhouse gas emissions of certain industries and sectors were capped and the market participants could trade in emission allowances.[126] The respective allowances are allocated according to national allocation plans. The Scheme explicitly allows for the use of Credits earned under the flexibility mechanisms of the Kyoto Protocol, such as the Clean Development Mechanism. Despite being the biggest and most important regional trading scheme, the European Emissions Trading Scheme is not the only one.[127]

Such cap-and-trade systems exemplify both the risks and the potential of the implementation of regulation relating to climate change: The capping element, coupled with permit requirements, potentially impacts on an existing investment by a foreign investor. The former freedom of the investor to pollute is restricted through the implementation of such a cap: the schemes aim to consecutively reduce the emission allowance of each polluter to reach an overall reduction in emissions. Accordingly, levels of greenhouse gas emissions that were formerly freely available to the investor will commence to cost money. On the other hand, the trading aspect of such a scheme – as well as the creation of tradable Credits under the Clean Devel-

---

124 See for a comprehensive discussion of the nature of Certified Emission Reductions in relation to the categories of 'commodity' or 'currency', *Weber*, Rolf H./*Darbellay*, Aline, 'Regulation and Financial Intermediation in the Kyoto Protocol's Clean Development Mechanism', 22 Georgetown International Environmental Law Review 2010, 271 (286–290). A brief overview of the current state of secondary or spot carbon market is provided by *Kossoy*, Alexandre/*Ambrosi*, Philippe, State and Trends of the Carbon Market 2010 (2010) pp. 14–15.

125 The European Union as a whole as well as its member states individually are obliged to meet their respective emission targets, *Posser*, Herbert/*Altenschmidt*, Stefan, 'European Union Emissions Trading Directive', 23 Journal of Energy & Natural Resources Law 2005, 60 (61–62).

126 Directive 2003/87/EC of the European Parliament and the Council of 13 October 2003, establishing a scheme for greenhouse gas emission allowance trading within the Community and amending Council Directive 96/61/EC, amended through Directive 2009/29/EC of the European Parliament and of the Council of 23 April 2009. See for a comprehensive overview, *Posser*, Herbert/*Altenschmidt*, Stefan, 'European Union Emissions Trading Directive', 23 Journal of Energy & Natural Resources Law 2005, 60–72.

127 Similar schemes exist, for example, in New Zealand, in Northeastern States of the U.S. (called Regional Greenhouse Gas Initiative), and in New South Wales (Australia). A voluntary system is the Chicago Climate Exchange. See for an overview of further initiatives *Kossoy*, Alexandre/*Ambrosi*, Philippe, State and Trends of the Carbon Market 2010 (2010) pp. 23–35.

opment Mechanism – opens up new investment possibilities to foreign investors. Tradable carbon credits, in the primary and in the secondary carbon market, can be considered as investment qualifying for protection under investment treaties.[128] Practically, investment in certain energy projects will become more economically interesting. However, in the context of investment in carbon credits or in their production, a multitude of possible conflicts can arise.[129]

In addition to the rather technical considerations relating to cap-and-trade schemes and systems regulating the allocation of carbon credits, the international initiatives to prevent climate change and mitigate its consequences have further practical implications for foreign investment. States will aim to promote low-carbon industries and to support the development of energy-efficient technologies and of technical equipment which is less reliant on fossil fuels.[130] The offer of subsidies or other incentives for such industries can have implications both for foreign investors in industries not fulfilling the criteria for such support and for foreign investors investing because of the implementation of such a support scheme. Finally, a more practical

---

128 *Bennett*, Lisa, 'Are tradable Carbon Emissions Investments? Characterization and Ramifications under International Investment Law', 85 New York University Law Review 2010, 1581 (1609–1610).

129 Regarding the creation of carbon credits in the primary carbon market, relevant risks for the investor relate to possible interference by the host state: Although the procedure for the verification is independent of the host state, the state obviously has the possibility to hinder and restrict the activity of the investor in a way that the low-carbon activity is less efficient than it was planned to be. This could result in a relevant impact on the amount of Credits allocated at the end of the project.

Nevertheless, the rules of procedure laid down in the Marrakech Accords require the host state to give its prior agreement to the project which cannot be withdrawn unilaterally afterwards. It also appears that there is little incentive for a host state to hinder the success of such a project, since the host state has to consider the project as contribution to sustainable development prior to its acceptance.

More important are regulations relating to the secondary carbon market, which states are at more liberty to introduce. This could be regulation that discounts the value of certain emission reduction credits. Alternatively, the market could become less attractive due to changes in rules and regulations. These issues will be addressed in hypothetical scenarios in the following chapters.

130 Several states have adopted regulation to partly subsidise investments in renewable energies. In Germany, for example, a wide range of technologies, like solar panels or biogas plants are eligible for subsidies (see, for example, Bundesrepublik Deutschland, Richtlinien zur Förderung von Maßnahmen zur Nutzung erneuerbarer Energien im Wärmemarkt, 20 July 2012). For more commercial purposes, states often use feed-in tariffs for energy created through low-carbon technology. This offers investors a guaranteed payment from an electricity supplier for the electricity they generate.

point should be mentioned: One effect of the restriction of greenhouse gas emissions in industrialised countries was the outsourcing of greenhouse gas intensive production to developing countries, where it would not face similar restrictions.[131] Thus, it is probable that the Kyoto Protocol – as an unintended by-effect – has caused a further influx of foreign investment in developing countries.

The global fight against climate change has not been concluded with the adoption of the Kyoto Protocol, which remains to date the most important legally binding international convention in this context. Following-up initiatives did not have the success hoped for.[132] Whereas the Protocol and its mechanisms have their deficiencies, the most important limitation to effectiveness is that too few countries committed to reductions and that the commitments undertaken are not onerous enough. With the ending of the first commitment period, the Protocol had to be extended to 2020 – for lack of agreement on a new instrument. With the prospects for the future of the Protocol being unclear, there are twofold consequences for foreign investment. First, foreign investors in any industry connected to the emission of greenhouse gases are to expect new and differing regulation regarding their investment activity. Second, investments connected to the carbon market or incentivised for promoting low-carbon technology are confronted with a specific and potentially dangerous degree of uncertainty.

IV. Intermediate Summary

Environmental law is an agglomeration of diverse subject areas. Varied as these areas may be, they are tied together by the interconnectedness of the 'environment' itself: Because of its holistic nature, environmental degradation cannot be sufficiently protected against by focusing on distinct impacts and dangers. The conservation of biological diversity, the regulation of toxic substances and the safeguarding of the climate are three examples

131 *Birnie*, Patricia/*Boyle*, Alan/*Redgwell*, Catherine, International Law and the Environment (2009) pp. 357–358. The phenomenon is referred to as "carbon leakage", which means that an emission-causing activity is relocated from a place with emissions-restrictions to a place without a similar policy. See for more detail, *Peretz*, Neil, 'Carbon Leakage under the European Union Emissions Trading Scheme: Is It a Major Policy Concern?', 23 Tulane Environmental Law Journal 2009, 57–91.

132 The sixteenth session of the Conference of the Parties to the UNFCCC and the sixth session of the Conference of the Parties serving as the Meeting of the Parties to the Kyoto Protocol took place in Cancun, Mexico in November 2010 has not provided a coherent follow-up mechanism for the Kyoto Protocol. See for the modest outcome of the conference, FCCC/KP/CMP/2010/12/Add.1 of 15 March 2011.

of areas of environmental concern. They exemplify that environmental protection has to take account of the multiple directions from which an environmental good is threatened.

However, the portrayed international agreements also demonstrate that regulating threats to the environment always goes in hand with a restriction of freedom. International environmental agreements restrict a state party's liberty to pollute and to let its subjects go about their business without supervision and control. Implementing environmental regulation requires an institutional effort that a state is generally only willing to undertake when its benefits outweigh the negative consequences. This is why international agreements are easier to reach in some subject areas than in others. Nevertheless, international as well as national regulation of environmental aspects is continuously increasing. Environmental regulation, such as bans, restriction or permit requirements, affects the economic activity of every individual in a given state. Consequently, the freedom foreign investors enjoy in planning and executing their investment activities is increasingly restricted.

D. Fundamental Principles of Environmental Law

This section provides an overview over three fundamental principles of international environmental law.[133] The first principle is the concept of sustainable development, which aims to reconcile environmental, economic, and social factors. Part of its relevance stems from its incorporation into a multitude of international – not only environmental – agreements. It is, for example, referred to in several investment agreements.[134] The second principle is the precautionary principle, which provides guidance as to the implementation of protective measures in the light of scientific uncertainty. Third, the polluter-pays principle and its implications are portrayed. These principles of international environmental law can influence the interpretation of the scope of the rules of investment protection. The impact of these principles depends on several factors, like the status of the respective principle in customary international law, or the existence of a specific reference in the underlying investment treaty. Otherwise, the content of such a principle could simply be reflected in a national environmental regulation of the host state.

---

133 See *Sands*, Philippe/*Peel*, Jacqueline, Principles of International Environmental Law (2012) pp. 187–237, for a comprehensive overview of principles and rules of international environmental law.

134 See the portrayal in 'Chapter 2 – The Influence of Environmental Concepts on the Interpretation of Investment Provisions', pp. 106 *et seq*.

I. Sustainable Development

The concept of sustainable development incorporates the understanding that economic activity and environmental considerations are intertwined and should be approached in a holistic manner. References to sustainable development have been included in a myriad of international resolutions and instruments and in international environmental agreements for over two decades.[135] Nevertheless, sustainable development is not a clearly defined and precise concept. It encapsulates several notions, which differ in significance according to the context in which the principle is invoked. Given the multiple dimensions of sustainable development, definitions tend to

---

135 The term 'sustainable development' was first prominently used in the Report of the *World Commission on Environment and Development*, 'Our Common Future – the Brundtland Report' (1987) Annex to UN Doc A/42/427. It defined sustainable development as development which meets the needs of the present generation without compromising the needs of future generations (Part 1, Chapter 2, para 1).

Sustainable development featured markedly in the United Nations Conference on Environment and Development in 1992. The adopted Rio Declaration sets forth a multitude of principles dealing with sustainable development. Furthermore, Agenda 21 describes elements of sustainable development in more detail. For example, it highlights the goal of 'mutual supportiveness' of trade and environment (Section 1, Chapter 2).

Sustainable development is also one of the key concepts of the General Assembly Resolution, 'United Nations Millennium Declaration', UN Doc. A/RES/55/2, 18 September 2000. Also, the World Summit on Sustainable Development, 'Plan of Implementation of the World Summit on Sustainable Development', UN Doc. A/CONF.199/20, 4 September 2002 dealt with specific challenges to sustainable development and, inter alia, devoted a section to sustainable development in a globalising world, where the interaction with the world's trade regime was discussed (paras 47–52). A further detailed attempt at identifying principles relevant to the concept of sustainable development was made by the *International Law Association*, 'New Delhi Declaration of Principles of International Law Relating to Sustainable Development', 2 April 2002, 2 International Environmental Agreements: Politics, Law and Economics 2002, 211–216. It identified sustainable development as a key element of the framework of United Nations activities (para 10). It further recognised the "three components of sustainable development – economic development, social development and environmental protection – as interdependent and mutually reinforcing pillars" (para 48).

For a more detailed description of the above, see *Barstow Magraw*, Daniel/*Hawke*, Lisa D., 'Sustainable Development', in: The Oxford Handbook of International Environmental Law (Bodansky, Daniel et al. (Eds.) 2007) 613 (614–618).

In addition to these reports and resolutions aiming to capture the content of the concept of sustainable development, the concept was referenced in a multitude of international agreements. Prominent examples are the 1992 UNFCCC and its 1997 Kyoto Protocol, the 1992 Convention on Biological Diversity and its 2000 Cartagena Protocol, and the 1994 Marrakesh Agreement Establishing the World Trade Organisation.

focus on the human, environmental, or economic dimension or a combination thereof.[136]

Despite the lack of one commonly accepted definition, it has been suggested that all approaches show common characteristics which specifically stress the "linkage between economic development and environmental standards in the context of human social conditions".[137] In this light, commentators have identified four characterising elements of sustainable development, which are

- the principle of inter-generational equity, which seeks to take the needs of future generations into account;
- the principle of intra-generational equity, which implies that the needs of other states and especially those of the world's poor have to be considered;
- the principle of sustainable use, which aims to preserve natural resources at a significant level; and
- the principle of integration, which aims to consolidate economic, environmental and social policies.[138]

For the scope of this study,[139] the relevant impact of the principle of sustainable use and of the principle of inter-generational equity can be plainly translated into the basic perception that the environment has to be

---

136 *Sands*, Philippe, 'International Law in the Field of Sustainable Development', 65 British Yearbook of International Law 1994, 303 (317).

137 *Sands*, Philippe, 'International Law in the Field of Sustainable Development', 65 British Yearbook of International Law 1994, 303 (318). See also General Assembly Resolution, 'World Summit Outcome', UN Doc. A/RES/60/1, 24 October 2005, para 48, which stresses the interdependence and mutual reinforcement of the three components – economic development, social development, and environmental protection.

138 *Sands*, Philippe/*Peel*, Jacqueline, Principles of International Environmental Law (2012), pp. 215–217; *Barstow Magraw*, Daniel/*Hawke*, Lisa D., 'Sustainable Development', in: The Oxford Handbook of International Environmental Law (Bodansky, Daniel et al. (Eds.) 2007) 613 (619); *Birnie,* Patricia/*Boyle,* Alan/*Redgwell,* Catherine, International Law and the Environment (2009) pp. 116–123.

139 More subtle implications of the principle of sustainable use and of the principle of inter-generational equity are largely outside the scope of this study. Such notions could be used as justifications for the implementation of an environmental policy at the national level which aims to protect certain resources. Accordingly, they could also feature as a philosophical basis to defend a specific environmental regulation in an investment dispute. A state could argue that it has to protect certain areas of its land or specific species to the detriment of the foreign investor, because the use that the investor intended would not be sustainable and impact on the ability to leave a substantial level of the said resource for future generations. However, to my knowledge, such an argument has not yet been made in an investment dispute.

protected. In the words of Principle 11 of the 1992 Rio Declaration on Environment and Development this understanding is framed as follows:

> "States shall enact effective environmental legislation. Environmental standards, management objectives and priorities should reflect the environmental and development context to which they apply [...]."[140]

Accordingly, states are obliged to adopt and apply environmental legislation. What meets the requirements of this principle will depend on the individual conditions prevailing in each state: the environmental context, i.e. the environmental resources and species differ and might require different forms and degrees of protection. Also, a highly developed country can be expected to devote more resources to the aim of protecting the environment than a country that struggles to fulfil the most basic needs of its citizens. The formulation used by Principle 11 also emphasises the understanding that the environmental standards applied by a state are subject to change. The level of protection required is influenced by changing factors inherent in the environmental and development progress. This element of volatility is important for the overall amelioration of environmental protection, but is also a reason for potential tensions between a national environmental legislation and the regime for the protection of foreign investments, of which stability and predictability are important factors.

This tension is envisaged in the principle of integration, which is the most significant[141] of the above elements in the context of this study:[142] Integration aims to reconcile environmental considerations with economic

---

[140] Principle 11 1992 Rio Declaration.

[141] *Sands*, Philippe/*Peel*, Jacqueline, Principles of International Environmental Law (2012) p. 215, believe that this element in many ways is the most significant and legalistic of the elements of sustainable development. Similarly, *Lowe*, Vaughan, 'Sustainable Development and Unsustainable Arguments', in: International Law and Sustainable Development: Past Achievements and Future Challenges (Boyle, Alan et al. (Eds.) 1999) 19 (26), states that the idea of reconciliation is "clearly central" to sustainable development. See also ICJ Case Concerning the Gabčíkovo-Nagymaros Project (Hungary/Slovakia) Separate Opinion of Judge Weeramantry, ICJ Reports 1997, 88 (90), stating that the principle of sustainable development essentially is the principle of reconciliation.

[142] The remaining principle of intra-generational equity is unlikely to become relevant in a specific conflict between the rules of investment protection and environmental protection. It appears, however, that this element could function as an argumentative tool for the modification of the rules of investment protection, to give more leeway to developing states. Such a need is acknowledged – without express reference to the principle of inter-generational equity – by *Mayeda*, Graham, 'International Investment Agreements Between Developed and Developing Countries: Dancing With the Devil? Case Comment on the Vivendi, Sempra and Enron Awards', 4 Mc Gill International Journal of Sustainable Development Law and Policy 2008, 189–230.

development, so that the respective conflicting needs are taken into account in the decision-making process. The premise is that neither economic development – of which foreign investment is undoubtedly a component –[143] nor environmental protection should be assessed independently of each other. The concept of integration is portrayed in Principle 4 of the 1992 Rio Declaration, which reads as follows:

> "In order to achieve sustainable development, environmental protection shall constitute an integral part of the development process and cannot be considered in isolation from it."[144]

It has been commentated that this provision "creates the possibility of moving environmental considerations and objectives from the periphery of international relations to the economic core".[145] Understood in this way, the principle of integration calls for environmental protection to be considered in economic activity related to development. It thus demands that decision makers in an economic context – like arbitrators in an investment dispute – conceive their subject area as not being isolated from environmental protection.

Sustainable development is considered the root of a number of substantial principles that influence states in their decision-making process: Even though there may not be an obligation for development itself to be sustainable, there is a requirement for development decisions to be the outcome of a process promoting sustainable development.[146] Principles and techniques to be applied in this context are, inter alia: environmental impact assessments,[147] the duty to co-operate to mitigate transboundary and global

---

143 The preambles of BITs regularly mention that the flow of investment will "stimulate the economic development" of the parties, that it will "increase the prosperity" of both nations, or use a different expression to this end. See for the former formulation 2004 Model U.S. BIT, for the latter, for example, 2008 German Model BIT; Germany-Bosnia and Herzegovina BIT; Germany-Albania BIT; 2007 Colombia Model BIT; 1991 Argentina-Chile BIT.

See also General Assembly Resolution, 'World Summit Outcome', UN Doc. A/RES/60/1, 24 October 2005, para 25. Furthermore, the importance of, inter alia, foreign investment for achieving sustainable development is acknowledged in Agenda 21, para 2.23.

144 Principle 4 Rio Declaration.

145 *Sands*, Philippe, 'International Law in the Field of Sustainable Development', 65 British Yearbook of International Law 1994, 303 (334).

146 *Birnie*, Patricia/*Boyle*, Alan/*Redgwell*, Catherine, International Law and the Environment (2009) pp. 126–127.

147 Principle 17 Rio Declaration; ICJ Case Concerning Pulp Mills on the River Uruguay (Argentina/Uruguay) Judgment of 20 April 2010, ICJ Reports 2010, 14 (83) para 204, stating that "it may now be considered a requirement under general international law to undertake an environmental impact assessment where there is a

environmental risks,[148] public participation,[149] the precautionary principle[150] and the polluter-pays principle[151].

The increasing recognition of existing linkages between subject areas addressed in international treaties counters the perception of areas of public international law as being self-contained and in isolation from each other.[152]

---

risk that the proposed industrial activity may have a significant adverse impact in a transboundary context, in particular, on a shared resource."

Case Concerning the Gabčíkovo-Nagymaros Project (Hungary/Slovakia) Judgment of 25 September 1997, ICJ Reports 1997, 7 (78) para. 140, expressing that the "need to reconcile economic development with protection of the environment" required the states involved to "look afresh at the effects on the environment of the operation of the Gabčíkovo power plant"; Case Concerning the Gabčíkovo-Nagymaros Project (Hungary/Slovakia) Separate Opinion of Judge Weeramantry, ICJ Reports 1997, 88 (111–113).

ECtHR Case of Hatton and Others v. United Kingdom (Application no. 36022/97) Grand Chamber Judgment of 8 July 2003, para 128; ECtHR Case of Taşkin and Others v. Turkey (Application no. 46117/99) Judgment of 10 November 2004, para 119; *Barstow Magraw*, Daniel/*Hawke*, Lisa D., 'Sustainable Development', in: The Oxford Handbook of International Environmental Law (Bodansky, Daniel et al. (Eds.) 2007) 613 (635–637).

148 Principle 27 1992 Rio Declaration; ITLOS MOX-Plant Case, Case No 10 (Ireland v. United Kingdom) Order of 3 December 2001, para 89 and the relating MOX Plant Case, Case No 10 (Ireland v. United Kingdom) Order No 3 of 24 June 2003, paras 66, 67; Arbitration Regarding the Iron Rhine Railway (Ijzeren Rijn) (Belgium/Netherlands) Decision of 24 May 2005, paras 59, 222, 223; ITLOS, Southern Bluefin Tuna Case, Cases No 3 and 4 (New Zealand, Australia v. Japan) Order of 27 August 1999, para 78.

149 Principle 10 Rio Declaration; UNECE Convention on Access to Information, Public Participation in Decision-Making and Access to Justice in Environmental Matters (1998 Aarhus Convention); Article 9 1992 Convention for the Protection of the Marine Environment of the North-East Atlantic (OSPAR-Convention); Principle 5 *International Law Association*, 'New Delhi Declaration of Principles of International Law Relating to Sustainable Development', 2 April 2002, 2 International Environmental Agreements: Politics, Law and Economics 2002, 211 (213). ECtHR Case of Taşkin and Others v. Turkey (Application no. 46117/99) Judgment of 10 November 2004, paras 118–199; ECtHR Case of Guerra v. Italy (Application no. 116/1996/735/932) Grand Chamber Judgment of 19 February 1998; *Barstow Magraw*, Daniel/*Hawke*, Lisa D., 'Sustainable Development', in: The Oxford Handbook of International Environmental Law (Bodansky, Daniel et al. (Eds.) 2007) 613 (633–635); see for further details *Birnie*, Patricia/*Boyle*, Alan/*Redgwell*, Catherine, International Law and the Environment (2009) pp. 288–298.

150 Principle 15 Rio Declaration; *Barstow Magraw*, Daniel/*Hawke*, Lisa D., 'Sustainable Development', in: The Oxford Handbook of International Environmental Law (Bodansky, Daniel et al. (Eds.) 2007) 613 (631–632).

151 Principle 16 Rio Declaration; *Sands*, Philippe, 'International Law in the Field of Sustainable Development', 65 British Yearbook of International Law 1994, 303 (338).

152 See in 'Chapter 2 – The Influence of Environmental Concepts on the Interpretation of Investment Provisions', p. 95 *et seq.*; *Sands*, Philippe, 'Sustainable

Sustainable development – and especially its principle of integration – is an explicit manifestation of the existence of such linkages between areas of international law relating to economic, environmental, and social influences. The recognition of these subject areas as being mutually reinforcing, integral concepts results in a duty to prevent, or at least mitigate harm done to the environment through development – a duty that arguably has attained the status of a 'principle of general international law'.[153]

Despite references to sustainable development in multiple international documents and international decisions, there remains considerable debate as to its legal status. While some commentators believe that the concept is part of customary international law,[154] it was also argued that sustainable development lacks the fundamentally norm-creating character essential for a "primary rule of international law".[155] However, even such an appreciation does not render sustainable development meaningless: practice shows that the principle and its elements are important components for states to take account of in the implementation and application of their economic undertakings as well as in the interpretation and development process of international agreements and general international law.[156] One commentator termed

---

Development: Treaty, Custom and the Cross-Fertilization of International Law', in: International Law and Sustainable Development: Past Achievements and Future Challenges (Boyle, Alan et al. (Eds.) 1999) 39 (43–45).

153 Arbitration Regarding the Iron Rhine Railway (Ijzeren Rijn) (Belgium/Netherlands) Decision of 24 May 2005, para 59. Expressing the same duty without a reference to the legal status of the principle, Case Concerning the Gabčíkovo-Nagymaros Project (Hungary/Slovakia) Judgment of 25 September 1997, ICJ Reports 1997, 7 (78) para. 140; Case Concerning Pulp Mills on the River Uruguay (Argentina/Uruguay) Provisional Measures Order of 13 July 2006, ICJ Reports 2006, 113 (133) para 80; Case Concerning Pulp Mills on the River Uruguay (Argentina/Uruguay) Judgment of 20 April 2010, ICJ Reports 2010, 14 (75) para 177.

154 *Sands*, Philippe/*Peel*, Jacqueline, Principles of International Environmental Law (2012) p. 208.

155 *Lowe*, Vaughan, 'Sustainable Development and Unsustainable Arguments', in: International Law and Sustainable Development: Past Achievements and Future Challenges (Boyle, Alan et al. (Eds.) 1999) 19 (24–31). Lowe argues that the implications deriving from sustainable development – which he sees as a "convenient umbrella term to label a group of congruent norms" – cannot create precise rights and obligations. Sustainable development could not express itself in normative language.

In my opinion, it appears that this perceived incapacity is the direct result of the reconciling nature of sustainable development, to which the absence of absolute prohibitions or obligations – which Lowe seems to require – is intrinsic.

Critical of Lowe's assessment, *Beyerlin*, Ulrich, 'Different Types of Norms in International Environmental: Policies, Principles and Rules', in: The Oxford Handbook of International Environmental Law (Bodansky, Daniel et al. (Eds.) 2007) 425 (445).

sustainable development a 'metaprinciple' which – through "pushing and pulling the boundaries of true primary norms" – exercised "a kind of interstitial normativity".[157] In the context of dispute resolution, sustainable development accordingly works as a "prism" through which economic disputes are viewed – disallowing their resolution without consideration of the broader environmental context in which they appear.[158] In application of such an understanding, other commentators suggest that the role of sustainable development may be similar to that of a preamble.[159]

Recent decisions of international courts and tribunals imply that sustainable development is roughly utilised as such a 'metaprinciple' or 'prism' in cases involving tension between economic and environmental considerations.[160] This apprehension of sustainable development is also closely con-

---

156 *Birnie*, Patricia/*Boyle*, Alan/*Redgwell*, Catherine, International Law and the Environment (2009) p. 127.

157 *Lowe*, Vaughan, 'Sustainable Development and Unsustainable Arguments', in: International Law and Sustainable Development: Past Achievements and Future Challenges (Boyle, Alan et al. (Eds.) 1999) 19 (31–35). Expressing a similar understanding, namely considering sustainable development to be a "guiding general principle for the consideration of environmental and developmental issues", Case Concerning Pulp Mills on the River Uruguay (Argentina/Uruguay) Separate Opinion of Judge Cançado Trindade to Judgment of 20 April 2010, ICJ Reports 2010, 135 (187) para 139.

158 *Lowe*, Vaughan, 'Sustainable Development and Unsustainable Arguments', in: International Law and Sustainable Development: Past Achievements and Future Challenges (Boyle, Alan et al. (Eds.) 1999) 19 (34, 36).

159 *Barstow Magraw*, Daniel/*Hawke*, Lisa D., 'Sustainable Development', in: The Oxford Handbook of International Environmental Law (Bodansky, Daniel et al. (Eds.) 2007) 613 (625).

160 United States – Import Prohibition of Certain Shrimp and Shrimp Products, DS58/AB/R, WTO Appellate Body Report of 12 October 1998 – albeit in the light of the preambular reference to sustainable development, para 129, stating that treaty provisions had to be interpreted "in the light of contemporary concerns of the community of nations about the protection and conservation of the environment" in a manner which is aware "of the importance and legitimacy of environmental protection as a goal of national and international policy" and para 153, stating that the objective of sustainable development must "add colour, texture and shading" to the interpretation.

Case Concerning the Gabčíkovo-Nagymaros Project (Hungary/Slovakia) Judgment of 25 September 1997, ICJ Reports 1997, 7 (78) para 140, expressing that the "need to reconcile economic development with protection of the environment" required the states involved to "look afresh at the effects on the environment of the operation of the Gabčíkovo power plant".

Case Concerning Pulp Mills on the River Uruguay (Argentina/Uruguay) Provisional Measures Order of 13 July 2006, ICJ Reports 2006, 113 (133) para 80, stating that due to sustainable development "account must be taken of the need to safeguard the continued conservation of the river environment and the rights of

nected with the concept of 'mutual supportiveness', which is used in some environmental and trade agreements and decisions by international judicial bodies to describe the relationship between economic and environmental requirements.[161] It is argued that mutual supportiveness constitutes the interpretative pillar of sustainable development.[162] Either way, the interpretative impact of both concepts appears to be identical and accurately captured in the understanding set forth above. It can thus be concluded that sustainable development has a fundamental impact on the understanding of international law – irrespective of the precise categorisation of the legal status of the principle.

II. Precautionary Principle

The precautionary principle seeks to guide the application and development of environmental law in cases of scientific uncertainty that require the assessment of relevant risks. If the scientific assessment indicates an important risk for the occurrence of environmental harm, the precautionary principle mandates that the environment profits from the benefit of the doubt. This core understanding is enshrined in Principle 15 of the Rio Declaration, which provides as follows:

> "In order to protect the environment, the precautionary approach shall be widely applied by States according to their capabilities. Where there are threats of serious or irreversible damage, lack of full scientific certainty shall not be used as a reason for postponing cost-effective measures to prevent environmental degradation."[163]

---

economic development of the riparian States". Case Concerning Pulp Mills on the River Uruguay (Argentina/Uruguay) Judgment of 20 April 2010, ICJ Reports 2010, 14 (74) para 177, stating that sustainable development mandated the equitable and reasonable utilisation of the shared resource, which required the taking into account of the "interests of the other riparian State in the shared resource and the environmental protection of the latter".

161 Preambular clause 8 1998 Rotterdam Convention on the Prior Informed Consent Procedure for Certain Hazardous Chemicals and Pesticides in International Trade; preambular clause 9 2000 Cartagena Protocol; Section 1, Chapter 2, paras 2.3 lit b, 2.9 lit d 1992 Agenda 21; see also Doha Ministerial Declaration, WT/MIN(01)/DEC/1, 14 November 2001, paras 6, 31; Arbitration Regarding the Iron Rhine Railway (Ijzeren Rijn) (Belgium/Netherlands) Decision of 24 May 2005, para 59.

162 *Pavoni*, Riccardo, 'Mututal Supportiveness as a Principle of Interpretation and Law-Making: A Watershed for the "WTO-and-Competing-Regimes" Debate?', 21 European Journal of International Law 2010, 649 (662). Similarly aligning the two concepts in the understanding that sustainable development "favour[ed] reconciliation over conflict", *Barstow Magraw*, Daniel/*Hawke*, Lisa D., 'Sustainable Development', in: The Oxford Handbook of International Environmental Law (Bodansky, Daniel et al. (Eds.) 2007) 613 (625).

163 Principle 15 Rio Declaration.

The principle is widely endorsed by the international community and features in slightly differing terminology – namely as precautionary principle, approach, or measures – in a multitude of international agreements.[164] The frequent insertion of references to the principle in international agreements indicates wide acceptance of its general tenets. This assumption is further underlined by national states' embrace of the principle – through application and implementation at the national level,[165] as well as through its utilisation as a legal argument at the international level[166].

However, the precise implications of the principle are less clear.[167] The three relevant notions of the precautionary principle relate to the threat of environmental harm, scientific uncertainty, and the resulting action of the

---

164 See preamble and Article 1 2000 Cartagena Protocol; Preamble, Articles 1 and 8 2001 Stockholm Convention on Persistent Organic Pollutants; Article 4 para 3 1991 Bamako Convention on the Ban of the Import into African and the Control of Transboundary Movement and Management of Hazardous Wastes Within Africa; Preamble, Article 2 1992 OSPAR Convention; Preamble of the 1996 Syracuse Protocol for the Protection of the Mediterranean Sea Against Pollution From Land-Based Sources and Activities; Article 2 1992 Convention on the Protection and Use of Transboundary Watercourses and International Lakes; Article 4 1999 Convention on the Protection of the Rhine; Preamble to 2001 International Convention on the Control of Harmful Anti-fouling Systems on Ships; Preamble to 1994 Oslo Protocol on Further Reduction of Sulphur Emissions to the 1979 Convention on Long-Range Transboundary Air Pollution; Preamble to 1998 Protocol on Heavy Metals to the 1979 Convention on Long-Range Transboundary Air Pollution; Article 3 1992 UNFCCC; Preamble 1992 Convention on Biological Diversity, repeating the words of principle 15 of the Rio Declaration, but not using the term 'precautionary'; Articles 5, 6 1995 Agreement for the Implementation of the Provisions of the United Nations Convention on the Law of the Sea of 10 December 1982 Relating to the Conservation and Management of Straddling Fish Stocks and Highly Migratory Fish Stocks. See also Article 191 Treaty on the Functioning of the European Union; Article 19 Energy Charter Treaty.

165 See as examples for recognition in judicial proceedings Indian Supreme Court decision in Vellore Citizens' Welfare Forum v. Union of India (1996), AIR1996SC2715; Supreme Court of Pakistan, Shehla Zia v. WAPDA (1994), SC 693. See also *Zander*, Joakim, The Application of the Precautionary Principle in Practice: Comparative Dimensions (2010) pp. 293–296 for a portrayal of the restrictive position in the U.S.

166 See references to the endorsement of precaution by Hungary and Slovakia in ICJ, Case Concerning the Gabčíkovo-Nagymaros Project (Hungary/Slovakia) Judgment of 25 September 1997, ICJ Reports 1997, 7 (62, 68) paras 97, 130; endorsement of the principle by Uruguay and Argentina in Case Concerning Pulp Mills on the River Uruguay (Argentina/Uruguay) Separate Opinion of Judge Cançado Trindade to Judgment of 20 April 2010, ICJ Reports 2010, 135 (156) para 51; ITLOS, Southern Bluefin Tuna Case, Cases No 3 and 4 (New Zealand, Australia v. Japan) Order of 27 August 1999.

167 See for a concise overview of controversial issues, *Wiener*, Jonathan B., 'Precaution', in: The Oxford Handbook of International Environmental Law (Bodansky, Daniel et al. (Eds.) 2007) 597 (602–604).

state.[168] Abstractly, it appears that the more detrimental the potential harm, the less likely would its occurrence have to be to justify precautionary actions. Thus, the risk assessment mandates that science indicates the likelihood of the occurrence of a relevant harm. If there are reasonable grounds to assume the occurrence of such harm, actions can be taken in spite of scientific uncertainty or – rather – irrespective of it.[169] The resulting action of the state has to be a proportional measure which effectively safeguards the endangered environmental good to fulfil the purpose of the principle.[170]

Uncertainties surrounding these parameters are at the heart of the continuing discussion about the legal status of the precautionary principle. Academics and practitioners differ in their legal appreciation of the precautionary principle: According to some, it has attained the status of customary international law[171] or constitutes a principle of international law[172]. Others

---

168 *Trouwborst*, Arie, Precautionary Rights and Duties of States (2006), pp. 37–158. See also Case Concerning Pulp Mills on the River Uruguay (Argentina/Uruguay) Separate Opinion of Judge Cançado Trindade to Judgment of 20 April 2010, ICJ Reports 2010, 135 (162 *et seq.*) paras 69–92.

169 *Trouwborst*, Arie, Precautionary Rights and Duties of States (2006) pp. 91–96.

170 *Trouwborst*, Arie, 'The Precautionary Principle in General International Law: Combatting the Babylonian Confusion', 16 Review of European Community and International Environmental Law 2007, 185 (189), refers to the following criteria for an appropriate state action: it has to be timely introduced, fitting for the specific circumstances, in place as long as necessary – but not longer, and not substituting one risk with another risk of the same or bigger dimensions. See also *Wiener*, Jonathan B., 'Precaution', in: The Oxford Handbook of International Environmental Law (Bodansky, Daniel et al. (Eds.) 2007) 597 (608–610), voicing concern as to whether the potential risks of precautionary measures themselves are correctly assessed in reality.

171 *Trouwborst*, Arie, 'The Precautionary Principle in General International Law: Combatting the Babylonian Confusion', 16 Review of European Community and International Environmental Law 2007, 185 (187–188); *de Sadeleer*, Nicholas, 'The Precautionary Principle in International Law', in: The Transformation of International Environmental Law (Kerbrat, Yann et al. (Eds.) 2011) 73–88; Mox Plant Case – Dispute Concerning Access to Information under Article 9 of the OSPAR Convention (Ireland/United Kingdom) Dissenting Opinion of Gavan Griffith to Final Award of 2 July 2003, 23 UN Reports of International Arbitral Awards 119, para 73.

172 European Commission, 'Communication on the Precautionary Principle', COM(2000) 1 final, 2 February 2000, para 4; Case Concerning Pulp Mills on the River Uruguay (Argentina/Uruguay) Separate Opinion of Judge Cançado Trindade to Judgment of 20 April 2010, ICJ Reports 2010, 135 especially (177) para 113. Similarly, Case Concerning Pulp Mills on the River Uruguay (Argentina/Uruguay) Dissenting Opinion of Judge ad hoc Vinuesa to Order on Provisional Measures, ICJ Reports 2006, 147 (152), describing the precautionary principle as "not an abstraction or an academic component of desirable soft law, but a rule of law within general international law". See also discussion by *Freestone*, David, 'International Fisheries Law Since Rio: The Continued Rise of the Precautionary Principle', in:

express valid doubts whether the principle has attained such a status in the international sphere.[173] The remaining academic discussion predominantly circles around three contentious issues: When does the precautionary principle entail a right to precautionary measures, when does a duty to implement such measures exist, and does the principle shift the burden of proof onto the proponent of the potentially dangerous activity?[174]

In the context of this work, it is not possible to profoundly discuss these issues. It suffices to state that adjudicators of international law can adopt

---

International Law and Sustainable Development: Past Achievements and Future Challenges (Boyle, Alan et al. (Eds.) 1999) 135 (136–137), arguing that principles in international law are guidelines and do not impose concrete obligations, so that a debate surrounding the exact content and application of a principle does not – as the example of the principle of self-determination demonstrates – preclude the possibility of it being a principle of international law.

173 *Birnie*, Patricia/*Boyle*, Alan/*Redgwell*, Catherine, International Law and the Environment (2009) pp. 159–164, expressing doubt because of a lack of sufficient authoritative determination by international tribunals, because the principle has not been universally applied to all environmental scenarios and because treaty references rely on different thresholds of harm. See also European Communities – Measures Concerning Meat and Meat Products (Hormones), DS26/AB/R, WTO Appellate Body Report of 16 January 1998, para 123, stating "that the precautionary principle, at least outside the field of international environmental law, still awaits authoritative formulation." See also the evaluation of the limits of the principle in judicial review at the European level by *Zander*, Joakim, The Application of the Precautionary Principle in Practice: Comparative Dimensions (2010) pp. 108 *et seq.*, cumulating in the statement that "the application of the precautionary principle as an independent legal instrument in the EU is still in its infancy" (151).

The ITLOS, Southern Bluefin Tuna Case, Cases No 3 and 4 (New Zealand, Australia v. Japan) Order of 27 August 1999, paras 77, 79, 80, which relied on scientific uncertainty is not evidence for the acceptance of a customary principle of precaution. It is not clear whether the order relied on such a precautionary approach (Separate Opinion of Judge ad hoc Shearer), the applied precaution was "inherent in the very notion of provisional measures" (Separate Opinion of Judge Treves, para 9), or is derived from UNCLOS, the underlying treaty, which incorporates a precautionary approach, that allows for more flexibility than the precautionary principle. There is not sufficient evidence to determine its alleged status in customary international law (Separate Opinion of Judge Laing, paras 16–19).

174 *Trouwborst*, Arie, 'The Precautionary Principle in General International Law: Combatting the Babylonian Confusion', 16 Review of European Community and International Environmental Law 2007, 185 (188, 192). Trouwborst suggests that under international law a state has a right to take precautionary action if there are reasonable grounds for concern that significant harm to the environment may be caused. If there are reasonable grounds for concern that the harm would be serious and/or irreversible, the state has a duty to take effective and proportional action to prevent such harm. See also the critical assessment by *Wiener*, Jonathan B., 'Precaution', in: The Oxford Handbook of International Environmental Law (Bodansky, Daniel et al. (Eds.) 2007) 597 (604–607).

either position. It should be kept in mind that in connection with investment arbitration the precautionary principle, like other environmental principles, will most certainly become relevant through measures adopted by the host state to regulate certain potentially dangerous activities of the investor. If there are scientific uncertainties relating to the environmental harmfulness of such activities, the investor may argue that measures preventing it from pursuing or continuing the activity violate its protected rights. In such a situation, the host state may explicitly or implicitly base its national measures on the precautionary approach. In an investment dispute brought by the investor, the state could rely on the precautionary principle as an ideological basis for the adopted measure.

It has to be kept in mind that international law recognises the use of the principle for adopting precautionary measures. This general assertion is not affected by the discussion regarding the legal status of the precautionary principle. As can be seen above, this uncertainty does not stem from an absence of the general acceptance of the principle as such, but relates to its precise implications and the acknowledgment that the principle has not been applied in connection with all potential environmental dangers.

Nevertheless, the potential shift of the burden of proof should briefly be addressed here. If the precautionary principle brought about a change in the burden of proof, this could influence the rules concerning the burden of proof in investment arbitration proceedings. Though favoured by some proponents of the precautionary principle,[175] there is not sufficient evidence that the precautionary principle as such entails a shift of the burden of proof.[176] However, it appears uncontested that international agreements in their application of a precautionary intention can introduce such a shift of the burden of proof.[177] The same is true for the national sphere.[178] In sum,

175 Mox Plant Case – Dispute Concerning Access to Information under Article 9 of the OSPAR Convention (Ireland/United Kingdom) Dissenting Opinion of Gavan Griffith to Final Award of 2 July 2003, para 72.

176 *Trouwborst*, Arie, 'The Precautionary Principle in General International Law: Combatting the Babylonian Confusion', 16 Review of European Community and International Environmental Law 2007, 185 (192); *Birnie*, Patricia/*Boyle*, Alan/*Redgwell*, Catherine, International Law and the Environment (2009) p. 158. See also the Case Concerning Pulp Mills on the River Uruguay (Argentina/Uruguay) Judgment of 20 April 2010, ICJ Reports 2010, 14 (71) para 164, where the ICJ held that "while a precautionary approach may be relevant in the interpretation and application of the [relevant treaty], it does not follow that it operates as a reversal of the burden of proof". See also European Commission, 'Communication on the Precautionary Principle', COM(2000) 1 final, 2 February 2000, para 6.4.

177 See Article 4 1988 Convention on the Regulation of Antarctic Mineral Resource Activities (which, however, has not entered into force); Annex 4 to 1994 Resolution Conf. 9.24 (Rev. CoP14), amended, 'Criteria for Amendment of Appen-

even though international environmental law does not require a shift of the burden of proof in connection with the precautionary principle, it does not disallow it. Accordingly, a national measure implementing such an onus onto a foreign investor should not be considered 'unfair'. The impact of such reasoning is most likely to become relevant in national rules requiring the use of environmental impact assessment.

Hence, the precautionary principle underscores the host state's margin of appreciation to introduce regulation. The host state is not restricted to introducing environmental regulation when the environmental impact of an economic activity unquestionably brings about environmental harm. It can also do so when a scientific assessment only indicates a risk. In general terms, it thus suffices to acknowledge the environmentalist onus of the principle. The question if the accurate level of risk for the introduction of the respective measure exists, will be subject to discussion in each specific case. In this sense, the precautionary principle goes hand-in-hand with the 'preventive principle', which also aims at preventing environmental harm and degradation.[179]

III. Polluter-Pays Principle

The polluter-pays principle is the application to the environment of a basic economic understanding: the negative externalities[180] of a productive or consumptive process have to be reflected in the price of the product or

dices I and II', June 2007 (regarding the possibility of delisting species from the relevant annexes); Guiding Principle 10 of Decision V/8 of the COP 5, 'Alien species that threaten ecosystems, habitats or species', May 2000, explicitly stating that the "burden of proof that a proposed introduction is unlikely to cause such harm should be with the proposer of the introduction". See also Annex 2 Article 3 para 3 lit c to the OSPAR Convention.

178 See for the context of German administrative law: *Calliess*, Christian, 'Vorsorgeprinzip und Beweislastverteilung im Verwaltungsrecht', Das Deutsche Verwaltungsblatt 2001, 1725 (1732–1733).

179 Case Concerning Pulp Mills on the River Uruguay (Argentina/Uruguay) Separate Opinion of Judge Cançado Trindade to Judgment of 20 April 2010, ICJ Reports 2010, 135 (170) para 95. Similarly, *Trouwborst*, Arie, 'The Precautionary Principle in General International Law: Combatting the Babylonian Confusion', 16 Review of European Community and International Environmental Law 2007, 185 (191–192), arguing that the precautionary principle has absorbed the preventive principle. See also *Wiener*, Jonathan B., 'Precaution', in: The Oxford Handbook of International Environmental Law (Bodansky, Daniel et al. (Eds.) 2007) 597 (603–604), pointing to the difficulty to reasonably distinguish between the two concepts.

180 Negative externalities are external costs. In this context, it means environmental problems, like the degradation of the environment, which are caused by a process of production or similar activity. An example is the emission of toxins from a pro-

process for the market to function properly.[181] Accordingly, the polluter-pays principle mandates that polluters bear and internalise the costs of their pollution.[182] In this sense, the polluter-pays principle is a cost allocation principle, built on the equitable premise that polluters, but not the society-at-large, have to bear the costs of the pollution and that individual polluters bear the responsibility for their share of contribution to a specific pollution problem.[183] The intended economic effects of this obligation are waste reduction through an efficient use of resources as well as the development of increasingly effective pollution abatement technologies.[184]

At its outset, the polluter-pays principle was understood to oblige polluters to bear the costs of pollution control and abatement.[185] These costs are

---

duction plant. See for an introduction, *de Sadeleer*, Nicholas, Environmental Principles: From Political Slogans to Legal Rules (2002) pp. 21–22.

A productive process can also have positive externalities, which are external benefits. An appropriate example is the absorption of greenhouse gases by sinks, such as forests. Such effects are obviously less frequent and less problematic from an environmental perspective. However, states could aim to induce such externalities through subsidies. See *Kim*, Hyung-Jin, 'Subsidy, Polluter Pays Principle and Financial Assistance among Countries', 34 Journal of World Trade 2000, 115 (120–121, 132).

181 According to the economic theory of externalities, the negative impacts of production have to be reflected in the price of the product, so that the price reflects the true costs of the product. Otherwise, the market does not function properly. See *de Sadeleer*, Nicholas, Environmental Principles: From Political Slogans to Legal Rules (2002) pp. 21–22.

182 *Sands*, Philippe/*Peel*, Jacqueline, Principles of International Environmental Law (2012) p. 228; *de Sadeleer*, Nicholas, Environmental Principles: From Political Slogans to Legal Rules (2002) p. 21; *Nash*, Jonathan Remy, 'Too Much Market? Conflict Between Tradable Pollution Allowances and the "Polluter Pays" Principle', 24 Harvard Environmental Law Review 2000, 465 (468); *Gaines*, Sanford E., 'The Polluter-Pays Principle: From Economic Equity to Environmental Ethos', 26 Texas International Law Journal 1991, 463 (465–466).

183 *Nash*, Jonathan Remy, 'Too Much Market? Conflict Between Tradable Pollution Allowances and the "Polluter Pays" Principle', 24 Harvard Environmental Law Review 2000, 465 (476–477).

184 *Nash*, Jonathan Remy, 'Too Much Market? Conflict Between Tradable Pollution Allowances and the "Polluter Pays" Principle', 24 Harvard Environmental Law Review 2000, 465 (468).

185 The polluter-pays principle was first mentioned in a legal context in Organisation for Economic Co-operation and Development (OECD), 'Council Recommendations on Guiding Principles Concerning the International Economic Aspects of Environmental Policies', C(72)128, 26 May 1972, Annex, para 4. This reference reads in relevant part as follows: "This principle means that the polluter should bear the expenses of carrying out [pollution prevention and control measures] decided by public authorities to ensure that the environment is in an acceptable state. In other words, the cost of these measures should be reflected in the cost of goods and services which cause pollution in production and/or consumption. Such measures

considered to be at the heart of the polluter-pays principle.[186] However, the scope of application of the principle was consecutively broadened. In addition to the abatement costs, the polluter-pays principle is increasingly considered to encompass costs arising from accidental pollution as well as the response costs arising from environmental damage.[187] This shift to an extension of the principle to include ex-post costs in the sense of a liability regime is prominent in regulations by the European Union.[188] However, it is less clear how far the understanding of the principle has developed outside the European context.

The polluter-pays principle was endorsed by the United Nations Conference on Environment and Development and found its way into Rio Principle 16, which reads as follows:

> "National authorities should endeavour to promote the internalisation of environmental costs and the use of economic instruments, taking into account the approach that the polluter should, in principle, bear the cost of pollution, with due regard to the public interest and without distorting international trade and investment."[189]

This description of the principle focuses on the internalisation of environmental costs and does not refer to costs for environmental degradation. The

---

should not be accompanied by subsidies that would create significant distortions in international trade and investment."

[186] *Gaines*, Sanford E., 'The Polluter-Pays Principle: From Economic Equity to Environmental Ethos', 26 Texas International Law Journal 1991, 463 (473–475). This author mentions, in addition to the control and abatement costs at the individual pollution source, ancillary and administrative costs incurred by the public to make environmental protection and control work to the extent that these are directly linked to control or prevention measures.

[187] See *Gaines*, Sanford E., 'The Polluter-Pays Principle: From Economic Equity to Environmental Ethos', 26 Texas International Law Journal 1991, 463 (481–487) and *de Sadeleer*, Nicholas, Environmental Principles: From Political Slogans to Legal Rules (2002) pp. 26–32 for a description of this development.

[188] Article 15 1991 Waste Framework Directive (Directive 91/156/EC of 18 March 1991), which broadly establishes the polluter-pays principle for the context of waste disposal; European Commission, 'White Paper on Environmental Liability' COM(2000) 66 final, 9 February 2000. See for portrayal of this development, *de Sadeleer*, Nicholas, Environmental Principles: From Political Slogans to Legal Rules (2002) pp. 28–31. See also European Court of Justice, Commune de Mesquer v. Total France SA, C-188/07, Judgment of 24 June 2008, paras 72, 82 for an illustration of the far-reaching implications of the polluter-pays principle for the liability for oil pollution damage.

[189] Principle 16 Rio Declaration. Para 15 lit b) 'Plan of Implementation of the World Summit on Sustainable Development', UN Doc. A/CONF.199/20, 4 September 2002 asked states, inter alia, to implement the principle as described in Principle 16. The underlying economic rationale of the polluter-pays principle is also reflected in paragraphs 2.14 and 30.3 of Agenda 21.

language used for mandating action required by national authorities – "should endeavour to promote" the principle – falls remarkably short of introducing a strong obligation. Furthermore, the reference to the public interest gives leeway for exceptions to a strict implementation of the principle.[190] In addition, the relevance of the clause stating that the principle should not distort international trade and investment is not exactly clear: the application of a similar cost allocation model, such as the polluter-pays principle, by all states serves international economic equity.[191] A society which decides for externalised environmental costs to be borne by the general public and not by the polluter gains a competitive advantage over countries which apply the polluter-pays principle – which leads to trade and investment distortions.[192]

Despite its catchy name, the precise implications arising from the polluter-pays principle are not self-evident: The principle requires the identification of who is the relevant polluter,[193] the establishment of the kinds of pollution or risks of pollution for which the polluter is liable,[194] as well as a regulation to deal with scenarios of excessive risks, costs and respective limitation[195]. Another issue that continues to attract debate even in states most inclined to the implementation of the polluter-pays principle is its relationship with subsidies.[196] The payment of subsidies to industry to facilitate the use of more environmentally friendly technologies may be help-

---

190 Similarly, *Birnie*, Patricia/*Boyle*, Alan/*Redgwell*, Catherine, International Law and the Environment (2009) p. 323.

191 *Gaines*, Sanford E., 'The Polluter-Pays Principle: From Economic Equity to Environmental Ethos', 26 Texas International Law Journal 1991, 463 (470).

192 *Gaines*, Sanford E., 'The Polluter-Pays Principle: From Economic Equity to Environmental Ethos', 26 Texas International Law Journal 1991, 463 (470); *de Sadeleer*, Nicholas, Environmental Principles: From Political Slogans to Legal Rules (2002) p. 25.

193 See *de Sadeleer*, Nicholas, Environmental Principles: From Political Slogans to Legal Rules (2002) pp. 38–42, for an introduction to the issues relating to the identification of the polluter.

194 See *de Sadeleer*, Nicholas, Environmental Principles: From Political Slogans to Legal Rules (2002) pp. 42–44, for an overview.

195 *Sands*, Philippe/*Peel*, Jacqueline, Principles of International Environmental Law (2012) pp. 232–233; *Birnie*, Patricia/*Boyle*, Alan/*Redgwell*, Catherine, International Law and the Environment (2009) pp. 324–325.

196 *de Sadeleer*, Nicholas, Environmental Principles: From Political Slogans to Legal Rules (2002) p. 42, states that the "polluter-pays principle was originally strictly defined to exclude subsidies for pollution and prevention measures financed by polluters." See for a discussion of the relationship between subsidies and the polluter-pays principle at the European level and in some individual European states, *Gaines*, Sanford E., 'The Polluter-Pays Principle: From Economic Equity to Environmental Ethos', 26 Texas International Law Journal 1991, 463 (477–481).

ful to the environmental cause; however, it tends to conflict with the polluter-pays principle.[197] Furthermore, it is observed that there is little support for the application of the polluter-pays principle in state-to-state relations.[198] In relation to other states, payment for environmental degradation appears to depend on the economic capacity rather than on the contribution to the polluting event.[199]

While the permeation of environmental law by the polluter-pays principle is rather comprehensive at the level of the European Union[200] and is reflected in national legislation,[201] the same cannot be said for international environmental law as such. Even though the polluter-pays principle is re-

---

197 Three exceptions to the general prohibition on subsidies for polluters are generally acknowledged, namely (1) assistance for technological innovation, (2) exceptions for transitional periods, and (3) aid to a specific industry or to an industry in a special situation. See *Gaines*, Sanford E., 'The Polluter-Pays Principle: From Economic Equity to Environmental Ethos', 26 Texas International Law Journal 1991, 463 (476–477).

See for a detailed discussion of subsidies and the polluter-pays principle, *Kim*, Hyung-Jin, 'Subsidy, Polluter Pays Principle and Financial Assistance among Countries', 34 Journal of World Trade 2000, 115 (117–129).

198 *Sands*, Philippe/*Peel*, Jacqueline, Principles of International Environmental Law (2012) p. 229; *Birnie*, Patricia/*Boyle*, Alan/*Redgwell*, Catherine, International Law and the Environment (2009) p. 325.

199 *Kim*, Hyung-Jin, 'Subsidy, Polluter Pays Principle and Financial Assistance among Countries', 34 Journal of World Trade 2000, 115 (129). See this article for a detailed discussion of financial assistance among states and their accordance with the polluter-pays principle (130–141).

A telling example is the financial assistance under the 1990 Adjustments and Amendments to the Montreal Protocol on Substances that Deplete the Ozone Layer (London Amendment), which introduced a multilateral fund to provide less developed countries with the means to comply with the relevant control measures, Article 10. The receiving of such funds by polluting entities would constitute a violation of the polluter-pays principle. However, it was also suggested that the implementation of this fund in which the main producers of CFCs pay for other countries to meet the relevant criteria was a reflection of the polluter-pays principle on an abstract level, *Gaines*, Sanford E., 'The Polluter-Pays Principle: From Economic Equity to Environmental Ethos', 26 Texas International Law Journal 1991, 463 (493–494).

200 Article 191 para 2 Treaty on the Functioning of the European Union. *Sands*, Philippe/*Peel*, Jacqueline, Principles of International Environmental Law, p. 229, imply that the polluter-pays principle has reached the status of a generally applicable rule of customary international law in relation to states in the EU, the UNECE and the OECD.

201 *de Sadeleer*, Nicholas, Environmental Principles: From Political Slogans to Legal Rules (2002) pp. 32–33; *Larson*, Eric Thomas, 'Why Environmental Liability Regimes in the United States, the European Community, and Japan Have Grown Synonymous With the Polluter-Pays Principle', 38 Vanderbilt Journal of Transnational Law 2005, 541 (550–563).

ferred to in a multitude of international agreements – with references ranging from calling it a "guiding principle",[202] mandating its application,[203] or calling on states "to take the principle into account"[204] – there is little evidence that the polluter-pays principle as such has reached the status of a general principle of international law: The generality of the references to the principle, the lack of a determinable common understanding and most importantly, the absence of consistent state practice imply that the polluter-pays principle has not yet reached a legally binding status.[205]

---

202 Article 2 para 5 lit b) 1992 Convention on the Protection and Use of Transboundary Watercourses and International Lakes; Article 3 para 2 lit d) 1994 Agreement on the Protection of the (River) Meuse; Article 3 para 2 lit d) 1994 Agreement on the Protection of the River Scheldt. Similarly, Article 2 para 4 1994 Convention on Cooperation for the Protection and Sustainable Use of the River Danube.

203 Article 2 para 2 lit b) 1992 OSPAR Convention; Article 3 para 4 1992 Convention on the Protection of the Marine Environment of the Baltic Sea Area; Article 2 para 1 1991 Alpine Convention. Similarly, Article 10 lit d) 1985 ASEAN Agreement on the Conservation of Nature and Natural Resources.

204 Article 4 lit d) 1999 Convention on the Protection of the Rhine; Article 3 para 2 1996 Protocol to the Convention on the Prevention of Marine Pollution by Dumping of Wastes and Other Matter of 29 December 1972. In addition, the principle is taken into account in the preambles of several environmental conventions: Preambular clause 6 1993 Convention on Civil Liability for Damage Resulting from Activities Dangerous to the Environment; preambular clause 7 1990 International Convention on Oil Pollution Preparedness, Response and Co-Operation; premabular clause 9 1992 Convention on the Transboundary Effects of Industrial Accidents; preambular clause 3 2003 Protocol on Civil Liability and Compensation for Damage Caused by the Transboundary Effects of Industrial Accidents on Transboundary Waters to the 1992 Convention on the Protection and Use of Transboundary Watercourses and International Lakes and to the 1992 Convention on the Transboundary Effects of Industrial Accidents.

205 Affaire concernant l'apurement des comptes entre le royaume des Pays-Bas et la république Française en application du protocole du 25 Septembre 1991 additionnel à la Convention relative à la protection du Rhin contre la pollution par les chlorures du 3 Décembre 1976 (Netherlands/France), Award of 12 March 2004, para 103: "Le tribunal observe que ce principe figure dans certains instruments internationaux, tant bilatéraux que multilatéraux, et se situe à des niveaux d'effectivité variables. Sans nier son importance en droit conventionnel, le Tribunal ne pense pas que ce principe fasse partie du droit international général." Expressing a similar understanding, *Birnie*, Patricia/*Boyle*, Alan/*Redgwell*, Catherine, International Law and the Environment (2009) p. 322.

This understanding is not impaired by the preambles of international agreements declaring the polluter-pays principle to be a general principle of international environmental law, such as preambular clause 7 1990 International Convention on Oil Pollution Preparedness, Response and Co-Operation; premabular clause 9 1992 Convention on the Transboundary Effects of Industrial Accidents; preambular clause 3 2003 Protocol on Civil Liability and Compensation for Damage Caused by the Transboundary Effects of Industrial Accidents on Transboundary Waters to the 1992 Convention on the Protection and Use of Transboundary Watercourses and Interna-

Nevertheless, the polluter-pays principle is not devoid of impact. First, it is a generally accepted principle for the allocation of costs for negative externalities and, as such, it can be legitimately implemented by states.[206] For the context of my study, this means that a foreign investor would generally have to accept the host state imposing such costs on the investor for its polluting activity. Accordingly, in certain situations the principle can function as an additional justification for the implementation of an environmental measure. Tensions are particularly relevant in situations in which the level of costs to be borne for a polluting activity is increased to a level that makes the investment activity no longer economically viable.

Furthermore, the polluter-pays principle can be relevant as an argumentative tool in connection with supporting schemes introduced by states to further investments in environmentally friendly activities – as well as with regard to the discontinuance of such a supporting scheme in cases in which the environmental value of the supported activity is later called into question. Thirdly, the polluter-pays principle can be a factor in the context of the calculation of compensation for a breach of an investment protection obligation by the host state. In cases in which the investor is a polluter, having externalised the costs of its pollution or having caused environmental degradation, as a result of which the host state interferes, the rationale of the polluter-pays principle can potentially have a reducing influence on the level of compensation to be paid by the host state. Such a scenario could, for example, occur in cases of direct expropriation, in which the state intends to retrieve a piece of land from the investor to protect it environmentally.[207]

---

tional Lakes and to the 1992 Convention on the Transboundary Effects of Industrial Accidents.

206 This derives from the above overview. It was explicitly recognised in United States – Tax on Petroleum and Certain Imported Substances, L/6175 – 34S/136, GATT Panel Report adopted on 17 June 1987, para 5.2.5, which stated that the rules on tax adjustment gave a party the possibility to follow the polluter-pays principle, but that they did not oblige it to do so.

Commentators suggested that states and courts "can and should take account of the principle in the development of environmental law and policy, but that they are in no way bound by international law to make polluters pay", *Birnie*, Patricia/*Boyle*, Alan/*Redgwell*, Catherine, International Law and the Environment (2009) p. 323.

207 See, for example, the decisions in *Compañía del Dessarollo de Santa Elena S.A. v. Republic of Costa Rica* and in *Marion Unglaube and Reinhard Unglaube v. Republic of Costa Rica*, as portrayed in 'Chapter 5 – Expropriation'.

IV. Intermediate Summary

International environmental law is a conglomerate of conventions, declarations and other instruments with differing legal impact. Principles of environmental law constitute an important part of the developing core of customary environmental law. Even though the legal status of the principle of sustainable development, the precautionary principle and the polluter-pays principle is not clear in international law, these principles are significant for both national environmental legislation and other areas of international law.[208] In both of these norm-creating areas, environmental principles will influence the evaluation of foreign investment activities.

E. Scenarios of Potential Conflict

The interests and rights of a foreign investor can be implicated by regulation of the host state intending to protect the environment. This section portrays four scenarios in an abstract manner, the parameters of which can be applied to several situations. The above portrayal of environmental issues has already hinted at some of these situations. The following chapters, which cover the protective scope of investment treaties, will apply the scenarios to specific situations to determine potential conflicts between the two sets of legal provisions.

I. Scenario No 1: Introduction and Application of Environmental Regulation

The first scenario concerns the classical issue of conflict between investment protection and norms implemented for the sake of the environment. Since an investor generally has to accept the regulation of the host state as it stands when it makes its investment, this scenario is most relevant with regard to environmental regulation introduced after the investment has been made. There is a myriad of possible examples for such a line-up: They range from the prohibition of certain activities for environmental reasons,

---

[208] To borrow the words of the arbitration panel in the Arbitration Regarding the Iron Rhine Railway (Ijzeren Rijn) (Belgium/Netherlands) Decision of 24 May 2005, para 58: "There is considerable debate as to what, within the field of environmental law, constitutes "rules" or "principles"; what is "soft law"; and which environmental treaty law or principles have contributed to the development of customary international law. [...]The emerging principles, whatever their current status, make reference to conservation, management, notions of prevention and of sustainable development, and protection for future generations."

over the implementation of new environmental standards for activities, to the requirement of employing specific measures to target specific emissions.

In the portrayal of international environmental law above a number of such possible conflicts has been mentioned. Examples include the prohibition of using an acquired piece of land for the intended construction of a hotel, the prohibition of further use of certain chemical substances – rendering the production of the substance useless – and the imposition of a cap-and-trade regime for the control of certain emissions. These subsequent rules all have one aspect in common: the regulations lead to the investor facing increased costs or even finding the investment no longer economically viable.[209] There is also potential for conflict when it comes to the implementation of pre-existing environmental rules: the investor's need to acquire a permit for its activity on the basis of the environmental regulation in force constitutes a particularly crucial situation for the impact of both investment and environmental protection.

As a whole, this group of host state measures is the most obvious source of conflicts between both circles of regulation: The foreign investor has invested in the host state with the awareness of the prevailing investment conditions. Then, after the investment has been made, the investor is confronted with restrictions it has not calculated. In how far the position of the foreign investor in such a situation conflicts with the interest of the home state to introduce and apply regulation for a public purpose is the main point of discussion in this survey.

II. Scenario No 2: Subsidies or Other Advantages for Environmentally Friendly Investments as Potential Violation of Other Investments

The following three scenarios are connected to economic mechanisms that the host state introduces to support an environmental purpose. Economic mechanisms, such as those which help reduce the costs of compliance, are legislative tools adopted by states to induce compliance with obligations arising under international environmental law. Although conflicts with provisions on investment protection in this situation are numerically

[209] *Johnson*, Lise, 'International Investment Agreements and Climate Change: The Potential for Investor-State Conflicts and Possible Strategies for Minimizing It', 39 Environmental Law Reporter News & Analysis 2009, 39 Envtl. L. Rep. News & Analysis 11147 (11149), using examples such as the obligation to employ carbon capture and storage technology for fossil fuel fired power plants, the imposition of strict energy efficiency requirements or emission standards on energy-intensive industries, or an obligation of certain land use requirements as adaptation measures.

less likely to occur, the strong connection of such mechanisms with environmental objectives requires a detailed look at potential tensions. A relevant economic support system offers incentives for the investment in specific technologies or production measures that are considered environmentally friendly. For the context of this survey, the concept of support systems is understood broadly and the concept can take different forms: a financial subsidy, a regulative framework that guarantees a favourable price for created products, or a favourable tax regime.

The scenario relates to all support schemes introduced by a state to further investment in environmentally friendly technologies. However, the overview of international environmental law emphasises the importance bestowed upon the prevention of climate change. Economic mechanisms are developed with the aim to reduce the emission of greenhouse gases, such as CO_2. Accordingly, several states financially encourage investment in the sector of renewable energy. Tools utilised to this end are, for example, feed-in-tariffs, where electricity from qualifying sources is paid a fixed minimum price guaranteed for a certain amount of time.[210] In addition, more elaborated concepts are developed, like the creation of carbon credits under the Clean Development Mechanism of the Kyoto Protocol.[211] This mechanism is closely connected to the reduction of carbon emissions, but it also offers advantages to investors in carbon-reduced projects or industries. The creation of carbon credits and the rules relating to their evaluation and trading in the carbon market will fall within the broad concept of support systems.

The second scenario considers the position of participants of the relevant market that do not qualify for the support system. It analyses whether the introduction of such a scheme constitutes a violation of the rights to investment protection of investors falling outside of the scope of application of the scheme. The impact of the scheme on existing, non-qualifying investments is most significant. This scenario will be considered in connection with all the relevant rights of investment protection; however, it is obvious that the core of the issue resides in the concept of non-discrimination. Does a scheme supporting, for example, environmentally friendly produced en-

---

210 *Boute*, Anatole, 'Combating Climate Change and Securing Electricity Supply: The Role of Investment Protection Law', 16 European Environmental Law Review 2007, 227 (238); *Boute*, Anatole, 'The Potential Contribution of International Investment Protection Law to Combat Climate Change', 27 Journal of Energy & Natural Resources Law 2009, 333 (341); European Commission, 'Communication on the support of electricity from renewable energy sources', COM(2005) 627 final, 7 December 2005, pp. 4–5. Other examples used are certificate schemes, where tradable certificates are linked to an obligation for electricity suppliers to hold a certain amount of such certificates.

211 See the portrayal above at pp. 56 *et seq.*

ergy discriminate against energy produced without reliance on these standards? The final product – energy – is identical, but the investors are treated differently because of the way the energy is produced.

III. Scenario No 3: Withdrawal of or Reductions in a Scheme Favouring Environmentally Friendly Investments

The remaining two scenarios concern implications arising from alterations to support schemes for environmentally friendly investments: The host state[212] has introduced a scheme to encourage investments in an environmentally friendly industry or measure of production, which it later withdraws or alters. The withdrawal of a promised economic support or a significant reduction in the anticipated financial advantage has an impact on investments made in reliance on the scheme. In how far such an alteration violates the protection guaranteed to foreign investors is the subject of the two remaining scenarios.

In the third scenario, the reason for the alteration is not related to the environmental objective for which the scheme was originally implemented. The rationale for the withdrawal or substantial limitation of the subsidising support scheme is of an economic or political nature. Practical examples for the relevant reasons can be an unexpected large number of participants in the scheme – placing a high financial burden upon the host state – or pressure from other participants in the market calling for the limitation. The specific connotation of this scenario lies in the fact that the interests of the investor and of the environment point to the same direction: Both the arguments for investment protection and for environmental protection desire the unaltered maintenance of the support scheme. The scenario shows that investment protection rights can go hand in hand with the aims of investors in green technologies.

One illustrative example for this scenario is the devaluation of carbon credits generated from investment in low-carbon projects due to a cap-and-trade system. The financial support represented by the emission credits arguably constitutes an important economic foundation of the investment.[213]

---

212 Problems relating to the accountability of other institutions, to which the state has derogated powers, like the EU which introduces and revokes decisions, are outside the scope of this survey. For the purpose of the survey, it does not matter whether the host state introduced the scheme out of its own initiative or because it forms part of an organisation or group of states requiring the adoption of such a scheme.

213 *Boute*, Anatole, 'The Potential Contribution of International Investment Protection Law to Combat Climate Change', 27 Journal of Energy & Natural Resources Law 2009, 333 (363).

Similarly, the carbon credits themselves can qualify for investment protection deriving from investment treaties.[214] However, their value stems from the carbon trading system within which they are marketed. If the host state found that the credits' value was based on an exaggerated view of their emission-reducing benefit, it could depress the price by flooding the market with additional credits.[215] The host state could also choose to abandon the emissions trading scheme altogether in favour of some other mode of regulation.[216] It could also withdraw carbon credits which it earlier accorded to an investor. Another relevant aspect in this context is the guarantee of explicit tariffs for furthering investment in renewable energies. The unilateral alteration of tariff structures has recently been the subject in a variety of investment decisions. Although this did not occur in an environmental context, these arbitral decisions provide some guidance to determine this issue.

IV. Scenario No 4: Withdrawal of Support Scheme Because Investment Affects the Environmental Objective

The fourth scenario differs from the third only in the reasoning for which the support scheme is altered or withdrawn: The investment project is eligible for receiving economic support because it is considered to further an environmental objective. After the investment has been made, an evaluation of the project casts doubt upon its helpfulness to the environmental cause – or finds that the project is harmful to the intended or another important environmental objective. The national authority withdraws the support given to the investor due to these considerations. In this scenario, the reasons for which the support is withdrawn are justified with environmental considerations: Environmental reasoning potentially weighs both in favour of the investment and against it.

Such a combination might appear artificially constructed, but it is not. In reality, the construction of support schemes for environmentally advantageous industries or projects is difficult. First, it is difficult to incorporate market-driven elements into environmental regulation, which requires peri-

---

214 *Bennett*, Lisa, 'Are tradable Carbon Emissions Investments? Characterization and Ramifications under International Investment Law', 85 New York University Law Review 2010, 1581 (1581,1592).

215 *Bennett*, Lisa, 'Are tradable Carbon Emissions Investments? Characterization and Ramifications under International Investment Law', 85 New York University Law Review 2010, 1581 (1602).

216 *Bennett*, Lisa, 'Are tradable Carbon Emissions Investments? Characterization and Ramifications under International Investment Law', 85 New York University Law Review 2010, 1581 (1602).

ods of practical testing and adjustment.[217] Second, environmental protection is a sensitive field due to the virtual inter-connection of all environmental sectors with each other.[218] The state has to ensure that the implemented support scheme really furthers its environmental goals: The schemes should be neither ineffective nor harmful to the intended or another important environmental objective. However, it is likely that certain aspects of the scheme have undesired effects, which only become visible retrospectively. This portrayal does not focus on the strength of the scientific evidence indicating the detrimental effects of the investment. Issues relating to the notions of precaution and scientific proof cannot be assessed in the abstract. Scenario No 4 can arise in the context of all support schemes intended to further environmental objectives. Two practical examples are portrayed in the following.

1. Creation of a 'Perverse Incentive'

One example illustrating the difficulty to foresee all environmental impact of supported investment projects stems from the Clean Development Mechanism of the Kyoto Protocol. The Clean Development Mechanism is a method which allows Annex B Parties to the Kyoto Protocol to offset a part of their domestic emissions with projects that reduce emissions in Non-Annex I Parties.[219] Such projects earn Certified Emission Reductions, which can be calculated against the domestic emissions of the Annex B Party. Under the Kyoto regime, the applicable six greenhouse gases are classified according to their global warming potential.[220] The Certified Emission Re-

---

[217] See *Wara*, Michael, 'Measuring the Clean Development Mechanism's Performance and Potential', 55 UCLA Law Review 2008, 1759 (1770, 1802) on the example of the specific challenges characterising the Clean Development Mechanism under the Kyoto Protocol: the absence of a cap on emissions for designated parties, the covering of multiple pollutants and their conversion into one common currency and the complex registration process stemming from it being based on projects.

[218] Examples of unforeseen negative consequences of environmental regulation in one area on another environmental good are manifold. One example is the substitution of ozone depleting substances through the Montreal Protocol with substances that have a high global warming potential, thus contributing to climate change. See *Roberts*, Mark W./*Grabiel*, Peter M., 'A Window of Opportunity: Combating Climate Change by Amending the Montreal Protocol to Regulate the Production and the Consumption of HFCs and ODS Banks', 22 Georgetown International Environmental Law Review 2009, 99 (105–106, 108).

[219] See above, pp. 56 *et seq.*

[220] The relevant greenhouse gases are listed in Annex A to the 1998 Kyoto Protocol. The respective factors are taken from the evaluation of the IPCC (Intergovernmental Panel on Climate Change), as stated in Article 5 para 3 Kyoto Protocol, and can be found in Intergovernmental Panel on Climate Change (IPCC), Working

ductions are accredited to reflect the differing global warming potential of the respective gas.[221] Accordingly, a one-unit reduction in a 'super-pollutant' will lead to the issuance of emission credits equalling the reduction of thousands of units of CO_2.[222]

One group of these 'super-pollutants' are hydrofluorcarbons, such as HFC-23, which is a very long-lived and potent greenhouse gas.[223] HFC-23 is a by-product of the production of HCFC-22, which is used as a more ozone layer friendly air-conditioner refrigerant or as a feedstock in the production of Teflon.[224] Because of the potency of HFC-23, the abatement of one metric ton of HFC-23 earns the equivalent to the abatement of several thousand metric tons of CO_2. The costs of the abatement of HFC-23 are relatively low since the technical process is simple.[225] When factoring in the substantial value for one Certified Emissions Reduction, the manufacturing of HCFC-22 can be economically viable solely because of the subsidies earned through

---

Group I Fourth Assessment Report: The Physical Science Basis (2007) para 2.10. *Schatz*, Andrew, 'Discounting the Clean Development Mechanism', 20 Georgetown International Environmental Law Review 2008, 703 (705); *Pillai*, Bharathi, 'Moving Forward to 2012: An Evaluation of the Clean Development Mechanism', 18 New York University Environmental Law Journal 2010, 357 (384).

221 See the list of the global warming potential of greenhouse gases at http://unfccc.int/ghg_data/items/3825.php. For use within the Kyoto system, all values are converted to the value for 1 ton to CO_2. Other gases have significantly higher values, like 56 for methane and 9100 for HFC-23.

222 *Schatz*, Andrew, 'Discounting the Clean Development Mechanism', 20 Georgetown International Environmental Law Review 2008, 703 (705).

223 The global warming potential of HFC-23 is 9100. In comparison, the value for CO_2 is 1. See http://unfccc.int/ghg_data/items/3825.php.

224 *Wara*, Michael, 'Measuring the Clean Development Mechanism's Performance and Potential', 55 UCLA Law Review 2008, 1759 (1778–1779); *Schatz*, Andrew, 'Discounting the Clean Development Mechanism', 20 Georgetown International Environmental Law Review 2008, 703 (721); *Roberts*, Mark W./*Grabiel*, Peter M., 'A Window of Opportunity: Combating Climate Change by Amending the Montreal Protocol to Regulate the Production and the Consumption of HFCs and ODS Banks', 22 Georgetown International Environmental Law Review 2009, 99 (119). Because of its less destructive effect on the ozone layer, the use of HCFC-22 instead of other gases was encouraged by the Montreal Protocol.

225 *Wara*, Michael, 'Measuring the Clean Development Mechanism's Performance and Potential', 55 UCLA Law Review 2008, 1759 (1783–1784); *Roberts*, Mark W./*Grabiel*, Peter M., 'A Window of Opportunity: Combating Climate Change by Amending the Montreal Protocol to Regulate the Production and the Consumption of HFCs and ODS Banks', 22 Georgetown International Environmental Law Review 2009, 99 (119); *Schatz*, Andrew, 'Discounting the Clean Development Mechanism', 20 Georgetown International Environmental Law Review 2008, 703 (720); *Pillai*, Bharathi, 'Moving Forward to 2012: An Evaluation of the Clean Development Mechanism', 18 New York University Environmental Law Journal 2010, 357 (385).

the Clean Development Mechanism.[226] The support scheme thus creates a 'perverse incentive' to manufacture a gas not to use it productively, but to earn money from the abatement of a by-product of the production. Accordingly, the Clean Development Mechanism creates an incentive to produce more HCFC-22 than there would be in the absence of the subsidy.[227]

This example illustrates the difficulty to create a market mechanism to support greener technologies in the intended way without any negative impacts or side effects. While this incentive is especially extreme, the parameters were also witnessed in connection with the parallel problem of adipic acid, which is the feedstock for the production of nylon 6-6, which releases N_2O as a by-product.[228] To further the overall environmental aim – namely the prevention of global climate change – states could be willing to alter the rules for which Emission Reduction Credits are earned, or discount their value in trading.[229] This concrete example from the context of

---

226 See detailed calculation by *Wara*, Michael, 'Measuring the Clean Development Mechanism's Performance and Potential', 55 UCLA Law Review 2008, 1759 (1783–1785). The author calculated, inter alia, that a developing world producer of HFCF-22 could earn twice as much from the subsidy of the Clean Development Mechanism as it could earn from the sale of its primary product.

227 *Wara*, Michael, 'Measuring the Clean Development Mechanism's Performance and Potential', 55 UCLA Law Review 2008, 1759 (1785–1786); *Roberts*, Mark W./*Grabiel*, Peter M., 'A Window of Opportunity: Combating Climate Change by Amending the Montreal Protocol to Regulate the Production and the Consumption of HFCs and ODS Banks', 22 Georgetown International Environmental Law Review 2009, 99 (119–120); *Pillai*, Bharathi, 'Moving Forward to 2012: An Evaluation of the Clean Development Mechanism', 18 New York University Environmental Law Journal 2010, 357 (386); *Schatz*, Andrew, 'Discounting the Clean Development Mechanism', 20 Georgetown International Environmental Law Review 2008, 703 (721). Wara (1785–1789) additionally points to two related incentives counterproductive to the environmental goals intended by the Clean Development Mechanism: (1) The fraction of the by-product HFC-23 within the production of HCFC-22 can be minimised through a modification of the conditions under which the chemical synthesis takes place. Since the occurrence of the by-product is wasteful in terms of energy and materials, there would be a normal incentive to optimise these conditions. However, the subsidy for the abatement creates an incentive to the opposite, so that it encourages the construction of inefficient plants. (2) Environmental regulators in the respective developing countries have no incentive to implement regulation that prescribes maximum levels for the by-product to occur, since it is more profitable to heavily tax the earnings of the plant owners.

Furthermore, Wara (1789) and Roberts and Grabiel (116) found that the abating of HFC-23 emissions through the Clean Development Mechanism was extremely costly, while it could be achieved at a fraction of these costs.

228 *Wara*, Michael, 'Measuring the Clean Development Mechanism's Performance and Potential', 55 UCLA Law Review 2008, 1759 (1778).

229 In June 2011, the European Commission has formally adopted a ban on the use of industrial gas credits in the EU Emissions Trading System (EU ETS) as of

the Clean Development Mechanism points to a possible problem in creating very complicated economic support schemes: Not all problematic consequences of the scheme can be properly foreseen and assessed when it is first implemented.[230]

2. Neglect of Impacts on Other Environmental Sectors

A further illustration of the forth scenario – an investment that was expected to be beneficial to the environment is subsequently raising concerns as to its sustainability – is the promotion of certain types of biofuels, such as bioethanol and biodiesel.[231] Bioethanol is a petrol substitute, mainly produced from sugar cane and corn.[232] Biodiesel is a diesel fuel derived from agricultural feedstock, such as rapeseed, soybeans and palm oil.[233] The introduction of biofuels was first enthusiastically seen as a measure to, inter alia, reduce the emissions of greenhouse gases and to improve local air quality in comparison with the combustion of fossil fuels.[234] To further these alleged

May 2013. The ban began on 1 January 2013 with a phase-out period of 4 months until 30 April 2013 for credits from existing projects. See http://ec.europa.eu/clima/news/articles/news_2011060801_en.htm.

230 The host state in which the investment takes place may generally not be unhappy about investment activity, even if the environmental goal is not furthered. As described above, the host state of a project under the Clean Development Mechanism does not have to accept a proposed project and has to be explicitly satisfied that the conditions for sustainable development are met. As was described for China, the possibility to heavily tax at 65% the revenue generated from Certified Emission Reductions by such investments makes the scheme so economically attractive for the host state that it is unlikely to demand an alteration of the scheme. See *Wara*, Michael, 'Measuring the Clean Development Mechanism's Performance and Potential', 55 UCLA Law Review 2008, 1759 (1788).

231 See for an overview of types and classifications of biofuels: *United Nations Environment Programme*, 'Towards Sustainable Production and Use of Resources: Assessing Biofuels' (2009), pp. 25–27. For the present purpose, the term biofuel will be understood to include liquid and solid fuels derived from agricultural feedstock, i. e. those that are commonly referred to as first generation biofuels.

232 *United Nations Environment Programme*, 'Towards Sustainable Production and Use of Resources: Assessing Biofuels' (2009) pp. 25–26; *Powers*, Melissa, 'King Corn: Will the Renewable Fuel Standard Eventually End Corn Ethanol's Reign?', 11 Vermont Journal of Environmental Law 2010, 667 (675); *Smaling*, Rudolf M., 'Environmental Barriers to Widespread Implementation of Biofuels', 2 Environmental & Energy Law & Policy Journal 2008, 287 (289).

233 *United Nations Environment Programme*, 'Towards Sustainable Production and Use of Resources: Assessing Biofuels' (2009) pp. 25–26; *Smaling*, Rudolf M., 'Environmental Barriers to Widespread Implementation of Biofuels', 2 Environmental & Energy Law & Policy Journal 2008, 287 (290–291).

234 *Hahn*, Robert W., 'Ethanol: Law, Economics and Politics', 19 Stanford Law and Policy Review 2008, 434 (435, 446); *Hughes*, Sara/*Partzsch*, Lena/*Gaskell*,

environmental advantages, domestic subsidies and other support schemes were implemented for the growing and production of biofuels.[235]

However, evidence increasingly points to the negative environmental consequences of these first-generation biofuels, thus implicating the harmfulness of larger reliance on them. The main area of concern relates to the process of growing such crops, which requires substantial amounts of land and drives the need to convert more soil into arable land. This leads to the conversion of rainforests, peatland and other land not yet used for agricultural production, which brings about an irreversible loss of biodiversity as well as the emission of substantial amounts of greenhouse gases so far contained in the natural cover and the soil.[236] Furthermore, these crops are mainly grown in monocultures and the high intensity of the farming requires substantial amounts of energy and fertilizers – resulting in significant greenhouse gas emissions, the pollution of water courses and loss of biodiversity.[237] The extensive amount

Joanne, 'The Development of Biofuels in the Context of the Global Water Crisis', 7 Sustainable Development Law & Policy 2007, 58 (58); *Smaling*, Rudolf M., 'Environmental Barriers to Widespread Implementation of Biofuels', 2 Environmental & Energy Law & Policy Journal 2008, 287 (288). Other advantages associated with the use of biofuels are the reduction of the dependence on foreign crude oil imports, the reduction of oil prices, and the establishment of an attractive opportunity for the development of local communities in developing countries, see *Ottinger*, Richard L., 'Biofuels: Potential, Problems & Solutions', 19 Fordham Environmental Law Review 2009, 253 (253–254).

235 On the level of the EU, Directive 2003/30/EC of 8 May 2003 on the promotion of the use of biofuels or other renewable fuels for transport, implemented the aim of increasing the market share of biofuels. According to Directive 2003/96/EC of 27 October 2003, member states granted tax exemptions or tax rebates for biofuels. Further, many developing countries benefit from duty-free and quota-free access to the EU for ethanol. Mandatory blend requirements further constitute an economic advantage for producers. See for a detailed and critical assessment, *Kutas*, Géraldine/*Lindberg*, Carina/*Steenblik*, Ronald, Biofuels – At What Cost? Government Support for Ethanol and Biodiesel in the European Union (2007).

236 *United Nations Environment Programme*, 'Towards Sustainable Production and Use of Resources: Assessing Biofuels' (2009) pp. 53–55; *Smaling*, Rudolf M., 'Environmental Barriers to Widespread Implementation of Biofuels', 2 Environmental & Energy Law & Policy Journal 2008, 287 (299–300); *Powers*, Melissa, 'King Corn: Will the Renewable Fuel Standard Eventually End Corn Ethanol's Reign?', 11 Vermont Journal of Environmental Law 2010, 667 (687–688).

237 *Hahn*, Robert W., 'Ethanol: Law, Economics and Politics', 19 Stanford Law and Policy Review 2008, 434 (447–448); *Ottinger*, Richard L., 'Biofuels: Potential, Problems & Solutions', 19 Fordham Environmental Law Review 2009, 253 (256); *Smaling*, Rudolf M., 'Environmental Barriers to Widespread Implementation of Biofuels', 2 Environmental & Energy Law & Policy Journal 2008, 287 (296–298).

of water required for the growing can also be problematic for the global water resources.[238]

Another great concern relates to the use of edible plants for the production of biofuels: It points to the direct competition of feedstock with its use as a food source and is considered a factor leading to an increase in food prices and facilitating food shortages.[239] Further concerns stem from the sizeable amounts of energy involved in the process of the production of the respective fuel from its agricultural feedstock as well as its transportation.[240] The data on the environmental advantages of the combustion of biofuels in comparison with fossil fuels are mixed. While several emissions are reduced, some studies indicate that biofuels, depending on the respective feedstock, lead to an increase in emissions of nitrogen oxides.[241]

The case of biofuels is a classic example of projects and investments that were first hailed as environmental improvements. However, reality has shown that the intended environmental advantages will often not be realised. Biofuels can be outright detrimental to the environment and cause human rights concerns. The resulting question is how a state can react that has implemented support schemes to further investment in such activities. Can the state revoke such assistance given that the environmental advantage will not be achieved by a specific project? Practical examples could be the investment in a palm oil plantation in Indonesia or the building of an energy plant run on palm oil in a European country.

---

[238] *Hughes*, Sara/*Partzsch*, Lena/*Gaskell*, Joanne, 'The Development of Biofuels in the Context of the Global Water Crisis', 7 Sustainable Development Law & Policy 2007, 58 (60); *Hahn*, Robert W., 'Ethanol: Law, Economics and Politics', 19 Stanford Law and Policy Review 2008, 434 (448).

[239] *Rotman*, David, 'The Price of Biofuels', 111 Technology Review 2008, 42, pp. 42–51 (42, 45); *Smith*, David N., 'The Way We Think: Ethics, Health and the Environment in International Business', 5 Asian Journal of WTO & International Health Law and Policy 2010, 25 (30, 43); *Ottinger*, Richard L., 'Biofuels: Potential, Problems & Solutions', 19 Fordham Environmental Law Review 2009, 253 (255); *Powers*, Melissa, 'King Corn: Will the Renewable Fuel Standard Eventually End Corn Ethanol's Reign?', 11 Vermont Journal of Environmental Law 2010, 667 (685–686).

[240] *Rotman*, David, 'The Price of Biofuels', 111 Technology Review 2008, 42 (44); *Smith*, David N., 'The Way We Think: Ethics, Health and the Environment in International Business', 5 Asian Journal of WTO & International Health Law and Policy 2010, 25 (30); *Powers*, Melissa, 'King Corn: Will the Renewable Fuel Standard Eventually End Corn Ethanol's Reign?', 11 Vermont Journal of Environmental Law 2010, 667 (687).

[241] *Hahn*, Robert W., 'Ethanol: Law, Economics and Politics', 19 Stanford Law and Policy Review 2008, 434 (447–448); *Smaling*, Rudolf M., 'Environmental Barriers to Widespread Implementation of Biofuels', 2 Environmental & Energy Law & Policy Journal 2008, 287 (301, 303–304).

The problem that supposedly environmentally friendly technologies have side effects that are – at least allegedly – detrimental to the environment is a frequently occurring feature of progress in technology. Problematic implications which are about to gain more recognition are, for example, carbon capture and storage technology,[242] or the use of neodymium in wind turbines[243]. It has to be taken into account that environmental implications deriving from one supposedly environmentally friendly technology or concept frequently lead to the creation of better technologies with fewer negative impacts. For environmental technologies or economic support schemes to be "standing on the shoulders of giants", there will often have been a lot of trial and error in prior generations of the technology. Accordingly, the state has to be able to adjust incentive regimes implemented for such technologies.

V. Intermediate Summary

The four scenarios describe possible situations in which the standards of treatment accorded to foreign investors conflict or interact with the objective of the host state to protect the environment. The scenarios do not intend to capture all combinations of conflict which could occur. The aim is to typify certain scenarios in which a conflict is most likely. Scenario No 1 describes the most obvious potential for conflict and it has already featured in several investment decisions. For the other scenarios, investment awards give indications as to how arbitral tribunals are likely to evaluate the tension between both sets of rights. The subsequent chapters are to establish guidelines deriving from investment treaties and awards as to how the scenarios are likely to be evaluated in an investment dispute.

---

242 The most likely risks of carbon capture and storage are consequences of a potential leakage of the captured CO_2 . Such leakage has a negative impact on the global climate – releasing the greenhouse gases it was supposed to store and may cause asphyxiation, the contamination of ground water and the death of vegetation. See *Langlet*, David, 'Safe Return to the Underground? The Role of International Law in Subsurface Storage of Carbon Dioxide', 18 Review of European Community & International Environmental Law 2009, 286–303. The issue of carbon capture and storage is likely to receive more attention now that carbon capture storage projects are eligible for credits under the Clean Development Mechanism.

243 Rare-earth materials are essential for many green energy technologies. However, the mining of these rare-earth materials can cause environmental damage, *Percival*, Robert V., 'China's "Green Leap Forward" Toward Global Environmental Leadership', 12 Vermont Journal of Environmental Law 2011, 633 (648).

F. Conclusion

Human alteration of the natural environment is accompanied by negative implications for ecosystems, freshwater, air, soil, fauna, flora and human beings. The increasing recognition of the impact of human activity on the environment has resulted in the imposition of restrictions on degrading activity: Slowly, but steadily states have created and implemented national and international environmental regulation in a wide range of subject areas. The exact contours of the obligation to protect the environment differ from state to state. However, a multitude of environmental issues are recognised and legally addressed in an increasing number of states.

The prevalence of environmental restrictions in specific context is exemplified by international conventions and agreements regarding certain subject matters: States have agreed on binding rules and restrictions to address environmental problems. Further, targets set up for implementation in the national jurisdictions have been adopted. In addition, international environmental law has seen the creation of a set of environmental principles that is to influence the further development of international law as well as the approach of national legislation towards upcoming environmental issues.

The increasing level of environmental regulation has an impact on economic activities such as foreign investment projects, as it constitutes a restriction on economic activity. Foreign investment activities are clearly affected by such regulation, as they have to conform to regulation in place in the host state. With the corpus of environmental law being in motion, the potential for conflicts with the interests of foreign investors – which are primarily interested in stability – is high. The potential for conflict between both sets of rules and interests can be typified in certain scenarios. Most importantly, the introduction of an environmental rule that was not anticipated can counter the interest of the investor. Similarly, the actual application of national regulation – for example with regard to the granting of a necessary permit – can be contested. Further problems can stem from the introduction of economic support schemes to further allegedly environmental technologies and processes. The scenarios which have been portrayed in this chapter will be further scrutinised in connection with the respective standards of investment protection in the subsequent chapters.

Chapter 2

The Influence of Environmental Concepts on the Interpretation of Investment Provisions

Interpretation of documents is to some extent an art, not an exact science.
Sir Humphrey Waldock, 1964

The constant increase in the numbers of international agreements and respective institutions has resulted in an intensified specialisation of different areas of international law. This specialisation leads to concerns regarding the coherence of the system as a whole, mainly with respect to the interaction and interdependence of the different, more or less specialised branches of international law – a phenomenon commonly referred to as fragmentation.[1] International investment law, and – to a lesser extent – international environmental law, embody characteristics and principles which set them apart from the more general body of international law. Investment law, especially due to its distinct dispute settlement process that focuses on the rights of an individual, the investor, can be considered a special or self-contained regime of international law. Conceiving investment law as a

---

[1] See for a comprehensive overview of the phenomenon of fragmentation, *International Law Commission*, Fragmentation of International Law: Difficulties arising from the Diversification and Expansion of International Law, Report of the Study Group of the International Law Commission of 13 April 2006 (A/CN.4/L.682), finalised by Martti Koskenniemi, paras 7–17.

Highlighting and evaluating different aspects of fragmentation such as 'competition' of potentially applicable norms and differing interpretations of the same norms through different international courts and tribunals, *Higgins*, Rosalyn, 'A Babel of Judicial Voices? Ruminations from the Bench', 55 International and Comparative Law Quarterly 2006, 791–804.

Stating that fragmentation concerns the separation of a specialised state-controlled system like the system of the World Trade Organization (WTO system) from a more general state-controlled system, namely the system of public international law, so that the specialised system can be analysed within the realm of the general system, *Klabbers*, Jan, 'Reluctant Grundnormen: Articles 31 (3) (C) and 42 of the Vienna Convention on the Law of Treaties and the Fragmentation of International Law', in: Time, History and International Law (Craven, Matthew et al. (Eds.) 2007) 141 (157). Klabbers further mentions the fragmentation involved in non-state centred regulation as an additional threat (158).

self-contained regime amplifies the issue of its relationship with other areas of international law, such as environmental law. Does the distinctness of international investment law materially isolate it from international environmental law?

It is a truism that a legal arrangement cannot exist completely independent from the system of law from which it derives its validity – or it would be devoid of any meaning.[2] Accordingly, no regime is truly 'self-contained'. Investment law, like any other special branch of international law, is still part of the overall system of international law and requires the application of the basic tenets of the system. In addition to these fundamental tenets, which give relevance to the existence and observance of treaty obligations as such, there is a visible desire of the system of international law to maintain a certain material coherence. It is in this sense that international courts and tribunals express the thought that self-contained regimes of international law do not exist in a legal vacuum, but are "to be interpreted as far as possible in harmony with other principles of international law".[3] In the absence of a hierarchy of norms, it is this principle of the harmonisation of norms[4] which counters the impact of fragmentation by

---

[2] See for a comprehensive discussion of the issue *International Law Commission*, Fragmentation of International Law: Difficulties arising from the Diversification and Expansion of International Law, Report of the Study Group of the International Law Commission of 13 April 2006 (A/CN.4/L.682), finalised by Martti Koskenniemi, paras 172–185.

[3] See for the human rights system under the European Convention on Human Rights (ECHR) the decisions of the ECtHR: Case of McElhinney v. Ireland (Application no. 31253/96) Grand Chamber Judgment of 21 November 2001, para. 36; Case of Al-Adsani v. United Kingdom (Application no. 35763/97) Grand Chamber Judgment of 21 November 2001, para. 55. Similarly, Case of Loizidou v. Turkey (Application no. 15318/89) Grand Chamber Judgment of 18 December 1996, para 43. For the WTO system, see United States – Standards for Reformulated and Conventional Gasoline, DS2/AB/R, WTO Appellate Body Report of 29 April 1996, stating that the GATT "is not to be read in clinical isolation from public international law". See also, more generally, Legal Consequences for States of the Continued Presence of South Africa in Namibia (South West Africa) notwithstanding Security Council Resolution 276 (1970), Advisory Opinion of 21 June 1971, ICJ Reports 1971, 16 (31), para 53.

[4] The principle of harmonious interpretation is considered to be a customary means of treaty interpretation, which mandates that a treaty should be read consistent with other customary or conventional international law, see *Van Damme*, Isabelle, 'Some Observations about the ILC Study Group Report on the Fragmentation of International Law: WTO Treaty Interpretation against the Background of Other International Law', XVII Finnish Yearbook of International Law 2006, 21 (24, 38). *Contra, Orakhelashvili*, Alexander, 'Recent Practice on the Principles of Treaty Interpretation', in: 40 Years of the Vienna Convention on the Law of Treaties (Orakhelashvili, Alexander et al. (Eds.) 2010) 117 (149), stating that interpretative no-

addressing potential normative conflicts, thus aiming to make the system of international law more coherent.

The extent to which provisions of investment protection contained in investment treaties conflict with environmental norms and measures is the core issue of the subsequent chapters. This chapter focuses on the impact that environmental norms can have in the interpretative context of investment treaties. First, it discusses the concept of 'conflict' and introduces common principles of interpretation. Second, the chapter provides an overview of environmental references contained in investment treaties and attempts to determine the effect they can have as 'interpretative context'. The survey presents and distinguishes preambular references and provisions in the operative part of a treaty, along with assessing their relevance in the light of the general rules of treaty interpretation. Finally, further possible points of entry are portrayed and assessed as to their potential for introducing notions of environmental law to an investment dispute, in the absence of a specific reference in the investment treaty.

A. Conflicts of Norms and Interpretation

Conflicts of norms arise when two or more norms are applicable to the same factual situation. If each set of norms offers a different solution to the factual situation, the sets of norms are *prima facie* in conflict. There are primarily two scenarios of normative conflicts: norms of international law can be logically incompatible, so that observing one norm results in breaching the other norm.[5] If this is the case, a reconciliation of both norms is impossible. Logical incompatibility requires a solution to the conflict which gives one rule precedence over the other. In the case of potential conflicts between international investment law and international environmental law, no general hierarchy of either set of norms can be determined. Investment treaties as such are not more elevated in the hierarchy of norms than international environmental law.[6] Second, there can be a more indirect incompat-

---

tions like 'harmonious interpretation' "are not really part of the law of treaty interpretation".

[5] *International Law Commission*, Fragmentation of International Law: Difficulties arising from the Diversification and Expansion of International Law, Report of the Study Group of the International Law Commission of 13 April 2006 (A/CN.4/L.682), finalised by Martti Koskenniemi, para 24; *Kammerhofer*, Jörg, 'The Theory of Norm Conflict Solutions in International Law', in: Sustainable Development in World Investment Law (Cordonier Segger, Marie-Claire et al. (Eds.) 2011) 83 (85).

[6] In international law, there is no fixed hierarchical relationship between different norms. Nevertheless, *jus cogens* norms, *erga omnes* norms and norms falling

ibility, which occurs when one treaty frustrates the goal of the other treaty.[7] This relationship is a categorisation of different regimes of law more than of individual norms opposing each other.[8] Indirect incompatibility can generally be adjusted through a harmonising interpretation of the treaty provisions.

Whether the relationship of the respective norms is one of logical incompatibility is to be determined by applying the respective norms in conflict and evaluate their interaction. It is preferable that the interpreter, amongst the possible ways of interpretation of a norm, chooses the way which renders both norms compatible with each other.[9] If this is possible, a situation of logical incompatibility does not exist. If the result suggests that there is indirect incompatibility, the solution to the conflict is to be found in the way in which the relevant norms are interpreted. The previous chapter has demonstrated that international environmental law relies on principles and tools of non-obligatory character to achieve its goals. It rarely imposes concrete obligations on states. Accordingly, a conflict with international environmental norms and standards is usually one of indirect incompatibility. Adjudicators should attempt to solve potential clashes with obligations stemming from international environmental law primarily through means of interpretation.

---

within the scope of Article 103 Charta of the United Nations are generally considered to take precedence over other obligations. See for a detailed discussion, *International Law Commission*, Fragmentation of International Law: Difficulties arising from the Diversification and Expansion of International Law, Report of the Study Group of the International Law Commission of 13 April 2006 (A/CN.4/L.682), finalised by Martti Koskenniemi, paras 324–409. Investment law does not fall into these categories. This does not mean that there could not be interpretative rules establishing a hierarchy of investment obligations in a specific case, like the *lex specialis* or the *lex posterior* rule.

On a more practical note, however, it is possible that the 'procedural primacy' of investment law is relevant. The well-established dispute resolution procedure constitutes a sharp contrast to environmental agreements, which practically do not have a specialised court or forum. Undoubtedly, the numeric mass of arbitral decisions which has the concerns of investment law at its heart has an impact on the relations of the two fields of law from the perspective of an adjudicator.

[7] *International Law Commission*, Fragmentation of International Law: Difficulties arising from the Diversification and Expansion of International Law, Report of the Study Group of the International Law Commission of 13 April 2006 (A/CN.4/L.682), finalised by Martti Koskenniemi, para 24.

[8] *International Law Commission*, Fragmentation of International Law: Difficulties arising from the Diversification and Expansion of International Law, Report of the Study Group of the International Law Commission of 13 April 2006 (A/CN.4/L.682), finalised by Martti Koskenniemi, para 24.

[9] *Viñuales*, Jorge E./*Jesko* Langer, Magnus, 'Managing Conflicts Between Environmental and Investment Norms in International Law', in: The Transformation of International Environmental Law (Kerbrat, Yann et al. (Eds.) 2011) 171 (174).

A substantial part of international environmental considerations becomes effective through environmental measures and regulation at the national level. The foreign investor is most likely to perceive the national measure, which openly impacts on its investment activity, as being in direct conflict with the obligations of the investment treaty. In reality, the issue thus evolves into a 'legitimacy conflict' between a norm of international law and one of national law.[10] Even though then the conflicting norms are apparently not on the same level of hierarchy,[11] the national environmental measure will often be inspired by international environmental conventions and the aims set forth therein. Even if international environmental law does not oblige the state to take the specific measure affecting the investor, the host state may be obliged to take measures to further the overall environmental objective by adopting respective regulation and measures. Further, the sovereign right of the host state to adopt regulation for application within its territory is relevant. Accordingly, a legitimacy conflict requires the har-

---

[10] *Viñuales*, Jorge E./*Jesko* Langer, Magnus, 'Managing Conflicts Between Environmental and Investment Norms in International Law', in: The Transformation of International Environmental Law (Kerbrat, Yann et al. (Eds.) 2011) 171 (176) use this categorisation "legitimacy conflict" for conflicts between an obligation arising from international investment law and a national measure "based on environmental considerations other than an obligation stemming from international environmental law". In my understanding, the differentiation that the authors make between norms based on an *obligation* stemming from international environmental law and measures based on other environmental considerations cannot practically be maintained. First, the categorisation provides no real distinction. The differentiation relies on whether a party involved claims that the measure derives from an international obligation (176–177). Whether a national environmental measure actually reflects an international obligation of the host state will be a central part of the discussion in every scenario, since the extent to which a national norm is shaped by international environmental consideration can constitute a factor in determining the legitimacy of the exercise of the state's authority to regulate. Second, whether there really is an international obligation to adopt the specific measure is influenced by the scope and precision of the underlying international convention. Generally, only rarely do conventions impose specific measures for the state to adopt, so that an environmental target set by the international instrument can be achieved through a set of different measures. In the light of the sovereignty of the national state, I am not convinced that the precision with which international environmental law obliges a state to adopt one specific measure is a constructive criterion for differentiation. Therefore, I apply the term 'legitimacy concept' to characterise all conflicts between national environmental measures and international obligations of investment protection.

[11] See Article 27 1969 Vienna Convention on the Law of Treaties (VCLT), which prescribes that in the international legal order, international law obligations prevail over national law. This determination for the sphere of international law is correct, even if Article 27 VCLT does not implement the general superiority of international law, see *Corten*, Olivier/*Klein*, Pierre (Eds.) The Vienna Convention on the Law of Treaties, A Commentary (2011) Article 27 para 17 (Schaus, Annemie).

monisation of both conflicting subject areas. Interpretation can constitute an appropriate tool.

Logically, the base for interpreting provisions in international treaties is the actual text of the respective treaty. Some investment treaties do already express the understanding that investment law is not to be understood in isolation from environmental law. Not being oblivious of the development of national and international environmental law and the alleged potential for collision, references to environmental concepts and to the relationship between both areas of law can be found in investment treaties and in free trade agreements containing provisions on investment protection. Although such references are frequent in more recent investment agreements, their absolute number is small in comparison to the overwhelmingly large number of investment treaties that have been concluded to date. Nevertheless, these references are relevant for two reasons: First, on a general level, they indicate areas of concern identified by states and potentially give guidance to how states perceive the relationship between norms from both areas of law. Second, on a more concrete level, such references can influence the interpretation of other provisions and obligations contained in the treaty.

In this chapter, the focus is on the influence which environmental norms and principles have on the interpretation of investment treaties. The interpretation of international treaties follows the rules of the 1969 Vienna Convention on the Law of Treaties (VCLT).[12] The VCLT prescribes the

---

[12] The fundamental guideline for the interpretation of international treaties is the VCLT. Today, the rules contained in the VCLT are generally considered to be applicable to the interpretation of all treaties. See *Gardiner*, Richard, Treaty Interpretation (2008) p. 7; *McLachlan*, Campell, 'The Principle of Systematic Integration and Article 31 (3) (c) of the Vienna Convention', 54 International & Comparative Law Quarterly 2005, 279 (293). The relevance of the VCLT is further underlined by the *International Law Commission*, Fragmentation of International Law: Difficulties arising from the Diversification and Expansion of International Law, Report of the Study Group of the International Law Commission of 13 April 2006 (A/CN.4/L.682), finalised by Martti Koskenniemi, paras 177–178, which finds that there is no evidence of any rule-regime claiming to be operative independently of the VCLT.

More specifically, commentators maintain that investment tribunals established under the aegis of ICSID, have applied the rules of the VCLT as a statement of the applicable interpretative regime. See *Gardiner*, Richard, Treaty Interpretation (2008), p. 119; *Schreuer*, Christoph, 'Diversity and Harmonization of Treaty Interpretation in Investment Arbitration', in: Treaty Interpretation and the Vienna Convention on the Law of Treaties: 30 Years On (Fitzmaurice, Malgosia et al. (Eds.) 2010) 129 (129); *Fauchald*, Ole Kristian, 'The Legal Reasoning of ICSID Tribunals: An Empirical Analysis', 19 European Journal of International Law 2008, 301 (314). However, Fauchald finds that the references to the VCLT in arbitral decisions are of a rather superficial nature and that relatively few tribunals make active use of the wording of a treaty in their reasoning (314, 322). See as an example for non-ICSID

body of material to be taken into account and how it has to be approached – thereby creating an inherent logical consequence:[13] According to these rules, a treaty first and foremost has to be interpreted in good faith. The object is to establish the intention of the parties as the true meaning of the treaty.[14] In this quest, all relevant elements prescribed by Articles 31 to 33 VCLT for the interpretation of a treaty are thrown into an 'interpretative crucible', so that their interaction leads to the legally relevant interpretation.[15] In the adjudication of an investment case, interpretation will especially be important to determine the scope of the protective guarantees owed to the investor. In the process of establishing the material borders of these concepts, environmental law can have an interpretative influence.

Accordingly, it is important to determine what exactly the interpretative influence of environmental references in investment treaties consists of. This issue requires a portrayal and evaluation of the existing clauses and provisions. In the absence of specific environmental references in the text of an investment treaty, international environmental law can become relevant as part of the international legal system, in which the treaty is rooted. The system, which arguably strives for coherence as far as possible,[16] foresees certain openings in the interpretative process to other areas of international law. One of these entry points is Article 31 paragraph 3 lit c VCLT, which provides that "any relevant rules of international law applicable in the relations between the parties" shall be taken into account in the interpretation of a treaty. Another potential entry for international law is Article 42 paragraph 1 sentence 2 ICSID Convention, which permits the application of rules of international law to the dispute in the absence of an agreement of the parties on the applicable rules of law.

---

tribunals the intense consideration of the VCLT by the tribunal in Methanex v. United States, Partial Award of 7 August 2002, paras 97–102 and Award of 3 August 2005, Part II, Chapter B, paras 15–23.

[13] *Gardiner*, Richard, Treaty Interpretation (2008) p. 9.

[14] *Gardiner*, Richard, Treaty Interpretation (2008) p. 6; *Corten*, Olivier/*Klein*, Pierre (Eds.) The Vienna Convention on the Law of Treaties, A Commentary (2011) Article 31 para 48 (Sorel, Jean-Marc/Boré Eveno, Valérie).

[15] The approach taken by the VCLT is best illustrated with the words of the *International Law Commission*: "All the various elements, as they were present in any given case, would be thrown into the crucible, and their interaction would give the legally relevant interpretation", United Nations Conference on the Law of Treaties, 'Official Records: Documents of the Conference' (1971), A/CONF.39/11/Add.2, p. 39, para 8.

[16] *International Law Commission*, Fragmentation of International Law: Difficulties arising from the Diversification and Expansion of International Law, Report of the Study Group of the International Law Commission of 18 July 2006 (A/CN.4/L.702), paras 10–12.

B. Preambular Clauses

According to the principles incorporated in Article 31 VCLT, a treaty is to be interpreted "in accordance with the ordinary meaning to be given to the terms of the treaty in their context and in the light of its object and purpose".[17] In addition to the ordinary meaning of the terms, which constitutes the starting point for the interpretation, the 'context' and the 'object and purpose' of the treaty are relevant. The preamble of a treaty can be relevant to both of these notions: First, Article 31 paragraph 2 VCLT specifies that the preamble – as element of the integral text of the treaty – forms part of the context of the treaty, against which a specific norm has to be interpreted. Second, international courts and tribunals often establish the object and purpose of a treaty with reference to its preamble.[18] This is also the case for investment tribunals.[19] Although the preamble of a treaty is not the appropriate place for stating obligations, it sometimes contains components with regard to which the parties could not agree on whether they were significant enough to insert them into the operative part.[20] The preambular clauses are relevant as interpretative tools for the meaning of terms used in the substantive provisions, because they set forth the underlying motivation, aims and considerations of the treaty.[21]

---

[17] Article 31 para 1 VCLT.

[18] See, for example, ICJ, Reservations to the Convention on the Prevention and Punishment of the Crime of Genocide, Advisory Opinion of 28 May 1951, ICJ Reports 1951, 15 (23); Case Concerning Military and Paramilitary Activity in and against Nicaragua, (Nicaragua/United States of America), Judgment on the Merits of 27 June 1986, ICJ Reports 1986, 14 (138), para 275; ECtHR Case of Golder v. United Kingdom (Application no. 4451/70) Judgment of 21 February 1975, para 34.

[19] See SGS Société Générale de Surveillance S.A. v. Republic of the Philippines, ICSID Case No. ARB/02/6, Decision on Objections to Jurisdiction of 29 January 2004, para 116; Plama Consortium Limited v. Bulgaria, ICSID Case No. ARB/03/24, Decision on Jurisdiction of 8 February 2005, para 193; LG&E v. Argentina, ICSID Case No. ARB/02/1, Decision on Liability of 3 October 2006, para 124; Compañiá de Aguas del Aconquija S.A. and Vivendi Universal v. Argentine Republic, ICSID Case No. ARB/97/3, Award of 20 August 2007, para 7.4.4.; Saluka Investments BV (The Netherlands) v. The Czech Republic, Award of 17 March 2006, paras 299–300; Ioan Micula, Viorel Micula, S.C. European Food S.A, S.C. Starmill S.R.L. and S.C. Multipack S.R.L. v. Romania, ICSID Case No. ARB/05/20, Award of 11 December 2013, paras 513–516.

See also *Schreuer*, Christoph, 'Diversity and Harmonization of Treaty Interpretation in Investment Arbitration', in: Treaty Interpretation and the Vienna Convention on the Law of Treaties: 30 Years On (Fitzmaurice, Malgosia et al. (Eds.) 2010) 129 (131) suggesting that investment tribunals most frequently seek guidance from the preamble of the respective treaty when identifying its object and purpose.

[20] *Suy*, Eric, 'Le Préambule' in: Liber Amicorum Judge Mohammed Bedjaoui (Yakpo, Emile et al. (Eds.) 1999) 253 (260).

I. Bilateral Investment Treaties

The preambles of current bilateral investment treaties set forth differing and multiple aims to be achieved through the treaty. The most dominant objectives set forth in these treaties emphasise the aims of encouraging foreign investment and of extending and intensifying the parties' economic relations. In this sense, the preambles in investment treaties are frequently used to underline the importance of stability and favourable conditions for investments. In addition to these reasons for the conclusion of the investment treaty, however, several states use preambular clauses to formulate policy goals that are not intrinsically connected to the furthering of economic co-operation. Clauses emphasising the concern for environmental objectives are a case in point.

Although the numeric occurrence of preambular clauses referring to environmental objectives is marginal in comparison with the overall number of bilateral investment treaties, these clauses deserve attention due to their prevalence in recent bilateral investment treaties. The focus of these preambular clauses in recent bilateral treaties is predominantly on one issue: the concern that the state's desire to attract foreign investment will lead, inter alia, to a decrease in the adoption and implementation of environmental rules. Especially highly-regulated states fear the negative effects of the so-called regulatory 'race-to-the-bottom'.[22] A rather frequently used formulation for a preambular clause is the following:

> "The Governments of [...]
> Agreeing that these objectives can be achieved without relaxing health, safety and environmental measures of general application [...]
> Have agreed as follows: [...]"

This reference can be found in a multitude of more recent bilateral investment treaties concluded by the United States of America (U.S.),[23] in

---

21 Similarly, *Gardiner*, Richard, Treaty Interpretation (2008) p. 186; *Suy*, Eric, 'Le Préambule' in: Liber Amicorum Judge Mohammed Bedjaoui (Yakpo, Emile et al. (Eds.) 1999) 253 (254–255).

22 The fear of a regulatory 'race-to-the-bottom' is further the object of references in substantive clauses in investment treaties. The relevance of this concern will be discussed in more detail below, pp. 119 *et seq.*

23 Preambular clause 5 U.S.-Honduras BIT; preambular clause 5 U.S.-Georgia BIT; preambular clause 5 U.S.-Azerbaijan BIT; preambular clause 5 U.S.-Albania BIT; preambular clause 5 U.S.-Bolivia BIT; preambular clause 5 U.S.-El Salvador BIT; preambular clause 5 U.S.-Jordan BIT; preambular clause 5 U.S.-Mozambique BIT; preambular clause 5 U.S.-Trinidad and Tobago BIT; preambular clause 5 U.S.-Bahrain BIT; preambular clause 5 U.S.-Croatia BIT; preambular clause 5 U.S.-Nicaragua BIT; preambular clause 5 U.S.-Uzbekistan BIT.

most of the more recent bilateral investment treaties concluded by Finland[24] and in some other bilateral investment treaties.[25] The reference stresses that the overall economic objectives of the respective investment treaty,[26] like greater economic co-operation between the states, stimulation of economic development, and improvement of living standards can be achieved without relaxing environmental measures of general application. Although a 'measure' may not be precisely defined, it is generally considered to encompass a wide array of legislative and administrative concepts, such as regulation, laws, and procedures.[27] According to the U.S., which is supposedly a driving force behind the insertion of the formulation[28], the clause has to be understood broadly as aiming at the maintenance of environmental regulation.[29] In the light of the concern that was supposed to be addressed, namely the alleged race-to-the-bottom with regard to environmental legislation, it is not surprising that the preamble appears to focus on the phase of attracting investment. Its wording does not give guidance on the relationship of investment protection and environmental measures once the investment has been successfully attracted.

The same objective was inserted in some more recent investment treaties with a slightly different wording. This preambular clause, which has so far not been used frequently, reads as follows:

---

[24] Preambular clause 6 Finland-Nicaragua BIT; preambular clause 5 Finland-Bosnia and Herzegovina BIT; preambular clause 6 Finland-Armenia BIT; preambular clause 6 Finland-Belarus BIT; preambular clause 6 Finland-Ethiopia BIT; preambular clause 6 Finland-Tanzania BIT; preambular clause 6 Finland-Zambia BIT; preambular clause 6 Finland-Nigeria BIT; preambular clause 5 Finland-Guatemala BIT; preambular clause 6 Finland-Kyrgyzstan BIT.

[25] Preambular clause 4 China-Trinidad and Tobago BIT; preambular clause 3 Spain-Trinidad and Tobago BIT.

[26] The over-riding goals of the treaty mentioned in the antecedent preambular clauses of the above-referenced BITs to which the U.S. are a party are the following: Promote greater economic co-operation; stimulate the flow of private capital and the economic development of the Parties; maximise effective utilisation of economic resources and improve living standards; development of economic and business ties.

The BITs with participation of Finland contain very similar language.

[27] See Article 1 2004 U.S. Model BIT, defining 'measure' to include "any law, regulation, procedure, requirement, or practice". See also identical Article 201 1993 North American Free Trade Agreement (NAFTA).

[28] These BITs are modelled after the 1994 U.S. Model BIT.

[29] The Letter of Submittal by the U.S. Department of State attached to the respective BITs, p. 2, understands the respective preambles to set forth, inter alia, the following goals: "[…] the stimulation of economic development; higher living standards […] and maintenance of health, safety, and environmental measures".

> “[…] Desiring to achieve these objectives in a manner consistent with the protection of health, safety, and the environment, and the promotion of internationally recognized labor rights […]”[30]

This clause is more aspirational than the previously-cited version. It refers to ‘protection of the environment’ and thus arguably inserts a more far-reaching objective of its own right. Furthermore, the wording implies that the over-reaching objectives are meant to be achieved “in a manner consistent” with environmental protection, so that it has a broader scope than existing environmental measures, which could be relaxed to attract investment. Thus, the clause can be interpreted as a more general statement on the relationship and co-existence of environmental and investment protection. However, the value of this core statement of the clause is reduced since it is the expression of a ‘desire’ and not of an ‘agreement’.

As a last example of a preambular clause in this context, a clause with a different objective is portrayed. It reads as follows:

> “[…] Recognizing also the increasing need for measures to protect the environment […]”[31]

This clause does not address the fear of the regulatory race-to-the-bottom, but implies a mandate for the state parties to maintain and strengthen their environmental regulation. The formulation goes so far as to state a need for future regulation in environmental matters. It does not expressly link environmental measures to the achievement of over-reaching goals of the investment treaty, but the fact that this clause forms part of a preamble to an investment agreement indicates that the state parties wish to give weight to environmental protection in the light of their wish to reciprocally encourage and protect investments. Thus, the clause underlines the acceptance of this notion by the state parties.

This overview indicates that most bilateral investment treaties referring to environmental concerns in their preambles do so in fear of the regulatory race-to-the-bottom. In general, few bilateral investment treaties contain such a preambular clause[32] and the insertion of such clauses appears to be driven by a small set of states. The review suggests that in earlier decades

---

30 In these words, preambular clause 5 U.S.-Rwanda BIT; with the addition of the “promotion of consumer protection”, preambular clause 5 U.S.-Uruguay BIT.

31 Preambular clause 5 Germany-Trinidad and Tobago BIT.

32 A complete analysis of the preambles of all BITs was not feasible in this study. My research is limited to a review of approximately 250 bilateral investment treaties. Problems that might have prevented the identification of more relevant investment treaties are, first, that not all BITs are comprehensively available in the public domain. Second, the majority of BITs was concluded before the mid-1990s, when referencing to the ‘environment’ first started in bilateral investment treaties.

there was no sufficient realisation of the potential environmental impact of foreign investment. But even with the increasing awareness, few states appear to perceive the preamble of bilateral investment treaties a relevant place to address the concern.

II. Free Trade Agreements Containing Provisions on Investment Protection

States increasingly conclude free trade agreements, which contain provisions on investment protection.[33] The provisions on investment protection generally constitute one whole chapter in the free trade agreement, which roughly encompasses the same elements as a bilateral investment treaty. In such free trade agreements, the preamble to the whole treaty gives indications for the interpretation of the investment-related provisions. In comparison to the rather limited references to environmental considerations in the preambles of bilateral investment treaties, the preambles of free trade agreements contain references to more diverse environmental aspects and more agreements tend to incorporate references.

An example of a clause, which describes the inter-relationship between environmental ideas and the creation of the envisaged free trade area, reads as follows:

> "[...] Promote economic development in accordance with the protection and conservation of the environment, as well as sustainable development; [...]"[34]

The formulation expresses the aim of promoting economic development in a manner which is not to the detriment of the protection and conservation

---

Third, however, even after this point in time, few states seem to be interested in inserting environmental notions into the preambles of bilateral investment treaties.

[33] For the context of the study, those free trade agreements are considered to "contain provisions on investment protection", which have a section that roughly follows the basic template of a BIT. At least they provide for protection comprising national treatment, most-favoured nation treatment, fair and equitable treatment and against expropriation.

[34] Preambular clause 11 Taiwan-El Salvador and Honduras FTA; preambular clause 14 Mexico-El Salvador, Guatemala, Honduras FTA; preambular clause 12 Colombia-El Salvador, Honduras, Guatemala FTA. With a similar wording in: preambular clause 11 Panama-Taiwan FTA; preambular clause 8 Chile-Australia FTA; preambular clause 13 Chile-Peru FTA.

See also the text of the slightly differing preamble of the earlier NAFTA. Its preambular clauses 13 and 14 read as follows: "[...]Promote sustainable development; Strengthen the development and enforcement of environmental laws and regulations [...]". This clause clearly states three environmental aims without explicitly connecting them to the creation of the free trade area, which is the overall purpose of the agreement (see Articles 101, 102 NAFTA).

of the environment. The clause also mentions sustainable development as an objective worthy of promotion. However, the clause could be perceived to indicate a distinction between economic development in accordance with environmental standards and sustainable development. Despite the unusual wording, this was probably not the intention of the drafters. Since sustainable development is a concept that itself incorporates notions of economic development,[35] it would be impossible to construct an opposition of the two concepts.

Several states have inserted into the preambles of the free trade agreements they concluded an explicit reference to environmental concepts and aims, which have to be considered in the process of implementing the economic objective.[36] Differing wordings enumerate environmental aims and expressly connect them to the implementation of the respective agreement. An example of a preamble which aims to introduce a comprehensive set of environmental ideas is the following:

> "[...] Implement this Agreement in a manner consistent with environmental protection and conservation, promote sustainable development, and strengthen their cooperation on environmental matters;
> Protect and preserve the environment and enhance the means for doing so, including through the conservation of natural resources in their respective territories; [...]"[37]

---

[35] See the detailed portrayal in 'Chapter 1 – Environmental Norms and Principles' at pp. 63 *et seq.*

[36] Language used to this end in recent years by the U.S. is the following:
"[...] Desiring to strengthen the development and enforcement of labor and environmental laws and policies, promote basic workers' rights and sustainable development, and implement this Agreement in a manner consistent with environmental protection and conservation; [...]". It can be found in preambular clause 7 U.S.-Korea FTA; preambular clause 13 U.S.-Morroco FTA; preambular clause 10 U.S.-Oman FTA, without reference to labour laws and workers' rights in this clause.
This formulation clearly emphasises the need for the implementation of the economic and trade impact in accordance with environmental aspects and additionally sets forth further, not strictly related environmental goals. It could, however, be argued that the wording "desiring to strengthen" puts less stress on the states' intent than the use of the word "strengthen" does, which was used in the NAFTA clause.
Another version, apparently more popular with Asian state parties to a free trade agreement reads as follows:
"[...] Recognizing that this Agreement should be implemented with a view toward raising the standard of living, creating new job opportunities, and promoting sustainable development in a manner consistent with environmental protection and conservation; [...]". It can be found in preambular clause 4 China-Pakistan FTA; preambular clause 7 Peru-China FTA; preambular clause 5 Korea-Chile FTA.

[37] Preambular clauses 16 and 17 CAFTA-DR; preambular clauses 17 and 18 U.S.-Panama FTA; preambular clauses 17 and 18 Taiwan-Nicaragua FTA; with a very similar wording and meaning: preambular clauses 13–15 U.S.-Chile FTA. Con-

This accumulation of environmental notions is rather extensive for the preamble of a free trade agreement. While it expressly links the implementation of the agreement to environmental protection, the preamble additionally states a multitude of other environmental objectives without connecting them to the economic objective. The clauses emphasise the desire for a comprehensive environmental perspective, irrespective of the construction of the free trade area.

The above-cited examples of preambular clauses in free-trade agreements mention a diverse set of environmental concepts, which constitutes a contrast to the preambles of bilateral investment treaties, as cited above, which primarily aim to address the specific concern of a regulatory race-to-the-bottom. The diversity of environmental concepts mentioned and encouraged in the preambles of free-trade agreements becomes even more evident when a larger set of agreements is evaluated. To this end, I have analysed the preambles of 51 free trade agreements which contain investment provisions that were concluded after 1994.[38]

My analysis of these agreements finds that all, except for 13,[39] contain a preambular reference to an environmental concept. Thus, a large majority of

taining only the first clause: preambular clause 13 U.S.-Colombia FTA; preambular clause 12 U.S.-Peru FTA. Containing similar language to only the first clause, but referring to the strengthening of development and enforcement of environmental legislation instead of environmental co-operation: preambular clauses 14–16 Mexico-Nicaragua FTA; preambular clauses 13, 15, 16 Mexico-Costa Rica FTA; preambular clauses 15–17 Mexico-Bolivia FTA.

[38] The purpose of this exercise is to identify – irrespective of subtle differences in phrasing – those concepts, if any, that are most widely accepted as relevant environmental references in a preamble. The analysis further reflects on the geographic prevalence of the respective reference. The informative value of the analysis is limited, however, by the set of agreements, fulfilling the above-mentioned criteria, which I have been able to identify in the public domain. The 50 treaties analysed are the following: NAFTA, U.S.-Panama FTA, U.S.-Chile, U.S.-Colombia FTA, U.S.-Korea FTA, U.S.-Morocco FTA, CAFTA-DR, Chile-Japan FTA, Japan-Philippines FTA, Japan-Brunei Darussalam FTA, Taiwan-Nicaragua FTA, Chile-Colombia FTA, Peru-Singapore FTA, Chile-Australia FTA, U.S.-Oman FTA, Taiwan-El Salvador and Honduras FTA, Mexico-El Salvador and Honduras and Guatemala FTA, Chile-Colombia FTA, Mexico-Bolivia FTA, Taiwan-Panama FTA, Chile-Mexico FTA, Mexico-Nicaragua FTA; Mexico-Costa Rica FTA, Japan-Thailand FTA, Japan-Mexico FTA, Colombia-El Salvador and Honduras and Guatemala FTA, Peru-Chile FTA, India-Singapore FTA, Canada-Peru FTA, Central America-Panama FTA, Korea-Singapore FTA, U.S.-Australia FTA, U.S.-Singapore FTA, Japan-Malaysia FTA, Malaysia-New Zealand FTA, New Zealand-China FTA, Peru-China FTA, Korea-Chile FTA, China-Pakistan FTA, EFTA-Singapore FTA, Central America-Dominica FTA, ASEAN-Australia, New Zealand FTA, Thailand-New Zealand FTA; Thailand-Australia FTA; Australia-Singapore FTA, Pakistan-Malaysia FTA, New Zealand-Singapore FTA, Panama-Singapore FTA, Japan-Singapore FTA.

the analysed preambles include such references. The support is strongest for the concepts of 'sustainable development' (36 treaties) and the 'protection and conservation of the environment' (35 treaties), for which support is measurable in all regional areas.[40] The analysis further shows that the inclusion of these two concepts is prevalent in preambles of free trade agreements concluded by Middle and South American as well as North American states. Among Asian states, there seems to be some acceptance of the reference to the above-mentioned concepts; but the data also indicates that the majority of agreements without any reference to environmental concepts were concluded with Asian participation. The two concepts enjoy support in Australia and New Zealand, despite an apparent preparedness of these states to enter into agreements which do not contain such a reference in their preambles. There is no conclusive evidence for Europe[41], the Gulf region or Africa[42] due to the insufficient number of identified agreements.

The other six reoccurring environmental concepts were included in substantially fewer treatments. They focused on strengthening environmental co-operation (8 treaties); the enforcement (7 treaties) or the development (7 treaties) of environmental laws, policies and/or regulation; the enhancement of means of protection or preservation of the environment (5 treaties); the creation of conservation or protection areas and measures in the state's own territory (4 treaties); and on the conclusion of multilateral environmental agreements (2 treaties). The results suggest that states deem these concepts less relevant in the preamble of a free trade agreement. The evaluation has to take into account that the exact wording of free trade agreements, like that of bilateral investment treaties, frequently relies – at least to a substantial extent – on a model agreement. Although a lot of states use model treaties in negotiations, the extent to which the concluded treaty relies on such a model will depend on the respective bargaining power of the states, on whether both states have a model agreement they wish to see reflected, and on the specific circumstances of the negotiations.[43]

---

39 Of these, six contain an article within their investment chapter which specifically refers to the environment.

40 The different regional areas looked at are North America, Middle and South America, Asia, Australia and New Zealand, Europe, and North Africa and the Gulf region.

41 The European Union has concluded a significant number of free-trade and similar agreements. However, they do not contain relevant provisions on investment. CETA is the first.

42 The two analysed treaties with participation from Northern Africa and the Gulf region are both free trade agreements concluded with the U.S. and are obviously relying on U.S. model language.

43 See expressly for investment treaties, *Schreuer*, Christoph, 'Diversity and Harmonization of Treaty Interpretation in Investment Arbitration', in: Treaty Inter-

Nevertheless, the analysis has indicated that the wide acceptance of some of the concepts is not simply a result of an economically weaker party having to accept certain formulations and references. Rather, it seems logical and laudable that the concept of sustainable development, which aims at reconciling environmental, social and economic perspectives is so frequently mentioned. As for the remaining environmental concepts which do not have a direct implication for economic activity, it is no surprise that the very general idea of 'protection and conservation of the environment' is more frequently used than more specific and detailed notions.

Finally, the overview suggests that states are more likely to incorporate preambular references to environmental protection in an agreement that creates a free trade zone, rather than in a treaty which exclusively concerns foreign investment. One potential reason for this difference could be that the potential for conflict between environmental values and free trade has been apparent for a longer period and consequently has received more attention.[44] Furthermore, the negotiating process of free trade agreements is more intense due to the diverse subject areas covered so that the concerned public is more likely to take note. Accordingly, the inclusion of preambular clauses which intend to address these potential conflicts may be an attempt to mitigate concerns. Another reason for the more significant prevalence of environmental clauses in free trade agreements as opposed to bilateral investment treaties probably is the moment of their conclusion: Free-trade agreements containing provisions on investment protection are relatively recent treaties, all concluded at a point in time when environmental concerns were more commonly acknowledged, whereas the vast majority of bilateral investment treaties have been concluded throughout the last five decades.

pretation and the Vienna Convention on the Law of Treaties: 30 Years On (Fitzmaurice, Malgosia et al. (Eds.) 2010) 129 (136–137).

44 Environmental problems transcend borders especially easily if they are connected to a product which falls within the free trade regime of the World Trade Organisation (WTO). The famous 1991 dispute between the U.S. and Mexico, which related to the harvest of tuna with methods affecting dolphins, emphasised potential environmental implications of free trade rules. Other famous WTO cases, concerning asbestos, hormones in beef or shrimps and turtles followed suit. The WTO addressed the issue by declaring environmental protection to be a goal of the WTO regime. If the attempt at harmonisation has been successful is open to debate. See the overly enthusiastic record of the WTO, available at: https://www.wto.org/english/tratop_e/envir_e/envt_intro_e.htm, last visited 30 June 2014.

III. Multilateral Investment Treaties

In addition to the treaties portrayed above, there have been attempts to conclude multilateral investment treaties. A successful multilateral investment treaty is the 1994 Energy Charter Treaty (ECT). The ECT is not reduced in terms of territorial application, but is thematically restricted to investment in the energy sector.[45] Against this background, it is not surprising that two of its preambular clauses expressly address environmental concerns connected with the production and use of energy. The relevant clauses read as follows:

> "Recalling the United Nations Framework Convention on Climate Change, the Convention on Long-Range Transboundary Air Pollution and its protocols, and other international environmental agreements with energy-related aspects; and
> Recognizing the increasingly urgent need for measures to protect the environment, including the decommissioning of energy installations and waste disposal, and for internationally-agreed objectives and criteria for these purposes, [...]"[46]

In clear contrast to any of the preambular clauses analysed before, the first of the two clauses specifically refers to important international environmental agreements, such as the UNFCCC. The second clause addresses very specific environmental concerns related to energy production and consumption, the increasing urgency of which it expressly recognises. The specific scope of the treaty has led to the inclusion of more specific environmental references regarding the use and exploitation of energy resources. The clauses send clear signals for the recognition of environmental impacts of relevant investments – signals that are more precise than those found in other investment treaties.[47] Since a conflict between an investor's interests and the governmental aim to protect the environment is more likely to appear in the energy sector than in several other sectors, such a protective language could prove to be relevant in interpreting the provisions of the treaty in case of a dispute.

Although there are no other multilateral investment treaties in force,[48] this overview would be incomplete without a look at the draft of the Mul-

---

[45] Article 2 1994 Energy Charter Treaty (ECT).

[46] Preambular clauses 14 and 15 ECT.

[47] See also *Sussman*, Edna, 'The Energy Charter Treaty's Investor Protection Provisions: Potential to Foster Solutions to Global Warming and Promote Sustainable Development, 14 ILSA Journal of International and Comparative Law 2008, 391 (403), suggesting that the preambular environmental reference is an element relevant to an interpretation following Article 31 VCLT and specifically so for the understanding of the covered investments.

[48] The Agreement of Trade-Related Investment Measures (TRIMS), which was concluded within the system of the World Trade Organisation, is no investment

tilateral Agreement on Investment (MAI)[49], which was thoroughly negotiated within the Organisation for Economic Co-operation and Development (OECD), but failed in 1998 due to the discontinuation of the negotiations.[50] While the first draft of the MAI did not contain any environmental reference,[51] a multitude of environmental concepts was later on discussed for insertion into the preamble. Among these were the notions of sustainability, the protection and preservation of the environment, references to the 1992 Rio Declaration and the Agenda 21, the polluter-pays principle, and the precautionary approach.[52] Although ultimately no agreement was reached, the elements indicate that the states involved in the negotiations took the task of referring to environmental concepts in the preamble of the treaty seriously. In addition, there was a particular discussion about inserting a clause stating that the states resolved "to implement the agreement in accordance with international law", which some delegations objected to for fear of establishing a hierarchy within international law – with environmental agreements taking precedence over the MAI.[53] There was also discus-

---

treaty in this sense. According to Article 1 TRIMS it only applies to investment measures related to trade in goods and therefore falls short of the scope of content and protection of an investment treaty. Its aim is to facilitate the application of the 1994 GATT.

49 See for negotiating text and background information, http://www.oecd.org/document/22/0,3343,en_2649_33783766_1894819_1_1_1_1,00.html.

50 The treaty was intended to be a non-sector related multilateral investment treaty, open to both OECD members and non-members.

51 *Kolo*, Abba/*Wälde*, Thomas, 'Environmental Regulation, Investment Protection and "Regulatory Taking" in International Law', 50 International and Comparative Law Quarterly 2001, 811 (818).

52 The different elements discussed for insertion into the intended preambular clause of the Draft MAI:

[Recognising that investment, as an engine of economic growth, can play a key role in ensuring that economic growth is sustainable, when accompanied by appropriate environmental policies to ensure it takes place in an environmentally sound manner] [Recognising that appropriate environmental policies can play a key role in ensuring that economic development, to which investment contributes, is sustainable], and resolving to [desiring to] implement this agreement [in accordance with international environmental law and] in a manner consistent with sustainable development, as reflected in the Rio Declaration on Environment and Development and Agenda 21, [including the protection and preservation of the environment and principles of the polluter pays and the precautionary approach].

Brackets signify different version. No agreement was reached by the time of the discontinuation of the negations. Other more individual preferences existed regarding certain elements.

53 The footnote accompanying this phrase of the Draft MAI (footnote 8 to the clause) reads as follows:

"This phrase raises the questions whether the MAI intends to set a presumption that multilateral environmental agreements have precedence and over it, and, if so, wheth-

sion about the need to specifically state that "environmental policies shall not constitute a means of disguised restriction on international trade and investment" and the question if such language belonged into the preamble of the treaty.[54]

IV. Interpretative Value of Preambular Clauses

The interpretative value of preambular clauses containing environmental references primarily derives from the general impact a preamble has in the context of treaty interpretation. As shown above, the preamble can contribute, first, to the determination of the object and purpose of the treaty and, second, constitute an element of the 'context' of a specific treaty provision. Even though it has been suggested that the preambles in bilateral treaties, such as bilateral investment treaties, would not be of great use for the purpose of interpretation, since they were generally very short and systematically used the same wording,[55] the bilateral format does obviously not prevent the state parties from expressing relevant notions in more extensive preambular clauses. Accordingly, preambles incorporating elements additive to the most obvious tenets of an investment or free trade agreement, such as references to environmental standards, have to be considered in the interpretation of the treaty provisions.

To establish the potential interpretative impact of environmental preambular references with regard to the object and purpose of the investment treaty, it is first necessary to determine the implications of the 'object and purpose'. While the duality of the notion could imply a differentiation between 'object' – meaning the immediate goals of the treaty – and 'purpose' – relating to more distant and general aims – commentators purport that this differentiation is not helpful and not supported by international doctrine and practice.[56] Accordingly, the 'object and purpose' is to characterise the intentions the parties pursued with the conclusion of the respective treaty. These intentions are to be distilled from the majority of the substantive

er a preambular reference establishes that presumption. One delegation is strongly opposed to the inclusion of this phrase because it is impossible to define precisely."

[54] Footnote 10 accompanying the relevant clause of the Draft MAI.

[55] *Suy*, Eric, 'Le Préambule' in: Liber Amicorum Judge Mohammed Bedjaoui (Yakpo, Emile et al. (Eds.) 1999) 253 (255).

[56] *Klabbers*, Jan, 'Some Problems Regarding the Object and Purpose of Treaties', VIII Finnish Yearbook of International Law 1997, 138 (144–145). Especially the deliberations of the Vienna Conference on the Law of Treaties indicate that the two terms refer to one single notion (147–148). Generally, *Villiger*, Mark E., Commentary on the 1969 Vienna Convention on the Law of Treaties (2009) Article 31 para 11.

provisions relating to a specific topic, the preamble, and the title of the treaty.[57] Therefore, establishing the object and purpose of a treaty requires a holistic approach towards the whole material available.[58]

The environmental clauses, as portrayed above, in comparison with the remainder of the respective treaties are not significant enough to relevantly influence the determination of the object and purpose, overall. One environmental reference within a multitude of preambular clauses referring to other objectives, surrounded by substantive provisions which do not focus on environmental issues, and without a reflection in the title cannot generally be understood as the object and purpose of the treaty. Even if it is true, as a commentator has assessed, that a majority of investment tribunals has not referred to any source for their statements concerning object and purpose,[59] it is unlikely that such a less systematic approach will give weight to environmental references contained in the preamble. The object and purpose of investment treaties or free trade agreements is too closely connected to economic considerations for environmental considerations to be relevant on a *prima facie* basis. However, the evaluation could be different with regard to the concept of sustainable development. This concept, with its close connection to economic development, could affect the object and purpose in so far as it influences the manner in which the economic relationship is to be handled.

The assessment that environmental references in the preamble may not be relevant for the determination of the object and purpose of the treaty does not mean that they lack any interpretative impact. They are relevant because they form part of the 'context' to the provision that is interpreted.[60] The aims and objectives stated in the preamble are part of the apparatus for selecting and modifying the ordinary meaning of terms that are used in the

---

[57] Similarly, *Klabbers*, Jan, 'Some Problems Regarding the Object and Purpose of Treaties', VIII Finnish Yearbook of International Law 1997, 138 (155–158). However, Klabbers cautions against an "undue reliance on the text alone" in the establishment of the object and purpose of the treaty (157).

[58] Others maintain that a treaty can have several objects and purposes. See, for example, *Villiger*, Mark E., Commentary on the 1969 Vienna Convention on the Law of Treaties (2009) Article 31 para 11. I concur with Klabbers, Jan, 'Some Problems Regarding the Object and Purpose of Treaties', VIII Finnish Yearbook of International Law 1997, 138–160 that the object and purpose of a treaty is a more singular concept. Otherwise, the concept would offer little help in the interpretative exercise.

[59] Empirically analysing 98 decisions of investment tribunals operating under the ICSID Convention: *Fauchald*, Ole Kristian, 'The Legal Reasoning of ICSID Tribunals: An Empirical Analysis', 19 European Journal of International Law 2008, 301 (322).

[60] See Article 31 para 2 VCLT.

substantive provisions, so that in cases of doubt over the meaning of a substantive provision, the preamble may justify a wider or more restrictive interpretation.[61] In this sense, the case can be made for environmental references in the preamble to subtly influence the balance of the treaty when interpreting a specific provision:[62] The preambular suggestion that the economic obligations should be implemented in a manner that reflects certain environmental objectives sets some limits to the interpretation of the economic object of the treaty.

Accordingly, environmental preambular clauses can have a balancing effect on the interpretation of a specific substantive provision. Support for the understanding of environmental preambular references influencing the interpretation of substantive provisions in this manner also comes from the Appellate Body of the World Trade Organisation (WTO). In a dispute before it, the WTO Appellate Body had to evaluate the interpretational value of a preambular clause that referred to sustainable development and to the protection of the environment. It stated that preambular references to environmental concepts "must add colour, texture and shading" to the interpretation of the material provisions of the treaty, which have to be "read with the perspective embodied in the [...] preamble".[63] It is in this sense that environmental concepts mentioned in the preamble influence and limit the interpretation of substantive provisions in investment treaties.

C. References Within the Substantive Provisions of the Respective Treaties

Another technique employed in investment agreements that aim to reconcile the obligation of investment protection with environmental concepts is the inclusion of specific references as part of the substantive provisions. In the operative part of free trade agreements, these references sometimes oc-

61 *Gardiner*, Richard, Treaty Interpretation (2008) p. 186–187.

62 See the argumentation in Saluka Investments BV (The Netherlands) v. The Czech Republic, Award of 17 March 2006, para 300, in which the tribunal looks at all preambular clauses and establishes an inter-connectivity of the elements. The tribunal finds that the collection of preambular clauses "calls for a balanced approach" to the interpretation of the substantive provisions of the treaty.

63 United States – Import Prohibition of Certain Shrimp and Shrimp Products, DS58/AB/R, WTO Appellate Body Report of 12 October 1998, para. 153. The Appellate Body held: „As this preambular language reflects the intentions of negotiators of the WTO Agreement, we believe it must add colour, texture and shading to our interpretation of the agreements annexed to the WTO Agreement, in this case, the GATT 1994. We have already observed that Article XX(g) of the GATT 1994 is appropriately read with the perspective embodied in the above preamble."

cur in the form of a separate chapter on environmental objectives. The insertion of such articles within the substantive provisions is more readily used in free trade agreements than in exclusive investment treaties. The following section will provide an overview of such substantive articles, determine what environmental issues are covered, and assess their potential impact on conflicts of values. A distinction will be drawn between singular environmental provisions within the provisions on investment and separate chapters dedicated to environmental issues.

I. Articles Referring to the Environment Within the Investment Provisions

Environmental references in the substantive investment provisions of free trade and bilateral investment agreements predominantly address two areas of concern: The first issue relates to the legal capacity of each state party to adopt, maintain, and enforce environmental regulation. The second issue concerns, once again, the fear of a regulatory race-to-the-bottom, which could result in the creation of pollution havens. A relevant example of a provision which addresses these two issues in a joint manner reads as follows:

> "1. Nothing in this Chapter shall be construed to prevent a Party from adopting, maintaining or enforcing any measure otherwise consistent with this Chapter that it considers appropriate to ensure that investment activity in its territory is undertaken in a manner sensitive to environmental concerns.
>
> 2. The Parties recognize that it is inappropriate to encourage investment by relaxing domestic health, safety or environmental measures. Accordingly, a Party should not waive or otherwise derogate from, or offer to waive or otherwise derogate from, such measures as an encouragement for the establishment, acquisition, expansion or retention in its territory of an investment of an investor. If a Party considers that another Party has offered such an encouragement, it may request consultations with the other Party and the two Parties shall consult with a view to avoiding any such encouragement."[64]

---

[64] Article 1114 NAFTA; Article 9.15 Chile-Mexico FTA; Article 10.18 Chile-Korea FTA; Article G-14 Canada-Chile FTA; Article II para 5, Article XII para 2 Canada-Latvia BIT. See also Article 12 U.S.-Urugay BIT, with paragraphs in reverse order and a slightly different wording for the obligation not to relax the standard, most importantly "measures" are substituted by "laws"; Article 12 U.S.-Rwanda BIT, with the same wording as the above-mentioned BIT. This wording can also be found in the 2004 U.S. Model BIT.

1. Adopting, Maintaining and Enforcing Environmental Measures

The first paragraph of the provision addresses the capacity of the state to adopt and enforce its environmental regulation as far as there are implications for investment activity undertaken in its territory. Although the paragraph ostensibly emphasises the sovereignty of states to adopt and implement such rules, it is tainted by the use of concepts which are not very clear. While the range of 'measures' supported is understood broadly,[65] and the notion 'sensitive to environmental concerns' opens a wide margin of appreciation for the state parties, the impact of the paragraph is significantly restricted by referring to patterns 'otherwise consistent' with investment protection obligations. The textual interpretation of this phrase indicates that it applies to environmental measures which are in complete coherence with the requirements of investment protection. However, this interpretation raises questions as to the purpose of the insertion of the provision: It goes without saying that measures which do not contravene the guarantees set forth in the treaty can be adopted. There is no need to expressly stipulate that measures consistent with the investment provisions can be implemented.

However, this paragraph may also be interpreted as to add to the discussion more than to confirm that the signatory states acknowledged the potential for conflict between environmental protection and investment activity. Apparently, the governments of Canada and the U.S. understood this provision as a means to adopt and implement those measures that are necessary in achieving a respective level of environmental protection, but not to hinder the protection of foreign investment more than necessary to achieve the environmental objective.[66] This wider understanding was also embraced by one arbitrator in *S.D. Myers Inc. v. Canada*, who perceived the provision as a general expression of the necessity to reconcile environmental measures with environmental objectives – so that the host state is free to adopt environmental measures, as long as these do not unnecessarily distort trade and investment.[67]

---

[65] See already above at p. 104 and the far-reaching definition in Article 201 NAFTA. Accordingly, a 'measure' could be any product of state activity, such as a law or an administrative regulation, and the term would also capture less typical instruments, such as incentive schemes for certain behaviour or public campaigns to raise information and awareness.

[66] *Kinnear*, Meg N./*Björklund*, Andrea K./*Hannaford*, John F.G. (Eds.) Investment Disputes under NAFTA, An Annotated Guide to NAFTA Chapter 11 (2006) 6–1114, with reference to the Statement on Implementation and Statement of Administrative Action.

[67] S.D. Myers Inc. v. Canada, Separate Opinion by Arbitrator Bryan Schwartz, 12 November 2000. Arbitrator Schwartz states the following: "I view Article 1114 as acknowledging and reminding interpreters of Chapter 11 (Investment) that the

The paragraph, in its incorporation in the first paragraph of Article 1114 NAFTA, has been discussed in an arbitral decision. The tribunal in *Metalclad Corporation v. United Mexican States*[68] held that its finding of an improper behaviour of the defendant state was not altered by the requirements contained in the provision. In line with its prior findings that the environmental requirements for the approval of the landfill in question were incorporated in the permits granted by the federal state and not subject to municipal construction permits, the tribunal had no difficulty to conclude that – since a state agency had issued the permits necessary to work the landfill –"Mexico was satisfied that this project was consistent with, and sensitive to, its environmental concerns."[69] The tribunal thus expresses the understanding that the environmental concerns the host state may have had are incorporated in the legislation of the state, so that there is no room for further consideration. Accordingly, the paragraph has not become relevant.

In this light, it is not clear whether the paragraph strengthens the capacity of host states to implement environmental measures if these impact on investment protection rights. It is unlikely to constitute a substantial factor in cases of a collision of norms. In no way does the paragraph establish a hierarchy of environmental norms and investment protection. Despite the arguably limited impact of the paragraph, its language – but not that of the second paragraph – is also endorsed by other investment agreements, which repeat it either verbatim[70] or with modifications[71]. Further agreements express the underlying idea with a different wording[72].

---

parties take both the environment and open trade very seriously and that means should be found to reconcile these two objectives and, if possible, to make them mutually supportive. I have already indicated that the context of NAFTA as a whole clearly provides the basic approach that should be followed: parties are free to choose high environmental standards, but should adopt and apply them in a way that avoids barriers to trade that are not necessary in order to achieve the environmental purpose."

68 See the portrayal of the facts and the decision in 'Chapter 4 – Standards of Fair Treatment' at pp. 261 *et seq*.

69 Metalclad Corporation v. United Mexican States, ICSID Case No. ARB(AF)/97/1, Award of 30 August 2000, para 98.

70 Article 10.8 Peru-Singapore FTA; Article 10.11 Nicaragua-Taiwan FTA; Article 15.10 U.S.-Singapore FTA; Article 10.11 U.S.-Peru FTA; Article 10.10 U.S.-Oman FTA; Article 10.10 U.S.-Morocco FTA; Article 11.11 U.S.-Australia FTA; Article 11.13 Chile-Peru FTA; Article 10.12 U.S.-Chile FTA; Article 9.13 Chile-Colombia FTA; Article 10.18 Korea-Singapore FTA; Article 10.11 CAFTA-DR. Modified to fit the format of a bilateral investment treaty: Annex I, Nr. 3 para 1 Canada-Croatia BIT; Article XVII para 2 Canada-Trinidad and Tobago BIT; Article XVII para 2 Canada-Barbados BIT. The latter two additionally contain a general exception clause as para 3. The implication of such a clause is discussed below at pp. 123 *et seq*.

2. Regulatory Race-to-the-Bottom

The second paragraph of the cited Article addresses the concern of a regulatory race-to-the-bottom to the economic detriment of states which maintain a high level of environmental regulation. It thus relates to the encouragement and attraction of foreign investment, i.e. to the pre-establishment phase in the host country. The paragraph states that the state parties "recognise" that it is inappropriate to attract investment through the weakening of environmental regulation and that they "should not" derogate from such regulation in order to attract investment. In addition, the paragraph provides for a consultation scheme: A state which believes that another state has encouraged investment through the derogation from environmental regulation can request consultations with that state. A commentator suggests that this paragraph contains "extraordinarily weak language" which "imposes no real legal obligation on the parties".[73]

According to the race-to-the-bottom theory, countries adopt sub-optimal environmental policies and lower their standards to not disadvantage their industries[74] – or to make their own jurisdiction more attractive to potential investors. The fear of a regulatory race-to-the-bottom is closely connected to the pollution haven hypothesis. Pollution haven hypothesis is the prediction that liberalisation leads to a relocation of polluting industries from high income countries with stringent environmental regulation to low income countries with lax environmental regulation.[75] Research suggests that there is little empirical evidence for the occurrence of pollution havens.[76] More

---

71 Article 12.16 Colombia-El Salvador, Guatemala, Honduras FTA, refers to ensuring that the investment activity is undertaken in a manner observing the "ecological and environmental legislation".

72 Article 6.10 India-Singapore FTA; Article 6.10 EFTA-Singapore FTA, both with a reference to measures "consistent with this chapter".

73 *Knox*, John H., 'The Neglected Lessons of the NAFTA Environmental Regime', 45 Wake Forest Law Review 2010, 391 (395).

74 *Esty*, Daniel C./*Geradin*, Damien, 'Environmental Protection and International Competitiveness' 32 Journal of World Trade 1998, 5 (16).

75 *Ederington*, Josh, 'NAFTA and the Pollution Haven Hypothesis', 35 Policy Studies Journal 2007, 239 (239). Criticising the pollution haven hypothesis as simplistic, due to its focusing on one particular factor while leaving out other relevant factors and differences between countries, *Cole*, Matthew A./*Elliott*, Robert J.R., 'FDI and the Capital Intensity of "Dirty" Sectors: A Missing Piece of the Pollution Haven Puzzle', 9 Review of Development Economics 2005, 530 (541–542); *Eskeland*, Gunnar S./*Harrison*, Ann E., 'Moving to Greener Pastures? Multinationals and the Pollution Haven Hypothesis', 70 Journal of Development Economics 2003, 1 (21).

76 Specifically for the context of NAFTA: *Ederington*, Josh, 'NAFTA and the Pollution Haven Hypothesis', 35 Policy Studies Journal 2007, 239 (241, 243), rely-

specifically, researchers have neither found a systematic impact of abatement costs on the distribution of foreign investment nor an overall positive correlation between levels of specific emissions and the pattern of foreign investment.[77] Suggested reasons for the absence of pollution havens include the realisation that even in the sector of polluting industries pollution abatement costs do not have a systematic impact on the costs of production,[78] and that countries with more stringent environmental regulation generally offer the capital and sufficiently skilled workers required by polluting industries.[79]

---

ing on patterns of emissions and energy consumption. Stating that the findings relating to abatement costs and industrial relocation are ambiguous, *Eskeland*, Gunnar S./*Harrison*, Ann E., 'Moving to Greener Pastures? Multinationals and the Pollution Haven Hypothesis', 70 Journal of Development Economics 2003, 1 (4). Similarly, *Cole*, Matthew A./*Elliott*, Robert J.R., 'FDI and the Capital Intensity of "Dirty" Sectors: A Missing Piece of the Pollution Haven Puzzle', 9 Review of Development Economics 2005, 530 (531) with further references. More general *Esty*, Daniel C./*Geradin*, Damien, 'Environmental Protection and International Competitiveness' 32 Journal of World Trade 1998, 5 (13).

See, however, *Tienhaara*, Kyla, Expropriation of Environmental Governance: Protecting Foreign Investors at the Expense of Public Policy (2009) pp. 23–24, who finds that more recent research indicates the existence of significant pollution haven effects. One reason given for these findings is a serious increase in environmental cost in the most hazardous industries during the last two decades.

77 *Eskeland*, Gunnar S./*Harrison*, Ann E., 'Moving to Greener Pastures? Multinationals and the Pollution Haven Hypothesis', 70 Journal of Development Economics 2003, 1 (9, 13, 21). The authors find an insignificant or even negative correlation between foreign investment and both water pollution and total toxic release. However, a positive correlation has been detected between foreign investment and air pollution for the countries in the survey. But the authors also find that foreign ownership is associated with lower levels of energy use, thus has a positive influence on the pollution level (17–18).

78 *Esty*, Daniel C./*Geradin*, Damien, 'Environmental Protection and International Competitiveness' 32 Journal of World Trade 1998, 5 (10). Similarly, *Cole*, Matthew A./*Elliott*, Robert J.R., 'FDI and the Capital Intensity of "Dirty" Sectors: A Missing Piece of the Pollution Haven Puzzle', 9 Review of Development Economics 2005, 530 (531, 533).

79 *Cole*, Matthew A./*Elliott*, Robert J.R., 'FDI and the Capital Intensity of "Dirty" Sectors: A Missing Piece of the Pollution Haven Puzzle', 9 Review of Development Economics 2005, 530 (533, 535). These authors demonstrate that the sectors which face the greatest pollution abatement costs are typically more capital intensive (as opposed to being labour intensive) than sectors, which are less pollution intensive. They have also found that the countries with the highest capital-labour ratio generally also have the most stringent environmental regulation. They suggest that the scarcity and cost of physical capital in countries with more relaxed environmental standards is the reason for polluting industries to rather invest in countries with stringent environmental regulation. The authors conclude that potential gains from more lax environmental regulation are not enough to compensate for the low capital-labour ratio in such countries, overall.

While evidence – other than anecdotal – for the existence of an actual lowering of environmental regulation is scarce,[80] commentators have suggested that the – at least perceived – economic impact stemming from stringent environmental regulation leads to 'regulatory chill', inciting states not to elevate their environmental standards.[81] The reasons for states not to tighten environmental regulation are obviously difficult to assess. For the context of the evaluation of environmental references in investment treaties, it is important to note that this issue does not fall within the scope of the paragraph discussed. The provision expressly refers to a relaxation of environmental measures only. With this limitation and its focus on the state's activity prior to the establishment of foreign investment, the paragraph provides no guidance regarding the solution of potential conflicts between specific, established investments and the state's desire to regulate for environmental concerns. Irrespective of this fact, several investment agreements have enclosed its language in a provision – without incorporating the content of the first paragraph.[82] Some agreements use different language, for example without referring to the obligation to consult,[83] or embrace a different connotation[84].

---

[80] *Esty*, Daniel C./*Geradin*, Damien, 'Environmental Protection and International Competitiveness' 32 Journal of World Trade 1998, 5 (17–19), pointing to examples of amendments to environmental statutes benefiting forestry, mining and agrobusiness industries in Ontario (Canada), legislative efforts in Germany, and the legislative framework in the European Union.

[81] *Esty*, Daniel C./*Geradin*, Damien, 'Environmental Protection and International Competitiveness' 32 Journal of World Trade 1998, 5 (7, 19–21), mentioning as anecdotal evidence the reluctance of industrialised states to systematically control and reduce their emissions of greenhouse gases in the context of climate change; *Clapp*, Jennifer, 'What the Pollution Havens Debate Overlooks', 2 Global Environmental Politics 2002, 11 (16–17); *Tienhaara*, Kyla, Expropriation of Environmental Governance: Protecting Foreign Investors at the Expense of Public Policy (2009) pp. 25–26.

[82] Article 74 Agreement Between Japan and the United Mexican States for the Strengthening of the Economic Partnership; Article 809 Canada-Peru FTA. See also 2004 Canada Model BIT.

[83] Article 74 Japan-Indonesia FTA; Article 87 Chile-Japan FTA; Article 71 Japan-Brunei Darussalam FTA.

[84] Article 17.13 Mexico-Columbia FTA states that "no party will eliminate domestic measures applicable to health, safety or environmental measures or offer to waive their application to the investment of an investor of any country, as a means to encourage the establishment, acquisition, expansion or retention of the investment in its territory. If a Party considers that another Party has offered such an encouragement, it may request consultations with the other Party." [My translation from Spanish original].

A very condensed (and not very precise) version of the basic idea of the paragraph can be found in Article 90 Japan- Malaysia FTA. It provides that "[e]ach

In addition to investment agreements that refer to the concepts set forth in one of the two clauses cited above, there is also a substantial amount of treaties that embrace both of them but have introduced alterations to the formulation. The most notable provision demands that investment activity be "undertaken under [a Party's] ecological or environmental laws", instead of referring to a sensitivity to environmental concerns. Further, that provision alters the second paragraph, so that it does not refer to the obligation of the two parties to consult with a view to avoiding the undesired encouragement.[85] Other free trade agreements limit the scope of the consultations even further[86] or do not refer to such consultations at all[87].

The reference to the capacity of the host state to ensure that investment undertaken in its territory accords to its ecological or environmental laws is decidedly more precise than the vague concept of being "sensitive to environmental concerns". The formulation also reflects the way in which the respective provision of the NAFTA was understood by the tribunal in *Metalclad Corporation v. United Mexican States*[88]. However, the wording leaves little room for arguing that the provision expresses anything more than the remaining sovereignty of the state to impose and apply laws which could impact on foreign investors. The omission of the state's possibility to oblige another party to participate in consultations regarding a possible encouragement of investment through the relaxation of environmental standards further reduces the potential impact of the provision. Yet, it is unlikely that the consultation mechanism has ever had a relevant effect.[89] Nevertheless, the idea of prescribing consultation schemes in which participation is not mandatory for the party concerned cannot be seen as a helpful tool of treaty-making. Rather, it can be perceived as a reinforcement

---

Country shall not encourage investments by investors of the other Country by relaxing its environmental measures."

[85] Article 10.15 Panama-Taiwan FTA. With very similar alterations: Article 14.16 Mexico-El Salvador, Guatemala, Honduras FTA; Article 16.14 Mexico-Nicaragua FTA; Article 13.15 Mexico-Costa Rica FTA; Article 10.15 Centralamerica-Panama FTA; Article 15.14 Bolivia-Mexico FTA; Article 10.15 Panama-El Salvador FTA.

[86] Article 10.16 Taiwan-El Salvador, Honduras FTA, limiting the consultations to those "within the Committee of Investment and Cross-border Trade in Services".

[87] Article 111 Japan-Thailand FTA, only stating the inappropriateness of relaxing "environmental measures" to encourage investment and that therefore the parties "shall not waive or otherwise derogate from such environmental measures" as a way to encourage investment. Article 102 Japan-Philippines FTA contains a very similar wording.

[88] See in 'Chapter 4 – Standards of Fair Treatment' at p. 263.

[89] The overview of research into the creation of pollution havens indicates that the anticipated concerns have not constituted an issue in reality. Accordingly, there has probably never been any case of consultation in this regard.

of state sovereignty regarding the possibility to attract investment activity to the detriment of environmental protection.

3. General Exception Provisions

A further technique applied in some investment treaties is the use of a general exception clause. These clauses are modelled on Article XX 1994 General Agreement on Tariffs and Trade (GATT) or Article XIV General Agreement on Trade in Services (GATS). A typical clause, which adopts the approach for application in an investment treaty, reads as follows:

> "Subject to the requirement that such measures are not applied in a manner that would constitute arbitrary or unjustifiable discrimination between investments or between investors, or a disguised restriction on international trade or investment, nothing in this Agreement shall be construed to prevent a Party from adopting or enforcing measures necessary:
>
> (a) to protect human, animal or plant life or health;
>
> (b) o ensure compliance with laws and regulations that are not inconsistent with the provisions of this Agreement; or
>
> (c) for the conservation of living or non-living exhaustible natural resources.[90]"

In contrast to the clauses and provisions portrayed above, a general exception does not aim at subtly influencing the interpretation of a specific provision or treatment standard. Rather, it aims to exempt certain measures from further scrutiny in the investment context. A measure, which is non-discriminatory, does not restrict international investment in a disguised manner and which was adopted for one of the enumerated reasons does not violate the host state's obligation under the investment treaty. On the face of it, this provision accords states significant policy space. Accordingly, commentators have argued that such an exception would offer the most

---

[90] Article 10 para 1 2004 Canadian Model BIT. Similarly, Article XVII para 3 Canada-Trinidad and Tobago BIT; Article XVII para 3 Canada-Barbados BIT; Annex 1, Article 3 Canada-El Salvador BIT; Article 18 Jordan-Singapore BIT (with further non-environmental policy objectives). See also the more general formulation adopted in Article 22 para 1 2007 COMESA Investment Agreement.

Furthermore, some FTAs rely on the technique of incorporating, by reference, the general exception of Article XX GATT and/or XIV GATS, mutatis mutandis, into the investment provisions of the agreement, see Article 20.2 para 2 lit c Korea-Singapore FTA; Article 20.2 para 2 lit c 2003 Panama-Taiwan FTA; Article 200 China-New Zealand FTA.

See also the clause contained in the draft CETA (Canada-EU) free trade agreement. It states that for the purpose of, inter alia, the investment chapter "GATT 1994 Article XX is incorporated into and made part of this Agreement." The unadjusted language of the trade context is no helpful addition to the investment provisions.

balanced protection of environmental regulation and investor interests.[91] In practice, however, the measure would have to be scrutinized to determine in how far the measure is 'non-discriminatory', not a 'disguised restriction on investment' and 'necessary' for the pursuit of the policy objective. There remains considerable uncertainty as to how investment tribunals would understand such an exception clause.[92]

Investment tribunals tend to interpret exceptions in treaties narrowly.[93] Generally, a state invoking an exception bears the burden of proving that the exception applies and that its criteria are met.[94] Whereas the criteria of non-discrimination are rather straight forward, the other elements of the chapeau of the provision, namely the concept of a disguised restriction on investment and, even more so, the necessity of the measure are less clear. In my understanding, the approach to determining what is necessary – a contribution to achieving the aim or absolute necessity –[95] is crucial for the practical impact of the measure.

Further uncertainty stems from the formulation of the policy objectives. The objectives in lit a and lit c can be interpreted broadly and provide a good basis for balancing the factors to determine the necessity of the measure[96]. The same, however, cannot be said with regard to "ensuring compli-

---

91 *Bennett*, Lisa, 'Are tradable Carbon Emissions Investments? Characterization and Ramifications under International Investment Law', 85 New York University Law Review 2010, 1581 (1617).

92 *Newcombe*, Andrew, 'General Exceptions in International Investment Agreements', in: Sustainable Development in World Investment Law (Cordonier Segger, Marie-Claire et al. (Eds.) 2011) 355 (357, 369).

93 Enron Corporation and Ponderosa Assets, L.P. v. Argentine Republic, ICSID Case No. ARB/01/3, Award of 22 May 2007, para 331; Sempra Energy International v. The Argentine Republic, ICSID Case No. ARB/02/16, Award of 28 September 2007, para 373; Canfor Corporation v. United States of America; Terminal Forest Products Ltd. v. United States of America, Decision on Preliminary Questions of 6 June 2006, para 187.

94 *Newcombe*, Andrew, 'General Exceptions in International Investment Agreements', in: Sustainable Development in World Investment Law (Cordonier Segger, Marie-Claire et al. (Eds.) 2011) 355 (362–363).

95 *Newcombe*, Andrew, 'General Exceptions in International Investment Agreements', in: Sustainable Development in World Investment Law (Cordonier Segger, Marie-Claire et al. (Eds.) 2011) 355 (364–365) draws from the jurisprudence of the WTO on Article XX 1994 GATT that the meaning of 'necessary' is to be found between those two extreme positions.

96 The Appellate Body of the WTO applies a balancing approach to determine the legitimacy of measures adopted to protect one of the policy objectives listed in the corresponding provision of the 1994 GATT. See, for example, Brazil – Measures Affecting Imports of Retreated Tyres, DS332/AB/R, WTO Appellate Body Report of 3 December 2007, para 210.

ance with laws and regulations that are not inconsistent with the treaty". Whether regulation is consistent with the treaty will often be the issue in cases of conflict with environmental aims. The last concern raised in connection with general exception clauses is whether they could be construed to restrict the policy space of the state by limiting it to the closed list of exceptions.[97] However, even if it is not entirely clear how investment tribunals will understand the regulatory scope of the general exception provisions, the provisions will provide guidance as to the policy objectives that the state parties consider predominantly important. Accordingly, they can also constitute context for the interpretation of other provisions of the investment section. The objectives enumerated in the general exceptions provisions may be seen as highlighting limitations imposed by public international law on the interpretation of investment protection provisions.[98]

II. Separate Chapters or Provisions on the 'Environment'

In addition to the environmental references discussed so far, which primarily focus on two aspects of potential collision between the investment target and environmental values, other provisions set forth more detailed rules promoting environmental values. These are found as complete chapters within certain free trade agreements containing investment provisions. The insertion of a complete chapter on the 'environment' is largely a reaction to public criticism relating to the alleged detrimental effect on the environment of earlier agreements.[99] In addition, a small set of investment treaties contain such more detailed provisions. While the specific environmental procedures contained in these chapters cannot be comprehensively reviewed in the context of this study, the most prominent substantial concepts are portrayed in the following.

---

97 *Newcombe*, Andrew, 'General Exceptions in International Investment Agreements', in: Sustainable Development in World Investment Law (Cordonier Segger, Marie-Claire et al. (Eds.) 2011) 355 (366).

98 *Newcombe*, Andrew, 'General Exceptions in International Investment Agreements', in: Sustainable Development in World Investment Law (Cordonier Segger, Marie-Claire et al. (Eds.) 2011) 355 (370). Newcombe, however, does not believe that the substantive investment protections are to be understood fundamentally differently in a treaty which contains such a general exception from one which does not contain one.

99 *Hunt*, Nathaniel Hemmerick, 'One Step Forward, Two Steps Back: The Central American Free Trade Agreement and the Environment', 35 Georgia Journal of International and Comparative Law 2007, 545 (554), for the example of the relevant chapter of the CAFTA-DR as a reaction to harsh public criticism of the NAFTA.

1. Provisions Setting Forth Environmental Regime

a) North American Agreement on Environmental Co-operation

The NAFTA, which has served as a model of free-trade agreements containing investment provisions, was negotiated and implemented in parallel with an environmental side agreement, the North American Agreement on Environmental Co-operation (NAAEC). It was created to address environmental concerns stemming from trade and investment implications, to promote sustainable development regionally, and to address transboundary impacts of the economic provisions.[100] In addition to setting forth certain substantive obligations relating to environmental protection,[101] the NAAEC, most notably, has established a Commission for Environmental Co-operation (CEC)[102]. The governing body of the CEC, the Council, is in charge of, inter alia, encouraging environmental enforcement and co-operation.[103] The CEC further administers two compliance procedures, one of which can be triggered by non-governmental organisations or individuals,[104] and one which is at the disposal of the state parties[105].

With the NAAEC being a side agreement independent of the NAFTA, its implications for the interpretation of the latter differ from the effect of clauses within the treaty itself: The NAAEC is not part of the treaty itself, nor is it part of the context of the treaty as envisaged in Article 31 paragraph 2 VCLT. Despite the less restricted wording of the clause,[106] only agreements on the interpretation of the respective treaty fall into this category.[107] Theoretically, this may restrict the potential impact of ideas and principles promulgated in the NAAEC on the interpretation of NAFTA

---

100 See the environmental objectives set forth in Article 1 NAAEC. It contains multiple references to sustainability (lit a, b) and co-operation (lit c, f) as well as to trade and economic implications (lit e, i) and refers to compliance and pollution prevention (lit g, j). See for a comprehensive overview of the NAFTA environmental regime, *Knox*, John H., 'The Neglected Lessons of the NAFTA Environmental Regime', 45 Wake Forest Law Review 2010, 391 (394).

101 Articles 2, 5 NAAEC.

102 Part 4 NAAEC.

103 Article 10 NAAEC.

104 Article 14 NAAEC.

105 Article 22 NAAEC.

106 Article 31 para 2 lit a VCLT extends the context of the treaty to "any agreement relating to the treaty which was made between all the parties in connection with the conclusion of the treaty".

107 *Gardiner*, Richard, Treaty Interpretation (2008) p. 204; *Villiger*, Mark E., Commentary on the 1969 Vienna Convention on the Law of Treaties (2009) Article 31 paras 17, 18.

obligations – which are only to be "taken into account together with the context", as prescribed by Article 31 paragraph 3 lit c VCLT. However, the arbitral tribunal in *S.D. Myers Inc. v. Canada*, which refers to the NAAEC in its interpretative undertaking, does not draw such a distinction. It indiscriminately has drawn upon the preamble of the NAFTA, the NAAEC, and the international agreements confirmed in the NAAEC to establish three principles, in the light of which the substantive provisions of the NAFTA were to be interpreted.[108] The tribunal went on to state that the principles thus determined were consistent with the express provisions of other environmental agreements that were relevant to its decision.[109] It determined that the logical corollary of all those principles was that in a situation in which "a state can achieve its chosen level of environmental protection through a variety of equally effective and reasonable means, it is obliged to adopt the alternative that is most consistent with open trade".[110] Further in the award, the tribunal explicitly states that the principles distilled amongst others from the NAAEC provisions, constitute the "legal context" of the investment treaty obligation of national treatment.[111] In the light of such an indiscriminate understanding, it appears overly academic to distinguish sharply between environmental references contained in the investment treaty itself and those contained in a separate, but connected agreement.

The formal relationship between the NAFTA and the NAAEC has been criticised for inherently separating environmental and trade aspects, since the formal links are kept to a legal and institutional minimum.[112] Further-

---

[108] S.D. Myers Inc. v. Canada, Partial Award on the Merits, 13 November 2000, para 220. After having portrayed several provisions of the NAAEC (paras 217–219), the tribunal states the following:

"The Preamble to the NAFTA, the NAAEC and the international agreements affirmed in the NAAEC suggest that specific provisions of the NAFTA should be interpreted in light of the following general principles:

- Parties have the right to establish high levels of environmental protection. They are not obliged to compromise their standards merely to satisfy the political or economic interests of other states;
- Parties should avoid creating distortions to trade;
- environmental protection and economic development can and should be mutually supportive."

[109] See the portrayal of the arbitral decision in 'Chapter 3 – Standards of Non-Discriminatory Treatment' at pp. 176 *et seq*.

[110] S.D. Myers Inc. v. Canada, Partial Award on the Merits, 13 November 2000, para 221.

[111] S.D. Myers Inc. v. Canada, Partial Award on the Merits, 13 November 2000, para 247.

[112] *Johnson*, Pierre Marc/*Beaulieu*, André, The Environment and NAFTA: Understanding and Implementing the New Continental Law – Why a North American Agreement on Environmental Cooperation? (1996) pp. 126, 128. The authors illus-

more, to the extent that there existed a formal relationship between the NAFTA and the NAAEC, the latter was found to be "almost always subordinate".[113] The assessment of the practical implications of the environmental regime suggests that its most important effect relates to the promotion of sustainable development.[114] In contrast, it is suggested that the practical impact of the treaty in addressing concerns relating to the relationship between trade and environmental obligations is "weak".[115] But despite its shortcomings, the environmental regime of the NAFTA constitutes the main model for the environmental chapters contained in later free trade agreements.[116] A large set of these common elements will now be analysed.

b) Environmental Chapters in Post-NAFTA Agreements

The environmental chapters of free trade agreements – or articles in bilateral investment treaties – stipulate several relevant provisions such as the following: (1) the right of each state to determine its own level of environmental protection while ensuring, at the same time, that national regulations encourage high levels of environmental protection and aim at improving national regulations in that respect;[117] (2) the obligation of each state not to fail persistently in enforcing its national environmental laws, and the under-

trate this separation by stating that the CEC does not have a mandate to enforce or even clarify Article 1114 NAFTA with regard to relaxation of environmental standards to attract investment.

113 *Johnson*, Pierre Marc/*Beaulieu*, André, The Environment and NAFTA: Understanding and Implementing the New Continental Law – Why a North American Agreement on Environmental Cooperation? (1996) p. 129. Similarly, *Royalty*, Kent W./*Ross*, Dianna, 'NAFTA Chapter 11: "Tantamount to Expropriation": Tantamount to Explosive', 21 The International Trade Journal 2007, 299 (308, 315, 323).

114 *Knox*, John H., 'The Neglected Lessons of the NAFTA Environmental Regime', 45 Wake Forest Law Review 2010, 391 (392). See pp. 408–412 for a detailed account of the rules relating to the promotion of sustainable development.

115 *Knox*, John H., 'The Neglected Lessons of the NAFTA Environmental Regime', 45 Wake Forest Law Review 2010, 391 (405). Similarly, *Royalty*, Kent W./*Ross*, Dianna, 'NAFTA Chapter 11: "Tantamount to Expropriation": Tantamount to Explosive', 21 The International Trade Journal 2007, 299 (309), calling it a "weakly enforced pledge".

116 *Knox*, John H., 'The Neglected Lessons of the NAFTA Environmental Regime', 45 Wake Forest Law Review 2010, 391 (413–414), criticising the uniformity of environmental provisions in post-NAFTA agreements as well as the lack of learning lessons from the inadequacies of the environmental regime of the NAFTA.

117 Article 17.1 CAFTA-DR; Article 17.1 U.S.-Oman FTA; Article 18.1 U.S.-Peru FTA; Article 19.1 Nicaragua-Taiwan FTA; Article 19.1 U.S.-Chile FTA; Article 19.1 U.S.-Australia FTA; Article 5 para 1 Belgium-Luxembourg-Madagascar BIT; Article 5 para 1 Belgium-Luxembourg-Guinea BIT; Article 5 para 1 Belgium-Luxembourg-Sudan BIT. See also Article 1701 para 1 Canada-Peru FTA in connec-

standing that trade and investment shall not be encouraged by a weakening of environmental regulation;[118] (3) the possibility for each state to introduce certain incentives and flexible mechanisms to achieve environmental protection;[119] (4) the recognition by the state parties that environmental co-operation is important to achieve environmental protection – such as the promotion of sustainable development – and their commitment to expanding such co-operation;[120] (5) the right of each state to request consultations with another state regarding any matter under the chapter, while setting forth a procedure to be followed which opens a road to dispute settlement under the agreement for certain issues;[121] and (6) the recognition by the state parties that multilateral environmental agreements to which they are all party and the implementation of the respective obligations play an important role in achieving the environmental objectives of the chapter[122].

---

tion with the provisions of the accompanying Agreement on the Environment between Canada and the Republic of Peru.

[118] Article 17.2 CAFTA-DR; Article 17.2 U.S.-Oman FTA; Article 18.3 U.S.-Peru FTA; Article 19.2 Nicaragua-Taiwan FTA; Article 19.2 U.S.-Chile FTA; Article 19.2 U.S.-Australia FTA. Similarly, Article 5 para 2 Belgium-Luxembourg-Madagascar BIT; Article 5 para 2 Belgium-Luxembourg-Guinea BIT; Article 5 para 2 Belgium-Luxembourg-Sudan BIT. The provisions contained in the BITs state "that it is inappropriate to encourage investment by relaxing domestic environmental legislation" and that each party "shall strive to ensure that it does not waive or otherwise derogate from, or offer to waive or otherwise derogate from, such legislation as an encouragement for the establishment, maintenance or expansion in its territory of an investment".

[119] Article 17.4 CAFTA-DR; Article 17.4 U.S.-Oman FTA; Article 18.5 U.S.-Peru FTA; Article 19.4 Nicaragua-Taiwan FTA; Article 19.4 U.S.-Australia FTA.

[120] Article 17.9 CAFTA-DR; Article 17.7 U.S.-Oman FTA; Article 18.10 U.S.-Peru FTA; Article 19.8 and Annex 19.8 Nicaragua-Taiwan FTA; Article 19.5 and Annex 19.3 U.S.-Chile FTA; Article 19.6 U.S.-Australia FTA. Similarly, Article 5 para 4 Belgium-Luxembourg-Madagascar BIT; Article 5 para 4 Belgium-Luxembourg-Guinea BIT; Article 5 para 4 Belgium-Luxembourg-Sudan BIT. With the exception of the latter, these BITs provide for a consultation scheme according to which each party can request the reunion of the parties to discuss matters falling within the scope of the environmental provision. See also Article 1702 Canada-Peru FTA in connection with Article 7 Agreement on the Environment between Canada and the Republic of Peru.

[121] Article 17.10 CAFTA-DR; Article 18.12 U.S.-Peru FTA; Article 19.9 Nicaragua-Taiwan FTA; Article 17.8 U.S.-Oman FTA; Article 19.6 U.S.-Chile FTA; Article 19.7 U.S.-Australia FTA.

[122] Article 17.12 CAFTA-DR; Article 17.9 U.S.-Oman FTA; Article 18.13 and Article 18.2 with Annex 18.2 U.S.-Peru FTA; Article 19.10 Nicaragua-Taiwan FTA; Article 19.8 U.S.-Australia FTA. Similarly, Article 5 para 3 Belgium-Luxembourg-Madagascar BIT; Article 5 para 3 Belgium-Luxembourg-Guinea BIT; Article 5 para 3 Belgium-Luxembourg-Sudan BIT, with which the parties "reaffirm their commitments under the international environmental agreements, which they have accepted" and "shall strive to ensure that such commitments are fully recognised and implemented by their domestic legislation."

The first element, which relates to the level of environmental protection within the national jurisdiction of the state parties, supports high levels of environmental protection and aims to increase stringency. While the sovereignty of the national state in implementing its environmental targets is confirmed,[123] the provision enshrines the desire to augment environmental standards. Given a certain lack of clarity as to what constitutes a "high level" of environmental protection or an "improvement" of national laws and policies, the wording suggests that the provision is primarily stating an ambition. Nevertheless, the provision expressly emphasises the right of a state to introduce national regulation to increasingly protect its environment. Even in the absence of a direct reference to a potential conflict with economic rights, the ambition to increase environmental standards would have to be considered a relevant factor in an interpretative exercise if opposing objectives clashed.

The second element relates to the potential impact of environmental regulation on the competitiveness of countries and their industries. As far as the provisions dismiss the possibility of weakening environmental regulation to attract investment, they mirror the fear of a regulatory race-to-the-bottom and of the creation of pollution havens, which has been discussed above. The same concerns are addressed by the additional obligation for states not to fail persistently in enforcing their environmental obligations.[124] The formulation shows that the provision focuses on the non-enforcement of environmental regulation as far as it affects the trade between the parties. Thus, environmental regulation is not an end in itself. In the Central American Free Trade Agreement (CAFTA), the respective provision is the only norm in the environmental chapter that opens recourse for another state to dispute resolution procedures,[125] – which reinforces the importance attached to it in comparison to the consultation scheme contained in the more limited provision of the NAAEC.[126] In the light of the reluctance of states to use intergovernmental compliance procedures,[127] however, the practical impact of the mechanism remains questionable.

---

123 See *Hunt*, Nathaniel Hemmerick, 'One Step Forward, Two Steps Back: The Central American Free Trade Agreement and the Environment', 35 Georgia Journal of International and Comparative Law 2007, 545 (556), who considers this explicit reference to be an overstatement of the national sovereignty of the states involved. I cannot share this assessment, since the sovereignty of a national state regarding its national laws is a clear fact in the absence of an express commitment to the contrary.

124 According to Article 17.2.1 (a) CAFTA-DR, a state "shall not fail to effectively enforce its environmental laws, through a sustained or recurring course of action or inaction, in a manner affecting trade between the Parties [...]".

125 Article 17.10.6-8 CAFTA-DR.

126 The provision is similar to the one contained in Article 22 NAAEC.

127 *Knox*, John H., 'The Neglected Lessons of the NAFTA Environmental Regime', 45 Wake Forest Law Review 2010, 391 (397) evaluates the similar procedure

The third element relates to the implementation of certain incentives and flexible mechanisms to achieve environmental protection. The explicit mentioning of incentive schemes and flexible mechanisms in addition to underlining the sovereignty of states with respect to their environmental legislation could be explained by the potential impact of such rules on the substantive standards of investment protection. The restrictive effect of, for example, a cap-and-trade system to create incentives for the reduction of certain emissions will be discussed in subsequent chapters. In cases of conflict, this provision arguably underscores the margin of appreciation of the legislating state. While the majority of mechanisms in the non-enumerative lists refer to very subtle approaches of the state, the reference to programs demanding the exchange of permits encompasses emission trading schemes or similar approaches.

The reference to environmental co-operation, the fourth element mentioned above, features the promotion of sustainable development in concert with the strengthening of investment relations. The detailed incorporation gives weight to those notions which have already been identified above as elements of some environmental preambular clauses in investment treaties. Specifically, the parties identify priority areas for environmental co-operation and protection, and they expressly recognise the importance of conserving and improving the environment. Further, the parties recognise that the achievement of their common environmental goals may lead to an increase in investment into environmental goods and services. In the spirit of co-operation, the fifth element sets forth a standardised system for consultations amongst the state parties, which relates to each of the questions relevant to the environmental chapter as a whole.

The sixth element deals with the relevance of international environmental agreements to which all parties to the respective economic agreement are a party, too. The element confirms the importance of such environmental agreements and their domestic implementation for environmental protection. It expresses the parties' recognition that the environmental package contained in the respective economic agreement can contribute to the goals of international environmental agreements. Some of the treaties containing this element, however, go further and insert a mandate for the parties to "consult, as appropriate, with respect to negotiations on environmental issues of mutual interest".[128] Ascribing specific importance to seven enumerated in-

---

under Article 22 NAAEC and finds that no country has ever brought a complaint to this dispute resolution mechanism and that the lack of interest of the participant states has been so succinct that they have never even negotiated the relevant rules of procedure.

128 Article 18.13 para 2 U.S.-Peru FTA; Article 18.13 para 2 U.S.-Colombia FTA; Article 20.10 para 2 U.S.-Korea FTA.

ternational environmental agreements,[129] these treaties oblige state parties to "adopt, maintain, and implement laws, regulations, and all other measures to fulfil [their respective] obligations".[130] Additionally, provisions in some treaties reinforce the importance of other international environmental obligations undertaken by each state[131]. Furthermore, some environmental chapters expressly call for the protection of biological diversity.[132] As far as provisions relating to this sixth element focus on the relationship of international environmental agreements and economic obligations, they will be reviewed in the context of the following section.

In addition to these aspects, several post-NAFTA free trade agreements contain provisions aiming at the establishment of certain legislative standards[133] and of an Environmental Affairs Council to monitor implementation of measures, to share best practices, and to provide for complaint mechanisms for the general public, triggering an institutionalised procedure[134]. These provisions largely mirror elements of the earlier NAAEC. Although the regulation of certain environmental aspects, the creation of an

---

129 In the case of the U.S.-Colombia FTA, the U.S.-Peru FTA, the U.S.- Korea FTA and the U.S.-Panama FTA these are the 1973 Convention on International Trade in Endangered Species of Wild Fauna and Flora, the 1987 Montreal Protocol on Substances that Deplete the Ozone Layer, the 1978 London Protocol to the 1973 Convention on the Prevention of Pollution from Ships, the 1971 Ramsar Convention on Wetlands of International Importance Especially as Waterfowl Habitat, the 1980 Convention on the Conservation of Antarctic Marine Living Resources, the 1946 International Convention For the Regulation of Whaling, the 1949 Convention for the Establishment of an Inter-American Tropical Tuna Commission.

130 Article 18.2 U.S.-Peru FTA; Article 18.2 U.S.-Colombia FTA; Article 17.2 U.S.-Panama FTA; Article 20.2 U.S.-Korea FTA.

131 The clause states that "each party recogni[s]es the importance to it of the multilateral environmental agreements to which it is a party", Article 18.13 para 3 U.S.-Peru FTA; Article 18.13 para 3 U.S.-Colombia FTA.

132 Article 18.11 U.S.-Peru FTA; Article 18.11 U.S.-Colombia FTA. See also Article 1702 Canada-Peru FTA in connection with Article 5 Agreement on the Environment between Canada and the Republic of Peru.

133 Article 17.3 CAFTA-DR establishes the obligation of each state party to have judicial and administrative proceedings in place to sanction or remedy violations of environmental laws, together with a possibility for interested persons to request the competent authorities to investigate alleged violations. Similar provisions in Article 19.3 Nicaragua-Taiwan FTA; Article 18.4 U.S.-Peru FTA; Article 17.3; U.S.-Oman FTA; Article 19.8 U.S.-Chile FTA; Article 19.3. U.S.-Australia FTA.

134 The Environmental Affairs Council and its tasks and procedures are enshrined in Articles 17.5-8 CAFTA-DR; Articles 18.6-9 U.S.-Peru FTA. An environmental Affairs Council which lacks the institutionalised procedure is established by Articles 19.6-7 Nicaragua-Taiwan FTA; Articles 19.3-4 U.S.-Chile FTA. Enshrining a joint committee lacking an institutionalised procedure Articles 17.5-6 U.S. Oman FTA; Article 19.5 U.S.-Australia FTA.

environmental committee, and the possibility of public participation mirror basic aspects and are positively assessed by commentators, the overall regime is considered insufficient for real environmental protection.[135]

2. Provisions on Relationship with Environmental Agreements

As already mentioned, the sixth element of the environmental package found in some post-NAFTA free trade agreements specifically elaborates on the relationship between economic obligations and international environmental agreements. As there is potential for conflicts for a state party to both investment protection provisions and international environmental agreements – especially if the environmental convention mandates concrete measures that can influence investment activity – respective provisions addressing the potential normative conflict deserve particular attention.

The first example of such a norm is Article 104 NAFTA. This provision states that in the event of inconsistency between the NAFTA and the "specific trade obligations set out in [three multilateral and two bilateral expressly listed treaties] such obligations shall prevail to the extent of the inconsistency", provided that the party chooses the least inconsistent measure among equally effective and reasonable means.[136] While the effect of this conflict norm is already doubtful in the trade context,[137] the explicit

[135] Commentators have found such provisions to be insufficient, primarily because of a lack of enforcement provisions and of references to an absolute standard of protection, see *Hunt*, Nathaniel Hemmerick, 'One Step Forward, Two Steps Back: The Central American Free Trade Agreement and the Environment', 35 Georgia Journal of International and Comparative Law 2007, 545 (557, 558); *Jenkins*, Benjamin W., 'The Next Generation of Chilling Uncertainty: Indirect Expropriation under CAFTA and Its Potential Impact on Environmental Protection', 12 Ocean and Coastal Law Journal 2007, 269 (281–283). *Knox*, John H., 'The Neglected Lessons of the NAFTA Environmental Regime', 45 Wake Forest Law Review 2010, 391 (421–422) focuses his criticism on the implementation being entirely left to the governments. He further points to the importance of independence of the secretariat from the environmental council in receiving citizen submissions.

[136] Article 104 para 1 NAFTA. The multilateral environmental agreements incorporated are the 1973 Convention on International Trade in Endangered Species of Wild Fauna and Flora, the 1987 Montreal Protocol on Substances that Deplete the Ozone layer and the 1989 Basel Convention on the Control of Transboundary Movements of Hazardous Wastes and Their Disposal. The bilateral agreements are a 1986 Canadian- U.S. Agreement on the Transboundary Movement of Hazardous Waste and a 1983 U.S.-Mexican Agreement on the Cooperation for the Protection and Improvement of the Environment in the Border Area (see Annex 104.1). Para 2 of the provision allows for the future insertion of further environmental agreements upon unanimous consent of the parties.

[137] Criticism relates to the application being restricted to trade obligations stemming from international environmental agreements, thus excluding national legisla-

wording of the provision suggests that it does not apply to potential differences between investment obligations and international environmental agreements. The wording reduces relevant conflicts to those of trade obligations within the NAFTA and in the enumerated environmental agreements.

However, this has not deterred the arbitral tribunal in *S.D. Myers Inc. v. Canada* from indicating that the rule contained in Article 104 NAFTA can be applied to an investment dispute. It concludes from the provision that if there is an alternative for the state party to fulfil its obligations under the Basel Convention – which does not involve a breach of the NAFTA – this way has to be followed.[138] The tribunal does not even mention the explicit connection of Article 104 NAFTA to trade obligations. The general understanding pronounced by the tribunal is not controversial. The tribunal found that since the Basel Convention was yet to be ratified and the state could respect its environmental obligations without violating its investment obligations, there was no conflict of existing obligations.[139] Hence, the potential prevalence of the environmental obligation does not have to be considered. The express reference to trade obligations in the provision suggests that the parties did not foresee any relevant conflicts between investment obligations and environmental obligations contained in international environmental agreements – or they would also have mentioned those in the provision.

Some more recent free trade agreements contain virtually the same provision, which refers to an upated list of relevant multilateral environmental agreements.[140] Like Article 104 NAFTA, these provisions state that in the event of any inconsistency between the free trade agreement and specific

---

tion. Further, it has been suggested that the improbability of a state party arguing that it has accepted two mutually exclusive obligations contravenes the relevance of the provision. See in more detail, *Knox*, John H., 'The Neglected Lessons of the NAFTA Environmental Regime', 45 Wake Forest Law Review 2010, 391 (400–401). A more enthusiastic, yet not uncritical assessment is made by *Housman*, Robert, 'The North American Free Trade Agreement's Lessons For Reconciling Trade and the Environment', 30 Stanford Journal of International Law 1994, 379 (398–400), who describes the Article as "one of the agreement's most aggressive attempts to advance the trade and environment debate".

[138] S.D. Myers Inc. v. Canada, Partial Award on the Merits, 13 November 2000, para 215.

[139] S.D. Myers Inc. v. Canada, Partial Award on the Merits, 13 November 2000, paras 215, 255.

[140] Article 103 Canada-Peru FTA; Article 103 Canada-Colombia FTA. The respective environmental Agreements listed in the Annex are (i) the 1979 Convention on International Trade in Endangered Species of Wild Fauna and Flora, (ii) the 1990 Montreal Protocol on Substances that Deplete the Ozone Layer, (iii) the 1989 Basel Convention on the Control of Transboundary Movements of Hazardous Wastes and Their Disposal, (iv) the 1998 Rotterdam Convention on the Prior Informed Consent Procedure for Certain Hazardous Chemicals and Pesticides in International Trade

trade obligations set out in one of the listed environmental agreements, the environmental obligation prevails if the state has adopted the alternatively possible measure which is the least inconsistent with the provisions of the free trade agreement. An investment tribunal that is confronted with such a conflict is very likely to follow the guidance given by the provision.[141] However, the provision is rather narrow in scope – since primacy is only accorded to environmental trade obligations and not to all environmental obligations contained in the listed agreements. The express regulation for this specific situation also establishes an implicit hierarchy to the detriment of other environmental agreements and the non-trade-specific provisions in the listed agreements.[142] Third, the provision puts an investment tribunal in a position to decide, whether the host state has chosen the measure that is the least inconsistent with the treaty obligations – a question which may not be easy to assess. Accordingly, such a provision is of very limited assistance for the host state in implementing its environmental obligations.

In contrast, other post-NAFTA free trade agreements contain more general statements on the relationship between economic and environmental agreements than explicit conflict of norms provisions. Such rules provide that the parties "shall continue to seek means to enhance the mutual supportiveness of multilateral environmental agreements to which they are all party and trade agreements to which they are all party"[143]. The formulation underlines that the provision makes a general statement on the relationship between environmental agreements and trade agreements, but does not create a hierarchy of potentially contradicting obligations. While the element ascribes an additional value to environmental treaties that could have a contextual influence, its express limitation to environmental agreements to

(and, in the Canada-Peru FTA additionally the 2001 Stockholm Convention on Persistent Organic Pollutants).

141 See, however, the very systematic argument by *Kammerhofer*, Jörg, 'The Theory of Norm Conflict Solutions in International Law', in: Sustainable Development in World Investment Law (Cordonier Segger, Marie-Claire et al. (Eds.) 2011) 83 (97), that provisions like Article 103 Canada-Peru FTA and Canada-Columbia FTA are not in a position to derogate, because they are provisions found in the same treaty as the conflicting provisions. Since the Article is on the same hierarchical level, it cannot establish a preference based in law.

142 Article 102 para 2 Canada-Peru FTA; Article 102 para 2 Canada-Colombia FTA expressly state that "in the event of any inconsistency between this Agreement and any other such agreements, this Agreement shall prevail to the extent of the inconsistency, except as otherwise provided in this Agreement."

143 Exact wording of Article 17.12 para 1 CAFTA-DR. The exclusive applicability of the provision to trade obligations is further strengthened through the reference to "ongoing negotiations in the WTO regarding multilateral environmental agreements" in para 2 of the provision.

which all states are parties reduces its potential scope the more state parties are included. However, the provision emphasises the concept of 'mutual supportiveness', which is a helpful tool in aligning economic and environmental obligations.[144] The textual connection of the endorsement with "trade agreements" does not prevent the application of the provision in connection with foreign investment, since this term is significantly broader in scope than the "specific trade obligations" discussed above.

Some of the more recent free trade agreements contain additional provisions concerning the relationship of their economic obligations with environmental agreements. The rationale set forth prescribes the balancing of the opposing obligations. Such a provision reads as follows:

> "In the event of any inconsistency between a Party's obligations under this Agreement and a covered agreement, the Party shall seek to balance its obligations under both agreements, but this shall not preclude the Party from taking a particular measure to comply with its obligations under the covered agreement, provided that the primary purpose of the measure is not to impose a disguised restriction on trade."[145]

This provision refers to inconsistencies between any economic obligation and those of covered environmental agreements, which are enumerated in an appendix to the respective agreement[146]. Accordingly, it is not explicitly restricted to conflicts of rules regarding trade and the environmental agreements cover a broad range of issues. The states' duty to balance their respective obligations underlines the understanding that the state parties have not intended to establish a hierarchy of norms. The reconciliatory, balancing approach is closer to the idea of 'mutual supportiveness'. The balancing approach is not meant to preclude a state party from taking a specific measure to comply with its obligations under a covered environmental agree-

---

144 'Mutual supportiveness', like harmonisation or systematic integration, aims at a harmonious balance of norms. See in detail, *Matz-Lück*, Nele, 'Harmonization, Systemic Integration, and 'Mutual Supportiveness' as Conflict-Solution Techniques: Different Modes of Interpretation as a Challenge to Negative Effects of Fragmentation?', XVII Finnish Yearbook of International Law 2006, 39 (43).

145 Article 18.13 para 4 U.S.-Peru FTA; Article 18.13 para 4 U.S.-Colombia FTA; Article 17.13 para 3 U.S.-Panama FTA; Article 20.10 para 3 U.S.-Korea FTA.

146 In the case of the U.S.-Colombia FTA, the U.S.-Peru FTA, the U.S.-Korea FTA and the U.S.-Panama FTA these are the 1973 Convention on International Trade in Endangered Species of Wild Fauna and Flora, the 1987 Montreal Protocol on Substances that Deplete the Ozone Layer, the 1978 London Protocol to the 1973 Convention on the Prevention of Pollution from Ships, the 1971 Ramsar Convention on Wetlands of International Importance Especially as Waterfowl Habitat, the 1980 Convention on the Conservation of Antarctic Marine Living Resources, the 1946 International Convention For the Regulation of Whaling, the 1949 Convention for the Establishment of an Inter-American Tropical Tuna Commission.

ment, as long as the measure does not constitute a disguised restriction on trade. Accordingly, a genuine environmental measure that is not a disguised restriction of a legitimate investment activity is accepted under the provision, even if it negatively impacts on the investment. Thus, the provision gives considerable weight to the values enshrined in the covered environmental agreements. The "importance of balancing trade obligations and environmental obligations" and the understanding that economic obligations and environmental tenets are "mutually supportive" are also recognised in provisions of other free-trade agreements.[147]

Even though most formulations expressly refer to trade, but not to investment obligations, the reconciliatory approach should also be understood as a guideline for the interpretation of investment law. Since a hierarchy of norms has not been established – and an investment tribunal has not been deterred from deriving principles for the investment context from a rule expressly relating to trade obligations –[148] there is nothing to prevent adherence to the reconciliatory principle in the investment context. This is all the more the case since the notion of 'mutual supportiveness' is a concept closely connected to sustainable development[149] and it is one of the principles distilled from a set of environmental references by the investment tribunal in *S.D. Myers Inc. v. Canada*.[150] Accordingly, emphasising the interconnection of subject areas and attempting to integrate them in cases of conflict is the interpretative approach to be derived from such a provision. However, its scope of application is limited by the exclusive reference to a specific set of environmental treaties. These norms cannot be invoked in cases of conflict with other environmental obligations, because the state parties have chosen an exhaustive enumeration of relevant environmental treaties.

---

147 Article 1703 para 1 Canada-Peru FTA, Article 1703 Canada-Colombia FTA, specifically referring to the environmental notions incorporated in the Agreement on the Environment between Canada and the Republic of Peru – or with the Republic of Colombia, respectively.

148 See above at pp. 126 *et seq.*

149 *Pavoni*, Riccardo, 'Mututal Supportiveness as a Principle of Interpretation and Law-Making: A Watershed for the "WTO-and-Competing-Regimes" Debate?', 21 European Journal of International Law 2010, 649 (661). See for the principle of sustainable development, the detailed portrayal in 'Chapter 1 – Environmental Norms and Principles' at pp. 63 *et seq.*

150 S.D. Myers Inc. v. Canada, Partial Award on the Merits, 13 November 2000, paras 220, 247.

III. Sector Specific References

Article 19 paragraph 1 ECT provides an example of a provision in an investment treaty that contains environmental references connected to a specific economic sector. The provision mentions sustainable development in connection with obligations arising out of international environmental agreements as overreaching goals – in pursuit of which the minimisation of environmental impacts stemming from operations within the energy cycle should be aimed at. To this end, the parties are called upon to integrate precautionary measures in their policies and actions. The provision further emphasises the economic efficiency of protective measures, the polluter-pays principle, and the non-distortion of international investment and trade. In addition to the abstract enumeration of these principles, the provision suggests that the state parties undertake several concrete activities. It mentions the implementation of environmental principles in national energy policies, a fuller reflection of environmental costs and benefits throughout the energy cycle, the promotion of renewable and cleaner energy sources, the promotion of respective awareness, and the participation in research, development, and technology transfer.

Article 19 paragraph 1 ECT thus expressly confirms the importance of several fundamental environmental concepts for the context of the covered investments and in detail proposes specific fields of application. However, these references are closely tied to general policies of the state, so that it is not clear which impact they can have with regard to a specific investment activity. Since the provision sets certain environmental parameters for states to implement in their national energy policies, it supports national legislation which treats energy investments differently according to their environmental impact, thus favouring more environmentally advantageous projects over others.[151] Such a distinction obviously does not relieve the state of acting in a transparent manner in its assessment of differing energy projects.[152]

In this way, the ECT accords a distinct place to environmental protection and provides each state party with a tool for implementing a strategy fitting its own requirements. It merits pointing out that the ECT considers the

---

[151] See – especially – Article 19 para 1 lit b ECT, stipulating to "promote […] a fuller reflection of environmental costs and benefits throughout the Energy Cycle", and lit d, stipulating "have particular regard to Improving Energy Efficiency, to developing and using renewable energy sources, to promoting the use of cleaner fuels and to employing technologies and technological means that reduce pollution".

[152] See Article 19 para 1 lit i ECT, stipulating to "promote the transparent assessment at an early stage and prior to decision, and subsequent monitoring, of Environmental Impacts of environmentally significant energy investment projects".

application and interpretation of the above provision relevant enough to provide for a special, subordinate dispute settlement forum – namely a review by the Charter Conference – as long as no other appropriate forum exists.[153] While the ECT has been hailed by some commentators as having broken "new ground" by its emphasis on the importance of environmental protection in the energy industry,[154] the proper interpretative impact of its environmental references remains unclear. Article 19 ECT certainly could be relied on – especially in the interpretation and assessment of national environmental measures of the host state – but it remains to be seen whether investment tribunals will support such an approach.

IV. Interpretative Value of Environmental Provisions

The portrayal of environmental references within the substantive provisions of investment agreements has shown that a limited set of stipulations has been adopted in a significant number of agreements, within the small group – in absolute numbers – of agreements that contain such references. The resemblance of the provisions portrayed and the fact that they predominantly feature in agreements concluded by a similar set of member states – most notably the U.S. and Canada – suggest that they reflect model treaty language. The reliance on model treaty language, however, does not influence the interpretative value of a stipulation, nor does it reduce its importance in comparison to a specifically negotiated clause. The final text has to be interpreted in its integrity and is not to be differentiated according to the effort that has been put into the negotiation of the respective provision – which is often difficult to discern.[155]

---

153 Article 19 para 2 ECT provides as follows: "At the request of one or more Contracting Parties, disputes concerning the application or interpretation of provisions of this Article shall, to the extent that arrangements for the consideration of such disputes do not exist in other appropriate international fora, be reviewed by the Charter Conference aiming at a solution."

154 *Kolo*, Abba/*Wälde*, Thomas, 'Environmental Regulation, Investment Protection and "Regulatory Taking" in International Law', 50 International and Comparative Law Quarterly 2001, 811 (817). See also the assessment by *Sussman*, Edna, 'The Energy Charter Treaty's Investor Protection Provisions: Potential to Foster Solutions to Global Warming and Promote Sustainable Development, 14 ILSA Journal of International and Comparative Law 2008, 391 (403) which concludes that the application of the ECT to climate change solutions is well-grounded in its original intention and in its provisions.

155 The idea that a particular provision, which in contrast to most of the remainder of the agreement was specifically negotiated, should have a greater weight in the interpretation of the treaty was dismissed in investment arbitration. See Siemens A.G. v. Argentine Republic, ICSID Case No. ARB/02/8, Decision on Jurisdiction, 3 August 2004, para 106.

The stipulations portrayed in this section take the form of material treaty provisions. The above depiction has attempted to evaluate their relevance as directly applied provisions. It has pointed to specific formulations which render them more or less significant for the situation they purport to address. The overview has indicated that these material references fall short of establishing clear-cut solutions to situations of conflicts between investment obligations and environmental concepts. Their interpretative value, however, is not restricted to their direct application. They can possibly help to determine the 'object and purpose' of the treaty as well as constitute 'context' for the interpretation of other material provisions. The environmental references can arguably influence these two components by demonstrating that investment law is not isolated from environmental concepts.

The interpretative approach to determining the object and purpose of a treaty have been discussed above.[156] Even though free trade agreements that dedicate a complete chapter to the 'environment' could be seen as furthering, amongst others, the object and purpose of environmental protection, I hold that to classify such references in this sense would be overstating the effect accorded to them by the state parties. While investment tribunals may be tempted to determine an object and purpose for parts of a treaty or even for singular provisions in the interpretative process, there is the danger that the intentions of the parties are confused, if an object and purpose for specific parts or provisions is determined which is distinct from the object and purpose of the treaty as a whole.[157] Furthermore, the VCLT does not prescribe the singling out of objects and purposes of sections or single provisions. For the purpose of interpretation, only one – admittedly broad – object and purpose of a treaty should be distilled and, in the light of the factors to be taken into account in the case of free trade agreements, this is unlikely to be 'environmental protection'.[158]

---

156 See above at pp. 113 *et seq.*

157 *Klabbers*, Jan, 'Some Problems Regarding the Object and Purpose of Treaties', VIII Finnish Yearbook of International Law 1997, 138 (151–152).

158 See, however, *Alvarez*, José E., 'The Return of the State', 20 Minnesota Journal of International Law 2011, 223 (237), who argues with regard to the 2004 U.S. Model BIT that the treaty's object and purpose is not really clear and that the combination of the changes to its preamble, the more restricted investor rights and the expansive list of state exceptions "suggests that its object and purpose now includes the right of the host states to regulate as they please".

See also the discussion surrounding the 2007 Draft Norway Model BIT (available at: http://www.asil.org/ilib080421.cfm). Norway intended to create a model BIT which satisfied the needs of foreign investors as well as strengthened the capacity of the state to regulate (Article 12), inter alia, for environmental reasons. This balanced approach of the template, however, ended up being criticised by both interest groups for being insufficient. Norway finally abandoned the proposal.

Accordingly, the most important interpretative influence of the environmental provisions consists in providing 'context' for the interpretation of specific provisions on the substantive scope of investment protection. There is no basis for abstractly distinguishing between environmental provisions with relation to their position within a given treaty. They all constitute the relevant interpretative context for cases with an environmental connotation. Although a strict application of the rules of the VCLT indicates that a separate environmental side agreement does not belong to the interpretative context,[159] investment tribunals may consider the context more broadly.[160] However, since the portrayal has indicated that environmental references are more likely to be included in the treaty itself, the issue of separate agreements is not of great importance.[161]

As the terms used in a treaty do not necessarily have one single ordinary meaning,[162] the set of possible meanings is informed by its context. Whenever an environmental reference forms part of the interpretative context, its practical impact will depend on the content of the respective reference itself. While all of these norms can be relevant as a clear embrace of environmental values, the portrayal above has shown that the clarity and sharpness of such references differ which clearly influences the interpretative value of the references. Article 1114 NAFTA, the model of an environmental reference within the investment provisions of a treaty, was hailed by early commentators as evidence that modern economic agreements could "provide both the material resources and the legal means to raise environmental standards of practice".[163] In the light of the deficiencies that have been pointed out above, this appreciation appears to be overly optimistic. So far, such provisions have not had a meaningful interpretative influence on investment proceedings. Given that one of the elements of the provision – the one that relates to the right of the state to introduce environmental measures – explicitly refers to measures "otherwise consistent" with the investment obligations, and that the other element – which relates to the regulatory

---

159 See Article 31 paras 2, 3 VCLT; *Gardiner*, Richard, Treaty Interpretation (2008) p. 204.

160 See above at pp. 126 *et seq.*

161 In cases in which a separate format is chosen, an express reference to both treaties being 'mutually supportive' can also call for an interpretation of both treaties hand in hand, so that the separate agreement is arguably drawn within the context of the other. See the example of Article 1703 para 3 Canada-Peru FTA and the Agreement on the Environment between Canada and the Republic of Peru as well as Article 1703 Canada-Colombia FTA and the respective environmental agreement.

162 *Gardiner*, Richard, Treaty Interpretation (2008) p. 164.

163 *Kolo*, Abba/*Wälde*, Thomas, 'Environmental Regulation, Investment Protection and "Regulatory Taking" in International Law', 50 International and Comparative Law Quarterly 2001, 811 (818).

race-to-the-bottom – has no logical connection to existing investment, its implications for an interpretative context are very limited.

The six elements contained in environmental chapters of free trade agreements, which have been portrayed above, constitute significant environmental context for the interpretation of investment provisions. Their emphasis is not reduced by their lack of express connections to investment activity. The reference to sustainable development, the state parties' recognition of the importance of improving national regulation and enforcement, and the endorsement of flexible mechanisms to achieve environmental protection all provide for interpretative 'context'. If a provision on investment protection is interpreted within this context, legitimate environmental concerns or policies of the state will probably be accredited with more significance.[164] The environmental context is even more concise in the sector-specific provisions contained in the ECT. The environmental principles and rules relating to the energy sector provide for rather precise environmental context, within which the legitimacy of regulatory activity of the state is to be interpreted.

Additionally, the provisions concerning the conflict of norms between economic obligations and environmental agreements can be relevant as interpretative context. Insofar as they focus on balancing economic with environmental obligations, they underline that neither regime of international law is distinct from the other. As the discussion above indicates, it can be argued that even those clauses that expressly refer to trade obligations can contribute – with regard to the interpretation of norms of investment protection – towards a reconciliation with rivalling environmental values. The balancing, reconciliatory approach set forth in these provisions is also mirrored in the notion of sustainable development, which underlines that international investment law is not self-contained in the sense that it is isolated from environmental considerations.

However, it is not possible to determine the practical impact of these provisions in an interpretative exercise undertaken by an investment tribunal. The influence of the interpretative context cannot be abstractly assessed for a specific case. First, its impact depends on the clarity of the textual interpretation of the investment provisions under scrutiny.[165] Second, the

---

164 The above-cited example of the NAFTA-decision *S.D. Myers Inc. v. Canada* illustrates how tribunals attempt to incorporate environmental provisions in interpreting the other provisions of an investment treaty.

165 See for an assessment of the relevance of textual interpretation in the jurisprudence of the ICJ, *Corten*, Olivier/*Klein*, Pierre (Eds.) The Vienna Convention on the Law of Treaties, A Commentary (2011) Article 31 para 31 (Sorel, Jean-Marc/Boré Eveno, Valérie).

respective impact will depend on the facts of the individual case. It is to be hoped that investment tribunals will apply a technique of balancing economic and environmental obligations. There is little reason for concern that investment tribunals will overstretch the borders of such harmonisation, namely losing sight of the principle of effectiveness[166] in interpretation and frustrate the object and purpose of the investment treaty. Hence, a harmonising interpretation aiming at a balanced understanding of conflicting provisions is clearly desirable.

V. Intermediate Summary

The overview of provisions containing environmental references – be it in the preamble, in the operative text or in a separate chapter designated to the environment – underscores that states have increasingly perceived the need to address environmental concepts in investment treaties. Even though this discussion has highlighted the inadequacies or limitations of the different types of references, the fact that certain environmental concepts receive support in the investment treaty itself is likely to have an impact in the case of a conflict between an investment and environmental objective. Since such a conflict is rather going to be a legitimacy conflict than a situation of direct incompatibility between two obligations under international law, it does not appear problematic that agreements generally do not construct a proper hierarchy of obligations. The environmental concepts mentioned in the treaty constitute interpretative 'context' that can subtly influence the interpretation of the scope of the substantive investment protection obligations. For practical purposes, the incorporation of the substantive notion of sustainable development – which may even influence the object and purpose of the treaty – as well as the procedural approach of 'mutual supportiveness' appear to be the most helpful tools to achieve a balance of the different objectives that oppose each other.

---

166 See generally for the principle of effectiveness or effet utile in international law, *Corten*, Olivier/*Klein*, Pierre (Eds.) Les conventions de Vienne sur le droit des traités : commentaire article par article (2006) Article 31 para 52 (Sorel, Jean-Marc). The principle of effectiveness in the interpretation of treaty provisions is expressly confirmed by investment tribunals. See SGS Société Générale de Surveillance S.A. v. Republic of the Philippines, ICSID Case No. ARB/02/6, Decision on Objections to Jurisdiction of 29 January 2004, para 116; Salini Costruttori S.p.A. and Italstrade S.p.A. v. Jordan, ICSID Case No. ARB/02/13, Decision on Jurisdiction of 9 November 2004, para 95; Noble Ventures, Inc. v. Romania, ICSID Case No. ARB/01/11, Award of 12 October 2005, paras 50, 52.

D. Further Points of Entry for Relevant Rules of International Law

The large majority of investment agreements do not contain any express reference to environmental concepts or values. However, even these investment agreements do not exist detached from environmental developments and internationally set standards. Since different regimes of public international law operate within one legal system, states are likely to be parties to investment agreements as well as to international environmental agreements. The following section will assess the extent to which rules of international environmental law influence the application or interpretation of investment agreements irrespective of explicit environmental references.

I. Additionally Taking Relevant Rules of International Law into Account

The interpretation of provisions in investment treaties can be influenced by environmental concepts to the extent that these concepts fall within the scope of application of Article 31 paragraph 3 lit c VCLT. This norm provides that "there shall be taken into account, together with the context: […] any relevant rules of international law applicable in the relations between the parties." The article can be understood to enshrine the principle of systematic integration.[167] Thus, it does not only underline the understanding that every specialised regime of law derives its validity from the general system of international law, but even advocates the interpretation of specific norms against a comprehensive background of other material provisions of international law. Accordingly, the provision of the VCLT obliges the adjudicator to integrate a "sense of coherence and meaningfulness" into the process of legal reasoning.[168]

The relevance of the understanding enshrined in Article 31 paragraph 3 lit c VCLT has repeatedly been acknowledged by international courts and tribunals. In this sense, the International Court of Justice (ICJ) has expressed that a specific treaty provision under consideration is "not intended to oper-

---

[167] International Law Commission, Fragmentation of International Law: Difficulties arising from the Diversification and Expansion of International Law, Report of the Study Group of the *International Law Commission* of 13 April 2006 (A/CN.4/L.682), finalised by Martti Koskenniemi, paras 413, 465.

[168] *International Law Commission*, Fragmentation of International Law: Difficulties arising from the Diversification and Expansion of International Law, Report of the Study Group of the International Law Commission of 13 April 2006 (A/CN.4/L.682), finalised by Martti Koskenniemi, para 419.

ate wholly independently" of other relevant rules of international law and that those rules relating to the question under consideration form "an integral part of the task of interpretation".[169] Even more pronounced is the formulation chosen by the European Court of Human Rights (ECtHR), which declared with regard to the European Convention on Human Rights (ECHR) that it "should so far as possible be interpreted in harmony with other rules of international law of which it forms part [...]"[170]. This endorsed harmonisation of different rules of international law is similar to the balancing approach called for by some of the environmental references in investment treaties, as portrayed above. Like those specific references, Article 31 paragraph 3 lit c VCLT is part of a larger interpretation process, but it will not always be applicable and so only play a role in particular instances.[171] Accordingly, the conditions and the scope of the application of the rule have to be assessed in more detail. Most notably, the 'rules of international law' that fall within the scope of application and issues of intertemporality are of importance.

1. Rules of International Law

It appears that the term 'international law' is apt to include all the sources of international law, including custom, general principles and, where

---

169 ICJ Case Concerning Oil Platforms (Islamic Republic of Iran/United States of America), Judgment of 6 November 2003, ICJ Reports 2003, 161 (182) para 41, with regard to the rules of international law on the use of force. See also ICJ, Legal Consequences for States of the Continued Presence of South Africa in Namibia (South West Africa) notwithstanding Security Council Resolution 276 (1970), Advisory Opinion of 21 June 1971, ICJ Reports 1971, 16 (31) para 53, emphasising the need to interpret and apply an international instrument "within the framework of the entire legal system prevailing at the time of the interpretation".

170 ECtHR Case of Al-Adsani v. United Kingdom, (Application no. 35763/97), Grand Chamber Judgment of 21 November 2001 para. 55; ECtHR Case of McElhinney v. Ireland (Application no. 31253/96) Grand Chamber Judgment of 21 November 2001, para. 36, referring to the rules of international law on state immunity. Similarly, ECtHR Case of Loizidou v. Turkey (Application no. 15318/89) Grand Chamber Judgment of 18 December 1996, para 43. See also ECtHR Case of Bosphorus Hava Yolları Turizm ve Ticaret Anonim Şirketi v. Ireland (Application no. 45036/98) Grand Chamber Judgment of 30 June 2005, para 150, expressing the need to secure the proper functioning of international organisations.

171 *Van Damme*, Isabelle, 'Some Observations about the ILC Study Group Report on the Fragmentation of International Law: WTO Treaty Interpretation against the Background of Other International Law', XVII Finnish Yearbook of International Law 2006, 21 (26), stating that the provision will often not be needed, because the interpretation pursuant to the antecedent paragraphs of Article 31 VCLT would have resulted in a proper understanding of the term being interpreted. Similarly, *Gardiner*, Richard, Treaty Interpretation (2008) p. 259.

applicable, other treaties.[172] There seems to be little discussion about the fact that customary law and general principles of law do qualify as rules in the present context.[173] Concerning the application of custom or general principles, the real difficulty lies in ascertaining that the concepts considered do really constitute 'rules', and are not just broader principles or considerations that have not yet attained the status of 'rules'[174]. The difficulties of such categorisation – which requires the establishment of both state practice and *opinio iuris* – have been highlighted in the prior chapter for the subject area of international environmental law.[175] In this sense, international tribunals have had to determine the legal status of notions of international environmental law in order to consider them in accordance with Article 31 paragraph 3 lit c VCLT.[176]

---

172 Article 38 para 1 Statute of the International Court of Justice. See also *McLachlan*, Campell, 'The Principle of Systematic Integration and Article 31 (3) (c) of the Vienna Convention', 54 International & Comparative Law Quarterly 2005, 279 (290); *Gardiner*, Richard, Treaty Interpretation (2008) p. 267; European Communities – Measures Affecting the Approval and Marketing of Biotech Products, DS291-3/R, WTO Panel Report of 29 September 2006, para 7.67.

173 The ICJ in its above-cited decision in the *Case Concerning Oil-Platforms* as well as the ECtHR in the cases of *Al-Adsani* and *McElhinney* made reference to uncontested concepts of customary law.

International Law Commission, Fragmentation of International Law: Difficulties arising from the Diversification and Expansion of International Law, Report of the Study Group of the International Law Commission of 13 April 2006 (A/CN.4/L.682), finalised by Martti Koskenniemi, paras 463–469.

174 *McLachlan*, Campell, 'The Principle of Systematic Integration and Article 31 (3) (c) of the Vienna Convention', 54 International & Comparative Law Quarterly 2005, 279 (290).

175 See the portrayal in 'Chapter 1 – Environmental Norms and Principles' at pp. 62 *et seq*.

176 International tribunals came to differing conclusions: In the Mox Plant Case – Dispute Concerning Access to Information under Article 9 of the OSPAR Convention (Ireland/United Kingdom) Final Award of 2 July 2003, 23 UN Reports of International Arbitral Awards 59, para 101, the tribunal found that it could not apply the environmental notions invoked by Ireland due to them being *in statu nascendi*. The Panel in European Communities – Measures Affecting the Approval and Marketing of Biotech Products, DS291-3/R, WTO Panel Report of 29 September 2006, para 7.89 found that the legal status of the precautionary principle remained unsettled and therefore did not apply it. In Affaire concernant l'apurement des comptes entre le royaume des Pays-Bas et la république Française en application du protocole du 25 Septembre 1991 additionnel à la Convention relative à la protection du Rhin contre la pollution par les chlorures du 3 Décembre 1976 (Netherlands/France), Award of 12 March 2004, para 103, the tribunal found that it could not apply the polluter-pays principle because it was not part of "droit international général". In the Arbitration Regarding the Iron Rhine Railway (Ijzeren Rijn) (Belgium/Netherlands) Decision of 24 May 2005, para 59, the tribunal found that the duty for development

Given that few environmental principles are unequivocally understood to constitute customary international law, they can only be relevant in the context of systematic integration if they are enshrined in provisions which are 'applicable' rules of international law in the sense of the provision. Principles of environmental law can aid a harmonisation of the two areas of law, if they are found in environmental agreements that are considered applicable "in the relations between the parties" of an investment dispute. Accordingly, the understanding of the term 'party' is a crucial point.

According to a narrow understanding, all parties to the treaty, which is being interpreted, are also parties to all other treaties that are potentially 'applicable' in the sense of the provision. While this approach has been endorsed by some international bodies,[177] it leads to an important problem: The higher the number of parties to the agreement being interpreted is, the less likely all its parties are also bound by the agreement that could offer interpretative context. Accordingly, those agreements with a high number of parties – which are generally more significant treaties – would be increasingly isolated from rules established in other areas of law, since it would be inherently unlikely to identify relevant treaties to which each of these states is also a party.[178] Such an understanding would not be helpful in countering the tendency of fragmentation in international law. A more inclusive understanding requires all parties to the pending dispute to be parties to the other treaties complementing the interpretative undertaking.[179]

---

to prevent, or at least mitigate harm to the environment "has now become a principle of general international law."

177 This approach was used by the WTO panel in European Communities – Measures Affecting the Approval and Marketing of Biotech Products, DS291-3/R, WTO Panel Report of 29 September 2006, para 7.68 and 7.71. A similar view, albeit without a specific reference to Article 31 para 3 lit c VCLT, was expressed by the GATT Panel in United States – Restrictions on Imports of Tuna, DS29/R, GATT Panel Report adopted on 16 June 1994, para 5.19.

178 *International Law Commission*, Fragmentation of International Law: Difficulties arising from the Diversification and Expansion of International Law, Report of the Study Group of the International Law Commission of 13 April 2006 (A/CN.4/L.682), finalised by Martti Koskenniemi, para 471.

179 Proposal advocated by *McLachlan*, Campell, 'The Principle of Systematic Integration and Article 31 (3) (c) of the Vienna Convention', 54 International & Comparative Law Quarterly 2005, 279 (314); *International Law Commission*, Fragmentation of International Law: Difficulties arising from the Diversification and Expansion of International Law, Report of the Study Group of the International Law Commission of 13 April 2006 (A/CN.4/L.682), finalised by Martti Koskenniemi, para 472.

Approach seems to have been adopted by a penal in further proceedings to the United States-Shrimp dispute. United States – Import Prohibition of Certain Shrimp and Shrimp Products (Malaysian Recourse to Article 21.5), DS58/RW, WTO Panel

This approach broadens the range of treaties possibly relevant as additional interpretative material. However, it entails the risk that the same provision in a treaty is interpreted differently in disputes involving different parties – depending on the treaties to which the respective states are parties. Thus, there is a danger of disintegration of the content of the respective treaty.[180]

These two opposing approaches indicate that there is no solution without drawbacks to the issue. In the adjudication of a dispute under a bilateral investment treaty, the solution is identical because both state parties are automatically those involved in the dispute. In contrast, there are likely to be differences in the case of a dispute arising under a multilateral investment agreement. Nevertheless, the issue does not appear to pose as substantial a problem in investment cases as it does in the trade context, because even those agreements with a high number of parties – like the ECT or the CAFTA-DR – do not have as high and heterogeneous a membership as other international treaties, for example the GATT. I would also argue that a potential disintegrative effect does not pose a threat to international investment law. It is a distinctive feature of international investment law to stem from a multitude of different agreements, which tend to differ slightly from each other in certain aspects and wording. However, investment tribunals aim to interpret investment protection provisions, as far as possible, in a concurrent way and rely on interpretations made with regard to different treaties. Decisions and treaties are distinguished when the respective tribunals consider it appropriate. Disintegration does not appear a significant risk due to the multitude of different treaties and the frequent cross-fertilisation of investment treaties.

The issue cannot be decided in the context of this study. For the present purpose it suffices to demonstrate that Article 31 paragraph 3 lit c VCLT can be an entry point to ask investment tribunals to "take relevant conventions into account" when interpreting provisions of investment protection. In this sense, the content of international environmental agreements can constitute a relevant background for understanding provisions in investment treaties. For a complete appreciation of the apparatus of applicable environmental treaties it is, however, necessary to address the thorny issue of inter-temporality.

Report of 15 June 2001, at para 5.57; United States – Import Prohibition of Certain Shrimp and Shrimp Products, DS58/AB/R, WTO Appellate Body Report of 12 October 1998, paras 130–132.

180 See for detailed discussion *McLachlan*, Campell, 'The Principle of Systematic Integration and Article 31 (3) (c) of the Vienna Convention', 54 International & Comparative Law Quarterly 2005, 279 (315).

2. Issues of Inter-Temporality

The issue of inter-temporality concerns the question whether an international agreement has to be interpreted in the light of the legal environment existent at the time of its conclusion or in force at the time of the interpretative exercise. In the context of this study, the question is specifically relevant, since a multitude of investment treaties was concluded prior to the entry into force of several potentially relevant environmental agreements. Earlier investment treaties pre-date significant developments in the context of international environmental law. If these treaties were to be interpreted exclusively in the light of the international law relevant at the time of their conclusion, the application of Article 31 paragraph 3 lit c VCLT could not constitute an environmental background for the interpretation of their provisions.

Since the intentions of the parties guide the interpretation of a treaty, the traditional rule is that of 'contemporaneity', which relies on the international law existent at the time when the treaty was concluded.[181] The rationale is that when states enter into an agreement, they bear in mind the state of the law at the time of the formation of their relationship. Nevertheless, the parties are aware that their formed legal relationship will be affected by time. Accordingly, a completely static interpretation of terms in a treaty would frequently not serve the intentions of the parties, which wanted to create an agreement significant for a substantive period of time. Whether the parties wanted the utilised legal terms to remain unaltered throughout time, or whether they anticipated changes and intended the treaty to evolve alongside such changes, has to be determined through interpretation. The intention of the parties is the key in this regard.[182]

The starting point for the determination of the respective intention is the language used in the treaty. For the context of this study it suffices to distinguish two broad scenarios: First, the treaty may contain terms which are "not static, but evolutionary".[183] This is the case when a term can be clas-

---

[181] In Island of Palmas (Netherlands/U.S.A.) Award of 24 April 1928, 2 UN Reports of International Arbitral Awards 829 (845), the arbitrator stated that "[a] judicial fact must be appreciated in the light of the law contemporary with it, and not the law in force at the time when a dispute in regard to it arises or falls to be settled".

[182] See *Higgins*, Rosalyn, 'Some Observations on the Inter-Temporal Rule in International Law', in: Theory of International Law at the Threshold of the 21st Century. Essays in Honour of Krzysztof Skubiszewski (Markarczyk, Jerzy (Ed.) 1996) 173 (181). In the same sense, *McLachlan*, Campell, 'The Principle of Systematic Integration and Article 31 (3) (c) of the Vienna Convention', 54 International & Comparative Law Quarterly 2005, 279 (311).

[183] ICJ Legal Consequences for States of the Continued Presence of South Africa in Namibia (South West Africa) notwithstanding Security Council Resolution 276

sified as 'generic' – accommodating for an evolving meaning and not maintaining its own idiosyncratic meaning.[184] Accordingly, 'generic' terms are to be interpreted against the background of international law as it stands at the time of the dispute. Similarly, the incorporation of obligations in very general terms, which necessitates a consideration of changing circumstances, indicates the adjustment of their application according to the situation as it develops over time.[185] Terms like 'fair and equitable treatment', or 'due process', which are regularly found in investment treaties – in the absence of a specific, fixating definition contained in the respective treaty – can certainly be considered as 'generic' in this sense.

Second, the intention of the parties that the terms in a treaty do evolve can be derived from reading the terms against the object and purpose of the treaty. The object and purpose can indicate that the parties have committed themselves to continuous progressive development. This understanding is most commonly accepted in the evolutionary interpretation of human rights treaties. These treaties are seen as "living instruments", which require an interpretation of uncertain provisions in the light of contemporary ideas and morals.[186] This reflects the intention of the parties which wanted to create dynamic protection. It has been observed that such an understanding is now

(1970), Advisory Opinion of 21 June 1971, ICJ Reports 1971, 16 (31) para 53. The ICJ enumerates the concepts of 'strenuous conditions of the modern world', 'the well-being and development' and of the 'sacred trust of civilisation' and concludes that they have to be "applied within the framework of the entire legal system prevailing at the time of the interpretation". Equally, United States – Import Prohibition of Certain Shrimp and Shrimp Products, DS58/AB/R, WTO Appellate Body Report of 12 October 1998, para. 130. The Appellate Body stated that "from the perspective embodied in the preamble of the WTO Agreement […] the generic term 'natural resources' in Article XX(g) is not 'static' in its content or reference but is rather 'by definition, evolutionary'".

[184] Case Concerning Aegean Sea Continental Shelf (Greece/Turkey) Judgment of 19 December 1978, ICJ Reports 1978, 3 (32) para 77, stating that when a term in a treaty can be classified as generic, there is a presumption "that its meaning was intended to follow the evolution of the law and to correspond with the meaning attached to the expression by law in force at any time given". The ICJ referred to the term 'continental shelf'.

[185] *McLachlan*, Campell, 'The Principle of Systematic Integration and Article 31 (3) (c) of the Vienna Convention', 54 International & Comparative Law Quarterly 2005, 279 (317–318), stating that while the broad meaning of the general terms remains the same, the actual content of the obligation is influenced by factual changes over time.

[186] ECtHR Case of Tyrer v. United Kingdom (Application no. 5856/72) Judgment of 25 April 1978, para 31; ECtHR Case of Matthews v. United Kingdom (Application no. 24833/94) Grand Chamber Judgment of 18 February 1999, para. 39; Inter-American Court of Human Rights, Interpretation of the American Declaration of the Rights and Duties of Man Within the Framework of Article 64 of the

also applied more widely in other areas of law.[187] Possible examples are references to general environmental obligations, like an obligation to ensure the non-impairment of the quality of water or the protection of nature. In the *Case Concerning the Gabčíkovo-Nagymaros Project*, the ICJ found that these references indicated the recognition of the parties of a potential necessity to adapt their project, so that the treaty "is not static, and is open to adapt to emerging norms of international law".[188] In another case, a tribunal – intensely relying on the object and purpose of the treaty – applied the evolutionary approach to take into account new technical developments, which the parties could not foresee when concluding the treaty.[189] This exercise of "breath[ing] future economic life into the sparse textual provisions"[190] was necessary to accommodate the underlying intentions of the parties.

Accordingly, in the context of investment arbitration, an evolutionary interpretation is in order, when the object and purpose of the respective treaty show a respective intention of the parties. As has been explained above, environmental references – even if they exist – are unlikely to be prominent enough in an investment treaty to influence its object and purpose. However, this is not what is required in this context. While investment tribunals frequently understand the object and purpose of these treaties as narrowly focused on the 'promotion and protection of investments',[191] a

American Convention on Human Rights, Advisory Opinion OC-10/89 of 14 July 1989, paras 37, 38, 43.

[187] *Higgins*, Rosalyn, 'A Babel of Judicial Voices? Ruminations from the Bench', 55 International and Comparative Law Quarterly 2006, 791 (797–798). See also ICJ Case Concerning Pulp Mills on the River Uruguay (Argentina/Uruguay) Separate Opinion of Judge Cançado Trindade to Judgment of 20 April 2010, ICJ Reports 2010, 135, para 99, indiscriminately referring to treaties as 'living instruments' and arguing for the consideration of international law as evolved at the moment of interpretation.

[188] Case Concerning the Gabčíkovo-Nagymaros Project (Hungary/Slovakia) Judgment of 25 September 1997, ICJ Reports 1997, 7 (67–78) para 112. The ICJ went on to state that the environmental obligations through "impos[ing] a continuing – thus necessarily evolving – obligation on the parties" prescribed that current standards had to be taken into consideration in the evaluation of environmental risks (para 140).

[189] Arbitration Regarding the Iron Rhine Railway (Ijzeren Rijn) (Belgium/Netherlands) Decision of 24 May 2005, paras 79, 80.

[190] *Higgins*, Rosalyn, 'A Babel of Judicial Voices? Ruminations from the Bench', 55 International and Comparative Law Quarterly 2006, 791 (798).

[191] See, for example, the reasoning in LG&E v. Argentina, ICSID Case No. ARB/02/1, Decision on Liability of 3 October 2006, para 124; CMS Gas Transmission Company v. The Argentine Republic, ICSID Case No. ARB/01/8, Award of 12 May 2005, para 274. See also criticism expressed by tribunal in Noble Ventures,

more holistic approach would not assess this promotion and protection as an end in itself. The overall aim of investment treaties is to intensify economic co-operation and to increase the prosperity or living standards of both nations.[192] If these elements are understood to be constituent parts of the object and purpose of an investment agreement, they allow for an evolutionary interpretation: notions like 'prosperity' and 'development' are prone to reflect changing attitudes. A pertinent example is 'development', which is increasingly understood as 'sustainable development' in international agreements.

3. Interpretative Effect and Relevance of Article 31 Paragraph 3 lit c VCLT

Article 31 VCLT prescribes a hierarchy of the elements which have to be taken into account in the interpretative process. Accordingly, Article 31 paragraph 3 lit c VCLT is subsidiary to the steps described in paragraph 1, so that it only becomes relevant when the prior interpretative undertaking has not yielded satisfactory results. Thus, the most relevant hindrance to environmental concepts influencing the interpretation of investment provisions via this route is that there may be no room for the application of the provision. It is questionable whether an investment tribunal tasked with interpreting standards relating to the protection of foreign investments, will conclude – despite the existing significant body of case law – that the

---

Inc. v. Romania, ICSID Case No. ARB/01/11, Award of 12 October 2005, para 52, stating that "it is not permissible, as is too often done regarding BITs, to interpret clauses exclusively in favour of investors […]".

[192] Saluka Investments BV (The Netherlands) v. The Czech Republic, Award of 17 March 2006, paras 299–300; Suez, Sociedad General de Aguas de Barcelona S.A., and InterAguas Servicios Integrales del Agua S.A. v. The Argentine Republic, ICSID Case No. ARB/03/17, Decision on Liability of 30 July 2010, paras 198–200; Suez, Sociedad General de Aguas de Barcelona, S.A. and Vivendi Universal, S.A. v. Argentine Republic, ICSID Case No. ARB/03/19, Decision on Liability of 30 July 2010, paras 215–218, analysing that the parties "pursue the broader goals of heightened economic cooperation between the two States concerned with a view toward achieving increased economic prosperity or development". Arguing for a "balanced interpretation", which "takes into account the totality of the treaty's purpose", Plama Consortium Limited v. Bulgaria, ICSID Case No. ARB/03/24, Award of 27 August 2008, para 167; El Paso Energy International Company v. The Argentine Republic, ICSID Case No. ARB/03/15, Decision on Jurisdiction of 27 April 2006, para 70.

The increase in prosperity or living standards features prominently in a multitude of preambles of investment treaties. See, for example, a myriad of investment treaties concluded by Germany, containing preambular clause 3 2008 Germany Model BIT; preambular clause 3 U.S.-Korea FTA; preambular clause 3 U.S.-Rwanda BIT.

proper interpretation of these standards requires recourse to a background of other international law.

One commentator suggests that "nothing prohibits tribunals from dealing with the underlying conflicts of investment law with other special areas of international law through interpretational means such as balancing [...] by using non-investment law through Article 31 paragraph 3 lit c VCLT".[193] However, it has to be kept in mind that the task of an investment tribunal is the adjudication of the dispute before it. It has to interpret the treaty before it in good faith to give weight to the intentions of the parties. In contrast, it is not the task of the tribunal to contribute to the harmonisation of clashing regimes of international law as an end in itself.[194] However, tribunals cannot choose to apply the provision at will, as its application is not voluntary when its conditions are fulfilled.[195] In practical terms, Article 31 paragraph 3 lit c VCLT provides for the relevant rules of international law to be "taken into account". Arguably, this formulation requires more than a mere 'taking into consideration' of the relevant norm, but less than 'applying' it.[196] Accordingly, the treaty retains its primary role, with

---

193 *van Aaken*, Anne, 'Fragmentation of International Law: The Case of International Investment Law', XVII Finnish Yearbook of International Law 2006, 91 (108). Similarly for the context of environmental regulation on climate change, *Boute*, Anatole, 'The Potential Contribution of International Investment Protection Law to Combat Climate Change', 27 Journal of Energy & Natural Resources Law 2009, 333 (374), stating that the provision could be applied to use international rules like the Kyoto Protocol as 'interpretative context', so that its 'systemic integration' enabled arbitral tribunals to acknowledge the police powers of the host country in the implementation of climate policies.

194 See, however, *Brown*, Chester, 'Bringing Sustainable Development Issues before Investment Tribunals', in: Sustainable Development in World Investment Law (Cordonier Segger, Marie-Claire et al. (Eds.) 2011) 175, who discusses the procedural possibility for investment tribunals to raise issues of sustainable development *proprio motu* in an investment dispute when the parties have not raised arguments as to obligations stemming, for example, from international environmental agreements (184–185). The author bases the tribunal's capacity on the principle *jura novit curia*. Nevertheless, the dividing line remains the relevance of the provisions for the settlement of the dispute.

195 Similarly, *Van Damme*, Isabelle, 'Some Observations about the ILC Study Group Report on the Fragmentation of International Law: WTO Treaty Interpretation against the Background of Other International Law', XVII Finnish Yearbook of International Law 2006, 21 (28), arguing that the provision should only be applied to the extent necessary for the purpose of treaty interpretation.

196 *Sands*, Philippe, 'Treaty, Custom, and the Cross-Fertilization of International Law', 1 Yale Human Rights and Development Law Journal 1998, 85 (103). See also, *Sands*, Philippe/*Commission*, Jeffrey, 'Treaty, Custom and Time: Interpretation/Application?', in: Treaty Interpretation and the Vienna Convention on the Law of Treaties: 30 Years On (Fitzmaurice, Malgosia et al. (Eds.) 2010) 39 portraying

the relevant norm of international law being interpreted into the convention and not being applied instead of it.[197] The exact influence of an interpretation of an investment provision by reference to an environmental norm cannot be evaluated abstractly, because it will depend on the circumstances of the specific case. The tribunal in the *Arbitration Regarding the Iron Rhine Railway* formulated this aspect eloquently in stating that

> "[t]he mere invocation of such matters does not, of course, provide the answers […] to what may or may not be done, where, by whom and at whose costs."[198]

Irrespective of that statement, the analysis above suggests that in cases in which the application of Article 31 paragraph 3 lit c VCLT is warranted, investment provisions can be interpreted by reference to an environmental background. Several concepts used in investment treaties have a generic connotation so that they are subject to changing perceptions and therefore influenced by international law as it stands at the time of interpretation. Even more than the assessment of the inter-temporality of a singular clause, the 'object and purpose' of the investment treaty – insofar as it relates to the 'development' of the state parties – is receptive to an evolutionary approach which accommodates to sustainability.

To conclude, Article 31 paragraph 3 lit c VCLT can serve as a vehicle to invoke the wider corpus of international environmental law when interpreting substantive norms of investment treaties. The impact of the provision, however, is unlikely to be ample. The analysis of decisions of WTO panels and its Appellate Body suggests that the provision has occasionally been applied, but considered to be of subsidiary value.[199] Irrespective of the differences between the regimes of international trade and international investment, this finding indicates that adjudicators in supposedly self-contained regimes tend not to emphasise potential impacts deriving from other treaty regimes. Similarly, in the investment sphere, the relevance will depend on the perspective of the respective investment tribunal. Likewise, the evaluation of the norm as an answer to the threat of systematic fragmentation is

---

the opposing approaches to the question at what point the interpretation of a treaty by reference to other rules of international law becomes an application of those other rules in relation to the *Oil Platforms* decision of the ICJ and other international decisions.

197 *Sands*, Philippe, 'Treaty, Custom, and the Cross-Fertilization of International Law', 1 Yale Human Rights and Development Law Journal 1998, 85 (102).

198 Arbitration Regarding the Iron Rhine Railway (Ijzeren Rijn) (Belgium/Netherlands) Decision of 24 May 2005, para 60.

199 See detailed analysis of *Van Damme*, Isabelle, 'Some Observations about the ILC Study Group Report on the Fragmentation of International Law: WTO Treaty Interpretation against the Background of Other International Law', XVII Finnish Yearbook of International Law 2006, 21 (30–38).

not apparent: Despite its possibilities – and the effect it has so far had in judicial decisions – commentators caution against too much optimism about the overall integrating impact of the provision.[200]

II. 'International Law' as Applicable Law to the Dispute

So far, this chapter has approached the issue of influences of environmental law on the interpretation of concepts of investment protection from a substantive angle, by portraying potential interpretative impacts on investment protection provisions. In addition, international environmental law can have an effect via the procedural points of entry if 'international law' is designated as law applicable to an investment dispute. Such a determination arguably opens the special regime of investment law to the wider corpus of international law. The choice of the substantive law applicable to a dispute resides primarily within the freedom of the parties. The following section briefly portrays two resulting scenarios, namely, first, the designation of 'international law' as governing an arising dispute in the investment treaty itself and, second, the determination of the law applicable by a tribunal in accordance with Article 42 paragraph 1 sentence 2 ICSID Convention[201] – in cases in which the parties have not reached a respective agreement.

---

200 *Higgins*, Rosalyn, 'A Babel of Judicial Voices? Ruminations from the Bench', 55 International and Comparative Law Quarterly 2006, 791 (802–804). The author uses, inter alia, the application of the provision in the ICJ *Oil Platforms* case to caution that the invocation of the provision possibly "brings with it as many problems as it resolves".

Similarly critical, *Klabbers*, Jan, 'Reluctant Grundnormen: Articles 31 (3) (C) and 42 of the Vienna Convention on the Law of Treaties and the Fragmentation of International Law', in: Time, History and International Law (Craven, Matthew et al. (Eds.) 2007) 141 (159–160). Klabbers expresses that if the provision is used to approach fragmentation as a unifying trait, in the application of which any rule of law can be taken into consideration, it risks moving from a mode of treaty interpretation to a "quasi-legislative exercise" in search of the best way to maintain the system intact. This would not be what the parties to the respective treaty had in mind.

201 In disputes not falling within the scope of the ICSID Convention, the applicable law is determined by a similar rule of the respective applicable regime. A further relevant example is Article 35 para 1 sentence 2 2010 UNCITRAL Arbitration Rules, which provides that in the absence of a respective designation by the parties, "the arbitral tribunal shall apply the law which it determines to be appropriate". This clause leaves the determination to the arbitral tribunal, which is free to apply rules of international law. Because of the lack of a specific reference to 'international law', the cause will not be discussed any further.

1. Designation of 'International Law' as Applicable Law Within the Treaty

States can use the investment treaty to designate the law applicable to a potential dispute. While it is not the purpose of this survey to comprehensively establish how frequently this technique has been used, it appears that the number of investment treaties addressing the issue of the law governing an arising dispute is significant.[202] Typically, such provisions set forth that the dispute is to be decided in accordance with the investment treaty itself and the 'applicable rules of international law' or 'the principles of international law'[203]. Some bilateral treaties also refer to the laws of the host state – with formulations mirroring the language of Article 42 paragraph 1 sentence 2 ICSID Convention.[204] Accordingly, these investment treaties constitute a point of entry for the application of other international law in an investment dispute. Whether 'international law' plays a primary or only subsidiary role in deciding a dispute depends on the exact wording used in the investment treaty.[205]

2. Applicable Law Through Article 42 Paragraph 1 Sentence 2 ICSID Convention

When the parties have not agreed on the rules of law applicable to the dispute, Article 42 paragraph 1 sentence 2 of the ICSID Convention prescribes that the tribunal shall apply the law of the state party to the dispute "and such rules of international law as may be applicable". The 'rules of

---

[202] See, *Kreindler*, Richard H., 'The Law Applicable to International Investment Disputes', in: Arbitrating Foreign Investment Disputes: Procedural and Substantive Legal Aspects (Horn, Norbert (Ed.) 2004) 401, who finds that an "[investment] treaty invariably refers in some manner to principles of public international law – either standing alone or in some stipulated or non-stipulated symbiosis with a body of rules of national law" (403–404).

[203] Article 1131 para 1 NAFTA; Article 26 para 6 ECT; Article 10.22 para 1 CAFTA-DR (for those claims alleging the breach of the investment treaty); Article 40 para 1 2004 Canada Model BIT; Article 10 para 5 2007 Colombia Model BIT, referring to "principles of international law applicable to the subject matter".

[204] See, for example, Article 10 para 4 Argentina-Canada BIT; Article 8 para 3 China-Bosnia and Herzegovina BIT.

[205] Furthermore, international law can also apply to an investment dispute as a component of the domestic law that is chosen as applicable. For further elaboration, see *Schreuer*, Christoph, The ICSID Convention: A Commentary (2001) Article 42 para 60; *Kreindler*, Richard H., 'The Law Applicable to International Investment Disputes', in: Arbitrating Foreign Investment Disputes: Procedural and Substantive Legal Aspects (Horn, Norbert (Ed.) The Hague: Kluwer Law International, 2004) 401 (413–415).

international law' are understood in the sense given by Article 38 paragraph 1 Statue of the ICJ.[206] Accordingly, treaties, customary law, general principles of international law, and relevant international decisions are encompassed. The particular wording "as may be applicable" does not restrict the body of rules of law, but prescribes that the relevant rules of international law are to be applied.[207] As such, the provision indiscriminately allows the application of relevant international law, without restricting it to norms related to investment protection.

More difficult to discern, however, is the determination of the function of international law with regard to the law of the state party. A traditional understanding of this relationship ascribed to international law a subsidiary function, according to which it was used to fill existing lacunae of the state law or had a corrective function, if the law of the state did not conform to international law.[208] This understanding is deeply grounded in decisions relating to 'contract claims' – as opposed to the 'treaty claims' of modern investment treaties.[209] For those disputes alleging the violation of an investment agreement – especially since the investment treaty itself forms part of international law – international law is assigned a function on par with the law of the state: Article 42 paragraph 1 sentence 2 ICSID Convention is understood as opening a direct recourse to the substantive norms of public international law.[210] Accordingly, ICSID tribunals are free to identify – in

---

[206] *Gaillard*, Emmanuel/*Banifatemi*, Yas, 'The Meaning of 'and' in Article 42(1), Second Sentence, of the Washington Convention: The Role of International Law in the ICSID Choice of Law Process', 18 ICSID Review Foreign Investment Law Journal 2003, 375 (397); *Schreuer*, Christoph, The ICSID Convention: A Commentary (2001) Article 42 para 106.

[207] *Schreuer*, Christoph, The ICSID Convention: A Commentary (2001) Article 42 para 129.

[208] Klöckner Industrie-Anlagen GmbH v. United Republic of Cameroon, ICSID Case No. ARB/81/2, Annulment Decision of 3 May 1985, para 69; Amco Asia Corporation and others v. Republic of Indonesia, ICSID Case No. ARB/81/1, Decision on the Application for Annulment of 16 May 1986, 1 ICSID Reports 1993, 509 (515).

[209] *Parra*, Antonio R., 'Applicable Law in Investor-State Arbitration', in: Contemporary Issues in International Arbitration and Mediation: The Fordham Papers 2007 (Rovine, Arthur W. (Ed.) 2007) 3 (6–7).

[210] Wena Hotels Ltd. v. Arab Republic of Egypt, ICSID Case No. ARB/98/4, Decision of the Ad Hoc Committee on the Application for Annulment of 28 January 2002, paras 39, 40; Middle East Cement Shipping and Handling Co. S.A. v. Arab Republic of Egypt, ICSID Case No. ARB/99/6, Award of 12 April 2002, para 87; Siemens A.G. v. Argentine Republic, ICSID Case No. ARB/02/8, Award of 6 February 2007, para 77; CMS Gas Transmission Company v. The Argentine Republic, ICSID Case No. ARB/01/8, Award of 12 May 2005, paras 116–117; *Gaillard*, Emmanuel/*Banifatemi*, Yas, 'The Meaning of 'and' in Article 42(1), Second Sentence,

international law as well as in the law of the host state – the proper rules for the adjudication of the disputes brought before them.[211] This freedom aligns the competence of ICSID tribunals with that of other international arbitration tribunals.[212]

Accordingly, the provision authorises investment tribunals to apply 'international law'. It is not surprising that the overwhelming majority of the international law relied upon in this context is investment law – stretching from investment treaties, over customary rules and general principles, to decisions of other investment tribunals and judicial writings[213]. Additionally, the VCLT, as mentioned above, and the customary rules on the responsibility of a state are frequently invoked[214]. A commentator assesses that very few ICSID tribunals apply the wider corpus of public international law.[215] Although the determinations of the 1972 Convention Concerning the Protection of the World Cultural and Natural Heritage (UNESCO Convention) influenced the findings in one case, in conjunction with

---

of the Washington Convention: The Role of International Law in the ICSID Choice of Law Process', 18 ICSID Review Foreign Investment Law Journal 2003, 375 (407–409).

[211] Parra states that this freedom should not be perceived as allowing tribunals too much discretion in their choice of the applicable rules, since their choice will have to be justified in each case, "with each law applied in its own ambit", *Parra*, Antonio R., 'Applicable Law in Investor-State Arbitration', in: Contemporary Issues in International Arbitration and Mediation: The Fordham Papers 2007 (Rovine, Arthur W. (Ed.) 2007) 3 (12).

[212] See the complete freedom to determine the applicable law in the absence of the designation by a party in Article 35 para 1 sentence 2 2010 UNCITRAL Arbitration Rules. Similarly, *Gaillard*, Emmanuel/*Banifatemi*, Yas, 'The Meaning of 'and' in Article 42(1), Second Sentence, of the Washington Convention: The Role of International Law in the ICSID Choice of Law Process', 18 ICSID Review Foreign Investment Law Journal 2003, 375 (411).

[213] See examples enumerated in *Schreuer*, Christoph, The ICSID Convention: A Commentary (2001) Article 42 paras 107–118. See also the assessment by *Di Pietro*, Domenico, 'Applicable Law Under Article 42 of the ICSID Convention and the Case of Amco v. Indonesia' in: International Investment Law and Arbitration: Leading Cases from the ICSID, NAFTA, Bilateral Treaties and Customary International Law (Weiler, Todd (Ed.) 2005) 223 (258).

[214] See the comprehensive portrayal by *Fauchald*, Ole Kristian, 'The Legal Reasoning of ICSID Tribunals: An Empirical Analysis', 19 European Journal of International Law 2008, 301 (310–312). See, for example, Southern Pacific Properties (Middle East) Limited v. Egypt, ICSID Case No. ARB/84/3, Award of 20 May 1992, para 85; Asian Agricultural Products Ltd. v. Republic of Sri Lanka, ICSID Case No. ARB/87/3, Award of 27 June 1990, paras 72–78, 86.

[215] *Leeks*, Annie, 'The Relationship Between Bilateral Investment Treaty Arbitration and the Wider Corpus of International Law: The ICSID Approach', 65 University of Toronto Faculty of Law Review 2007, 1 (33).

other reasons,[216] substantive treaty law other than investment law appears to be considered relevant very rarely.

Significant concepts of customary international law have more frequently been relied on in some recent investment decisions, which dealt with the invocation of the defence of necessity by the host state. In this context, several investment tribunals thoroughly assessed if the requirements of the customary standard of necessity were fulfilled.[217] Even though some of the relevant investment treaties contained a treaty provision on necessity, three of the tribunals did not engage in much discussion as to the treaty standard, but rather contended themselves with finding that the customary standard was not fulfilled.[218] The lack of independent deliberation of the treaty standard and the assessment of the customary standard has led to criticism and in two cases even to the annulment of the decisions.[219] It is a curious coincidence that the situation in which investment tribunals were inclined to

---

[216] Parkerings-Compagniet AS v. Lithuania, ICSID Case No. ARB/05/8, Award of 11 September 2007, paras 392, 396. In Southern Pacific Properties (Middle East) Limited v. Egypt, ICSID Case No. ARB/84/3, Award of 20 May 1992, para 154, the UNESCO Convention was also considered to be relevant, but the tribunal found that the international obligation of the respondent to protect the designated site, which was the subject of the dispute, only became binding on the respondent at a later point.

[217] Suez, Sociedad General de Aguas de Barcelona S.A., and InterAguas Servicios Integrales del Agua S.A. v. The Argentine Republic, ICSID Case No. ARB/03/17, Decision on Liability of 30 July 2010, paras 229–243; CMS Gas Transmission Company v. The Argentine Republic, ICSID Case No. ARB/01/8, Award of 12 May 2005 paras 315–331; Sempra Energy International v. The Argentine Republic, ICSID Case No. ARB/02/16, Award of 28 September 2007, paras 344–355; Enron Corporation and Ponderosa Assets, L.P. v. Argentine Republic, ICSID Case No. ARB/01/3, Award of 22 May 2007, paras 304–313; LG&E v. Argentina, ICSID Case No. ARB/02/1, Decision on Liability of 3 October 2006, paras 248–259.

See also UNCITRAL tribunals, AWG Group Ltd. v. The Argentine Republic, Decision on Liability of 30 July 2010, paras 249–265; National Grid plc v. The Argentine Republic, Award of 3 November 2008, paras 256–262.

[218] Enron Corporation and Ponderosa Assets, L.P. v. Argentine Republic, ICSID Case No. ARB/01/3, Award of 22 May 2007, paras 333, 339–341; Sempra Energy International v. The Argentine Republic, ICSID Case No. ARB/02/16, Award of 28 September 2007, para 344; CMS Gas Transmission Company v. The Argentine Republic, ICSID Case No. ARB/01/8, Award of 12 May 2005, para 315.

[219] Considering the alignment of the treaty standard with the standard under customary law to be an error of law, CMS Gas Transmission Company v. The Argentine Republic, ICSID Case No. ARB/01/8, Annulment Proceeding, Decision of 25 September 2007, paras 130–134. Annulment of the awards in: Enron Corporation and Ponderosa Assets, L.P. v. Argentine Republic, ICSID Case No. ARB/01/3, Annulment Proceeding, Decision on the Application for Annulment of the Argentine Republic of 30 July 2010, para 405; Sempra Energy International v. The Argentine

profoundly discuss and base their findings on general international law, it was to restrict[220] the possibility of a state to be excused for failing in its investment obligations. It is striking, however, that the determinations related to the application and interpretation of general international law have been subject to such intense criticism by *ad hoc* committees. Whereas the respective decisions of the tribunals and committees can be seen as reflecting uneasiness with the application of international law outside those rules most closely connected to investment protection, it still seems more likely that the difficulties stemmed from the particularities of the concept of necessity in international law.[221]

Republic, ICSID Case No. ARB/02/16, Annulment Proceeding, Decision of 29 June 2010, para 159.

220 I do not argue that the proper application of the emergency provision in the underlying BITs of Argentina should have resulted in a different finding on the merits. This assessment is outside of the scope of this study. Nevertheless, the conditions of the customary standard on necessity arguably require an even more restrictive understanding than those contained in the respective treaties.

221 Necessity has long been a recognised defence in public international law. It aims to avoid an overly rigid application of legal obligations in circumstances where these conflict with other values, (see *Heathcote*, Sarah, 'Circumstances Precluding Wrongfulness in the ILC Articles on State Responsibility: Necessity', in: The Law of International Responsibility (Crawford, James et al. (Eds.) 2010) 491 (491)). The conceptual roots of the necessity defence thus are intermingled with those of the defences of self-defence and *force majeure*. Necessity involves voluntary action on the part of the state breaching its international obligation, whereas *force majeure* applies to a scenario in which the state is physically unable to comply with its obligation (*International Law Commission*, Second Report on State Responsibility, Addendum of 30 April 1999 (A/CN.4/498/Add.2), by Special Rapporteur James Crawford, paras 251–252). Necessity is today recognised as a defence established in customary international law (ICJ Case Concerning the Gabčíkovo-Nagymaros Project (Hungary/Slovakia) Judgment of 25 September 1997, ICJ Reports 1997, 7 (40) para 51; Legal Consequences of the Construction of a Wall in the Occupied Palestinian Territory, Advisory Opinion of 9 July 2004, ICJ Reports 2004, 136 (195) para 140). The effect of the successful invocation of the defence is that it "preclud[es] the wrongfulness of an act not in conformity with an international obligation". In the light of the interest of the international community of abidance by its obligations, it is logical that such a ground for precluding wrongfulness can only be granted on an "exceptional basis" and "under certain strictly defined conditions which must be cumulatively satisfied" (ICJ, Case Concerning the Gabčíkovo-Nagymaros Project (Hungary/Slovakia) Judgment of 25 September 1997, ICJ Reports 1997, 7 (40) para 51). This restrictive understanding has to guide the application of the principle in each specific case.

3. Evaluation

This portrayal has shown that there exist further – more procedural – openings for general international law to be applied in investment disputes. Rules of international law which are relevant to a specific case can be considered by the adjudicators – in cases in which 'international law' is either part of the agreed governing law or has a function to play in the absence of an express agreement. The relevance of these points of entry for the application of international environmental law cannot be comprehensively assessed. The jurisprudence evaluated, however, suggests that investment tribunals perceive the concept of 'applicable rules of international law' in a rather restrictive manner. Only very rarely has international law – other than the most fundamental principles of the law of treaties or of the responsibility of states – been applied. Therefore, it is doubtful whether these entries will be used by tribunals to provide an entry for environmental treaties in the absence of more specific or material opening clauses.[222] It also has to be kept in mind that investment tribunals rather apply general international law to increase the scope of investment protection. To the extent that investment tribunals apply international law in a corrective function to the law of the host state, it is likely to be used to extend this protective scope.[223] As a result, the application of international law in such a dispute potentially decreases the impact of national environmental rules. Either way, a national environmental measure which violates standards of investment protection would not be upheld in an investment dispute – irrespective of the input of international law in addition to the investment treaty.

E. Conclusion

This chapter has shown that the protection of foreign investment in investment treaties is not segregated from environmental considerations. Several investment treaties positively promulgate the connection of both areas of law through their environmental references. Even though this survey has pointed to the limitations in substance of most of these references, with few clauses having the capacity to solve potentially arising conflicts

[222] Similarly, *Boute*, Anatole, 'The Potential Contribution of International Investment Protection Law to Combat Climate Change', 27 Journal of Energy & Natural Resources Law 2009, 333 (372), stating that the extent to which Article 42 ICSID Convention allows for the application of extraneous rules of international law remains unclear.

[223] See examples enumerated by *Schreuer*, Christoph, The ICSID Convention: A Commentary (2001) Article 42 paras 143–148.

between the two sets of norms, it has highlighted the relevance of environmental references as 'interpretative context' for investment protection provisions. Further, general international law is relevant for the interpretation of investment provisions as law applicable to a dispute. Even though the limitations of this more subsidiary impact on international environmental law have been portrayed, the respective rules underline that investment agreements are not to be understood in isolation of other aspects of international law.

The chapter has illustrated a multitude of potential interpretative influences furthering the reconciliation of environmental and investment protection standards. It has shown that a balancing approach in the interpretation of investment protection provisions can be useful to diminish existing conflicts with other norms, and can this way counter the fragmentation of international law. A concept that appropriately embodies this reconciliatory notion is the principle of sustainable development. It typifies the understanding that economic, environmental, and societal considerations are mutually supportive. Without overstating the verifiable acceptance of this concept outside the realm of international environmental law, the above findings have indicated that among the investment treaties recognising the possibility of tensions with environmental aims, it enjoys measurable support.

The perception of economic factors and conditions is subject to change over time. It can be argued that the appreciation of 'development' has evolved throughout the last decades and is now increasingly embracing notions of environmental and social relevance. An indication of such a change is the increase in initiatives setting standards of social corporate responsibility.[224] In this light, the furthering of the development of both state parties, which constitutes the underlying purpose of investment treaties, should be interpreted through the 'prism' of sustainable development – i. e. in a way which takes environmental aspects into account. Applying the principle of sustainable development as a 'metaprinciple' – as it is done in the interpretative undertakings of international dispute resolution bodies – could add a relevant interpretative background to terms stemming from investment treaties that are devoid of environmental references.

It remains to be seen if investment tribunals will adopt this approach. A commentator observed that investment tribunals were "rather hesitant" to integrate rules of law in the sense of the principle of sustainable develop-

[224] See for example the United Nations-backed initiative on Principles for Responsible Investment (http://www.unpri.org/); the development of the ISO 14000 family on environmental management (http://www.iso.org/iso/theiso14000family_2009.pdf).

ment.[225] The analysis in this chapter suggests that investment tribunals do rarely undertake detailed considerations of international law outside of the broader scope of investment law. In addition, investment tribunals may have a certain bias to interpret the terms contained in investment treaties primarily to the advantage of the foreign investor. Nonetheless, all participants in arbitral proceedings should be aware that the interpretative power regarding investment treaties does not exclusively rest with the arbitral tribunal. The state parties to the investment treaty also have a legitimate role to play.[226] As far as it is their intention that considerations of sustainability be taken into account in the application of investment treaties, they can express this view – in interpretative notes, pleadings in arbitral proceedings, and in the text of newly-adopted investment treaties.

At its outset, this chapter has pointed to two diverging perceptions of conflicts of norms: A direct conflict, featuring the logical incompatibility of two opposing obligations, and an indirect conflict, which exists when the fulfilment of one obligation frustrates the aim of another treaty. The existence of a conflict in the narrow sense is only established if the opposition of the two norms cannot be reconciled through interpretation. The interpretative tools portrayed in this chapter illustrate that generally there is ample possibility to mitigate existing scenarios of conflict. Unless the international environmental agreement enlists specific sites or species to be protected, or prohibits the production and use of certain substances that are part of the investment activity of an investor, a direct conflict of rules is rare. As the considerations in this chapter have shown, a tension between a national environmental measure and a protective obligation owed to the foreign investor is most likely a scenario of indirect incompatibility. The following chapters will analyse the relationship between the most important provisions of investment protection and international and national environmental norms and measures.

---

225 *Kentin*, Esther, 'Sustainable Development in International Investment Dispute Settlement: The ICSID and NAFTA Experience', in: International Law and Sustainable Development: Principles and Practice (Schrijver, Nico et al. (Eds.) 2004) 309 (325). See also *Mayeda*, Graham, 'International Investment Agreements Between Developed and Developing Countries: Dancing With the Devil? Case Comment on the Vivendi, Sempra and Enron Awards', 4 Mc Gill International Journal of Sustainable Development Law and Policy 2008, 189 (204) arguing for the application of a 'sustainable development analysis' in investment arbitration in reliance on Article 31 para 3 lit c VCLT. This understanding is based on the consideration of sustainable development as constituting customary international law.

226 See for a comprehensive assessment of the dual role of states in investment arbitrations and especially in relation to interpretation, *Roberts*, Anthea, 'Power and Persuasion in Investment Treaty Arbitration: The Dual Role of States', 104 American Journal of International Law 2010, 179–225.

Chapter 3

Standards of Non-Discriminatory Treatment

Discrimination does not cease to be discrimination, nor to attract the international liability stemming therefrom, because it is undertaken to achieve a laudable goal or because the achievement of that goal can be described as necessary.

Tribunal in Corn Products International, Inc. v. United Mexican States, 2008

Modern investment treaties contain several provisions guaranteeing different levels of treatment to foreign investors. These treatment standards can be broadly divided into two categories: standards providing for an absolute level of protection and standards incorporating a relative level of protection. The former are those standards which reflect and strengthen elements of the customary international minimum standard of treatment, thus establishing protective guarantees independent of the treatment received by others. The latter category of standards, which provides for a relative level of protection, compares the treatment of the foreign investor to the treatment of other investors. Detectable differences in treatment require legitimate reasons, whereas the nationality of the investor is no valid distinguishing criterion. Thus, the treatment standards – all from a different angle – prescribe guarantees of the protection accorded to foreign investors and their investments.

This chapter focuses on those standards which promote the non-discrimination of investors or investments, entailing a relative level of protection. The non-discrimination of the foreign investor on grounds of its nationality is a fundamental pillar of the investment protection enshrined in modern investment treaties. Whereas notions of non-discrimination may influence all treatment standards, they are predominant in the widely recognised standards of national treatment and of most-favoured-nation treatment. These standards require that the foreign investor be treated at least as favourably as national investors or investors of third states are, respectively. In addition, some investment treaties explicitly prohibit subjecting foreign investors to 'arbitrary or discriminatory measures'. This standard, arguably, does not only prohibit discrimination closely connected to the nationality of the investor, but also captures discrimination on other grounds. Its reference to arbitrariness, however, incorporates an absolute standard and potentially overlaps with the standard of fair and equitable treatment.

In addition to these specific treatment standards, some investment treaties contain further provisions disallowing discrimination of foreign investors. Relevant examples are provisions restricting the use of performance requirements. A performance requirement is an obligation for the investor to meet certain specified goals in connection with the operations of its investment in the host state. The purpose of performance requirements is to ensure that the investment has positive effects on the development of the host state, for example through the use of local content or labour in certain industries. However, some investment treaties do specifically prohibit certain performance requirements for being discriminatory,[1] because they distinguish between national and foreign companies, products or workforces. As instruments to promote public benefits of investment, performance requirements can also further environmental objectives, such as implementing an obligation for an investment project to undertake an environmental impact assessment[2]. Although environmental performance requirements are specifically embraced in some investment treaties,[3] this study will not further focus on this standard. Environmental measures adopted can, but do not need to take the form of performance requirements. The questions that environmental measures pose with regard to investment protection are therefore not

---

1 See, for example, Article 1106 NAFTA; Article 10.9 CAFTA-DR; Article 10.9 U.S.-Peru FTA; Article 807 Canada-Peru FTA; Article 7 2004 Canada Model BIT. See for an overview of different techniques applied by investment agreements to limit the use of performance requirements, *Falsafi*, Alireza, 'Regional Trade and Investment Agreements: Liberalizing Investment in a Preferential Climate', 36 Syracuse Journal of International Law and Commerce 2008, 43 (55, 56).

2 See generally on environmental impact assessment, *Craik*, Neil, The International Law of Environmental Impact Assessment (2008). See the detailed description of the environmental impact assessment in Peru in *UNCTAD*, 'Foreign Investment and Performance Requirements: New Evidence from Selected Countries' (2003), UNCTAD/ITE/IIA/2003/7, pp. 64–66. The also the determination by the tribunal in Maffezini v. Spain, ICSID Case No. ARB/97/7, Award on the Merits of 13 November 2000, para 65, which found that an environmental impact assessment "is basic for the adequate protection of the environment and the application of appropriate preventive measures".

3 See Article 1106 para 6 NAFTA, stating that measures which are not applied in an arbitrary or unjustifiable manner and do not constitute a disguised restriction on international investment can generally be maintained, including, inter alia, measures "necessary to protect human, animal or plant life or health" or measures "necessary for the conservation of living or non-living exhaustible natural resources".

This language is modelled after Article XX GATT. See also Article 10.9 para 3 lit c CAFTA-DR, implementing the same rule, but containing a more comprehensive scope, as it refers to measures "related to the conservation of living or non-living exhaustible natural resources".

relevantly determined by the form in which they are adopted. Therefore, this study approaches the issue in an abstract manner. The fundamental question is whether environmental measures conflict with non-discrimination obligations. If they do, the protection of the investor is not significantly altered by them taking the form of performance requirements.

To determine potential conflicts between environmental measures and the protective standards against discrimination, this chapter first portrays the standard of national treatment. To this end, it depicts how investment tribunals understand the material content of this standard and how they approach environmental issues. Second, the survey portrays the protective scope of the standard of most-favoured-nation treatment. Third, it appreciates the content of the prohibition of arbitrary and discriminatory measures. The chapter is to point to the common features of all three standards and to the importance of the determination of a suitable comparator. It further focuses on the evaluation of the justifiability of differential treatment. In this context, the evaluation of measures allegedly introduced by states to further a public purpose is of particular relevance. Finally, this chapter assesses the relevance of the portrayed treatment standards with regard to the scenarios of conflicts with environmental protection, as described in the first chapter.

A. National Treatment

The obligation to grant foreign investors national treatment is implemented in the overwhelming majority of modern investment treaties. It essentially obliges the host state to accord to the other party's investors and their investments treatment that is no less favourable than the treatment bestowed upon its own national investors or investments.[4] The requirement for national treatment originates from the *Calvo* doctrine originally favoured by Latin-American states, which sought to ascertain that the treatment guaranteed to foreign investors did not go beyond the level of protection accorded to nationals – to the detriment of an objective minimum protection standard for foreign investors.[5] With the increase in domestic treatment standards in developing host countries, which now often exceed

---

[4] See, for example, Article 4 para 1 2006 France Model BIT; Article 4 para 1 2003 India Model BIT; Article 4 para 1 2007 Columbia Model BIT; Article 10.3 paras 1–2 CAFTA-DR; Article 1102 paras 1–2 NAFTA. See also Dolzer, Rudolf, 'National Treatment: New Developments', OECD Conference Paper, Paris 2005, available at: http://www.oecd.org/investment/internationalinvestmentagreements/36055356.pdf, p. 1.

[5] *DiMascio*, Nicholas/*Pauwelyn*, Joost, 'Nondiscrimination in Trade and Investment Treaties: Worlds Apart or Two Sides of the Same Coin?', 102 American Journal of International Law 2008, 48 (52); *Zhou*, Jian, 'National Treatment in Foreign

the original benchmark set by the international minimum standard, the guarantee of national treatment has steadily risen to the level of an important protection for foreign investors.[6]

The obligation of national treatment is an expression of the concept of non-discrimination.[7] Applying the prohibition of discrimination based on nationality, it disallows discrimination both *de jure* and *de facto*.[8] The former refers to measures that openly treat relevant entities differently, whereas the latter includes measures which are neutral on their face, but which result in differential treatment.[9] The standard of national treatment seeks to provide protection only against discrimination on the grounds of nationality, not against discrimination on other grounds.[10] With the standard not being owed to investors under customary international law, the scope of application of the obligation derives from the respective investment treaty.[11] Resulting differences, for example, relate to the applicability of the obligation

---

Investment Law: A Comparative Study from a Chinese Perspective', 10 Touro International Law Review 2000, 39 (85–86).

6 *DiMascio*, Nicholas/*Pauwelyn*, Joost, 'Nondiscrimination in Trade and Investment Treaties: Worlds Apart or Two Sides of the Same Coin?', 102 American Journal of International Law 2008, 48 (67).

7 Archer Daniels Midland Company and Tate & Lyle Ingredients Americas, Inc. v. United Mexican States, ICSID Case No. ARB (AF)/04/5, Award of 21 November 2007, para 193; Corn Products International, Inc. v. United Mexican States, ICSID Case No. ARB(AF)04/01, Partial Award of 15 January 2008, para 109; Parkerings-Compagniet AS v. Lithuania, ICSID Case No. ARB/05/8, Award of 11 September 2007, para 367; *DiMascio*, Nicholas/*Pauwelyn*, Joost, 'Nondiscrimination in Trade and Investment Treaties: Worlds Apart or Two Sides of the Same Coin?', 102 American Journal of International Law 2008, 48 (48).

8 Archer Daniels Midland Company and Tate & Lyle Ingredients Americas, Inc. v. United Mexican States, ICSID Case No. ARB (AF)/04/5, Award of 21 November 2007, para 193; Corn Products International, Inc. v. United Mexican States, ICSID Case No. ARB(AF)04/01, Partial Award of 15 January 2008, para 115; ADF Group Inc. v. United States, ICSID Case No. ARB (AF)/00/1, Award of 9 January 2003, para 157.

9 Archer Daniels Midland Company and Tate & Lyle Ingredients Americas, Inc. v. United Mexican States, ICSID Case No. ARB (AF)/04/5, Award of 21 November 2007, para 193; *Ortino*, Federico, 'Non-Discriminatory Treatment in Investment Disputes', in: Human Rights in International Investment Law and Arbitration (Dupuy, Pierre-Marie et al. (Eds.) 2009) 344 (349–350).

10 Pope & Talbot Inc. v. Canada, Award on the Merits of Phase 2 of 10 April 2001, para 79; Loewen Group, Inc. and Raymond L. Loewen v. United States, ICSID Case No. ARB(AF)/98/3, Award of 26 June 2003, para 139; *DiMascio*, Nicholas/*Pauwelyn*, Joost, 'Nondiscrimination in Trade and Investment Treaties: Worlds Apart or Two Sides of the Same Coin?', 102 American Journal of International Law 2008, 48 (72).

11 *Congyan*, Cai, 'China-US BIT Negotiations and the Future of Investment Treaty Regime: A Grand Bilateral Bargain with Multilateral Implications', 12 Journal of International Economic Law 2009, 457 (471).

during the phase of establishment of the investment,[12] or to the determination of the organisational level within a federal state, at which the treatment has to be evaluated.[13] These specific issues are, however, not part of this survey. Its foremost task is to give an insight into the three elements that investment tribunals analyse to determine the relevant protection owed to the investor, namely (a) to which national investor the foreign investor must be compared; (b) whether the foreign investor was treated less favourably; and (c) which factors could justify a differential treatment.[14]

I. Definition of the Comparator

The crucial element for finding out whether the investor was granted national treatment is establishing the correct comparator: The foreign investor has to be compared to the correct class of national investors for the standard to offer meaningful protection. To ascertain that differences in treatment are connected to the nationality of the foreign investor, only investors raising similar public policy concerns should be compared.[15] In the jurisprudence of investment tribunals this issue is frequently subsumed under the headline of whether the foreign and the national investor are 'in like circumstances' or 'in like situations' – which reflects the language contained in several investment treaties.[16]

---

[12] In some modern investment treaties the obligation to provide for national treatment explicitly applies "with respect to the establishment, acquisition, expansion [...] of investments", thus extending to the pre-establishment phase, see, for example, Article 10.3 paras 1–2 CAFTA-DR; Article 1102 paras 1–2 NAFTA. The diverging policies and practice in this respect are portrayed in *Congyan*, Cai, 'China-US BIT Negotiations and the Future of Investment Treaty Regime: A Grand Bilateral Bargain with Multilateral Implications', 12 Journal of International Economic Law 2009, 457 (469–473).

[13] Some investment treaties state that the relevant level of treatment accorded to national investors is determined by the respective federal state or the province with which the foreign investor deals, see, for example, Article 10.3 para 3 CAFTA-DR; Article 1102 para 3 NAFTA.

[14] Archer Daniels Midland Company and Tate & Lyle Ingredients Americas, Inc. v. United Mexican States, ICSID Case No. ARB (AF)/04/5, Award of 21 November 2007, para 196; Bayindir Insaat Turizm Ticaret Ve Sanayi A.S. v. Islamic Republic of Pakistan, ICSID Case No. ARB/03/29, Award of 27 August 2009, para 399.

[15] *DiMascio*, Nicholas/*Pauwelyn*, Joost, 'Nondiscrimination in Trade and Investment Treaties: Worlds Apart or Two Sides of the Same Coin?', 102 American Journal of International Law 2008, 48 (72).

[16] See, for example, Article 10.3 para 1 CAFTA-DR; Article 1102 NAFTA; Article 4 para 1 U.S.-Rwanda BIT. However, other investment treaties do not use the likeness-criterion, see Article 10 para 7 ECT; Article 3 para 1 Germany-Bosnia and Herzegovina BIT.

Given the linguistic similarity of 'like circumstances' to the wording of the obligation to national treatment in Article III GATT, which contains the term 'like products', investment tribunals have discussed whether the respective understanding of WTO panels constitutes a relevant guideline for understanding the terminology in investment law: In the trade law context, the relevant criterion is the competitive relationship between the national and foreign product.[17] While, in contrast, only few investment tribunals explicitly refer to the competitive element when determining the relevant comparator,[18] arbitral decisions indicate that investment tribunals are influenced by the trade law approach: An apparent majority of investment decisions discussing a violation of the standard of national treatment compare the foreign investment to a domestic investment 'in the same business or economic sector'.[19] The relevance of the investors' presence in the same business sector was only explicitly rejected by few investment tribunals.[20]

---

[17] European Communities – Measures Affecting Asbestos and Asbestos Containing Products, DS135/AB/R, WTO Appellate Body Report of 12 March 2001, para. 99; Korea – Measures Affecting Imports of Fresh, Chilled and Frozen Beef, DS161/AB/R, WTO Appellate Body Report of 11 December 2000, para. 137.

[18] Archer Daniels Midland Company and Tate & Lyle Ingredients Americas, Inc. v. United Mexican States, ICSID Case No. ARB (AF)/04/5, Award of 21 November 2007, para 202; Corn Products International, Inc. v. United Mexican States, ICSID Case No. ARB(AF)04/01, Partial Award of 15 January 2008, para 126; S.D. Myers Inc. v. Canada, Partial Award on the Merits, 13 November 2000, para 251. See, in contrast, the express embracing of the 'competition' element in academic writing: *Grierson-Weiler*, Todd/*Laird*, Ian A., 'Standards of Treatment', in: The Oxford Handbook of International Investment Law (Muchlinski, Peter (Ed.) 2008) 259 (291–293); *Kurtz*, Jürgen, 'The Use and Abuse of WTO Law in Investor-State Arbitration: Competition and Its Discontents', 20 European Journal of International Law 2009, 749 (759, 766); *Swan*, Alan C., 'NAFTA Chapter 11 – "Direct Effect" and Interpretative Method: Lessons From Methanex v. United States', 64 University of Miami Law Review 2009, 21 (52, 59); *Howse*, Robert/*Chalamish*, Efraim, 'The Use and Abuse of WTO Law in Investor-State Arbitration: A Reply to Jürgen Kurtz', 20 European Journal of International Law 2009, 1087 (1092, 1093).

[19] Pope & Talbot Inc. v. Canada, Award on the Merits of Phase 2 of 10 April 2001, para 78; S.D. Myers Inc. v. Canada, Partial Award on the Merits, 13 November 2000, para 250; Archer Daniels Midland Company and Tate & Lyle Ingredients Americas, Inc. v. United Mexican States, ICSID Case No. ARB (AF)/04/5, Award of 21 November 2007, para 198; Champion Trading Company, Ameritrade International, Inc., James T. Wahba, John B. Wahba, Timothy T. Wahba v. Egypt, ICSID Case No. ARB/02/9, Award of 27 October 2006, para 130; Feldman v. Mexico, ICSID Case No. ARB(AF)/99/1, Award of 16 December 2002, para 171; Corn Products International, Inc. v. United Mexican States, ICSID Case No. ARB(AF)04/01, Partial Award of 15 January 2008, para 120.

[20] Bayindir Insaat Turizm Ticaret Ve Sanayi A.S. v. Islamic Republic of Pakistan, ICSID Case No. ARB/03/29, Award of 27 August 2009, para 402; Occidental Exploration and Production Company v. The Republic of Ecuador, LCIA Case No. UN3467, Award of 1 July 2004, para 173.

The tribunal in *Occidental v. Ecuador*, concerned with a regulation for VAT refunds not granted to exporters of oil, declared that the 'like situation' "can relate to all investors that share a relevant condition",[21] thus convincingly focusing on the absence of any legitimate reason to differentiate between foreign and domestic investments in the particular circumstances surrounding the rules for VAT refunds.[22]

The identification of the relevant 'business or economic sector' can be impeded by the facts of the specific case. For instance, businesses concerned with very similar tasks do not necessarily operate in the same business sector.[23] Furthermore, the understanding of the concept of 'business sector' in a narrow or broad sense may intensely influence the identification of the relevant comparator. The tribunal in *Methanex v. United States* – at the restrictive end of the spectrum – decided to compare the foreign investor only with companies that were "identical", as the tribunal found it to be "perverse to ignore identical comparators if they were available and to use comparators that were less 'like'".[24] Commentators have dismissed this approach as being too narrow, stating that the foreign investor could have been discriminated against with respect to some other, not completely identical, domestic investment.[25] Similarly, most other tribunals perceived the relevant business sector more broadly. Investment tribunals have furthermore demonstrated that the determination of the business sector as such is

---

21 Occidental Exploration and Production Company v. The Republic of Ecuador, LCIA Case No. UN3467, Award of 1 July 2004, para 176.

22 *DiMascio*, Nicholas/*Pauwelyn*, Joost, 'Nondiscrimination in Trade and Investment Treaties: Worlds Apart or Two Sides of the Same Coin?', 102 American Journal of International Law 2008, 48 (85).

23 United Parcel Service of America Inc. v. Government of Canada, Award of 24 May 2007, paras 117–119, which details that the existing difference in rules and regulations for courier and postal traffic leads to them not being in 'like circumstances'.

24 Methanex v. United States, Award of 3 August 2005, Part IV Chapter B para 17. See also the similar narrow understanding of the business sector in Feldman v. Mexico, ICSID Case No. ARB(AF)/99/1, Award of 16 December 2002, para 171, which held that only firms in the business of reselling/exporting cigarettes were in a like situation to claimant in this situation, in which the investor challenged a tax regime for exports.

25 *DiMascio*, Nicholas/*Pauwelyn*, Joost, 'Nondiscrimination in Trade and Investment Treaties: Worlds Apart or Two Sides of the Same Coin?', 102 American Journal of International Law 2008, 48 (84–85); *Kurtz*, Jürgen, 'The Use and Abuse of WTO Law in Investor-State Arbitration: Competition and Its Discontents', 20 European Journal of International Law 2009, 749 (766–768); *Swan*, Alan C., 'NAFTA Chapter 11 – "Direct Effect" and Interpretative Method: Lessons From Methanex v. United States', 64 University of Miami Law Review 2009, 21 (58, 59).

not sufficient to find out whether a foreign investor is in 'like circumstances' with domestic investors belonging to the business sector, since the specific circumstances of the respective case can indicate obvious, factual differences between investors within the same business sector.[26]

The case law indicates that the identification of the correct 'comparator' is crucial for finding discrimination of the investor. The concept gives investment tribunals substantial leeway to point the case into a specific direction: First, tribunals have to decide whether the facts before them warrant reliance on the concept of the business sector or whether a different comparison is more appropriate.[27] Second, the identification of the respective business sector allows for a certain amount of latitude in understanding the broadness of the sector. These differences indicate that the choice of the relevant comparator is more strongly influenced by a tribunal's understanding of the specific facts of the case than by absolute and objectively defined borders of the concept. It follows that the choice of the correct comparator sets the course for the resulting evaluation.

II. Treatment No Less Favourable

As a second step, the tribunal has to establish whether the foreign investor was treated less favourably than comparable domestic investors: Investment tribunals compare the treatment accorded to the foreign investor to the best treatment bestowed upon one domestic investor falling within the category of

---

[26] Generally, further differentiation between investors in the same business sector stems from justifications for differential effects because of legitimate policy reasons. But it is nevertheless possible for investment tribunals to further distinguish among investors operating within the same business sector. See Champion Trading Company, Ameritrade International, Inc., James T. Wahba, John B. Wahba, Timothy T. Wahba v. Egypt, ICSID Case No. ARB/02/9, Award of 27 October 2006, para 154, in which the tribunal stated that the differences between companies buying cotton at specific points at fixed rates and those buying in the free market were too significant to compare them. In International Thunderbird Gaming Corporation v. Mexico, Award of 26 January 2006, paras 181–182, the foreign investor and a domestic owner of gambling facilities could not be compared, because the latter had legally battled against the intended closure of the facilities.

[27] *Grierson-Weiler*, Todd/*Laird*, Ian A., 'Standards of Treatment', in: The Oxford Handbook of International Investment Law (Muchlinski, Peter (Ed.) 2008) 259 (292–293) suggest that the non-appreciation of a competitive situation by the tribunal in *Loewen Group, Inc. and Raymond L. Loewen v. United States* was incorrect. The tribunal found that the investor, which had been denied justice in local court proceedings in the U.S. initiated by the competitor, could not be compared with this competitor, since "their circumstances as litigants were very different", Loewen Group, Inc. and Raymond L. Loewen v. United States, ICSID Case No. ARB(AF)/98/3, Award of 26 June 2003, para 140.

relevant comparators.[28] Accordingly, the treatment of the investor was less favourable if one domestic investor was treated more favourably. The trade law-inspired approach favoured by respondent states, according to which a violation of the treatment standard requires that the majority of comparable domestic investors be treated more favourably than the foreign investor, is not considered suitable.[29] Similarly, the argument that a violation cannot occur when other comparable non-national investors have received treatment more favourable has also been rejected.[30] That this is correct derives from the general understanding of investment law as protecting the rights of each individual investor.[31] The individual investor is not concerned with the overall treatment of a sector or a group, but with its own financial loss.

The treatment is less favourable if its result produces an adverse effect on the foreign investor or the foreign investment.[32] In contrast, investment tribunals do mainly not focus on the motivation underlying the treatment. It appears that the general understanding is that discriminatory intent is not a pre-requisite,[33] but a significant, additional indication[34] for the finding of a

28 Feldman v. Mexico, ICSID Case No. ARB(AF)/99/1, Award of 16 December 2002, para 181; Methanex v. United States, Award of 3 August 2005, Part IV Chapter B para 21; Pope & Talbot Inc. v. Canada, Award on the Merits of Phase 2 of 10 April 2001, para 42.

29 Pope & Talbot Inc. v. Canada, Award on the Merits of Phase 2 of 10 April 2001, paras 46–67.

30 Feldman v. Mexico, ICSID Case No. ARB(AF)/99/1, Award of 16 December 2002, para 175.

31 *Grierson-Weiler*, Todd/*Laird*, Ian A., 'Standards of Treatment', in: The Oxford Handbook of International Investment Law (Muchlinski, Peter (Ed.) 2008) 259 (293); *DiMascio*, Nicholas/*Pauwelyn*, Joost, 'Nondiscrimination in Trade and Investment Treaties: Worlds Apart or Two Sides of the Same Coin?', 102 American Journal of International Law 2008, 48 (78).

32 *Grierson-Weiler*, Todd/*Laird*, Ian A., 'Standards of Treatment', in: The Oxford Handbook of International Investment Law (Muchlinski, Peter (Ed.) 2008) 259 (293); *Weiler*, Todd, 'Saving Oscar Chin: Non-Discrimination in International Investment Law', in: International Investment Law and Arbitration: Leading Cases from the ICSID, NAFTA, Bilateral Treaties and Customary International Law (Weiler, Todd (Ed.) 2005) 557 (570–571); *Miles*, Kate, 'Sustainable Development, National Treatment and Like Circumstances in Investment Law', in: Sustainable Development in World Investment Law (Cordonier Segger, Marie-Claire et al. (Eds.) 2011) 265 (270).

33 Consortium R.F.C.C. v. Kingdom of Morocco, ICSID Case No. ARB/00/6, Award of 22 December 2003, para 74; Occidental Exploration and Production Company v. The Republic of Ecuador, LCIA Case No. UN3467, para 177; Corn Products International, Inc. v. United Mexican States, ICSID Case No. ARB(AF)04/01, Partial Award of 15 January 2008, para 138.

34 Archer Daniels Midland Company and Tate & Lyle Ingredients Americas, Inc. v. United Mexican States, ICSID Case No. ARB (AF)/04/5, Award of 21 November

violation of the treatment standard. Only rarely has it been indicated that intent to discriminate against the foreign investor has to be established.[35]

In accordance with the general rules, the burden of proof rests on the investor to establish a *prima facie* case of discrimination. Some commentators argue that if discrimination is established on a *prima facie* basis, the burden of proof shifts onto the state to prove that the difference in treatment is not connected to the nationality of the investor.[36] Other investment tribunals express the understanding that the burden of proof is on the investor for all aspects of the claim and that it does not shift to the state.[37] Commentators suggest that while the evidence of a different treatment should count in favour of the investor, it should not lead to shifting the burden of proof.[38] This understanding underlines the importance of the regulatory autonomy of states and does not treat the government as "guilty until proven innocent" due to a possible discrepant effect of a legitimate regula-

2007, paras 209–210; S.D. Myers Inc. v. Canada, Partial Award on the Merits, 13 November 2000, para 254, in which the tribunal states that "[i]ntent is important, but protectionist intent is not necessarily decisive on its own", because the word "treatment" suggests the need for a practical impact of the measure. An opposing view is taken by the tribunal in Corn Products International, Inc. v. United Mexican States, ICSID Case No. ARB(AF)04/01, Partial Award of 15 January 2008, para 138, stating that where intent was shown it was sufficient to demonstrate treatment less favourable. This far-reaching approach, however, probably reflects the clear-cut intent of the respondent state, which expressly stated that the regulatory measure was meant to constitute a counter-measure against the state of origin of the investor.

35 Methanex v. United States, Award of 3 August 2005, Part IV Chapter B para 12. See also Genin and others v. Estonia, ICSID Case No. ARB/99/2, Award of 25 June 2001, para 369 in the context of the standard prohibiting discriminatory measures.

36 Feldman v. Mexico, ICSID Case No. ARB(AF)/99/1 (NAFTA), Award 16 December 2002, paras 176–177; Pope & Talbot Inc. v. Canada, Award on the Merits of Phase 2 of 10 April 2001, para 78; *Grierson-Weiler*, Todd/*Laird*, Ian A.,'Standards of Treatment', in: The Oxford Handbook of International Investment Law (Muchlinski, Peter (Ed.) 2008) 259 (295).

37 United Parcel Service of America Inc. v. Government of Canada, Award of 24 May 2007, para 84; Methanex v. United States, Award of 3 August 2005, Part IV Chapter B para 12; International Thunderbird Gaming Corporation v. Mexico, Award of 26 January 2006, paras 176–177.

38 *DiMascio*, Nicholas/*Pauwelyn*, Joost, 'Nondiscrimination in Trade and Investment Treaties: Worlds Apart or Two Sides of the Same Coin?', 102 American Journal of International Law 2008, 48 (86). See also the tribunal in Corn Products International, Inc. v. United Mexican States, ICSID Case No. ARB(AF)04/01, Partial Award of 15 January 2008, para 122, stating that a violation of the national treatment of the GATT in a case where the alleged violation of a national treatment clause in an investment treaty directly concerned the said product, was a "very strong indication" of a violation of the standard in investment law.

tion.[39] On the other hand, it should be relatively easy for a government to justify a legitimate regulation that has a discrepant effect – whereas proving the opposite could be very difficult for the investor. Either way, the state would have to give reasons to justify differential treatment.

III. Justification of Differential Treatment

Unlike the provision of national treatment in the GATT,[40] in bilateral and multilateral investment treaties the standard is generally not coupled with provisions guiding a possible justification of less favourable treatment. In the light of the right of a state to regulate, however, it is understood that the treatment standard does not prohibit measures aimed at implementing legitimate policy considerations. Accordingly, the less favourable treatment of a foreign investor can be justified if the differentiation is connected to a legitimate public policy[41] – so that the less favourable treatment of a foreign investor is only a by-effect of this regulation. Investment tribunals often use such distinguishing reasoning to find that the foreign investor and the comparator were, after all, not in a 'like situation'.[42]

The conditions set by investment tribunals for such public policy justification are twofold: the public policy furthered by the treatment has to

---

[39] *DiMascio*, Nicholas/*Pauwelyn*, Joost, 'Nondiscrimination in Trade and Investment Treaties: Worlds Apart or Two Sides of the Same Coin?', 102 American Journal of International Law 2008, 48 (86).

[40] With its Article XX, the GATT contains a 'general exceptions' provision, enlisting objectives for which measures can be adopted and enforced – provided that the measures are necessary to protect an objective and that they are not means for arbitrary or unjustifiable discrimination or constitute a disguised restriction on international trade.

[41] *Ortino*, Federico, 'Non-Discriminatory Treatment in Investment Disputes', in: Human Rights in International Investment Law and Arbitration (Dupuy, Pierre-Marie et al. (Eds.) 2009) 344 (360).

[42] In Gami Investments, Inc. v. Mexico, Award of 15 November 2004, para 114, the tribunal found that sugar mills operating in conditions of effective insolvency were not in a 'like situation' to financially secure sugar mills. In Parkerings-Compagniet AS v. Lithuania, ICSID Case No. ARB/05/8, Award of 11 September 2007, para 420, in which the same criteria were used to establish a violation of the most-favoured-nation treatment, claimant was not in a 'like situation' to another investor wanting to pursue a similar land development project because of differences in the contracts each had proposed to conclude with the city. See further below at pp. 189 *et seq*.

See also *Moloo*, Rahim/*Jacinto*, Justin, 'Environmental and Health Regulation: Assessing Liability under Investment-Treaties', 29 Berkeley Journal of International Law 2011, 1 (58–59), arguing that as a matter of treaty interpretation and policy, regulatory distinctions have to be discussed under the umbrella of the 'like circumstances'.

constitute a legitimate goal and the measure has to bear a reasonable relation to the policy.[43] Although so far only few investment tribunals have dealt with what constitutes a legitimate public policy,[44] it is safe to assume that the concept is understood broadly. Environmental considerations and policies can qualify. With regard to the relationship between the measure and the policy, the existing case law does not clearly indicate how strong the connection has to be to meet the criterion. The strength of the nexus is described as a "plausible connection"[45] or, more strictly, as a "reasonable nexus"[46]. Commentators suggest that the nexus between the measure and the policy objective varies according to the circumstances of the case and the importance of the policy objectives pursued.[47] This appears to be a workable suggestion for balancing the opposing interests: The more important the public policy concern is, the more can it be tolerated that the measure happens to negatively affect a foreign investor – even if it does not affect a national, comparable investor. However, with governmental motivations for the adoption and implementation of specific measures rarely being singular,[48] there will often be a host of open and hidden reasons for the introduction of a measure, some of them more laudable than others. Accordingly, it has to be ascertained that a legitimate public policy is not used as a smokescreen to cover discriminatory treatment.[49]

---

[43] S.D. Myers Inc. v. Canada, Partial Award on the Merits, 13 November 2000, paras 246, 255; Pope & Talbot Inc. v. Canada, Award on the Merits of Phase 2 of 10 April 2001, para 102. Feldman v. Mexico, ICSID Case No. ARB(AF)/99/1, Award of 16 December 2002, para 182, referring to a "rational justification".

[44] *Ortino*, Federico, 'Non-Discriminatory Treatment in Investment Disputes', in: Human Rights in International Investment Law and Arbitration (Dupuy, Pierre-Marie et al. (Eds.) 2009) 344 (361) provides an overview of policies which were held to be legitimate.

[45] Gami Investments, Inc. v. Mexico, Award of 15 November 2004, para 114.

[46] Pope & Talbot Inc. v. Canada, Interim Award of 26 June 2000, para 81. See also discussion of the criterion by *Ortino*, Federico, 'Non-Discriminatory Treatment in Investment Disputes', in: Human Rights in International Investment Law and Arbitration (Dupuy, Pierre-Marie et al. (Eds.) 2009) 344 (362–363).

[47] *DiMascio*, Nicholas/*Pauwelyn*, Joost, 'Nondiscrimination in Trade and Investment Treaties: Worlds Apart or Two Sides of the Same Coin?', 102 American Journal of International Law 2008, 48 (88), referring to the tribunal in Parkerings-Compagniet AS v. Lithuania, ICSID Case No. ARB/05/8, Award of 11 September 2007, paras 368, 371. Similairly, with reference to the WTO exemptions, *Weiler*, Todd, 'Saving Oscar Chin: Non-Discrimination in International Investment Law', in: International Investment Law and Arbitration: Leading Cases from the ICSID, NAFTA, Bilateral Treaties and Customary International Law (Weiler, Todd (Ed.) 2005) 557 (575, 577).

[48] See the discussion of governmental motivation in S.D. Myers Inc. v. Canada, Partial Award on the Merits, 13 November 2000, paras 161–162.

[49] There can only be a justification of a differential treatment, not of discrimination, i.e. of measures which specifically target foreign investors either *de facto* or

IV. Analysis of Case Law Concerning Environmental Measures

The portrayal of the standard of national treatment foremost points to two aspects of increased relevance in cases in which an allegedly environmental measure potentially results in differential treatment of the foreign investor: First, the foreign investor has to be compared to the correct comparator. The breadth of the interpretative scope of this criterion grants investment tribunals significant leeway. The probability of finding a violation of the standard increases or decreases in correlation with how broadly or narrowly the concept of a 'like situation' is understood. Second, possible justifications of differential treatment of the foreign investor, which derive from the implementation of a legitimate policy objective, are particularly relevant. In this context, the problematic issue is not so much whether environmental considerations reflect a reasonable public policy, but rather whether the respective measure is in reality motivated and informed by the alleged policy objective. The existing case law on the standard of national treatment containing an environmental nexus is limited. It primarily consists of two cases, *S.D. Myers v. Canada* and *Methanex v. United States*, which will now be portrayed in more detail below.

1. S.D. Myers v. Canada

a) Portrayal of the Arbitral Decision

In *S.D. Myers v. Canada*, the tribunal had to decide if a Canadian ban on the export of polychlorinated biphenyl (PCB) to the U.S. violated the obligation of granting national treatment with regard to the U.S. investor. Canada, the responding state, argued that the export ban constituted a uniform regulatory regime under which all were treated equally[50] and that the measure was introduced for environmental reasons. Prior to assessing the violation of the standard of national treatment, the tribunal detachedly analysed the environmental arguments brought forward by Canada for implementing the ban. The reasons are closely connected to the 1989 Basel Convention,[51] which Canada had ratified and the U.S. had signed, but not

---

de jure. See also Corn Products International, Inc. v. United Mexican States, ICSID Case No. ARB(AF)04/01, Partial Award of 15 January 2008, para 142.

50 S.D. Myers Inc. v. Canada, Partial Award on the Merits, 13 November 2000, para 241.

51 S.D. Myers Inc. v. Canada, Partial Award on the Merits, 13 November 2000, para 121.

ratified[52]. The Convention, inter alia, aims to reduce transboundary movement of hazardous waste and further obliges state parties to ensure the existence of local disposal facilities for hazardous waste.[53]

In its assessment of the relevant 'like circumstances' to determine the relevant comparator, the tribunal emphasised the need to "keep in mind the overall legal context"[54] and referred to a host of different legal material which it considered to be part of this legal context. The tribunal developed a set of environmental principles, which it distilled from principles enshrined or affirmed in the NAAEC, such as the principles of the Rio Declaration.[55] The arbitrators summarised the legal context to determine the likeness of circumstances as "including both [the] concern with the environment and the need to avoid trade distortions that are not justified by environmental concerns"[56], and to conclude that the foreign investor was in the same business sector and in competition with Canadian companies providing PCB waste remediation services, thus in a like situation.[57]

Having identified the relevant comparators, the tribunal assessed whether the export ban denied the foreign investor national treatment. It states that, although protectionist intent was important, the treatment had to have a

---

52 S.D. Myers Inc. v. Canada, Partial Award on the Merits, 13 November 2000, paras 105–108, 210.

53 Article 4 para 2 lit d mandates the reduction of transboundary movements of hazardous waste. Article 4 para 2 lit b Basel Convention obliges state parties to take the appropriate measures to "[e]nsure the availability of adequate disposal facilities, for the environmentally sound management of hazardous wastes and other wastes, that shall be located, to the extent possible, within it, whatever the place of their disposal." See the portrayal of the Basel Convention in 'Chapter 1 – Environmental Norms and Principles' at pp. 50 *et seq*. See also portrayal of the Basel Convention by the tribunal, S.D. Myers Inc. v. Canada, Partial Award on the Merits, 13 November 2000, paras 210–213.

54 S.D. Myers Inc. v. Canada, Partial Award on the Merits, 13 November 2000, para 245.

55 S.D. Myers Inc. v. Canada, Partial Award on the Merits, 13 November 2000, para 247. The tribunal expressly pointed to the following concepts: " – states have the right to establish high levels of environmental protection. They are not obliged to compromise their standards merely to satisfy the political or economic interests of other states; – states should avoid creating distortions to trade; – environmental protection and economic development can and should be mutually supportive." See also, in 'Chapter 1 – Environmental Norms and Principles' the portrayal of the diverse principles of the 1992 Rio Declaration.

56 S.D. Myers Inc. v. Canada, Partial Award on the Merits, 13 November 2000, para 250.

57 S.D. Myers Inc. v. Canada, Partial Award on the Merits, 13 November 2000, para 251.

"practical impact" on the investor to find a violation.[58] The tribunal was convinced of the existence of the latter criterion without further consideration; however, the tribunal's prior conclusion – that the export ban was motivated by protectionist intent – was central to its overall assessment of the treatment standard: the evaluation of the protectionist intent is at the heart of the tribunal's assessment of the state's environmental argumentation against other evidence at its disposal. The discourse features the environmental merits of the ban and the obligations deriving from the Basel Convention alleged by Canada. The tribunal held that a protectionist motivation and not the environmental reasoning was really tipping the scales.

The tribunal did not find fault with Canada's argument that its 1989 policy to destroy Canadian PCBs in Canada reflected the understanding underlying the Basel Convention.[59] However, the tribunal focuses on evidence that the decision makers had altered their perception of this policy, which meant that PCB waste should be disposed of "in Canada by Canadians", when the export ban was introduced.[60] In portraying detailed evidence on the clear protectionist intent,[61] the tribunal illustrates the governmental appreciation of the matter, detailing how environmental argumentation was used to find reasons for the introduction of an export ban. That the export ban was lifted only several months after its implementation, further supported the assessment of the tribunal that the ban was motivated by protectionist intent rather than by valid environmental reasons.[62]

The tribunal refrained from assessing the environmental merit of any of the concerns brought forward by Canada. One concern related to whether the U.S. would comply with the regulations of the Basel Convention in the

---

58 S.D. Myers Inc. v. Canada, Partial Award on the Merits, 13 November 2000, para 254.

59 S.D. Myers Inc. v. Canada, Partial Award on the Merits, 13 November 2000, paras 108, 182.

60 S.D. Myers Inc. v. Canada, Partial Award on the Merits, 13 November 2000, paras 116, 162, 169, 171.

61 The facts described by the tribunal suggest that as a result of being heavily lobbied by the Canadian waste disposal industry, Canadian government officials made commitments to their domestic industry that they would prevent the exports of PCBs, S.D. Myers Inc. v. Canada, Partial Award on the Merits, 13 November 2000, paras 168, 172, 174, 176, 178.

62 Only a few months after its implementation, the export ban was lifted by Canada. Canada then expressed that it welcomed the open border in the interests of expediting the elimination of PCBs from the environment, provided that any risks associated with exporting PCB waste to the U.S. were minimised through proper regulations and safeguards, S.D. Myers Inc. v. Canada, Partial Award on the Merits, 13 November 2000, para 162.

case of an export. The tribunal correctly established that the Basel Convention allowed exports to non-party states when guided by bilateral agreements containing provisions not less stringent than those of the Convention itself.[63] The tribunal was satisfied that the existing bilateral Transboundary Agreement between Canada and the U.S. fulfilled the relevant criteria,[64] so that the consistency of the Agreement and the Basel Convention was not called into question.[65] Another concern voiced by Canada questioned whether the PCB waste would be disposed of in an environmentally sound manner in the U.S., in accordance with obligations of the Basel Convention. The tribunal recalled that it had been the Canadian position at a conference of the parties to the Basel Convention that the use of disposal facilities in other OECD countries assured hazardous wastes would be managed in an environmentally sound manner.[66] It also took note of the investor's proposal that Canada should make environmental disposal conditions a requirement for export.[67] Furthermore, the tribunal was not convinced that the export ban fulfilled the conditions required by national law for an 'interim order', as which it was introduced – i.e. for a tool to provide immediate action against a 'significant danger to the environment and to human life and health'.[68]

---

[63] S.D. Myers Inc. v. Canada, Partial Award on the Merits, 13 November 2000, para 106, with reference to Article 11 Basel Convention.

[64] The tribunal mentioned that the Transboundary Agreement pronounced the understanding that the use of the nearest disposal facility for hazardous waste could be across the border – as was the case for the PCBs the investor intended to export, S.D. Myers Inc. v. Canada, Partial Award on the Merits, 13 November 2000, paras 103, 112. The tribunal was further satisfied that the Agreement was applicable to PCBs, S.D. Myers Inc. v. Canada, Partial Award on the Merits, 13 November 2000, paras 190, 205–207.

[65] S.D. Myers Inc. v. Canada, Partial Award on the Merits, 13 November 2000, paras 190, 213.

[66] S.D. Myers Inc. v. Canada, Partial Award on the Merits, 13 November 2000, para 182. The tribunal also referenced the framework adopted by the OECD, para 99.

[67] S.D. Myers Inc. v. Canada, Partial Award on the Merits, 13 November 2000, para 192.

[68] The tribunal did not call the high toxicity and the harmfulness to human health and the environment of PCBs into question, S.D. Myers Inc. v. Canada, Partial Award on the Merits, 13 November 2000, para 153. However, the tribunal considered that Canada could have easily amassed the relevant implications stemming from the opening of the border by the U.S. prior to the pending opening, so that such a measure would not have been necessary, S.D. Myers Inc. v. Canada, Partial Award on the Merits, 13 November 2000, paras 120, 190. Furthermore, the tribunal found no evidence that the existence of a relevant danger had been properly assessed, S.D. Myers Inc. v. Canada, Partial Award on the Merits, 13 November 2000, para 187.

The tribunal's discussion of legitimate goals to justify the differential treatment of investors is intermingled with the portrayal of the intent of discrimination on the part of governmental officials, which cannot be clearly distinguished. There is only one environmental argument presented by Canada that the tribunal wholeheartedly accepted as such: Canada's concern to ensure the viability of its domestic hazardous waste disposal facilities to continue being able to treat PCBs even if the U.S. decided to re-close its border. The tribunal recognised that this was – also under the rules of the Basel Convention – an important aspect.[69] However, the tribunal stated that this reason could not justify the introduction of the export ban. It held that

> "[t]here were a number of legitimate ways by which Canada could have achieved it, but preventing [the investor] from exporting PCBs for processing in the USA [...] was not one of them. [...T]he method contravened Canada's international commitments under the NAFTA. Canada's right to source all government requirements and to grant subsidies to the Canadian industry are but two examples of legitimate alternative measures. The fact that the matter was addressed subsequently and the border re-opened also shows that Canada was not constrained in its ability to deal effectively with the situation."[70]

In focusing on alternate possibilities for the state to achieve its environmental objective, the tribunal invoked the gist of Article 104 of the NAFTA and the environmental principles distilled from NAAEC, the international agreements confirmed by it, and the preamble of NAFTA to conclude that "when a state can achieve its chosen level of environmental protection through a variety of equally effective and reasonable means, it is obliged to adopt the alternative that is most consistent with open trade".[71] This approach was expressly found to be "consistent with the language and the case law arising out of the WTO family of agreements".[72] The tribunal's finding that the legitimate aim of safeguarding domestic PCB disposal facilities could have been pursued with "legitimate, alternative measures" resulted in the determination that the export ban was not justified. Thus, the ban violated the standard of national treatment.

[69] S.D. Myers Inc. v. Canada, Partial Award on the Merits, 13 November 2000, paras 195, 255.

[70] S.D. Myers Inc. v. Canada, Partial Award on the Merits, 13 November 2000, para 255.

[71] S.D. Myers Inc. v. Canada, Partial Award on the Merits, 13 November 2000, paras 214, 215, 221.

[72] S.D. Myers Inc. v. Canada, Partial Award on the Merits, 13 November 2000, para 221.

b) Evaluation

From a systematic perspective, the decision poses some difficulties. Although the identification of the relevant comparators is convincing, the tribunal did not address to what extent the investor was treated differently. With the ban being a uniform measure relating to all exports of PCBs, the foreign investor was not treated differently on a factual basis. Nonetheless, only the foreign investor wanted to export PCB wastes, so that there is no doubt that the ban differentiated between the investors on a *de facto* basis. The central part of the decision undoubtedly focuses on the issue of protectionist intent. Even though the tribunal deemed the intent not to be decisive on its own, it used a considerable part of its findings for this issue. However, this discussion is intermingled with the portrayal of grounds for the justification of the measure. It also precedes the legal analysis of the elements of the standard of national treatment, thereby impeding a structured assessment of the tribunal's findings.

One concern deriving from the tribunal's approach relates to the focus on the government's intent. Even though the detailed record of the governmental appreciation of the issue is a forceful indication of the existence of protectionist intent, the fixation on intent is problematic: In a democratic society, several legislative players and other interested groups interact in the process of adopting a specific regulatory measure, so that a multitude of considerations will have been voiced in the legislative process. It may be possible that some of these interested parties voice protectionist ideas to underline their demand for a certain regulation. Does this mean that – for example – an environmental legislative measure cannot be justified even if it truly furthers a legitimate public policy?

The tribunal, nevertheless, addressed the environmental reasoning put forward by the Canadian government. In this context, the tribunal attempted not to substitute considerations of the Canadian government for its own assessment of the environmental risks: The evidentiary record quoted in the award exposed how some of the alleged concerns did not exist for the Canadian decision makers at the time of the implementation of the ban. In addition, the tribunal relied on the clear language of the Basel Convention and – for its conclusion that the Transboundary Agreement was consistent with the Convention – it further referred to a report issued by NAFTA's Commission for Environmental Cooperation.[73] In this light, the tribunal also accepted the legitimacy of one leg of the environmental argumentation put forward – namely of the need to safeguard the viability of domestic

---

[73] S.D. Myers Inc. v. Canada, Partial Award on the Merits, 13 November 2000, para 213 and accompanying footnote 36.

PCB disposal facilities – which reflected notions contained in the Basel Convention. Overall, the tribunal thus refrained from making its own environmental assessment and relied on information that the respondent government had at its disposal at the time the ban was implemented.[74]

The tribunal clearly took note of the environmental material that informed the interpretation of the treatment standards in this context, namely of the NAAEC, and the environmental rules confirmed in it, the environmental references in the preamble of the NAFTA and the Basel Convention. The methodological problems of the tribunal's interpretative approach to developing the set of environmental rules that characterise the understanding of the investment protection standards have been outlined above.[75] Nevertheless, the tribunal's material focus on the 'mutual supportiveness' of, inter alia, environmental protection and economic development is to be applauded. The approach can prove to be a relevant aspect for the adjudication of future disputes.

This set of rules concerning the relationship between environmental and economic considerations and especially the gist of Article 104 NAFTA also inspired the tribunal's finding that a state which can choose from a host of possible measures to protect a legitimate public purpose has to adopt the measure that has the least negative impact on international investment. However, this understanding can prove to be rather problematic, since it obliges the tribunal to assess how far the host state had other legitimate measures at its disposal which would have been as effective in furthering the environmental aim.[76] Evaluating the environmental effectiveness of several environmental measures could exceed the competence of an investment tribunal, as it should generally refrain from substituting the considerations of the state for its own. Also, it may be difficult for a tribunal to assess the feasibility and legitimacy of alternate measures: It is possible that

[74] Exceptions to this statement were concerns whether PCBs were covered by the Transboundary Agreement and whether they were considered as hazardous waste under U.S. legislation. In this regard, the tribunal found that an authoritative answer could have been swiftly and easily obtained, as was later the case, S.D. Myers Inc. v. Canada, Partial Award on the Merits, 13 November 2000, para 190.

[75] See 'Chapter 2 – The Influence of Environmental Concepts on the Interpretation of Investment Provisions' at pp. 126 *et seq*.

[76] See, *Kurtz*, Jürgen, 'A General Investment Agreement in the WTO? Lessons from Chapter 11 of NAFTA and the OECD Multilateral Agreement on Investment', 23 University of Pennsylvania Journal of International Economic Law 2002, 713 (749–750) who, in this context, criticises decisions of WTO panels for ignoring the realities of the regulatory decision-making process when determining the 'least trade-restrictive measure'.

the subsidies for the domestic PCB disposal industry endorsed by the tribunal in *S.D. Myers v. Canada* would have violated free trade obligations.[77]

In sum, the analysis of the decision suggests that environmental grounds abstractly qualify as legitimate public policy objectives and that they can be used to justify a discrepant effect of an adopted measure. However, the main task of the investment tribunal was to consider whether the measure resulting in differential treatment – i.e. the export ban – was strongly enough informed by the purported public policy. The evidentiary record set forth by the tribunal indicates that the real purpose of the ban was not the furthering of environmental objectives, but protectionist motivation masqueraded as legitimate regulation. The issue points to the core of the conflict between environmental and investment protection: Are environmental objectives used as a smokescreen for discrimination by the state – or do investment tribunals consider legitimate environmental regulation as "hidden protectionism"[78], jeopardising environmental policies? Although there is no definite answer to this question, the specific circumstances in *S.D. Myers v. Canada* suggest that the assessment of the tribunal was correct.

2. Methanex v. United States

The second relevant case involving a claim of breach of the standard of national treatment due to an environmental measure is *Methanex v. United States*. In this case, the tribunal had to decide whether the Californian ban on MTBE – a petrol additive – for environmental reasons violated the treatment standard. The foreign investor, a producer of the MTBE-feedstock methanol, complained that the regulation favoured the domestic ethanol industry with which he was competing, since ethanol can be used as a petrol additive instead of MTBE.

The focus of the decision relates to the identification of the relevant comparator. The tribunal expressed the understanding – as already mentioned above – that if there were any entrepreneurs identical to the investor in every aspect but nationality, only those should be considered as com-

---

77 The WTO aims to discipline the use of subsidies by its member states. In supporting national disposal facilities, a subsidy could have had adverse effects on interests of another state. It is remarkable that the tribunal did not consider it necessary to evaluate whether the host state could have adopted the measure without breaching other obligations.

78 Evaluating the decision in *S.D. Myers v. Canada* in this way, *Boute*, Anatole, 'Combating Climate Change and Securing Electricity Supply: The Role of Investment Protection Law', 16 European Environmental Law Review 2007, 227 (244).

parators.[79] In the case at hand, the foreign investor was not the only methanol producer in California; there were other domestic methanol producers. The tribunal held that only these domestic methanol producers were in 'like circumstances' with the investor.[80] Selecting these comparators, the tribunal had effectively ended the considerations of the merits of this claim: Since the ban uniformly applied to all MTBE produced, the treatment of the foreign investor was not less favourable. The tribunal stated:

> "The California ban does not differentiate between foreign investors or investments and various MTBE producers in California or, if it is relevant, methanol feedstock producers in the United States."[81]

In addition, the tribunal elaborated on the likeness of methanol and ethanol, which had been alleged by the investor. It stated that there was an important difference between the uses of these two products, since ethanol is an oxygenate, i. e. a petrol additive in its own right, whereas methanol is not used as a petrol additive, but only functions as a feedstock for MTBE, the oxygenate.[82] Accordingly, the tribunal found that ethanol and methanol products were not in competition, since the binary choice was between MTBE and other lawful and practicable oxygenates.[83] By way of obiter dictum, the tribunal further expressed its understanding that the terminology of 'like circumstances' is not to be interpreted in conformity with trade law provisions referring to 'any like, directly competitive or substitutable goods', so that the tribunal rejected seeking guidance from decisions of WTO panels on the interpretation of the likeness-criterion in the context of investment law.[84]

The decision to disregard a trade law-inspired interpretation of the likeness-criterion is extensive[85] – however, the complete exclusion of investors

---

79 Methanex v. United States, Award of 3 August 2005, Part IV Chapter B para 17. In the words of the tribunal it would be "perverse to ignore identical comparators if they were available and to use comparators that were less 'like'".

80 Methanex v. United States, Award of 3 August 2005, Part IV Chapter B paras 18–19.

81 Methanex v. United States, Award of 3 August 2005, Part IV Chapter B para 21.

82 Methanex v. United States, Award of 3 August 2005, Part IV Chapter B para 28.

83 Methanex v. United States, Award of 3 August 2005, Part IV Chapter B para 28.

84 Methanex v. United States, Award of 3 August 2005, Part IV Chapter B paras 29–37.

85 The tribunal highlights the wording enshrined in the parts of NAFTA which contain trade rules as opposed to the investment provisions, using different terminology. Therefore, in the understanding of the tribunal, the interpretation of the standard of national treatment is primarily guided by the wording contained in the

producing easily substitutable and therefore competitive products from the group of comparable investors appears too formalistic to accommodate the concerns of the investor. It can be assumed that the tribunal's decision to narrowly define the group of comparators results from the fact that the tribunal saw no indication of any malign intent on the part of the Californian authorities to discriminate against foreign producers of methanol, as the investor had centrally claimed.[86] Had the evidentiary record indicated that the protection of domestic industries was a central reason for the introduction of the ban, the tribunal would probably not have chosen the investors in 'like circumstances' as narrowly in such a light-hearted manner. It appears that the assessment of whether the regulating authority was motivated by protectionist intent is a central factor in the evaluation of the standard of national treatment, even if it is not explicitly mentioned.

Finding that there was no differential treatment, the tribunal relieved itself of assessing whether the MTBE-ban was warranted from an environmental perspective: the question of a legitimate justification did not arise. The decision indicates reluctance by tribunals to profoundly assess reasons for the justification of measures leading to differential treatment. Whereas the tribunal in this case concluded that the ban of MTBE was based on the "reasonable scientific grounds that MTBE contaminated groundwater and was difficult and expensive to clean up,"[87] it refrained from expressing an opinion on the environmental merit of the evidence before it. It is also questionable whether such an evaluation would have been in order, if the issue of justification had been relevant. In a case like this, where the tribunal finds that reasonable scientific evidence is relied on in a transparent legislative process, there is no reason for the tribunal to substitute the state's findings with its own evaluation.

---

provision itself and not by wording found in other treaties, Methanex v. United States, Award of 3 August 2005, Part IV Chapter B paras 29–37. This discussion of WTO law has been harshly criticised by commentators: *Swan*, Alan C., 'NAFTA Chapter 11 – "Direct Effect" and Interpretative Method: Lessons From Methanex v. United States', 64 University of Miami Law Review 2009, 21 (59–65); *Kurtz*, Jürgen, 'The Use and Abuse of WTO Law in Investor-State Arbitration: Competition and Its Discontents', 20 European Journal of International Law 2009, 749 (766–768); *Kurtz*, Jürgen, 'The Use and Abuse of WTO Law in Investor-State Arbitration: Competition and Its Discontents: A Rejoinder to Robert Howse and Efraim Chalamish', 20 European Journal of International Law 2009, 1095 (1097).

[86] The discussion of the alleged malign intent of the authorities is a central part of the decision. The core findings are summarised in Methanex v. United States, Award of 3 August 2005, Part III Chapter A para 102, a detailed assessment of the allegations can be found at Part III Chapter B paras 1–60.

[87] Methanex v. United States, Award of 3 August 2005, Part III Chapter A para 102.

3. Ethyl Corporation v. Government of Canada

The decision in *Methanex v. United States* eased fears of environmentalists stirred by the earlier case *Ethyl Corporation v. Government of Canada*. That case concerned a Canadian ban on all international and inter-provincial trade in methylcyclopentadienyl manganese tricarbonyl (MMT), a fuel additive providing octane enhancement. The investor was the sole importer of MMT into Canada, where the chemical produced in the U.S. was blended with fuel and distributed nationwide.[88] The host state alleged that the ban was necessary to protect the health of Canadians, the cleanness of air in the light of the precautionary principle;[89] however, the substance itself was not banned, due to insufficient evidence regarding its toxicity.[90] The case was settled between the parties after a Canadian panel on inter-provincial trade found that the government could have achieved its objective through a less trade restrictive measure.[91] Accordingly, the investment tribunal did not decide on the merits of the case.[92]

---

[88] Ethyl Corporation v. Canada, Statement of Claim of 2 October 1997, paras 8, 9.

[89] Ethyl Corporation.v. Canada, Statement of Defence of 27 November 1997, paras 30, 36–43; 59–60.

[90] Ethyl Corporation v. Canada, Statement of Claim of 2 October 1997, paras 17, 18.

[91] *Gaines*, Sanford E., 'Environmental Policy Implications of Investor-State Arbitration under NAFTA Chapter 11', 7 International Environmental Agreements: Politics, Law and Economics 2007, 171 (183). The host state paid U.S. $ 13 million to the investor. The background to this case illustrates that an economic interest was significant: The automobile industry favoured a ban of MMT because the substances reduces the efficacy of pollution control equipment in vehicles (182). See also *Soloway*, Julie A., 'Environmental Regulation as Expropriation: The Case of NAFTA's Chapter 11', 33 Canadian Business Law Journal 2000, 92 (119), who portrays how the import ban was partly based on "mixed scientific evidence as to the harmfulness of MMT" as well as meant as support for the national automobile and ethanol industry "in order to develop an alternate fuel strategy".

[92] The investor alleged the violation of the standard of national treatment, expropriation and the imposition of performance requirements.

In the light of subsequent decisions, it appears rather likely that an investment tribunal would have considered the treatment of the investor as a violation of its rights: A ban on the importation of a substance, the use of which is not prohibited because of insufficient evidence of environmental harm appears problematic. Similarly, *Soloway*, Julie A., 'Environmental Regulation as Expropriation: The Case of NAFTA's Chapter 11', 33 Canadian Business Law Journal 2000, 92 (119).

V. Intermediate Summary

The limited case law available illustrates the significant freedom that investment tribunals have when applying the standard of national treatment in scenarios involving environmental measures. There is no open battle between both sets of legal norms. Rather, tribunals implicitly assess the credibility of the environmental justification alleged by the respondent state for the differential treatment. In this context, it is important how the host state reached its environmental assessment, not whether the material assessment is correct. Indices of protectionist intent weigh against the plausibility of the environmental assessment. The overall impression of the process applied by the host state influences the choice of the relevant comparator or – likewise – the justification stage of the standard.

B. Most-Favoured Nation Treatment

The obligation to accord most-favoured nation treatment to a foreign investor is an element found in the vast majority of modern investment treaties. A typical clause provides that "neither Contracting State shall in its territory subject investments owned or controlled by investors of the other Contracting State or investors of the other Contracting State, as regards their activity in connection with investments, to treatment less favourable than it accords to investments or investors of any third State".[93] Such most-favoured nation clauses are generally reciprocal, unconditional and indeterminate in nature.[94] Since the exact wording in the respective agreements differ, it has been convincingly argued that slight differences in the wording of such clauses do not alter their function.[95]

Historically, most-favoured nation clauses operated predominantly in matters relating to trade, although their use has never been restricted to any

93 Slightly altered version of Article 3 2008 German Model BIT. See also Article 10. 4 CAFTA-DR; Article 1103 NAFTA, requiring parties to "accord to investors of another Party and to their investment treatment no less favourable than that it accords, in like circumstances, to investors of any other Party or of any non-Party with respect to the establishment, acquisition, expansion, management, conduct, operation, and sale or other disposition of investments in its territory."

94 *Schill*, Stephan W., 'Multilateralizing Investment Treaties through Most-Favored-Nation Clauses', 27 Berkley Journal of International Law 2009, 496 (501). See also the differentiated discussion by *Ziegler*, Andreas R., 'Most-Favoured-Nation (MFN) Treatment', in: Standards of Investment Protection (Reinisch, August (Ed.) 2008) 59 (65–66).

95 *Schill*, Stephan W., 'Multilateralizing Investment Treaties through Most-Favored-Nation Clauses', 27 Berkley Journal of International Law 2009, 496 (503).

subject area.[96] The fundamental working way of a most-favoured nation clause is that it introduces into the relationship between state A and B – the two states party to the agreement containing the clause – a benefit that state A has accorded by treaty to state C. State B can benefit from such a provision, although the benefit is not foreseen in the treaty concluded between state A and B. This phenomenon has been described as "drafting by reference",[97] because the clause automatically incorporates benefits granted to third states without requiring any further consent to this end. Accordingly, the most relevant function of most-favoured nation clauses is to disable states from entering into bilateral quid pro quo bargains, which extend preferential treatment to certain states and exclude others from it.[98] A commentator suggests that the clauses thus function as vehicles for the 'multilateralisation' of investment law.[99]

Accordingly, most-favoured nation provisions have been used to incorporate more favourable substantive investment protection provisions into a treaty. There is a host of issues connected with this incorporation of substantive standards in investment treaties. The debate focuses on restrictions on integration stemming from the subject matter, the temporal dimension, the personal applicability, and on possibilities for circumventing such restrictions.[100] These questions, however, are not relevant for this study. The relationship between substantive investment protection provisions and environmental norms and standards is the same, no matter whether the respective standard is literally contained in the treaty or if it is incorporated into the scope of an agreement via a most-favoured nation clause. Similarly, the intensely debated subject of most-favoured nation clauses constituting vehicles for the incorporation of more favourable procedural provisions[101] falls outside the scope of this survey.

---

96 *Ziegler*, Andreas R., 'Most-Favoured-Nation (MFN) Treatment', in: *Standards of Investment Protection* (Reinisch, August (Ed.) 2008) 59 (61–64); *Schill*, Stephan W., 'Multilateralizing Investment Treaties through Most-Favored-Nation Clauses', 27 Berkley Journal of International Law 2009, 496 (506, 509).

97 *Schwarzenberger*, Georg, International Law as Applied by International Courts and Tribunals (1957) p. 243.

98 *Schill*, Stephan W., 'Multilateralizing Investment Treaties through Most-Favored-Nation Clauses', 27 Berkley Journal of International Law 2009, 496 (502–503).

99 See generally *Schill*, Stephan W., 'Multilateralizing Investment Treaties through Most-Favored-Nation Clauses', 27 Berkley Journal of International Law 2009, 496–569.

100 See discussion in *Schill*, Stephan W., 'Multilateralizing Investment Treaties through Most-Favored-Nation Clauses', 27 Berkley Journal of International Law 2009, 496 (521 *et seq*); *Ziegler*, Andreas R., 'Most-Favoured-Nation (MFN) Treatment', in: Standards of Investment Protection (Reinisch, August (Ed.) 2008) 59 (74–84).

Accordingly, the analysis of the standard of most-favoured nation treatment is restricted to its basic substantive content. In this sense, the standard disallows treating a foreign investor from state B less favourably than an investor from state C. The thematic congruence of the standard of most-favoured nation treatment with the standard of national treatment – as well as the frequent systematic position of the two standards in the same clause – makes a strong case for interpreting both standards along the same lines: First, a comparator has to be identified – in the context of the most-favoured nation treatment a national of a third state. Second, it must be assessed whether the foreign investor has been treated less favourably than the investor of the third state was. Third, it has to be determined whether there is a legitimate policy to justify the discrepant effect of the measure.

I. Parkerings-Compagniet AS v. Lithuania

Although the standard of most-favoured nation treatment is not frequently invoked in this connotation in investment treaty arbitration, *Parkerings-Compagniet AS v. Lithuania* exemplifies the application of the standard in a case connected to environmental considerations. The case concerned a foreign investor that had taken part in a tender for the building of parking facilities near the old town of Vilnius. The investor complained, inter alia, that it had not been accorded most-favoured nation treatment because the authorities had not concluded a cooperation agreement with it and it was not allowed to build its proposed project, whereas another foreign investor was authorised by agreement to build its project on the site.[102]

In assessing the merits of the claim of the violation of most-favoured nation treatment, the tribunal first established that both investors were foreign investors from different countries.[103] Since both investors were engaged in similar activities – namely in the construction and management of parking garages – and competed for the same project, they were readily found

---

[101] See generally for the procedural implications of MFN-clauses, *Radi*, Yannick, 'The Application of the Most-Favoured Nation Clause to the Dispute Settlement Provisions of Bilateral Investment Treaties: Domesticating the "Trojan Horse"', 18 European Journal of International Law 2007, 757–774. See also *Ziegler*, Andreas R., 'Most-Favoured-Nation (MFN) Treatment', in: Standards of Investment Protection (Reinisch, August (Ed.) 2008) 59 (84–86).

[102] Parkerings-Compagniet AS v. Lithuania, ICSID Case No. ARB/05/8, Award of 11 September 2007, para 363.

[103] Parkerings-Compagniet AS v. Lithuania, ICSID Case No. ARB/05/8, Award of 11 September 2007, para 372.

to operate in a similar economic or business sector.[104] The different treatment of the two investors was also determined without difficulties, since the other investor was authorised to build its proposed project and had become party to a cooperation agreement, whereas the complaining investor was not. The final – and most important – test related to possible justifications for the difference in treatment:

First, the tribunal dealt with the denial of authorisation to build the proposed project. In this context, the tribunal intensively discussed differences between the two proposed projects. It established that the project proposed by claimant was considerably bigger than that of the other investor, but did not feel that this was a decisive difference.[105] However, the project proposed by claimant extended significantly into the 'old town' as defined by the UNESCO Convention and stretched especially near the historical site of the cathedral.[106] The tribunal took note of the concerns voiced within the administration of the respondent state in the planning phase, relating to a possible direct and indirect environmental impact of planned works, increased traffic in the old town, the impact of the building site on cultural properties – possibly causing the destruction of large areas of unexplored cultural layer and further architectural and archaeological concerns, such as the construction work constituting a violation of archaeological conventions signed by the state.[107] In this light, the tribunal decided that the extension of the building project into the old town proposed by claimant was a decisive difference between the two proposed projects.[108] It stated that:

> "the fact that [claimant's] project [...] extended significantly more into the Old Town as defined by the UNESCO, is decisive. Indeed, the record shows that the opposition raised against [claimant's project] were important and contributed to the Municipality decision to refuse such a controversial project. *The historical and archaeological preservation and environmental protection could be and in this case were a justification for the refusal of the project.* The potential negative impact of [claimant's project] in the Old Town was increased by its considerable size and its proximity with the culturally sensitive area of the Cathedral. Conse-

---

[104] Parkerings-Compagniet AS v. Lithuania, ICSID Case No. ARB/05/8, Award of 11 September 2007, para 373.

[105] Parkerings-Compagniet AS v. Lithuania, ICSID Case No. ARB/05/8, Award of 11 September 2007, paras 380, 391.

[106] Parkerings-Compagniet AS v. Lithuania, ICSID Case No. ARB/05/8, Award of 11 September 2007, para 385.

[107] Parkerings-Compagniet AS v. Lithuania, ICSID Case No. ARB/05/8, Award of 11 September 2007, paras 385–388.

[108] Parkerings-Compagniet AS v. Lithuania, ICSID Case No. ARB/05/8, Award of 11 September 2007, paras 392, 395–396.

quently, [claimant's project] was not similar with the [project] constructed by [the other investor]."[109] [Emphasis added.]

Thus the tribunal found that the differences in size and extension of the two projects were significant enough for the projects not to be in 'like circumstances', so that the municipality had legitimate grounds to distinguish between the two projects. Hence, with claimant failing to prove that the other investor had received treatment more favourable with respect to administrative procedures,[110] the refusal to authorise claimant's project was "justified by various concerns, especially in terms of historical and archaeological preservation and environmental protection".[111] With regard to the second incident of different treatment – the non-conclusion of a cooperation agreement –[112] the tribunal focused on the conditions contained in the agreements offered, which differed significantly. It emphasised the party autonomy of the public entity, which uses the defence of the public interest as its main benchmark and therefore normally does not discriminate when choosing to contract with one party and not another.[113] Thus, the tribunal found no breach of the treatment standard.

The tribunal effectively applied the test for the standard of most-favoured nation treatment as set forth above. In line with the formulations used by investment tribunals when assessing an alleged violation of the standard of national treatment, the tribunal concluded – after establishing that existing differences were justified – that the two competing investors were, after all, not in 'like circumstances'. In line with the approach chosen by tribunals adjudicating claims relating to a violation of the standard of national treatment, the tribunal did not profoundly assess the merits of the environmental and cultural concerns raised by the authorities: By confirming that the position and expansion of the proposed projects differed and by subsequently accepting that the arguments opposing claimant's project were important,

---

[109] Parkerings-Compagniet AS v. Lithuania, ICSID Case No. ARB/05/8, Award of 11 September 2007, para 392.

[110] Parkerings-Compagniet AS v. Lithuania, ICSID Case No. ARB/05/8, Award of 11 September 2007, para 393.

[111] Parkerings-Compagniet AS v. Lithuania, ICSID Case No. ARB/05/8, Award of 11 September 2007, para 396.

[112] Parkerings-Compagniet AS v. Lithuania, ICSID Case No. ARB/05/8, Award of 11 September 2007, para 409.

[113] Parkerings-Compagniet AS v. Lithuania, ICSID Case No. ARB/05/8, Award of 11 September 2007, para 411. The tribunal furthermore pointed to the differences between the two contracts: It summarised that the contract of the other investor foresaw for the relevant land to be bought by the municipality, whereas claimant had proposed the leasing of the land, with it remaining the owner of the land, Parkerings-Compagniet AS v. Lithuania, ICSID Case No. ARB/05/8, Award of 11 September 2007, para 420.

the tribunal assessed the justification for the measure in terms of coherence,[114] but did not review it materially. In a case comparing the treatment of two foreign investors, it is not so much the allegation of 'protectionist intent' that is important – in contrast to the decisions relating to the standard of national treatment. However, any form of malign intent would be treated just the same.

A very remarkable feature of the decision is that it indicates that cultural heritage and environmental concerns constitute components of the likeness-criterion: The ecological impact of an investment project can be a distinguishing criterion. Commentators applaud this finding in the award as a "break-through ruling"[115] and express the understanding that this approach could and should be transposed to other cases in which investment projects have differing impacts on the environment.[116] This approach allows legislators and administrators to adopt differing rules for similar investment projects – depending on their environmental impact. Furthermore, it is interesting that in the passage quoted, the tribunal seems to suggest that it is sufficient that environment-inspired concerns "contributed" to the refusal decision. This leaves interpretative scope for reflections that a regulatory measure can be justified, if environmental considerations are part of, but not the exclusive reason for, adopting the measure. However, the tribunal also ascertains that the environmental and cultural reasons were "determinant" and not "built up",[117] so that their impact has to be rather significant.

---

114 The tribunal expressly states that „[i]n the record, nothing convincing would show that such concerns were not determinant or were built up to reject [claimant's] project", Parkerings-Compagniet AS v. Lithuania, ICSID Case No. ARB/05/8, Award of 11 September 2007, para 396.

115 *Miles*, Kate, 'International Investment Law and Climate Change: Issues in the Transition to a Low-Carbon World', Society of International Economic Law, Working Paper No. 27/08, 2008, p. 31.

116 *Viñuales*, Jorge E., 'Access to Water in Foreign Investment Disputes', 21 Georgetown International Law Review 2009, 733 (757), mentioning as possible examples different treatment justified by the preservation of the quality or the availability of freshwater resources – when the pollution levels of the projects or their needs with regard to freshwater differ. *Miles*, Kate, 'International Investment Law and Climate Change: Issues in the Transition to a Low-Carbon World', Society of International Economic Law, Working Paper No. 27/08, 2008, p. 32, expresses the hope that other tribunals will follow the approach of the tribunal in *Parkerings-Compagniet AS v. Lithuania.*

117 Parkerings-Compagniet AS v. Lithuania, ICSID Case No. ARB/05/8, Award of 11 September 2007, para 396.

II. Intermediate Summary

To the extent reviewed in this survey, the standard of most-favoured nation treatment is very similar to the standard of national treatment. The limited case law available demonstrates that the approach to reconciling the treatment standard with environmental considerations is similar: The plausibility of the host state implementing the allegedly violating measure for environmental reasons is paramount. In the absence of any indices for malign motivation, the host state has not breached its obligation. However, there is no clean-cut approach as to whether this is a determination at the level of comparable circumstances or at the level of justification for differential treatment.

C. Prohibition Against Arbitrary and Discriminatory Measures

The third standard countering the discrimination of foreign investors is the prohibition of arbitrary or discriminatory measures. Although this standard is not as frequently enshrined in investment treaties as the two non-discrimination standards described above, it is prevalent enough to have been discussed in a multitude of investment decisions. The formulations used in investment treaties generally prohibit subjecting foreign investors to 'arbitrary or discriminatory measures'[118] or to 'unreasonable or discriminatory measures'[119] in the management, maintenance, use, enjoyment or disposal of their investments. As the wording underlines, the standard contains two separate protective scopes: One countering arbitrary measures and the other countering discriminatory measures. Despite the logical connection of these two protective notions, a measure does not have to be arbitrary and discriminatory to violate the standard. The standard is closely connected to the standard of fair and equitable treatment, from which it cannot always be clearly distinguished: Some arbitral tribunals focus on the overlap of the protective scope of both standards,[120] whereas others concentrate on their

---

[118] See, for example, Article 2 para 3 lit b U.S.-Ecuador BIT; Article 2 para 2 lit b U.S.-Argentina BIT.

[119] See, for example, Article 10 para 1 ECT; Article 3 para 1 Netherlands-Czech Republic BIT; Article 3 para 1 Netherlands-Estonia BIT.

[120] MTD Equity Sdn. Bhd. & MTD Chile S.A. v. Chile, ICSID Case No. ARB/01/7, Award of 25 May 2004, para 196; Rumeli Telekom A.S. and Telsim Mobil Telekomunikasyon Hizmetleri A.S. v. Kazakhstan, ICSID Case No. ARB/05/16, Award of 29 July 2008, para 681; Joseph Charles Lemire v. Ukraine, ICSID Case No. ARB/06/18, Decision on Jurisdiction and Liablity of 14 January 2010, para 259; Victor Pey Casado and President Allende Foundation v. Republic of

distinction and defined the standards separately.[121] In practice, it appears that the notion of non-arbitrariness is closely aligned with the standard of fair and equitable treatment, whereas the notion of non-discrimination is more akin to the standard of national treatment.

I. Elements of the Standard

A relevant understanding of the standard was developed by the ICJ in *Elettronica Sicula S.p.A.* When defining arbitrariness, the ICJ stated that this was "something opposed to the rule of law", namely "a wilful disregard of due process of law, an act which shocks, or at least surprises, a sense of juridical propriety."[122] In this context, the Court also asked whether the respective measures were "unreasonable or merely capricious".[123] Several investment tribunals relied on this understanding in their determination of the scope of the standard:[124] Underlining that these elements closely resemble the ordinary meaning of 'arbitrary',[125] tribunals identify the 'disre-

---

Chile, ICSID Case No. ARB/98/2, Award of 8 May 2008, paras 671-3; CMS Gas Transmission Company v. The Argentine Republic, ICSID Case No. ARB/01/8, Award of 12 May 2005, para 290; PSEG Global, Inc., The North American Coal Corporation, and Konya Ingin Electrik Uretim ve Ticaret Limited Sirketi v. Turkey, ICSID Case No. ARB/02/5, Award of 19 January 2007, para 261.

[121] Plama Consortium Limited v. Bulgaria, ICSID Case No. ARB/03/24, Award of 27 August 2008, para 184; Duke Energy Electroquil Partners & Electroquil S.A. v. Republic of Ecuador, ICSID Case No. ARB/04/19, Award of 18 August 2008, para 377. See also, *Schreuer*, Christoph, 'Protection against Arbitrary and Discriminatory Measures', in: The Future of Investment Arbitration (Rogers, Catherine A. et al. (Eds.) 2009) 183 (192).

[122] ICJ Case Concerning Elettronica Sicula S.p.A. (ELSI) (United States of America/Italy), Judgment of 20 July 1989, ICJ Reports 1989, 15 (76) para 128.

[123] ICJ Case Concerning Elettronica Sicula S.p.A. (ELSI) (United States of America/Italy), Judgment of 20 July 1989, ICJ Reports 1989, 15 (76) para 129.

[124] Duke Energy Electroquil Partners & Electroquil S.A. v. Republic of Ecuador, ICSID Case No. ARB/04/19, Award of 18 August 2008, para 378; Joseph Charles Lemire v. Ukraine, ICSID Case No. ARB/06/18, Decision on Jurisdiction and Liablity of 14 January 2010, para 262; Noble Ventures, Inc. v. Romania, ICSID Case No. ARB/01/11, Award of 12 October 2005, para 176; Azurix v. Argentine Republic, ICSID Case No. ARB/01/12, Award of 14 July 2006, para 392; Siemens A.G. v. Argentine Republic, ICSID Case No. ARB/02/8, Award of 6 February 2007, para 318. See also Genin and others v. Estonia, ICSID Case No. ARB/99/2, Award of 25 June 2001, para 371, albeit controversially emphasising the notion of 'bad faith'.

[125] Azurix v. Argentine Republic, ICSID Case No. ARB/01/12, Award of 14 July 2006, para 392; Siemens A.G. v. Argentine Republic, ICSID Case No. ARB/02/8, Award of 6 February 2007, para 318.

gard or substitution of the rule of law'[126] and the 'impropriety of the measure'[127] as most relevant criteria.

However, several investment tribunals had to apply a treaty standard prohibiting 'unreasonable or discriminatory measures'. It is not clear whether 'unreasonableness' in this context is understood as equalling 'arbitrariness'. Some tribunals explicitly found that the standards were identical,[128] whereas others understood the provision prohibiting unreasonable measures to have a wider protective scope.[129] While the issue of the correct interpretation of this diverging formulation of the standard cannot be decided in the context of this study, it has to be pointed out that a broader understanding of the protective scope further reduces the distinctiveness of the standard: Reasonableness of treatment is practically akin to fair and equitable treatment.[130]

With regard to what a 'discriminatory measure' is, the ICJ in *Elettronica Sicula S.p.A* developed a test according to which it is an intentional measure taken against a foreign investor – to favour a national investor – which is not taken under similar circumstances against another national.[131] Invest-

---

126 LG&E v. Argentina, ICSID Case No. ARB/02/1, Decision on Liability of 3 October 2006, para 162; Azurix v. Argentine Republic, ICSID Case No. ARB/01/12, Award of 14 July 2006, para 392; Siemens A.G. v. Argentine Republic, ICSID Case No. ARB/02/8, Award of 6 February 2007, para 318; Joseph Charles Lemire v. Ukraine, ICSID Case No. ARB/06/18, Decision on Jurisdiction and Liablity of 14 January 2010, para 263.

127 Enron Corporation and Ponderosa Assets, L.P. v. Argentine Republic, ICSID Case No. ARB/01/3, Award of 22 May 2007, para 281; Sempra Energy International v. The Argentine Republic, ICSID Case No. ARB/02/16, Award of 28 September 2007, para 318.

128 National Grid plc v. The Argentine Republic, Award of 3 November 2008, para 197; Plama Consortium Limited v. Bulgaria, ICSID Case No. ARB/03/24, Award of 27 August 2008, para 184, both focusing on whether something was done "capriciously, without reason". The equation of 'unreasonable' with 'arbitrary' measure is also, albeit indirectly, undertaken by the tribunal in EDF (Services) Limited v. Romania, ICSID Case No. ARB/05/13, Award of 8 October 2009, para 303.

129 BG Group Plc v. Argentina, Award of 24 December 2007, paras 341, 342, explicitly distinguishing between the two notions and stating that the expectations of the parties were guiding the interpretation of 'reasonableness'. AES Summit Generation Limited and AES-Tisza Erömü Kft v. The Republic of Hungary, ICSID Case No. ARB/07/22 (ECT), Award of 23 September 2010, paras 10.3.8, 10.3.9 stating that to be reasonable, a measure required a rational policy aimed at addressing a matter of public interest and furthermore, there had to be an appropriate correlation between this public policy objective and the measure adopted.

130 Biwater Gauff (Tanzania) Ltd. v. United Republic of Tanzania, ICSID Case No. ARB/05/22, Award of 24 July 2008, para 692; Saluka Investments BV (The Netherlands) v. The Czech Republic, Award of 17 March 2006, paras 309, 460.

131 ICJ Case Concerning Elettronica Sicula S.p.A. (ELSI) (United States of America/Italy), Judgment of 20 July 1989, ICJ Reports 1989, 15 (72–73) para 122.

ment tribunals rely on this definition of discrimination to determine whether the standard of non-discrimination was violated.[132] The elements established by the ICJ indicate the similarity of the prohibition of discriminatory measures with the standards of national and most-favoured nation treatment. This close connection is also recognised by investment tribunals.[133] There is, however, room for an important difference between these standards: The prohibition of discriminatory measures is not logically restricted to the discrimination based on the nationality of the investor. While some investment tribunals did focus on the nationality of the investor as distinguishing criterion,[134] others understood the protective scope more broadly and assessed whether differences in treatment existed, irrespective of the nationality of the comparators.[135] Accordingly, specific targeting of the foreign investor is not a prerequisite for finding a violation. It suffices that inves-

See also ICJ Asylum Case (Colombia/Peru) Judgment of 20 November 1950, ICJ Reports 1950, 266 (284).

[132] Biwater Gauff (Tanzania) Ltd. v. United Republic of Tanzania, ICSID Case No. ARB/05/22, Award of 24 July 2008, para 695; Rumeli Telekom A.S. and Telsim Mobil Telekomunikasyon Hizmetleri A.S. v. Kazakhstan, ICSID Case No. ARB/05/16, Award of 29 July 2008, para 680; BG Group Plc v. Argentina, Award of 24 December 2007, para 359; LG&E v. Argentina, ICSID Case No. ARB/02/1, Decision on Liability of 3 October 2006, para 146.

[133] BG Group Plc v. Argentina, Award of 24 December 2007, para 355, 356; Lauder v. Czech Republic, Award of 3 September 2001, para 220; Parkerings-Compagniet AS v. Lithuania, ICSID Case No. ARB/05/8, Award of 11 September 2007, para 291.

[134] Biwater Gauff (Tanzania) Ltd. v. United Republic of Tanzania, ICSID Case No. ARB/05/22, Award of 24 July 2008, para 695; Lauder v. Czech Republic, Award of 3 September 2001, para 220; Noble Ventures, Inc. v. Romania, ICSID Case No. ARB/01/11, Award of 12 October 2005, para 180; Rumeli Telekom A.S. and Telsim Mobil Telekomunikasyon Hizmetleri A.S. v. Kazakhstan, ICSID Case No. ARB/05/16, Award of 29 July 2008, para 680.

[135] AES Summit Generation Limited and AES-Tisza Erömü Kft v. The Republic of Hungary, ICSID Case No. ARB/07/22 (ECT), Award of 23 September 2010, para 10.3.53; BG Group Plc v. Argentina, Award of 24 December 2007, para 357; LG&E v. Argentina, ICSID Case No. ARB/02/1, Decision on Liability of 3 October 2006, para 148; Consortium R.F.C.C. v. Kingdom of Morocco, ICSID Case No. ARB/00/6, Award of 22 December 2003, para 51; Enron Corporation and Ponderosa Assets, L.P. v. Argentine Republic, ICSID Case No. ARB/01/3, Award of 22 May 2007, para 282; Sempra Energy International v. The Argentine Republic, ICSID Case No. ARB/02/16, Award of 28 September 2007, para 319; National Grid plc v. The Argentine Republic, Award of 3 November 2008, para 200; Marion Unglaube and Reinhard Unglaube v. Republic of Costa Rica, ICSID Case No. ARB/08/1, ICSID Case No. ARB/09/20, Award of 16 May 2012, para 263; Plama Consortium Limited v. Bulgaria, ICSID Case No. ARB/03/24, Award of 27 August 2008, para 184; Ulysseas, Inc. v. The Republic of Ecuador, Award of 12 June 2012, para 293; Merrill & Ring Forestry L.P. v. Canada, Award of 31 March 2010, para 94 (with regard to national treatment).

tors in like situations are treated differently without reasonable or justifiable grounds.

Shifting the focus away from different treatment due to the nationality of the investor, the test of discriminatory measures requires, first, the identification of a comparator, second, the application of a measure with detrimental effect on the foreign investor, but not the comparator, and, third, the absence of reasons justifying the difference in treatment. Accordingly, the determination of a violation of the protective standard closely resembles the test for finding a violation of national treatment. In both situations, the choice of the sector to look for a suitable comparator is very important. Abstractly, it is clear that one can only "compare like with like"[136]. However, to identify investors which are 'like' the foreign investor is bound to be difficult in practice.

The standard against discriminatory measures was applied in *Nykomb Synergetics Technology Holding AB v. Latvia*. This case concerned a foreign investor constructing a modern cogeneration plant in Latvia. For the construction, the investor had relied on legislation and a contract guaranteeing the payment of a double tariff for the produced energy and heat for the duration of eight years from the start of the production.[137] Despite the fact that the ecological advantages of the cogeneration technology were undisputed,[138] the state-owned energy company refused to pay the double tariff upon completion of the plant.[139] However, it continued to pay this double tariff to two domestic operators of cogeneration plants.[140]

In assessing the merits of the claim of a violation of the standard prohibiting discriminatory and arbitrary measures – which were considered as part

---

136 Nykomb Synergetics Technology Holding AB v. Latvia, Arbitration Institute of the Stockholm Chamber of Commerce (ECT), Award of 16 December 2003, para 4.3.2. See also on the importance of identifying the correct sector for comparing, National Grid plc v. The Argentine Republic, Award of 3 November 2008, para 200; Metalpar S.A. and Buen Aire S.A. v. Argentine Republic, ICSID Case No. ARB/03/5, Award of 6 June 2008, para 162.

137 Nykomb Synergetics Technology Holding AB v. Latvia, Arbitration Institute of the Stockholm Chamber of Commerce (ECT), Award of 16 December 2003, para 3.8.

138 Nykomb Synergetics Technology Holding AB v. Latvia, Arbitration Institute of the Stockholm Chamber of Commerce (ECT), Award of 16 December 2003, para 3.1.

139 Nykomb Synergetics Technology Holding AB v. Latvia, Arbitration Institute of the Stockholm Chamber of Commerce (ECT), Award of 16 December 2003, para 4.1.

140 Nykomb Synergetics Technology Holding AB v. Latvia, Arbitration Institute of the Stockholm Chamber of Commerce (ECT), Award of 16 December 2003, para 4.3.2.

of the standard of fair and equitable treatment – the tribunal implicitly perceived the domestic investors to function as relevant comparators to the foreign investor. Further, paying double tariffs to domestic investors, the state-owned energy company had treated the foreign investor differently. The – albeit short – debate of the tribunal focused on whether the foreign investor was 'like' the domestic energy suppliers. The respondent state argued that there were significant differences between the companies; however, it failed to identify any criteria allowing the application of different methodology in the calculation of tariffs. The tribunal finds that all the information available to it "suggests that the three companies are comparable, and subject to the same laws and regulations" and that in such a situation, the burden of proof lies on the state to prove that no discrimination has taken place.[141] Accordingly, the tribunal found that the state had not satisfied this burden and held that the investor had been subjected to discriminatory measures, thus finding a violation.

The discussion of the standard in the decision is brief. The only element emphasised by the tribunal relates to the shift of the burden of proof onto the respondent state to rebut the impression that the different energy suppliers are comparable. Although there are arguments against a shift of the burden of proof onto the respondent state as mentioned above, the decision of finding a violation in this case is convincing: The state had not provided evidence for its assertion that there were significant differences between the foreign and domestic investors. The main relevance of the award, however, does not lie in the methodological application of the standard, but more in the underlying interests at stake: In *Nykomb Synergetics Technology Holding AB v. Latvia* it is the investor that profits from regulation furthering environmentally friendlier technology, so that the protective interest of the investor and the furthering of environmental policies go hand in hand.

II. Intermediate Summary

Even though the list of illegitimately distinguishing criteria is not limited to the nationality of the investor, the prohibition against discriminatory measures largely poses the same questions as the two standards portrayed above. There is no case law describing a real conflict between these standards and environmental measures. However, there is no reason why an investment tribunal should approach such a conflict over discriminatory

141 Nykomb Synergetics Technology Holding AB v. Latvia, Arbitration Institute of the Stockholm Chamber of Commerce (ECT), Award of 16 December 2003, para 4.3.2.

measures differently than tribunals have done with regard to national and most-favoured nation treatment.

D. The Environmental Relevance of Standards of Non-Discrimination

Having established the protective scope of the standard of national treatment, of most-favoured nation treatment and of the prohibition against arbitrary and discriminatory measures as well as analysed respective cases containing environmental components, this study is going to identify criteria relevant for their application to situations involving environmental measures. As a second step, the criteria developed will be applied to environmental scenarios to raise the awareness for and illustrate potential conflicts. Since the overview has shown that the tests applied by tribunals adjudicating cases involving these standards are similar across all three standards, the study does not focus on potential differences: The protection against non-discrimination of investors is at the heart of the discussion, notwithstanding subtle differences among the standards. However, the notion of arbitrariness as contained in the standard prohibiting arbitrary or discriminatory measures will not be further considered in this context. As it is particularly closely connected to the standard of fair and equitable treatment, it is later reviewed in that context.

I. Criteria for Standards of Non-Discrimination in Environmental Context

As the analysis shows, a claim for the violation of one of the standards of non-discrimination requires the fulfilment of three elements, namely the identification of a relevant comparator, the different treatment of the investor and the comparator, and the absence of legitimate grounds for the justification of this difference. Whereas the portrayed case law indicates that all of these criteria can be influenced by environmental considerations, I maintain that it serves the environmental purpose of the potentially violating measure best to concisely evaluate the environmental legitimacy of a measure at the third step of the analysis – when assessing grounds for justifying the discrepant effect of a measure.

1. No Restrictive Comparator Test

Methanex v. United States exemplified how the conflict concerning the ban of a chemical implemented for environmental reasons can be "solved" through a narrow choice of comparators: The restrictive understanding of investors in 'like circumstances' led to the desired result, making a discussion about the environmental objective as ground for justification unnecessary. In this specific case, I am confident that the narrow concept of comparators did not alter the final decision. However, commentators have convincingly argued that in a situation in which the competition of two products is immediately obvious, the restriction of possible comparators does not do the protective standard justice.[142] While there is merit in discussing the different use and chemical characteristics of two substances that are considered to be in 'like circumstances', I maintain that the concept of the 'same business or economic sector' – as it is frequently applied by investment tribunals – offers all the necessary flexibility to determine an appropriate comparator. Had the tribunal in *Methanex v. United States* focused on the 'business sector' concept, it could easily have found that the relevant sector related to "products used to produce 'reformulated gasoline'[143]", thereby addressing the investor's primary concern.

Purposely restricting the group of possible comparators to avoid addressing the investor's concerns appears to be an easy solution. Ultimately, it does not help the legitimacy of the process: An investor that has extensively brought forward arguments regarding the competitive relationship between its product and a similar product cannot feel satisfied with a decision that is largely leaving this concern out of the discussion. A substantive discussion of the environmental reasons that justify a differentiating measure will also help to draw the line between legitimate public policy interests of the state and the protection of foreign investors. It makes the decision more comprehensible for the individual investor and – at the same time – furthers the consistency of the respective case law.

Environmentally minded commentators hailed the restrictive approach to determining the standard of national treatment by the tribunal in *Methanex v. United States*. They correctly point out that every claim, even a frivolous one, requires that the state allocate funds for the adjudicative pro-

---

142 *Kurtz*, Jürgen, 'The Use and Abuse of WTO Law in Investor-State Arbitration: Competition and Its Discontents', 20 European Journal of International Law 2009, 749 (768, 769); *Swan*, Alan C., 'NAFTA Chapter 11 – "Direct Effect" and Interpretative Method: Lessons From Methanex v. United States', 64 University of Miami Law Review 2009, 21 (59, 67, 68).

143 'Reformulated gasoline' is petrol with an added oxygenate. It fulfils environmental standards set by the U.S. 1990 Clean Air Act. The requirement for added oxygenates was repealed by the U.S. Congress in the 2005 National Energy Policy Act. See for the legislative developments, *Gaines*, Sanford E., 'Environmental Policy Implications of Investor-State Arbitration under NAFTA Chapter 11', 7 International Environmental Agreements: Politics, Law and Economics 2007, 171 (195).

cess.[144] Yet, the pre-emptive reduction of the potential success of the claim is not the right approach, either, because it risks ignoring cases of real discrimination[145]. Fortunately, not all investment cases afford the opportunity to decide on the merits by restrictively defining the relevant comparators. This argument against the restriction of the comparator-test, however, does not mean that investors never attempt to construct a comparison artificially. An investment tribunal predominantly relying on the 'business sector' test is well-situated to address legitimate concerns.

2. Relevance of Protectionist Intent

Case law indicates that with regard to the second element – the differences in treatment – a differential effect on the comparable investors is a requirement.[146] An effect on the investor will generally be measurable; otherwise, the investor would not have brought the dispute. In the environmental cases portrayed, the question of protectionist intent played an important role. Investment tribunals generally found a violation when there were clear indices of protectionist intent, even if its decisiveness was denied. The identification of protectionist or other malign intent generally seems to result in the finding of a violation of the respective standard.

The argumentation in *S.D. Myers Inc. v. Canada* illustrates a problem stemming from the focus on potential protectionist intent: To what extent is the environmental legitimacy of a measure tainted or annihilated by one person in the legislative process who is driven by a protectionist agenda? In a democratic legislative body, it is possible that some participants desire a measure to support domestic industries, whereas others are motivated by support for the genuine environmental background of the measure. This fact underlines that establishing protectionist intent cannot absolve the tribunal from independently assessing the environmental merit of a measure: The

144 *Dougherty*, Kara, 'Methanex v. United States: The Realignment of NAFTA Chapter 11 with Environmental Regulation', 27 Northwestern Journal of International Law and Business 2007, 735 (746, 749).

145 Unwarranted claims should be addressed in the distribution of costs. An investment tribunal has discretion in allocating costs, see, for example, Article 42 2010 UNCITRAL Arbitration Rules. Accordingly, a tribunal can determine that the costs of the arbitration be borne by the unsuccessful party. The tribunal in Methanex v. United States, Award of 3 August 2005, Part V, paras 12, 13 made such an allocation.

146 As phrased by the tribunal in Marion Unglaube and Reinhard Unglaube v. Republic of Costa Rica, ICSID Case No. ARB/08/1, ICSID Case No. ARB/09/20, Award of 16 May 2012, para 267: "While evidence of discriminatory intent may be relevant, and may reinforce such a finding, it is the fact of unequal treatment which is key."

fact that somebody involved in the administrative process of adopting the measure in question has expressed protectionist intent cannot lead to a complete disregard of reasons for environmental justification.

Whether the expression of protectionist ideas is on the record is – arguably – coincidental and influenced by a multitude of factors, such as the transparency of the legislative process. Accordingly, the ease with which it can be established cannot be decisive for the evaluation of the legitimacy of the measure. How far protectionist intent has tainted a measure will depend on the appreciation of the specific factors of each case: Even in *S.D. Myers Inc. v. Canada*, where the tribunal found protectionist intent to be a driving force behind the implementation of the export ban, the tribunal summarily assessed whether the environmental justifications brought forward by the respondent state had merit. The overall process to adopt the measure has to be evaluated.

3. Justification

The third element of the test relates to the justification for the differential treatment, to the effect that the comparators are – after all – not in a 'like situation'. This requires, first, that the measure be based on a legitimate policy which the state wanted to further. As was stated above, investment tribunals appreciate the legitimacy of the underlying policy in broad terms. Every state retains the competence to legislate and implement measures to further the policy aims it considers relevant – provided they are not countering the aims underlying the investment treaty. Accordingly, there is little doubt that environmental policies do qualify abstractly. However, an investment tribunal will not have to evaluate the general notion of 'furthering environmental protection', but may have to assess more precisely, whether the particular elements of an environmental reason justify a discrepant effect.

a) Deference

States have sovereignty to determine policy objectives. This material competence is reflected in the level of deference accredited to the state by investment tribunals reviewing adopted measures: The tribunal is not placed to substitute its own assessment of an environmental problem for that of the state, so that the review of an environmental measure by an investment tribunal can only be summary. Accordingly, I find that an investment tribunal should determine, whether the environmental reasons invoked by the state to justify a measure are cogent, by applying a control of coherence.

The tribunal in *Parkerings-Compagniet AS v. Lithuania* applied such a 'coherence review' to the differences between the two planned projects: It established that the alleged differences in size and location between the projects existed and simply concluded that in the light of these differences the state could treat the projects differently. Accordingly, the tribunal refrained from independently assessing the impact and relevance of the existing distinction between the projects.

The tribunal in *S.D. Myers Inc. v. Canada* was not so brief, since the decision against the respondent state required a more profound assessment of the alleged environmental reasons: The deference owed to the state necessitated dealing with the complex environmental arguments brought forward by the state. However, the tribunal refrained from substituting the state's environmental rationale and renounced the possibility to determine the 'correct' interpretation of the environmental norms at issue. The assessment is restricted to arguments used and voiced by the respondent state itself – to establish that the environmental concerns could not have been the real motivation for the export ban. In the light of the visible protectionist intent connected to the adoption of the ban, the tribunal emphasised the lack of legitimate concerns for the introduction of this measure. It considered the overall assessment as tainted.

As an expression of deference owed to the state, tribunals assert restraint in independently assessing the scientific evidence on which the respective state relied when implementing the measure. For example, the tribunal in *Methanex v. United States* satisfied itself with summarily asserting that there were reasonable scientific grounds that the banned oxygenate contaminated groundwater, necessitating expensive clean ups. The reluctance of tribunals to extensively analyse the scientific evidence on which the state based its policy measure is to be welcomed, because a tribunal placing a different emphasis on the evidence relied on by the state in its regulatory process would encroach on the policy space of the state.

b) Reasonable Nexus

Further, there has to be a 'reasonable nexus' between the measure and the policy objective. As asserted above, tribunals have so far not succeeded in establishing criteria for the strength of the required nexus. Accordingly, there is merit in basing the assessment of the nexus on the following formula: the more important the policy objective, the less strong the connection between the policy and the measure has to be. In the light of the deference owed to the state, tribunals should not impose their judgment concerning the essentiality of a certain measure, but should rationally assesses the risks and dangers combated by the policy. The connection between the policy and the measures is one of 'reasonableness'. This requirement underlines the margin of appreciation that the state has in choosing the specific measures it attempts to adopt.

In any case, 'reasonableness' requires a connection which is less close than 'necessity'. 'Necessity' is the strength required for the relevant nexus in the 'general exceptions' clauses in WTO law.[147] In WTO law, a necessary measure is appropriately described as being "located significantly closer to the pole of 'indispensable' than to the opposite pole of simply 'making a contribution to'" on the "range of degrees of necessity".[148] It appears that the 'reasonable nexus' requirement of investment law, in contrast, spans the whole width of the described range of degrees of necessity. A reasonable nexus exists when the measure makes a – perhaps significant – contribution to furthering the policy objective. A further test applied in the WTO context is whether any alternative – that is not impacting on the rights of other states – is "reasonably available" for the state to achieve its desired level of protection regarding the pursued objective.[149]

There appears to be a strong intention on the part of practitioners and academics to accord the interpretation of requirements in international investment law to WTO law.[150] However, in my opinion – at least in the context of assessing the justification for differential treatment – this intention should not be followed. The first reason is that investment treaties generally do not contain an express 'general exceptions' clause requiring the nexus to be 'necessary'. There is no rule in international law which requires immanent grounds for justification to be narrower than those grounds expressly contained in the text of a treaty – even less so if different treaties are concerned. Second, the differences between the two systems indicate that states should be granted a wider margin of appreciation in investment proceedings. Trade law relates to measures which restrict goods and ser-

---

[147] Article XX GATT, with the exception of certain objectives, for which it is enough that the measures are "relating to" the objectives, such as "the conservation of exhaustible natural resources".

[148] Korea – Measures Affecting Imports of Fresh, Chilled and Frozen Beef, DS161/AB/R, WTO Appellate Body Report of 11 December 2000, para 161.

[149] United States – Measures Affecting the Cross-Border Supply of Gambling and Betting Services, DS285/AB/R, WTO Appellate Body Report of 7April 2005, para 308.

[150] See, for example, *Kurtz*, Jürgen, 'The Use and Abuse of WTO Law in Investor-State Arbitration: Competition and Its Discontents', 20 European Journal of International Law 2009, 749–771 and *Grierson-Weiler*, Todd/*Laird*, Ian A.,'Standards of Treatment', in: The Oxford Handbook of International Investment Law (Muchlinski, Peter (Ed.) 2008) 259 (295).

vices originating in one state from being freely distributed in another state. Accordingly, a measure that bans the import of certain goods lacking or possessing certain characteristics has impacts on the legislative territory of the state of origin. The trade measure thus has characteristics of imposing the policy concerns of the importing state onto the state of origin, which effectively is an extraterritorial application of environmental or other policy concerns. This territoriality issue does not arise when a state adopts a measure for application in its own territory – as is the case in the investment context. Here, the measure is more closely connected to the legislation within the host state and the state is to be restricted in its autonomy to regulate as little as possible.[151] Accordingly, the requirement that the measure be close to 'indispensable' – an understanding that investment tribunals have adopted in assessing the standard of necessity in customary international law –[152] would be too intense a restriction of the legitimate pursuit of adopting public policy measures.

c) Alternative, Less Disruptive Measures

The issue of other 'reasonably available' measures – albeit without expressly relying on WTO law – was central to the decision in *S.D. Myers Inc. v. Canada*. Probably inspired by the similar wording of Article 104 NAFTA, the tribunal held that whenever a state can achieve its chosen level of environmental protection through a variety of equally effective and reasonable means, it is obliged to adopt the alternative that is most consistent with "open trade".[153] The tribunal did not consider the question

---

151 In my understanding, it is important to keep in mind that the starting point for the assessment of an environmental measure in investment law differs from that taken in international trade law. Therefore, investment tribunals should be cautious when taking guidance from trade law. For example, the WTO Agreement on the Application of Sanitary and Phytosanitary Measures (SPS Agreement) expresses the understanding that the state needs to justify the introduction of such measures. Measures shall be "applied only to the extent necessary to protect [the respective, limited set of policies]" (Article 2 para 2). The express aim of the SPS Agreement is to bring about a harmonisation of standards and this makes it necessary for any state to accept the standards of other states as equivalent. This, however, is not the premise in investment law, where the state remains free to set any level of protection for any reason it considers relevant. As long as that level has been set prior to the investment, it does not require any justification. The SPS Agreement, on the contrary, states that a measure shall "not [be] maintained without sufficient scientific evidence" (Article 2 para 2). Similarly, for measures introduced later, the level of scrutiny also differs.

152 Continental Casualty Company v. Argentina, ICSID Case No. ARB/03/9, Award of 5 September 2008, paras 196–199.

153 *Antal*, Edit, 'Lessons From NAFTA: The Role of the North American Commission for Environmental Cooperation in Conciliating Trade and Environment', 14

whether a rule referring to 'open trade' should be guiding the outcome of an investment dispute. The final determination was based on the finding that the respondent state had not chosen the measure that was least disruptive of international trade, since the tribunal identified two measures that – in its opinion – could have furthered the state's legitimate policy without violating its investment protection obligations.

Obliging a state to adopt the measure 'least disruptive of international investment' to further a legitimate policy objective goes beyond the proportionality approach commonly applied by national courts in proceedings. Such a requirement would not allow a state to choose from a variety of equally effective measures, but narrows the choice down so that only one measure remains legitimate. In my opinion, an investment tribunal should not engage in such an in-depth assessment of other potential measures. First, it is doubtful if an international tribunal is adequately positioned to assess other measures a state could have legitimately adopted: Whereas a national court, as part of the judicial system and accordingly familiar with the national and international obligations of the state, is set up to properly oversee and evaluate the whole legal order within which the entity of the state has acted, an international tribunal is not in the same situation. An investment tribunal is not necessarily familiar with the relevant material to correctly assess other international obligations and internal competences to conclude which alternative measures the public entity could have taken. The decision in *S.D. Myers Inc. v. Canada* itself is a case in point. Whether the subsidies for the national PCB disposal facilities suggested by the tribunal would have been legal under the state's trade obligations, is open to debate.

Especially in cases concerning complex environmental issues, it may not be easy for an investment tribunal to find out which other measures a state could have legitimately taken without violating other international obligations. This issue is interconnected with the more practical problem for a tribunal to assess the environmental benefit of different measures. Such an assessment requires an individual evaluation of the scientific evidence relied upon by the state, which would significantly broaden the scope of review in comparison to the standard invoked above. An example is provided by the facts underlying the decision in *Methanex v. United States*. In this case, the investor argued that the ban of MTBE was not the most efficient measure to further the environmental objective, namely to prevent the pollution of groundwater. It argued that repairing and controlling the leaking under-

---

Michigan State Journal of International Law 2006, 167 (176) evaluates the approach taken as an "arbitrary interpretation". Also critical, *Moloo*, Rahim/*Jacinto*, Justin, 'Environmental and Health Regulation: Assessing Liability under Investment-Treaties', 29 Berkeley Journal of International Law 2011, 1 (36).

ground storage tanks in which petrol was stored was effectively less disruptive to its investment.[154] A tribunal seeking to identify the measure equally efficient, but least disruptive of international investment would have had to assess these arguments and – effectively – substitute the state's considerations with its own understanding of a practicable solution.

In my opinion, this assessment would be outside the scope of review of a tribunal. It would also significantly reduce the freedom of the state to choose how to implement its policy objectives.[155] In the example, the state should decide whether a – potentially labour-and cost-intensive – control system is as secure as a ban of MTBE, unless factors indicate that the assessment undertaken by the state is flawed by inappropriate considerations. An investment tribunal should control the process of the evaluation of evidence by the state, but not independently assess this evidence. The restricted competence of review of an investment tribunal is arguably reflected in its limited capacity regarding the type of relief it can grant. The tribunal's competence is restricted to deciding whether the investor receives compensation for its loss, but the tribunal cannot challenge, stop or prohibit the respective measure as such. This reduced competence indicates that international law does not foresee for investment tribunals to independently assess which measures a state should adopt. It would be an anachronism for investment tribunals to indirectly make such a determination when considering whether standards of non-discrimination were violated. Tribunals should restrict their analysis to the evaluation whether the assessment process of the state was flawed – especially with regard to the position of the foreign investor.

4. Burden of Proof

It has been demonstrated above that it is contentious – once the investor has established a *prima facie* case of discrimination – if the burden of proof shifts to the respondent state to prove that the apparent discrimination is only a discrepant effect of a legitimate measure furthering a public policy.[156] Some commentators, inter alia relying on a comparison of the invest-

---

[154] Methanex v. United States, Claimant Methanex Corporation's Reply to the Amicus Curiae Submissions of Earthjustice and the International Institute for Sustainable Development of 23 April 2004, paras 9–10.

[155] Similarly sceptical of investment tribunals evaluating the effectiveness of governmental measures because of its potential to restrict the host state's margin of appreciation, *Romson*, Åsa, 'International Investment Law and the Environment', in: Sustainable Development in World Investment Law (Cordonier Segger, Marie-Claire et al. (Eds.) 2011) 37 (44–45).

[156] See above at pp. 173 *et seq.*

ment regime with the WTO system, strongly argue in favour of a shifting of the burden of proof.[157] Without intending to conclusively determine the issue for all situations, I maintain that shifting the burden of proof in cases involving environmental measures unduly conflicts with the deference owed to the state.

This does not mean that the alleged or real reasons relied on by the state in the adoption of the respective environmental measure would not coherently be evaluated. It is my understanding that a tribunal will evaluate all the material before it – with some elements indicating that the measure is discriminatory and others indicating that the measure is legitimate. It has been demonstrated that the finding of protectionist intent, for example, forcefully signals the absence of the legitimacy of the measure – an allegation which the state would have to comment on. In its process of evaluation, a tribunal can draw disadvantageous conclusions from the lack of reasoning or participation on the part of the state irrespective of a shift of the burden of proof. The impact of the burden of proof only becomes relevant in a situation of *non liquet*, i.e. in a situation, when – despite argumentation on the merits by both parties – it remains unclear whether the measure constitutes a legitimate policy consideration. In such a situation, the state – in recognition of its regulatory authority – should be able to profit from the benefit of the doubt.[158]

II. Application of Criteria to Different Scenarios

The criteria developed for assessing violations of the standards of non-discrimination in situations involving environmental regulation are now applied to several specific scenarios. The broad notions of potential conflicts were portrayed in the first chapter on environmental norms and standards.[159]

---

[157] *Grierson-Weiler*, Todd/*Laird*, Ian A., Ian A.,'Standards of Treatment', in: The Oxford Handbook of International Investment Law (Muchlinski, Peter (Ed.) 2008) 259 (295); *Wyllie*, Candice A., 'A Comparative Analysis of Nondiscrimination in Multilateral Agreements: North American Free Trade Agreement (NAFTA), Energy Charter Treaty (ECT), and General Agreement on Tariffs and Trade (GATT)', 18 Willamette Journal of International Law and Dispute Resolution 2010, 64 (68, 107).

[158] Similarly, the solution favoured by *Moloo*, Rahim/*Jacinto*, Justin, 'Environmental and Health Regulation: Assessing Liability under Investment-Treaties', 29 Berkeley Journal of International Law 2011, 1 (59). They argue – in line with their interpretation of the standard in close connection to its wording – that the burden is on the investor to prove that it is in 'like circumstances' with a comparator. Accordingly, whether "a legitimate regulatory distinction precludes a finding of 'like circumstances' is a factor to be taken into account by the tribunal in determining whether the claimant has met its burden".

[159] See, in 'Chapter 1 – Environmental Norms and Principles' at pp. 82 *et seq*.

The described scenarios are only examples which give an indication of potential conflicts, but they do not represent a comprehensive overview. The purpose of this application is to raise awareness for potential practical conflicts between environmental measures and investment protection standards.

1. Scenario No 1: Introduction and Application of Environmental Regulation

The first set of scenarios concerns the classical cases of conflicts between environmental measures and standards of non-discrimination of foreign investors and investments: Due to allegedly environmental considerations, the state introduces or implements regulation negatively affecting some, but not all investors. A foreign investor complains that it is targeted by the respective environmental measure, whereas other comparable domestic or foreign investors are not affected in the same way. Accordingly, the investment tribunal has to apply the standards of national or most-favoured nation treatment and those prohibiting discriminatory measures in order to differentiate between measures legitimately furthering environmental objectives and those using a 'green disguise' to discriminate against foreign investors.

a) Establishment of the Investment – Refusal of Permits

It is the general rule that foreign investors have to accept the regulatory framework of the host state as it stands when they start their investment activity.[160] This acceptance obviously encompasses environmental norms and standards in force in the host state. Accordingly, the potential for conflicts between environmental norms and investment protection rights is limited in the establishment phase. However, *Parkerings-Compagniet AS v. Lithuania* exemplified that the foreign investors' rights of non-discrimination can be at stake, if the implementation of one investment project is allowed, whereas the necessary permits for a similar, but foreign investment are refused. To set this issue aside from the general question of whether a respective investment treaty grants foreign investors a right to establishment,[161] the focus of the scenario is on situations in which the foreign investor has undertaken preparatory works or taken part in a tender. Such a component

---

160 This rule is reflected in the expression in many investment treaties that the 'investment' must be made in accordance with the laws of the host state or that 'investment' is defined in reliance on the laws of the host state. See also, Gami Investments, Inc. v. Mexico, Award of 15 November 2004, para 93.

161 See on the right to establishment, *Sornarajah*, M., The International Law on Foreign Investment (2010) pp. 96 *et seq.*

of preparation for the commencement of the proper investment is the starting point of the analysis.

The scenario is embedded in the general issue whether differing environmental impacts of investment projects constitute a reason to treat the projects differently. Abstractly, this question can clearly be answered in the affirmative. No investment tribunal will find fault with a host state demanding the fulfilment of different requirements for the construction or operation of investment projects in different ecological surroundings: A state, for example, can restrict the settlement of investment projects in designated environmental protection areas or subject them to tighter emission standards. That the geographic location and stretch of a project with regard to a designated protection zone – and therefore its environmental and cultural impact – is a legitimate ground to differentiate between two otherwise similar investment projects, is also supported by the decision in *Parkerings-Compagniet AS v. Lithuania.*

The environmental impact of a project is not exclusively defined by its location, but also by a multitude of other factors. The results of studies of environmental impact assessment[162] are relevant instruments to further differentiate between investment projects. Environmental impact assessment is mandatory in many states and can result in the conclusion that the intended project of a foreign investor will not receive the necessary permits because its disadvantageous impact on the environment is too big. Even if a similar project is granted the necessary permits at the same time, the differential treatment will be found to be justified, as long as it reflects differing results in the environmental impact assessment. The decision in *Parkerings-Compagniet AS v. Lithuania* further demonstrates that the standards of non-discrimination in this line-up do not only protect against potential material discrimination. A foreign investor is also protected against 'procedural discrimination', i. e. against being held to higher administrative standards or obtaining relevance clearance more difficultly.[163] In applying these findings, which can be compared to the process determining the – environmental – impact of the respective investment projects, an investor can also claim a procedural violation of a standard of non-discrimination: It would have to show that its comparators benefited from a more lenient application of the administrative requirements relating to the environmental impact assessment.

162 See generally on environmental impact assessment, *Craik*, Neil, The International Law of Environmental Impact Assessment (2008). The author identifies various different strands of environmental impact assessment commitments. The relevant criteria in a specific case, however, will be determined by the laws of the host state.

163 Parkerings-Compagniet AS v. Lithuania, ICSID Case No. ARB/05/8, Award of 11 September 2007, paras 393, 394.

b) Introduction of Environmental Restrictions After Investment Has Been Placed

The highest potential for conflicts between environmental regulation and the protection of investment arises when environmental restrictions are introduced after the investment has been made. In this case, the investor based its calculations on a regulatory framework, which is retrospectively adjusted. However, the potentially frustrated expectations of the investor are not central in the context of potential violations of the standard of non-discrimination. Rather, the introduction of environmental restrictions is at the heart of the issue: Does the introduction of a specific environmental measure or restriction or the way in which it is introduced discriminate against the foreign investor?

The evaluation of whether a respective measure is discriminatory is clearly closely connected to the specific measure under consideration. However, this overview attempts to illustrate a few connectors for potential discrimination. Obviously, a tightening of restrictions on emissions or on the use of certain substances affecting the environment is more onerous for industries that use or produce these substances or for those that have more significant emissions than for industries not relying on the respective substances. However, factual differences in impact alone do not result in such measures being discriminatory. The measures will only be considered discriminatory if the intense impact is intended or when the restrictive measure is not based on sound environmental justification. It follows, for example, that climate change mitigation measures generally do not constitute discrimination of carbon-intensive industries, even though those will have to bear the brunt of a strengthening of emission reduction targets.[164]

The introduction of new – and innovative – schemes aiming at environmental protection can pose questions relating to discrimination in their introductory phase. An example is a cap-and-trade system like the European Emissions Trading Scheme. A system based on an absolute overall number of allowances requires an objective process of allocation based on a coherent baseline: the limited pool of allowances has to be allocated untainted by discrimination. In their basic tenets, innovative environmental schemes accordingly do not pose questions completely different from traditional administrative set-ups. The same is true for the treatment of 'new' investments created

---

164 Generally, *Schill*, Stephan W., 'Do Investment Treaties Chill Unilateral State Regulation to Mitigate Climate Change?', 24 Journal of International Arbitration 2007, 469 (470, 477). *Contra*, *Miles*, Kate, 'International Investment Law and Climate Change: Issues in the Transition to a Low-Carbon World', Society of International Economic Law, Working Paper No. 27/08, 2008, p. 33.

through the implementation of emission trading schemes. Whether there are legitimate reasons to differentiate between, for example, entities owning carbon credits to comply with their own environmental obligations and entities owning carbon credits purely for investment purposes[165] would have to be decided in the application of the general rules as portrayed above. However, the favouring of some market sectors over others – due to the administrative practicalities arising from the implementation of the European Emissions Trading Scheme – will more intensely be scrutinised below.

In the realm of WTO law, commentators have pointed to the potential of climate change mitigation measures violating trade obligations, for example with regard to the introduction of emission trading schemes implementing the Kyoto Protocol.[166] Specifically, one commentator argues that the rules implementing the European Emissions Trading Scheme, which disallows the participation of emission allowance brokers from a country not party to the Kyoto Protocol, constitute unjustified discrimination on the basis of nationality.[167] Whereas potential implications of the Kyoto Protocol for the standard of non-discrimination in the investment context have been highlighted elsewhere,[168] there is so far little evidence that nationality restrictions in the context of an emissions trading scheme are in reality likely to conflict with investment protection obligations. The creation of carbon credits or the allocation of allowances is closely connected to location – rather than nationality – and will generally be guided by rules implemented by the host state of the respective investment. There is no rule in the Marrakech Accords to suggest that emission reduction to obtain carbon credits cannot be effectuated by a foreign investor from a country not party to the Kyoto Protocol.[169]

165 See for this and similar examples relating to investment in carbon credits, *Bennett*, Lisa, 'Are tradable Carbon Emissions Investments? Characterization and Ramifications under International Investment Law', 85 New York University Law Review 2010, 1581 (1605).

166 *Green*, Andrew, 'Climate Change, Regulatory Policies and the WTO: How Constraining are Trade Rules?', 8 Journal of International Economic Law 2005, 143 (151, 187–189); *Martin*, Marisa, 'Trade Law Implications of Restricting Participation in the European Union Emissions Trading Scheme', 19 Georgetown International Environmental Law Review 2007, 437–474.

167 *Martin*, Marisa, 'Trade Law Implications of Restricting Participation in the European Union Emissions Trading Scheme', 19 Georgetown International Environmental Law Review 2007, 437 (439).

168 *Werksman*, Jacob/*Baumert*, Kevin A./*Dubash*, Navroz K., 'Will International Investment Rules Obstruct Climate Protection Policies? An Examination of the Clean Development Mechanism', 3 International Environmental Agreements: Politics, Law and Economics 2003, 59 (71–75).

169 The parties of the Kyoto Protocol had the legitimate intention to point out that states not party to the Protocol should not profit from the implemented systems. However, the Protocol is quiet on the role of private – investing – entities. See also

The Protocol relates to states reducing emissions, and not to the entity implementing the actual reduction project. Even though the Kyoto Protocol differentiates between several categories of states – parties and non-parties, Annex I and non-Annex I parties, parties in compliance and non-compliant parties – there is no obligation to expand this understanding to investors coming from these states.[170] There may be political arguments for restricting investors from non-party home states in this context, so that their home states do not indirectly profit from the regime. In reality, however, the ease with which joint ventures can lead to a different nationality of an investor as well as the assumption that the recipient states of Joint Implementation or CDM projects consider such investment as advantageous, in my opinion results in little interest in restricting the goup of potential participants. Accordingly, I do not share the opinion that the nationality of an investor does pose a significant problem in this context.

aa) Restrictive Regulation of Some, but Not All Business Sectors

The potential for conflicts between environmental regulation and investment protection is elevated after the investment has been made. A relevant example for the present context is the adoption of the environmental regulation of some industrial sectors, but not of all sectors. The targeting of some industries, but not of others, first invokes the question of the comparability of the different sets of industrial sectors. Whereas I argued above that the assessment of potential clashes between environmental regulation and investment protection should generally not be resolved in the context of identifying a comparator, claims of investors in one business sector regarding an allegedly more favourable treatment of another business sector necessitate a rigid comparison of both sets of sectors.

Different business or industrial sectors by definition have distinguishing characteristics, so that a comparison between the treatment of one sector and the treatment of the other sector requires the establishment of funda-

---

Werksman, Jacob/*Baumert*, Kevin A./*Dubash*, Navroz K., 'Will International Investment Rules Obstruct Climate Protection Policies? An Examination of the Clean Development Mechanism', 3 International Environmental Agreements: Politics, Law and Economics 2003, 59 (71).

170 This rather straight-forward analysis, however, does not prevent commentators from assuming that host states would choose such an approach. The reliance on this hypothesis obviously leads to the determination of starker potential for conflict than would be necessary. See, for example, *Baetens*, Freya, 'The Kyoto Protocol in Investor-State Arbitration: Reconciling Climate Change and Investment Protection Objectives', in: Sustainable Development in World Investment Law (Cordonier Segger, Marie-Claire et al. (Eds.) 2011) 683 (699–701).

mental similarities, which disallow reliance on existing divergences for differential treatment. Existing similarities or differences between business sectors have already been discussed in investment awards in connection with the standard against discriminatory measures, albeit not in connection with environmental regulation. Some tribunals found the distinctness of characteristics of the different sectors to be crucial,[171] so that the application of different solutions to differing sectors did not constitute a singling out of a specific sector.[172] Other tribunals found, for example, that public utility sectors – electricity, water or gas distribution – were similar enough to make differences in treatment difficult to explain.[173]

This case law underlines that it is not the abstract similarity of the sectors which is determining, but their similarity with regard to the connecting factor of the respective measure. In an environmental context, the comparability of different business sectors was invoked by the investor in *Pac Rim Cayman LLC v. Republic of El Salvador*. The investor alleges as part of its argument that it, as a mining company, is not accorded national treatment and most-favoured nation treatment since "other industries whose operations raise similar environmental concerns, such as power plants, dams, ports, and fishing operations, have received environmental permits", whereas it was not issued with environmental permits.[174] Even though the arbitral tribunal has found that it does not have jurisdiction regarding the investor's claims under the CAFTA,[175] the underlying facts portray a relevant situation of conflict.

A relevant example, in which the participants in one industrial sector compare the treatment of their sector with the treatment of another sector,

---

[171] National Grid plc v. The Argentine Republic, Award of 3 November 2008, para 201; Metalpar S.A. and Buen Aire S.A. v. Argentine Republic, ICSID Case No. ARB/03/5, Award of 6 June 2008, paras 161, 162.

[172] Enron Corporation and Ponderosa Assets, L.P. v. Argentine Republic, ICSID Case No. ARB/01/3, Award of 22 May 2007, para 282; Sempra Energy International v. The Argentine Republic, ICSID Case No. ARB/02/16, Award of 28 September 2007, para 319.

[173] LG&E v. Argentina, ICSID Case No. ARB/02/1, Decision on Liability of 3 October 2006, para 148. Similarly, CMS Gas Transmission Company v. The Argentine Republic, ICSID Case No. ARB/01/8, Award of 12 May 2005, paras 293, 294.

[174] Pac Rim Cayman LLC v. Republic of El Salvador, ICSID Case No. ARB/09/12, Notice of Intent of 9 December 2008, para 35; Pac Rim Cayman LLC v. Republic of El Salvador, ICSID Case No. ARB/09/12, Claimant's Response to Respondent's Preliminary Objections of 26 February 2010, paras 184, 187.

[175] Pac Rim Cayman LLC v. Republic of El Salvador, ICSID Case No. ARB/09/12, Decision on the Respondent's Jurisdictional Objections of 1 June 2012, para 7.1.

is the introduction of an emission reduction scheme. The introduction of such a scheme can serve as a relevant example of differential treatment of the participants in one or another industrial sector. The European Emissions Trading Scheme is the archetype of such an emission allowance scheme. Consequently, one can assume that issues arising in the context of its introduction illustrate potential problems with regard to the standards of non-discrimination in investment cases. One aspect that led to a series of claims of discrimination in the European context related to the fact that one set of industries had to participate in the scheme, whereas other arguably comparable industries were left out – at least in the initial phase of the scheme. Those industries that had to participate in the scheme were obliged, first, to hold a permit to emit greenhouse gases and, second, to surrender emission allowances that equal their emissions during a specified period on pain of financial sanctions.[176]

The company that brought the dispute at the European level was a major steel producer. It argued that the application of the scheme to the sector of steel manufacturing, but not to the competing non-ferrous metal and chemical product sectors – which were responsible for comparable or even higher emissions of CO_2 – violated the Union's principle of equal treatment.[177] The question was whether the unequal treatment of comparable situations[178] was justified. The European Court of Justice (ECJ) applied the standard of equal treatment under European Law,[179] and found that the al-

[176] European Court of Justice, Société Arcelor Atlantique et Lorraine and Others v. Premier ministre, Ministre de l'Écologie et du Développement durable, Ministre de l'Économie, des Finances et de l'Industrie, C-127/07, Judgment of 16 December 2008, para 42; European General Court, Arcelor SA v. European Parliament and Council of the European Union, T-16/04, Judgment of 2 March 2010, para 168.

[177] European General Court, Arcelor SA v. European Parliament and Council of the European Union, T-16/04, Judgment of 2 March 2010, para 162. The absolute level of emissions of the sectors were contentious: In creating the directive the legislative organs had relied on CO_2 emissions in 1990, which were 174.8 million tonnes for the steel sector, 26.2 million tonnes for the chemical sector and 16.2 million tonnes for the non-ferrous metal sector. The correctness of these numbers was contested by claimant, European Court of Justice, Société Arcelor Atlantique et Lorraine and Others v. Premier ministre, Ministre de l'Écologie et du Développement durable, Ministre de l'Économie, des Finances et de l'Industrie, C-127/07, Judgment of 16 December 2008, paras 52, 55.

[178] The ECJ stated that the competition of the sectors and potentially differing levels of emissions did not make the sets of sectors incomparable, European Court of Justice, Société Arcelor Atlantique et Lorraine and Others v. Premier ministre, Ministre de l'Écologie et du Développement durable, Ministre de l'Économie, des Finances et de l'Industrie, C-127/07, Judgment of 16 December 2008, paras 36, 37.

[179] "A difference in treatment is justified if it is based on an objective and reasonable criterion, that is, if the difference relates to a legally permitted aim pursued

lowance scheme could only help achieving its environmental objective – i.e. combating climate change by reducing greenhouse gas emissions – if the scheme functioned properly and its establishment was not impeded by involving too great a number of participants.[180] The aim of initialising a functioning system, so that the experience gained in its implementation could be used to further increase the circle of participating industries, was considered to justify the different treatment of the sectors.

The facts underlying the decision of the ECJ illustrate an environmental conflict between an investor and the introduction of an emission allowance scheme. Two sets of sectors were compared, which both emitted relevant levels of greenhouse gases but significantly differed in relation to the number of emitting installations. In discussing the justification of the differential treatment, the ECJ primarily focuses on the administrative hurdles and practical difficulties, which the inclusion of the chemical product sector would have induced. The justification thus focuses on the capabilities of the administration when handling the newly implemented scheme. It is completely detached from the environmental impact of the different sectors. Accordingly, the case underlines the wide margin of appreciation the ECJ accords to the legislative organs of the European Union.

Would an investment tribunal confronted with a claim of discrimination based on similar facts reach the same conclusion? The tribunal would have to assess whether the underlying environmental objective – the overall reduction of greenhouse gas emissions at the lowest possible costs – is a le-

---

by the legislation in question, and it is proportionate to the aim pursued by the treatment," European Court of Justice, Société Arcelor Atlantique et Lorraine and Others v. Premier ministre, Ministre de l'Écologie et du Développement durable, Ministre de l'Économie, des Finances et de l'Industrie, C-127/07, Judgment of 16 December 2008, para 47.

[180] European Court of Justice, Société Arcelor Atlantique et Lorraine and Others v. Premier ministre, Ministre de l'Écologie et du Développement durable, Ministre de l'Économie, des Finances et de l'Industrie, C-127/07, Judgment of 16 December 2008, paras 60–65. The particularity about the chemical product sector was that it contained roughly 34 000 installations which – in contrast to the whole scheme, applying to 10 000 installations – was a very high number.

See also the unsuccessful challenge of a national allocation plan – implementing the European Directive, Arrêt n° 92/2006 of the Cour d'Arbitrage Belge of 7 June 2006, rejecting the request to annul the decree of the Walloon region of 10 November 2004, Moniteur Belge of 23 June 2006, p. 32159. The Belgian Court rejected the claim that the implemented system was discriminatory, focusing on the environmental objective of the system, which it considered to participate in a "superior public interest" (B.15). See for a critical assessment of the strong will of the Court to confirm the national measures in the light of this superior interest, *Pâques*, Michel, 'L'*emission trading* à la Cour d'Arbitrage', Aménagement-Environnement 2006, 181–190.

gitimate policy concern. In my opinion, the tribunal would find that it is a legitimate environmental reason, as there is a near-international consensus on the need to mitigate global climate change, irrespective of the willingness of states to actively curb their emissions.[181] The determining issue of the evaluation would be the closeness of the nexus between the measure and the underlying policy. Although the establishment of the allowance scheme is closely connected to the underlying environmental objective, it is clear that not the allowance scheme as such decreases the targeted emissions: Only the successful implementation and application of the scheme, which continuously reduces emission levels over time, can further the environmental policy.

Due to the complexity of such a scheme, investment tribunals should not demand that the nexus between the measure and the environmental policy be very close: If the nexus between the measure and the environmental objective it intends to facilitate is required to be too close and evident, the establishment of more sophisticated environmental schemes is rendered impractical. The example of the European Emissions Trading Scheme also illustrates that a complex environmental scheme cannot be held to a standard of perfection from the very beginning. Administrative realities can require an initial phase that is not fair to all participants in the market.

This line-up is further evidence that the approach adopted by the tribunal in *S.D. Myers v. Canada* is not practicable, according to which a state has to adopt the measure which has the least impact on foreign investment. Sophisticated environmental schemes make it impossible to determine whether they constitute the measure that is 'least disruptive of international trade' and investment. States must have the liberty to adopt such a scheme or another less direct measure to further an environmental objective. Due to the complexity of such a scheme, an investment tribunal cannot possibly assess the environmental effect of the scheme and compare it to alternate measures. Additionally, an investment tribunal is not well situated to analyse and evaluate the complex considerations flowing into the creation of more sophisticated environmental schemes. The reasoning of the ECJ also indicates that it may be necessary to accept that a complex scheme – at least in its initial phase – has discrepant effects on comparable investments. This is even more the case since a sophisticated allowance system is ultimately implemented to minimise the economic impact of environmental protection.

181 See, however, *Miles*, Kate, 'Sustainable Development, National Treatment and Like Circumstances in Investment Law', in: Sustainable Development in World Investment Law (Cordonier Segger, Marie-Claire et al. (Eds.) 2011) 265 (278), who sees the reason for the decisions of the ECJ in that Court's political obligation to support the ETS – a constraint under which an investment tribunal would not be.

bb) Universal Regulation

The third situation to be considered in the context of this scenario relates to measures of universal application, which have a disproportionately higher impact on some investors than on others. The cases *S.D. Myers v. Canada* and *Methanex v. United States* exemplified that the adoption of a universal measure – i.e. the ban of a certain activity or substance – can constitute a violation of the standards of non-discrimination: In both cases, a universal ban more significantly affected the foreign investor that intended to export PCBs or that produced methanol for the production of MTBE, respectively. The superficially equal treatment of investors in differing situations is discriminatory, if the more significant effect of the measure on one foreign investor is not justified.

General regulation tends to have discrepant effects on different subjects. Factual differences amongst affected investors generally do not indicate discrimination. When instituting an environmental measure, a state wants to target investors with an intense polluting impact as much as investors that only marginally contribute to the problem. The fact that one foreign investor is more economically affected by the measure is on its own not enough to constitute discrimination.[182] Case law, like the decision *S.D. Myers v. Canada*, indicates that a specific set of facts is required to reveal discrimination, which demonstrates the specific targeting – especially for protectionist reasons – of the foreign investor.

2. Scenario No 2: Subsidies or Other Advantages for Environmentally Friendly Investments as Potential Violation of Other Investments

The second scenario concerns the introduction of an incentive scheme for investments which are considered environmentally advantageous. The central issue in this context relates to the impact of such a scheme on other investments, primarily those which do not fulfil the criteria to participate in

---

182 See also the similar finding of the European General Court, Arcelor SA v. European Parliament and Council of the European Union, T-16/04, Judgment of 2 March 2010, para 170. The European General Court did not find that the steel sector was in a specific situation with regard to the establishment of the European Emissions Trading Scheme. It did not differ from the other sectors falling into the scope of application of the scheme to an extent that would have disallowed to subject it to the same rules on permits and consequent emissions reductions. The Court expressed its opinion that – specifically with regard to the overall environmental aim of emissions reduction and the polluter-pays principle – all targeted emitting sectors were in the same situation. Accordingly, the claim of equal treatment of sectors in differing situations was dismissed.

the scheme. Can a state legitimately differentiate between investments due to their environmental impact? The question at the heart of the issue is whether investors in environmental advantageous projects are in 'like circumstances' to investors in projects involving conventional technologies.

An illustrative example of such support systems are guaranteed tariffs for energy produced from renewable sources at a level significantly above the tariffs paid for energy or electric current from conventional sources. The arising question is whether the tariff discriminates against producers of conventional energy, which cannot profit from the scheme. The energy or electric current as an end product is the same, no matter how it was produced. Yet, one product – namely energy produced from renewable sources – is guaranteed a more favourable tariff. Environmentally minded commentators express concern that investment tribunals could find that the production of energy is a 'like' activity irrespective of the source from which it is produced and – in line with the interpretation of the likeness criterion in WTO law – could be reluctant to allow the application of environmental criteria for distinction.[183]

The application of the criteria developed above suggests that at the first step of the test – the level of suitable comparators – installations relating to the creation of energy are probably considered to be in the same business sector. Energy from renewable and conventional sources has identical characteristics and thus is an indistinguishable final product. Although two comparators are treated differently, I assume that investment tribunals would accept that the underlying environmental reasons constitute a legitimate justification for the differential treatment:[184] The tribunal in *Parkerings-Compagniet AS v. Lithuania* made it obvious that the environmental impact of different investment projects can constitute a legitimate reason for distinguishing between these investments. The understanding that investment – especially in the energy sector – and environmental protection are not mutually exclusive is furthermore directly reflected in the provisions of the ECT.[185] The aims of the UNFCCC and its Kyoto Protocol, foremost the halting of

---

183 *Werksman*, Jacob/*Baumert*, Kevin A./*Dubash*, Navroz K., 'Will International Investment Rules Obstruct Climate Protection Policies? An Examination of the Clean Development Mechanism', 3 International Environmental Agreements: Politics, Law and Economics 2003, 75; *Miles*, Kate, 'International Investment Law and Climate Change: Issues in the Transition to a Low-Carbon World', Society of International Economic Law, Working Paper No. 27/08, 2008, p. 31.

184 Similarly, *Boute*, Anatole, 'The Potential Contribution of International Investment Protection Law to Combat Climate Change', 27 Journal of Energy & Natural Resources Law 2009, 333 (371).

185 See Article 19 ECT. See above in 'Chapter 2 – The Influence of Environmental Concepts on the Interpretation of Investment Provisions' at pp. 138 *et seq*.

global climate change, are overwhelmingly accepted at the international level – even in the absence of the willingness of some states to actively reduce emissions. Supporting the generation of energy from renewable sources also strengthens national energy security by reducing dependence on depleting resources. These two reasons have been relied on by national and European courts which hold that states have a legitimate interest in regulation: the national legislation obliging energy companies to feed-in energy from renewable sources at non-competitive prices was found not to violate fundamental rights.[186]

In my opinion, an investment tribunal would not reach a different conclusion. Tribunals are aware of the policy space accorded to states to formulate general policies and implement rules furthering them. That the need to prevent climate change is a widely accepted policy concern is demonstrated in a significant number of international conventions and resolutions. It is difficult to imagine that an investment tribunal – against the background of systematic integration – would declare a measure so closely connected to the furthering of non-emitting technologies to be discriminatory.

3. Scenario No 3: Withdrawal of, or Reductions in, a Scheme Favouring Environmentally Friendly Investments

The third scenario concerns subsequent alterations to schemes that were implemented to induce investment in environmentally friendly technologies. Frequently, the investment in more environmentally friendly technology is only economically interesting or even viable if the investor receives certain financial aides. The financial assistance is frequently not a one-off subsidy to kick-start the investment, but is accredited to the investor over a longer period after its investment has been made. The host state may later withhold the originally guaranteed assistance, thus attempting to alter the conditions of the investment.

Relevant examples of such a scheme are guaranteed tariffs for energy produced in an environmental advantageous or renewable way. Several states have decided to further the renewable sector by guaranteeing tariffs

186 See for the compatibility of the German Stromeinspeisungsgesetz and the Erneuerbare Energien Gesetz with European Law and the German Basic Law, European Court of Justice, PreussenElektra AG v. Schleswag AG, C-379/98, Judgment of 13 March 2001, paras 4, 73, 74, 76, 80, 81; Bundesgerichtshof, Stromeinspeisung II, KZR 19/95, Judgment of 22 October 1996, paras 43, 47, 50, 52–75; Bundesgerichtshof, VIII ZR 160/02, VIII ZR 161/02, VIII ZR 322/02, Judgment of 11 June 2003, paras 18–20, 30–41. These decisions concern disputes brought by energy companies which had to accept the feeding-in of energy and had to compensate the producers of renewable energy at higher prices.

to investors producing energy from renewable sources, well above the tariffs that are paid for traditionally produced energy. The non-payment of such guaranteed tariffs was the issue in *Nykomb Synergetics Technology Holding AB v. Latvia*. The state-owned energy company refused to pay the double-tariffs contractually agreed to before the plant of the investor had been built. The tribunal made it clear that as long as other operators comparable to the foreign investor were paid these tariffs, the refusal to pay them to the investor was discriminatory. The focus of the decision on the element of non-discrimination embraced by the standard of fair and equitable treatment allowed the tribunal to easily find a violation of the rights of the investor:[187] It was in the comfortable situation that comparable operators received the agreed-on tariffs.

The approach underlines that the standards against non-discrimination are only helpful in this context, if several producers of environmentally advantageous energy are treated differently. Obviously, every measure affecting one investor, but not another investor exhibiting significant parallels, potentially poses questions of discrimination: An investor can argue that alterations to the scheme under which it invested were discriminatory, because comparable schemes in a comparable business sector were not affected. Likewise, alterations made to the allocation of carbon credits for environmentally advantageous projects can be partial and discriminatory. However, these differences in treatment are not connected to the core of the respective assistance scheme: The real underlying issue of alterations to an assistance scheme is not connected to discrimination.

4. Scenario No 4: Withdrawal of Support Scheme Because Investment Affects the Environmental Objective

Like the third scenario, the fourth scenario relates to changes made to a scheme that supports environmentally friendly investments. In this scenario, the changes are motivated by environmental reasons – because the state has realised that the supported investments have, in fact, a harmful impact on the environment. Like in the third scenario, standards prohibiting discrimination of foreign investors do not challenge the core of such an alteration to an assistance scheme.

A practical example is a scheme that financially supports the production of alternative fuel. A foreign investor invested in plants to produce biodiesel

---

187 See for a critical assessment of the solution adopted by the tribunal – characterised as "elegantly skirt[ing] around every issue that had been theoretically contested" –, *Wälde*, Thomas W./*Hobér*, Kaj, 'The First Energy Charter Treaty Arbitral Award', 22 Journal of International Arbitration 2005, 83 (95–97).

from palm oil. This source for fuel production was originally considered environmentally friendly, but there are now doubts as to its desirability stemming from the destruction of vast areas of rain forest to create cultivable land. Therefore, the host state excludes the foreign investor from the scheme and stops paying subsidies, whereas other participants – those producing fuel from other regenerative sources – continue to receive support. As the investor is treated differently, the host state may argue that the withdrawal of the support scheme for some investors is justified because of environmental policy considerations. At this level, the legal discussion does not differ from the discussion portrayed in Scenario No 1: A tribunal has to determine whether the investors are comparators and – most importantly – whether the difference in treatment is justified as furthering an environmental aim. Depending on the specific circumstances of the case, the host state can rely on a host of environmental rules and policies. In application of the general understanding of deference owed to the state, it appears that distinguishing the different sets of investors can be justified in reliance on environmental policies. This, however, does not answer the question whether the state can alter a contractually agreed support scheme to the detriment of the foreign investor: Other standards of protection come into play for the investor.

III. Summary Assessment

The analysis of the investment decisions and the portrayal of the scenarios show that tribunals can apply the standards of non-discrimination in a way that allows states to set their own level of environmental protection, without neglecting the protection of foreign investors. To this end, the relevant class of comparators should not be defined too restrictively. The concept has to accommodate the concerns of investors. Current investment decisions indicate that the process which led to the implementation of the environmental measure is crucial for the assessment. Tainting the process with protectionist or other malign intent reduces the legitimacy of the measure. As regards the scientific foundation of the measure, the plausibility of both the process and the result is important.

The portrayed scenarios have pointed to directions of potential conflicts occurring in investment disputes. In this context, the findings of the ECJ and of national courts dealing with the respective issues indicate ways in which investment tribunals could assess certain problems. If investment tribunals followed these examples, the deference owed to the host state would remain at the heart of the assessment of the measure. They would also safeguard valid positions of foreign investors. At present, it is nevertheless not foreseeable if – and how – the hypothetical scenarios will be filled with life.

E. Summary

The assessment of standards prohibiting discrimination – the standards of national and most-favoured nation treatment as well as the prohibition of discriminatory measures – has shown that these standards do not only robustly protect the interests of foreign investors: They can also be understood to accord states the necessary leeway to introduce measures legitimately furthering an environmental policy. The investment decisions rendered so far in connection with environmental issues underline that investment tribunals are not oblivious to the importance of environmental protection and do not leave its effects out of the solution of cases. Although elements of the approaches applied by investment tribunals have been criticised, the overall resolution of these disputes does not raise any concerns.

Even though investment tribunals do not always systematically address the relevant elements of the standard, the main aspect is the justification of an environmental measure. Two criteria can be discerned namely (1) whether there is a legitimate environmental aim that the state intends to further and (2) whether there is a sufficiently reasonable nexus between the policy and the measure. The study has emphasised that investment tribunals generally respect the deference owed to the state. In this sense, investment tribunals should only engage in a coherence review of the assessment of scientific evidence undertaken by the state and refrain from substituting the state's assessment with their own evaluation of the evidentiary record. This is all the more the case if more flexible environmental concepts are adopted that aim to achieve environmental objectives in a less direct way. Further, I have argued that the deference should prevent investment tribunals from finding that a measure violates the standard of non-discrimination, because another measure would have been the 'least disruptive of international investment'. In my opinion, the deference accorded to the state is ill-reflected if the burden of proof is shifted onto the state.

Despite good reasons for such an interpretation, it cannot be assessed whether investment tribunals will follow the understanding developed above. The composition of each tribunal varies and the respective facts underlying each case will raise different concerns. On a general note, commentators found more recent investment tribunal decisions to adopt a rather "hands-off interpretation" of the standard of national treatment in favour of regulating governments.[188] It remains to be seen whether this is a continuous trend. Either way, the decision in *Parkerings-Compagniet AS v. Lithu-*

---

[188] *DiMascio*, Nicholas/*Pauwelyn*, Joost, 'Nondiscrimination in Trade and Investment Treaties: Worlds Apart or Two Sides of the Same Coin?', 102 American Journal of International Law 2008, 48 (78).

ania indicates that investment tribunals are prepared to acknowledge discrepancies in the environmental impact of investment projects as grounds for differentiation: An investment project more intensely affecting the environment is not in a 'like situation' to a project with less relevant impact. How and where an investment tribunal draws the line between a legitimate environmental measure and one using environmental protection as a disguise for discrimination, will be influenced by a myriad of factors in each case.

Chapter 4

Standards of Fair Treatment

While administration, like legislation,
can be likened to sausage making,
this episode goes well beyond the glitches and
innocent mistakes that may typify the process.
Tribunal in Pope & Talbot v. Canada, 2001

Fairness is one of the fundamental notions underlying the system of the protection of foreign investments. As a concept, it permeates the protective scope of all standards of treatment and – to varying degrees – influences their interpretation. Most notably, the notion of fairness in treatment is enshrined in the standard of fair and equitable treatment, an absolute standard of investment protection, which is routinely contained in investment agreements. Today, there is reason to believe that the standard of fair and equitable treatment is the most important protective standard, with the majority of breaches of investment agreements acknowledged by investment tribunals being linked to a violation of this standard.

Nevertheless, the exact scope of the standard of fair and equitable treatment is not precisely defined. With 'fairness' constituting a very broad – yet difficult to describe – concept, investment tribunals have focused on different notions. This has lead to a host of diverging approaches to interpretation. Prior interpretation by arbitral tribunals influences subsequent interpretative efforts. In addition, the interpretation differs according to the respective wording and terminology in each treaty. Specifically, some investment treaties link the scope of the standard of fair and equitable treatment to that of the customary international minimum standard. This way, the difficulties arising from defining the content of customary law impact on the understanding of fair and equitable treatment.

Furthermore, given the vastness of the notion of fairness, it is difficult – and maybe even impossible – to clearly distinguish the protective scope of the standard of fair and equitable treatment from other concepts protecting the interests of foreign investors. A multitude of specific protective notions related to the idea of fairness are enshrined as independent standards in some investment treaties, triggering the question of how far they are meant to constitute an integral part of the standard of fair and equitable treatment in treaties in which they are not separately mentioned. Examples of specific notions are the protection against denial of justice and the maxim *pacta sunt servanda*.

Though the portrayal of a myriad of specific protective notions of fairness is not relevant in the context of this study and therefore remains outside its remit, three different absolute standards of treatment will be considered in more detail: The first to be looked at is the standard of constant protection and security, which is closely related to fair and equitable treatment. The second standard, the standard of fair and equitable treatment, is at the centre of this chapter. Its diverse connotations will be thoroughly investigated. The third standard is the protection against arbitrary and discriminatory measures – as far as the standard deals with arbitrariness. Following the portrayal of how these standards are generally understood by investment tribunals, the relevance of the specific standard relating to potential conflicts with environmental measures will be assessed. This will be followed by a portrayal of arbitral decisions in cases in which environmental measures were at stake. These implications will be used to establish criteria for drawing the line between the legitimate interest of the state to regulate and interests of foreign investors. Finally, the developed criteria will be applied to the potential scenarios of conflicts developed in the first chapter.

A. Full Protection and Security

The obligation for the host state to accord full – or constant – protection and security to the investment of the foreign investor is a standard notion in investment treaties. It is usually found in the same provision that obliges the host state to accord fair and equitable treatment to investments.[1] Nevertheless, there is no uniform formulation of the obligation: References range from an obligation to accord investments 'full' or 'constant' protection and security to an obligation to accord 'protection'. Irrespective, investment tribunals rarely understood different wordings to imply different concepts of protection.[2] Despite the differences in the exact wording of the obligation in different investment treaties, it appears to be a common per-

---

1 Article 1105 para 1 NAFTA; Article 2 para 2 2008 German Model BIT; Article 5 para 1 2004 Canada Model BIT; Article 3 para 3 2007 Columbia Model BIT.

2 Parkerings-Compagniet AS v. Lithuania, ICSID Case No. ARB/05/8, Award of 11 September 2007, para 354, finds no relevant difference between the term 'protection' and the notion of 'full protection and security'. Conversely, Siemens A.G. v. Argentine Republic (ICSID Case No. ARB/02/8), Award of 6 February 2007, para 303, expressing that the reference to 'legal security' in the relevant BIT implied a different scope of the protection.

ception that these provisions do not set forth interpretative elements beyond purely referencing to the standard.[3] The following section will – by way of overview – touch upon the scope of protection of the obligation, then illustrate two opposing approaches to interpreting the standard and discuss the relationship of the standard with the standard of fair and equitable treatment. It will conclude by setting forth reasons why the standard does not require a distinct scrutiny into its relationship with environmental norms and standards.

I. Scope of Protection

The standard of full protection and security reflects the basic duty of states to take appropriate measures to protect the physical integrity of installations and persons associated with the foreign investment from attacks attributable to the states, attacks by third parties and civil unrest. The traditional understanding of the standard as protecting foreign investment against physical harm is uncontested.[4] The obligation is overwhelmingly understood as requiring due diligence of the host state.[5] Accordingly, investors' arguments

3 A potential exception to this rule are more recent treaties, which express – concurrent with restrictive tendencies relating to the interpretation of the standard of fair and equitable treatment – the understanding that the standard does not require protection beyond that accorded under the international minimum standard of treatment, such as Article 3 para 4 2007 Columbia Model BIT. The consequences of such express limitations will be discussed in the context of the fair and equitable treatment standard, but are not relevant in the context of portraying the obligation to provide full protection and security. See portrayal of the discussion as to the 'international standard', *Cordero Moss*, Giuditta, 'Full Protection and Security', in: Standards of Investment Protection (Reinisch, August (Ed.) 2008) 131 (136–137).

4 See portrayal by *Cordero Moss*, Giuditta, 'Full Protection and Security', in: Standards of Investment Protection (Reinisch, August (Ed.) 2008) 131 (138–142).

5 Asian Agricultural Products Ltd. v. Republic of Sri Lanka, ICSID Case No. ARB/87/3, Award of 27 June 1990, para 53; AWG Group Ltd. v. The Argentine Republic, Award on Liability of 30 July 2010, para 164; Jan de Nul N.V. and Dredging International N.V. v. Arab Republic of Egypt, ICSID Case No. ARB/04/13, Award of 6 November 2008, para 269; Lauder v. Czech Republic, Award of 3 September 2001, para 308; Noble Ventures, Inc. v. Romania, ICSID Case No. ARB/01/11, Award of 12 October 2005, para 164; Pantechniki S.A. Contractors & Engineers v. Republic of Albania, ICSID Case No. ARB/07/21, Award of 30 July 2009, para 81; Suez, Sociedad General de Aguas de Barcelona S.A., and InterAguas Servicios Integrales del Agua S.A. v. The Argentine Republic, ICSID Case No. ARB/03/17, Award of 30 July 2010, para 158; Waguih Elie George Siag and Clorinda Vecchi v. The Arab Republic of Egypt, ICSID Case No. ARB/05/15, Award of 1 June 2009; para 447; Saluka Investments BV (The Netherlands) v. The Czech Republic, Award of 17 March 2006, para 484; Rumeli Telekom A.S. and Telsim Mobil Telekomunikasyon Hizmetleri A.S. v, Kazakhstan, ICSID Case No.

that the standard imposes a regime of strict liability appear to have constantly been rejected by arbitral tribunals.[6] Arbitral tribunals have additionally clarified that the protection of physical integrity "may also include an obligation to provide adequate mechanisms and legal remedies for prosecuting the State organs or private parties responsible for the injury caused to the investor"[7], which embraces the existence of appropriate fora for the investor to claim compensation for violations of the investment's physical integrity[8].

Whereas the standard uncontroversially protects against attacks on the physical integrity of the investment, recent arbitral decisions voiced the idea that the obligation to provide full protection and security offered broader protection than the traditional understanding. It was suggested that the standard was not limited to protecting physical integrity,[9] but that it encom-

ARB/05/16, Award of 29 July 2008, para 668; Plama Consortium Limited v. Bulgaria, ICSID Case No. ARB/03/24, Award of 27 August 2008, para 179; Pantechniki S.A. Contractors & Engineers v. Republic of Albania, ICSID Case No. ARB/07/21, Award of 30 July 2009, para 81; Ulysseas, Inc. v. The Republic of Ecuador, Award of 12 June 2012, para 272.

6 Asian Agricultural Products Ltd. v. Republic of Sri Lanka, ICSID Case No. ARB/87/3, Award of 27 June 1990, paras 47–53; AES Summit Generation Limited and AES-Tisza Erömü Kft v. The Republic of Hungary, ICSID Case No. ARB/07/22, Award of 23 September 2010, para 13.3.2; AWG Group Ltd. v. The Argentine Republic, Award on Liability of 30 July 2010, para 164; Lauder v. Czech Republic, Award of 3 September 2001, para 308; Noble Ventures, Inc. v. Romania, ICSID Case No. ARB/01/11, Award of 12 October 2005, para 164; Técnicas Medioambientales Tecmed, S.A. v. United Mexican States, ICSID Case No. ARB (AF)/00/2, Award of 29 May 2003, para 177; Suez, Sociedad General de Aguas de Barcelona S.A., and InterAguas Servicios Integrales del Agua S.A. v. The Argentine Republic, ICSID Case No. ARB/03/17, Award of 30 July 2010, para 158; Waguih Elie George Siag and Clorinda Vecchi v. The Arab Republic of Egypt, ICSID Case No. ARB/05/15, Award of 1 June 2009; para 447; Saluka Investments BV (The Netherlands) v. The Czech Republic, Award of 17 March 2006, para 484; Rumeli Telekom A.S. and Telsim Mobil Telekomunikasyon Hizmetleri A.S. v, Kazakhstan, ICSID Case No. ARB/05/16, Award of 29 July 2008, para 668; Plama Consortium Limited v. Bulgaria, ICSID Case No. ARB/03/24, Award of 27 August 2008, para 181; Tulip Real Estate and Development Netherlands B.V. v. Republic of Turkey, ICSID Case No. ARB/11/28, Award of 10 March 2014, para 430.

7 AWG Group Ltd. v. The Argentine Republic, Award on Liability of 30 July 2010, para 173; Suez, Sociedad General de Aguas de Barcelona S.A., and InterAguas Servicios Integrales del Agua S.A. v. The Argentine Republic, ICSID Case No. ARB/03/17, Award of 30 July 2010, para 167. Implicitly, Wena Hotels Ltd. v. Arab Republic of Egypt, ICSID Case No. ARB/98/4, Award of 8 December 2000, paras 94, 95.

8 Parkerings-Compagniet AS v. Lithuania, ICSID Case No. ARB/05/8, Award of 11 September 2007, para 355.

9 Siemens A.G. v. Argentine Republic (ICSID Case No. ARB/02/8), Award of 6 February 2007, para 303. It has to be noted, however, that the relevant BIT of the Argentine Republic explicitly referred to "legal security".

passed notions such as the stability of the legal and business framework or environment.[10] Accordingly, investment tribunals found that physical damage of the investment – in the light of the wording 'protection', especially in addition to the adjective 'full' –[11] was not a pre-requisite for finding a breach of the standard.[12] It was also argued that an intended limitation of the protective scope to physical safety could easily have been reflected in the chosen formulation.[13]

Several other investment tribunals rejected such an expansive interpretation of the standard. Some tribunals explicitly rejected the idea that the standard extended to an obligation to maintain a stable and secure legal and commercial environment.[14] Others applied the standard as relating to physical security without explicitly depicting the scope of the material protection[15] or – noting both the traditional stance on the standard and broader

---

[10] Azurix v. Argentine Republic, ICSID Case No. ARB/01/12, Award of 14 July 2006, para 408; Biwater Gauff (Tanzania) Ltd. v. United Republic of Tanzania, ICSID Case No. ARB/05/22, Award of 24 July 2008, para 729. Referring to the regulatory framework, National Grid plc v. The Argentine Republic, Award of 3 November 2008, para 190.

[11] Azurix v. Argentine Republic, ICSID Case No. ARB/01/12, Award of 14 July 2006, para 408; Biwater Gauff (Tanzania) Ltd. v. United Republic of Tanzania, ICSID Case No. ARB/05/22, Award of 24 July 2008, para 729.

[12] Azurix v. Argentine Republic, ICSID Case No. ARB/01/12, Award of 14 July 2006, para 406; Compañiá de Aguas del Aconquija S.A. and Vivendi Universal v. Argentine Republic, ICSID Case No. ARB/97/3, Award of 20 August 2007; para 7.4.15; National Grid plc v. The Argentine Republic, Award of 3 November 2008, para 187.

[13] Compañiá de Aguas del Aconquija S.A. and Vivendi Universal v. Argentine Republic, ICSID Case No. ARB/97/3, Award of 20 August 2007; para 7.4.15.

[14] AWG Group Ltd. v. The Argentine Republic, Award on Liability of 30 July 2010, para 176; Suez, Sociedad General de Aguas de Barcelona S.A., and InterAguas Servicios Integrales del Agua S.A. v. The Argentine Republic, ICSID Case No. ARB/03/17, Award of 30 July 2010, para 170. BG Group Plc v. Argentina, Award of 24 December 2007, para 326, stating that it considers it "inappropriate" to depart from the originally understood standard.

[15] Eureko B.V. v. Republic of Poland, Partial Award of 19 August 2005, paras 236–237; Noble Ventures, Inc. v. Romania, ICSID Case No. ARB/01/11, Award of 12 October 2005, paras 164–165; Pantechniki S.A. Contractors & Engineers v. Republic of Albania, ICSID Case No. ARB/07/21, Award of 30 July 2009, paras 82–84; Técnicas Medioambientales Tecmed, S.A. v. United Mexican States, ICSID Case No. ARB (AF)/00/2, Award of 29 May 2003, para 177; Waguih Elie George Siag and Clorinda Vecchi v. The Arab Republic of Egypt, ICSID Case No. ARB/05/15, Award of 1 June 2009, para 448; Saluka Investments BV (The Netherlands) v. The Czech Republic, Award of 17 March 2006, para 484; Rumeli Telekom A.S. and Telsim Mobil Telekomunikasyon Hizmetleri A.S. v, Kazakhstan, ICSID Case No. ARB/05/16, Award of 29 July 2008, para 668; EDF (Services) Limited v. Romania, ICSID Case No. ARB/05/13, Award of 8 October 2009,

interpretations – did not have to decide the issue.[16] Further approaches consisted of the statement that only an "exceptional situation" could extend the protection to encompass non-physical violations,[17] or of the application of the traditional interpretation while stating that the correctness of a broader understanding could not be excluded "as a matter of principle" for all other situations.[18]

Tribunals rejecting a more expansive interpretation emphasise the standard's traditional association with situations compromising the physical security of foreign investment, or argue that requiring stability of the legal and business framework would make the protective obligation akin to a stabilisation clause[19]. The most convincing argument against an extensive interpretation of the standard, however, is that it is not helpful, as it does not broaden the overall protection of the investor: The extension of the protective scope of the standard of full protection and security is neither necessary nor desirable in the light of the interpretative scope of the standard of fair and equitable treatment.[20] Tribunals also express concern over the resulting lack of distinction between the two concepts.[21] Although proponents of the extension of the interpretative scope of the standard of full

---

para 300; Toto Costruzioni Generali S.p.A. v. Republic of Lebanon, ICSID Case No. ARB/07/12, Award of 7 June 2012, para 228.

16 Plama Consortium Limited v. Bulgaria, ICSID Case No. ARB/03/24, Award of 27 August 2008, para 180; SAUR International SA v. Republic of Argentina, ICSID Case No. ARB/04/4, Decision on Jurisdiction and Liability of 6 June 2012, para 501.

17 PSEG Global, Inc., The North American Coal Corporation, and Konya Ingin Electrik Uretim ve Ticaret Limited Sirketi v. Turkey, ICSID Case No. ARB/02/5, Award of 19 January 2007, para 258.

18 Enron Corporation and Ponderosa Assets, L.P. v. Argentine Republic, ICSID Case No. ARB/01/3, Award of 22 May 2007, paras 286–287; Sempra Energy International v. The Argentine Republic, ICSID Case No. ARB/02/16, Award of 28 September 2007, para 323–324.

19 AES Summit Generation Limited and AES-Tisza Erömü Kft v. The Republic of Hungary, ICSID Case No. ARB/07/22, Award of 23 September 2010, para 13.3.5.

20 AWG Group Ltd. v. The Argentine Republic, Award on Liability of 30 July 2010, para 174; Suez, Sociedad General de Aguas de Barcelona S.A., and Inter-Aguas Servicios Integrales del Agua S.A. v. The Argentine Republic, ICSID Case No. ARB/03/17, Award of 30 July 2010, para 168; BG Group Plc v. Argentina, Award of 24 December 2007, para 326.

21 Enron Corporation and Ponderosa Assets, L.P. v. Argentine Republic, ICSID Case No. ARB/01/3, Award of 22 May 2007, para 286; PSEG Global, Inc., The North American Coal Corporation, and Konya Ingin Electrik Uretim ve Ticaret Limited Sirketi v. Turkey, ICSID Case No. ARB/02/5, Award of 19 January 2007, para 258.

protection and security found that the two guarantees could overlap[22] or that the standard was automatically breached in the case of a breach of the standard of fair and equitable treatment,[23] the approach of the opponents of the extension is more straightforward: An overlapping of the two standards is neither necessary nor desirable.[24]

II. Evaluation of the Relevance of this Standard for this Study

From this portrayal of the protective content of the standard of full protection and security, I conclude that a separate discussion of the standard in this study is not necessary. If the standard is understood in its traditional scope – an understanding I favour – a tension with environmental norms and standards is unthinkable: A genuine environmental norm and its implementation cannot collide with a host state's obligation to protect investments from physical interference or with judicial procedures that remedy such physical damage or punishing offenders. Environmental objectives can never be legitimately achieved through means of physical attacks or the toleration of civil unrest.[25]

But even if the more extensive interpretative approach of the standard is applied, a separate discussion of its elements is not necessary for assessing potential conflicts with environmental standards. The extension of the standard of full protection and security leads to an overlap of its protective scope with that of the standard of fair and equitable treatment. The concept of the stability of the legal and regulatory framework constitutes an element

---

[22] Jan de Nul N.V. and Dredging International N.V. v. Arab Republic of Egypt, ICSID Case No. ARB/04/13, Award of 6 November 2008, para 269.

[23] Occidental Exploration and Production Company v. The Republic of Ecuador, LCIA Case No. UN3467, Award of 1 July 2004, para 187; Azurix v. Argentine Republic, ICSID Case No. ARB/01/12, Award of 14 July 2006, para 408.

[24] AWG Group Ltd. v. The Argentine Republic, Award on Liability of 30 July 2010, para 174; Suez, Sociedad General de Aguas de Barcelona S.A., and Inter-Aguas Servicios Integrales del Agua S.A. v. The Argentine Republic, ICSID Case No. ARB/03/17, Award of 30 July 2010, para 168.

[25] This assessment is not countered by the fact that public opposition to an investment project can lead to citizens of the host state demonstrating against it or blocking the activity. Even though the host state has to respect the right to protest of its citizens, it is irrespectively obliged to protect the physical integrity of the investment. The destruction of property is no legitimate way to protest or demand higer environmental standards. Accordingly, a conflict between both interests cannot occur at this level. Should the protests have other negative consequences on the investment, the standard of fair treatment is relevant to assess the alleged violation.

of the standard of fair and equitable treatment.[26] Investment tribunals that favour the extensive interpretation have not tried or succeeded in distinguishing the two standards. At least, as far as it does not relate to physical interference, the standard of full protection and security is not additive to the standard of fair and equitable treatment. Accordingly, there is no need for an independent analysis.

B. Fair and Equitable Treatment

The protective scope of the standard of fair and equitable treatment is rather vague and cannot easily be defined. Due to this lack of precision, investment tribunals have applied different protective scopes and embraced distinct interpretations. To overcome the resulting shortcomings, the tribunals stress the flexibility of the standard of fair and equitable treatment, emphasising the need to find individual solutions with regard to the facts in each individual case.[27] Helpful as such an approach may be to ascertain the legitimacy of each decision, it cannot relieve those involved in international investment activities of the burden of establishing parameters within which the conduct of a host state is evaluated in relation to fairness and equitability. Especially host states need to be able to appreciate beforehand whether their legislative, regulatory or other activities fulfil these requirements.

Although it is not the purpose of this study to describe the standard of fair and equitable treatment in all its connotations and subtleties, a broad picture of how investment tribunals understand the protective scope of the standard will be developed. Starting from an analysis of the approaches taken to interpret the standard, the study portrays the material contours by way of overview. Before establishing the material elements of the standard of fair and equitable treatment, the study points to the relationship with the customary minimum standard. After these elements have been described, their relationship with, and implications for, environmental norms and standards will be assessed.

---

[26] The notion of stability of the legal and business framework is discussed in more detail below at pp. 247 *et seq*.

[27] AWG Group Ltd. v. The Argentine Republic, Decision on Liability of 30 July 2010, para 188; Jan Oostergetel and Theodora Laurentius v. The Slovak Republic, Award of 23 April 2012, para 221.

I. Interpretative Approaches to Fair and Equitable Treatment

With investment treaties lacking precise descriptions of what is fair and equitable treatment, the task of distilling the protective scope of the concept is largely left to investment tribunals. In contrast to other protective standards, the concept of fair and equitable treatment has not been subjected to the same level of scrutiny through interpretation and application in other international or national fora.[28] At the outset, investment tribunals had little external guidance in interpreting the standard. Accordingly, the general rules of treaty interpretation as enshrined in Article 31 VCLT were particularly relevant: Investment tribunals aimed to distil the ordinary meaning of the terms 'fair' and 'equitable' – and found that the meaning is encapsulated in the synonyms 'just, even-handed, unbiased, and legitimate'.[29] Other tribunals correctly observed that this approach was not very helpful to discern the protective scope of the standard due to the equal vagueness of the synonyms.[30] Pursuant to Article 31 VCLT, tribunals further aimed to identify object and purpose by relying on the preambular clauses of the respective investment treaties. Some tribunals used specific terms contained in the preamble to identify elements of the standard of fair and equitable treatment.[31] Other tri-

---

[28] The concept of protection against expropriation has been shaped and applied by a significant amount of international decisions, most notably those of the Iran-U.S. Claims Commission. (See portrayal in 'Chapter 5 – Expropriation' at p. 50.) Provisions prohibiting discrimination are common at the international level and investment tribunals, as was portrayed above, were influenced by the interpretation of provisions on non-discrimination by panels in the WTO arena. (See portrayal in 'Chapter 3 – Standards of Non-Discriminatory Treatment' at p. 169).

[29] Azurix v. Argentine Republic, ICSID Case No. ARB/01/12, Award of 14 July 2006, para 360; MTD Equity Sdn. Bhd. & MTD Chile S.A. v. Chile, ICSID Case No. ARB/01/7, Award of 25 May 2004, para 113; Siemens A.G. v. Argentine Republic, ICSID Case No. ARB/02/8, Award of 6 February 2007, para 290. Similarly, National Grid plc v. The Argentine Republic, Award of 3 November 2008, para 168; Tulip Real Estate and Development Netherlands B.V. v. Republic of Turkey, ICSID Case No. ARB/11/28, Award of 10 March 2014, para 401.

[30] AWG Group Ltd. v. The Argentine Republic, Decision on Liability of 30 July 2010; para 213; Saluka Investments BV (The Netherlands) v. The Czech Republic, Award of 17 March 2006, para 297; Ioan Micula, Viorel Micula, S.C. European Food S.A, S.C. Starmill S.R.L. and S.C. Multipack S.R.L. v. Romania, ICSID Case No. ARB/05/20, Award of 11 December 2013, para 504.

[31] CMS Gas Transmission Company v. The Argentine Republic, ICSID Case No. ARB/01/8, Award of 12 May 2005, para 274; Enron Corporation and Ponderosa Assets, L.P. v. Argentine Republic, ICSID Case No. ARB/01/3, Award of 22 May 2007, paras 259–260; LG&E v. Argentina, ICSID Case No. ARB/02/1, Decision on Liability of 3 October 2006, para 124, concluding that maintaining a stable legal and business environment was an element of fair and equitable treatment. Joseph Charles Lemire v. Ukraine, ICSID Case No. ARB/06/18, Decision on Jurisdiction

bunals gathered a general understanding of how to interpret the standard from taking a more holistic approach to the preambular clauses.[32] Emphasis was put on the aim of promoting and protecting investments.

In line with the rules of treaty interpretation portrayed in the second chapter,[33] I maintain that a preamble should be perceived in its entirety to identify the object and purpose of the treaty – which cannot be effectuated by relying on isolated preambular clauses. Furthermore, it was argued above that – in line with the understanding expressed by the tribunal in *Saluka Investments BV (The Netherlands) v. The Czech Republic* – preambles frequently do not mention the protection of investments as an end in itself, but as a necessary element alongside the "overall aim of encouraging foreign investment and extending and intensifying the parties' economic relations".[34] While it is obvious that investment treaties intend to protect foreign investments, this protection necessitates considering the overreaching purpose of investment treaties: Foreign investment aims to intensify the economic relations between two states to improve the living standards in both states.[35]

---

and Liability of 14 January 2010, para 264, concluding that legitimate expectations were an important part of the standard.

32 Azurix v. Argentine Republic, ICSID Case No. ARB/01/12, Award of 14 July 2006, para 360; MTD Equity Sdn. Bhd. & MTD Chile S.A. v. Chile, ICSID Case No. ARB/01/7, Award of 25 May 2004, para 113; Siemens A.G. v. Argentine Republic, ICSID Case No. ARB/02/8, Award of 6 February 2007, para 290. All three decisions conclude from the objectives cited that the treatment should be "conducive to fostering the promotion of foreign investment" – thus underlining the obligation of the host state to be positive or proactive about foreign investment. Similarly, Compañiá de Aguas del Aconquija S.A. and Vivendi Universal v. Argentine Republic, ICSID Case No. ARB/97/3, Award of 20 August 2007, para 7.4.4. National Grid plc v. The Argentine Republic, Award of 3 November 2008, para 170, emphasising the deriving obligation of the host state to encourage and create favourable conditions for foreign investors.

33 See in 'Chapter 2 – The Influence of Environmental Concepts on the Interpretation of Investment Provisions' at pp. 100 *et seq.*

34 Saluka Investments BV (The Netherlands) v. The Czech Republic, Award of 17 March 2006, para 300, stating that the statement of aims is "more subtle and balanced" than is sometimes appreciated. The decision also pointed out that an interpretation which exaggerated the protection to be accorded to foreign investments could dissuade host states from admitting foreign investments which would negatively impact on the mutual economic relations. Similairly, Ioan Micula, Viorel Micula, S.C. European Food S.A, S.C. Starmill S.R.L. and S.C. Multipack S.R.L. v. Romania, ICSID Case No. ARB/05/20, Award of 11 December 2013, paras 515–516.

35 Even though the preambles of investment agreements can differ significantly, the intention to improve the economic conditions in all state parties is frequently mentioned. See for the spectrum of preambular clauses the portrayal in 'Chapter 2 – The Influence of Environmental Concepts on the Interpretation of Investment Provisions' at pp. 102 *et seq.*

Such arguably mutual gain cannot be achieved if the protection of foreign investment is overstated and granted at the expense of legitimate regulatory interests of the host state.

To date, the differing approaches to interpretation have not resulted in a common understanding of the standard of fair and equitable treatment. However, with the surge in investment treaty arbitration, prior investment awards have become a significant point of reference in subsequent decisions. One determination that has been cited with approval by a multitude of investment tribunals[36] is the formula pronounced by the tribunal in *Waste Management II v. United Mexican States*. The tribunal summarised the findings of other tribunals on the protective scope of the standard as follows:

> "[...T]he minimum standard of treatment of fair and equitable treatment is infringed by conduct attributable to the State and harmful to the claimant if the conduct is arbitrary, grossly unfair, unjust or idiosyncratic, is discriminatory and exposes the claimant to sectional or racial prejudice, or involves a lack of due process leading to an outcome which offends judicial propriety – as might be the case with a manifest failure of natural justice in judicial proceedings or a complete lack of transparency and candour in an administrative process.
> [...]".[37]

Though it is undisputed that the conduct reflected in this categorisation constitutes a breach of the standard of fair and equitable treatment, it is under debate whether interference of a lesser degree breaches the protective standard. The quote additionally points to a major obstacle to developing a

---

36 Azurix v. Argentine Republic, ICSID Case No. ARB/01/12, Award of 14 July 2006, para 370; BG Group Plc v. Argentina, Award of 24 December 2007; para 292; Biwater Gauff (Tanzania) Ltd. v. United Republic of Tanzania, ICSID Case No. ARB/05/22, Award of 24 July 2008, para 597; Gami Investments, Inc. v. Mexico, Award of 15 November 2004, para 89; Glamis Gold, Ltd. v. The United States of America, Award of 8 June 2009, para 559; Jan de Nul N.V. and Dredging International N.V. v. Arab Republic of Egypt, ICSID Case No. ARB/04/13, Award of 6 November 2008, para 187; Methanex v. United States, Award of 3 August 2005, Part IV, Chapter C, para 12; Victor Pey Casado and President Allende Foundation v. Republic of Chile, ICSID Case No. ARB/98/2, Award of 8 May 2008, para 670; Siemens A.G. v. Argentine Republic, ICSID Case No. ARB/02/8, Award of 6 February 2007, para 297; Deutsche Bank AG v. Democratic Socialist Republic of Sri Lanka, ICSID Case No. ARB/09/2, Award of 31 October 2012, para 420; Railroad Development Corporation v. Republic of Guatemala, ICSID Case No. ARB/07/23, Award of 29 June 2012, para 219; Antoine Abou Lahoud and Leila Bounafeh-Abou Lahoud v. Democratic Republic of the Congo, ICSID Case No. ARB/10/4, Award of 7 February 2014, paras 439, 440; Mobil Investments Canada Inc. and Murphy Oil Corporation v. Canada, ICSID Case No. ARB(AF)/07/4, Decision on Liability and on Principles of Quantum of 22 May 2012, paras 141, 152.

37 Waste Management II v. United Mexican States, ICSID Case No. ARB(AF)/00/3 (NAFTA), Award of 30 April 2004, para 98.

common understanding of fair and equitable treatment: Investment tribunals evaluate the relationship between the standard of fair and equitable treatment and the customary minimum standard of treatment differently. The respective approach significantly influences the understanding of the protective scope of the standard of fair and equitable treatment.

II. The Relationship Between Fair and Equitable Treatment and the International Minimum Standard of Treatment

The international minimum standard of treatment, an obligation stemming from customary international law, is the protection the host state owes to any foreigner, irrespective of the existence of an investment treaty.[38] Questions regarding the relationship of both standards first surfaced in the interpretation of Article 1105 NAFTA, a provision entitled 'Minimum Standard of Treatment', which expressly links the standard of fair and equitable treatment to "international law".[39] In their interpretation, the state parties to the NAFTA – in their capacity as Free Trade Commission – declared, inter alia, that the standard of fair and equitable treatment did not require protection in addition to what was required by the customary international minimum standard.[40] Although this interpretation was only authoritative in investment disputes arising out of the NAFTA,[41] the issue was also keenly discussed in other investment disputes. This was due to the numeric prevalence of NAFTA disputes and especially relevant in connection with other investment treaties linking the standard of fair and equitable treatment to

38 *Sornarajah*, M., The International Law on Foreign Investment (2010), p. 122.

39 Article 1105, para 1 NAFTA reads as follows: "Each Party shall accord to investments of investors of another Party treatment in accordance with international law, including fair and equitable treatment and full protection and security."

40 Interpretation of the Free Trade Commision of 31 July 2001 (FTC Interpretation). The complete text relating to Article 1105 NAFTA, the NAFTA provision on fair and equitable treatment reads as follows:

"1. Article 1105(1) prescribes the customary international law minimum standard of treatment of aliens as the minimum standard of treatment to be afforded to investments of investors of another Party. 2. The concepts of "fair and equitable treatment" and "full protection and security" do not require treatment in addition to or beyond that which is required by the customary international law minimum standard of treatment of aliens. 3. A determination that there has been a breach of another provision of the NAFTA, or of a separate international agreement, does not establish that there has been a breach of Article 1105(1)."

41 After the issuance of the FTC Interpretation, the question whether this interpretation was in fact binding on the interpretation of the standard by NAFTA tribunals was intensely discussed. See, for example, Pope & Talbot Inc. v. Canada, Award in Respect of Damages, 31 May 2002, paras 17–24. More recent decisions accept its binding character without further elaborating on the issue.

'international law'. Furthermore, to date there has been an increasing number of investment agreements which explicitly limit the protective scope of fair and equitable treatment in this way.[42]

However, equating the standard of fair and equitable treatment with the customary minimum standard does not in itself define the scope of protection promised to foreign investments, since the material content of the international minimum standard has to be ascertained. The determination in the *Neer* Claim (1926)[43] is widely considered to reflect the international minimum standard as it traditionally stood.[44] The test invoked in this decision is whether the authorities "acted in an outrageous way, in bad faith, in wilful neglect of their duties, or in a pronounced degree of improper action".[45] For the present purpose, it is assumed that this test reflects the material content of the international minimum standard at the time the decision was rendered – despite valid arguments that the statement of the *Neer* Claim has never been a general statement encapsulating the duties of a host state owed to a foreign investor.[46]

---

42 Article 5 para 2 U.S.- Uruguay BIT; Article 10.5 para 2 U.S.- Oman FTA; Article 15.5 para 2 U.S.- Singapore FTA; Article 10.5 para 2 CAFTA-DR; Article 5 para 2 2004 Canada Model BIT; Article 3 para 4 2007 Colombia Model BIT.

43 L. F. H. Neer and Pauline Neer (U.S.A./United Mexican States) Arbitral Decision of 15 October 1926, 4 UN Reports of International Arbitral Awards 60-66.

44 Azurix v. Argentine Republic, ICSID Case No. ARB/01/12, Award of 14 July 2006, para 365; Compañiá de Aguas del Aconquija S.A. and Vivendi Universal v. Argentine Republic, ICSID Case No. ARB/97/3, Award of 20 August 2007; para 7.4.46; Glamis Gold, Ltd. v. U.S.A., Award of 8 June 2009, para 616; Siemens A.G. v. Argentine Republic, ICSID Case No. ARB/02/8, Award of 6 February 2007, para 293.

45 L. F. H. Neer and Pauline Neer (U.S.A./United Mexican States) Arbitral Decision of 15 October 1926, 4 UN Reports of International Arbitral Awards 60 (62), para 5.

46 It is argued that the test expressed in the *Neer* Claim was confined to the context it dealt with, namely the specific situation of attaints to the physical integrity of the alien by non-state actors which were not attributable to the state and the consequent denial of justice and lack of due process. See ADF Group Inc. v. United States, ICSID Case No. ARB (AF)/00/1, Award of 9 January 2003, paras 180–181; Mondev International Ltd. v. United States of America, ICSID Case No. ARB(AF)/99/2, Award of 11 October 2002, para 115; Merrill & Ring Forestry L.P. v. Canada, Award of 31 March 2010, paras 197, 201, 204. See also *Kill*, Theodore, 'Don't Cross the Streams: Past and Present Overstatement of Customary International Law in Connection With Conventional Fair and Equitable Treatment Obligations', 106 Michigan Law Review 2008, 853 (868).

See also Railroad Development Corporation v. Republic of Guatemala, ICSID Case No. ARB/07/23, Award of 29 June 2012, para 216, demonstrating that the decision in *Neer* is based on the opinions of commentators, going further than an analysis of State practice followed because of a sense of obligation at the time.

It is under debate whether the content of the customary standard has changed its basic substantial tenets since it was first described. A restrictive approach – while recognising that the material content of the international minimum standard is not frozen in time, but can evolve –[47] argues that the threshold for finding a violation of the standard remains high.[48] In the light of this understanding, it is upon the foreign investor to prove that and to what extent the material protection under customary law has evolved over time[49], failing that the international minimum standard in the sense of the *Neer* Claim is applied.[50] Similarly, tribunals stated that the protective scope of the standard of fair and equitable treatment was broader than the customary minimum standard.[51] The opposing approach argues that the international minimum standard has substantially evolved over time, to the extent that it is now "substantially similar" to the standard of fair and equitable treatment.[52] Accordingly, the latter standard is considered to form part of

---

47 ADF Group Inc. v. United States, ICSID Case No. ARB (AF)/00/1, Award of 9 January 2003, para 179; Chemtura Corporation v. Government of Canada, Award of 2 August 2010, paras 121–122; CMS Gas Transmission Company v. The Argentine Republic, ICSID Case No. ARB/01/8, Award of 12 May 2005, para 284; International Thunderbird Gaming Corporation v. Mexico, Award of 26 January 2006, para 194; Merrill & Ring Forestry L.P. v. Canada, Award of 31 March 2010, paras 192–193; Mondev International Ltd. v. United States of America, ICSID Case No. ARB(AF)/99/2, Award of 11 October 2002, paras 119, 123; Railroad Development Corporation v. Republic of Guatemala, ICSID Case No. ARB/07/23, Award of 29 June 2012, para 218.

48 International Thunderbird Gaming Corporation v. Mexico, Award of 26 January 2006, para 194.

49 ADF Group Inc. v. United States, ICSID Case No. ARB (AF)/00/1, Award of 9 January 2003, paras 183–185; Glamis Gold, Ltd. v. U.S.A., Award of 8 June 2009, paras 601–604, 610–614.

50 Glamis Gold, Ltd. v. U.S.A., Award of 8 June 2009, para 604, stating that it is effectively the standard manifested in *Neer*, namely the standard of egregiousness that constitutes the international minimum standard today.

51 Enron Corporation and Ponderosa Assets, L.P. v. Argentine Republic, ICSID Case No. ARB/01/3, Award of 22 May 2007, para 258; Sempra Energy International v. The Argentine Republic, ICSID Case No. ARB/02/16, Award of 28 September 2007, para 302.

52 Azurix v. Argentine Republic, ICSID Case No. ARB/01/12, Award of 14 July 2006, para 361. Similarily, Biwater Gauff (Tanzania) Ltd. v. United Republic of Tanzania, ICSID Case No. ARB/05/22, Award of 24 July 2008, para 592; CMS Gas Transmission Company v. The Argentine Republic, ICSID Case No. ARB/01/8, Award of 12 May 2005, para 284; Duke Energy Electroquil Partners & Electroquil S.A. v. Republic of Ecuador, ICSID Case No. ARB/04/19, Award of 18 August 2008, para 337; Occidental Exploration and Production Company v. The Republic of Ecuador, LCIA Case No. UN3467, Award of 1 July 2004, para 190; Rumeli Telekom A.S. and Telsim Mobil Telekomunikasyon Hizmetleri A.S. v. Kazakhstan, ICSID Case No. ARB/05/16, Award of 29 July 2008, para 611; Deutsche Bank AG

customary international law, so that today's minimum standard cannot be correctly mirrored with the *Neer* test.[53] Thus, both standards are identical at an elevated level of protection.

I am not convinced that the international minimum standard requires so exalted a level of protection that it is materially identical to the standard of fair and equitable treatment. The majority of arbitral awards which equate both standards do so with little analysis of the state of customary international law.[54] It is difficult to agree that all the subtle notions of the protective scope of the standard of fair and equitable treatment that tribunals detected constitute customary international law; i.e. that they constitute the relevant level of protection for foreign investors even in the absence of an investment treaty.[55] However, the purpose of this chapter is to establish the protective scope of the treaty standard of fair and equitable

---

v. Democratic Socialist Republic of Sri Lanka, ICSID Case No. ARB/09/2, Award of 31 October 2012, para 419; SAUR International SA v. Republic of Argentina, ICSID Case No. ARB/04/4, Decisison on Jurisdiction and Liability of 6 June 2012, para 494.

[53] Merrill & Ring Forestry L.P. v. Canada, Award of 31 March 2010, paras 211, 213.

[54] See for a notable exception Merrill & Ring Forestry L.P. v. Canada, Award of 31 March 2010, paras 184 *et seq.*, which demonstrates that the developments of alien protection in public international law were more pronounced in the sphere of the protection of foreign property than in other contexts.

[55] There is little evidence to suggest that the protective standard of customary international law stretches this far. Applying the general criteria for the establishment of a norm of customary law, the following arguments and observations speak against it: (1) the absence of international decisions properly establishing a customary standard at such a level (2) such a customary standard – or its development – was not mentioned in *Elettronica Sicula S.p.A.*, the latest decision of the ICJ on investment issues in 1989 (3) the failure of initiatives to create a multilateral investment treaty partly due to differing understanding as to the obligations of states (4) the history of resolutions and discussions between developing and developed countries with regard to the scope of investment protection (5) the arguments brought forward by respondent states in investment arbitrations, which cannot be disregarded as devices of interpretation (see, for the importance of state contributions for interpretation, *Roberts*, Anthea, 'Power and Persuasion in Investment Treaty Arbitration: The Dual Role of States', 104 American Journal of International Law 2010, 179 (218 *et seq.*)) (6) the absence of any statement by any state that the standard of customary law has reached the level granted under investment treaties (AWG Group Ltd. v. The Argentine Republic – Suez, Sociedad General de Aguas de Barcelona S.A., and InterAguas Servicios Integrales del Agua S.A. v. The Argentine Republic, ICSID Case No. ARB/03/17 – Suez, Sociedad General de Aguas de Barcelona, S.A. and Vivendi Universal, S.A. v. Argentine Republic, ICSID Case No. ARB/03/19, Common Separate Opinion of Arbitrator Pedro Nikken to Decision on Liability of 30 July 2010, para 7) and (7) the fact that the country that is arguably most intensely favouring investor rights, namely the U.S., tries to limit and reduce

treatment.[56] To this end, the following portrayal establishes criteria referenced by investment tribunals in their quest to determine the protective scope of fair and equitable treatment. Although the international minimum standard in my opinion is less onerous on the host state, this does not preclude reliance on arbitral awards purportedly applying the minimum standard of treatment, since the prerequisites of the customary standard are encompassed by the standard of fair and equitable treatment.

III. Conceptual Notions of the Standard of Fair and Equitable Treatment

Despite differing approaches to treaty interpretation and to the relationship with customary international law, investment tribunals have identified several notions of the standard of fair and equitable treatment, on which decisions are frequently based – despite the commonly confirmed flexibility of the standard. The most prevalent notions in this context are (1) legitimate expectations of the investor, (2) the stable and predictable legal framework, (3) transparency and (4) due process. A further notion identified by scholars is the 'obligation of vigilance and protection'[57], relating to the physical security of the investor and its investment, thus being interlocked with the standard of full protection and security.[58] Like the standard of full

---

the scope of the standard of fair and equitable treatment, because it feels that findings in that regard have been excessive.

See also the critical approach of *Kill*, Theodore, 'Don't Cross the Streams: Past and Present Overstatement of Customary International Law in Connection With Conventional Fair and Equitable Treatment Obligations', 106 Michigan Law Review 2008, 853 (864–869) towards converging the two standards, with the effect that elements identified through a broad interpretation of the standard of fair and equitable treatment – without further analysis – are declared to form part of customary international law.

[56] The correct consequence of the above finding would be to differentiate at least between two treatment standards: One in which fair and equitable treatment is restricted to the customary minimum standard, and a broader independent treaty standard of fair and equitable treatment. However, this distinction would not reflect the practice of investment tribunals in interpreting treaties.

See also *Mayeda*, Graham, 'Playing Fair: The Meaning of Fair and Equitable Treatment in Bilateral Investment Treaties', 41 Journal of World Trade 2007, 273 (289) who argues that 'fairness' should be understood to have a procedural, but not a substantive meaning in the standard of fair and equitable treatment.

[57] *Yannaca-Small*, Katia, 'Fair and Equitable Treatment Standard: Recent Developments', in: Standards of Investment Protection (Reinisch, August (Ed.) 2008) 111 (118–119); *Tudor*, Ioana, The Fair and Equitable Treatment Standard in the International Law of Foreign Investment (2008) pp. 156 *et seq.*

[58] *Yannaca-Small*, Katia, 'Fair and Equitable Treatment Standard: Recent Developments', in: Standards of Investment Protection (Reinisch, August (Ed.) 2008) 111 (118).

protection and security itself, this notion is not relevant in a study relating to conflicts with legislative and administrative measures of the host state.

The following thorough portrayal of the four notions of the standard detailed above does not attempt to construct elements as exclusive categories. Being part of one undividable treatment standard, these notions are interlinked with each other. They will be discussed distinctively to better illustrate the parameters following which investment tribunals assess whether a measure introduced by a state violates the standard of fair and equitable treatment.[59] The insight gained into the understanding of the scope of the treatment standard will subsequently be applied to potential areas of conflict with environmental norms and standards.

1. Legitimate Expectations

A multitude of investment tribunals refer to the legitimate expectations of the investor as an element of the standard of fair and equitable treatment by.[60] It is also acknowledged by scholars that legitimate expectations play

---

[59] It is not the aim of this overview to define a precise and unquestionable framework for analysing the standard of fair and equitable treatment. In the light of the ongoing debate about the protective scope, the identified notions solely reflect the intersection of findings in a multitude of investment decisions applying the standard.

[60] ADF Group Inc. v. United States, ICSID Case No. ARB (AF)/00/1, Award of 9 January 2003, para 189; AES Summit Generation Limited and AES-Tisza Erömü Kft v. The Republic of Hungary, ICSID Case No. ARB/07/22, Award of 23 September 2010, paras 9.3.6 *et seq.*; AWG Group Ltd. v. The Argentine Republic, Award on Liability of 30 July 2010; paras 222 *et seq.*; Walter Bau v. Thailand, Award of 1 July 2009, paras 11.7, 12.1; Bayindir Insaat Turizm Ticaret Ve Sanayi A.S. v. Islamic Republic of Pakistan, ICSID Case No. ARB/03/29, Award of 27 August 2009, paras 178 *et seq.*; Biwater Gauff (Tanzania) Ltd. v. United Republic of Tanzania, ICSID Case No. ARB/05/22, Award of 24 July 2008, paras 602 *et seq.*; BG Group Plc v. Argentina, Award of 24 December 2007, para 294; CME Czech Republic B.V. v. Czech Republic, Partial Award of 13 September 2001, para 611; Chemtura Corporation v. Government of Canada, Award of 2 August 2010, para 179; CMS Gas Transmission Company v. The Argentine Republic, ICSID Case No. ARB/01/8, Award of 12 May 2005, para 277; Continental Casualty Company v. Argentina, ICSID Case No. ARB/03/9, Award of 5 September 2008, para 260; Duke Energy Electroquil Partners & Electroquil S.A. v. Republic of Ecuador, ICSID Case No. ARB/04/19, Award of 18 August 2008, para 340; Enron Corporation and Ponderosa Assets, L.P. v. Argentine Republic, ICSID Case No. ARB/01/3, Award of 22 May 2007, para 262; Glamis Gold, Ltd. v. U.S.A., Award of 8 June 2009, paras 620–622; International Thunderbird Gaming Corporation v. Mexico, Award of 26 January 2006, para 147; Jan de Nul N.V. and Dredging International N.V. v. Arab Republic of Egypt, ICSID Case No. ARB/04/13, Award of 6 November 2008, para 186; Joseph Charles Lemire v. Ukraine, ICSID Case No. ARB/06/18, Decision on Jurisdiction and Liability of 14 January 2010, paras 267–268; LG&E v. Argentina, ICSID Case No. ARB/02/1, Decision on Liability of 3 October 2006, pa-

a central role in the understanding of fair and equitable treatment.[61] The cited decisions exemplify that the legitimate expectations of the investor are

---

ras 127–128, 130; Merrill & Ring Forestry L.P. v. Canada, Award of 31 March 2010, para 233; Metalclad Corporation v. United Mexican States, ICSID Case No. ARB(AF)/97/1, Award of 30 August 2000, paras 87, 89; Metalpar S.A. and Buen Aire S.A. v. Argentine Republic, ICSID Case No. ARB/03/5, Award of 6 June 2008, para 185; National Grid plc v. The Argentine Republic, Award of 3 November 2008, para 173; Parkerings-Compagniet AS v. Lithuania, ICSID Case No. ARB/05/8, Award of 11 September 2007, paras 330–331; Plama Consortium Limited v. Bulgaria, ICSID Case No. ARB/03/24, Award of 27 August 2008, paras 175–176; PSEG Global, Inc., The North American Coal Corporation, and Konya Ingin Electrik Uretim ve Ticaret Limited Sirketi v. Turkey, ICSID Case No. ARB/02/5, Award of 19 January 2007, paras 240–241; Rumeli Telekom A.S. and Telsim Mobil Telekomunikasyon Hizmetleri A.S. v. Kazakhstan, ICSID Case No. ARB/05/16, Award of 29 July 2008, para 609; Saluka Investments BV (The Netherlands) v. The Czech Republic, Award of 17 March 2006, para 302; Waguih Elie George Siag and Clorinda Vecchi v. The Arab Republic of Egypt, ICSID Case No. ARB/05/15, Award of 1 June 2009, para 450; Suez, Sociedad General de Aguas de Barcelona S.A., and InterAguas Servicios Integrales del Agua S.A. v. The Argentine Republic, ICSID Case No. ARB/03/17, Decision on Liability of 30 July 2010, para 203; Técnicas Medioambientales Tecmed, S.A. v. United Mexican States, ICSID Case No. ARB (AF)/00/2, Award of 29 May 2003, para 154; Waste Management II v. United Mexican States, ICSID Case No. ARB(AF)/00/3 (NAFTA), Award of 30 April 2004, para 98; EDF (Services) Limited v. Romania, ICSID Case No. ARB/05/13, Award of 8 October 2009, para 216; Toto Costruzioni Generali S.p.A. v. Republic of Lebanon, ICSID Case No. ARB/07/12, Award of 7 June 2012, para 159; Jan Oostergetel and Theodora Laurentius v. The Slovak Republic, Award of 23 April 2012, para 222; Ioan Micula, Viorel Micula, S.C. European Food S.A, S.C. Starmill S.R.L. and S.C. Multipack S.R.L. v. Romania, ICSID Case No. ARB/05/20, Award of 11 December 2013, para 529; Franck Charles Arif v. Republic of Moldova, ICSID Case No. ARB/11/23, Award of 8 April 2013, para 532.

Opposing the notion of legitimate expectations: AWG Group Ltd. v. The Argentine Republic – Suez, Sociedad General de Aguas de Barcelona S.A., and Inter-Aguas Servicios Integrales del Agua S.A. v. The Argentine Republic, ICSID Case No. ARB/03/17 – Suez, Sociedad General de Aguas de Barcelona, S.A. and Vivendi Universal, S.A. v. Argentine Republic, ICSID Case No. ARB/03/19, Common Separate Opinion of Arbitrator Pedro Nikken to Decision on Liability of 30 July 2010, paras 2–4, 22–27.

61 *Yannaca-Small*, Katia, 'Fair and Equitable Treatment Standard: Recent Developments', in: Standards of Investment Protection (Reinisch, August (Ed.) 2008) 111 (125); *von Walter*, André, 'The Investor's Expectations in International Investment Arbitration', in: International Investment Law in Context (Reinisch, August et al. (Eds.) 2008) 173 (182); *Dolzer*, Rudolf, 'Fair and Equitable Treatment: A Key Standard in Investment Treaties', 39 International Lawyer 2005, 87 (103); *Tudor*, Ioana, The Fair and Equitable Treatment Standard in the International Law of Foreign Investment (2008) p. 165. See also International Thunderbird Gaming Corporation v. Mexico, Separate Opinion to Award of 26 January 2006 by Arbitrator Thomas Wälde, paras 37, 44, arguing that the breach of legitimate expectations created by specific assurances now constitutes a self-standing subcategory of the fair and equitable treatment standard.

considered relevant in the determination of whether the host state breached the treatment standard in disputes based on the international minimum standard as well as in disputes relying on an independent treaty standard. Accordingly, the determination of the kind of expectations an investor legitimately or reasonably holds is relevant.

Investment tribunals generally express the opinion that expectations can only be created at the time the investment is decided and made.[62] Subsequent agreements are not considered to be relevant.[63] It appears to be undisputed that expectations preceding or coinciding with investing are determinant, although the determination of the relevant point in time can be difficult in practice[64]. This approach is instructed by the concept of causation: An investor can only rely on expectations and invest accordingly, if it held these expectations prior to the investment activity. In this sense, several tribunals highlighted the necessity of the investor's reliance on promises or expectations in making its investment.[65]

---

[62] AES Summit Generation Limited and AES-Tisza Erömü Kft v. The Republic of Hungary, ICSID Case No. ARB/07/22, Award of 23 September 2010, paras 9.3.8–13; Bayindir Insaat Turizm Ticaret Ve Sanayi A.S. v. Islamic Republic of Pakistan, ICSID Case No. ARB/03/29, Award of 27 August 2009, paras 190–191; Duke Energy Electroquil Partners & Electroquil S.A. v. Republic of Ecuador, ICSID Case No. ARB/04/19, Award of 18 August 2008, paras 340, 365; AWG Group Ltd. v. The Argentine Republic, Decision on Liability of 30 July 2010, para 228; LG&E v. Argentina, ICSID Case No. ARB/02/1, Decision on Liability of 3 October 2006, para 130; National Grid plc v. The Argentine Republic, Award of 3 November 2008, para 173; Parkerings-Compagniet AS v. Lithuania, ICSID Case No. ARB/05/8, Award of 11 September 2007, para 331; Plama Consortium Limited v. Bulgaria, ICSID Case No. ARB/03/24, Award of 27 August 2008, para 176; Jan Oostergetel and Theodora Laurentius v. The Slovak Republic, Award of 23 April 2012, para 254.

[63] Duke Energy Electroquil Partners & Electroquil S.A. v. Republic of Ecuador, ICSID Case No. ARB/04/19, Award of 18 August 2008, para 365.

[64] See, for example, determination in AES Summit Generation Limited and AES-Tisza Erömü Kft v. The Republic of Hungary, ICSID Case No. ARB/07/22, Award of 23 September 2010, paras 9.3.13 *et seq.*

[65] AWG Group Ltd. v. The Argentine Republic, Decision on Liability of 30 July 2010, para 226; Biwater Gauff (Tanzania) Ltd. v. United Republic of Tanzania, ICSID Case No. ARB/05/22, Award of 24 July 2008, para 602; CME Czech Republic B.V. v. Czech Republic, Partial Award of 13 September 2001, para 611; Enron Corporation and Ponderosa Assets, L.P. v. Argentine Republic, ICSID Case No. ARB/01/3, Award of 22 May 2007, para 262; International Thunderbird Gaming Corporation v. Mexico, Award of 26 January 2006, para 147; Técnicas Medioambientales Tecmed, S.A. v. United Mexican States, ICSID Case No. ARB (AF)/00/2, Award of 29 May 2003, para 154; Ioan Micula, Viorel Micula, S.C. European Food S.A, S.C. Starmill S.R.L. and S.C. Multipack S.R.L. v. Romania, ICSID Case No. ARB/05/20, Award of 11 December 2013, para 672.

The most important aspect of the notion relates to the nature of the expectations themselves and to the criteria according to which they are considered 'reasonable' or 'legitimate'. The investment tribunal in *Técnicas Medioambientales Tecmed, S.A. v. United Mexican States* stated that the standard of fair and equitable treatment required the host state "to provide to international investments treatment that does not affect the basic expectations that were taken into account by the foreign investor to make the investment."[66] This approach appears to base the relevance of the expectations of an investor – and accordingly the host state's liability under the heading of fair and equitable treatment – on the subjective viewpoint of the investor. This understanding was correctly criticised:[67] Not all subjective expectations the investor may have held when investing are relevant, but only those that stand against a test of objectivity.

Accordingly, it is "relevant that the treatment is in breach of representations made by the host [s]tate which were reasonably relied on by the claimant."[68] Such a test is akin to asking what a reasonable investor in the

---

66 Técnicas Medioambientales Tecmed, S.A. v. United Mexican States, ICSID Case No. ARB (AF)/00/2, Award of 29 May 2003, para 154. Several investment tribunals relied on this quote in forming their understanding of the concept of legitimate expectations: Azurix v. Argentine Republic, ICSID Case No. ARB/01/12, Award of 14 July 2006, para 371; Enron Corporation and Ponderosa Assets, L.P. v. Argentine Republic, ICSID Case No. ARB/01/3, Award of 22 May 2007, para 262; Eureko B.V. v. Republic of Poland, Partial Award of 19 August 2005, para 235; Jan de Nul N.V. and Dredging International N.V. v. Arab Republic of Egypt, ICSID Case No. ARB/04/13, Award of 6 November 2008, para 186; L.E.S.I. S.p.A. et ASTALDI S.p.A. v. Algeria, ICSID Case No. ARB/05/3, Award of 12 November 2008, para 151; LG&E v. Argentina, ICSID Case No. ARB/02/1, Decision on Liability of 3 October 2006, para 127; MTD Equity Sdn. Bhd. & MTD Chile S.A. v. Chile, ICSID Case No. ARB/01/7, Award of 25 May 2004, para 114; National Grid plc v. The Argentine Republic, Award of 3 November 2008, para 173; Occidental Exploration and Production Company v. The Republic of Ecuador, LCIA Case No. UN3467, Award of 1 July 2004, para 185; PSEG Global, Inc., The North American Coal Corporation, and Konya Ingin Electrik Uretim ve Ticaret Limited Sirketi v. Turkey, ICSID Case No. ARB/02/5, Award of 19 January 2007, para 240; Saluka Investments BV (The Netherlands) v. The Czech Republic, Award of 17 March 2006, para 302; Sempra Energy International v. The Argentine Republic, ICSID Case No. ARB/02/16, Award of 28 September 2007, para 298; Siemens A.G. v. Argentine Republic, ICSID Case No. ARB/02/8, Award of 6 February 2007, para 298.

67 MTD Equity Sdn. Bhd. & MTD Chile S.A. v. Chile, ICSID Case No. ARB/01/7, Decision on Annulment of 21 March 2007, para 67, emphasising that not the investor's expectations are the source of the obligations of the host state, but the relevant treaty. L.E.S.I. S.p.A. et ASTALDI S.p.A. v. Algeria, ICSID Case No. ARB/05/3, Award of 12 November 2008, para 151.

68 Waste Management II v. United Mexican States, ICSID Case No. ARB(AF)/00/3 (NAFTA), Award of 30 April 2004, para 98. This decision was used by several investment tribunals to determine the importance of legitimate expectations: BG

situation of the investor would have trusted to be able to rely on.[69] In this context, the conduct of the host state is particularly important, since the expectations of the investor have to be created by the host state or its agents or other entities whose conduct is attributable to the state in question.[70] With the exact content of the input of the host state being subject to debate, the tribunal in *Parkerings-Compagniet AS v. Lithuania* found the following formula:

> "The expectation is legitimate if the investor received an explicit promise or guaranty from the host-State, or if implicitly, the host-State made assurances or representation that the investor took into account in making the investment. Finally, in the situation where the host-State made no assurance or representation, the circumstances surrounding the conclusion of the agreement are decisive to determine if the expectation of the investor was legitimate. In order to determine the legitimate expectation of an investor, it is also necessary to analyse the conduct of the State at the time of the investment."[71] [Footnote omitted]

This approach encompasses the elements that investment tribunals frequently discuss in this context. Tribunals have expressed the understanding that expectations require rather explicit promises from the host state, like clear assurances or contractual undertakings.[72] However, these decisions

---

Group Plc v. Argentina, Award of 24 December 2007, para 294; EDF (Services) Limited v. Romania, ICSID Case No. ARB/05/13, Award of 8 October 2009, para 216; LG&E v. Argentina, ICSID Case No. ARB/02/1, Award of 3 October 2006, para 128; National Grid plc v. The Argentine Republic, Award of 3 November 2008, para 173; Saluka Investments BV (The Netherlands) v. The Czech Republic, Award of 17 March 2006, para 302; Siemens A.G. v. Argentine Republic, ICSID Case No. ARB/02/8, Award of 6 February 2007, para 297.

69 AWG Group Ltd. v. The Argentine Republic, Award on Liability of 30 July 2010, para 228.

70 ADF Group Inc. v. United States, ICSID Case No. ARB (AF)/00/1, Award of 9 January 2003, para 189; Ioan Micula, Viorel Micula, S.C. European Food S.A, S.C. Starmill S.R.L. and S.C. Multipack S.R.L. v. Romania, ICSID Case No. ARB/05/20, Award of 11 December 2013, para 669.

71 Parkerings-Compagniet AS v. Lithuania, ICSID Case No. ARB/05/8, Award of 11 September 2007, para 331.

72 Walter Bau v. Thailand, Award of 1 July 2009, paras 11.10-1, 12.1; Biwater Gauff (Tanzania) Ltd. v. United Republic of Tanzania, ICSID Case No. ARB/05/22, Award of 24 July 2008, para 615; Continental Casualty Company v. Argentina, ICSID Case No. ARB/03/9, Award of 5 September 2008, paras 260–262; Duke Energy Electroquil Partners & Electroquil S.A. v. Republic of Ecuador, ICSID Case No. ARB/04/19, Award of 18 August 2008, paras 340, 360; Glamis Gold, Ltd. v. U.S.A., Award of 8 June 2009, paras 620–622; Jan de Nul N.V. and Dredging International N.V. v. Arab Republic of Egypt, ICSID Case No. ARB/04/13, Award of 6 November 2008, paras 263, 265; Metalpar S.A. and Buen Aire S.A. v. Argentine Republic, ICSID Case No. ARB/03/5, Award of 6 June 2008, paras 186–187; National Grid plc v. The Argentine Republic, Award of 3 November 2008, paras 173, 177–178 (main decision relates to the regulatory framework and the fact that Argentina solicited the investment); Plama Consortium Limited v. Bulgaria, ICSID Case

illustrate that the line is difficult to draw between a promise and an inducement to invest stemming from the underlying legal framework. Some decisions seem to imply that the existence of certain laws and rules suffices as a basis for relevant expectations.[73] Another tribunal found that "general legislative statements engender reduced expectations".[74] Thus, the inter-connection of the legitimate expectations of the investor and the notion of stability of the legal framework becomes obvious.

Although the specific circumstances of each case are decisive, expectations should only be acknowledged to a lesser extent, in my opinion. The reason is that – in the absence of an umbrella clause – the non-compliance with a contractual undertaking cannot be equated with the violation of the treaty.[75] The general distinction in international law would be disregarded if a state's breach of commitments that might not even reach the level of a contractual undertaking were considered to constitute a breach of the treaty – via the notion of legitimate expectations. The parameters of the notion of legitimate expectations make it obvious that surrounding factors have to be taken into account. Amongst these factors are the political, socioeconomic, cultural, and historical conditions prevailing in the host state.[76] Further,

---

No. ARB/03/24, Award of 27 August 2008, para 176; PSEG Global, Inc., The North American Coal Corporation, and Konya Ingin Electrik Uretim ve Ticaret Limited Sirketi v. Turkey, ICSID Case No. ARB/02/5, Award of 19 January 2007, para 241 (referring to a promise of the administration on which the investor relied when making the investment); Waste Management II v. United Mexican States, ICSID Case No. ARB(AF)/00/3 (NAFTA), Award of 30 April 2004, para 98.

73 AWG Group Ltd. v. The Argentine Republic, Award on Liability of 30 July 2010, paras 222, 226, referring to "laws, regulations, declared policies, and statements" of the host state; the decision on the merits, however, relates to a sector-specific tariff structure and specific guarantees the investor had asked for, paras 231, 234; Joseph Charles Lemire v. Ukraine, ICSID Case No. ARB/06/18, Decision on Jurisdiction and Liability of 14 January 2010, paras 267–268 referring to the expectations the investor had regarding the regulatory framework for the broadcasting industry. Merrill & Ring Forestry L.P. v. Canada, Award of 31 March 2010, para 233, which refers to the expectation of an investor to conduct its business "in a normal framework free of interference from government regulations which are not underpinned by appropriate public policy objectives."

74 Continental Casualty Company v. Argentina, ICSID Case No. ARB/03/9, Award of 5 September 2008, para 261. A commentator suggests that the more specific the assurances given are, the more likely they are to constitute the basis for a claim because of frustration of legitimate expectations, *Yannaca-Small*, Katia, 'Fair and Equitable Treatment Standard: Recent Developments', in: Standards of Investment Protection (Reinisch, August (Ed.) 2008) 111 (126).

75 Duke Energy Electroquil Partners & Electroquil S.A. v. Republic of Ecuador, ICSID Case No. ARB/04/19, Award of 18 August 2008, paras 342, 358.

76 Bayindir Insaat Turizm Ticaret Ve Sanayi A.S. v. Islamic Republic of Pakistan, ICSID Case No. ARB/03/29, Award of 27 August 2009, para 192; Duke En-

tribunals have underlined the fact that the state's legitimate right to regulate economic life and other aspects of public life in the public interest have to be considered.[77]

2. Stable and Predictable Legal Framework

A second protective notion of the standard of fair and equitable treatment is the obligation of the host state to create and maintain a stable and predictable legal framework. Myriad investment tribunals have readily identified this obligation.[78] Stability, predictability and consistence enable foreign investors to plan their investment according to the legal framework of the

---

ergy Electroquil Partners & Electroquil S.A. v. Republic of Ecuador, ICSID Case No. ARB/04/19, Award of 18 August 2008, para 340; Suez, Sociedad General de Aguas de Barcelona S.A., and InterAguas Servicios Integrales del Agua S.A. v. The Argentine Republic, ICSID Case No. ARB/03/17, Decision on Liability of 30 July 2010, para 209; National Grid plc v. The Argentine Republic, Award of 3 November 2008, para 180; Toto Costruzioni Generali S.p.A. v. Republic of Lebanon, ICSID Case No. ARB/07/12, Award of 7 June 2012, para 165.

In this sense, a commentator suggested that an investor investing in a developing country could not expect the same level of stability and administrative efficiency that it could expect in a developed country, *Tudor*, Ioana, The Fair and Equitable Treatment Standard in the International Law of Foreign Investment (2008) pp. 164–165.

[77] Saluka Investments BV (The Netherlands) v. The Czech Republic, Award of 17 March 2006, paras 305–306; EDF (Services) Limited v. Romania, ICSID Case No. ARB/05/13, Award of 8 October 2009, para 209; Ulysseas, Inc. v. The Republic of Ecuador, Award of 12 June 2012, para 249.

[78] CMS Gas Transmission Company v. The Argentine Republic, ICSID Case No. ARB/01/8, Award of 12 May 2005, para 274; Duke Energy Electroquil Partners & Electroquil S.A. v. Republic of Ecuador, ICSID Case No. ARB/04/19, Award of 18 August 2008, para 339; Enron Corporation and Ponderosa Assets, L.P. v. Argentine Republic, ICSID Case No. ARB/01/3, Award of 22 May 2007, para 260; Joseph Charles Lemire v. Ukraine, ICSID Case No. ARB/06/18, Decision on Jurisdiction and Liability of 14 January 2010, para 284; L.E.S.I. S.p.A. et ASTALDI S.p.A. v. Algeria, ICSID Case No. ARB/05/3, Award of 12 November 2008, para 151; LG&E v. Argentina, ICSID Case No. ARB/02/1, Decision on Liability of 3 October 2006, paras 124-5, 127, 131; Merrill & Ring Forestry L.P. v. Canada, Award of 31 March 2010, para 232; Occidental Exploration and Production Company v. The Republic of Ecuador, LCIA Case No. UN3467, Award of 1 July 2004, paras 183, 191; Plama Consortium Limited v. Bulgaria, ICSID Case No. ARB/03/24, Award of 27 August 2008, para 173 (explicitly for the context of the ECT); PSEG Global, Inc., The North American Coal Corporation, and Konya Ingin Electrik Uretim ve Ticaret Limited Sirketi v. Turkey, ICSID Case No. ARB/02/5, Award of 19 January 2007, para 253; Sempra Energy International v. The Argentine Republic, ICSID Case No. ARB/02/16, Award of 28 September 2007, para 300; Jan Oostergetel and Theodora Laurentius v. The Slovak Republic, Award of 23 April 2012, para 222.

host state.[79] In investment awards, this notion is often intertwined with the discussion of the investor's legitimate expectations. The stability of the legal framework is essential, since the investor analyses the feasibility and profitability of its undertaking under the laws and regulations of the host state before taking the decision to invest – especially with regard to long-term investments. Accordingly, both notions relate to expectations that the investor had at the time of making its investment with regard to the comportment of the host state. It appears, however, as if the notion of legitimate expectations rather relates to precise and specific promises the host state made to the individual investor, whereas the notion of legal stability more generally relates to the laws and regulations in force in the host state.[80]

Given the importance of legal continuity for investors, it would be unfair for a host state to encourage investors to invest by means of a very generous legal framework – only to substantially alter this framework to the investors' disadvantage once the investment has been made. On the other hand, the investor cannot expect the legal framework to remain unchanged indefinitely. The practical question is how stable the legal framework has to remain: Investment tribunals point to the fact that the notion of the stability of the legal framework is materially different from a stabilisation clause.[81] They also emphasise that the legal framework does not 'freeze',

---

79 *Yannaca-Small*, Katia, 'Fair and Equitable Treatment Standard: Recent Developments', in: Standards of Investment Protection (Reinisch, August (Ed.) 2008) 111 (123).

80 Investment tribunals tend not to clearly distinguish between these two notions. See, for example, Parkerings-Compagniet AS v. Lithuania, ICSID Case No. ARB/05/8, Award of 11 September 2007, para 329 (discussing whether the investor had "any legitimate expectation in the stability of the legal system"). Also, whether specific promises as to the guarantees implemented in the legal framework had or had not been given to the putative investor – so as to trigger a relating expectation – is a question considered by tribunals in their decisions: For such a specific promise see CMS Gas Transmission Company v. The Argentine Republic, ICSID Case No. ARB/01/8, Award of 12 May 2005, para 277; LG&E v. Argentina, ICSID Case No. ARB/02/1, Decision on Liability of 3 October 2006, para 133. For an evaluation of the absence of a specific guarantee see Glamis Gold, Ltd. v. U.S.A., Award of 8 June 2009, para 813; Plama Consortium Limited v. Bulgaria, ICSID Case No. ARB/03/24, Award of 27 August 2008, para 219; AES Summit Generation Limited and AES-Tisza Erömü Kft v. The Republic of Hungary, ICSID Case No. ARB/07/22, Award of 23 September 2010, para 9.3.31.

81 AES Summit Generation Limited and AES-Tisza Erömü Kft v. The Republic of Hungary, ICSID Case No. ARB/07/22, Award of 23 September 2010, paras 9.3.29, 9.3.31; EDF (Services) Limited v. Romania, ICSID Case No. ARB/05/13, Award of 8 October 2009, para 218; Parkerings-Compagniet AS v. Lithuania, ICSID Case No. ARB/05/8, Award of 11 September 2007, paras 332; Ioan Micula, Viorel Micula, S.C. European Food S.A, S.C. Starmill S.R.L. and S.C. Multipack S.R.L. v. Romania, ICSID Case No. ARB/05/20, Award of 11 December 2013, para 529. See

since the host state retains its regulatory power, thus having the sovereign right to adapt its legal framework to changing circumstances.[82] In the context of environmental regulation, it is a major concern that the notion of stability impacts on the host states' ability to adopt new legislation to strengthen their domestic regimes of environmental protection.[83]

Tribunals found a violation of the stability and predictability notion when the legal and business framework, under which the investment was made, had been 'entirely transformed' or 'dispensed with all together'.[84] They specifically pointed to the fact that predictable frameworks had been transferred into 'ambiguous, unreliable systems'[85] or that the new legal framework remained in itself 'inconsistent', with the content of its rules being

---

for a brief portrayal of stabilisation clauses, *Sornarajah*, M., The International Law on Foreign Investment (2010) pp. 281–284.

[82] AES Summit Generation Limited and AES-Tisza Erömü Kft v. The Republic of Hungary, ICSID Case No. ARB/07/22, Award of 23 September 2010, paras 9.3.29; Enron Corporation and Ponderosa Assets, L.P. v. Argentine Republic, ICSID Case No. ARB/01/3, Award of 22 May 2007, para 261; CMS Gas Transmission Company v. The Argentine Republic, ICSID Case No. ARB/01/8, Award of 12 May 2005, para 277; EDF (Services) Limited v. Romania, ICSID Case No. ARB/05/13, Award of 8 October 2009, para 217; Plama Consortium Limited v. Bulgaria, ICSID Case No. ARB/03/24, Award of 27 August 2008, para 177; Saluka Investments BV (The Netherlands) v. The Czech Republic, Award of 17 March 2006, para 305; Jan Oostergetel and Theodora Laurentius v. The Slovak Republic, Award of 23 April 2012, para 224; Mobil Investments Canada Inc. and Murphy Oil Corporation v. Canada, ICSID Case No. ARB(AF)/07/4, Decision on Liability and on Principles of Quantum of 22 May 2012, para 153; Ioan Micula, Viorel Micula, S.C. European Food S.A, S.C. Starmill S.R.L. and S.C. Multipack S.R.L. v. Romania, ICSID Case No. ARB/05/20, Award of 11 December 2013, para 673.

Similarily, Continental Casualty Company v. Argentina, ICSID Case No. ARB/03/9, Award of 5 September 2008, para 258 stating that "it would be unconscionable for a country to promise not to change its legislation as time and needs change".

[83] *Miles*, Kate, 'International Investment Law and Climate Change: Issues in the Transition to a Low-Carbon World', Society of International Economic Law, Working Paper No. 27/08, 2008, p. 20.

[84] CMS Gas Transmission Company v. The Argentine Republic, ICSID Case No. ARB/01/8, Award of 12 May 2005, para 277. Similarly, LG&E v. Argentina, ICSID Case No. ARB/02/1, Decision on Liability of 3 October 2006, para 139.

[85] In this sense, several of the cases concerning the Argentinean financial crisis 2000–2002: Enron Corporation and Ponderosa Assets, L.P. v. Argentine Republic, ICSID Case No. ARB/01/3, Award of 22 May 2007, para 266; Sempra Energy International v. The Argentine Republic, ICSID Case No. ARB/02/16, Award of 28 September 2007, para 303; LG&E v. Argentina, ICSID Case No. ARB/02/1, Decision on Liability of 3 October 2006, paras 136–138. Also, PSEG Global, Inc., The North American Coal Corporation, and Konya Ingin Electrik Uretim ve Ticaret Limited Sirketi v. Turkey, ICSID Case No. ARB/02/5, Award of 19 January 2007, paras 250, 254.

unclear[86]. The latter finding potentially implies the absence of valid policy reasons for altering the legal framework. Other tribunals found that the regulatory authority was reduced by the existing regulatory framework, so that the measures taken were outside the scope of the legitimate right to regulate and constituted an abuse of regulatory discretion.[87] One tribunal also held that even though the investor had to expect alterations to the legal framework, it did not have to expect the specific changes implemented, because they were discriminatory.[88]

3. Transparency

A multitude of investment tribunals identified transparency as a further notion of the protective scope of the standard of fair and equitable treatment. While it is undeniable that transparency is considered to play an important role in international economic relations,[89] investment treaties rarely explicitly tie transparency to this treatment standard[90]. In the context of fair and equitable treatment, transparency is considered a significant element for the protection of both the legitimate expectations of the investor and the stability of the legal framework.[91]

Arbitral decisions dealing extensively with the notion of transparency predominantly had to determine whether a certain process or procedure ap-

---

86 Occidental Exploration and Production Company v. The Republic of Ecuador, LCIA Case No. UN3467, Award of 1 July 2004, para 184.

87 Suez, Sociedad General de Aguas de Barcelona S.A., and InterAguas Servicios Integrales del Agua S.A. v. The Argentine Republic, ICSID Case No. ARB/03/17, Decision on Liability of 30 July 2010, para 217; AWG Group Ltd. v. The Argentine Republic, Award on Liability of 30 July 2010, para 237.

88 Saluka Investments BV (The Netherlands) v. The Czech Republic, Award of 17 March 2006, para 357–358.

89 See transparency provisions in investment treaties: Article 10, 11 2004 U.S. Model BIT; Article 19 2004 Canada Model BIT; Article 102 NAFTA; Chapter 18 CAFTA-DR. For the concept of transparency in international economic law, see UNCTAD, 'Transparency' (2004), UNCTAD/ITE/IIT/2003/4. See also *Kotera*, Akira, 'Regulatory Transparancy', in: The Oxford Handbook of International Investment Law (Muchlinski, Peter et al. (Eds.) 2008) 617, pp. 617 *et seq.* on the development of transparency in international economic law and on pp. 625 *et seq.* more specifically on developments in the context of investment treaties and arbitrations.

90 See, for an exception, Article 10 para 1 ECT, which explicitly obliges states to create, inter alia, "transparent" conditions for investors and states that such conditions shall include a commitment to accord fair and equitable treatment.

91 Plama Consortium Limited v. Bulgaria, ICSID Case No. ARB/03/24, Award of 27 August 2008, para 178.

plied by the host state was transparent.[92] These awards indicate that the notion of transparency is closely related to the concept of due process, but they also demonstrate that the underlying notion of transparency is not precisely defined. One approach to the required level of transparency demands that "all relevant legal requirements for the purpose of initiating, completing and successfully operating investments made, or intended to be made under an investment treaty should be capable of being readily known to all affected investors."[93] Another definition goes further and requires the state to act "totally transparently", which means that the foreign investor should not only be in a position to "know beforehand any and all rules and regulations that will govern its investments", but also "the goals of the relevant policies and administrative practices or directives, to be able to plan its investment and comply with such regulations".[94]

Demanding transparency in terms of the latter definition appears excessive. To know the goals of applicable policies – in so far as they do not derive from the applicable rules themselves – goes beyond the requirements set by norms expressly requiring transparency in international investment agreements[95]. Such a definition would, literally understood, disallow all changes to the regulatory framework that could potentially affect the investment, thus literally freezing the relevant legislation. A commentator stated that this understanding could hold host states in a regulatory "time warp", excluding the possibility to tighten regulation to accommodate to advances in scientific knowledge or shifts in social values.[96]

However, the discussions of transparency in investment awards are not particularly refined: Tribunals indiscriminately refer to both definitions set

---

[92] No violation was found in L.E.S.I. S.p.A. et ASTALDI S.p.A. v. Algeria, ICSID Case No. ARB/05/3, Award of 12 November 2008, paras 155, 159, 160. A violation was found in Rumeli Telekom A.S. and Telsim Mobil Telekomunikasyon Hizmetleri A.S. v. Kazakhstan, ICSID Case No. ARB/05/16, Award of 29 July 2008, paras 617–618; Siemens A.G. v. Argentine Republic, ICSID Case No. ARB/02/8, Award of 6 February 2007, para 308; Saluka Investments BV (The Netherlands) v. The Czech Republic, Award of 17 March 2006, paras 420, 499; Metalclad Corporation v. United Mexican States, ICSID Case No. ARB(AF)/97/1, Award of 30 August 2000, paras 88, 99.

[93] LG&E v. Argentina, ICSID Case No. ARB/02/1, Decision on Liability of 3 October 2006, para 128; Metalclad Corporation v. United Mexican States, ICSID Case No. ARB(AF)/97/1, Award of 30 August 2000, para 76.

[94] Técnicas Medioambientales Tecmed, S.A. v. United Mexican States, ICSID Case No. ARB (AF)/00/2, Award of 29 May 2003, para 154.

[95] See e.g. Articles 10, 11 2004 U.S. Model BIT; Article 11 U.S.-Rwanda BIT.

[96] *Miles*, Kate, 'International Investment Law and Climate Change: Issues in the Transition to a Low-Carbon World', Society of International Economic Law, Working Paper No. 27/08, 2008, p. 20.

forth above[97] – as well as to a third award, according to which the fair and equitable treatment standard may be infringed by conduct amounting to "a complete lack of transparency and candour in an administrative process"[98]. Those decisions that found a breach of the standard of fair and equitable treatment did so without clearly positioning themselves on the scope of transparency.

4. Due Process

Several investment tribunals identified the obligation for the host state to act in accordance with due process as a further notion of fair and equitable treatment.[99] Generally, the notion of due process can be an expression of the concept of 'denial of justice' or it can be understood more broadly as an element of procedural fairness.[100] The concept of 'denial of justice',[101]

---

97 See, for example, CMS Gas Transmission Company v. The Argentine Republic, ICSID Case No. ARB/01/8, Award of 12 May 2005, paras 278, 279; Occidental Exploration and Production Company v. The Republic of Ecuador, LCIA Case No. UN3467, Award of 1 July 2004, para 185.

98 Waste Management II v. United Mexican States, ICSID Case No. ARB(AF)/00/3 (NAFTA), Award of 30 April 2004, para 98.

99 AES Summit Generation Limited and AES-Tisza Erömü Kft v. The Republic of Hungary, ICSID Case No. ARB/07/22 (ECT), Award of 23 September 2010, para 9.3.38; Bayindir Insaat Turizm Ticaret Ve Sanayi A.S. v. Islamic Republic of Pakistan, ICSID Case No. ARB/03/29, Award of 27 August 2009, paras 178, 344; Chemtura Corporation v. Government of Canada, Award of 2 August 2010, para 162; Glamis Gold, Ltd. v. U.S.A., Award of 8 June 2009, paras 616, 627; Jan de Nul N.V. and Dredging International N.V. v. Arab Republic of Egypt, ICSID Case No. ARB/04/13, Award of 6 November 2008, para 187; Merrill & Ring Forestry L.P. v. Canada, Award of 31 March 2010, paras 208, 213; Middle East Cement Shipping and Handling Co. S.A. v. Arab Republic of Egypt, ICSID Case No. ARB/99/6, Award of 12 April 2002, para 143; Rumeli Telekom A.S. and Telsim Mobil Telekomunikasyon Hizmetleri A.S. v. Kazakhstan, ICSID Case No. ARB/05/16, Award of 29 July 2008, para 609; Saluka Investments BV (The Netherlands) v. The Czech Republic, Award of 17 March 2006, paras 303, 308; Waguih Elie George Siag and Clorinda Vecchi v. The Arab Republic of Egypt, ICSID Case No. ARB/05/15, Award of 1 June 2009, para 450; Waste Management II v. United Mexican States, ICSID Case No. ARB(AF)/00/3 (NAFTA), Award of 30 April 2004, para 98; Jan Oostergetel and Theodora Laurentius v. The Slovak Republic, Award of 23 April 2012, para 221; TECO Guatemala Holdings, LLC v. Republic of Guatemala, ICSID Case No. ARB/10/23, Award of 19 December 2013, para 711.

100 *Tudor*, Ioana, The Fair and Equitable Treatment Standard in the International Law of Foreign Investment (2008) pp. 157 *et seq.*

101 For a comprehensive study on denial of justice, see *Paulsson*, Jan, Denial of Justice in International Law (2005). Investment tribunals frequently define denial of justice by reference to the decision of the ICJ in the *Elettronica Sicula S.p.A.*. Accordingly, they ask whether the measures in question amount to "a wilful disregard

which is frequently considered to form a part of the protective scope of the standard of fair and equitable treatment,[102] is not relevant in this study as it protects investors against the denial of basic rights in judicial proceedings. It is unthinkable that the denial of these basic rights is connected to conflicts between protection owed to foreign investors and environmental regulation implemented by the host state. Therefore, 'denial of justice' is not discussed in this study.

In the current context, the notion of due process is of interest insofar as it embraces – in close connection with the notion of transparency – a concept of procedural fairness[103]. It is particularly relevant for the evaluation of administrative procedures. However, investment awards have not defined a clear-cut scope of the standard. It can be argued that the notion requires that fair procedures be in place, since the absence of participatory procedures does not release the host state from fair conduct towards the investor.[104] However, similarly to the rather narrow understanding of 'denial of

---

of due process of law, an act which shocks, or at least surprises, a sense of juridical propriety". ICJ, Case Concerning Elettronica Sicula S.p.A. (ELSI) (United States of America/Italy), Judgment of 20 July 1989, ICJ Reports 1989, 15 (76) para 128.

[102] International Thunderbird Gaming Corporation v. Mexico, Award of 26 January 2006, para 194; Loewen Group, Inc. and Raymond L. Loewen v. United States, ICSID Case No. ARB(AF)/98/3, Award of 26 June 2003, para 129; Jan de Nul N.V. and Dredging International N.V. v. Arab Republic of Egypt, ICSID Case No. ARB/04/13, Award of 6 November 2008, paras 188, 196; Mondev International Ltd. v. United States of America, ICSID Case No. ARB(AF)/99/2, Award of 11 October 2002, para 127; Victor Pey Casado and President Allende Foundation v. Republic of Chile, ICSID Case No. ARB/98/2, Award of 8 May 2008, paras 656–658; Rumeli Telekom A.S. and Telsim Mobil Telekomunikasyon Hizmetleri A.S. v. Kazakhstan, ICSID Case No. ARB/05/16, Award of 29 July 2008, para 651; Waste Management II v. United Mexican States, ICSID Case No. ARB(AF)/00/3 (NAFTA), Award of 30 April 2004, paras 98, 132.

It has to be taken note, however, that the concept of denial of justice with this definition is not only discussed in the context of fair and equitable treatment, but also under the heading of arbitrary and discriminatory treatment. See LG&E v. Argentina, ICSID Case No. ARB/02/1, Decision on Liability of 3 October 2006, para 157; Duke Energy Electroquil Partners & Electroquil S.A. v. Republic of Ecuador, ICSID Case No. ARB/04/19, Award of 18 August 2008, para 378.

[103] *Tudor*, Ioana, The Fair and Equitable Treatment Standard in the International Law of Foreign Investment (2008) p. 162 *et seq.*

[104] Middle East Cement Shipping and Handling Co. S.A. v. Arab Republic of Egypt, ICSID Case No. ARB/99/6, Award of 12 April 2002, para 143 ("a matter as important [...] should have been notified by a direct communication [...] irrespective of whether there was a legal duty or practice to do so [...]"); Metalclad Corporation v. United Mexican States, ICSID Case No. ARB(AF)/97/1, Award of 30 August 2000, para 88 (holding that, inter alia, the "absence of any established practice or procedure as to the manner of handling applications for a municipal construction permit" violates the obligations of the host state).

justice', tribunals have also expressed that the notion of due process is only considered to be infringed, if the

> "state's acts or procedural omissions are, on the facts and in the context [...] manifestly unfair or unreasonable (such as would shock, or at least surprise a sense of juridical propriety)."[105]

IV. Intermediate Summary

The standard of fair and equitable treatment is a broad standard of the treatment of foreign investment. Even though decisions of investment tribunals do not apply a common clear-cut scope of protection, they point to a set of protective notions of the standard. To determine what fair treatment means in a specific situation, the investor's legitimate expectations, the stability of the legal framework, the notions of transparency and due process are significant points of reference. In contrast, it appears that attempts to narrow the protective scope to that of the traditional understanding of the international minimum standard have not been influential.

C. Analysis of Case Law Concerning Environmental Measures

The portrayal of the standard of fair and equitable treatment indicates that two aspects are predominantly relevant for the introduction of an allegedly environmental measure: First, the evaluation of promises or guarantees that were given to the investor prior to its investment. Second, the degree to which existing structures, on which the investor relied when making its investment, can be altered to accommodate for better protection of environmental objectives. Both aspects require balancing of the investor's right to be protected against changes in the promises and the framework on which it relied with the state's right to regulate in the public interest. A further relevant aspect in this context relates to fairness in the application of administrative and legislative procedures. This issue, though being relevant for cases in which measures are applied and implemented for environmental

---

105 AES Summit Generation Limited and AES-Tisza Erömü Kft v. The Republic of Hungary, ICSID Case No. ARB/07/22 (ECT), Award of 23 September 2010, para 9.3.40. Similarly, Glamis Gold, Ltd. v. U.S.A., Award of 8 June 2009, paras 770, 771 which requires "complete lack of due process" (albeit on the international minimum standard) and Genin and others v. Estonia, ICSID Case No. ARB/99/2, Award of 25 June 2001, para 371 stating that "any procedural irregularity that may have been present would have to amount to bad faith, a wilful disregard of due process of law or an extreme insufficiency of action" (albeit in the context of arbitrariness).

reasons, is not so strongly connected to the right of the state to further environmental objectives. Due process in proceedings is independent of the objectives behind the measure in question. The following section will portray decisions in which investment tribunals were confronted with conflicts over measures introduced to further an environmental objective and the right of a foreign investor to be treated fairly and equitably.

I. Chemtura Corporation v. Canada

1. Portrayal of the Arbitral Decision

The case of *Chemtura Corporation v. Government of Canada* concerned an investor generating products for pest control which contained lindane, a pesticide, to be used, inter alia, on canola seeds. Because of risks associated with lindane, its use was prohibited in the U.S. and steps to restrict its use had been taken at the international level over the last decades.[106] The dispute before the tribunals concerned the legitimacy of several measures taken by Canadian government authorities to stop the use of lindane-based products on canola seeds. The measures complained of were the termination of the registration of lindane-based products for use on canola seeds, the prohibition of planting lindane-treated seeds, the alleged frustration of a review of the registration process, and allegedly unfair treatment of the investor in the process of registering replacement products.

Having stated at the outset that the customary international minimum standard – taking account of its evolution – was the relevant standard of treatment,[107] the NAFTA tribunal evaluated Canada's review process of lindane. The tribunal noted that it was not its task to determine whether certain uses of lindane were dangerous.[108] In portraying the broader factual context, the tribunal found "that lindane has raised increasingly serious concerns both in other countries and at the international level since the 1970s"[109] and mentioned that lindane was included in the list of chemicals designated for elimination under the 2001 Stockholm Convention on Persis-

---

106 See the portrayal of the respective international law in 'Chapter 1 – Environmental Norms and Principles' at pp. 48 *et seq.*

107 Chemtura Corporation v. Government of Canada, Award of 2 August 2010, para 122.

108 Chemtura Corporation v. Government of Canada, Award of 2 August 2010, para 134.

109 Chemtura Corporation v. Government of Canada, Award of 2 August 2010, para 135, where the tribunal enlists a detailed set – namely 22 – of examples provided by respondent.

tent Organic Pollutants[110] in May 2009.[111] The tribunal further referred to evidence that the review of lindane was prompted by commitments undertaken by Canada during the negotiations of the Aarhus Protocol[112],[113] as well as by concerns relating to the long-range transboundary impact of the agrochemical in the Arctic environment.[114] In the light of this evidence and the description by experts, according to whom the decision to ban lindane was decided after the data had been objectively evaluated,[115] the tribunal saw no basis for the investor's allegations that the review was a trade irritant or for the implied bad faith on the part of the host state.[116]

The tribunal further assessed whether the review process as a whole was compromised by procedural impropriety or bad faith on the part of the respondent state. Given the complexity of the review regulations, the tribunal found that it had to "appraise any procedural deficiency in the light of the mechanisms provided by the Respondent itself to manage such potential occurrences" before establishing a breach.[117] Consequently, the tribunal found that the note announcing the special review and the related process did not reach the threshold of relevant violations.[118] With regard to the investor's allegation that the review was scientifically flawed, the tribunal

---

110 See in 'Chapter 1 – Environmental Norms and Principles' at pp. 48 *et seq.*

111 Chemtura Corporation v. Government of Canada, Award of 2 August 2010, para 136.

112 1998 Aarhus Protocol to the 1979 UNECE Convention on Long-Range Transboundary Air Pollution on Persistent Organic Pollutants.

113 Chemtura Corporation v. Government of Canada, Award of 2 August 2010, para 139.

114 Chemtura Corporation v. Government of Canada, Award of 2 August 2010, para 140.

115 Chemtura Corporation v. Government of Canada, Award of 2 August 2010, paras 139, 141–142.

116 Chemtura Corporation v. Government of Canada, Award of 2 August 2010, paras 137–138, 143. The tribunal stated in that respect that "the standard of proof for allegations of bad faith or disingenuous behavio[u]r is a demanding one."

117 Chemtura Corporation v. Government of Canada, Award of 2 August 2010, para 145.

118 Chemtura Corporation v. Government of Canada, Award of 2 August 2010, paras 147, 148. The tribunal decided that the note announcing the special review, which claimant contended was unspecific and insufficient, had to be assessed against the legitimate regulatory concerns prompting the review and other steps taken by the relevant regulatory agency – the Pest Management Regulatory Agency of Canada – to convey the rationale and focus of the review. Additionally, the tribunal pointed to the fact that the investor was a sophisticated registrant experienced in a highly-regulated industry, thus being familiar with the re-evaluation policy of the regulatory agency, Chemtura Corporation v. Government of Canada, Award of 2 August 2010, para 149.

emphasised that the circumstances surrounding the review pointed to a genuine regulatory concern and it repeated the understanding that it was not within the review scope of the tribunal to judge the correctness or adequacy of the scientific results.[119] Similarly, the tribunal found neither relevant improper influencing or thwarting of the process of setting up a board of review[120] nor a need to question the participation of experts of the regulatory agency in the re-evaluation note at the end of the review process.[121] It specifically stated that the re-evaluation note was not a biased exercise conducted for litigation purposes, as the investor contended.[122]

The second issue the tribunal addressed was whether the prohibition of planting canola seeds treated with chemicals containing lindane after a specific deadline[123] violated the investor's legitimate expectations and the obligation to maintain a transparent regulatory environment.[124] The tribunal found that the deadline stemmed from a voluntary withdrawal agreement, which was an industry-led initiative, only involving the Canadian regulatory agency.[125] Furthermore, the tribunal held that the investor had no legitimate expectation to be treated more favourably than foreseen by the withdrawal agreement, given that the equal treatment of all registrants by the regulatory agency was an expression of regulatory transparency.[126] As a third aspect, the tribunal evaluated the cancellation of the investor's lindane registrations in February 2002.[127] The tribunal found that the regulatory agency followed its standard regulatory practice with respect to the investor[128] and that there was no legal obligation to grant a phase-out through

---

119 Chemtura Corporation v. Government of Canada, Award of 2 August 2010, para 153.

120 Chemtura Corporation v. Government of Canada, Award of 2 August 2010, paras 159, 160.

121 Chemtura Corporation v. Government of Canada, Award of 2 August 2010, para 162.

122 Chemtura Corporation v. Government of Canada, Award of 2 August 2010, para 162.

123 The deadline was 1 July 2001.

124 Chemtura Corporation v. Government of Canada, Award of 2 August 2010, paras 164, 166.

125 Chemtura Corporation v. Government of Canada, Award of 2 August 2010, para 169.

126 Chemtura Corporation v. Government of Canada, Award of 2 August 2010, para 179.

127 In this regard, the investor alleged that it was unfairly deprived of a phase-out right and that this denial constituted a punitive measure, Chemtura Corporation v. Government of Canada, Award of 2 August 2010, para 182.

128 Chemtura Corporation v. Government of Canada, Award of 2 August 2010, paras 191, 192.

voluntary discontinuation.[129] Furthermore, the allegation of a punitive measure was found to be "obviously unfounded".[130]

Lastly, the tribunal evaluated whether the investor was not accorded the expeditious treatment it expected in the registration process of its new lindane replacement product, Gaucho CS FL. The tribunal found that the regulatory agency had not committed to an expedited registration process for all replacement products, but it had committed to working in good faith to achieve a swift registration of the products without jeopardizing the standard of review for each registration.[131] In evaluating the alleged delay in processing the application, the tribunal declared that it had to

> "take into account the obvious fact that the operation of complex administrations is not always optimal in practice and that the mere existence of delays is not sufficient for a breach of the international minimum standard of treatment. This is not to say that a violation must be outrageous in order to breach such standard."[132]

It found that the responsibility for the delay which occurred could not be attributed in its entirety either to the investor or to the regulatory agency[133] and that in the light of the circumstances the delays that were attributable to the agency did not constitute a breach of the international minimum standard.[134]

2. Assessment

The arbitral decision addresses the concerns of the investor in a systematic and detailed manner, thereby providing a good overview of the tribunal's assessment of the protective scope of the treatment standard. The tri-

---

129 Chemtura Corporation v. Government of Canada, Award of 2 August 2010, para 190.

130 Chemtura Corporation v. Government of Canada, Award of 2 August 2010, paras 190, 192.

131 Chemtura Corporation v. Government of Canada, Award of 2 August 2010, para 207. Further, the tribunal found that Gaucho CS FL did not fall within the scope of the expedited registration process since it was only submitted at a later stage, Chemtura Corporation v. Government of Canada, Award of 2 August 2010, para 211.

132 Chemtura Corporation v. Government of Canada, Award of 2 August 2010, para 215.

133 Chemtura Corporation v. Government of Canada, Award of 2 August 2010, para 218.

134 Chemtura Corporation v. Government of Canada, Award of 2 August 2010, para 219. To underline this finding, the tribunal further looked to the registration of the products in the U.S. and found that the time spans required in that legislation were roughly similar, para 220.

bunal accredited the host state with broad regulatory authority. While stating that the scope of the protective standard was not abstractly reduced by a margin of appreciation granted to domestic regulatory agencies operating in highly specialised domains,[135] the tribunal considered such a margin when reviewing the concrete measures complained of by the investor. Accordingly, the tribunal emphasised that the review of scientific evidence on which the state relied in implementing the environmental measure was restricted. It balanced the evidence before it and found that this "suggest[ed]" that the review of the toxin "was launched out of legitimate regulatory concerns and in accordance with Canada's international commitments".[136]

A major part of the determination is dedicated to the evaluation of administrative processes and procedural requirements. The tribunal underscores that the state will not be held against a standard of perfection: A few procedural inadequacies do not violate the notion of due process, if the whole process is not relevantly impacted. In scrutinising the whole procedure, the tribunal takes the surrounding circumstances – including the procedural knowledge and contribution of the investor – into account. Although this standard of review appears adequate for the treaty standard of fair and equitable treatment, it is questionable whether the applied level of scrutiny correctly reflects the customary standard of international law. This is especially the case with regard to the assessment of the registration process of the lindane replacement product. Here, the tribunal analyses whether a process that takes roughly double the time of what is normally foreseen violates the standard. Nevertheless, the assessment correctly captures "the fundamental character and purpose" of the standard of fair and equitable treatment and may be seminal in illustrating the limitations on compensation for the consequences of legitimate regulatory conduct.[137]

II. Methanex v. United States

The award in *Methanex v. United States* predominantly dealt with an alleged discrimination due to the ban on the oxygenate, for which the investor produced a feedstock.[138] Discussing a potential violation of the standard of

135 Chemtura Corporation v. Government of Canada, Award of 2 August 2010, para 123.

136 Chemtura Corporation v. Government of Canada, Award of 2 August 2010, para 147.

137 *Moloo*, Rahim/*Jacinto*, Justin, 'Environmental and Health Regulation: Assessing Liability under Investment-Treaties', 29 Berkeley Journal of International Law 2011, 1 (65).

138 See for a portrayal of the facts, 'Chapter 3 – Standards of Non-Discriminatory Treatment' at pp. 183 *et seq.*

fair and equitable treatment under the NAFTA, the tribunal – when applying a literal interpretation of the relevant provision – found that 'discrimination' was not an element of this standard[139] and that a prohibition of discrimination did not form part of the international minimum standard.[140] Since the investor had not demonstrated a relevant development of the protective scope of the international minimum standard,[141] the tribunal found no violation. Due to this narrow understanding of the protective scope, the environmental component of the claim is not discussed in this context.

III. S.D. Myers Inc. v. Canada

As portrayed in the third chapter, the focus of the decision in *S.D. Myers Inc. v. Canada* was on whether the export ban on PCBs violated the standard of national treatment,[142] but not on a potential breach of the standard of fair and equitable treatment. In connection with the latter standard, the tribunal stated that the respective standard contained in the treaty was a "floor below which treatment of foreign investors must not fall", irrespective of discrimination.[143] Most importantly, the tribunal emphasised the "high measure of deference that international law generally extends to the right of domestic authorities to regulate matters within their own borders".[144] In this context, the tribunal stated that it was not its task to "second-guess government decision-making" and that potential errors in the appreciation of facts by the tribunal were to be remedied through internal political processes, but not in the context of arbitration.[145] Irrespective of this finding,

---

139 Methanex v. United States, Award of 3 August 2005, Part IV Chapter C paras 14, 16.

140 Methanex v. United States, Award of 3 August 2005, Part IV Chapter C para 25.

141 Methanex v. United States, Award of 3 August 2005, Part IV Chapter C para 26. The tribunal intensely looked at the decision in *Waste Management v. Mexico*, to which the investor had referred as encapsulating a broader understanding of the scope of the international minimum standard. The tribunal declared that even this scope would not help claimant, since there was no "sectional or racial prejudice" in the alleged discrimination.

142 See for a portrayal of the facts, 'Chapter 3 – Standards of Non-Discriminatory Treatment' at pp. 176 *et seq.*

143 S.D. Myers Inc. v. Canada, Partial Award on the Merits, 13 November 2000, para 259.

144 S.D. Myers Inc. v. Canada, Partial Award on the Merits, 13 November 2000, para 263.

145 S.D. Myers Inc. v. Canada, Partial Award on the Merits, 13 November 2000, para 261. The tribunal stated verbatim that a "tribunal does not have an open-ended mandate to second-guess government decision-making. Governments have to make

the tribunal concluded by briefly stating that a violation exists when the treatment reaches a level which is "unacceptable from the international perspective", which it found to be the case.[146] Given the extensive discussion of the decision in the context of national treatment, a further evaluation at this stage would be repetitive. The tribunal's apprehension of the deference owed to the host state, however, deserves attention.

IV. Metalclad Corporation v. United Mexican States

1. Portrayal of the Arbitral Decision

Metalclad Corporation v. United Mexican States is a further case applying the standard of fair and equitable treatment to a measure allegedly implemented to address environmental concerns. The case related to the use of an acquired site as a hazardous waste disposal facility. The foreign investor had been granted all relevant permits, save for a municipal permit for the construction of the hazardous waste landfill, the necessity of which was disputed.[147] The investor completed its work on the facility – despite arising opposition to the project at the level of the state and the municipality. Ultimately, the municipality denied the investor the local construction permit for several reasons, inter alia, ecological concerns regarding the environmental impact on the site and on surrounding communities and the opposition of the local population; but none referring to any physical defects of the construction.[148] The denial of the permit occurred thirteen months after the investor's application in a meeting which was closed to the investor. Furthermore, the governor of the state issued an "Ecological Decree" declaring the area of the landfill to be a natural area for the protection of rare cacti.

The tribunal's discussion of the standard of fair and equitable treatment focused on the authority of the municipality to deny the municipal construc-

---

many potentially controversial choices. In doing so, they may appear to have made mistakes, to have misjudged the facts, proceeded on the basis of a misguided economic or sociological theory, placed too much emphasis on some social values over others and adopted solutions that are ultimately ineffective or counterproductive. The ordinary remedy, if there were one, for errors in modern governments is through internal political and legal processes, including elections."

[146] S.D. Myers Inc. v. Canada, Partial Award on the Merits, 13 November 2000, paras 263, 268.

[147] Metalclad Corporation v. United Mexican States, ICSID Case No. ARB(AF)/97/1, Award of 30 August 2000, paras 77–79.

[148] Metalclad Corporation v. United Mexican States, ICSID Case No. ARB(AF)/97/1, Award of 30 August 2000, paras 92–93.

tion permit as well as on the relevance of assurances given to the investor. At the outset, the tribunal pointed to the importance of the notion of transparency, albeit in a way independent of assessing the scope of the treatment standard. The tribunal understood 'transparency' to mean that – in addition to assuring that all relevant rules relating to the investment are "capable of being readily known" – the host state is obliged to act as soon as it becomes "aware of any scope for misunderstanding or confusion" relating to such legal requirements.[149]

To determine whether the municipality had the authority to deny the permit, the tribunal aimed to entangle the relevant competence of the municipality under Mexican law.[150] It found that – if an obligation for a municipal construction permit exists – the authority of the municipality does not extend beyond considerations of appropriate construction. Environmental considerations fell within the authority of the federal state, so that the denial of the permit was improper.[151] The tribunal raised several objections regarding procedural propriety and transparency, namely the lack of a clear rule as to whether a municipal construction permit was required, the absence of an established practice or procedure as to the manner of handling applications for such a permit, the denial occurring thirteen months after the investor's application at a time when the investor – with the knowledge of the municipality – had virtually completed the site, and the fact that the denial occurred in a meeting to which the investor was neither invited nor had a possibility to appear.[152] Furthermore, the tribunal considered that the activities of the municipality and the state following the denial of the permit indicated that the denial of the permit was improper.[153]

---

149 Metalclad Corporation v. United Mexican States, ICSID Case No. ARB(AF)/97/1, Award of 30 August 2000, para 76.

150 Metalclad Corporation v. United Mexican States, ICSID Case No. ARB(AF)/97/1, Award of 30 August 2000, paras 82–83.

151 Metalclad Corporation v. United Mexican States, ICSID Case No. ARB(AF)/97/1, Award of 30 August 2000, para 86. The tribunal concluded as follows: "Consequently, the denial of the permit by the Municipality by reference to environmental impact considerations in the case of what was basically a hazardous waste disposal landfill, was improper, as was the municipality's denial of the permit for any reason other than those related to the physical construction or defects in the site."

152 Metalclad Corporation v. United Mexican States, ICSID Case No. ARB(AF)/97/1, Award of 30 August 2000, paras 88, 90, 91.

153 Metalclad Corporation v. United Mexican States, ICSID Case No. ARB(AF)/97/1, Award of 30 August 2000, para 97. The tribunal criticised the following activities of the municipality: the attempt to challenge the agreement concluded between the investor and the respondent state allowing for the operation of the landfill (para 94) and the filing of an injunction to bar the landfill from operating (para 95). In this context, the tribunal also mentions the actions of the state regarding the is-

The tribunal additionally focused on the assurances by federal officials given to the investor, according to which the federal permits issued were the only permits necessary to construct and operate the landfill. The municipal permit would be issued if an application were filed.[154] The tribunal pointed out that the investor – relying on these representations – continued its work on the site with the knowledge of the federal, state, and municipal governments.[155] It held that the investor was entitled to rely on the representations by federal officials and to continue its work on the landfill.[156]

The tribunal does not assess whether the municipality and the state were motivated by legitimate environmental concerns to ban the operation of the hazardous waste facility. Only in passing does the tribunal refer to environmental considerations. It states as follows:

> "This conclusion is not affected by NAFTA Article 1114, which permits a Party to ensure that investment activity is undertaken in a manner sensitive to environmental concerns. The conclusion of the [Agreement allowing the operation of the landfill] and the issuance of the federal permits show clearly that Mexico was satisfied that this project was consistent with, and sensitive to, its environmental concerns."[157]

Accordingly, the tribunal was satisfied that the divisions of regulatory authority within the federal state did not require a review of environmental considerations, since the federal government had been satisfied with the environmental soundness of the landfill. Thus, the tribunal found a breach of the standard of fair and equitable treatment.[158]

---

suance of an ecological decree covering the area (para 96) despite its limited powers to regulate in environmental matters (para 84).

[154] Metalclad Corporation v. United Mexican States, ICSID Case No. ARB(AF)/97/1, Award of 30 August 2000, paras 80, 85, 88.

[155] Metalclad Corporation v. United Mexican States, ICSID Case No. ARB(AF)/97/1, Award of 30 August 2000, para 87.

[156] Metalclad Corporation v. United Mexican States, ICSID Case No. ARB(AF)/97/1, Award of 30 August 2000, para 89.

[157] Metalclad Corporation v. United Mexican States, ICSID Case No. ARB(AF)/97/1, Award of 30 August 2000, para 98.

[158] Metalclad Corporation v. United Mexican States, ICSID Case No. ARB(AF)/97/1, Award of 30 August 2000, paras 100–101. In para 99, the tribunal summarised its findings as follows: "The totality of these circumstances demonstrates a lack of orderly process and timely disposition in relation to an investor of a Party acting in the expectation that it would be treated fairly and justly in accordance with the NAFTA."

2. Assessment

The arbitral decision is tainted by a significant systematic flaw: The tribunal did not interpret Article 1105 NAFTA to determine the protective scope of the standard of fair and equitable treatment. Rather, it relied on the concept of 'transparency' to reach its conclusion – without discussing whether this concept is encompassed by the protection of the treatment standard.[159]

In the light of the reasoning of the tribunal, it is not clear whether the tribunal considered the relevant treatment standard to encompass the notion of transparency. Furthermore, the tribunal did not discuss whether the applicable standard was the international minimum standard or whether it related to a broader protective understanding.

Nevertheless, evaluated against the notions of the standard of fair and equitable treatment set forth above, it appears as if the tribunal's finding of a breach in reliance on transparency has merit. In my opinion it is doubtful whether the customary international minimum standard has attained a protective level encompassing the notion of transparency, whereas the treaty standard of fair and equitable treatment has done so.[160] While the abstract understanding of transparency adopted by the tribunal appears excessive, – due to the obligation of the host state to act as soon as it becomes "aware of any scope for misunderstanding or confusion" relating to legal requirements of the investment – the concrete circumstances merit the finding of a violation: It is not transparent behaviour to adopt a legal framework which is not clear as to the necessary permits and to observe the investor construct its facilities without indicating the lack of relevant permits. In the meantime, the findings in the award have resulted in Mexico aiming for more precision in its environmental laws and more transparency in its decision making.[161]

---

[159] The exclusive reliance on a concept of 'transparency' stemming from Article 102 NAFTA, but not discussed as element of the standard of fair and equitable treatment enshrined in Article 1105 NAFTA led the judge in the proceedings to set aside the award to reason that the tribunal had "decided a matter beyond the scope of the submission to arbitration", United Mexican States v. Metalclad, Supreme Court of British Columbia, Reasons for Judgment of the Honorable Mr. Justice Tysoe of 2 May 2001, paras 69, 70, 71, 73, 76.

[160] The arbitral decision in *Metalclad Corporation v. United Mexican States* was rendered before the FTC Interpretation became binding on tribunals in cases arising under the provisions of the NAFTA. Accordingly, the arbitral tribunal could have adopted a broader approach to the standard.

[161] *Gaines*, Sanford E., 'Environmental Policy Implications of Investor-State Arbitration under NAFTA Chapter 11', 7 International Environmental Agreements: Politics, Law and Economics 2007, 171 (180–181). The author paints an interesting

Similarly, the tribunal could have found a breach of the legitimate expectations of the investor because of the assurances by federal officials on which the investor relied. Although an investor cannot normally substitute permits with assurances that these permits are not relevant, the evaluation has to take account of the unclear regulatory framework, which lacks a precise determination of the necessary permits. In such a situation of uncertainty, the investor could legitimately rely on those representations. Unfortunately, the award lacks a systematic discussion of the protective scope of the standard with regard to the notions of transparency, due process and legitimate expectations.

Despite the environmental reasons set forth by the municipality for denying the construction permit, the tribunal did not address the validity of these environmental concerns at all. Such an approach appears correct as the issue is inseparably intertwined with the issue of federalism. As far as the national law of the host state contains a division of authority in the sense that federal entities are responsible to assess environmental implications of a project, it would be wrong for the tribunal to substitute its environmental assessment – or that of the municipality – for those of the competent entities. The tribunal correctly concluded that the issuance of the federal permits showed that environmental requirements were satisfied. Whereas the respondent state criticised the tribunal's approach to interpreting its national laws, it has to be maintained that the investor, on balance, would not have been dealt with fairly, even if the municipality had had the authority to deny its permit for environmental reasons: The lack of clarity regarding internal competencies within the host state cannot be held against the foreign investor.[162]

V. Glamis Gold, Ltd. v. U.S.A.

1. Portrayal of the Arbitral Decision

The public policy implications in *Glamis Gold, Ltd. v. U.S.A.* related to the cultural impact of a measure that was also arousing environmental concerns: The investor, a Canadian mining company, owned mining rights over a stretch of land in the south-eastern Californian desert. It sought approval

picture of the factual developments following the arbitral decision and finds, inter alia, that the award has not lead to 'regulatory chill' in Mexico, but to an amelioration of environmental laws.

[162] In a similar sense, see also the rule enshrined in Article 27 VCLT, according to which a state may not invoke the provisions of its internal law as justification for its failure to perform a treaty.

for a mining project to extract gold in the close vicinity of areas of special cultural concern to Native Americans, featuring three open pits, the excavation of 150 million tons of ore and 300 million tons of waste rock, and a subsequent complete backfill of only two of the pits. This project was ultimately not approved – and the investor claimed that Californian legislation introduced retrospectively and an unduly delay in considering the project rendered it economically unviable.

At the outset, the tribunal declared to base its assessment on the minimum standard of treatment in the sense of the *Neer* test, albeit emphasising the possibility of an evolution of the standard in the sense "that, as an international community, we may be shocked by State actions now that did not offend us previously".[163] The first measure the tribunal discussed was "a reasoned, complicated legal opinion" drafted by a solicitor of the U.S. Federal Department of the Interior, which changed a "decades-old rule and century-old regime" regarding the consequences of the discovery of Native American artefacts at a mining site – a regime on which the investor had based its expectations.[164] The tribunal found that such a change did not violate the rights of the investor, as the Opinion was neither arbitrary, nor exhibiting a manifest lack of reason, nor exhibiting blatant unfairness or evident discrimination against this particular investor.[165] The tribunal refused to analyse the requirement of due process, as potential procedural errors had been remedied by a subsequent Opinion which had swiftly replaced the first Opinion.[166]

With regard to the alleged legitimate expectations of the investor, the tribunal underlined that these would require at least a "quasi-contractual relationship, whereby the State has purposely and specifically induced the investment."[167] This was not the case, since the investor could not derive

163 Glamis Gold, Ltd. v. U.S.A., Award of 8 June 2009, para 616. The test the tribunal ostensibly applies throughout the award is whether the respective measure "is manifestly arbitrary, completely lacking in due process, exhibiting evident discrimination, or manifestly lacking in reasons".

164 Glamis Gold, Ltd. v. U.S.A., Award of 8 June 2009, paras 758, 761. The anterior regime was the "unnecessary or undue degradation" standard, according to which the discovery of such artefacts at a mining site could require mitigation, but would not lead to a denial of the mining project.

165 Glamis Gold, Ltd. v. U.S.A., Award of 8 June 2009, paras 763–765.

166 Glamis Gold, Ltd. v. U.S.A., Award of 8 June 2009, para 771. The tribunal also made it clear that it would not delve into the details of and justifications for domestic law (para 762), which had to be challenged in domestic courts and also considered the discussion of process requirements under national law not helpful, as they did not give guidance for the decision under international law (para 770).

167 Glamis Gold, Ltd. v. U.S.A., Award of 8 June 2009, para 766.

such far-reaching expectations from the regulatory framework. The tribunal stated:

> "First, Claimant was operating in a climate that was becoming more and more sensitive to the environmental consequences of open-pit mining. Second, although the [Opinion] came to a different result than a reasonable investor might expect under the mining regulatory regime as it stood, the federal government did not make specific commitments to induce Claimant to persevere with its mining claims. It did not guarantee Claimant approval of its claims, nor did it offer Claimant any benefits to pursuing such claims beyond the customary chance to exploit federal land for possible profit."[168]

Accordingly, the tribunal underlines that a long standing legal framework can be legitimately altered for environmental reasons, as long as state representatives have not given concrete commitments to the contrary to a foreign investor.

As to the alleged delay in reviewing the investor's mining project, the tribunal found that – despite a possible slowness – the review was proceeding diligently as it dealt with a particularly complicated, contested issue and the federal government was quite aware of the likelihood, if not imminence, of litigation.[169] Neither did the tribunal find a second cycle of the review to be lacking due process, which took place at the time the arbitration had already started.[170] Thirdly, the tribunal assessed the cultural review of the investor's mining project. It began by emphasising that it would not substitute the national authority's appreciation of the facts with its own.[171] Regarding the evaluation of the content of the cultural survey, the tribunal was satisfied with the host state's reasoning for the application of the specific – novel and never used before – methodology; namely the need to cover a vast area cost-efficiently.[172] Furthermore, the tribunal considered that the

---

168 Glamis Gold, Ltd. v. U.S.A., Award of 8 June 2009, para 767.

169 Glamis Gold, Ltd. v. U.S.A., Award of 8 June 2009, para 774.

170 Glamis Gold, Ltd. v. U.S.A., Award of 8 June 2009, para 776.

171 Glamis Gold, Ltd. v. U.S.A., Award of 8 June 2009, para 779. The tribunal stated the following: "In evaluating each of these arguments, the Tribunal is mindful of Respondent's statement that "[i]t is simply not this Tribunal's task to become archaeologists and ethnographers and to draw a definitive conclusion as to the location of the Trail of Dreams." The Tribunal agrees with this statement. It is not the role of this Tribunal, or any international tribunal, to supplant its own judgment of underlying factual material and support for that of a qualified domestic agency. Indeed, our only task is to decide whether Claimant has adequately proven that the agency's review and conclusions exhibit a gross denial of justice, manifest arbitrariness, blatant unfairness, a complete lack of due process, evident discrimination, or a manifest lack of reasons so as to rise to the level of a breach of the customary international law standard embedded in Article 1105."

172 Glamis Gold, Ltd. v. U.S.A., Award of 8 June 2009, para 782.

host state was justified in relying upon the opinion of the professionals engaged in the survey the way that it did.[173] It was also satisfied with the evidence the host state offered for having used a diligent review procedure.[174]

Regarding the initiatives of the government of California, such as the Senate bill, to implement mandatory backfilling requirements for all excavations,[175] the tribunal found that the bill did not specifically target the investor,[176] that none of the reasonable expectations of the investor was violated by changes to a predictable and transparent framework,[177] and that the bill was not arbitrary.[178] The tribunal highlighted that the mere appearance of arbitrariness was not sufficient – and that one bill could legitimately address only some concerns and not others, constituting a compromise between the conflicting desires and needs of the various parties affected.[179] Relying on similar reasoning the tribunal also denied a violation of the standard of treatment through the regulations of the State Mining and Geology Board: In the absence of specific assurances, there was no breach of the investor's legitimate expectations and the investor could not expect the

---

173 Glamis Gold, Ltd. v. U.S.A., Award of 8 June 2009, para 783. The tribunal emphasises the expertise of the engaged professionals, stating that it "is professionals such as these, with their technical background and expertise, not this Tribunal, who are the proper parties to determine" the technicalities of the technical review.

174 Glamis Gold, Ltd. v. U.S.A., Award of 8 June 2009, paras 784-7. Specifically, the tribunal was satisfied that the host state could reasonably rely on the evidence gathered, that the public hearings and site-visits were not shams, and that the review did not come to a pre-determined conclusion – so that the tribunal did not find evidence of arbitrariness.

175 Glamis Gold, Ltd. v. U.S.A., Award of 8 June 2009, para 166.

176 Glamis Gold, Ltd. v. U.S.A., Award of 8 June 2009, paras 792–796. The tribunal points to the difficulty to ascertain legislative intent. It uses the language and drafting history of the bill to conclude that claimant's project was not exclusively targeted, but that the bill addressed concerns that the legislator had regarding the potential damage to sacred sites caused by present and future open pit mines in general. Whether or not another project will be affected by the bill in the future, the tribunal could not determine, but this aspect was not relevant to its findings.

177 Glamis Gold, Ltd. v. U.S.A., Award of 8 June 2009, paras 799–802. The tribunal stressed the fact that relevant legitimate expectations of the investor required an active inducement of a quasi-contractual expectation by respondent. It pointed to the "highly regulated environment with respect to environmental measures in general, and mineral exploration in particular" and to the resulting atmosphere of regulation (para 800). The tribunal further emphasised that there would have to be a specific inducement of investment on the part of the state and referred to the categorisation of the assurances in *Metalclad*, which were "definitive, unambiguous and repeated" (para 802).

178 Glamis Gold, Ltd. v. U.S.A., Award of 8 June 2009, paras 803–805.

179 Glamis Gold, Ltd. v. U.S.A., Award of 8 June 2009, paras 803–805.

host state to refrain from passing legislation affecting it.[180] The regulation was based on sufficient scientific evidence and not arbitrary.[181] The tribunal also found that the use of emergency legislation was within the state's regulatory powers, since there was an existing threat to the sacred sites which the state could legitimately address temporarily.[182] Finally, the tribunal found that the cumulative effect of all measures taken together did not reach the level of a violation of the standard of treatment either.[183]

2. Assessment

Like most of the more recent NAFTA awards, this arbitral decision demonstrates systematic problems in determining the protective scope of the treatment standard.[184] Although the tribunal declared that it would apply the *Neer* test, some of its considerations – most notably the notion of legitimate expectations – are not rooted in the *Neer* standard.[185] From a doctrinal perspective, the tribunal should have demonstrated that this notion has evolved into customary international law. Irrespective, the applied protective scope appears fair to both the investor and the host state. Further, the findings of the tribunal are interesting regarding the juxtaposition of 'legitimate expectations' and the 'stability of the regulatory framework'. The tribunal's emphasis on the necessity of a "quasi-contractual relationship" underlines the diminished protection afforded by the notion of the 'regulatory framework'. Accordingly, public policy considerations – like environmental reasons – can lead to a legitimate alteration of the legal framework, unless the change is arbitrary or targets a specific investor.

Although the tribunal expressly doubted the applicability of domestic deference in international tribunals, it found that in the present case deference was contained in the restricted protective scope of the treatment stan-

---

180 Glamis Gold, Ltd. v. U.S.A., Award of 8 June 2009, paras 811, 813.

181 Glamis Gold, Ltd. v. U.S.A., Award of 8 June 2009, paras 817–818. Specifically, the tribunal found that the fact that non-metallic extractions were not included did not render the regulation arbitrary, because a legislator was not obliged to address all existing problems at the same time.

182 Glamis Gold, Ltd. v. U.S.A., Award of 8 June 2009, paras 813–815. The tribunal stated that "at least one project was known and presented a potential danger to Native American sacred sites, and the possibility existed of other potentially disruptive projects yet unknown, thus the regulation not being speculative" (para 814).

183 Glamis Gold, Ltd. v. U.S.A., Award of 8 June 2009, paras 824–828.

184 See portrayal above at pp. 236 *et seq.*

185 See the similar critical assessment of *Kahn*, Jordan C., 'Striking NAFTA Gold: Glamis Advances Investor-State Arbitration', 33 Fordham International Law Journal 2009, 101 (153).

dard, rather than being additive to it.[186] While this argument can have problematic implications – especially in cases not based on the *Neer* test – the practical assessment illustrates that the tribunal was very cautious not to supplant its appreciation of evidence for that of the host state. It declined to assess the cultural – and environmental – evidence on which the host state had based its measures. Likewise, such margin of appreciation was also granted to the host state with regard to the applied procedures and methodologies.

VI. Plama Consortium Limited v. Bulgaria

The case *Plama Consortium Limited v. Bulgaria* addressed several issues that the investor – a consortium that had acquired a refinery as part of the privatisation process – considered to be violating its right to fair and equitable treatment under the ECT. One of the complaints related to a change in the environmental law of the host state. The tribunal had to assess whether the law at the time the investment was made exonerated the investor from liability for prior environmental damage. Under the later amendments to the environmental law, the investor was – through the target of its investment – clearly liable for past environmental damage, as implemented exonerations were not applicable due to a specific deadline.

The tribunal found that the relevant rules of the environmental law prior to the amendment were not clear as to the liability for cleaning up past environmental damage.[187] Further, there was no evidence that the investor had successfully bargained for a clause in the privatisation agreement following which the state assumed liability for prior environmental damage.[188] In assessing the legitimacy of the changes in the law, the tribunal found no evidence that the change in the environmental law directly targeted or discriminated against the investor or favoured its main competitor; rather, the change was intended to create favourable conditions for investors.[189] Considering a potential violation of the investor's legitimate expectations, the tribunal emphasised that the underlying ECT did not protect investors against "any and all changes" in the host state's law and it found no promises or other representations that the host state had made in

---

186 Glamis Gold, Ltd. v. U.S.A., Award of 8 June 2009, para 617.

187 Plama Consortium Limited v. Bulgaria, ICSID Case No. ARB/03/24, Award of 27 August 2008, paras 212, 220.

188 Plama Consortium Limited v. Bulgaria, ICSID Case No. ARB/03/24, Award of 27 August 2008, para 213.

189 Plama Consortium Limited v. Bulgaria, ICSID Case No. ARB/03/24, Award of 27 August 2008, paras 218, 223.

this respect.[190] Additionally, the tribunal questioned the existence of any real harm for the investor, as there was neither evidence that the investor had paid or would have to pay in the future for cleaning, nor that outstanding liability made financing the investor's intended project impossible.[191]

This decision features a very specific factual situation, so that only limited conclusions can be drawn from it to determine the relationship between the standard of fair and equitable treatment and environmental measures. However, the case illustrates that an investor cannot derive legitimate expectations from unclear laws or agreements. The decision further seems to imply that uncertainty and vagueness in a relevant law do not generally constitute a detriment to the host state, arguably imposing on the investor an obligation to seek clarification of an unclear position. The decision also demonstrates that changes to an environmental law are not barred by a foreign investor that is negatively affected by them.

VII. Técnicas Medioambientales Tecmed, S.A. v. United Mexican States

Técnicas Medioambientales Tecmed, S.A. v. United Mexican States concerned a foreign investor that had acquired the majority in a company owning a landfill facility for hazardous waste, the operation of which necessitated a licence. The original licence of indefinite duration was substituted by a licence which required yearly renewal.[192] Subsequent to the acquisition of the landfill, the regulations for landfills – especially regarding the necessary distance to urban centres – were altered, imposing conditions which the facility did not fulfil.[193] Although the new regulations did not retrospectively apply to the facility, its closeness to the nearest town as well as the transportation of contaminated soil from another region to the landfill resulted in significant opposition by the local community.[194] Both the company and the municipality agreed on the relocation of the landfill. Before a new location was identified, the competent environmental authority declined the renewal of the li-

---

190 Plama Consortium Limited v. Bulgaria, ICSID Case No. ARB/03/24, Award of 27 August 2008, para 219.

191 Plama Consortium Limited v. Bulgaria, ICSID Case No. ARB/03/24, Award of 27 August 2008, para 225–226.

192 Técnicas Medioambientales Tecmed, S.A. v. United Mexican States, ICSID Case No. ARB (AF)/00/2, Award of 29 May 2003, paras 36, 38.

193 Técnicas Medioambientales Tecmed, S.A. v. United Mexican States, ICSID Case No. ARB (AF)/00/2, Award of 29 May 2003, para 106.

194 Técnicas Medioambientales Tecmed, S.A. v. United Mexican States, ICSID Case No. ARB (AF)/00/2, Award of 29 May 2003, paras 106, 108.

cence for the original site, despite the expectation of the investor to use the original facility until the relocation process was completed.[195] The stated reasons were not stemming from the way the facility was operated, but related to breaches of guidelines on the transportation of waste.[196]

Arguably, the arbitral decision primarily focuses on expropriation, with regard to which it finds a violation.[197] Nevertheless, the discussion of the standard of fair and equitable treatment is detailed, and – as is portrayed above – especially the tribunal's understanding relating to the relevance of the investor's legitimate expectations inspired a substantial number of subsequent investment tribunals.[198] Although the formulation of these expectations *in abstracto* is very broad, the application of the notion to the facts of the case is convincing. The tribunal relied on the fair expectation of the investor that the laws applicable to its investment "would be used for the purpose of assuring compliance with environmental protection, human health and ecological balance goals underlying such laws".[199] The tribunal found that, in agreeing to the relocation of the landfill, the investor had – and expressed – the legitimate expectation that it could operate the original facility until the relocation had taken place.[200] These expectations were violated by the non-renewal of the licence.

The tribunal determined that the refusal to renew the licence was primarily motivated by reasons which were not made transparent to the investor.[201] The infringements of regulations relating to the transport of waste had previously never been invoked as potential reasons to deny a renewal of the licence. The tribunal did not decide whether the environmental authority attempted to pressure the company to relocate swiftly at its own cost, or whether the aim was to unequivocally close the facility due to local opposition. Either way, the investor was not treated with the transparency it could have expected.[202] Further, the tribunal placed this incident in the context of

---

[195] Técnicas Medioambientales Tecmed, S.A. v. United Mexican States, ICSID Case No. ARB (AF)/00/2, Award of 29 May 2003, paras 110, 112.

[196] Técnicas Medioambientales Tecmed, S.A. v. United Mexican States, ICSID Case No. ARB (AF)/00/2, Award of 29 May 2003, paras 99, 107.

[197] See in more detail in 'Chapter 5 – Expropriation' at pp. 328 *et seq.*

[198] See above at p. 244.

[199] Técnicas Medioambientales Tecmed, S.A. v. United Mexican States, ICSID Case No. ARB (AF)/00/2, Award of 29 May 2003, para 157.

[200] Técnicas Medioambientales Tecmed, S.A. v. United Mexican States, ICSID Case No. ARB (AF)/00/2, Award of 29 May 2003, paras 158–160.

[201] Técnicas Medioambientales Tecmed, S.A. v. United Mexican States, ICSID Case No. ARB (AF)/00/2, Award of 29 May 2003, paras 161–164.

[202] Técnicas Medioambientales Tecmed, S.A. v. United Mexican States, ICSID Case No. ARB (AF)/00/2, Award of 29 May 2003, para 164. The tribunal further

the overall treatment of the investor. The investor was deprived of the opportunity to clearly assess the legal situation of its investment, so that the treatment could not be considered to be fair and equitable.[203]

The decision illustrates the duty of a host state to take into account the legitimate expectations of the investor in a transparent manner, when aiming to further environmental objectives. The intention of the municipality to accommodate the growing and outspoken concerns of the local population regarding the environmental impact of the investment is appropriate. The investor accepted the necessity to relocate the facility – for the position of which it was not responsible – and supported the process of finding a suitable location. Accordingly, the competent authorities could have achieved their environmental objective in a conjoint undertaking, acknowledging the expectations of the investor. However, by giving in to public pressure, the host state sought a solution that disregarded the investor's position. The tribunal correctly found that this was not a legitimate way to remedy prior inefficiencies in addressing the concerns. Both parties agreed that the evidence on which the national authority had relied did not relate to the operation of the landfill as such and that the breaches could be punished by fine,[204] so that the tribunal did not have to evaluate it. Therefore, the refusal to renew the relevant licence was not based on appropriate reasons and not connected to the existence of environmental concerns.

VIII. Vattenfall AB, Vattenfall Europe AG, Vattenfall Europe Generation AG & Co. KG v. The Federal Republic of Germany

The last case to be briefly portrayed in this context is *Vattenfall AB, Vattenfall Europe AG, Vattenfall Europe Generation AG & Co. KG v. The Federal Republic of Germany*, which was settled by agreement. This case concerned the conduct of local authorities relating to the issuance of permits for a new coal-fired plant that the investor intended to construct on the site

stated: "The refusal to renew the Permit in this case was actually used to permanently close down a site whose operation had become a nuisance due to political reasons relating to the community's opposition expressed in a variety of forms, regardless of the company in charge of the operation and regardless of whether or not it was being properly operated."

203 Técnicas Medioambientales Tecmed, S.A. v. United Mexican States, ICSID Case No. ARB (AF)/00/2, Award of 29 May 2003, paras 165–167, 173. The tribunal particularly emphasises the facts relating to the change of the original indefinite licence to one requiring yearly renewal, paras 168–171.

204 Técnicas Medioambientales Tecmed, S.A. v. United Mexican States, ICSID Case No. ARB (AF)/00/2, Award of 29 May 2003, paras 50, 99, 100, 107.

of a previously operated plant.[205] A change in the political composition of the federal government with participation of a green party, which had vowed in the election campaign to stop the building of the plant, allegedly influenced the subsequent actions of the competent authorities.

The local authorities competent to issue relevant permits finally issued a water use permit and an emission control permit, with what the investor claimed to be "extremely severe restrictions", which departed from a prior agreement.[206] The investor claimed that the imposed restrictions under the water use permit for using cooling water violated a prior agreement and that a "politically motivated delay of the administrative procedure" for the authorisation of the power plant breached the host state's obligation to treat the investor fairly and equitably under Article 10 ECT.[207] Unsurprisingly, the settlement agreement between the parties, as incorporated in the award, does not address these issues.[208] The parties agreed that the investor is issued a "modified water use permit" and that it is released from the obligation to "set up district heating pipelines and to build and operate a discharge cooler".[209] Although it is impossible to completely judge from the scarce material available in the public domain, it looks like the investor has significantly improved its situation through the settlement. It is impossible to estimate how far the environmental objectives purportedly furthered by the host state have been given up or whether they are now being addressed through a different channel. Accordingly, this case does not give much guidance for the subject of this study.

---

[205] Vattenfall AB, Vattenfall Europe AG, Vattenfall Europe Generation AG v. Federal Republic of Germany, ICSID Case No. ARB/09/6, Request for Arbitration of 30 March 2009, para 11.

[206] Vattenfall AB, Vattenfall Europe AG, Vattenfall Europe Generation AG v. Federal Republic of Germany, ICSID Case No. ARB/09/6, Request for Arbitration of 30 March 2009, paras 36–40.

[207] Vattenfall AB, Vattenfall Europe AG, Vattenfall Europe Generation AG v. Federal Republic of Germany, ICSID Case No. ARB/09/6, Request for Arbitration of 30 March 2009, para 54. The investor also complained about the fact that these restrictions were decided very swiftly over a delay of three days without granting the investor a hearing as well as about "the extension of the monitoring period of the fish-stair by one year to two years".

[208] Furthermore, the parties explicitly state that the agreement does in no way indicate their liability, obligation or admission of any fact, Vattenfall AB, Vattenfall Europe AG, Vattenfall Europe Generation AG v. Federal Republic of Germany, ICSID Case No. ARB/09/6, Award of 11 March 2011, para 12 incorporating Article 5 of the Agreement.

[209] Vattenfall AB, Vattenfall Europe AG, Vattenfall Europe Generation AG v. Federal Republic of Germany, ICSID Case No. ARB/09/6, Award of 11 March 2011, para 12 incorporating Article 2 of the Agreement.

IX. Intermediate Summary

The diverse facts underlying the portrayed investment decisions illustrate that aspects of fairness in the treatment of foreign investment can become relevant in a multitude of diverse conflicts with environmental regulation. The decisions indicate that 'fairness' has both a material and a procedural connotation. These two connotations are relevant for the tribunals' determination – and not the abstract question whether the environmental objective or foreign investment deserve more protection. Section E below will assess the environmental relevance of the standards of fairness which can be gathered from the portrayed decisions.

D. Prohibition Against Arbitrary or Unreasonable Measures

The prohibition against arbitrary and discriminatory measures – with a focus on the element of discrimination – has already been portrayed in the third chapter.[210] The portrayal shows that this standard is closely connected to, and cannot be clearly distinguished from, the standard of fair and equitable treatment, even more so if the standard is referred to as protection against 'unreasonable measures'. Further, it demonstrates that tribunals frequently base their understanding of the prohibition of arbitrariness on the decision of the ICJ in *Elettronica Sicula S.p.A*. Accordingly, a measure 'wilfully opposing or disregarding the rule of law' would be considered to violate the standard. As has been shown above, it is not clear whether a test of 'reasonableness' is identical with a test of 'arbitrariness'. Tribunals have also tested the 'reasonableness' of a measure. They required the measure to be based on a rational policy and to be reasonable in relation to this policy[211] – or, alternatively, they measured the 'reasonableness' against the expectations of the parties involved[212].

Above, it has been argued that the notions of non-arbitrariness and reasonableness considerably overlap with the standard of fair and equitable treatment. Even though it is certainly possible to establish differences in the respective protective scope, it is difficult to imagine a measure that would pass the test of being 'fair and equitable', though being 'arbitrary' or 'un-

210 See 'Chapter 3 – Standards of Non-Discriminatory Treatment' at pp. 193 *et seq*.

211 AES Summit Generation Limited and AES-Tisza Erömü Kft v. The Republic of Hungary, ICSID Case No. ARB/07/22 (ECT), Award of 23 September 2010, para 10.3.7.

212 BG Group Plc v. Argentina, Award of 24 December 2007, para 342.

reasonable'. It appears that a measure which opposes the rule of law and is not based on a rational policy cannot be considered 'fair'. Accordingly, the inter-connectedness of the standard with the obligation of fair and equitable treatment is generally acknowledged. As it is not the primary purpose of this study to identify subtle differences between protective notions, the standard of protection against arbitrary or unreasonable measures is not separately evaluated in the following. This approach is reinforced by the absence of tribunal decisions regarding environmental measures that specifically focus on the standard.

E. The Environmental Relevance of Standards of Fairness

The protective scopes of the absolute treatment standards portrayed in this chapter are rooted in the concept of 'fairness'. The portrayal has emphasised the broad protective scope of the treaty standard of fair and equitable treatment, which may encompass the protection offered by the prohibition of arbitrary or unreasonable measures and those elements additive to the traditional scope of the standard of full protection and security. This study does not aim at clearly differentiating between these standards, but focuses on potential conflicts between the concept of 'fairness' for the foreign investor and the state's regulatory interest in protecting the environment. Therefore, this section employs a unified 'standard of fairness', which is akin to a broad treaty standard of fair and equitable treatment. This standard of fairness encompasses – but is not restricted to – the protective notions of the investor's legitimate expectations, the stability of the regulatory framework, transparency and due process.

I. Criteria for Standards of Fairness in Environmental Context

The aim of this section is to identify factors to draw a line between the protection of the investor and the legitimate authority of the state to introduce measures for environmental protection. To this end, the study will first portray the substantive implications of the standard of fairness. With regard to the procedural component of the standard, it will describe the requirements of the scientific basis for a measure, before elaborating on aspects of procedural fairness and transparency. The investment decisions portrayed above and their implications for the protective scope of 'fairness' and the relationship with environmental norms and measures will instruct the following analysis.

1. Legitimacy of the Investor's Expectations

The substantive element of the standard of fair treatment relates to the protection of the investor's expectations and to the stability of the legal framework. The investor's expectations reflect the basis on which the economic viability of the investment activity was calculated, making them central pillars of protection. The host state's sovereign right to adopt and amend legislation for purposes of environmental protection is intrinsically opposed to them. Above, I have demonstrated that investment tribunals tend not to make a precise, terminological distinction between 'legitimate expectations' and 'stability of the legal framework'. Furthermore, some investment tribunals use the notion of 'legitimate expectations' extremely broadly in equating it to the investor being 'treated fairly and equitably'.[213] It follows that the identification of relevant criteria for assessing the dividing line between the investor's interest in stability and the host state's desire for latitude in adjusting regulation is not significantly influenced by terminology.

One of the relevant issues is the strength of the expectations the host state induces in the foreign investor. In the narrow sense of an intensified level of commitment, 'legitimate expectations' require that an additional assurance be given to the foreign investor, such as an explicit promise, guarantee, or at least a quasi-contractual relationship with the host state at the time the investment is made. Examples of relevant promises and guarantees are concession agreements, tenders, licences, and permits.[214] Furthermore, some tribunals identify expectations stemming from the regulatory framework, which set forth detailed tariff structures or comparably specific advantages.[215] A quasi-contractual relationship is created by unambiguous, definitive

[213] See, as one example, Joseph Charles Lemire v. Ukraine, ICSID Case No. ARB/06/18, Decision on Jurisdiction and Liability of 14 January 2010, para 267, where the tribunal found that the investor "could expect a regulatory system for the broadcasting industry which was to be consistent, transparent, fair, reasonable, and enforced without arbitrary or discriminatory decisions".

[214] Walter Bau v. Thailand, Award of 1 July 2009, para 12.9; Metalpar S.A. and Buen Aire S.A. v. Argentine Republic, ICSID Case No. ARB/03/5, Award of 6 June 2008, para 186. Suez, Sociedad General de Aguas de Barcelona S.A., and Inter-Aguas Servicios Integrales del Agua S.A. v. The Argentine Republic, ICSID Case No. ARB/03/17, Decision on Liability of 30 July 2010, para 212.

[215] BG Group Plc v. Argentina, Award of 24 December 2007, para 306; CMS Gas Transmission Company v. The Argentine Republic, ICSID Case No. ARB/01/8, Award of 12 May 2005, paras 275, 277; Enron Corporation and Ponderosa Assets, L.P. v. Argentine Republic, ICSID Case No. ARB/01/3, Award of 22 May 2007, para 264; LG&E v. Argentina, ICSID Case No. ARB/02/1, Decision on Liability of 3 October 2006, para 133; National Grid plc v. The Argentine Republic, Award of 3 November 2008, para 178; AWG Group Ltd. v. The Argentine Republic, Decision

and repeated representations by competent authorities of the host state. Vivid examples are the representations given by federal officials in *Metalclad Corporation v. United Mexican States*. The investor had been cautious about the necessity of permits from differing authorities and – prior to the purchase of the site as well as throughout the process of constructing the landfill – had received assurances from federal officials. Thus, the investor was made to believe that it had all necessary permits.

Likewise, the decision in *Glamis Gold, Ltd. v. U.S.A.* illustrates that 'legitimate expectations' require an element additive to the mere existence of a general regulatory framework. The tribunal found that the investor could not count on the long-standing mining regulatory regime to remain unchanged, because such an expectation had not been encouraged by specific commitments of the home state. The tribunal stated that the "upset of expectations [...] requires something greater than mere disappointment; it requires, as a threshold condition, the active inducement of a quasi-contractual expectation."[216] Hence, the tribunal emphasised the more protective scope of such expectations in contrast to the general interest in the stability of the regulatory framework. Similarly, the tribunal in *Plama Consortium Limited v. Bulgaria* stated that an investment treaty does not "protect investors against any and all changes in the host country's law", with protection requiring at least "reasonable and justifiable expectations".[217]

The particular facts surrounding the investment in the respective case have to be evaluated for the assessment of 'fairness'. In my opinion, a proper vehicle to do so is the assessment of the 'legitimacy' of the investor's expectations. Investment tribunals have pointed to the importance of the surrounding circumstances. The evaluation appreciates the inducement of the investor in the light of the "political, socioeconomic, cultural and historical conditions prevailing in the host state".[218] In sum, it consists of a

on Liability of 30 July 2010, para 222; Suez, Sociedad General de Aguas de Barcelona S.A., and InterAguas Servicios Integrales del Agua S.A. v. The Argentine Republic, ICSID Case No. ARB/03/17, Decision on Liability of 30 July 2010, para 212.

216 Glamis Gold, Ltd. v. U.S.A., Award of 8 June 2009, para 799.

217 Plama Consortium Limited v. Bulgaria, ICSID Case No. ARB/03/24, Award of 27 August 2008, para 219. The tribunal further stated that the change of the environmental law did not contravene any legitimate expectations of the investor as the host state had "not made any representations or promises to freeze its legislation".

218 Bayindir Insaat Turizm Ticaret Ve Sanayi A.S. v. Islamic Republic of Pakistan, ICSID Case No. ARB/03/29, Award of 27 August 2009, para 192; Duke Energy Electroquil Partners & Electroquil S.A. v. Republic of Ecuador, ICSID Case No. ARB/04/19, Award of 18 August 2008, para 340; Suez, Sociedad General de Aguas de Barcelona S.A., and InterAguas Servicios Integrales del Agua S.A. v. The Argentine Republic, ICSID Case No. ARB/03/17, Decision on Liability of 30 July

process of weighing the expectations of the investor against the legitimate regulatory interests of the host state.[219] Circumstances reducing the legitimacy of expectations are, for example, a situation when the host state is in a state of transition so that changes to the regulatory framework are immanent,[220] or the volatility of the prevailing political conditions.[221] Likewise, activity in a highly regulated industry is prone to be subjected to further restrictions.

The process gives the investment tribunal the possibility to balance the economic interest of the investor with the environmental interest of the host state in the regulation. Although this approach does not provide clear-cut solutions to existing conflicts, it constitutes a framework for assessing the

---

2010, para 211. Similarly, Saluka Investments BV (The Netherlands) v. The Czech Republic, Award of 17 March 2006, paras 304, 306; National Grid plc v. The Argentine Republic, Award of 3 November 2008, para 175; Parkerings-Compagniet AS v. Lithuania, ICSID Case No. ARB/05/8, Award of 11 September 2007, paras 331, 332; EDF (Services) Limited v. Romania, ICSID Case No. ARB/05/13, Award of 8 October 2009, para 219. See also Generation Ukraine, Inc. v. Ukraine, ICSID Case No. ARB/00/9, Award of 16 September 2003, para 20.37.

[219] Saluka Investments BV (The Netherlands) v. The Czech Republic, Award of 17 March 2006, para 306; AWG Group Ltd. v. The Argentine Republic, Decision on Liability of 30 July 2010, para 236, Suez, Sociedad General de Aguas de Barcelona S.A., and InterAguas Servicios Integrales del Agua S.A. v. The Argentine Republic, ICSID Case No. ARB/03/17, Decision on Liability of 30 July 2010, para 216; Toto Costruzioni Generali S.p.A. v. Republic of Lebanon, ICSID Case No. ARB/07/12, Award of 7 June 2012, para 165; Jan Oostergetel and Theodora Laurentius v. The Slovak Republic, Award of 23 April 2012, para 224. Supporting this approach, *Boute*, Anatole, 'The Potential Contribution of International Investment Protection Law to Combat Climate Change', 27 Journal of Energy & Natural Resources Law 2009, 333 (370). The decision in Joseph Charles Lemire v. Ukraine, ICSID Case No. ARB/06/18, Decision on Jurisdiction and Liability of 14 January 2010, para 285 points to further factors to be considered, namely, the investor's duty to perform an investigation before effecting the investment and the investor's conduct in the host state.

[220] Parkerings-Compagniet AS v. Lithuania, ICSID Case No. ARB/05/8, Award of 11 September 2007, para 335; Joseph Charles Lemire v. Ukraine, ICSID Case No. ARB/06/18, Decision on Jurisdiction and Liability of 14 January 2010, para 317; Saluka Investments BV (The Netherlands) v. The Czech Republic, Award of 17 March 2006, paras 357–358, albeit finding that the investor did not have to expect the discriminatory changes that were taken.

In contrast, the legitimacy of the expectations can be reinforced when the host state enacted legislation to attract foreign investment to counter a prior economic crisis, National Grid plc v. The Argentine Republic, Award of 3 November 2008, para 176.

[221] Bayindir Insaat Turizm Ticaret Ve Sanayi A.S. v. Islamic Republic of Pakistan, ICSID Case No. ARB/03/29, Award of 27 August 2009, para 193; Toto Costruzioni Generali S.p.A. v. Republic of Lebanon, ICSID Case No. ARB/07/12, Award of 7 June 2012, paras 165, 245.

fairness of a respective measure. The balancing exercise reflects the strength of the assurance that reared the investor's expectation as well as the sovereign right of the state to legislate for the protection of public interest: An investment induced through specific representations of the host state is more robustly protected than an investment made in the hope that a set of general laws will not change. Thus, the circumstances surrounding the investment activity in this balancing exercise are the more relevant, the less straight forward the respective assurance by the host state is. Further factors for consideration are the impact of alterations on the investment, attempts undertaken to mitigate negative implications for the investor, and the understanding that unilateral changes to contractual structures, which were implemented by the government to obtain financial resources, deserve more scrutiny.[222]

This balancing exercise is also applicable to cases dealing with environmental measures. The tribunal in *Glamis Gold, Ltd. v. U.S.A.* mentioned the "climate that was becoming more and more sensitive to the environmental consequences of open-pit mining" as one of the circumstances which the investor must have been aware of.[223] Accordingly, an investor cannot legitimately expect to continue certain industrial practices with a negative environmental impact in the light of increasing opposition. The example indicates that an investor cannot expect environmental legislation to remain unaltered or "frozen"[224], unless the host state has made an explicit promise to this effect. Given the high measure of deference accredited to host states by the tribunal in *S.D. Myers Inc. v. Canada*, their regulatory competence with regard to environmental policies subsists.[225] Further, the relevance of

---

222 Continental Casualty Company v. Argentina, ICSID Case No. ARB/03/9, Award of 5 September 2008, para 261, promulgating a detailed description of factors for balancing.

See also the – albeit not express – balancing of interests in *Técnicas Medioambientales Tecmed, S.A. v. United Mexican States*: The tribunal found that the investor's expectation to be able to operate the original facility until the relocation of the landfill – to which it had agreed – was legitimate in the light of the state's interest in a swift relocation and the respective co-operation of the investor, to which it was not legally obliged.

223 Glamis Gold, Ltd. v. U.S.A., Award of 8 June 2009, para 767.

224 Saluka Investments BV (The Netherlands) v. The Czech Republic, Award of 17 March 2006, para 305; EDF (Services) Limited v. Romania, ICSID Case No. ARB/05/13, Award of 8 October 2009, para 218, focusing on the obligation of fair and equitable treatment not serving the same purpose as a stabilisation clause. Similarly, AES Summit Generation Limited and AES-Tisza Erömü Kft v. The Republic of Hungary, ICSID Case No. ARB/07/22 (ECT), Award of 23 September 2010, paras 9.3.31, 9.3.34.

225 See also Marion Unglaube and Reinhard Unglaube v. Republic of Costa Rica, ICSID Case No. ARB/08/1, ICSID Case No. ARB/09/20, Award of 16 May 2012,

the environmental interest can be a determining factor in striking the balance. When making use of its right to regulate, the host state has to implement its policies *bona fide* – through conduct justified by public policies and with respect to the requirements of procedural fairness.[226] These procedural elements will be analysed separately below.

In my opinion, the balancing exercise to determine the legitimacy of the investor's expectations in the light of the circumstances is an appropriate tool to determine the 'fairness' of subsequent changes to the environmental regulatory framework. The sovereignty of the host state to freely alter relevant laws and regulations is restricted, if explicit promises to the contrary have been relied on by the investor. If the balance indicates that the investor has not been treated 'fairly', the implementation of the respective environmental measures requires compensation for the frustrated investor. Accordingly, the government of a host state is obliged to consider the implications stemming from potential promises, even before they are made to investors. The legislative and administrative areas affected by the respective assurance as well as the time length which the promise is made for have to be assessed carefully.[227]

---

para 258. More general, TECO Guatemala Holdings, LLC v. Republic of Guatemala, ICSID Case No. ARB/10/23, Award of 19 December 2013, paras 490–493.

226 Saluka Investments BV (The Netherlands) v. The Czech Republic, Award of 17 March 2006, para 307; Franck Charles Arif v. Republic of Moldova, ICSID Case No. ARB/11/23, Award of 8 April 2013, para 537.

227 Although it is unlikely that a host government explicitly assures investors that specific environmental legislation will not be amended, it is possible that assurances be given which indirectly require such stability.

Implications arising from long-term commitments are also problematic. It is difficult to estimate potential future environmental implications of assurances which cover a time span of several decades. Furthermore, conflicts can arise between long-term assurances and principles of democratic governance, when a subsequent democratically elected government is bound by promises made by a previous government. This problem is most relevant when the previous government itself was not democratically elected, but the issue can also arise when a government is changed in a democratic society due to opposition against the environmental impact of the respective investment project. Such a situation was underlying the case *Vattenfall AB, Vattenfall Europe AG, Vattenfall Europe Generation AG & Co. KG v. The Federal Republic of Germany*, in which the green party gained political influence, inter alia, because of outspoken opposition to the investor's power plant project. It was claimed that these reasons resulted in changes in the permits given to the investor. From an academic perspective, a decision by the investment tribunal would have furthered the understanding of the extent to which the regulatory capacity of the federal state was restricted by prior promises.

How far the mentioned democratic implications influence the legitimacy of the expectations depends on the respective circumstances in each case. If there are rifts relating to the appreciation of an investment project between the federal and the

In sum, balancing the circumstances that surround the investment with the expectations an investor may have, is a relevant means of assessing the legitimacy of the expectations. The regulatory capacity of the host state on the one hand and the investor's interest in stability on the other hand, are the main components to be taken into account in this balancing exercise. The surrounding circumstances reduce or increase the significance of these two components and allow investment tribunals to strike a fair balance. Accordingly, the expectations of the investor will be considered 'legitimate', if they prevail over the alleged interest of the host state.

2. Scientific Basis for Introducing Environmental Measure

The second element relates to the scientific reasons on which the host state bases its assessment of the desirability of the environmental measure. The host state is accorded significant latitude in choosing and evaluating reasons for the introduction of policy measures. The tribunal in *S.D. Myers Inc. v. Canada* emphasises the "high measure of deference" that international law generally accredits to domestic authorities for the regulation of matters within their borders. However, the standard of fairness mandates that there are scientific reasons for the introduction of the measure which at least fulfil the threshold of non-arbitrariness.[228] Moreover, it has to be ascertained that the environmental measure is not a disguised tool for protectionism or other illegitimate reasons.

In this light, the tribunal in *Chemtura Corporation v. Government of Canada* assessed whether the decision of the host state to review the use of

---

state government like in *Metalclad Corporation v. United Mexican States*, public international law generally does not reduce the responsibility of the state due to its internal construction or democratic constitution. Accordingly, these factors will be of little relevance in assessing the legitimacy of potential expectations.

228 As argued above (footnote 151 in 'Chapter 3 – Standards of Non-Discriminatory Treatment'), it is my understanding that approaches developed within international trade law should not be directly applied to the investment context. Even though one could assume that the rather detailed norm Article 5 SPS Agreement is a helpful tool to determine whether a measure adopted by a state has been based on good scientific practice, in my understanding, this provision constitutes too restrictive an approach to describe the regulatory powers of a state in the investment context. While a masure that meets all these criteria has certainly met the threshold, a measure falling short could not be automatically considered as violation of the protective standards. Investment tribunals rightly apply, for example, less stringent criteria for review where relevant scientific evidence is insufficient than Article 5 para 7 SPS Agreement, do not require the minimizing of costs or negative impact on investors (Article 5 paras 3, 4, 6 SPS Agreement), and do not impose the elements a review should apply (Article 5 para 2 SPS Agreement). The right of the state to regulate activities within its territory has to be understood more broadly.

the pesticide lindane was based on scientific reasons. Explicitly without evaluating whether the chemical was dangerous, the tribunal relied on a host of international undertakings aimed at the elimination of lindane and found that the initiation of the review process was legitimate. Similarly, the tribunal in *Glamis Gold, Ltd. v. U.S.A.* was satisfied that the cultural survey of the area in which the investor wanted to undertake its mining activity, was grounded on a solid scientific and archaeological basis. The tribunal further stated that it had no reason to doubt the applied methodology or the expertise of the engaged professionals, explicitly emphasising that it was not the task of the tribunal to determine the exact location of the culturally significant trail.

Accordingly, the tribunals' review of the scientific evidence on which the host state relied when adopting the respective measure is an assessment of the legitimacy of the scientific process, but does not extend to an independent evaluation of the data itself. Like in the context of the standard of non-discrimination, investment tribunals refrain from substituting their own environmental assessment for that of the host state. In my opinion, the conclusion that follows from the deference owed to the host state is that host states can choose the level of scientific certainty they require for the adoption of an environmental measure. Therefore, the host state is generally at liberty to rely on the precautionary principle in the assessment of environmental dangers.[229]

The analysis of the case law indicates that the verdict on an environmental measure as a disguised tool for protectionism or for furthering other, unrelated objectives is not determined by an isolated examination of the scientific reasons cited by the host state. Decisions in which the tribunal doubted whether the cited environmental reasons were pivotal to the measure – like in *Técnicas Medioambientales Tecmed, S.A. v. United Mexican States* or in *S.D. Myers Inc. v. Canada* – additionally identified other deficiencies in the treatment of the investor. Hence, there are valid reasons to assume that the evaluation of the scientific basis of the environmental measure is largely influenced by other indices of impropriety on the part of the host state. The high degree of deference owed to the host state impedes the finding of a violation in an isolated assessment.

229 Similarly, *Moloo*, Rahim/*Jacinto*, Justin, 'Environmental and Health Regulation: Assessing Liability under Investment-Treaties', 29 Berkeley Journal of International Law 2011, 1 (55).

3. Procedural Fairness and Transparency

The procedural aspect of the standard of fairness is closely connected to the assessment of the scientific reasons for a measure. Regulatory and administrative processes have to conform to the protective notions of procedural fairness and transparency. Accordingly, the introduction and implementation of environmental measures necessitate a transparent way that embraces due process – irrespective of the policy reasons underlying the measure. The situations in which the notion of procedural fairness is relevant are manifold and cannot be enumerated exhaustively. However, case law highlights certain aspects and guidelines.

In sum, the host state has to apply a due and transparent process, when it administratively alters or modifies the position of the foreign investor by implementing an environmental measure. According to circumstances, this can require the involvement of the investor. However, the host state is not held to a standard of perfection: The process applied by the host state does not have to be optimal, nor can the investor expect to be treated in a 'totally transparent'[230] way. The analysed awards further demonstrate that the procedural obligations are not influenced by the environmental reasons underlying the respective measure. A very important objective does not diminish the procedural obligations of the host state: Due process requirements have to be fulfilled by the host state in any case.

One procedural component relates to the transparency in the laws and regulations relevant to the investment activity. A relevant lack of transparent rules has been found in *Metalclad Corporation v. United Mexican States*, where the necessity to obtain a municipal permit for the landfill was unclear: the Mexican authorities assured the investor that the permit was at best a formality and would be granted upon application, which turned out not to be true. Furthermore, the municipality was found to withhold the permit for reasons outside its administrative authority. Irrespective of valid criticism of the tribunal's over-reliance on 'transparency',[231] the case illustrates the importance of applicable rules that are sufficiently clear for the investor to establish its rights and obligations. However, an investor cannot expect complete transparency, but is obliged to seek clarification.[232] The assurances given to the investor in this case aggravated the situation.

---

230 The case-law portrayed above and the application of the standard to the facts in *Técnicas Medioambientales Tecmed, S.A. v. United Mexican States* itself, does not conform to this very strict standard the tribunal abstractly described. See above at pp. 271 *et seq.*

231 See above at pp. 261 *et seq.*

A second – and more important – aspect of procedural fairness relates to procedural shortcomings within the general framework.[233] The decision making process within the state has to be fair and transparent with regard to respective powers and procedural requirements. The less straight forward the procedure is, the more relevant are attempts by the authorities of the host state to involve the investor.[234] In *Técnicas Medioambientales Tecmed, S.A. v. United Mexican States* the tribunal found fault with the lack of participatory involvement of the investor. The investor was not informed of any specific terms and conditions relating to the re-location, its contributions were not sufficiently addressed, and it was at no point warned that the breaches of transportation guidelines could lead to a revocation of the licence. The host state did not communicate any specific strategy to address the environmental issue and, in the end, made the investor bear the brunt of its own inefficiency at solving the problem. In furthering an environmental measure for which no procedure existed – the relocation of a hazardous waste facility – the host state completely disregarded the investor's position.

Regarding the procedural fairness of an administrative process, investment tribunals have stated the relevance of assessing the procedural process as a whole, inclusive of mechanisms offered by the host state to address potential procedural shortcomings. This aspect was emphasised by the decision in *Chemtura Corporation v. Government of Canada*. The tribunal found that the host state's review process of the pesticide lindane was not tainted by procedural impropriety or bad faith. With regard to the registration process of replacement products, the tribunal conceded that the operation of complex administrations could not always be expected to function in an optimal way. When assessing the delays that had occurred, the tribunal found that they were partly attributable to the investor. Thus, the threshold for finding an 'unfair' process was not reached. That the complexity of a review procedure legitimately influences the duration of the process was further acknowledged in *Glamis Gold, Ltd. v. U.S.A.* If individual compo-

---

232 In this sense, the tribunal in *Plama Consortium Limited v. Bulgaria* did not hold the lack of clarity of the original environmental law with regard to the investor's exemption for prior environmental damage of the acquired refinery against the host state. Although there was reason for the investor to believe in its exemption, there was no evidence of a specific provision in the privatisation agreement, which the investor had claimed to be central to its investment. In the light of this lack of allegedly sought clarification, the investor could not rely on the belief of being exempted.

233 Joseph Charles Lemire v. Ukraine, ICSID Case No. ARB/06/18, Decision on Jurisdiction and Liability of 14 January 2010, paras 315, 316.

234 See, for example, National Grid plc v. The Argentine Republic, Award of 3 November 2008, para 179, referring to the absence of "meaningful negotiations".

nents of the treatment of the investor do not reach the threshold of 'unfairness', investment tribunals further evaluate the record as a whole.[235]

One procedural aspect that deserves particular attention in future arbitral decisions is the evaluation of governmental officials who have expressed a negative opinion on the – for example environmental – performance of a foreign investor. It is questionable if such expressions taint the process. Situations in which there is public opposition to an investment project because of its social, health or environmental impact are not uncommon.[236] A line has to be drawn between governments expressing legitimate concerns and officials fuelling public fears for illegitimate reasons. However, in my opinion, the standard of procedural fairness should not restrict public discussions or the voicing of opinions in a democratic process. An investor with a poor performance in a vital service need not be protected from non-arbitrary, negative comments by officials.[237]

4. Conclusive Summary

The discussion has shown that the host state is granted a high measure of deference with respect to the introduction of environmental measures. Standards of fairness influence this latitude in a two-fold manner: The component of the substantive protection of the investor mandates that the investor's expectations be respected. These expectations derive their strength from specific investment-inducing activities of the host state. However, they are only 'legitimate' if the balance with the circumstances surrounding the

[235] Chemtura Corporation v. Government of Canada, Award of 2 August 2010, paras 216, 224; Glamis Gold, Ltd. v. U.S.A., Award of 8 June 2009, paras 824–828; Gami Investments, Inc. v. Mexico, Award of 15 November 2004, para 97.

[236] In addition to the cases concerning waste disposal facilities portrayed above, public opposition and protests have been particularly relevant in cases concerning the privatisation of former public services, such as freshwater and sewage services.

[237] In this sense, I believe that the tribunal's findings in Biwater Gauff (Tanzania) Ltd. v. United Republic of Tanzania, ICSID Case No. ARB/05/22, Award of 24 July 2008, paras 624–627, constitute too strong a restriction of the rights of government officials. In my understanding, publicly criticising an investor for its existing poor performance and stating that its contract was terminated, even though the contract was still valid at that point – but was to be terminated within a period of weeks – is not sufficiently unfair to find a breach.

In contrast, the overall portrayal of the conduct of government officials – which went beyond public criticism – in Compañiá de Aguas del Aconquija S.A. and Vivendi Universal v. Argentine Republic, ICSID Case No. ARB/97/3, Award of 20 August 2007, paras 7.4.19–7.4.45 merits the determination of procedural unfairness. The same can be said for the decision in Azurix v. Argentine Republic, ICSID Case No. ARB/01/12, Award of 14 July 2006, para 376 – where the governor repeatedly called on customers not to pay their bills.

investment indicates that the environmental measure would be unfair to the investor in the absence of compensation. The procedural component of the standard of fairness requires that the environmental measure be placed on a scientific footing and that the measure is adopted in a transparent and due process. As the host state is not held to a standard of procedural perfection, the procedural requirements are not balanced against the importance of the environmental objective: The basic tenets of a fair process have to be respected at all times.

II. Application of Criteria to Different Scenarios

The criteria developed for assessing violations of the standards of fairness in scenarios involving environmental regulation will now be applied to the scenarios, which were depicted and applied in the first and third chapters. The purpose is to further illustrate the factors investment tribunals may take into account when striking a balance between the investor's interests in stability and the host state's regulatory interest in adopting environmental measures. However, the scenarios described in the following only constitute examples, which give an indication of potential conflicts. They do not represent a comprehensive overview.

1. Scenario No 1: Introduction and Application of Environmental Regulation

The first scenario relates to the most obvious conflicts between environmental measures and the standard of fairness. An investor has commenced its investment activity in the host state before the state introduces regulation allegedly due to environmental considerations, which negatively affects the foreign investor. The foreign investor complains that the alteration of the regulatory framework or the introduction of a specific measure violates its guarantee of being treated fairly.

a) Refusal of Permits

It is crucial for the foreign investor to hold the relevant environmental permits to undertake its planned investment activity in the host state. The investor has to accept the legal order of the host state as it stands when the investment activity is started. Irrespective of potential limitations to investment protection during the establishment phase, an investor can begin its entrepreneurial undertaking on the understanding that it will be granted relevant permits or licenses in the case of successful preparatory works and studies. Relevant examples are expensive test drillings or the conduct of environmental impact assessment studies. In such a situation, the investor may have spent significant resources in reliance on a regulatory framework. The expenses are bereft of purpose if the host state alters the conditions for obtaining the respective permits.

The substantive component of the protection of fairness links the scenario to the legitimacy of the investor's expectations. A balancing test to determine the legitimacy of expecting immutability of the regulatory framework has to take account of the facts of the specific case, such as the – environmental – circumstances surrounding the preparations. Case law indicates that representations made to the investor are crucial in shaping the legitimacy of the investor's expectation to be granted a permit. The decision in *Metalclad Corporation v. United Mexican States* underlines the relevance of representations by state officials regarding the ease with which the investor can receive permits.[238] Similarly, the decision in *Glamis Gold, Ltd. v. U.S.A.* emphasises that in the absence of such specific representations by government officials, the legitimacy of the investor's expectation that a relevant permit will be issued in accordance with long-standing rules is reduced. In the absence of explicit promises, the regulatory authority has more latitude to alter the legal framework.

Furthermore, the procedural component of the standard of fairness cannot be neglected in the process of deciding on the allocation of permits or licences. The process has to reflect transparency and the notions of due process set forth above. It will depend on a multitude of factors whether the process can be described as 'fair'. Questions an investment tribunal will dwell on are, inter alia, the following: Does the process that amended the regulatory framework accord to the normal procedure for such changes? Have inappropriate considerations been implicated in the process? Have the

---

[238] The alleged specific commitment of a government is also at the heart of the pending investment case *Windstream Energy LLC v. Government of Canada*. The investor, that intended to develop an offshore wind energy project on Lake Ontario, alleges that the provincial government had promised that the investor would be able to apply for required regulatory approvals under a streamlined approvals process. However, the host state then allegedly delayed the approval process and finally imposed a moratorium on freshwater offshore wind energy production. See Windstream Energy LLC v. Government of Canada, Notice of Arbitration of 5 November 2013, paras 30, 40, 43. The host state focuses on the investor having been aware of the undeveloped regulatory environment and that it had willingly assumed this regulatory risk in investing. Furthermore, the host state relies on the need for further regulatory review and technical and environmental studies, indicating, inter alia, consequences for the drinking water in the region. See Windstream Energy LLC v. Government of Canada, Response to the Notice of Arbitration of 5 December 2013, paras 5, 6, 39, 52 *et seq*.

requirements of procedural propriety been adhered to? It is clear that a host state is not held to procedural perfection; nevertheless, the overall assessment of the procedure has to take account of all procedural implications.

Both the substantive and the procedural notions of the standard of fairness were invoked by the investor in *Pac Rim Cayman LLC v. Republic of El Salvador*. In this case, in which the tribunal has no jurisdiction concerning the treaty claim,[239] the investor alleges that it invested tens of millions of dollars on preparatory work in reliance on the mining and investment regulation as well as on specific representations – only to find the original framework replaced by a presidential imposition of a *de facto* ban on mining.[240] It seems obvious that the alleged representations of high-ranking officials as well as the process through which the regulatory framework was altered are central to the claim. Similarly, the investors in the ongoing case *William Ralph Clayton, William Richard Clayton, Douglas Clayton, Daniel Clayton and Bilcon of Delaware Inc. v. Government of Canada* claim that measures which were applied through the environmental impact assessment of their investment project were unfair. The investors argue that a multitude of measures imposed substantive restrictions which were materially unreasonable and that the applied process was highly irregular and too lengthy.[241] The host state maintains that it did not impose arbitrary or unreasonable criteria and that the process was in line with national laws and regulations, while delays were triggered by acts of the investor.[242]

b) Introduction of Environmental Restrictions After Investment Was Placed

The potential for conflicts between environmental regulation and the protection of investment is most significant in relation to environmental restrictions introduced after the investment has been made. In such cases,

---

239 Pac Rim Cayman LLC v. Republic of El Salvador, ICSID Case No. ARB/09/12, Decision on the Respondent's Jurisdictional Objections of 1 June 2012, para 7.1.

240 Pac Rim Cayman LLC v. Republic of El Salvador, ICSID Case No. ARB/09/12, Claimant's Response to Respondent's Preliminary Objections of 26 February 2010, para 139; Pac Rim Cayman LLC v. Republic of El Salvador, ICSID Case No. ARB/09/12, Notice of Arbitration of 30 April 2009, paras 90, 91.

241 William Ralph Clayton, William Richard Clayton, Douglas Clayton, Daniel Clayton and Bilcon of Delaware Inc. v. Government of Canada, Amended Statement of Claim of 3 December 2009, paras 13, 28, 36.

242 William Ralph Clayton, William Richard Clayton, Douglas Clayton, Daniel Clayton and Bilcon of Delaware Inc. v. Government of Canada, Amended Statement of Defence of 18 December 2009, paras 97, 98, 104.

the investor has based its calculations on a regulatory framework which is retrospectively adjusted. The parameters for assessing whether a retrospective adjustment of the legal framework is 'unjust' were portrayed above. Pursuant to these benchmarks, the investor's expectation that the legal framework remains stable is to be balanced with the right of the state to install environmental protection measures, inter alia.[243]

A relevant example in this context is the imposition of emission targets. If the host state decides to introduce or strengthen emission controls, it creates additional environmental obligations for the investor. In the light of the parameters set forth above, it is my understanding that investment tribunals will generally – i.e. unless explicit promises to the contrary have been made – find that the investor could not legitimately expect that its emission allowances would not decrease. An investor cannot but expect that emission allowances of diverse substances be reduced. The balancing act takes account of the host state's right to introduce regulation for a public policy in the light of the high degree of deference owed to the host state and the surrounding circumstances of each case. A relevant surrounding factor decreasing the legitimacy of the expectation of stability is well-known criticism of the environmental impact of the investment activity, as the decision in *Glamis Gold, Ltd. v. U.S.A.* demonstrates. Similarly, the political circumstances with regard to many toxins or emissions indicate approaches to stricter regulation, so that investors cannot legitimately expect to be forever freed from respective constraints. This is most notably the case with regard to carbon constraints, so that no investor can expect to be freed from them, not even the ones that invest in countries currently not bound by emission reduction obligations.[244]

The premise for assuming that the regulatory interest of the host state must generally prevail is obviously that the reasons for the introduction of the respective environmental measure are based on sound science and that the process of introducing the amendment of the regulation or the respective measure is characterised by the principles of procedural fairness and transparency. Against this background, the tribunals in *Methanex v. United States*

243 The pending – and confidential – proceedings in Vattenfall AB and others v. Federal Republic of Germany (ICSID Case No. ARB/12/12) might focus on this aspect. The case concerns the consequences of the decision of the host state to phase-out the production of nuclear energy more rapidly than previously agreed with the investor. Also, the investor was prohibited from restarting two of its power plants and this restriction did not directly translate into greater capacities for other plants. Unfortunately, the exact content of the claims is not in the public domain.

244 *Boute*, Anatole, 'The Potential Contribution of International Investment Protection Law to Combat Climate Change', 27 Journal of Energy & Natural Resources Law 2009, 333 (370).

and *Chemtura Corporation v. Government of Canada* held that a host state could phase out chemicals that were no longer seen as environmentally acceptable. Especially the latter decision exemplifies how a measure based on scientific grounds and implemented in an overall fair, albeit not perfect, procedure fulfils the requirements imposed by the standard of fairness in investment protection. In my understanding, these findings are applicable to other cases, in which the host states enact rules for the reduction of emissions of the investment activity – regardless of whether toxic components used by the investor are banned or restricted or the emissions of the activity are targeted.

Similarly, in my view, it follows that the investor's desire for the stability of the legal framework does not prevent the host state from introducing new – and innovative – schemes aiming at environmental protection. The example of a cap-and-trade system like the European Emissions Trading Scheme has already been discussed in this context in the prior chapter. Such a scheme is a prolonged process of phasing specific substances out. The scheme is meant to bring about the intended reduction in a way more protective of business interests than a direct imposition of emission limits and bans would be. Accordingly, the implementation of such a scheme is a generally acceptable tool for the host state to further a public policy.

Yet, a cap-and-trade system – as well as direct bans or restrictions – also has to comply with the exigencies of the procedural component of the standard of fairness. Accordingly, the specific way in which the respective cap-and-trade scheme is implemented could be problematic. In the prior chapter, I argued that the host state should be accredited with a broad margin of appreciation to decide, for example, which sectors were to participate in the scheme.[245] In my understanding, an investor would have difficulties to argue that it was 'unfair' for the host state to decide that the sector in which it was active had to participate in the scheme. If environmental reasons exist for the adoption of a scheme, the regulatory latitude in selecting sectors should be extensive, with the level of arbitrariness serving as an absolute barrier. Other, more specific, procedural requirements are difficult to assess in the abstract. It is clear that by establishing a cap-and-trade system the host state is obliged to respect the procedural requirements of the standard of fairness. However, the transparency of such a complex system will have its limits. This is true for the selection of market participants at the point of creating the parameters of the scheme and for the transparency of all future consequences of the scheme. With regard to the European Emissions Trading Scheme, the French Conseil d'État held that the fact that a company does not know the price of emission certificates in advance does

245 See 'Chapter 3 – Standards of Non-Discriminatory Treatment' at pp. 216 *et seq.*

not constitute a violation of the principle of legal certainty.[246] This decision, which holds that a complete foreseeability of all – financial – consequences of such a scheme is not required, indicates that an investment tribunal applying international law should come to a similar conclusion.

Another example of potential conflict in this scenario relates to restrictions on the use of land owned by an investor. The host state may restrict, for example, the building activity in a stretch of land that is important for the nesting of endangered species. In such a situation, the investor is more at risk, because the increased protection of respective areas is more specifically directed at the asset of the investor. The balancing exercise will have to take all surrounding circumstances into account: Thus, an investment tribunal will consider expectations held by the investor, the environmental interest of the host state, non-arbitrariness in selecting this specific part of land for protection and the applied process. Especially, attempts at involving the investor in finding a mutually acceptable solution can be indicative of whether the measure is really a good faith attempt at protecting environmental interests. At the end, the balance of the specific factors will indicate whether fairness requires a compensation for the rights of the investor.

2. Scenario No 2: Subsidies or Other Advantages for Environmentally Friendly Investments as Potential Violation of Other Investments

The second scenario concerns the introduction of an incentive scheme for investments which are considered environmentally advantageous. The issue here is whether such a scheme is 'unfair' for other competing investments, which do not fulfil the criteria for participation. First, the sovereign right of the host state to implement measures supporting environmentally advantageous industries has to be considered. A host state introducing schemes to support investments, for example, in renewable energy technology which impacts less on the global climate, will not find it difficult to demonstrate that these measures are based on sufficient scientific reasons.

In this situation, one cannot fail to notice that the potential competitive disadvantage deriving from an incentive scheme for other investors is an indirect impact stemming from the comparison with other investors. As it is closely connected to the differential treatment of different investors, it is predominantly an issue of potential discrimination. It has been shown above that the standards of fairness encompass the notion of protection against

---

[246] Conseil d'État (France), Société Arcelor Atlantique et Lorraine, Société Sollac Méditerranée, Société Ugitech et al., Arrêt N° 287110, Decision of 8 February 2007.

discrimination. Accordingly, the introduction or application of a scheme that is discriminatory also violates the notions of fairness and equitability. The task of identifying discriminatory elements is portrayed in detail in 'Chapter 3 – Standards of Non-Discriminatory Treatment'. That determination is equally valid in the context of 'fairness'.

In an isolated assessment of the scheme's substantive unfairness to a foreign investor that cannot participate, the investor's legitimate expectations are relevant. Relevant expectations are closely connected to specific assurances from the host state. But it is unlikely that the host state will have given such a promise to an investor that cannot participate because of the negative environmental impact of its investment. Also, the balancing of opposing interests would certainly not lead to the investor having a legitimate interest in the maintenance of the antecedent legal framework, which did not distinguish between different environmental impacts. This appreciation of the support scheme is based on the premise that the exclusion of the investor is grounded on environmental differences, and is not due to reasons unrelated to the environmental objective. It follows that the host state is obviously bound by the procedural element of the standard of fairness. The implementation of a support scheme requires a transparent framework. Further, the administrative evaluation of respective applications is to follow the rules of due process and be sufficiently speedy. A legitimate environmental support scheme cannot arbitrarily exclude certain investors.

3. Scenario No 3: Withdrawal of or Reductions in a Scheme Favouring Environmentally Friendly Investments

The third scenario relates to alterations to schemes that were implemented to induce investment in environmentally friendly technologies after these investments were made. In cases in which the investor has relied on a supporting scheme of financial assistance to be paid over a longer period, decisions of the host state to withhold or reduce the originally guaranteed assistance after the investment has been made can violate the standard of fairness. This section focuses on potential violations of the standard that do not require the comparison to the treatment of other investors. In contrast, the case of *Nykomb Synergetics Technology Holding AB v. Latvia*, in which the non-payment of contractually agreed tariffs was considered a violation of the standard of fair and equitable treatment through discrimination is discussed elsewhere.[247]

[247] See in 'Chapter 3 – Standards of Non-Discriminatory Treatment' at pp. 197 *et seq.*

Relevant examples of such a scheme are tariffs guaranteed for energy produced in an environmentally advantageous or renewable way. These tariffs can be incorporated in explicit contracts between the investor and the host state or they can derive from a precise, specialised regulatory framework. Such specific inducement of investments generates expectations of the investor: The more precise the tariff structure, the more weight do the expectations have that a foreign investor deduces from it. Changes to tariff structures contained in regulatory frameworks have been the subject of a multitude of investment decisions – albeit not in connection with environmental objectives. Tribunals that had to evaluate unilateral changes to such tariff assurances by the host state found a violation of the standard of fair and equitable treatment.[248] In the light of the decisions in these cases, it is safe to assume that expectations stemming from a precise tariff structure are legitimate. Accordingly, the investor is protected against unilateral changes and reductions of the tariffs, which would violate the standard of fairness.[249] For the assessment, the reasons for which the tariff structure was introduced make no difference, as tariff structures will always be used to induce specific investment by – foreign – investors.

---

[248] AWG Group Ltd. v. The Argentine Republic, Decision on Liability of 30 July 2010, paras 231, 237; BG Group Plc v. Argentina, Award of 24 December 2007, paras 306, 307; CMS Gas Transmission Company v. The Argentine Republic, ICSID Case No. ARB/01/8, Award of 12 May 2005, paras 275, 277, 281; Enron Corporation and Ponderosa Assets, L.P. v. Argentine Republic, ICSID Case No. ARB/01/3, Award of 22 May 2007, paras 266, 268; LG&E v. Argentina, ICSID Case No. ARB/02/1, Decision on Liability of 3 October 2006, paras 134, 136; National Grid plc v. The Argentine Republic, Award of 3 November 2008, paras 178, 179; Sempra Energy International v. The Argentine Republic, ICSID Case No. ARB/02/16, Award of 28 September 2007, paras 303, 304; Suez, Sociedad General de Aguas de Barcelona S.A., and InterAguas Servicios Integrales del Agua S.A. v. The Argentine Republic, ICSID Case No. ARB/03/17, Decision on Liability of 30 July 2010, paras 212, 218.

[249] Unilateral changes to the price structure for energy produced from renewable sources are at the heart of a multitude of investment disputes under the ECT. These cases – which are currently pending, but not public – concern regulation in Spain (see AES Solar and others v. Spain; RREEF Infrastructure (G.P.) Limited and RREEF Pan-European Infrastructure Two Lux S.à r.l. v. Kingdom of Spain, ICSID Case No. ARB/13/30; CSP Equity Investment Sarl v. Spain; Charanne (the Netherlands) and Construction Investments (Luxembourg) v. Spain; Isolux Infrastructure Netherlands B.V. v. Spain; Masdar Solar & Wind Cooperatief UA v. Spain) and in the Czech Republic (see Antaris Solar and Dr. Michael Göde v. Czech Republic; Natland Investment Group NV, Natland Group Limited, G.I.H.G. Limited, and Radiance Energy Holding S.A.R.L. v. Czech Republic; Voltaic Network GmbH v. Czech Republic; ICW Europe Investments Limited v. Czech Republic; Photovoltaik Knopf Betriebs-GmbH v. Czech Republic; WA Investments-Europa Nova Limited v. Czech Republic; Mr. Jürgen Wirtgen, Mr. Stefan Wirtgen, and JSW Solar (zwei) v. Czech Republic).

The creation of emission credits through schemes supporting environmentally advantageous investments leads to other relevant examples. An investor may be induced to invest in a specific emission abatement project because of the emission credits that will be generated. The Marrakech Accords foresee a detailed system for the certification of qualifying projects. An investor will legitimately rely on the application of these rules. Accordingly, unilateral and unexpected changes in the amount of emission credits before the end of a crediting period would conflict with these expectations. In the light of the standard of fairness, it appears that an investor in the primary carbon market has the legitimate expectation that the framework within which it places its investment remains stable.[250] Thus – depending on the circumstances of each case – it is likely that relevant changes would be found to violate the standard of fairness.

Other issues arise with regard to investment in the secondary carbon market, i. e. investment in emission credits as a commodity. A host state may depress the price of emission credits or it may abandon the emissions' trading scheme altogether and replace it with some alternate mode of emissions' regulation. In such a situation, it is less clear what kind of relationship an investor in the secondary carbon market has with the host state. As the value of carbon credits is bound to fluctuate – being a reflection of supply and demand – it is unlikely that expectations of the investor will be as precise as in other cases. In my understanding, the respective circumstances detailing the extent to which the investment has been encouraged and induced by the host state are relevant. Without any encouragement of the investment additive to the pure existence of an emissions trading scheme, the legitimacy of the expectation that the scheme will be maintained would not be substantial. In such a case, a non-arbitrary reason would be sufficient for the state to alter its respective framework. In either situation, the procedural influence of the standards of fairness is relevant: Amendments to, or alterations of, the existing framework have to be based on valid reasons and have to conform to the exigencies of procedural fairness. As such, amendments have to follow the rules of internal competence and procedural participation laid down by the host state.

---

[250] *Baetens*, Freya, 'The Kyoto Protocol in Investor-State Arbitration: Reconciling Climate Change and Investment Protection Objectives', in: Sustainable Development in World Investment Law (Cordonier Segger, Marie-Claire et al. (Eds.) 2011) 683 (701) argues that the legitimate expectations of an investor could be violated, if the non-compliance of its home state leads to a suspension of its investment projects.

Even though I find it unlikely that this connection would be made by the host state, it would not constitute a violation of the investor's expectations in my opinion, if this risk had been known to the investor. In this situation, the non-compliance of its home state would be nothing more than a general business risk.

4. Scenario No 4: Withdrawal of Support Scheme Because Investment Affects the Environmental Objective

Like the third scenario, the fourth scenario relates to changes made to a scheme supporting the adoption of environmentally friendly investments. In this scenario, the changes are motivated by environmental reasons – most notably by the realisation that the investments supported do, in fact, have a harmful impact on the environment. Some categories of investors that originally qualified for profiting from the scheme are subsequently excluded.

The portrayal of Scenario No 3 has demonstrated that the expectations of an investor in environmentally advantageous technology are protected by the standard of fairness, when they rely on specific guarantees or tariffs that form part of the regulatory framework. The protection of these expectations via the standard of fairness is not influenced by the reasons for which the host state implemented changes. The investment tribunals which had to decide the cases of unilateral alterations to tariff structures did not find that the reasons for which the state decided to alter a promised framework could attenuate the violation of the fairness standard.[251] The intention and motivation that lead the state to alter its regulatory framework are not decisive.

Even though some tribunals have recognised that the regulatory authority of the state persists, they stated that the investor as participant in a "regulated industry had the legitimate expectation that the [...] authorities would exercise that regulatory authority and discretion within the rules of the detailed legal framework that [the host state] had established".[252] This understanding effectively reduces the regulatory freedom of the host state. This assessment refers to changes in a tariff structure made in an attempt by the host state to come to terms with a fundamental economic crisis. Accordingly, it is doubtful whether an alteration because of a detected environmental problem would garner more support. It is obviously preferable for a state to remain within the original framework. However, in this Scenario No 4

251 The alterations to the framework were made by the Argentinean authorities in an attempt to mitigate the effects of the country's severe financial crisis. The tribunals did for the most part not find that this grave situation could affect the position of the foreign investor. Explicitly, the tribunals in Sempra Energy International v. The Argentine Republic, ICSID Case No. ARB/02/16, Award of 28 September 2007, para 304, Enron Corporation and Ponderosa Assets, L.P. v. Argentine Republic, ICSID Case No. ARB/01/3, Award of 22 May 2007, para 268 stated that there was a breach of the objective standard of fair and equitable treatment, even if the host state "was guided by the best of intentions".

252 AWG Group Ltd. v. The Argentine Republic, Decision on Liability of 30 July 2010, para 237; Suez, Sociedad General de Aguas de Barcelona S.A., and InterAguas Servicios Integrales del Agua S.A. v. The Argentine Republic, ICSID Case No. ARB/03/17, Decision on Liability of 30 July 2010, para 217.

the state cannot fulfill the environmental objective when remaining within the pre-existing framework. The environmental objective and the stability of the framework are mutually exclusive.

In my understanding, the expectations of the investor have to be balanced against the regulatory interest of the state in the light of the circumstances in which the investment has been made. The circumstances will obviously differ from case to case. Putatively, one could argue that the investor knew that it was financially supported, not as an end in itself, but because the host state had an interest in a specific technology – or energy generated in a way – that was friendly to the environment. This can reduce the legitimacy of the investor's expectations if its technology is, in fact, not really environmentally advantageous. The issue boils down to the question which party is 'responsible' for the environmental success of the respective technology – the investor or the host state. Even if the explicit promises in the tariff structure created a high level of expectations, it still appears difficult to oblige the host state to continue the support of a technology that is environmentally disadvantageous.

Practical examples of such scenarios have been portrayed in the first chapter.[253] In this way, the creation of carbon credits from superfluously fabricated abatement projects might get decimated or the credits can be discredited to represent a reduced value of carbon reduction. However, the Executive Board of the Clean Development Mechanism has looked into the non-additionality of HFC-23 abatement facilities,[254] but no decision to limit the capacities of the facilities has been taken. In the situation of the HFC-23 abatement from specifically produced plants, it is my understanding that it would be legitimate to at least reduce the value of the credits created, because the undertaking clearly undermines the idea of the Kyoto Protocol. It is in this sense that credits received from certain projects which destroy industrial gases, such as HFC-23, can no longer be used to offset emissions within the European Emissions Trading Scheme.[255]

---

253 See 'Chapter 1 – Environmental Norms and Principles' at pp. 86 *et seq.*

254 Clean Development Mechanism-Meth Panel, Note on AM0001: Incineration of HFC 23 Waste Streams, Report of 44th Meeting 2010, available at: http://cdm.unfccc.int/Panels/meth/meeting/10/044/mp44_an02.pdf. See also the corresponding consideration of the Executive Board of the Clean Development Mechanism, Report of the 58th Meeting of 26 November 2010, CDM-EB-58, para 28.

255 Press Release of the European Commission IP/11/56 dated 21 January 2011. The cut-off date was 30 April 2013.

5. Conclusive Summary

The portrayal of the scenarios and the existing case law indicates that the standard of fairness is apt to lead to arbitral decisions that take due account of the valid interests of both the investor and the host state. The legitimacy of the investor's expectations is established through a balancing exercise against the regulatory interest of the state and the circumstances surrounding the investment. In the absence of specific representations or promises made by the host state the investor's desire for the stability of regulation will usually not be as relevant as the authority of the state to regulate in the public interest.

Real conflicts may therefore arise when the state has given specific assurances to an investor from which it intends to withdraw for environmental reasons. In such a situation, the host state has to compensate the investor for its loss. Fairness mandates that the investor be protected. Accordingly, a host state is under a specific obligation to evaluate the potential environmental impact of assurances it gives to a foreign investor. In practical terms, this may be more difficult for states in which environmental legislation and processes are not very advanced, yet. The potential for conflicts is the higher, the more environmental regulation has to be amended retrospectively. Further, states in the process of development may not yet have adequate processes in place to fairly deal with upcoming difficulties. In such a situation, the requirements of the standard of fairness can clash with the desire of the host state to introduce environmental regulation.

F. Summary

Investment treaties contain differently phrased standards of protection, which require the host state to observe an absolute level of protection. Of these, the standard of constant protection and security, preserving the physical integrity of the investment and the investor, cannot provide guidance on conflicts stemming from the introduction of allegedly environmental regulation. In contrast, the standard of fair and equitable treatment and the protection against arbitrary and discriminatory measures are both material in this context. They are considered to form a comprehensive standard of fairness for the purpose of this study.

This standard of fairness is comprised of four fundamental pillars. The material cornerstones are the investor's legitimate expectations and the stability of the regulatory framework. The investor's interest in stable and predictable regulation is balanced against the state's right to amend regulation to further an environmental objective: The legitimacy of the investor's expectation of stability is the higher, the more precise promises the host state has given to this end. The procedural cornerstones of the protection are tied to the notions of transparency and due process. These notions have to be reflected in the way in which the host state approaches the evaluation of scientific evidence. An investment tribunal will assess the process which leads to the adoption of the environmental measure, but not the scientific evidence or the environmental objective as such. Furthermore, the procedural notions are to characterise the host state's dealing with the investor. However, investment tribunals will not hold the host state to procedural perfection.

The four pillars of the concept of fairness in investment proceedings indicate that the review of an environmental measure involves the balancing of several aspects. The protective notions also underscore the need for host states to act transparently when dealing with foreign investment. Fairness is a fluid concept that does not offer clear-cut answers. Taking account of the interests of two parties to a dispute in the manner detailed in this chapter can result in decisions which are fair and equitable for all involved.

Chapter 5

Expropriation

Predictability is one of the most important objectives of any legal system. It would be useful if it were absolutely clear in advance whether particular events fall within the definition of an "indirect" expropriation. [...] But there is no checklist, no mechanical test to achieve that purpose. The decisive considerations vary from case to case [...]. The outcome is a judgment, i. e. the product of discernment, and not the printout of a computer programme.

Tribunal in Generation Ukraine v. Ukraine, 2003

Protection against the expropriation of foreign investment is the best established safeguard of the interests of foreign investors. Despite significant historic differences between capital exporting and capital importing states in evaluating the components of the protection against expropriation, there is little doubt that its basic tenets have reached the status of customary international law.[1] Accordingly, the foreign investors' 'property' is protected against 'takings' by a governmental-type authority. Although investment treaties do not prohibit the expropriation of foreign investments, the legality of expropriation is linked to a restricted set of conditions, most notably the payment of compensation to the investor.

The evaluation of protection against expropriation at the international level is characterised by historic shifts, which cannot be portrayed in detail. For the present context, it suffices to recall the two main opposing groups of states. Capital importing countries focused on the sovereignty of states[2] and their right to nationalise foreign property, whereas capital exporting countries opposed acts of expropriation and stressed the importance of prompt, adequate and effective compensation in such cases.[3] Although no

---

[1] See for a historic overview and an evaluation of established differences between *opinio juris* and state practice, *Dolzer*, Rudolf, Eigentum, Enteignung und Entschädigung im geltenden Völkerrecht (1985) pp. 14–54 (esp. pp. 50–54).

[2] See General Assembly Resolution, 'Declaration on the Establishment of a New International Economic Order', UN Doc. A/RES/S-6/3201, 1 May 1974.

[3] The so-called Hull-formula, which requires 'prompt, adequate and effective compensation' in cases of expropriation was first demanded by the U.S. for specific cases of expropriation in Mexico. Capital exporting countries focused on it, whereas especially Latin American countries opposed it, see *Lowenfeld*, Andreas F., Inter-

formal agreement on these opposite opinions has ever been reached, the proliferation of investment treaties setting express requirements for expropriation has reduced the importance of the debate for conflicts rooted in treaty obligations.

Increasingly, the perception of what constitutes expropriation has broadened. Foreign investment is not only protected against scenarios in which the objective of the state is to acquire title to the investment or economic benefits from it, through acts of direct expropriation and nationalisation. Measures targeting the foreign investor less directly than an outright 'taking' can constitute expropriation. It is not decisive whether the host state has the intention of 'taking' the investment or whether the measure results in an economic benefit for the state. Rather, it is the effect of the measure on the investment that is at the heart of the issue. It follows for the context of this study that primarily indirect measures – namely those purportedly furthering an environmental aim – will be tested as to their potential negative effect on foreign investment. As the finding of an expropriatory act triggers the obligation of the host state to compensate, it is most important from the perspective of the investor whether a measure impairing its investment constitutes expropriation, i.e. whether the threshold of the impact is substantial enough. Accordingly, this chapter will focus on the criteria for finding expropriation.

This chapter first briefly portrays direct expropriation, before it turns to indirect expropriation. In this regard, it discusses the elements establishing the ambit of indirect expropriation by portraying findings in decisions in investment and other international law. As a third stage, the chapter describes investment decisions that concern alleged expropriation through environmental measures. The tribunals' findings and extensive academic commentary are used, in a fourth section, to establish the distinguishing line between indirect expropriation and regulation that has an impact on the investment, but does not require compensation. Fifth, the distinguishing line is applied to hypothetical scenarios, to shed light on the potential for conflict between environmental measures and the protection of investors' property against expropriation. Finally, the requirement for compensation is analysed to determine in how far an environmental reason or obligation leading to the expropriatory measure can reduce the level of payable compensation.

---

national Economic Law (2008) pp. 475–493; *Sornarajah*, M., The International Law on Foreign Investment (2010) pp. 127–128.

A. Direct Expropriation

The differentiation between 'direct' and 'indirect' expropriation, strictly speaking, is not significant for the protection of the foreign investor, as factors and requirements for legality are essentially the same. However, direct expropriation is explicit about what it is: It is an open, deliberate and acknowledged taking of property, such as an outright seizure or formal or obligatory transfer of title in favour of the host state.[4] Deprivation of title to property is inherent in direct expropriation.[5] Accordingly, in such a situation, the investor's loss of control over its investment will be obvious.

Nationalisations of foreign property were relevant in the 1960s and 1970s in connection with advocating national sovereignty over natural resources[6], post-colonialism and revolutionary changes[7]. Since then, outright nationalisation or direct expropriation has become significantly less frequent and is less likely today,[8] with a multitude of states recognising the importance of foreign investment for their own development purposes. The overwhelming majority of investment decisions today relates to measures potentially qualifying as indirect, not as direct expropriation.

In this light, it is not surprising that measures constituting direct expropriation are unlikely instruments for implementing environmental standards. Generally, environmental legislation regulates or restricts certain economic activities. To achieve a coherent protection of an environmental objective, it is necessary to implement environmental standards to be observed by all exercising the activity in question – but not the transfer of title over certain

---

[4] Metalclad Corporation v. United Mexican States, Award of 30 August 2000, para. 103; Glamis Gold v. U.S.A., Award of 8 June 2009, para 355.

[5] National Grid plc v. The Argentine Republic, Award of 3 November 2008, para 145.

[6] See General Assembly Resolution, 'Resolution on Permanent Sovereignty over Natural Resources', Resolution 1803 (XVII), UN Doc. A/5217 (1962), 14 December 1962; General Assembly Resolution, 'Declaration on the Establishment of a New International Economic Order', UN Doc. A/RES/S-6/3201, 1 May 1974. Lowenfeld, Andreas F., International Economic Law (2008) pp. 483–485.

[7] See for a description of nationalisation in the context of the Iranian revolution, *Aldrich*, George H., The Jurisprudence of the Iran-United States Claims Tribunal (1996) pp. 174, 188–196. The examples of cases demonstrate that banks, insurance companies and the petroleum industry were subjected to nationalisation or 'de facto' nationalisation.

[8] *Baughen*, Simon, 'Expropriation and Environmental Regulation: The Lessons and NAFTA Chapter 11', 18 Journal of Environmental Law 2006, 207 (209). There is, however, a very recent trend towards more nationalisation, especially in South America. Examples are the expropriation of Spanish-owned oil assets in Argentina and acts of expropriation in Venezuela.

investments. A transfer of title over an investment can only be required in few scenarios. One plausible scenario is that foreign property – most certainly land – constitutes a part of an environmental protection zone. Then, the government has an environmental reason to directly obtain the property.

Such a situation formed the factual basis of the decision in *Compañía del Dessarollo de Santa Elena S.A. v. Republic of Costa Rica.*[9] In this case, the host state had issued an expropriation decree for the investor's property with the purpose of including the land in an already existing nearby national park to maintain its conservationist objective.[10] The property was explicitly expropriated by decree, so that the issue of whether there was expropriation was not subject to debate. Thus, the case concerned a direct expropriation for an environmental purpose. The legitimacy of the measure as such was not at issue. The only contested issue was the amount of compensation that the host state had to pay to the investor.[11] The respective findings of the tribunal will be discussed in more substance below.[12]

For the investor it is most interesting whether a measure affecting its investment constitutes expropriation. If this is the case, the investor is owed compensation, irrespective of whether the expropriation is lawful or not. Even though the determination of compensation can differ in cases of lawful and unlawful compensation,[13] the principal economic interest of the investor is not connected to the legality of the measure. Nevertheless, a tribunal that has established that a measure constitutes expropriation will assess whether the requirements of a lawful expropriation – as found in many modern investment treaties –[14] have been fulfilled, namely, that the expropriation occurred (a) for a public purpose, (b) in a non-discriminatory

---

9 Compañía del Dessarollo de Santa Elena S.A. v. Republic of Costa Rica, ICSID Case No. ARB/96/1. However, the decision is not based on an investment treaty.

10 Compañía del Dessarollo de Santa Elena S.A. v. Republic of Costa Rica, ICSID Case No. ARB/96/1, Award of 17 February 2000, para 18, citing the 1978 decree expropriating the property.

11 Compañía del Dessarollo de Santa Elena S.A. v. Republic of Costa Rica, ICSID Case No. ARB/96/1, Award of 17 February 2000, para 56.

12 See below at pp. 346 *et seq.*, 374 *et seq.*

13 PCIJ Case Concerning the Factory at Chorzów (Germany/Poland) Judgment of 13 September 1928, (Series A, No 17, 3) (47); *Schreuer*, Christoph, 'The Concept of Expropriation under the ECT and Other Investment Protection Treaties', in: Investment Arbitration and the Energy Charter Treaty (Ribeiro, Clarisse (Ed.) 2006) 108 (158–159); *Marboe*, Irmgard, Calculation of Compensation and Damages in International Investment Law (2009), paras 2.101 *et seq.*

14 See, for example, Article 10.7. CAFTA-DR; Article 1110 NAFTA; Article 6 para 2 France-Bosnia and Herzegovina BIT. Similarly, also Article 6 para 1 United Kingdom-Ukraine BIT; Article 5 para 1 United Kingdom-Uganda BIT. Similarly, but

manner, (c) in accordance with due process of law, and (d) was accompanied by payment of compensation. These criteria are identical for both direct and indirect expropriation.[15]

The first requirement of a lawful expropriation is that the measure was adopted to further a public purpose. In the light of the deference generally accorded, states profit from considerable leeway in defining purposes that are meant to further a public objective. Therefore, the relevance of this requirement is practically limited to screening out measures that are adopted for purely private gain.[16] It follows that regulatory measures which are taken in pursuance of environmental objectives are considered to fulfil a 'public purpose', even if the measure is adopted to further several differing purposes. The second condition for lawful expropriation is its non-discriminatory nature. Discrimination is an issue whenever the impact is more intense on specific foreign investors for reasons of their nationality than it is on national or other third state investors. In this sense, the content of the requirement accords with the tenets of non-discrimination, as discussed above.[17] The third requirement prescribes the adoption of the measure in accordance with due process of law. The relevance of due process for the concept of fairness in investment law has been portrayed in the previous chapter.[18] Some investment treaties further emphasise this connection in linking the legitimacy of expropriation to the standard of fair and equitable treatment.[19] Whether this express intertwining of both protective standards

---

not mentioning factor (b), Article 4 para 2 Germany-Afghanistan BIT; Article 3 para 2 Germany-Bangladesh BIT; Article 3 para 2 Germany-Mauritius BIT.

15 However, it is unlikely that a measure that indirectly impacts on the investment, without the intention of 'taking' any property, is coupled with the payment of compensation. Accordingly, it will not be a lawful expropriation in the strict sense. See, *Reisman*, W. Michael/*Sloane*, Robert D., 'Indirect Expropriation and Its Valuation in the BIT Generation', 74 British Yearbook of International Law 2003, 115 (137); *Ripinsky*, Sergey/*Williams*, Kevin, Damages in International Investment Law (2008) p. 69.

16 *Higgins*, Rosalyn, 'The Taking of Property by the State: Recent Developments in International Law', Recueil des Cours 1982-III, 259 (371). *Griebel*, Jörn, Internationales Investitionsrecht (2008) p. 18 states that only measures, which are taken in private interest, in the interest of third states, or to put pressure on the investor's home state do not reflect a 'public purpose'. See, however, the scrutiny of the criterion in ADC Affiliate Limited and ADC & ADMC Management Limited v. Republic of Hungary, ICSID Case No. ARB/03/16, Award of 2 October 2006, paras 429–433.

17 See in 'Chapter 3 – Standards of Non-Discriminatory Treatment' at pp. 166 *et seq.*

18 See in 'Chapter 4 – Standards of Fair Treatment' at pp. 252 *et seq.*

19 See, for example, Article 1110 para 1 lit c NAFTA; Article 10.7 para 1 lit d CAFTA-DR, referring to the standard contained in the same treaty.

is helpful is open to debate.[20] For the present purpose, it suffices to note that 'due process' requires the measure to conform to national decision making processes and to involve the investor to the extent provided for by the regulatory framework.

As this brief portrayal indicates, the implications of the three criteria are not controversial. However, it should be mentioned that not all bilateral investment treaties do prescribe all these requirements for lawful expropriation. Especially some of the less recent investment treaties do not mention the 'due process' criterion. In contrast, the fourth criterion for lawful expropriation is mentioned in all investment treaties: The payment of compensation is the most relevant criterion. Because of the important implications of the payment and the calculation of compensation, this requirement will be discussed in more detail below.[21]

B. Indirect Expropriation

With states decreasingly taking foreign property by way of direct expropriation, the concept of 'indirect expropriation' has become increasingly relevant. An act of indirect expropriation is less obvious to detect and requires the evaluation of certain criteria. Modern investment treaties indicate that the concept of expropriation is not restricted to direct takings of foreign property: The relevant provisions frequently refer to measures 'having effect equivalent to' or 'tantamount to' expropriation or nationalisation.[22] Although

---

[20] The intertwining of protection standards, so that one requires the fulfilment of conditions of another standard reduces the distinctiveness of the different standards. Whether such approaches will ultimately lead to a merging of all investment protection provisions under the umbrella of one comprehensive tort of violation of investment protection remains to be seen. In this sense, *Wälde*, Thomas, 'International Disciplines on National Environmental Regulation: With Particular Focus on Multilateral Investment Treaties', in: International Investments and Protection of the Environment: The Role of Dispute Resolution Mechanisms (International Bureau of the Permanent Court of Arbitration (Ed.) 2001) 29 (61).

Since the genuine requirements for a legitimate expropriation are so close to the notion of fair and equitable treatment, it is not a big step to expressly read these conditions into the expropriation provision.

[21] See below at pp. 369 *et seq.*

[22] See, for example, Article 10. 7 CAFTA-DR; Article 5 2003 Indian Model BIT; Article 4 2004 Canadian Model BIT; Article 1110 NAFTA, Article 13 ECT; Article 4 2008 German Model BIT.

The "laconic wording" of descriptions of indirect expropriation in investment treaties has been criticised by *Dolzer*, Rudolf, 'Indirect Expropriation of Alien Property', 1 ICSID Review Foreign Investment Law Journal 1986, 41 (55). Dolzer states sharply: "If legal clarity and security is the proper yardstick for the evaluation of

the effect of these formulations has been subject to debate, it can be assumed that they capture those forms of dispossession which can be described as indirect expropriation. Specifically, provisions referring to measures 'tantamount' to expropriation do not broaden the scope of the concept of expropriation.[23]

Courts and tribunals have identified a host of forms of indirect expropriation. The applied terms encompass 'de facto expropriation', 'regulatory expropriation' and 'disguised expropriation'. However, these labels do not designate clearly distinguishable concepts and they are applied interchangeably.[24] In contrast, an act labelled as 'creeping expropriation' is characterised by a series of acts attributable to the host state, which culminate in the expropriatory taking of the investor's property over a period of time.[25] Despite this distinctive temporal quality, there is no need to distinguish between 'creeping expropriation' and other forms of indirect expropriation.[26] For the purpose of this study, it is assumed that 'indirect expropriation' is a generic term which covers all forms and measures of a taking in the absence of a direct transfer of property. The term is considered to be synonymous to the term 'taking', which is predominantly used by American jurists as a reflection of the takings doctrine in U.S. law.

---

technical craftsmanship of investment treaties, the clauses […] fall below the mark of acceptability." With regard to the more recent investment treaties, which contain annexes to illuminate relevant factors, his verdict might be less harsh.

23 S.D. Myers v. Canada, Partial Award, 13 November 2000, paras 285–286; Pope & Talbot Inc. v. Canada, Interim Award of 26 June 2000, paras 96, 104; Glamis Gold, Ltd. v. The United States of America, Award of 8 June 2009, para 355. Conversely, Waste Management II v. United Mexican States, ICSID Case No. ARB(AF)/00/3 (NAFTA), Award of 30 April 2004, paras 143–144.

24 *Hoffmann*, Anne K., 'Indirect Expropriation', in: Standards of Investment Protection (Reinisch, August (Ed.) 2008) 151 (153).

25 Generation Ukraine v. Ukraine, Award of 16 September 2003, ICSID Case No. ARB/00/9, para 20.22; *Kriebaum*, Ursula, Eigentumsschutz im Völkerrecht (2008) p. 228. See for detailed portrayal of this issue, *Reisman*, W. Michael/*Sloane*, Robert D., 'Indirect Expropriation and Its Valuation in the BIT Generation', 74 British Yearbook of International Law 2003, 115 (122–128); *Schreuer*, Christoph, 'The Concept of Expropriation under the ECT and Other Investment Protection Treaties', in: Investment Arbitration and the Energy Charter Treaty (Ribeiro, Clarisse (Ed.) 2006) 108 (126–133). If the process of relevant acts stops before it reaches the point at which its effect is to be considered expropriatory, adverse effects on the investment do not constitute expropriation, Siemens A.G. v. Argentine Republic, ICSID Case No. ARB/02/8, Award of 6 February 2007, para. 263.

26 Feldman v. Mexico, Award of 16 December 2002, Case No. ARB(AF)99/1, para 101; Generation Ukraine v. Ukraine, Award of 16 September 2003, ICSID Case No. ARB/00/9, para 20.22; S.D. Myers v. Canada, Partial Award, 13 November 2000, para 286.

To determine the protective scope of the provisions on expropriation, it is most relevant to establish the factors which constitute indirect expropriation. For the protection of the foreign investor, it is less relevant whether an act of a host state meets the criteria of legal expropriation.[27] Accordingly, this section emphasises the portrayal of the factors which investment tribunals consider to constitute expropriation. The factors thus determined will subsequently be used to carve out the division between indirect expropriation and simple regulatory measures.

I. Factors Establishing Indirect Expropriation

Although investment treaties generally refrain from enumerating the relevant factors for finding expropriation,[28] scholarly writing and arbitral decisions have identified a consolidating set of more or less commonly accepted factors. Despite not being completely congruent, the proposed factors indicate similar aspects as relevant to finding expropriation. The factors, which are portrayed and assessed in the following, are (1) the substantial deprivation of the investment, (2) the interference of the measure with reasonable investment-backed expectations, and (3) the character of the governmental measure, purpose and context.

---

27 Similarly, *Schreuer*, Christoph, 'The Concept of Expropriation under the ECT and Other Investment Protection Treaties', in: Investment Arbitration and the Energy Charter Treaty (Ribeiro, Clarisse (Ed.) 2006) 108 (111); *Hoffmann*, Anne K., 'Indirect Expropriation', in: Standards of Investment Protection (Reinisch, August (Ed.) 2008) 151 (152).

28 See for one exception to the general reluctance, Annex 10.C para 4 CAFTA-DR. The provision reads as follows: "The second situation addressed by Article 10.7.1 is indirect expropriation, where an action or series of actions by a Party has an effect equivalent to direct expropriation without formal transfer of title or outright seizure.

(a) The determination of whether an action or series of actions by a Party, in a specific fact situation, constitutes an indirect expropriation, requires a case-by-case, fact-based inquiry that considers, among other factors:

(i) the economic impact of the government action, although the fact that an action or series of actions by a Party has an adverse effect on the economic value of an investment, standing alone, does not establish that an indirect expropriation has occurred; (ii) the extent to which the government action interferes with distinct, reasonable investment-backed expectations; and (iii) the character of the government action.

(b) Except in rare circumstances, nondiscriminatory regulatory actions by a Party that are designed and applied to protect legitimate public welfare objectives, such as public health, safety, and the environment, do not constitute indirect expropriations."

1. Substantial Deprivation

The most commonly determined factor is the 'substantial deprivation' of the investor of its investment. This terminology is used as a requirement in a large quantity of investment awards dealing with indirect expropriation.[29] A multitude of other arbitral decisions express the same understanding in similar words.[30] However, investment awards do not embrace a uniform

---

[29] AWG Group Ltd. v. The Argentine Republic, Award on Liability of 30 July 2010, paras 134, 145; BG Group Plc v. Argentina, Award of 24 December 2007, para 271; Chemtura Corporation v. Government of Canada, Award of 2 August 2010, paras 244, 247, 249; CMS Gas Transmission Company v. The Argentine Republic, ICSID Case No. ARB/01/8, Award of 12 May 2005, para 263; Enron Corporation and Ponderosa Assets, L.P. v. Argentine Republic, ICSID Case No. ARB/01/3, Award of 22 May 2007, para 245; Fireman's Fund Insurance Company v. United Mexican States, ICSID Case No. ARB(AF)/02/1, Award of 17 July 2006; para 176; Merrill & Ring Forestry L.P. v. Canada, Award of 31 March 2010, para 145; Pope & Talbot Inc. v. Canada, Interim Award of 26 June 2000, para 102; Saipem S.p.A. v. The People's Republic of Bangladesh, ICSID Case No. ARB/05/07, Award of 30 June 2009, para 133; Sempra Energy International v. The Argentine Republic, ICSID Case No. ARB/02/16, Award of 28 September 2007, para 284; Suez, Sociedad General de Aguas de Barcelona S.A., and InterAguas Servicios Integrales del Agua S.A. v. The Argentine Republic, ICSID Case No. ARB/03/17, Award of 30 July 2010, para 123; Suez, Sociedad General de Aguas de Barcelona, S.A.and Vivendi Universal, S.A. v. Argentine Republic, ICSID Case No. ARB/03/19, Award of 30 July 2010, para 134; Tokios Tokelés v. Ukraine, ICSID Case No. ARB/02/18, Award of 26 July 2007, para 120; Burlington Resources Inc. v. Republic of Ecuador, ICSID Case No. ARB/08/5, Decision on Liability of 14 December 2012, para 397; Deutsche Bank AG v. Democratic Socialist Republic of Sri Lanka, ICSID Case No. ARB/09/2, Award of 31 October 2012, para 503; Bosh International, Inc and B&P Ltd Foreign Investments Enterprise v. Ukraine, ICSID Case No. ARB/08/11, Award of 25 October 2012, para 218; Railroad Development Corporation v. Republic of Guatemala, ICSID Case No. ARB/07/23, Award of 29 June 2012, para 151; Ulysseas, Inc. v. The Republic of Ecuador, Award of 12 June 2012, para 186; EDF International S.A., SAUR International S.A. and León Participaciones Argentinas S.A. v. Argentine Republic, ICSID Case No. ARB/03/23, Award of 11 June 2012, para 1113.

[30] Azurix v. Argentine Republic, ICSID Case No. ARB/01/12, Award of 14 July 2006, para 318; Walter Bau v. Thailand, Award of 1 July 2009, paras 10.16-7; Bayindir Insaat Turizm Ticaret Ve Sanayi A.S. v. Islamic Republic of Pakistan, ICSID Case No. ARB/03/29, Award of 27 August 2009, para 443; Biwater Gauff (Tanzania) Ltd. v. United Republic of Tanzania, ICSID Case No. ARB/05/22, Award of 24 July 2008, para 455; Compañiá de Aguas del Aconquija S.A. and Vivendi Universal v. Argentine Republic, ICSID Case No. ARB/97/3, Award of 20 August 2007; para 7.5.29; Corn Products International, Inc. v. United Mexican States, ICSID Case No. ARB(AF)04/01, Partial Award of 15 January 2008, para 92; Consortium R.F.C.C. v. Kingdom of Morocco, ICSID Case No. ARB/00/6, Award of 22 December 2003, para 68; Continental Casualty Company v. Argentina, ICSID Case No. ARB/03/9, Award of 5 September 2008, para 276; Generation Ukraine, Inc. v.

understanding as to the conditions under which an investor is 'substantially deprived' of its investment. Arbitral tribunals have determined mainly two obviously intertwined facets: The first facet focuses on the loss of control of the investor over its business. The second facet relates to the loss of economic benefits of the investment. Whether investment tribunals consider a deprivation to be 'substantial' is furthermore influenced by other aspects, relating to the duration and intensity of the impact on the investment.

Those tribunals focusing on the investor's 'loss of control' over its investment frequently rely on the host of criteria enumerated by the arbitral tribunal in *Pope & Talbot v. Canada*: the nationalisation of the investment, the imposed regime being confiscatory, the investor's not remaining in control over its investment, the investor's not directing the day-to-day operations of the investment, the detention of officers or employees, a taking from the company's proceeds other than taxes, the interference with management and shareholders' activities, the obstruction of the investment from paying dividends, the interference with the appointment of directors or management, or the taking of other action ousting the investor from full ownership and control of its investment.[31] A large number of arbitral decisions either explicitly apply or sanction the criteria by way of reference.[32]

Ukraine, ICSID Case No. ARB/00/9, Award of 16 September 2003, paras 20.32; Lauder v. Czech Republic, Award of 3 September 2001, para 202; LG&E v. Argentina, ICSID Case No. ARB/02/1, Award of 3 October 2006, para 191; M.C.I. Power Group L.C. and New Turbine, Inc. v. Ecuador, ICSID Case No. ARB/03/6, Award of 31 July 2007, para 300; Metalpar S.A. and Buen Aire S.A. v. Argentine Republic, ICSID Case No. ARB/03/5, Award of 6 June 2008, para 173; Olguín v. Paraguay, ICSID Case No. ARB/98/5, Award of 26 July 2001, para 84; Parkerings-Compagniet AS v. Lithuania, ICSID Case No. ARB/05/8, Award of 11 September 2007, para 455; Plama Consortium Limited v. Bulgaria, ICSID Case No. ARB/03/24, Award of 27 August 2008, para 193; Wena Hotels Ltd. v. Arab Republic of Egypt, ICSID Case No. ARB/98/4, Award of 8 December 2008, para 99; AES Summit Generation Limited and AES-Tisza Erömü Kft v. The Republic of Hungary, ICSID Case No. ARB/07/22, Award of 23 September 2010, para 14.3.1; Antoine Abou Lahoud and Leila Bounafeh-Abou Lahoud v. Democratic Republic of the Congo, ICSID Case No. ARB/10/4, Award of 7 February 2014, para 504.

31 Pope & Talbot Inc. v. Canada, Interim Award 26 June 2000, para 100.

32 Archer Daniels Midland Company and Tate & Lyle Ingredients Americas, Inc. v. United Mexican States, ICSID Case No. ARB (AF)/04/5, Award of 21 November 2007, para 245; Chemtura Corporation v. Government of Canada, Award of 2 August 2010, paras 245, 247; CMS Gas Transmission Company v. The Argentine Republic, ICSID Case No. ARB/01/8, Award of 12 May 2005, para 263; Enron Corporation and Ponderosa Assets, L.P. v. Argentine Republic, ICSID Case No. ARB/01/3, Award of 22 May 2007, para 245; Feldman v. Mexico, ICSID Case No. ARB(AF)/99/1, Award of 16 December 2002, para 151; Fireman's Fund Insurance Company v. United Mexican States, ICSID Case No. ARB(AF)/02/1, Award of 17 July 2006; para 176; Merrill & Ring Forestry L.P. v. Canada, Award of 31 March

These criteria which focus on the loss of control reflect earlier precedents that assessed the occurrence of expropriation under international law. Most notably, decisions rendered by the Iran-U.S. Claims Tribunal stressed on the required extent of interference with property rights[33] and with fundamental rights of ownership[34]. Although the facts underlying these decisions reflect a very specific situation in the aftermath of revolutionary changes, they illustrate the level of interference required for finding an act of expropriation. In that regard, a large number of investment tribunals have relied on decisions of the Iran-U.S. Claims Tribunal in their argumentation.[35]

2010, paras 145–147; National Grid plc v. The Argentine Republic, Award of 3 November 2008, para 150; PSEG Global, Inc., The North American Coal Corporation, and Konya Ingin Electrik Uretim ve Ticaret Limited Sirketi v. Turkey, ICSID Case No. ARB/02/5, Award of 19 January 2007, para 278; Walter Bau v. Thailand, Award of 1 July 2009, paras 10.16-7. Sempra Energy International v. The Argentine Republic, ICSID Case No. ARB/02/16, Award of 28 September 2007, para 284, explicitly considering the approach to be representative of the required legal standard for an indirect expropriation.

See, however, Gami Investments, Inc. v. Mexico, Award of 15 November 2004, para 130 criticising the reliance on this passage for constituting an inconclusive analysis.

33 Starret Housing Corp. v. Iran, Interlocutary Award of 19 December 1983, Award No. ITL-32-24-1, 4 Iran-US CTR 122 (154) held that "it is recognized by international law that measures taken by a State can interfere with property rights to such an extent that these rights are rendered so useless that they must be deemed to have been expropriated, even though [...] the legal title to the property formally remains with the original owner". The case concerned, inter alia, the appointment of Iranian managers by the Iranian government to the housing project of an American investor, which was evaluated to constitute an expropriation.

34 Tippetts, Abbett, McCarthy, Stratton v. TAMS-AFFA Consulting Engineers of Iran, Award of 22 June 1984, Award No. 141-7-2, 6 Iran-US CTR 219 (225). The tribunal decided that the conclusion that property has been taken by the government "is warranted whenever events demonstrate that the owner was deprived of fundamental rights of ownership and it appears that the deprivation is not merely ephemeral ...". In this case, it was not the appointing of Iranian managers to the investment as such that was considered to have expropriated the investment, but specific acts of these appointed managers.

See for a detailed scrutiny of the facts in which the Iran-U.S. Claims Tribunal found acts constituting expropriation, *Aldrich*, George H., The Jurisprudence of the Iran-United States Claims Tribunal (1996) pp. 174–206.

35 BG Group Plc v. Argentina, Award of 24 December 2007, para 261; Biwater Gauff (Tanzania) Ltd. v. United Republic of Tanzania, ICSID Case No. ARB/05/22, Award of 24 July 2008, para 509; Compañiá de Aguas del Aconquija S.A. and Vivendi Universal v. Argentine Republic, ICSID Case No. ARB/97/3, Award of 20 August 2007, para 7.5.16; Consortium R.F.C.C. v. Kingdom of Morocco, ICSID Case No. ARB/00/6, Award of 22 December 2003, para 67; Generation Ukraine, Inc. v. Ukraine, ICSID Case No. ARB/00/9, Award of 16 September 2003, paras 20.23–24; Plama Consortium Limited v. Bulgaria, ICSID Case No. ARB/03/24, Award of 27 August 2008, para 191; Siemens v. The Argentine Republic, ICSID

The loss of control over the investment is complementary to, and regularly intertwined with, the facet of 'loss of economic benefits', because the loss of control generally leads to an economic loss for the investor. The economic loss is considered the most decisive factor, so that a distinction between the two features is largely superfluous. Analysis indicates that the degree of interference with the property right can be determined by reference to the severity of the economic impact.[36] Accordingly, a multitude of investment tribunals focused on the economic impact of the enacted governmental measure, assessing whether the governmental action 'radically deprived' the investor of all or the most beneficial economic use of its investment.[37]

The facet of economic impact is also most significant in the U.S.-American 'takings doctrine', to which international tribunals draw parallels. The three criteria of a 'taking' set forth in the U.S. Supreme Court's decision *Penn Central Transportation Corp. v. New York City*[38] have been influential. Similarly, the understanding developed in decisions of the European Court of Human Rights (ECtHR) of what constitutes an act of expropriation has influenced other areas of international law. In this sense, investment

---

Case No. ARB/02/8, Award of 6 February 2007; para 269; Wena Hotels Ltd. v. Arab Republic of Egypt, ICSID Case No. ARB/98/4, Award of 8 December 2008, para 98.

36 See determination in *OECD*, '"Indirect Expropriation" and the "Right to Regulate" in International Investment Law', OECD Working Papers on International Investment (2004/4) p. 10 *et seq.*

37 Archer Daniels Midland Company and Tate & Lyle Ingredients Americas, Inc. v. United Mexican States, ICSID Case No. ARB (AF)/04/5, Award of 21 November 2007, paras 244, 246; AWG Group Ltd. v. The Argentine Republic, Award on Liability of 30 July 2010, para 134; Compañiá de Aguas del Aconquija S.A. and Vivendi Universal v. Argentine Republic, ICSID Case No. ARB/97/3, Award of 20 August 2007, paras 7.5.25–29; Consortium R.F.C.C. v. Kingdom of Morocco, ICSID Case No. ARB/00/6, Award of 22 December 2003, para 68; Feldman v, Mexico, Case No. ARB(AF)99/1, Award of 16 December 2002, para 103; Glamis Gold, Ltd. v. The United States of America, Award of 8 June 2009, paras 357, 358; L.E.S.I. S.p.A. et ASTALDI S.p.A. v. Algeria, ICSID Case No. ARB/05/3, Award of 12 November 2008, para 137; Técnicas Medioambientales Tecmed, S.A. v. United Mexican States, ICSID Case No. ARB (AF)/00/2, Award of 29 May 2003, para 115.

See also recent investment treaties focusing on "the economic impact of the government action" as one criterion, such as Annex 10.C para. 4 lit a (i) CAFTA-DR.

38 U.S. Supreme Court, Penn Central Transportation Corp. v. New York City, Decision of 26 June 1978, 438 U.S. 104 (1978). The criteria enumerated are the following: (i) economic impact of the regulation, (ii) reasonable investment-backed expectations, and (iii) character of the governmental action. In this decision, the U.S. Supreme Court held that the economic impact of the measure was not harsh enough to constitute a taking.

tribunals have discussed findings of the ECtHR,[39] despite the different mandate of the human rights' institution, which is safeguarding the right to enjoyment of property[40]. The complete deprivation of the economic value of the right is also one element of the expropriation-test applied by the ECtHR,[41] even though the discussion of 'substantial deprivation' is seldom at the heart of its decisions. Furthermore, the ECtHR is prone to setting the barriers to finding a relevant deprivation at a very elevated level.[42]

---

39 Azurix v. Argentine Republic, ICSID Case No. ARB/01/12, Award of 14 July 2006, para 312; Lauder v. Czech Republic, Award of 3 September 2001, para 200; Victor Pey Casado and President Allende Foundation v. Republic of Chile, ICSID Case No. ARB/98/2, Award of 8 May 2008, paras 605, 606; Técnicas Medioambientales Tecmed, S.A. v. United Mexican States, ICSID Case No. ARB (AF)/00/2, Award of 29 May 2003, para 116.

40 The right to the enjoyment of property is enshrined in Article 1 of Protocol 1 (1952) to the ECHR. The provision reads as follows:

"Every natural or legal person is entitled to the peaceful enjoyment of his possessions. No one shall be deprived of his possessions except in the public interest and subject to the conditions provided for by law and by the general principles of international law.

The preceding provisions shall not, however, in any way impair the right of a State to enforce such laws as it deems necessary to control the use of property in accordance with the general interest or to secure the payment of taxes or other contributions or penalties."

41 *Kriebaum*, Ursula, Eigentumsschutz im Völkerrecht (2008) p. 253. The author finds that the ECtHR uses a test comprising of the following three elements: (i) complete deprivation of the economic value of the right, (ii) no alternative possibility of use, and (iii) irreversibility of the measure.

42 A relevant example is the ECtHR Case of Sporrong and Lönnroth v. Sweden (Application no. 7151/75; 7152/75) Judgment of 23 September 1982. The applicants in this case owned property in an area in which the local community could use expropriation permits issued by the government when deemed necessary for the purposes of land-development. In addition, the applicants had been subjected to prohibitions on construction on their property. These measures left the right to use and dispose of the property intact; however, these rights were practically diminished (para 60). The ECtHR focused on the fact that – although it became more difficult to sell properties affected by expropriation permits and prohibitions on construction – the applicants could continue to utilise their possessions and that the possibility of selling subsisted, thus that the relevant right had not disappeared (para 63). The ECtHR concluded: "[A]lthough the right in question lost some of its substance, it did not disappear. The effects of the measures involved are not such that they can be assimilated to a deprivation of possessions." This reasoning takes into account all economically viable components of the property – specifically the possibilities to use and to sell it – so that only a complete deprivation of all of these components leads to the finding of an expropriation of the property in question.

The ECtHR nevertheless found a violation of the applicants' right as enshrined in Article 1 of Protocol 1 to the ECHR because they had to bear an "individual and excessive burden" (para. 73).

a) Duration of the Impact

The duration of the effect of the measure can be a criterion for assessing whether its impact on the property is severe enough to constitute expropriation.[43] In the abstract, there is an understanding that the deprivation must have permanent or lasting results,[44] so that the deprivation of the rights of ownership can "not merely [be] ephemeral"[45]. It follows that the expropriatory measure cannot have a temporary nature unless there is a specific context or circumstance[46], so that, for example, the investment's successful development depends on the realisation of certain activities at specific moments that may not endure variations[47]. However, the case law of investment tribunals is not coherent. The few decisions which identified relevant time frames found that the deprivation of fundamental rights of ownership for nearly a year[48] or the suspension of an export license for at least four months[49] were not merely ephemeral. In contrast, another tribunal considered that the postponement of the venture into another market for a

---

43 *OECD*, '"Indirect Expropriation" and the "Right to Regulate" in International Investment Law', OECD Working Papers on International Investment (2004/4) p. 14.

44 AWG Group Ltd. v. The Argentine Republic, Award on Liability of 30 July 2010, para 134; LG&E v. Argentina, ICSID Case No. ARB/02/1, Award of 3 October 2006, para 193; Fireman's Fund Insurance Company v. United Mexican States, ICSID Case No. ARB(AF)/02/1, Award of 17 July 2006, para 176; S.D. Myers v. Canada, First Partial Award of 13 November 2000, para. 283; Plama Consortium Limited v. Bulgaria, ICSID Case No. ARB/03/24, Award of 27 August 2008, para 193; Técnicas Medioambientales Tecmed, S.A. v. United Mexican States, ICSID Case No. ARB (AF)/00/2, Award of 29 May 2003, para 116. Generation Ukraine v. Ukraine, ICSID Case No. ARB/00/9, Award of 16 September 2003, para 20.32 refers to a "persistent obstacle".

45 Criterion invoked by the Iran-U.S. Claims Tribunal in Tippetts, Abbett, McCarthy, Stratton v. TAMS-AFFA Consulting Engineers of Iran, Award of 22 June 1984, Award No. 141-7-2, 6 Iran-US CTR 219. It is also reflected in investment decisions and scholarly writing. See, for example, *Hoffmann*, Anne K., 'Indirect Expropriation', in: Standards of Investment Protection (Reinisch, August (Ed.) 2008) 151 (159).

46 S.D. Myers v. Canada, First Partial Award of 13 November 2000, para. 283. See also, Consortium R.F.C.C. v. Kingdom of Morocco, ICSID Case No. ARB/00/6, Award of 22 December 2003, para 68, stating that the expropriation can be temporary if the substantial consequences are equivalent to a definitive loss.

47 LG&E v. Argentina, ICSID Case No. ARB/02/1, Award of 3 October 2006, para 193.

48 Wena Hotels Ltd. v. Arab Republic of Egypt, ICSID Case No. ARB/98/4, Award of 8 December 2008, para 99.

49 Middle East Cement Shipping and Handling Co. S.A. v. Arab Republic of Egypt, ICSID Case No. ARB/99/6, Award of 12 April 2002, para 107.

period of eighteen months was ephemeral.[50] In the same sense, a temporary denial of "short duration" was considered irrelevant.[51] It follows that the evaluation of the specific circumstances of the individual case prevents the setting of general time frames.[52] Not being a key factor in its own right,[53] the duration is only one – and probably not the most decisive – factor for the determination of the overall impact of the measure.

b) Intensity of the Impact

An expropriation substantially affects the investment of the investor. The determination of the necessary level of deprivation is relevant when the investor's investment has not been completely affected. In assessing the substantiality of the deprivation, investment tribunals have required a deprivation "in whole or in material – or significant – part"[54], a deprivation "of parts of the value of the investment"[55], a measure "destroying the business"[56], or pronounced that expropriation required a certain level of sacrifice of private property, so that minor losses are not sufficient[57]. More arithmetically, a tribunal stated that "a diminution of 5% of the investment's value will not be enough for a finding of expropriation, while a

[50] S.D. Myers v. Canada, First Partial Award of 13 November 2000, para. 284.

[51] Glamis Gold, Ltd. v. The United States of America, Award of 8 June 2009, para 360.

[52] Azurix v. Argentine Republic, ICSID Case No. ARB/01/12, Award of 14 July 2006, para 313; S.D. Myers v. Canada, First Partial Award of 13 November 2000, para. 283.

[53] See, for example, the reasoning in Archer Daniels Midland Company and Tate & Lyle Ingredients Americas, Inc. v. United Mexican States, ICSID Case No. ARB (AF)/04/5, Award of 21 November 2007, para 249, where the tribunal held that the significance of the length of the interference did not have to be evaluated because the measure had not been intense enough.

[54] Biwater Gauff (Tanzania) Ltd. v. United Republic of Tanzania, ICSID Case No. ARB/05/22, Award of 24 July 2008, para 455; Metalclad Corporation v. United Mexican States, ICSID Case No. ARB(AF)/97/1, Award of 30 August 2000, para 103; AES Summit Generation Limited and AES-Tisza Erömü Kft v. The Republic of Hungary, ICSID Case No. ARB/07/22, Award of 23 September 2010, para 14.3.1. See also in Gami Investments, Inc. v. Mexico, Award of 15 November 2004, paras 126–132, the discussion of whether a "partial destruction" of the value of the investment can be sufficient, which was ultimately not decided.

[55] Middle East Cement Shipping and Handling Co. S.A. v. Arab Republic of Egypt, ICSID Case No. ARB/99/6, Award of 12 April 2002, para 107.

[56] Corn Products International, Inc. v. United Mexican States, ICSID Case No. ARB(AF)04/01, Partial Award of 15 January 2008, para 93.

[57] Continental Casualty Company v. Argentina, ICSID Case No. ARB/03/9, Award of 5 September 2008, para 284.

diminution of 95% would likely be sufficient".[58] Interestingly, one tribunal explicitly stated that a substantial interference with the rights of the investor does not have to result in economic damage.[59] With each tribunal utilising terminology suited to the facts before it, the descriptions of the necessary level of deprivation differ. Given the importance of the individual facts, a 'substantial deprivation' cannot be abstractly determined by the calculation of a mathematical percentage. However, there is an understanding that the cumulative effect of several governmental measures affecting the investment has to be evaluated to determine the potential expropriatory effect.[60]

A particular issue that deserves attention in this context are alternate possibilities for the economic and viable use of the affected investment. One investment tribunal found that if the regulatory action had not deprived the investor of the control of its investment and the investor was consequently free to pursue other related lines of business, there was no expropriation.[61] Accordingly, the investor's loss of the effective ability to pursue a specific line of business was not sufficient, as long as the investment could be used for a substitutable business. The case indicates that the substitutability of lines of business can be understood very broadly. An even broader approach was adopted by the European Commission of Human Rights (ECommHR) in a case in which a national measure introduced to safeguard human health had fundamentally altered the market for beef meat, in which the applicants had specialised in the deboning of cattle heads. The ECommHR, satisfied that the specialised equipment – at least to some extent – could be used in related businesses or be sold, emphasised the impact on the state of the offal market as determining factor of the loss in value of the applicants'

---

58 Tokios Tokelés v. Ukraine, ICSID Case No. ARB/02/18, Award of 26 July 2007, para 120.

59 Biwater Gauff (Tanzania) Ltd. v. United Republic of Tanzania, ICSID Case No. ARB/05/22, Award of 24 July 2008, para 464: "A distinction must be drawn between (a) interference with rights and (b) economic loss. A substantial interference with rights may well occur without actually causing any economic damage which can be quantified in terms of due compensation." The tribunal goes on to hold that the host of measures in question constitutes an expropriation, irrespective of the absence of economic loss.

60 Azurix v. Argentine Republic, ICSID Case No. ARB/01/12, Award of 14 July 2006, para 313; Biwater Gauff (Tanzania) Ltd. v. United Republic of Tanzania, ICSID Case No. ARB/05/22, Award of 24 July 2008, para 455.

61 Feldman v. Mexico, Case No. ARB(AF)99/1, Award of 16 December 2002, para 152. The investor in this case had lost the "the effective ability to export cigarettes, and any profits derived therefrom". However, this was no expropriation as the investor was "free to pursue other continuing lines of export trading, such as exporting alcoholic beverages, photographic supplies, or other products".

assets.[62] Thus, expropriation was not found. The approach of the EComm-HR, which ostensibly did not recognise the element of specialisation in setting up a business in the deboning of cattle heads, has received criticism. One commentator suggests that an investment tribunal applying the expropriation provision of a modern investment treaty would come to a different conclusion.[63] In any case, the specific facts determine if an alternate economic use annihilates the impact of the measure.

c) *Economic Impact as Sole Criterion?*

It is undisputed that the economic impact is a very decisive factor in finding indirect expropriation. It is, however, less clear whether the economic impact of a regulatory measure is supposed to constitute the only relevant criterion in this assessment.[64] Such an approach, which has been termed 'sole

62 Case of Pinnacle Meat Processors v. United Kingdom (Application no. 33298/96) European Commission on Human Rights Decision of 21 October 1998. The national measure under review was introduced to combat the spread of Bovine Spongiform Encephalopathy, through, inter alia, the prohibition of the use of deboning techniques applied by the applicants. The European Commission on Human Rights (ECommHR) found that the loss of business suffered by the applicants resulted from the restrictions on the use of specified bovine material, but was no form of de facto expropriation. The interference with the applicants' possessions impacted on the "control of use" rather than constituting a "deprivation of possessions". With regard to the substitutability of the investment in equipment related directly to head deboning, the ECommHR held that "at least some of the specialised plant and tools will be useable in the context of other meat operations" and emphasised that the applicants "remain owners of all their tangible assets, and that those assets can either be used in new or related businesses, or they can be sold." With regard to goodwill elements of the applicants' businesses it was decided that they were real in the sense that they could be valued, but that their "value was always likely to fluctuate with the state of the market". The application was consequently deemed to be inadmissible.

63 *Baughen*, Simon, 'Expropriation and Environmental Regulation: The Lessons and NAFTA Chapter 11', 18 Journal of Environmental Law 2006, 207 (224, 228).

Although the argumentation of the commentator has merit, I am not convinced that an investment tribunal in this situation would have necessarily found an expropriation. The ECommHR has correctly found that the national measure was not the only impact on the value of the assets. The demand for meat produced from cattle heads had significantly decreased so that the value of the applicants' property was significantly reduced, irrespective of the influence of the prohibiting national order. Furthermore, the ECommHR could not establish that the equipment was exclusively of use for the deboning business, which prevented an accurate evaluation of the applicants' economic loss. These uncertainties as to the value of the investment activity correctly disadvantaged the applicants.

64 *OECD*, '"Indirect Expropriation" and the "Right to Regulate" in International Investment Law', OECD Working Papers on International Investment (2004/4) p. 14

effect doctrine'[65], can be traced back to judicial decisions at the international and national level[66]. Notable decisions in international law which expressly tied the finding of expropriation to any – not merely ephemeral – deprivation of the alien of fundamental ownership rights are the *Tippetts* case of the U.S.-Iran Claims Tribunal[67] and the arbitration decision in *Biloune v. Ghana*[68].[69] This rather exclusive focus on the economic impact is also reflected in some subsequent investment decisions.[70]

As the analysis of modern investment decisions suggests, the economic effect is not considered the exclusive criterion for establishing expropriation of foreign investment. Even the decisions named as proponents of the 'sole effect doctrine' did not go so far as to declare that all other factors were meaningless. While it is understood that the public purpose and the police

---

et seq; *Dolzer*, Rudolf, 'Indirect Expropriations: New Developments', 11 New York University Environmental Law Journal 2002, 64 (79–93).

65 Terminology used by *Dolzer*, Rudolf, 'Indirect Expropriations: New Developments', 11 New York University Environmental Law Journal 2002, 64 (79).

66 In the U.S.-American legal tradition, the 'sole-takings approach' is most notably found in U.S. Supreme Court, Lucas v. South Carolina Coastal Council, Decision of 29 June 1992, 505 U.S. 1003 (1993). In this decision, the Court reasons that regulations are compensable "where the government has deprived a landowner of all economically beneficial uses" (at 1018), thus finding an expropriation solely because of the "total" economic deprivation.

67 Tippetts, Abbett, McCarthy, Stratton v. TAMS-AFFA Consulting Engineers of Iran, Award of 22 June 1984, Award No. 141-7-2, 6 Iran-US CTR 219. The tribunal emphasises the relevance of the impact of the respective measure in stating that "the intent of the government is less important than the effects of the measure on the owner, and the form of the measures of control or interference is less important than the reality of their impact" (pp. 225–226).

68 Biloune and Marine Drive Complex Ltd v. Ghana Investments Centre and the Government of Ghana, Award on Jurisdiction and Liability, 27 October 1989, 95 I.L.R. (1989) 183. The tribunal found that it need not determine the motivations of the governmental authorities, because the measures had the effect of causing the irreparable cessation of work on the project (209). This was sufficient for finding expropriation.

69 See for discussion and evaluation of further case law, *Dolzer*, Rudolf, 'Indirect Expropriations: New Developments', 11 New York University Environmental Law Journal 2002, 64 (80–90).

70 Metalclad Corporation v. United Mexican States, ICSID Case No. ARB(AF)/97/1, Award of 30 August 2000, paras 108, 111; Compañía del Dessarollo de Santa Elena S.A. v. Republic of Costa Rica, ICSID Case No. ARB/96/1, Award of 17 February 2000, para 77. See also Compañiá de Aguas del Aconquija S.A. and Vivendi Universal v. Argentine Republic, ICSID Case No. ARB/97/3, Award of 20 August 2007, paras 7.5.20–21 and Bayindir Insaat Turizm Ticaret Ve Sanayi A.S. v. Islamic Republic of Pakistan, ICSID Case No. ARB/03/29, Award of 27 August 2009, para 459, focusing on the effect of the measure as the "critical factor" and declaring that governmental intent is less relevant.

powers for the introduction of the regulatory measure – as such – do not prevent the finding of expropriation, it can be argued that the public purpose is one of the elements used in distinguishing an expropriatory taking from a non-compensable regulation by the host state.[71] Decisions exclusively focusing on the economic impact and declaring governmental intent irrelevant are regularly the ones in which the economic threshold has not been reached.[72] The tribunals do not have to consider the governmental intent when the impact on the investor has not reached a relevant level. Even though this approach triggers the question when the economic threshold is high enough to require a consideration of other factors in the assessment of an allegedly expropriatory act,[73] it is helpful to refute the relevance of the 'sole effect doctrine'.

2. Interference with Reasonable Investment-Backed Expectations

A further criterion discussed in the context of indirect expropriation is the interference of the respective measure with the investor's reasonable investment-backed expectations. The notion of legitimate, investment-backed expectations of the investor deeply influences the evaluation of the expropriatory impact of measures in many national jurisdictions and, as a result, informs the discussion at the international level.[74] Several arbitral tribunals

---

[71] Fireman's Fund Insurance Company v. United Mexican States, ICSID Case No. ARB(AF)/02/1, Award of 17 July 2006; para 176; Saluka Investments BV (The Netherlands) v. The Czech Republic, Award of 17 March 2006, paras 263, 264. The study of the *OECD*, '"Indirect Expropriation" and the "Right to Regulate" in International Investment Law', OECD Working Papers on International Investment (2004/4) p. 15 also found that the approach of balancing several aspects was predominant in investment decisions.

[72] National Grid plc v. The Argentine Republic, Award of 3 November 2008, paras 147, 155; Bayindir Insaat Turizm Ticaret Ve Sanayi A.S. v. Islamic Republic of Pakistan, ICSID Case No. ARB/03/29, Award of 27 August 2009, para 459.

See also *Kahn*, Jordan C., 'Striking NAFTA Gold: Glamis Advances Investor-State Arbitration', 33 Fordham International Law Journal 2009, 101 (129–132), who terms the approach of focusing exclusively on the economic impact of the measure to eliminate the claim for alleged regulatory expropriation the "inverse Lucas standard", thus referring to the above-mentioned decision of the U.S. Supreme Court (above footnote 66).

[73] *Kahn*, Jordan C., 'Striking NAFTA Gold: Glamis Advances Investor-State Arbitration', 33 Fordham International Law Journal 2009, 101(133).

[74] The decision of the U.S. Supreme Court decision *Penn Central Transportation Corp. v. New York City*, expressly cites reasonable expectations as one of the three conditions for finding expropriation. However, *Been*, Vicki/*Beauvais*, Joel C.,'The Global Fifth Amendment? NAFTA's Investment Protections and the Misguided Quest for an International "Regulatory Takings" Doctrine', 78 New York University Law Review 2003, 30 (69–78) gather from a comparison of the notion

have expressed the understanding that the evaluation of the investor's expectations constitutes one factor in the evaluation of the measure's overall impact on the respective investment.[75] Also, recent investment treaties refer to 'reasonable investment-backed expectations' in defining indirect expropriation.[76]

Investment tribunals consider expectations as relevant in so far as they are objectified, i. e. the subjective expectations of the investor have been induced or foreseen and accepted by the host state. Accordingly, investment tribunals have relied on the investor's expectations to find expropriation, when these expectations stemmed from specific assurances by government officials or from ostensible characteristics and long-term perspectives of the investment that the host state clearly foresaw.[77] Yet, these parameters underscore that the investor cannot expect favourable business conditions to remain unchanged forever or to be protected against normal commercial risk.[78] Invest-

---

in U.S. takings jurisprudence and earlier NAFTA cases that the perception of 'investment-backed expectations' is much broader in NAFTA decisions. They assert that NAFTA tribunals "have shown little concern for the reasonableness of the [investors'] expectations" (70).

See the detailed portrayal of the concept in different jurisdictions and the resulting argument that the protection of legitimate expectations constitutes a general principle of law, *Snodgrass*, Elizabeth, 'Protecting Investors' Legitimate Expectations – Recognizing and Delimiting a General Principle', 21 ICSID Review Foreign Investment Law Journal 2006, 1–58. A discussion of possible legal foundations of the concept of legitimate expectations in international law can be found in *von Walter*, André, 'The Investor's Expectations in International Investment Arbitration', in: International Investment Law in Context (Reinisch, August et al. (Eds.) 2008) 173 (193–200).

[75] National Grid plc v. The Argentine Republic, Award of 3 November 2008, para 153; LG&E v. Argentina, ICSID Case No. ARB/02/1, Award of 3 October 2006, para 190; Azurix v. Argentine Republic, ICSID Case No. ARB/01/12, Award of 14 July 2006, para 316; Sempra Energy International v. The Argentine Republic, ICSID Case No. ARB/02/16, Award of 28 September 2007, para 288.

[76] See, for example, Annex 10.C para. 4 lit a (ii) CAFTA-DR ; Annex B para 4 lit a (ii) U.S.-Uruguay BIT; Annex B para 4 lit a (ii) U.S.-Rwanda BIT; Annex B para 2 lit b Canada-Latvia BIT; Annex B.13(1) lit b (ii) Canada-Peru BIT.

[77] Metalclad Corporation v. United Mexican States, ICSID Case No. ARB(AF)/97/1, Award of 30 August 2000, paras 103, 107; Técnicas Medioambientales Tecmed, S.A. v. United Mexican States, ICSID Case No. ARB (AF)/00/2, Award of 29 May 2003, para 150. The latter tribunal focuses on the investor's expectation that the business is to operate for a long term. See for discussion of these two sources of expectations, *Fietta*, Stephen, 'Expropriation and the "Fair and Equitable" Standard, The Developing Role of Investor's "Expectations" in International Investment Arbitration', 23 Journal of International Arbitration 2006, 375 (380, 382, 384–385).

[78] See Feldman v. Mexico, ICSID Case No. ARB(AF)/99/1, Award of 16 December 2002, para 112, stating that "[g]overnments, in their exercise of regulatory power, frequently change their laws and regulations in response to changing eco-

ment tribunals thus follow criteria developed by earlier international jurisprudence.[79]

Since the criterion of reasonable investment-backed expectations is rarely at the centre of the determination, its exact relevance for the assessment is open to debate. In my understanding, the expectations that the investor reasonably holds are a relevant factor in connection with the overall economic impact of the respective measure. Breaches of expectations concerning the profitability of the investment are relevant, precisely because they result in the investment being less profitable than the investor anticipated – or even economically unviable. In a similar sense, commentators have argued that the legitimate expectations constitute a "useful guiding principle",[80] which does not annihilate the importance of neutralising the investment's economic benefit.[81] It follows that the frustration of investor's expectations which does not

---

nomic circumstances or changing political, economic or social considerations. Those changes may well make certain activities less profitable or even uneconomic to continue." See also Azinian, Davitian, & Baca v. Mexico, ICSID Case No. ARB (AF)/97/2, Award of 1 November 1999, para 83; Waste Management II v. United Mexican States, ICSID Case No. ARB(AF)/00/3 (NAFTA), Award of 30 April 2004, para 177; Maffezini v. Spain, ICSID Case No. ARB/97/7, Award on the Merits of 13 November 2000, para 64; Generation Ukraine, Inc. v. Ukraine, ICSID Case No. ARB/00/9, Award of 16 September 2003, paras 20.37–38.

[79] See, for example, PCIJ The Oscar Chinn Case (Britain/Belgium) Judgment of 12 December 1934 (Series A/B No 63, 65) (88): "Favourable business conditions and goodwill are transient circumstances, subject to inevitable changes; the interests of transport undertakings may well have suffered as a result of the general trade depression and the measures taken to combat it. No enterprise […] can escape from the chances and hazards resulting from general economic conditions."

Starrett Housing Corp v. Iran, Award of 14 August 1987, Award No. 314-24-1, 4 Iran-USCTR 112 (156), stating that "[i]nvestors in Iran, like investors in all other countries, have to assume a risk that the country might experience strikes, lock-outs, disturbances, changes of economic and political system and even revolution. That any of these risks materialized does not necessarily mean that property rights affected by such events can be deemed to have been taken."

That investors cannot rely on the mere expectation that regulation will not change, because they have to bear the normal risks associated with doing business is also reflected by commentators: *Sampliner*, Gary H., 'Arbitration of Expropriation Cases under U.S. Investment Treaties – A Threat to Democracy or the Dog That Didn't Bark?', 18 ICSID Review Foreign Investment Law Journal 2003, 1 (14); *Fortier*, Yves L./*Drymer*, Stephen L., 'Indirect Expropriation in the Law of International Investment: I Know It When I See It, or Caveat Investor', 19 ICSID Review Foreign Investment Law Journal 2004, 293 (307).

[80] *Paulsson*, Jan/*Douglas*, Zachary, 'Indirect Expropriation in Investment Treaty Arbitrations, Indirect Expropriation in Investment Treaty Arbitrations', in: Arbitrating Foreign Investment Disputes, Procedural and Substantive Legal Aspects (Horn, Norbert et al. (Eds.) 145 (157).

[81] *Fietta*, Stephen, 'Expropriation and the "Fair and Equitable" Standard, The Developing Role of Investor's "Expectations" in International Investment Arbitra-

reach this economic threshold can be addressed in connection with the standard of fair and equitable treatment.[82]

3. Character of the Governmental Measure

The character of the measure – signifying the purpose for which, and the context in which, it is adopted – arguably also influences the characterisation of a measure as expropriation.[83] The underlying question is whether non-discriminatory measures adopted for a socially relevant 'public purpose' can constitute expropriation. The acceptance of the relevance of the character of the measure mirrors the understanding embraced by the opponents to the 'sole effect doctrine'. In this context, two issues are of particular relevance: First, the reasons for which the respective measure is adopted. Second, the impact of these factors on the overall assessment of the expropriatory nature of the measure.

The host state has the police powers to legitimately adopt regulation. They are of particular importance in connection with the reasons motivating the adoption of the measure. The American Law Institute asserts that "[a] State is not responsible for loss of property or for other economic disadvantage resulting from bona fide general taxation, regulation, forfeiture for crime, or other action of the kind that is commonly accepted as within the police power of States, if it is not discriminatory".[84] This statement has

---

tion', 23 Journal of International Arbitration 2006, 375 (383, 398–399). See also *Kolo*, Abba/*Wälde*, Thomas, 'Environmental Regulation, Investment Protection and "Regulatory Taking" in International Law', 50 International and Comparative Law Quarterly 2001, 811 (843), who argue that the breach of prior commitments should be a factor in assessing the proportionality of the measure. They further argue that a breach weighs more heavily if the commitment was only recently entered into and when the state could have anticipated the regulatory changes (844).

82 This assessment is without prejudice to the findings of *Fietta*, Stephen, 'Expropriation and the "Fair and Equitable" Standard, The Developing Role of Investor's "Expectations" in International Investment Arbitration', 23 Journal of International Arbitration 2006, 375 (387), who determines differences in the understanding of 'legitimate expectations' in the context of expropriation and of the standard of fair and equitable treatment. Fietta finds that in the context of the former standard, the expectations are more closely tied to the investment as such, whereas in connection with the latter standard, the expectations are more closely tied to the treatment of the investor. Nevertheless, it is my understanding that the concept of 'expectations' is largely congruent.

83 *OECD*, '"Indirect Expropriation" and the "Right to Regulate" in International Investment Law', OECD Working Papers on International Investment (2004/4) p. 16.

84 American Law Institute, 'Restatement of the Law (Third) of the Foreign Relations of the United States' Volume 1, 1987, Section 712, Comment g. The state-

been approvingly cited and relied upon by international tribunals, including investment tribunals.[85] It indicates that general, non-discriminatory *bona fide* regulation within the police powers of the state, does not constitute expropriation. It is frequently acknowledged that customary law accords states with significant discretion in restricting property rights to protect public morals and order, health and safety, and the environment.[86] However, the exact borders and implications of regulation within the police powers are "anything but clear".[87]

The legitimate power of a state to adopt a measure does not answer in itself the question of whether an affected investor is entitled to compensation. Otherwise, there would be no distinction between regulation and lawful expropriation, which is conditioned upon the payment of compensation. When determining respective measures, investment tribunals have assessed the validity and permissibility of the measure and whether it fell within the regulatory powers of the state[88] or they have balanced the causes and effects of the respective measure in their determination.[89] The consequences of

---

ment is preceded by the following statement: "A state is responsible as for an expropriation of property when it subjects alien property to taxation, regulation, or other action that is confiscatory, or that prevents, unreasonably interferes with, or unduly delays, effective enjoyment of an alien's property or its removal from the state's territory […]."

85 AWG Group Ltd. v. The Argentine Republic, Decision on Liability of 30 July 2010, para 139; LG&E v. Argentina, ICSID Case No. ARB/02/1, Decision on Liability of 3 October 2006, para 196; Pope & Talbot Inc. v. Canada, Interim Award of 26 June 2000, paras 99, 102; Saluka Investments BV (The Netherlands) v. The Czech Republic, Award of 17 March 2006, para 260; Suez, Sociedad General de Aguas de Barcelona S.A., and InterAguas Servicios Integrales del Agua S.A. v. The Argentine Republic, ICSID Case No. ARB/03/17, Decision on Liability of 30 July 2010, para 128.

See for acceptance of the Restatement by the Iran-U.S. Claims Tribunal, *Aldrich*, George H., The Jurisprudence of the Iran-United States Claims Tribunal (1996) pp. 208–211; Emanuel Too v. United States of America et al., Award of 29 December 1989, Award No. 460-880-2, 23 Iran-US CTR 378.

86 *Fortier*, Yves L./*Drymer*, Stephen L., 'Indirect Expropriation in the Law of International Investment: I Know It When I See It, or Caveat Investor', 19 ICSID Review Foreign Investment Law Journal 2004, 293 (298); *Newcombe*, Andrew, 'The Boundaries of Regulatory Expropriation in International Law', 20 ICSID Review Foreign Investment Law Journal 2005, 1 (38); *Dolzer*, Rudolf, 'Indirect Expropriation of Alien Property', 1 ICSID Review Foreign Investment Law Journal 1986, 41 (62).

87 *Newcombe*, Andrew, 'The Boundaries of Regulatory Expropriation in International Law', 20 ICSID Review Foreign Investment Law Journal 2005, 1 (29).

88 Saluka Investments BV (The Netherlands) v. The Czech Republic, Award of 17 March 2006, para 276.

89 LG&E v. Argentina, ICSID Case No. ARB/02/1, Decision on Liability of 3 October 2006, para 194; Técnicas Medioambientales Tecmed, S.A. v. United

such findings and the assessment of the dividing line between an ordinary application of regulatory powers and expropriation are at the heart of this chapter. Accordingly, this issue will be discussed in more detail below with regard to environmental regulation.

II. Intermediate Summary

Finding indirect expropriation requires first and foremost that the investor be substantially deprived of its investment. A substantial deprivation occurs when the investor loses the economic benefits or the control over its investment. The investor has to be deprived of its investment in whole or in significant part by a measure with a permanent effect that stretches over a considerable time frame. If such a deprivation cannot be established, there is no expropriation. Only if the economic threshold is reached, do the expectations that the investor legitimately had and the reasons for which the measure was adopted become relevant. The police powers of the state that adopts legitimate regulation play a part in determining the line between a regulatory measure and expropriation, for which the investor has to be compensated.

C. Analysis of Case Law Concerning Environmental Measures

The concept of expropriation points to two significant issues for this study: First, the economic impact of an adopted measure is of the outmost importance to finding expropriation. In the absence of a substantial deprivation of the economic benefits or of the control over the investment, there is no expropriation. Measures adopted to safeguard environmental values are more likely to have an 'economic impact' than to result in a 'loss of control' over the foreign investment, since the appointment of managers or similar interference with the administration of the investment are unlikely instruments for the implementation of an environmental measure.

Generally, decisions in investment disputes indicate that the threshold for finding a substantial economic deprivation is very high: Only very rarely have investment tribunals recently considered the economic impact of any measures – irrespective of their subject matter – as substantial enough. Regulatory measures enacted to benefit a societal aim have rarely substantially deprived foreign investors of their investment. Telling examples are

---

Mexican States, ICSID Case No. ARB (AF)/00/2, Award of 29 May 2003, para 122, embracing the notion of 'proportionality'.

the awards rendered with regard to the host of regulatory measures introduced by the Argentine Republic to address its economic crisis in the years 2001 to 2003. In most of the cases so far decided, the tribunals did not find expropriation.[90] The two cases in which tribunals found an expropriation featured specific governmental decrees terminating the contracts of the investors, rather than general measures.[91] Other investment decisions finding indirect expropriation featured the revocation of specific licenses or breaches of specific contractual obligations.[92]

The second significant aspect deriving from the relevant case law relates to the character of the respective measure: Which relevance do investment tribunals accredit the purpose and the context of the adopted measure with, when they assess a potentially expropriatory impact? In short, the indications by investment tribunals are important to distinguish between expropriation and an environmental regulation that does not require compensation. They will further the understanding of where the line between both types of measures is drawn. To illuminate the relevance of these two aspects with respect to environmental regulation, this section will portray investment decisions discussing expropriation in the context of measures adopted – allegedly – for environmental reasons.

I. Metalclad Corporation v. United Mexican States

Metalclad Corporation v. United Mexican States is one of the few investment awards, which found an expropriation in connection with measures allegedly adopted for an environmental purpose. The case[93] concerned the use of a site as facility for the disposal of hazardous waste. The foreign

---

[90] AWG Group Ltd. v. The Argentine Republic, Award on Liability of 30 July 2010; para 138, making reference to the decisions of the investment tribunals in LG&E v. Argentina, ICSID Case No. ARB/02/1, Award of 3 October 2006; CMS Gas Transmission Company v. The Argentine Republic, ICSID Case No. ARB/01/8, Award of 12 May 2005; Azurix v. Argentine Republic, ICSID Case No. ARB/01/12, Award of 14 July 2006; Enron Corporation and Ponderosa Assets, L.P. v. Argentine Republic, ICSID Case No. ARB/01/3, Award of 22 May 2007.

[91] Siemens A.G. v. Argentine Republic (ICSID Case No. ARB/02/8), Award of 6 February 2007; SAUR International SA v. Republic of Argentina, ICSID Case No. ARB/04/4, Decision on Jurisdiction and Liability of 6 June 2012.

[92] Biwater Gauff (Tanzania) Ltd. v. United Republic of Tanzania, ICSID Case No. ARB/05/22, Award of 24 July 2008; CME Czech Republic B.V. v. Czech Republic, Award of 13 September 2001; Middle East Cement Shipping and Handling Co. S.A. v. Arab Republic of Egypt, ICSID Case No. ARB/99/6, Award of 12 April 2002.

[93] See the portrayal in 'Chapter 4 – Standards of Fair Treatment' at pp. 261 *et seq.*

investor, which had been granted all relevant federal permits for the construction of the facility, could neither finalise nor operate the facility, because a municipal construction permit was denied, despite prior representations of federal officials to the contrary. The reasons for the denial of the permit were partly environmental. Further, the governor of the state by decree declared an area of 188,758 hectares – including the site of the landfill – to be a natural area for the protection of rare cacti, banning the operation of the facility.[94]

The investment tribunal relied on a broad definition of expropriation; namely, that the concept includes "covert or incidental interference with the use of property, which has the effect of depriving the owner, in whole or in significant part, of the use or reasonably-to-be-expected economic benefit of property, even if not necessarily to the obvious benefit of the host State".[95] The tribunal first considered the denial of the municipal construction permit. In this regard, it stated that the action taken by the municipality despite the federal approval of the landfill – which it had previously found to breach the standard of fair and equitable treatment – amounted to expropriation of the investor.[96] Reiterating its prior findings on the exclusive competence of the federal authorities to assess the environmental impact of hazardous landfill facilities, the tribunal focused on the lack of competence of the municipality to deny the municipal construction permit for reasons not connected to the physical construction of the facility.[97] It found that these circumstances, coupled with the representations by the officials of the federal government and the municipality's subsequent attempt to judicially challenge the underlying agreement with the investor, expropriated the investor.[98] Further, the tribunal mentioned that the underlying facts were alike to those of *Biloune v. Ghana*.[99]

As a second – and additional – ground for expropriation, the tribunal evaluated the Ecological Decree issued by the governor. The tribunal concluded that the Decree had the effect of "barring forever the operation of

---

94 Metalclad Corporation v. United Mexican States, ICSID Case No. ARB(AF)/97/1, Award of 30 August 2000, paras 59, 109.

95 Metalclad Corporation v. United Mexican States, ICSID Case No. ARB(AF)/97/1, Award of 30 August 2000, para 103.

96 Metalclad Corporation v. United Mexican States, ICSID Case No. ARB(AF)/97/1, Award of 30 August 2000, para 104.

97 Metalclad Corporation v. United Mexican States, ICSID Case No. ARB(AF)/97/1, Award of 30 August 2000, paras 104–106.

98 Metalclad Corporation v. United Mexican States, ICSID Case No. ARB(AF)/97/1, Award of 30 August 2000, para 107.

99 Metalclad Corporation v. United Mexican States, ICSID Case No. ARB(AF)/97/1, Award of 30 August 2000, para 108.

the landfill", because it, inter alia, prohibited any potentially polluting activities as well as activities requiring permits and licenses.[100] After stating that it "need not decide or consider the motivation or intent of the adoption of the Ecological Decree", the tribunal declared – without further discussion – that the implementation of the Decree, "in and of itself", constituted an act of indirect expropriation.[101]

The tribunal's discussion of expropriation is very brief and lacks methodology. With regard to the first ground – the denial of the municipal permit – the finding of expropriation is largely based on the earlier determined violation of the standard of fair and equitable treatment. No additional reasons are invoked for finding expropriation. Most notably, the tribunal does not expressly assess whether the investor was substantially deprived of the economic value of its investment – despite the tribunal's reliance on the 'sole effect doctrine'. The methodological problems connected to the discussion of the standard of fair and equitable treatment "infect" the analysis of expropriation,[102] and the tribunal does not assess the criteria for expropriation in an independent way. This lack of independent assessment is not compensated by the reference to the findings in *Biloune v. Ghana*.[103]

The second ground for finding expropriation – the Ecological Decree – has not been subjected to in-depth scrutiny, either. In three short paragraphs, the tribunal reaches its conclusion – which constitutes *obiter dicta*. The "extremely broad" definition applied by the tribunal is "sufficiently broad to encompass the legitimate rezoning of property by a municipality".[104] The tribunal did not assess whether the Decree constituted a legitimate

[100] Metalclad Corporation v. United Mexican States, ICSID Case No. ARB(AF)/97/1, Award of 30 August 2000, paras 109, 110.

[101] Metalclad Corporation v. United Mexican States, ICSID Case No. ARB(AF)/97/1, Award of 30 August 2000, para 111.

[102] United Mexican States v. Metalclad, Supreme Court of British Columbia, Reasons for Judgment of the Honourable Mr. Justice Tysoe of 2 May 2001, paras 78, 79, 93. Judge Tysoe criticised the arbitral tribunal for reliance on transparency obligations not falling within the scope of the submission to arbitration.

[103] See the assessment in United Mexican States v. Metalclad, Supreme Court of British Columbia, Reasons for Judgment of the Honorable Mr. Justice Tysoe of 2 May 2001, para 80. The decision correctly finds that in the light of the significant factual differences between the two cases, the reliance on *Biloune v. Ghana* is not an independent basis for concluding that the host state's actions constitute expropriation.

[104] United Mexican States v. Metalclad, Supreme Court of British Columbia, Reasons for Judgment of the Honorable Mr. Justice Tysoe of 2 May 2001, para 99.
A commentator finds that the standard applied by the tribunal constitutes an "excess of protection", *Subedi*, Surya P., International Investment Law: Reconciling Policy and Principle (2008) p. 138.

regulatory measure for protecting cacti, guided by environmental studies and respective evidence. Most interestingly, the tribunal did not assess whether the adoption of the decree was within the competence of the governor or excluded by prior representations of the government – despite its in-depth analysis of internal competencies in the context of the first count of expropriation.

The award's lack of discussion of potential environmental factors in connection with the denial of the construction permit is due to the division of competence within the federal host state:[105] Environmental concerns were audited[106] and considered prior to issuing the federal permits, so that the tribunal was correct in stating that "Mexico was satisfied that this project was consistent with, and sensitive to, its environmental concerns".[107] However, such a division of competence did – most certainly – not exist with regard to the Ecological Decree, which was not tested as an 'environmental measure' pursuant to Article 1114 NAFTA. There were reasons to assume that the Decree was issued to permanently ban the investor from operating the landfill – with the issuance directly after the commencement of the arbitration process and media statements allegedly given by officials[108] –, but the finding would have required a more profound evaluation of factors.

In conclusion, *Metalclad Corporation v. United Mexican States* is not very helpful for determining the two key aspects: First, the decision does not give any indication as to the threshold for the economic impact that constitutes a substantially relevant deprivation.[109] Second, the tribunal does not indicate parameters for differentiating between an expropriatory act and legitimate regulation for a public purpose, as it does not clearly discuss potentially relevant factors. In theory, the creation of the ecological zone could have been a legitimate exercise of police powers, based on scientific

105 The relevant Mexican provisions are cited in Metalclad Corporation v. United Mexican States, ICSID Case No. ARB(AF)/97/1, Award of 30 August 2000. paras 82–84, 86.

106 Metalclad Corporation v. United Mexican States, ICSID Case No. ARB(AF)/97/1, Award of 30 August 2000. para 48.

107 Metalclad Corporation v. United Mexican States, ICSID Case No. ARB(AF)/97/1, Award of 30 August 2000. para 98. The tribunal accordingly found that the conditions of Article 1114 NAFTA were fulfilled. See in 'Chapter 4 – Standards of Fair Treatment' at p. 263.

108 Metalclad Corporation v. United Mexican States, ICSID Case No. ARB(AF)/97/1, Award of 30 August 2000. paras 59–61, 69.

109 The award points out that the area could not be used for any potentially polluting activities after the Ecological Decree was issued (para 110). There is no mentioning of alternative uses for the site. However, the ecological condition of the site may have derogated due to previous use.

evidence, thus constituting a non-discriminatory measure[110]. Even though the overall context does not support this hypothesis,[111] the tribunal's discussion would have required more breadth.

II. Técnicas Medioambientales Tecmed, S.A. v. United Mexican States

The investor in *Técnicas Medioambientales Tecmed, S.A. v. United Mexican States* was the majority owner of a company which operated a landfill facility for hazardous waste.[112] The facility was located in such a proximity to a town that it contravened subsequent regulation, which, however, was not applied to the facility retrospectively. The location as well as the transportation of hazardous waste undertaken by the investor lead to significant political opposition to the facility from the local community. As a result, both the company and the municipality agreed on the relocation of the landfill. Before a new location was identified, the competent environmental authority adopted a resolution which declined the renewal of the licence for the original site, despite the expectation of the investor to use the original facility until the relocation process was completed.[113]

In assessing the claim for expropriation, the tribunal found that the depriving economic impact of the measure was more relevant than its 'regulatory' nature, since the non-renewal of the permit had led to a permanent and irrevocable closure of the landfill. The site would never be used again for the purposes of landfill due to its proximity to the nearest town. Because of contamination, no other economically viable use was imaginable, so that the economic value of the site was destroyed.[114] Whereas the tribunal mentioned that the exercise of legitimate police powers by the host state could

---

[110] The site of the landfill comprises of 814 hectares, whereas the reserve created for cacti encompasses 188.758 hectares (paras 28, 109). This significant difference in circumference points to the adoption of a general measure.

[111] The findings with regard to the denial of the municipal permit indicate the unfair treatment of the investor. Also, the lack of swift and precise management of the protected area for the cacti – as established by *Gaines*, Sanford E., 'Environmental Policy Implications of Investor-State Arbitration under NAFTA Chapter 11', 7 International Environmental Agreements: Politics, Law and Economics 2007, 171 (179) – casts doubt on the sincerity of the environmental objective.

[112] See already portrayal in 'Chapter 4 – Standards of Fair Treatment'at pp. 271 *et seq.*

[113] Técnicas Medioambientales Tecmed, S.A. v. United Mexican States, ICSID Case No. ARB (AF)/00/2, Award of 29 May 2003, paras 110, 112.

[114] Técnicas Medioambientales Tecmed, S.A. v. United Mexican States, ICSID Case No. ARB (AF)/00/2, Award of 29 May 2003, paras 116, 117.

lead to an economic damage which did not require compensation,[115] the tribunal also stated that

> "[W]e find no principle stating that regulatory administrative actions are per se excluded from the scope of the Agreement, even if they are beneficial to society as a whole – such as environmental protection–, particularly if the negative economic impact of such actions on the financial position of the investor is sufficient to neutralize in full the value, or economic or commercial use of its investment without receiving any compensation whatsoever."[116]

Consequently, the tribunal purported to test whether the measure was "proportional to the public interest presumably protected thereby and to the protection legally granted to investments."[117] The tribunal discussed several factors to be taken into account in the balancing exercise.[118] As its most important determination, the tribunal found that the reasons given for the non-renewal of the permit[119] were not the real reasons underlying the denial. The authorities' wish to terminate the investor's licence stemmed from the social and political pressure in the community to stop the operation of a facility that was closely located to a major city.[120] However, this pressure

---

115 Técnicas Medioambientales Tecmed, S.A. v. United Mexican States, ICSID Case No. ARB (AF)/00/2, Award of 29 May 2003, para 119.

116 Técnicas Medioambientales Tecmed, S.A. v. United Mexican States, ICSID Case No. ARB (AF)/00/2, Award of 29 May 2003, para 121, with reference to the decision in Compañía del Dessarollo de Santa Elena S.A. v. Republic of Costa Rica, ICSID Case No. ARB/96/1, Award of 17 February 2000, para 72 in which the tribunal states that "[e]xpropriatory environmental measures – no matter how laudable and beneficial to society as a whole – are [...] similar to any other expropriatory measures [...]."

117 Técnicas Medioambientales Tecmed, S.A. v. United Mexican States, ICSID Case No. ARB (AF)/00/2, Award of 29 May 2003, para 122. In expressly adopting the language used by the ECtHR, the tribunal also focuses on the reasonableness of the relationship between the two interests.

118 These factors mentioned are, inter alia, the lack of possibilities for political participation of foreign investors in the decision making of the host state (para 122); the profitability expectations of the investor (para 149); and the fact that the opposition connected to the transport of the waste did not trigger consequences by the competent authorities (paras 137, 138).

119 Técnicas Medioambientales Tecmed, S.A. v. United Mexican States, ICSID Case No. ARB (AF)/00/2, Award of 29 May 2003, para 99. The reasons stated relate to alleged restrictions on the material authorised for the landfill, the exceeding of the landfill limits of one landfill cell, the landfill acting as a transfer centre for waste that was stored at a different place, and liquid and biological-infectious waste being received despite a respective prohibition. Partly, these reasons were challenged by the investor (paras 100–102).

120 Técnicas Medioambientales Tecmed, S.A. v. United Mexican States, ICSID Case No. ARB (AF)/00/2, Award of 29 May 2003, paras 129, 132, 136–138, 140, 145.

did not reach the threshold of an emergency.[121] The minor breaches of conditions, primarily relating to the transport of hazardous waste, were found not to endanger public health or the protection of the environment. Accordingly, the tribunal decided that "it would be excessively formalistic [...] to understand that the resolution is proportional to such violations when such infringements do not pose a present or imminent risk to the ecological balance or to people's health".[122] In this light, it found that the non-renewal of the licence constituted expropriation.

The decision apparently aims to take into account both the interests of the investor and the regulatory interests of the state. The tribunal does not apply a different approach to evaluating economic deprivations in the form of regulation pursuing a public purpose. However, it embraces the idea that the deference owed to sovereign powers and the legitimate interests of the host state have to be considered additionally. Despite the intense discussion of the circumstances that led to the resolution not to renew the licence, it is not clear how the tribunal approaches the balancing exercise and what importance the specific factors are accredited with. Although it appears that the decision of finding expropriation due to the eradication of the economic value of the landfill is defensible, there is no indication which factors – other than the opposition to the facility reaching the level of emergency –[123] in the tribunal's understanding would have resulted in not finding expropriation.

III. S.D. Myers Inc. v. Canada

In *S.D. Myers v. Canada*,[124] the tribunal had to assess whether the export ban on PCB expropriated the foreign investor. The closure of the border for exports had the effect of delaying the investor's venture into the market of the host state by approximately eighteen months[125] – with the Canadian ban being in effect for approximately sixteen months. After the ban was lifted, the border was open for exports for roughly five months – before it was permanently closed by the importing state – allowing the investor to

---

[121] Técnicas Medioambientales Tecmed, S.A. v. United Mexican States, ICSID Case No. ARB (AF)/00/2, Award of 29 May 2003, paras 124, 144, 147.

[122] Técnicas Medioambientales Tecmed, S.A. v. United Mexican States, ICSID Case No. ARB (AF)/00/2, Award of 29 May 2003, para 149.

[123] Técnicas Medioambientales Tecmed, S.A. v. United Mexican States, ICSID Case No. ARB (AF)/00/2, Award of 29 May 2003, para 139.

[124] See portrayal in 'Chapter 3 – Standards of Non-Discriminatory Treatment' at pp. 176 *et seq.*

[125] S.D. Myers Inc. v. Canada, Partial Award on the Merits, 13 November 2000, para 284.

accomplish seven exports. The investor argued that the delay had eliminated its comparative advantage and that this constituted expropriation of the investment.

The tribunal first found that the scope of the expropriation provision in the relevant investment treaty had to be interpreted in line with the whole body of international law and that "the general body of precedent usually does not treat regulatory action as amounting to expropriation".[126] In the light of the investor being affected by regulatory measures, the tribunal stated that it was "unlikely" that "regulatory conduct by public authorities" was expropriatory.[127] It drew the following distinction:

> "Expropriations tend to involve the deprivation of ownership rights; regulations a lesser interference. The distinction between expropriation and regulation screens out most potential cases of complaints concerning economic intervention by a state and reduces the risk that governments will be subject to claims as they go about their business of managing public affairs."[128]

Applying this standard to the facts of the case, the tribunal focused on expropriation as generally being a lasting deprivation of the investor. However, this investor was only temporarily affected.[129] The tribunal did not consider the delay in the entrepreneurial opportunity to constitute a legally relevant 'taking' by the host state, and therefore did not find expropriation.[130]

The decision in *S.D. Myers v. Canada* sheds light on both the assessment of the substantiality of the deprivation and the differentiation between regulatory measure and expropriation. Regarding deprivation, the tribunal emphasises that a temporary restriction on the investment does generally not constitute expropriation – which requires a lasting effect. This finding on the merits appears correct, as the delay did not take anything assessably substantial away from the investor. Despite the protectionist intention of the host state, the investor's competitors did not gain an advantage, in the end. However, the distinction drawn between expropriation and regulatory measure obviously is superficial. Although it sets forth a helpful guideline for

---

126 S.D. Myers Inc. v. Canada, Partial Award on the Merits, 13 November 2000, paras 280, 281.

127 S.D. Myers Inc. v. Canada, Partial Award on the Merits, 13 November 2000, para 281.

128 S.D. Myers Inc. v. Canada, Partial Award on the Merits, 13 November 2000, para 282.

129 S.D. Myers Inc. v. Canada, Partial Award on the Merits, 13 November 2000, para 284.

130 S.D. Myers Inc. v. Canada, Partial Award on the Merits, 13 November 2000, paras 284, 287. The tribunal further states that neither the host state nor any of the investor's competitors realised a benefit from the export prohibition (para 287).

most cases, it does not offer concrete criteria for drawing the line in controversial cases. Accordingly, this distinction – focusing on the nature and purpose of the measure, rather than on its economic impact – has been subject to criticism.[131]

IV. Chemtura Corporation v. Canada

In *Chemtura Corporation v. Government of Canada* the tribunal had to assess the legitimacy of several measures preventing the use of lindane-based products on canola seeds.[132] The investor, a generator of products for pest control that contained the pesticide, alleged that the cancellation of its lindane registrations constituted an expropriation of its investment. With regard to the 'substantial deprivation' criterion, the tribunal stated that it would be guided by the host of criteria identified by the tribunal in *Pope & Talbot Inc. v. Canada*[133]. The tribunal also mentioned the controversy that had arisen from the broad definition of expropriation in *Metalclad Corporation v. United Mexican States*, but found that it did not need to take a position, since the determination of what is 'substantial deprivation' was too closely connected to the specific circumstances of each case to apply rigid rules.[134]

In its fact-sensitive assessment, the tribunal relied on quantum evidence, according to which the percentage of lindane-related sales constituted a relatively small part – roughly 10% – of the investor's overall sales and roughly 5% of its overall sales from the crop protection business.[135] Furthermore, the host state had not interfered with the management, daily operations, or payment of dividends of the investor.[136] Thus, the deprivation was not considered substantial. Before concluding that the cancellation was not expropriation, the tribunal stated the following:

---

131 Azurix v. Argentine Republic, ICSID Case No. ARB/01/12, Award of 14 July 2006, para 310, although relying on a quote wrongly attributed to the award in S.D. Myers v. Canada. For general criticism of using the 'purpose' of the measure as distinguishing criterion, *Higgins*, Rosalyn, 'The Taking of Property by the State: Recent Developments in International Law', Recueil des Cours 1982-III, 259 (331).

132 See also the portrayal in 'Chapter 4 – Standards of Fair Treatment'at pp. 255 *et seq*.

133 See above at pp. 309 *et seq*.

134 Chemtura Corporation v. Government of Canada, Award of 2 August 2010, paras 248, 249.

135 Chemtura Corporation v. Government of Canada, Award of 2 August 2010, paras 261–263.

136 Chemtura Corporation v. Government of Canada, Award of 2 August 2010, para 264.

"Irrespective of the existence of a contractual deprivation, the Tribunal considers in any event that the measures challenged by the Claimant constituted a valid exercise of the Respondent's police powers. [... The competent governmental agency] took measures within its mandate, in a non-discriminatory manner, motivated by the increasing awareness of the dangers presented by lindane for human health and the environment. A measure adopted under such circumstances is a valid exercise of the State's police powers and, as a result, does not constitute an expropriation."[137]

Although the findings of the tribunal on the substance clearly analyse the economic impact of the ban on lindane on the investor, the tribunal appears to – eventually – apprehend that the regulatory and non-discriminatory nature of the measure in its own right prevented a finding of expropriation. It is not clear from the passage whether the tribunal expresses the understanding that the regulatory activity – implementing the findings of the governmental risk assessment regarding the recognised dangers of the pesticide – would not even constitute an expropriation if it had a substantial impact on the investment. Either way, the decision points to the relevance of those factors that are outside the economic circumstances.

V. Methanex v. United States

In *Methanex v. United States*,[138] the tribunal had to assess whether the Californian ban on the petrol additive MTBE constituted an expropriation of the investor. The investor – a producer of the MTBE feedstock methanol – claimed that the ban had the effect of giving its market shares to the ethanol industry, thus causing a significant deprivation of its investment.[139] With regard to the threshold of the standard, the tribunal stated the following:

"[A]s a matter of general international law, a non-discriminatory regulation for a public purpose, which is enacted in accordance with due process and, which affects, inter alios, a foreign investor or investment is not deemed expropriatory and compensable unless specific commitments had been given by the regulating government to the then putative foreign investor contemplating investment that the government would refrain from such regulation."[140]

---

137 Chemtura Corporation v. Government of Canada, Award of 2 August 2010, para 266.

138 See portrayal in 'Chapter 3 – Standards of Non-Discriminatory Treatment' at pp. 183 *et seq*.

139 Methanex v. United States, Award of 3 August 2005, Part IV, Chapter D, para 5.

140 Methanex v. United States, Award of 3 August 2005, Part IV, Chapter D, para 7.

The tribunal focused on the lack of any specific commitments given to the investor regarding the absence of further regulation prior to its investment.[141] In this context, the tribunal particularly emphasised the investor's awareness of, and participation in, the political, regulatory process – inclusive of the influence of interested groups on regulation.[142] The investor, which had itself lobbied to further its business interests, did not offer conclusive evidence for the "conspiratorial thesis", with which it intended to prove its allegation of being discriminated against.[143] In the light of the orderly legislative process, which took account of scientific studies, public hearings, and the evaluation of assessment reports regarding the effect of methanol and ethanol-based additives to petrol, the tribunal concluded that the "ban was made for a public purpose, was non-discriminatory and was accomplished with due process" so that the ban constituted "a lawful regulation and not an expropriation" "from the standpoint of international law".[144] Further, the tribunal stated that the investor had not demonstrated the features associated with expropriation, as the investor's allegedly taken customer base, goodwill and market share, did not qualify as relevant investment.[145]

From a methodological stance, it is remarkable that the tribunal does not begin its assessment with the question of whether there is a substantial deprivation of the investor. In contrast, the tribunal considers the absence of specific commitments as relevant. The closing remarks do not allow insight into the tribunal's perception of the economic threshold, as it considers the allegedly expropriated elements not to qualify as investment. The decision focuses on the nature of the adopted ban – a non-discriminatory measure, serving a public purpose, and accomplished with due process.

---

141 Methanex v. United States, Award of 3 August 2005, Part IV, Chapter D, paras 9, 10.

142 Methanex v. United States, Award of 3 August 2005, Part IV, Chapter D, paras 9, 10. The tribunal states that the investor "entered a political economy in which it was widely known, if not notorious, that governmental environmental and health protection institutions at the federal and state level, operating under the vigilant eyes of the media, interested corporations, non-governmental organizations and a politically active electorate, continuously monitored the use and impact of chemical compounds and commonly prohibited or restricted the use of some of those compounds for environmental and/or health reasons."

143 Methanex v. United States, Award of 3 August 2005, Part IV, Chapter D, paras 9, 13, 14. The investor alleged that the ban was introduced as a result of intense lobbying by participants in the ethanol industry.

144 Methanex v. United States, Award of 3 August 2005, Part IV, Chapter D, paras 14, 15.

145 Methanex v. United States, Award of 3 August 2005, Part IV, Chapter D, paras 16, 17.

Thereby, the decision adopts the understanding that a regulatory measure which fulfils these criteria is not expropriatory. The brevity of the tribunal's discussion of the facts of the case is due to the investor's allegations which were dealt with before – when it was established that there was no discrimination. This approach, which so clearly differs from the 'sole effects doctrine', was welcomed by environmentally-minded commentators.[146]

VI. Glamis Gold, Ltd. v. U.S.A.

In *Glamis Gold, Ltd. v. U.S.A.*,[147] the investor owned mining rights over a stretch of land in the southeastern Californian desert. It sought approval for a mining project to extract gold – featuring three open pits, the excavation of 150 million tons of ore, and 300 million tons of waste rock, and a subsequent complete backfill of only two of the pits. Ultimately, this project was not approved because of environmental implications and its vicinity to areas of special cultural concern to Native Americans.

The tribunal found that the concept of expropriation had to be understood in line with customary international law, so that for all forms of expropriation, even for the "thorny issue" of regulatory expropriation, the threshold issue remained whether a property right of the investor was taken.[148] For this determination, the tribunal relied on the test of 'radical deprivation' of the investor of the economic value of its investment.[149] To determine that there was no substantial deprivation of the investor, the tribunal analysed the entitlement and value that remained with the investor after the enactment of the criticised measures.[150] In a very detailed and technical analysis, based on the investor's economic valuation method, the tribunal determined

146 *Miles*, Kate, 'International Investment Law and Climate Change: Issues in the Transition to a Low-Carbon World', Society of International Economic Law, Working Paper No. 27/08, 2008, p. 16. The author remains cautious and states that "although clearly a step in the right direction towards limiting the scope for challenges to environmental regulation, one decision in favour of the host state does not remedy systemic issues."

147 See also portrayal in 'Chapter 4 – Standards of Fair Treatment' at pp. 265 *et seq.*

148 Glamis Gold, Ltd. v. U.S.A., Award of 8 June 2009, paras 354, 356.

149 Glamis Gold, Ltd. v. U.S.A., Award of 8 June 2009, paras 357, 358.

150 Glamis Gold, Ltd. v. U.S.A., Award of 8 June 2009, paras 361–363. To come to a valid evaluation, the tribunal analysed several determining factors of the investor's valuation in detail. These were (i) the costs of the backfilling, (ii) the evaluation of the third pit for which complete backfilling was not intended, (iii) the gold price, (iv) the costs of financial assurances for implementing the post-backfilling requirements, and (v) the appropriate discount rate.

that the measures of the host state did not radically diminish the value of the investment.[151] Therefore, the investor was not expropriated.

The detailed discussion of the impact of the measure on the value of the investment emphasises the importance the tribunal attached to the criterion of 'substantial deprivation'. Having determined the significant remaining value of the investment, the tribunal dismissed the claim for expropriation without having to discuss a potential impact of the regulatory nature of the measures. However, in this respect it stated clearly that it considered the economic impact and not the nature of a measure to be determinative. Thus, the decision supports an approach which arguably inverses the idea of the 'sole effect doctrine': Only if a measure has the relevant economic impact, will it be considered whether the measure constitutes expropriation.[152]

VII. Marion Unglaube and Reinhard Unglaube v. Republic of Costa Rica

The consolidated cases of *Marion Unglaube and Reinhard Unglaube v. Republic of Costa Rica* concern the expropriation of beach-front property owned by the investors as part of an eco-tourism hotel complex. Costa Rica intended to create a national park to protect the nesting habitat of endangered leatherback turtles.[153] Neither the relevance of the protection of the endangered turtles nor the abstract right of the host state to expropriate was contested.[154] Rather, the non-stringent and potentially contradictory approach to the expropriation was at the heart of the dispute.

The dispute concerned two contiguous areas owned by the investors. In 1991, the host state had declared its intention to create a national marine park and in 1995 it passed a respective law. One part of the investor's property, a 75-meter by 100-meter land strip, was supposed to become part

---

151 Glamis Gold, Ltd. v. U.S.A., Award of 8 June 2009, paras 366, 534–536. The tribunal considered the post-backfilling valuation of the investment to exceed U.S. $ 20 million.

152 *Kahn*, Jordan C., 'Striking NAFTA Gold: Glamis Advances Investor-State Arbitration', 33 Fordham International Law Journal 2009, 101 (133–135) considers this approach as significant for giving governments the confidence to regulate, as they can assess whether the measure has such a substantial economic impact on a foreign investor or not.

153 Marion Unglaube and Reinhard Unglaube v. Republic of Costa Rica, ICSID Case No. ARB/08/1, ICSID Case No. ARB/09/20, Award of 16 May 2012, para 37.

154 Marion Unglaube and Reinhard Unglaube v. Republic of Costa Rica, ICSID Case No. ARB/08/1, ICSID Case No. ARB/09/20, Award of 16 May 2012, paras 163, 166, 205.

of this national park. However, due to an imprecise wording in the underlying national law and their understanding that the host state had agreed to their development plans in 1992, the investors disputed that the land strip was within the designated area of the national park.[155] Despite the national law, the host state made efforts to expropriate the respective property only in 2003. The remainder of the investors' property was not considered part of the national park. The investors claimed that the host state had nevertheless undertaken measures threatening the expropriation of all of their property, such as breaching agreements on how to cooperate, the Supreme Court declaring the area to be a buffer zone for the national park and the administration freezing permits to develop the area.[156]

With regard to the 75-meter by 100-meter land strip, the tribunal found a *de facto* expropriation of the property.[157] In analysing the criteria for lawful expropriation, the tribunal discusses the objective of protecting the endangered leatherback turtle and states that the host state could have directly expropriated the property lawfully.[158] However, the tribunal found that this is not what happened. Rather, – like in the comparable decision in *Compañía del Dessarollo de Santa Elena S.A. v. Republic of Costa Rica* – the property had been "seriously and negatively impacted" since the date of the passing of the decree in 1991, which first envisaged the creation of the national park.[159] Since then, there had been an impact on the saleability and use of the property, even though the host state had not begun to formally expropriate the property. That eight years passed until direct action for expropriation was taken by the host state, which was then fought by the investors, did not change this fact. Rather, the tribunal found that the host state had violated both national and international law by not providing for an adequate and timely expropriation process, including the proper and precise drafting of the relevant provisions of the national park

155 Marion Unglaube and Reinhard Unglaube v. Republic of Costa Rica, ICSID Case No. ARB/08/1, ICSID Case No. ARB/09/20, Award of 16 May 2012, paras 51, 58, 176.

156 Marion Unglaube and Reinhard Unglaube v. Republic of Costa Rica, ICSID Case No. ARB/08/1, ICSID Case No. ARB/09/20, Award of 16 May 2012, paras 79, 83, 86.

157 Marion Unglaube and Reinhard Unglaube v. Republic of Costa Rica, ICSID Case No. ARB/08/1, ICSID Case No. ARB/09/20, Award of 16 May 2012, para 209.

158 Marion Unglaube and Reinhard Unglaube v. Republic of Costa Rica, ICSID Case No. ARB/08/1, ICSID Case No. ARB/09/20, Award of 16 May 2012, para 210.

159 Marion Unglaube and Reinhard Unglaube v. Republic of Costa Rica, ICSID Case No. ARB/08/1, ICSID Case No. ARB/09/20, Award of 16 May 2012, paras 211, 219–221.

law in 1995.[160] Since the property had not even been formally expropriated at the date of the arbitral award and adequate compensation had not been paid within a reasonable period of time, the year-long interference with the property constituted unlawful expropriation.[161]

With regard to the remainder of the property, the tribunal found no expropriation or other violation of the rights of the investor. There was no expropriation, even though the authorities had for a brief period purported to expropriate parts of the remainder of the property, because it was a short-lived attempt that was considered ephemeral.[162] The tribunal also assessed the suspension of further development on the property by the Supreme Court of the host state. Notably, the tribunal found it "troubling, surprising and puzzling" that the Supreme Court had declared a stretch of land lying within 500 metres of the park to constitute a buffer zone without "any credible showing of a technical or scientific basis" and without any involvement of the affected landowners.[163] However, the tribunal did not consider this expropriatory since new legal guidelines for the affected properties were adopted nine months afterwards that did not alter the property rights of existing owners.[164]

The tribunal discussed the impact of suspensions stemming from legal actions brought by the investors and environmental activists, respectively. The tribunal did not accept the argument of the host state that the investors could be blamed for the delay which had occurred in the process, due to their attempts to challenge decisions in national courts.[165] Similarly, with regard to the petitions brought by third parties, the tribunal states that "such unplanned delays occasioned by citizens in exercise of their legal rights are

---

160 Marion Unglaube and Reinhard Unglaube v. Republic of Costa Rica, ICSID Case No. ARB/08/1, ICSID Case No. ARB/09/20, Award of 16 May 2012, paras 209, 219, 221, 223.

161 Marion Unglaube and Reinhard Unglaube v. Republic of Costa Rica, ICSID Case No. ARB/08/1, ICSID Case No. ARB/09/20, Award of 16 May 2012, paras 305, 316.

162 Marion Unglaube and Reinhard Unglaube v. Republic of Costa Rica, ICSID Case No. ARB/08/1, ICSID Case No. ARB/09/20, Award of 16 May 2012, paras 226, 227.

163 Marion Unglaube and Reinhard Unglaube v. Republic of Costa Rica, ICSID Case No. ARB/08/1, ICSID Case No. ARB/09/20, Award of 16 May 2012, paras 231, 233.

164 Marion Unglaube and Reinhard Unglaube v. Republic of Costa Rica, ICSID Case No. ARB/08/1, ICSID Case No. ARB/09/20, Award of 16 May 2012, paras 231–234.

165 Marion Unglaube and Reinhard Unglaube v. Republic of Costa Rica, ICSID Case No. ARB/08/1, ICSID Case No. ARB/09/20, Award of 16 May 2012, paras 210, 213–214.

a common occurrence in democracies with independent court systems" and, while causing delays which may be frustrating, have to be accepted as they are conducted in accordance with national laws.[166] Furthermore, the tribunal found that the outcome of the court proceedings, if not every step of the way, was reasonable.[167]

In stressing the deference owed to the host state in regulating matters within its borders,[168] the tribunal dismissed all other claims of the investors. With regard to the interpretation of the erroneous wording of the 1995 national park law, the tribunal emphasised that it "is not appropriate for this tribunal to substitute an opinion of its own" unless the authorities had acted in an arbitrary or otherwise shocking manner.[169] The tribunal found no arbitrary or discriminatory treatment.[170] Specifically, it found no discrimination in the fact that the property of an environmental non-governmental organisation that aimed to protect the sea turtles and helped in setting-up the national park, located close to the 75-meter land strip of the investors, had not yet been targeted for expropriation.[171] Neither did the tribunal find a frustration of legitimate expectations of the investors.

The decision of the tribunal emphasises the relevance of procedural propriety when a host state is regulating to further a societal aim. There would have been no finding of a violation of a treaty obligation, had the host state proceeded to expropriate the targeted land strip in a timely manner and paid

---

166 Marion Unglaube and Reinhard Unglaube v. Republic of Costa Rica, ICSID Case No. ARB/08/1, ICSID Case No. ARB/09/20, Award of 16 May 2012, paras 184, 286.

167 Marion Unglaube and Reinhard Unglaube v. Republic of Costa Rica, ICSID Case No. ARB/08/1, ICSID Case No. ARB/09/20, Award of 16 May 2012, para 278.

168 Marion Unglaube and Reinhard Unglaube v. Republic of Costa Rica, ICSID Case No. ARB/08/1, ICSID Case No. ARB/09/20, Award of 16 May 2012, paras 246, 258.

169 Marion Unglaube and Reinhard Unglaube v. Republic of Costa Rica, ICSID Case No. ARB/08/1, ICSID Case No. ARB/09/20, Award of 16 May 2012, para 253.
See, similarly, the express statement of the tribunal in Franck Charles Arif v. Republic of Moldova, ICSID Case No. ARB/11/23, Award of 8 April 2013, para 441, according to which "international tribunals must refrain from playing the role of ultimate appellate courts. They cannot substitute their own application and interpretation of national law to the application by national courts."

170 Marion Unglaube and Reinhard Unglaube v. Republic of Costa Rica, ICSID Case No. ARB/08/1, ICSID Case No. ARB/09/20, Award of 16 May 2012, para 258.

171 Marion Unglaube and Reinhard Unglaube v. Republic of Costa Rica, ICSID Case No. ARB/08/1, ICSID Case No. ARB/09/20, Award of 16 May 2012, para 264.

appropriate compensation. However, in the absence of procedural propriety, the impact on the property turns into an unlawful *de facto* expropriation, irrespective of the importance of the environmental objective that the host state intends to further. In the light of the clear intention of the state to take the property, there was no need to discuss the investor's degree of deprivation.

With regard to the remainder of the property, the decision underscores that a host state is not held to a standard of administrative perfection. Even measures that have a negative impact on the property of an investor are not expropriatory, as long as they are not permanent and mechanisms within the host state's administration remedy earlier failures. In such circumstances, the tribunal appears to be lenient with regard to measures – such as the declaration of a buffer zone – that are not based on scientific and procedural grounds. The findings of the tribunal emphasise that measures which do not permanently restrict ownership rights do not constitute expropriation, even if they have not been adopted in line with due process. However, the decision dealt with a situation in which the host state had taken actions to directly target specific property for expropriation. In this sense, it does not help to distinguish expropriation from regulatory activity which does not require payment of compensation.

VIII. Further Cases Alleging Expropriation

The general reluctance of investment tribunals to find expropriation in cases involving general regulatory measures does not prevent investors from – additionally – claiming that their investment has been expropriated. Sometimes this appears to be nothing more than taking a chance – with the core of the claim being a different protective standard.[172] In other cases the invocation appears more plausible. In *Ethyl Corp. v. Canada*[173] – settled by agreement – the banned trade in the petrol additive MMT made up over 50% of the business of the investor.[174] Losses in this order could well have been considered 'substantial deprivation' by an investment tribunal. In contrast, in *Vattenfall AB, Vattenfall Europe AG, Vattenfall Europe Generation*

[172] Costs in international arbitration are generally allocated in an 'en bloc' fashion – and not with regard to the individual claims which were lost. Accordingly, an unsuccessful expropriation claim is unlikely to have a negative impact on the investor. A further plus for the investor could stem from the host state feeling a stronger stigma when it allegedly expropriated the investor.

[173] See portrayal in 'Chapter 3 – Standards of Non-Discriminatory Treatment' at pp. 186 *et seq.*

[174] *Soloway*, Julie A., 'Environmental Regulation as Expropriation: The Case of NAFTA's Chapter 11', 33 Canadian Business Law Journal 2000, 92 (114–115).

AG v. Federal Republic of Germany[175] – also settled by agreement – in which the impact of the measures on the investment is not quantifiable from the material publicly available, it is more difficult to imagine that the investor was substantially deprived of its investment, since it was holding title to the site and the necessary permits for the construction and operation of the power plant.

With regard to pending cases claiming expropriation by a measure implemented to allegedly further an environmental objective, it is very difficult to speculate on the relevance of such a claim. In the case *Pac Rim Cayman LLC v. Republic of El Salvador*, as already mentioned before, the investor claims that both the denial of permits and changes to the mining law have resulted in a substantial deprivation of its investment, rendering it effectively worthless.[176] In the less intensely discussed *Vito G. Gallo v. Canada* – a case that concerned an investor that owned a decommissioned, open pit iron-ore mine and intended to turn it into a waste landfill site –[177] it is impossible to assess – from the information publicly available – whether the Ontarian bill, which prohibited the disposal of waste at the mine site and revoked all certificates and permits acquired by the investor[178], constituted expropriation, like the investor claimed[179] – or whether the investor was seeking compensation for a business failure, as the host state contended[180]. Inter alia, the enactment of the bill in accordance with due process[181] and its being non-discriminatory were in dispute, as the bill targeted the only

175 See portrayak in 'Chapter 4 – Standards of Fair Treatment' at pp. 273 *et seq*.

176 Pac Rim Cayman LLC v. Republic of El Salvador, ICSID Case No. ARB/09/12, Notice of Arbitration of 30 April 2009, para 91.

177 The investor intended to construct the landfill using the 'hydraulic containment measure'. Irrespective of whether this measure constitutes an effective solution for the collection and containment of leachate, opposition arose to the operation of the landfill – and the cities targeted to use the site contracted with other operators, so that the project did not start operations, Vito G. Gallo v. Canada, Statement of Claim of 23 June 2008, paras 37, 43; Vito G. Gallo v. Canada, Statement of Defence of 15 September 2009, paras 50–61.

178 Vito G. Gallo v. Canada, Statement of Claim of 23 June 2008, paras 80, 85–87; Vito G. Gallo v. Canada, Statement of Defence of 15 September 2009, paras 140–141.

179 Vito G. Gallo v. Canada, Statement of Claim of 23 June 2008, para 118 *et seq*.

180 Vito G. Gallo v. Canada, Statement of Defence of 15 September 2009, paras 1–7, 22–61, 71–82, 97–100. See also the assessment that there was no substantial deprivation because the investment did not have a relevant value before the adoption of the bill, paras 217–223. The host state further contends that the business would have required seven permits to start the operation of the waste disposal site, whereas it never held more than three – conditioned – permits. Vito G. Gallo v. Canada, Statement of Defence of 15 September 2009, paras 5, 45–49.

181 Vito G. Gallo v. Canada, Statement of Claim of 23 June 2008, paras 81–85; Vito G. Gallo v. Canada, Statement of Defence of 15 September 2009, paras 140–149.

landfill seeking approval in the area by revoking issued permits[182] and prevented the respective recourse to national courts.[183] The tribunal found that it had no jurisdiction to hear the claim.[184]

IX. Evaluating Summary

The arbitral decisions portrayed indicate that the economic impact of the respective measure is as relevant in the context of an environmental measure as it is in any other context. Even though the approach to this criterion by tribunals may not always be stringent, the relevance of the investor's deprivation is clearly recognisable. It is my understanding that in future cases the issue of whether an environmental measure constitutes expropriation will not be relevant unless the investor has been substantially deprived of its investment. The arbitral decisions in *Chemtura Corporation v. Government of Canada* and, more expressly, in *Glamis Gold, Ltd. v. U.S.A.* support this understanding. The approach applied by the latter tribunal focuses on the irrelevance of other influencing factors, unless the measure reaches the relevant economic threshold.

The notion of the deprivation of investment clearly constitutes the core of the determination. It will depend on the circumstances of the case what percentage of deprivation an investment tribunal considers sufficient. Either way, the threshold is high. Still, the portrayed cases show that there is no uniform approach to distinguishing expropriation from regulatory measures. Influenced by the respective facts before them, tribunals evidently put diverging emphasis on the elements and base their reasoning on different approaches. The different perception, as well as a host of academic commentary, will now be used to establish meaningful criteria for drawing the line between expropriation and environmental regulation.

D. Expropriation in the Environmental Context

The arbitral decisions portrayed above demonstrate that there is not one common formula to distinguish regulatory measures from expropriation. Case law indicates that in practice few regulatory measures constitute expropriation – because they do not result in a 'radical' or 'substantial' depri-

[182] Vito G. Gallo v. Canada, Statement of Claim of 23 June 2008, paras 85–91, Vito G. Gallo v. Canada, Statement of Defence of 15 September 2009, paras 141–142.

[183] Vito G. Gallo v. Canada, Statement of Claim of 23 June 2008, para 87; Vito G. Gallo v. Canada, Statement of Defence of 15 September 2009, para 143.

[184] Vito G. Gallo v. Canada, Award of 15 September 2011, para 359.

vation that meets the economic threshold. However, this practical point does not answer how to abstractly distinguish expropriation from environmental regulation. The cases set forth above emphasise the lack of a unified approach to this issue. The tribunals – like scholarly commentators – focus on different elements of the definitions of expropriation and regulation, respectively, to establish a dividing line.

One may be sceptical about the possibility to determine a valid border between expropriation and regulation. It has been asserted that the line cannot be drawn in an abstract manner, and that an approach to the issue on a case-by-case basis is prone to having the most accurate results.[185] The wealth of discussion and diverging opinions on this subject points to the difficulty of establishing criteria for 'drawing the line'. With the warning of the tribunal in *Feldman v. Mexico* in mind that "[n]o one has come up with a fully satisfactory means of drawing the line from valid regulation to a compensable taking when governmental action interferes with broadly defined property rights,"[186] it is not my ambition to establish an infallible solution to detecting 'regulatory expropriation'. Rather, this study is going to portray certain approaches and propose a solution which may give guidance without restricting the tribunals' capacity to take account of the specific facets of each case.

I. Blanket Exemption for Regulatory Measures from Scope of Expropriation

One approach to distinguishing expropriation from regulatory measures is to focus on their distinctive nature, and to categorically exempt regulation

[185] In this regard, Christie stated five decades ago that "[i]t is evident that the question of what constitutes a 'taking' under international law presents a situation where the common law method of case by case development is pre-eminently the best method, in fact probably the only method, of legal development". *Christie*, G.C., 'What Constitutes A Taking of Property under International Law?' 38 British Yearbook of International Law 1962, 307 (338). Contemporary commentators like to state that this quote is as accurate today as it was at the time of Christie's writing. See, for example, *Paulsson*, Jan/*Douglas*, Zachary, 'Indirect Expropriation in Investment Treaty Arbitrations, Indirect Expropriation in Investment Treaty Arbitrations', in: Arbitrating Foreign Investment Disputes, Procedural and Substantive Legal Aspects (Horn, Norbert et al. (Eds.) 2004) 145 (146).

See, however, the correct criticism by *Royalty*, Kent W./*Ross*, Dianna, 'NAFTA Chapter 11: "Tantamount to Expropriation": Tantamount to Explosive', 21 The International Trade Journal 2007, 299 (321), who argue that governments need clarity and that their authority to regulate in the public interest cannot be left unclear.

[186] Feldman v. Mexico, Award of 16 December 2002, Case No. ARB(AF)99/1, para 101.

from the scope of expropriation. It is a tenable position that 'regulation' and 'expropriation' are intrinsically different from each other. In this sense, the tribunal in *S.D. Myers v. Canada* found that both concepts differed, as 'expropriation' involved the deprivation of ownership rights, whereas 'regulation' involved lesser interference.[187] The tribunal's focus on the 'loss of control' as criterion for expropriation, rather than on the economic impact on the investor, probably emphasises the difference perceived between both concepts. Even though the difference between both concepts may be more significant from that perspective, the tribunal did not understand this differentiation to mean drawing a definite line. Rather, the tribunal felt that its approach would "screen[...] out most potential cases of complaint".[188]

Whereas the clear-cut exemption of regulatory measures from the scope of expropriation would serve the interests of host states in arbitration proceedings,[189] it would undermine the protection owed to foreign investors. As the notion of 'creeping expropriation' exemplifies, regulatory measures – such as taxation – can constitute expropriation. In this sense, the American Law Institute in its Restatement expresses the understanding that a state expropriates foreign property when it subjects it to "taxation, regulation, or other action that is confiscatory [...] or unreasonably interferes with [...] effective enjoyment of an alien's property".[190] The investor's interest in controlling the investment and retaining its economic benefits would not be given sufficient consideration if regulatory measures were per se excluded from scrutiny. In this sense, the tribunal in *Pope & Talbot Inc. v. Canada*, stated that a "blanket exception for regulatory measures would create a gaping loophole in international protections against expropriation."[191]

---

187 See quote cited above at p. 331.

188 S.D. Myers Inc. v. Canada, Partial Award on the Merits, 13 November 2000, para 282.

189 See as an example for a host state relying on this approach, Pope & Talbot Inc. v. Canada, Counter Memorial of 29 March 2000, paras 413, 415, 425. See also the correct assessment of *Coe*, Jack Jr./*Rubins*, Noah, 'Regulatory Expropriation and the Tecmed Case: Context and Contributions', in: International Investment Law and Arbitration: Leading Cases from the ICSID, NAFTA, Bilateral Treaties and Customary International Law (Weiler, Todd (Ed.) 2005) 597 (632, 633) who state that "the universe of viable claims would be small", if all regulation were to be exempt from the duty to compensate.

190 American Law Institute, 'Restatement of the Law (Third) of the Foreign Relations of the United States' Volume 1, 1987, Section 712, Comment g.

191 Pope & Talbot Inc. v. Canada, Interim Award of 26 June 2000, para 99. Similairly, Feldman v. Mexico, ICSID Case No. ARB(AF)/99/1, Award of 16 December 2002, para 110, stating that "[n]o one can seriously question that in some circumstances government regulatory activity can be a violation of [the protection against expropriation]."

In the light of the breadth of possible regulatory measures, the protection of the investor would be endangered if regulatory measures were not screened with regard to potential expropriatory effects.

II. Influence of Police Powers

Public international law recognises the necessity for states to adopt regulation within their recognised police powers. In this context, international law tolerates interference with foreign property for economic regulatory purposes "to a significant degree".[192] The understanding that non-discriminatory *bona fide* regulation within the accepted police powers of the state, such as "bona fide general taxation, regulation, forfeiture for crime", does not require the compensation of an investor that is negatively affected by the measure is also expressed in the Restatement of the American Law Institute.[193] Investment tribunals have explicitly stated that *bona fide* regulation within the recognised police powers of the state does not require compensation for affecting the investor's property, because this principle has attained the status of customary international law.[194]

See also *Royalty*, Kent W./*Ross*, Dianna, 'NAFTA Chapter 11: "Tantamount to Expropriation": Tantamount to Explosive', 21 The International Trade Journal 2007, 299 (317–318), calling such an exemption an "overly simplistic" approach.

[192] *Higgins*, Rosalyn, 'The Taking of Property by the State: Recent Developments in International Law', Recueil des Cours 1982-III, 259 (331). Similarly, *Dolzer*, Rudolf, 'Indirect Expropriation of Alien Property', 1 ICSID Review Foreign Investment Law Journal 1986, 41 (62), drawing upon indications from domestic legal orders.

[193] American Law Institute, 'Restatement of the Law (Third) of the Foreign Relations of the United States' Volume 1, 1987, Section 712, Comment g.

[194] Saluka Investments BV (The Netherlands) v. The Czech Republic, Award of 17 March 2006, para 262; Methanex v. United States, Award of 3 August 2005, Part IV, Chapter D, para 7; Lauder v. Czech Republic, Award of 3 September 2001, para 198; S.D. Myers v. Canada, First Partial Award of 13 November 2000, para. 281; Técnicas Medioambientales Tecmed, S.A. v. United Mexican States, ICSID Case No. ARB (AF)/00/2, Award of 29 May 2003, para 119; Chemtura Corporation v. Government of Canada, Award of 2 August 2010, para 266. See also *Ratner*, Steven R., 'Regulatory Takings in Institutional Context: Beyond the Fear of Fragmented International Law', 102 American Journal of International Law 2008, 475 (481), who describes it as a point of agreement among decision makers and scholars.

See also Sedco, Inc. v. National Iranian Oil Co, and the Islamic Republic of Iran, Interlocutory Award of 24 October 1984, Award No. ITL 55-129-3, 9 Iran-US CTR Rep 248 stating that "a State is not liable for economic injury which is a consequence of a bona fide 'regulation' within the accepted police power of states" and *Aldrich*, George H., 'What Constitutes a Compensable Taking of Property? The Decisions of the Iran-United States Claims Tribunal', 88 American Journal of Inter-

However, international law does not appear to definitively answer the question of what types of regulation exactly fall within the police powers of states so that they remain non-compensable.[195] It has to be taken into account that the existence of a legitimate reason for the adoption of the respective measure – as such – does not distinguish regulation from expropriation: Both regulation and lawful expropriation are adopted for a public purpose.[196] Otherwise, the existence of a public purpose for a measure could not constitute a requirement for lawful expropriation. Accordingly, the societal aim as the public purpose that the measure fulfils cannot be the distinguishing criterion.[197]

In the context of environmental regulation, the investment tribunal in *Técnicas Medioambientales Tecmed, S.A. v. United Mexican States* expressed the understanding that environmental regulation – irrespective of its beneficial effect on society – was not as such excluded from the scope of expropriation.[198] The methodological impact of this statement is tainted by its reliance on the findings of the tribunal in *Compañía del Dessarollo de Santa Elena S.A. v. Republic of Costa Rica*, which coined the often-cited phrase that "[e]xpropriatory environmental measures – no matter how laudable and beneficial to society as a whole – are [...] similar to any other expropriatory measures [...]."[199] That tribunal, however, dealt with an ex-

---

national Law 1994, 585 (609), gathering the rule from jurisprudence of the Iran-U.S. Claims Tribunal.

Contra, *Kriebaum*, Ursula, Eigentumsschutz im Völkerrecht (2008) pp. 369–373.

[195] In the words of the tribunal in Saluka Investments BV (The Netherlands) v. The Czech Republic, Award of 17 March 2006, para 263: "[I]nternational law has yet to identify in a comprehensive and definitive fashion precisely what regulations are considered "permissible" and "commonly accepted" as falling within the police or regulatory power of States and, thus, non-compensable. In other words, it has yet to draw a bright and easily distinguishable line between non-compensable regulations on the one hand and, on the other, measures that have the effect of depriving foreign investors of their investment and are thus unlawful and compensable in international law."

[196] See *Higgins*, Rosalyn, 'The Taking of Property by the State: Recent Developments in International Law', Recueil des Cours 1982-III, 259 (331); *Schreuer*, Christoph, 'The Concept of Expropriation under the ECT and Other Investment Protection Treaties', in: Investment Arbitration and the Energy Charter Treaty (Ribeiro, Clarisse (Ed.) 2006) 108 (144).

[197] Similarly, Azurix v. Argentine Republic, ICSID Case No. ARB/01/12, Award of 14 July 2006, para 310.

[198] The passage is quoted above at p. 329. Técnicas Medioambientales Tecmed, S.A. v. United Mexican States, ICSID Case No. ARB (AF)/00/2, Award of 29 May 2003, para 121.

[199] Compañía del Dessarollo de Santa Elena S.A. v. Republic of Costa Rica, ICISD Case No. ARB/96/1, Award of 17 February 2000, para 72.

plicit, direct expropriation for environmental reasons, for which it had to determine the correct amount of compensation. Accordingly, the decision does not attempt to differentiate between regulation and expropriation, so that the quote is of limited use for the current issue. Nevertheless, it appears that the extent to which society can require the alien investor to bear the costs of normative changes in the realm of environmental protection is not answered by the societal aim as such. Especially in the context of environmental regulation and land use planning, a precise definition of the types of action qualifying as 'commonly accepted' has to be found.[200]

In line with the general understanding that the differentiation between valid regulation and expropriation depends on the circumstances of the specific case, one tribunal suggests that the "context within which an impugned measure is adopted and applied is critical to the determination of its validity."[201] More precisely, commentators have focused on a science-based risk assessment as distinguishing criterion.[202] When a rational connection between a scientifically identified risk and the adopted measure exists, the possibility that the measure is meant to disguise other intentions is excluded. Although the depth of deference accredited to a state in international law is not in doubt,[203] it is suggested that investment law demand a relationship of 'reasonable necessity' and proportionality between the harm and the adopted measure.[204] Furthermore, the method of the regulation

---

200 *Sampliner*, Gary H., 'Arbitration of Expropriation Cases under U.S. Investment Treaties – A Threat to Democracy or the Dog That Didn't Bark?', 18 ICSID Review Foreign Investment Law Journal 2003, 1 (10).

201 Saluka Investments BV (The Netherlands) v. The Czech Republic, Award of 17 March 2006, para 264.

202 *Newcombe*, Andrew, 'The Boundaries of Regulatory Expropriation in International Law', 20 ICSID Review Foreign Investment Law Journal 2005, 1 (36–38); *Wagner*, J. Martin, 'International Investment, Expropriation and Environmental Protection', 29 Golden Gate University Law Review 1999, 465 (520–523); *Moloo*, Rahim/*Jacinto*, Justin, 'Environmental and Health Regulation: Assessing Liability under Investment-Treaties', 29 Berkeley Journal of International Law 2011, 1 (25, 30).

203 *Sampliner*, Gary H., 'Arbitration of Expropriation Cases under U.S. Investment Treaties – A Threat to Democracy or the Dog That Didn't Bark?', 18 ICSID Review Foreign Investment Law Journal 2003, 1 (17–18). See also *Christie*, G.C., 'What Constitutes A Taking of Property under International Law?' 38 British Yearbook of International Law 1962, 307 (338), stating that "if the reasons given [for the introduction of the measure] are valid and bear some plausible relationship to the action taken, no attempt may be made to search deeper to see whether the state was activated by some illicit motive."

204 *Newcombe*, Andrew, 'The Boundaries of Regulatory Expropriation in International Law', 20 ICSID Review Foreign Investment Law Journal 2005, 1 (38–39).

– namely the observance of the principle of due process – is relevant for assessing the legitimacy.[205]

Case law – such as the decision in *S.D. Myers v. Canada* – suggests that the stringency of scientific evidence is less readily accepted when factors additive to the environmental concerns have influenced the decision to adopt the regulatory measure. The same is probably true for scenarios with mixed scientific evidence, where the regulation has a substantial impact on a foreign investor, as was the case in *Ethyl Corp. v. Canada*.[206] In my understanding, these scenarios have to be distinguished from cases in which the regulatory measure has been adopted in application of the precautionary principle.[207] In such cases, a risk assessment has indicated a relevant likelihood, though no certainty, of the occurrence of a relevant environmental harm. Although it is not possible to predict how investment tribunals would address a measure based on the precautionary principle, I believe that – in the light of the deference owed to the host state – the risk assessment that determined a likelihood, albeit not a certainty of the occurrence of a relevant environmental harm would be sufficient for finding the measure squarely placed within the police powers of the state.[208]

---

205 *Newcombe*, Andrew, 'The Boundaries of Regulatory Expropriation in International Law', 20 ICSID Review Foreign Investment Law Journal 2005, 1 (39–40). See also the in-depth assessment of the relevance of due process in the context of regulatory expropriation in an environmental context in *Paparinskis*, Martins, 'Regulatory Expropriation and Sustainable Development', in: Sustainable Development in World Investment Law (Cordonier Segger, Marie-Claire et al. (Eds.) 2011) 299 (312–320). Paparinskis finds that focusing on the method as opposed to the purpose of the regulation is advantageous, as it fosters better regulation.

206 *Soloway*, Julie A., 'Environmental Regulation as Expropriation: The Case of NAFTA's Chapter 11', 33 Canadian Business Law Journal 2000, 92 (119) portrays how the import ban was partly based on "mixed scientific evidence as to the harmfulness of MMT" as well as meant as support for the national automobile and ethanol industry "in order to develop an alternate fuel strategy".

207 See the portrayal in 'Chapter 1 – Environmental Norms and Principles' at pp. 70 *et seq.*

208 Similarly, *Madalena*, Iganacio, 'Foreign Direct Investment and the Protection of the Environment: The Border Between National Environmental Regulation and Expropriation', 12 European Environmental Law Review 2003, 70 (75).

Contra, *Moloo*, Rahim/*Jacinto*, Justin, 'Environmental and Health Regulation: Assessing Liability under Investment-Treaties', 29 Berkeley Journal of International Law 2011, 1 (30), who state that "a precautionary measure resulting in a substantial deprivation of an investor's investment will more likely trigger the requirement of compensation than a measure based on science evidencing a legitimate concern. A state should be entitled to adopt precautionary regulations to protect against potential health or environmental threats, but where there is no evidence supporting a health or environmental measure, the state – and not the investor – should bear the costs of adopting that measure."

It follows from the above, that a non-discriminatory regulatory measure reflecting the police powers of the enacting state has to be analysed with "special care"[209]. In my opinion, the entirety of circumstances sheds light on the legitimacy of the respective measure. This context comprises of, inter alia, the reasons for the adopted measure and the process leading to the adoption of the measure itself. In this sense, it is my understanding that environmental regulation mirrors – at the outset – a legitimate societal cause within the police powers of the adopting state. The risk assessment of the host state has to be based on scientific evidence, so that some evidence of relevant harm can be discerned. When choosing the measure that is to be adopted, the host state has to take account of, and evaluate the impact of, the measure on individuals. The context of the adoption itself requires a transparent process in accordance with the respective national administrative or legislative procedures. Whereas the factors and their impact differ in each respective case, it is my understanding that the whole of the factors in each case will give a clear indication of whether the respective measure goes beyond the scope of *bona fide* regulation.

III. Proportionality

In the context of determining whether a measure is within the police powers of the host state, the proportionality of the measure can constitute one criterion. More explicit, some investment tribunals[210] and scholars[211]

With all due respect, I believe that this appreciation is based on a misrepresentation of the precautionary principle: The precautionary principle does not support measures that are based on "no evidence". Rather, the principle places a bigger emphasis on the risk of the occurrence of the – grave – danger for an environmental objective. A risk assessment is required to determine the relevant factors before formulating an appropriate response to manage the risk.

209 Pope & Talbot Inc. v. Canada, Interim Award of 26 June 2000, para 99.

210 Técnicas Medioambientales Tecmed, S.A. v. United Mexican States, ICSID Case No. ARB (AF)/00/2, Award of 29 May 2003, para 122; LG&E v. Argentina, ICSID Case No. ARB/02/1, Award of 3 October 2006, para 195; Azurix v. Argentine Republic, ICSID Case No. ARB/01/12, Award of 14 July 2006, paras 311–312; LG&E v. Argentina, ICSID Case No. ARB/02/1, Award of 3 October 2006, para 195; Siemens A.G. v. Argentine Republic, ICSID Case No. ARB/02/8, Award of 6 February 2007, para 354; Deutsche Bank AG v. Democratic Socialist Republic of Sri Lanka, ICSID Case No. ARB/09/2, Award of 31 October 2012, para 522.

211 *Kolo*, Abba/*Wälde*, Thomas, 'Environmental Regulation, Investment Protection and "Regulatory Taking" in International Law', 50 International and Comparative Law Quarterly 2001, 811 (827 *et seq*); Fortier, Yves L./Drymer, Stephen L., 'Indirect Expropriation in the Law of International Investment: I Know It When I See It, or Caveat Investor', 19 ICSID Review Foreign Investment Law Journal 2004, 293 (324–325); *Paparinskis*, Martins, 'Regulatory Expropriation and Sustain-

apply proportionality considerations to determine whether a measure expropriates foreign investment. The tribunal in *Técnicas Medioambientales Tecmed, S.A. v. United Mexican States* discussed whether the measure was "proportional to the public interest presumably protected thereby and to the protection legally granted to investments", with the significance of the financial impact playing a "key role" in the evaluation.[212] The size of the investor's ownership deprivation – as well as its alien status which deprived it of exercising certain political rights – were considered to be specifically relevant.[213] Those scholars and arbitrators supporting proportionality con-

---

able Development', in: Sustainable Development in World Investment Law (Cordonier Segger, Marie-Claire et al. (Eds.) 2011) 299 (323–324); *Ben Hamida*, Walid, 'La prise en compte de l'intérêt général et des impératifs de développement dans le droit des investissements', 135 Journal du Droit International 2008, 999 (1025). See also *Kentin*, Esther, 'Sustainable Development in International Investment Dispute Settlement: The ICSID and NAFTA Experience', in: International Law and Sustainable Development: Principles and Practice (Schrijver, Nico et al. 2004) 309 (329), who argues that balancing the investor's rights with the sovereignty of the state over its natural resources and its interest in environmental protection is fundamental for achieving sustainable development.

212 Técnicas Medioambientales Tecmed, S.A. v. United Mexican States, ICSID Case No. ARB (AF)/00/2, Award of 29 May 2003, para 122.

213 Técnicas Medioambientales Tecmed, S.A. v. United Mexican States, ICSID Case No. ARB (AF)/00/2, Award of 29 May 2003, para 122. Endorsed in Azurix v. Argentine Republic, ICSID Case No. ARB/01/12, Award of 14 July 2006, paras 311–312.

The tribunal's factoring in the reduced possibility for the investor to politically participate in the host state is not very convincing. In this regard, it relies on findings of the ECtHR in the Case of James and Others v. United Kingdom (Application no. 8793/79) Judgment of 21 February 1986, paras 58–66. One passage reads as follows: "[N]on-nationals are more vulnerable to domestic legislation: unlike nationals, they will generally have played no part in the election or designation of its authors nor have been consulted on its adoption. Secondly, although a taking of property must always be effected in the public interest, different considerations may apply to nationals and non-nationals and there may well be legitimate reason for requiring nationals to bear a greater burden in the public interest than non-nationals."

Simply conferring this general statement to investment law, however, is not necessarily helpful. It is oblivious to the lobbying potential of potent foreign corporations. It is rather likely that economically potent investors – which provide for example services and employment opportunities – have a higher degree of political influence than the majority of nationals of the host state. However, a further differentiating factor can be that foreigners may not profit from reciprocal advantages offsetting the negative impact of the measure in the long run, if their investments are short term. Accordingly, it is my understanding that the foreignness of the investor should not be specifically considered in the abstract, but be evaluated in the specific context when assessing the proportionality of an environmental measure. Similarly, *Newcombe*, Andrew, 'The Boundaries of Regulatory Expropriation in International Law', 20 ICSID Review Foreign Investment Law Journal 2005, 1 (47).

siderations in assessing expropriation – like this investment tribunal – seek guidance from the jurisprudence of the ECtHR, because the ECtHR focuses on proportionality in its adjudication.

In its role as international institution overseeing the unison of national legislative, administrative or other measures with the human rights enshrined in the European Convention on Human Rights (ECHR), the ECtHR accords the acting states a 'wide margin of appreciation' in the adoption of a measure.[214] At the heart of the ECtHR's determination is the question whether the measure "strikes a fair balance" between the rights of the individual and the general interest of the society at large.[215] Accordingly, a measure depriving a person of his or her property need not only pursue, on the facts as well as in principle, a legitimate aim in the public interest, "but there must also be a reasonable relationship of proportionality between the means employed and the aim sought to be realised".[216]

The case law of the ECtHR, which contains a multitude of cases involving alleged regulatory expropriations, indicates that whenever measures are adopted to protect important societal values – such as environmental protection – in a transparent manner, the underlying right to the enjoyment of property has generally not been violated. In the light of the wide margin of appreciation accorded to the state to establish the public interest, such national measures are frequently considered proportionate. For example, in two cases concerning restrictions on the commercial use of property for environmental reasons – *Fredin v. Sweden*[217] and *Pine Valley Developments*

---

214 The ECtHR adopts the opinion that the national authorities are in principle better placed than the international judge to appreciate what is in the public interest, because of their direct knowledge of their society and its needs. The ECtHR stresses that the margin of appreciation available to the legislature in implementing social and economic policies should be a wide one and that it will respect the relevant legislature's judgment, unless that judgment is manifestly without reasonable foundation. See, for example, Case of James and Others v. United Kingdom (Application no. 8793/79) Judgment of 21 February 1986, para 46.

215 ECtHR Case of Sporrong and Lönnroth v. Sweden (Application no. 7151/75; 7152/75) Judgment of 23 September 1982, para. 69; ECtHR Case of Mellacher and Others v. Austria (Application no. 10522/83; 11011/84; 11070/84) Judgment of 19 December, para 48; ECtHR Case of Fredin v. Sweden (Application no. 12033/86) Judgment of 18 February 1991, para 51; ECtHR Case of Katte Klitsche de la Grange v. Italy (Application no. 12539/86) Judgment of 19 September 1994, para 42.

216 ECtHR Case of James and Others v. United Kingdom (Application no. 8793/79) Judgment of 21 February 1986, para 50.

217 The ECtHR Case of Fredin v. Sweden (Application no. 12033/86) Judgment of 18 February 1991 concerned restrictions for environmental reasons on the extraction of gravel from a gravel pit owned by the applicants– specifically the revocation of an extraction permit in the light of prior lawfully imposed restrictions on the use of the pit. The ECtHR took into account the chronology of events as well as the

Ltd and Others v. Ireland[218] – the ECtHR found that the measures were not disproportionate in the light of the legitimacy of the environmental aims pursued.

The proportionality approach is an effective tool to take account of a multitude of – partially contrary – factors. This is true for the determination of expropriation in the ambit of foreign investment law and European human rights law, retrospectively, even though the protective mandates are not identical. The human rights decisions exemplify that the ECtHR – in making its assessment – considers elements largely similar to those relevant in investment decisions: the economic impact of the governmental measure, the circumstances bringing about the interference with the property right – like transparency in decision making and time spans – the legitimacy of expectations of the property owners, as well as the importance of the societal aim. This congruence constitutes a strong argument for the workability of a proportionality approach in investment arbitration.[219]

IV. Only in Rare Circumstances

The discussion of various factors to be considered in distinguishing a regulatory measure from an act of expropriation points to the following formula: "Except in rare circumstances", non-discriminatory regulatory

---

underlying restrictions on the use of the pit. It establishes that at the time the applicants made a significant investment, there were no governmental representations, which could have led to them reasonably expecting to be able to continue exploitation for a long period of time (para 54). In its decision on proportionality, the ECtHR specifically emphasises the legitimacy of the environmental aim of the governmental measure (para 55). It emphasises the importance of environmental concerns and recognises "for its part that in today's society the protection of the environment is an increasingly important consideration" (para 48).

218 The ECtHR Case of Pine Valley Developments Ltd and Others v. Ireland (Application no. 12742/87) Judgment of 29 November 1991 concerned the annulment of a planning permission for environmental reasons, preventing the applicants from developing ground they owned. The ECtHR found that the annulment of the permit without any remedial action was not disproportional, since the applicants were engaged in a commercial venture involving an element of risk and they were aware of zoning plans for the area as well as of the local authority's opposition to the project (para 59).

219 See, however, *Ratner*, Steven R., 'Regulatory Takings in Institutional Context: Beyond the Fear of Fragmented International Law', 102 American Journal of International Law 2008, 475 (499–501, 526, 527), arguing for general caution in incorporating case law of the ECtHR into foreign investment decisions, due to the differing purposes and institutional features of the respective institutions. See also the cautious reference in Fireman's Fund Insurance Company v. United Mexican States, ICSID Case No. ARB(AF)/02/1, Award of 17 July 2006, para 176 (j) in footnote 161.

measures which are "designed and applied to protect legitimate public welfare objectives, such as [...] the environment" and adopted in a way that respects due process, "do not constitute indirect expropriations".[220] This approach gives considerable weight to the police powers of the state and sets a valid framework within which a state can further social aims without endangering the position of the foreign investor. In most scenarios, the implementation of a non-discriminatory regulatory measure adopted to protect a legitimate public welfare objective, such as environmental protection, does not constitute expropriation. Only in exceptional cases may an opposing determination be warranted.

This formula has found the support of commentators.[221] Whether the approach represents customary international law is open to debate.[222] Whereas

---

[220] This understanding is found in annexes to some modern investment treaties. See Annex 10-C, para 4 lit b CAFTA-DR; Annex B, para 4 lit b U.S.-Rwanda BIT; Annex B, para 4 lit b U.S.-Uruguay BIT, Annex B, para 4 lit b 2004 U.S. Model BIT. See also the slightly different wording in Annex B para 3 Canada-Latvia BIT; Annex B.13(1) lit c 2004 Canada Model BIT. The wording contained in these treaties does not refer to the due process requirement.

[221] *Subedi*, Surya P., International Investment Law: Reconciling Policy and Principle (2008), pp. 200–201. Similarly, *Royalty*, Kent W./*Ross*, Dianna, 'NAFTA Chapter 11: "Tantamount to Expropriation": Tantamount to Explosive', 21 The International Trade Journal 2007, 299 (323–324); *Moloo*, Rahim/*Jacinto*, Justin, 'Environmental and Health Regulation: Assessing Liability under Investment-Treaties', 29 Berkeley Journal of International Law 2011, 1 (37).

Without reference to the exception in 'rare circumstances', *Krajewski*, Markus/*Ceyssens*, Jan, 'Internationaler Investitionsschutz und innerstaatliche Regulierung, Eine Untersuchung anhand der bilateralen Investitionsabkommen Deutschlands', 45 Archiv des Völkerrechts 2007, 180 (195–196); *Lawrence*, Jessica C., 'Chicken Little Revisited: NAFTA Regulatory Expropriations after Methanex', 41 Georgia Law Review 2006, 261 (305–306).

See, however, critical of the guidance the formula gives in a specific case, *Coe*, Jack Jr./*Rubins*, Noah, 'Regulatory Expropriation and the *Tecmed* Case: Context and Contributions', in: International Investment Law and Arbitration: Leading Cases from the ICSID, NAFTA, Bilateral Treaties and Customary International Law (Weiler, Todd (Ed.) 2005) 597 (642).

[222] Stating that the above-cited BIT clauses represent customary international law, *Newcombe*, Andrew, 'The Boundaries of Regulatory Expropriation in International Law', 20 ICSID Review Foreign Investment Law Journal 2005, 1 (40). *Contra*, *Paparinskis*, Martins, 'Regulatory Expropriation and Sustainable Development', in: Sustainable Development in World Investment Law (Cordonier Segger, Marie-Claire et al. (Eds.) 2011) 299 (325); *Subedi*, Surya P., International Investment Law: Reconciling Policy and Principle (2008), p. 200.

The formulation contained in modern investment treaties appears to rely on language suggested by countries that are traditionally in the role of home states to capital exporting investors. With such states giving weight to the regulatory interests of host states, one can speculate that the support of the approach is widespread: States traditionally in the role of host states are very likely to support the approach.

the clause contained in several more recent investment treaties has been criticised for its lack of recognition of the element of due process,[223] an approach which encompasses all of these components is helpful to draw the line between regulation and expropriation. The relevance of the observance of due process, however, should not be overstated in this context. First, the capacity of an international tribunal to review the process within the national state is limited.[224] Second, violations of the due process requirement are addressed in the context of violations of standards of fairness, such as the standard of fair and equitable treatment. The protection against expropriation is not the sole safeguard against imperfect processes.

The accuracy of the results yielded with this approach to drawing a line between regulation and expropriation is also supported by the cases portrayed above. The measures which were considered expropriatory – in *Técnicas Medioambientales Tecmed, S.A. v. United Mexican States* and *Metalclad Corporation v. United Mexican States* – did not fulfil the above set of requirements. In contrast, expropriation was not found in cases which concerned a non-discriminatory regulatory measure to further environmental protection. The measures underlying the decisions in *Chemtura Corporation v. Government of Canada* and *Methanex v. United States*, which the tribunals considered to meet this standard, did not constitute expropriation. The differentiation is further supported by the award in *Chemtura Corporation v. Government of Canada*, which expressly stated that general measures like the one it reviewed were legitimate regulation, and not expropriation.

However, this approach recognises that rare and unusual circumstances might require a different evaluation of a *bona fide* environmental regulation. But what factors lead to the categorisation of a regulatory measure as expropriation and trigger the payment of compensation? Several scenarios for such 'rare circumstances' are thinkable, one of which derives from the application of the proportionality approach as portrayed above. If the adopted *bona fide* environmental regulation does not reflect the striking of a fair balance between the societal aim pursued and the interest of the investor, the regulatory measure may be considered 'rare'.[225] Less abstractly, two

---

223 *Paparinskis*, Martins, 'Regulatory Expropriation and Sustainable Development', in: Sustainable Development in World Investment Law (Cordonier Segger, Marie-Claire et al. (Eds.) 2011) 299 (322).

224 See in 'Chapter 3 – Standards of Non-Discriminatory Treatment' at pp. 202 *et seq*. See also *Krajewski*, Markus/*Ceyssens*, Jan, 'Internationaler Investitionsschutz und innerstaatliche Regulierung, Eine Untersuchung anhand der bilateralen Investitionsabkommen Deutschlands', 45 Archiv des Völkerrechts 2007, 180 (196).

225 In this sense, the tribunal in LG&E v. Argentina, ICSID Case No. ARB/02/1, Award of 3 October 2006. It relies on the distinction between the general regulatory character of measures furthering a social purpose and expropriation and states

further scenarios will more closely be analysed. One scenario relates to the adoption of an environmental measure in breach of a respective commitment by the host state. The second scenario addresses measures with an extraordinary impact on the investment of one investor, thereby demanding a 'special sacrifice'.

1. Environmental Measure in Breach of Prior Commitment

The tribunal in *Methanex v. United States* formulated one exception, in which a non-discriminatory regulation enacted in accordance with due process to further a public purpose can constitute an expropriation – that is a situation when the regulating government has promised the investor to refrain from the respective regulation.[226] While the relevance of the investor's investment-backed expectations in assessing expropriation has already been portrayed above,[227] this criterion relies on assurances that are more specific. The authorities of the host state must have given a promise that the environmental measures, which were finally adopted, would not be taken.[228] Such a situation in which the investor legitimately expects the government to refrain from regulating significantly differs from usual circumstances.

In my understanding, a governmental authority promising to refrain from specific regulation constitutes a 'rare circumstance', so that the governmental promise constitutes an important factor in the overall assessment of the measure. However, it does not automatically result in a finding of expropriation. With the promise being closely connected to the notion of legitimate expectations of the investor, I believe that the best approach is to give weight to the disregarded assurance and factor it into a balancing exercise of opposing interests. It is in that sense that the ECtHR factors a prior

that rare circumstances are those where proportionality is missing. It pronounces as follows: "With respect to the power of the State to adopt its policies, it can generally be said that the State has the right to adopt measures having a social or general welfare purpose. In such a case, the measure must be accepted without any imposition of liability, except in cases where the State's action is obviously disproportionate to the need being addressed."(para 195).

226 Methanex v. United States, Award of 3 August 2005, Part IV, Chapter D, para 7.

227 See above at pp. 318 *et seq*.

228 The decision in *Methanex v. U.S.A.* does not indicate from which sources such an assurance can arise. Most likely, not only direct, explicit promises, but also assurances drawn from existing national legislation could qualify. See *Alvarez-Jiménez*, Alberto, 'The *Methanex* Final Award, An Analysis from the Perspective of Environmental Regulatory Authorities and Foreign Investors', 23 Journal of International Arbitration 2006, 427 (431).

commitment of the government into the overall assessment of a measure.[229] The breadth of the effect of such a promise depends on the specifics of the individual case – with regard to circumstances surrounding the promise. In this light, the breach of specific promises could be factored into an assessment of the overall proportionality of the measure.[230] To sum up, a prior promise not to change existing environmental regulation would have opened up the possibility to conceive the measure as expropriation, a category from which it would have been excluded if classified as a non-discriminatory measure enacted in accordance with due process to further a public purpose.

2. Imposition of Special Sacrifice

Another situation which could qualify as 'rare' is when one or very few investors have to bear an exceptional and disastrous burden resulting from the enacted regulation. The jurisprudence of the ECtHR reflects that restrictions on the use of property can be so intense that the balance between the rights of the individual and the societal aim is not fairly struck. The individual who is made to bear an "excessive burden"[231] has to be compensated. This approach is also a feature of German administrative and constitutional law – known as *Sonderopfer*[232] – and is reflected in decisions of

[229] According to the ECtHR, a prior commitment to regulation does not extinguish the authority of the government to enact new environmental norms. In this sense, the ECtHR in the Case of Katte Klitsche de la Grange v. Italy (Application no. 12539/86) Judgment of 19 September 1994: It decided that the prior agreement of the government council with the land development plans of the applicant, did not prevent the government from enacting partly opposing measures in the planning sphere. In determining the proportionality of the measure, the ECtHR also took into account that there was "never an absolute prohibition on building on the applicant's land" (para 46) and that the restrictions were temporary (para 47).

[230] See similarly, generally for the assessment of breaches of prior commitments, *Kolo*, Abba/*Wälde*, Thomas, 'Environmental Regulation, Investment Protection and "Regulatory Taking" in International Law', 50 International and Comparative Law Quarterly 2001, 811 (843–844).

[231] ECtHR Case of James and Others v. United Kingdom (Application no. 8793/79) Judgment of 21 February, para 50; ECtHR Case of Sporrong and Lönnroth v. Sweden (Application no. 7151/75; 7152/75) Judgment of 23 September 1982, para. 73.

[232] German administrative and constitutional law recognises different approaches to identifying whether the owner of a property has been made to endure a 'special sacrifice'. The approaches focus on the impact of economic deprivation or the prevailing circumstances, respectively: The recognition of an individual bearing a 'Sonderopfer' is connected to the impact of a – lawful or unlawful – restriction on property, not to the finding of expropriation. See for detailed description of the notion in German law, *Krumbiegel*, Peter, Der Sonderopferbegriff in der Rechtsprechung des Bundesgerichtshofes (1975).

the U.S. Supreme Court[233]. Accordingly, the understanding that an individual investor bearing an excessive burden is in a 'rare circumstance' can constitute a useful guideline for investment tribunals.[234]

The jurisprudence of the ECtHR gives guidance for determining the circumstances under which an individual is made to bear an excessive burden. In the case of *James and Others v. The United Kingdom*,[235] the Court found that the applicants, who were holding houses as trustees were not subjected to an excessive burden by enfranchisements of property rights that were substantially under the market value. Despite the financial impact, the consequences for the applicants were not excessively over and above the disadvantageous effects the scheme, which was set up under the leasehold reform legislation, generally had on landlords.[236] Accordingly, the requisite balance under the property protection of the ECHR was not destroyed. In the case of *Pinnacle Meat Processors v. United Kingdom*, the ECommHR did not find that the applicants suffered an "individual and excessive burden" through measures restricting their business as cattle head deboners.[237] For this determination, the ECommHR focused on the fact that the applicants had received some compensation and had remained owners of their tangible assets, which they could sell or use in other operations.[238]

---

233 U.S. Supreme Court, Mononghahela Navigation v. U.S., Decision of 27 March 1893, 148 U.S. 312 (1893), stating that the relevant 5th Amendment of the U.S. Constitution is designed to prevent "the public from loading upon one individual more than his just share of burden of government."

234 *Kolo*, Abba/*Wälde*, Thomas, 'Environmental Regulation, Investment Protection and "Regulatory Taking" in International Law', 50 International and Comparative Law Quarterly 2001, 811 (845–846).

235 In the ECtHR Case of James and Others v. United Kingdom (Application no. 8793/79) Judgment of 21 February 1986, the applicants, acting as trustees for houses of ground leaseholders, had been subjected to 80 enfranchisements of property rights over these houses. These enfranchisements were based on legislation intended to allow tenants to purchase the property they live in. The ECtHR found that the legislation was compatible with the right to enjoyment of property (para 69), – even though the vast majority of purchases relating to the trust were not made by tenants living in the houses, but by non-resident landlords at prices significantly under the market value.

236 ECtHR Case of James and Others v. United Kingdom (Application no. 8793/79) Judgment of 21 February 1986, para 69.

237 The Order complained of in the Case of Pinnacle Meat Processors v. United Kingdom (Application no. 33298/96) European Commission on Human Rights Decision of 21 October 1998, inter alia, targeted the production and sale of meat stemming from those body parts of cattle considered to be more likely to contain prion proteins, which spread the bovine spongiform encephalopathy. See the more detailed description of the case above at footnote 62.

238 Case of Pinnacle Meat Processors v. United Kingdom (Application no. 33298/96) European Commission on Human Rights Decision of 21 October 1998.

Conversely, in the case of *Sporrong and Lönnroth v. Sweden* the ECtHR found a violation of the protection of property. The applicants' property was subjected to expropriation permits which the community could choose to use. Furthermore, there were prohibitions of construction on the property. The Court found that the combined effects constituted an "individual and excessive burden". The inflexibility of the underlying Swedish law together with the long time span for which the measures under consideration were enacted – during which the applicants were in "complete uncertainty as to the fate of their properties" – and the practical problems encountered had not been taken into consideration by the Swedish authorities.[239] The Court held that the measures created a situation which upset the fair balance between the right to property and the requirements of the general interest, so that the applicants bore an individual and excessive burden.[240]

These cases underline that for the ECtHR it is not the eradication of the economic benefit of the property as such which constitutes the excessive burden. Rather, the question is whether the individual owner is affected in excess by the impact the general measure has on other proprietors within its scope of application. However, in the context of investment law, it has been suggested that *bona fide* regulation eradicating the economic benefit of the investment would place too high a burden on the investor for it not to be compensated.[241] In my understanding, the complete annihilation of the economic value of the investment is a situation which is 'rare' in the sense that it deserves intense scrutiny.

The assumption that the complete eradication of the economic value of the investment through regulation furthering a public purpose constitutes expropriation is countered by the economic impact relevant for any finding of expropriation: A substantial economic deprivation is required in any instance of expropriation. The differences between 'substantial' and 'complete' eradication are small; they are arguably not significant enough to alter the whole appraisal of the measure. Is an investor whose investment is affected

---

239 ECtHR Case of Sporrong and Lönnroth v. Sweden (Application no. 7151/75; 7152/75) Judgment of 23 September 1982, paras. 70, 72.

240 ECtHR Case of Sporrong and Lönnroth v. Sweden (Application no. 7151/75; 7152/75) Judgment of 23 September 1982, para. 73.

241 *Paulsson*, Jan/*Douglas*, Zachary, 'Indirect Expropriation in Investment Treaty Arbitrations, Indirect Expropriation in Investment Treaty Arbitrations', in: Arbitrating Foreign Investment Disputes, Procedural and Substantive Legal Aspects (Horn, Norbert et al. (Eds.) 2004) 145 (158); *Fortier*, Yves L./*Drymer*, Stephen L., 'Indirect Expropriation in the Law of International Investment: I Know It When I See It, or Caveat Investor', 19 ICSID Review Foreign Investment Law Journal 2004, 293 (319–320); *Christie*, G.C., 'What Constitutes A Taking of Property under International Law?' 38 British Yearbook of International Law 1962, 307 (331–332).

to a very significant extent really in a situation that is fundamentally different from that of the other investor whose investment has completely lost its value? In my understanding, such an approach would render the whole differentiation between regulation and expropriation largely insignificant, as the core of the evaluation would be based on the economic loss.

However, the complete annihilation of the economic value of the investment certainly deserves particular attention. In my understanding, it depends on the respective circumstances whether the economic impact will tip the scale in favour of finding expropriation. The proportionality approach is an appropriate tool to take account of these factors. The idea expressed in the case law of the ECtHR – that the investor has to be affected in excess of the general negative consequences of the regulatory measure – can constitute a helpful distinguishing criterion. Generally, regulatory measures are unlikely to have a devastating effect on an investment or property. Nevertheless, when specific permits or licenses are revoked, the impact may be more substantial. Also, an investment activity which is diametrically opposed to the environmental objective the regulation aims to achieve could be more significantly affected. In these situations, the notion of unjust enrichment by the host state can give an indication: If the deprivation of the investor corresponds with an acquisition by the host state, expropriation is more likely.[242] On the other hand, an investor conducting business in a manner detrimental to society cannot expect its position to remain unaltered.[243] A balancing of different factors can help to determine whether one investor is expected to bear a special sacrifice.

---

242 *Newcombe*, Andrew, 'The Boundaries of Regulatory Expropriation in International Law', 20 ICSID Review Foreign Investment Law Journal 2005, 1–57 considers the notion of unjust enrichment of the host state as a generally relevant distinguishing criterion between expropriation and regulation, because the community should not unduly benefit at the expense of an individual (5, 7, 8, 13, 55). He equates the appropriation of property by the host state to reneging on contractual rights and commitments (13). Furthermore, he expresses the understanding that the host state cannot rely on police powers when it acquires property for public purposes (32).

In my understanding, the fact that the host state appropriates something is a relevant factor in a balancing exercise. However, I do not share the opinion that every revocation of a licence or permit should be considered as appropriation. Otherwise, the concept of expropriation would lose its exceptional character. Most economic activities – in a regulated environment – require permits. If any regulation resulting in restrictions on such permits constituted expropriation, the capacity of the state to regulate would be significantly restricted. In the end, this would place too strong an emphasis on the expectations and contractual rights of the investor.

243 *Fortier*, Yves L./*Drymer*, Stephen L., 'Indirect Expropriation in the Law of International Investment: I Know It When I See It, or Caveat Investor', 19 ICSID Review Foreign Investment Law Journal 2004, 293 (298).

V. Evaluating Summary

Despite a wealth of academic commentary on the assessment of the borders between regulation and expropriation, there is not a definite approach to distinguishing the two concepts. The idea supported in this study focuses on the understanding that a non-discriminatory regulatory measure, which was adopted in accordance with due process to further a public purpose, does generally not constitute expropriation. A scrutiny of the measure is only necessary in circumstances which can be described as 'rare', such as when the entire economic value of the investment is eradicated. In a case which is unusual in this sense, the specific elements of the situation should be assessed in a balancing exercise that pays particular attention to the proportionality of the respective measure.

This approach allows findings similar to those of the case-law portrayed above. The decisions in *Metalclad Corporation v. United Mexican States* and *Técnicas Medioambientales Tecmed, S.A. v. United Mexican States* concerned measures which did not live up to the requirements of due process, did not take account of the investment-backed expectations of the investor and – arguably – targeted specific investment projects. In contrast, general measures such as the prohibition on the use of lindane, underlying the decision in *Chemtura Corporation v. Government of Canada*, are not found to be expropriatory. The latter tribunal supported a differentiation between regulation and regulatory expropriation, which is similar to the approach supported in this study.

In practice, the most important hurdle to finding expropriation is the economic threshold. Few regulatory measures 'substantially deprive' foreign investors of their investment. The cases portrayed indicate that cases are problematic which involve the withholding or revocation of governmental authorisation to engage in a specific economic activity. When permits or similar authorisations are cancelled, the economic impact is likely to be significant. This was the case with the hazardous waste facilities in both *Metalclad Corporation v. United Mexican States* and *Técnicas Medioambientales Tecmed, S.A. v. United Mexican States*. In such situations, – unless the measure is implicated in violations of due process – the regulatory measure deserves specific scrutiny, because of the possibly intense impact on one individual investor. The arising issues can be competently addressed with the proportionality approach.

Furthermore, the relevance for states to base their environmental regulatory measures on a scientific risk assessment which is grounded in scientific evidence cannot be overstated. Scientific risk assessment and risk management clearly emphasise the relevance of the measure for fulfilling the alleged public purpose. Investment tribunals have so far accepted scientific evidence supporting regulatory measures, even if the findings were not indisputable. Accordingly, expropriation was not found in cases fulfilling these requirements, whereas the measures in *Metalclad Corporation v. United Mexican States* and *Técnicas Medioambientales Tecmed, S.A. v. United Mexican States* were not expressly based on scientific evidence. In this light, the evaluation of the protection area created for rare cacti in *Metalclad Corporation v. United Mexican States* could have been different, if the implementing decree had been the result of a scientific risk assessment.

The different – but not mutually exclusive – approaches portrayed to determine the dividing line between regulatory measures and expropriation should be seen as different pieces of the same puzzle. Undeniably, in the assessment of whether a measure constitutes expropriation, the economic impact on the foreign investor is to be balanced with the police powers of the host state and the state's capacity to adopt regulatory measures that may negatively affect foreign investment. In this sense, the proportionality approach is an appropriate tool to evaluate the specific circumstances of each case. Whether investment tribunals applying the approach would accord host states the rather wide margin of appreciation regarding the purpose and means of the enacted measure that the ECtHR recognises for national states is open to debate. In any case, the application of the proportionality approach would not negate the relevance of the border between regulation and expropriation, as established above. This drawing of a line would allow the exclusion of certain measures from the scope of further scrutiny.

E. Application of Criteria to Different Scenarios

The criteria developed above for distinguishing regulation from expropriatory measures are now applied to the notions of potential conflicts, as portrayed in the first chapter of this study. The aim of this application to the specific scenarios is to give an indication of potential conflicts, not to establish a comprehensive overview.

I. Scenario No 1: Introduction and Application of Environmental Regulation

The situations embraced in the first scenario deal with the classical conflict between environmental regulation and the protection against expropriation. The investor complains that the environmental measure has such an intense impact on its investment that it constitutes expropriation.

1. Permits and Environmental Restrictions

The foreign investor has to hold the relevant environmental permits to undertake its planned investment activity in the host state. The state can interfere with the activity by either not granting the relevant permit or by withdrawing or not renewing the permit.

If the intended investment project cannot be started due to lack of the relevant environmental permits, there may not be a developed 'investment' that has been affected. However, as the complaint in *Pac Rim Cayman LLC v. Republic of El Salvador* demonstrates,[244] the investor can have invested significant sums to conduct expensive test drillings or undertake environmental impact assessment studies. Accordingly, the first issue that has to be determined is whether the denial of the permit constitutes a 'taking of the investment'. Even if the concept of 'investment' is broadly understood, it may be difficult – depending on the specific factual situation – to consider futile preparatory work as relevant investment. If a site or relevant material has been acquired, an investment has undoubtedly been made, which has to be protected. In such a case, all the factors leading to the denial of the permit have to be taken into consideration. At the outset, the investment activity has to meet the respective requirements set forth in the national law. The relevant national law has to meet the standards of procedural propriety set forth above. In this context, it has to be kept in mind that the host state is free to set a specific environmental standard in its national laws. If the national law meets these standards and is properly applied to the case of the investor, the denial of the permit will not constitute expropriation.

The second situation relates to the withdrawal of a permit for environmental reasons. In such a situation, the investor has commenced its investment activity. The withdrawal of a position that had previously been granted, substantially changes the business situation of the investor. The withdrawal of the permit can lead to the economic endeavour being no longer possible or economically viable. If, for example, an investor owning a site wants to extract mineral resources, but no longer holds the permit to do so, it is possible that the investor is substantially deprived of its investment, meeting the high economic threshold. The decision in *Técnicas Medioambientales Tecmed, S.A. v. United Mexican States* emphasises this point. Alternative uses of such a site, which has been used for an environmentally degrading activity, will often be infeasible.

In such a case, it is the task of an investment tribunal to evaluate whether the withdrawal of the permit was in fact a *bona fide* application of the

[244] Pac Rim Cayman LLC v. Republic of El Salvador, ICSID Case No. ARB/09/12, Notice of Arbitration of 30 April 2009, para 91.

national laws. Of course, permits can be revoked, especially if the regulated economic undertakings violate legal requirements or do no longer fulfil the relevant environmental criteria. Furthermore, the state has the right to make the environmental requirements for granting a permit more onerous. Accordingly, the criteria set forth above to determine the nature of the governmental measure have to be assessed. Does the withdrawal reflect a non-discriminatory strategy which is adopted in line with the principles of due process? Are changes in the requirements for granting the permit based on scientific assessments? If these questions are answered in the affirmative, the investor has not been specifically targeted and a balancing of the opposing interests will generally not consider the withdrawal of the permit to constitute expropriation.

The question whether the alleged withdrawal of permits constitutes expropriation is likely to remain a relevant issue in future investment decisions. The investor in the pending proceedings in *Lone Pine Resources Inc. v. The Government of Canada*, for example, argues that the revocation of its permits and approvals to mine for oil and gas constitutes expropriation. The province of Québec introduced, inter alia, a bill to limit certain shale gas exploration and production activities.[245] Similarly, the investor in the pending proceedings in *Infinito Gold Ltd. v. Costa Rica* claims that it had acquired all permits for the development of a gold mine project, but that the value of this investment had been expropriated by the withdrawal of the exploitation concession and the host state's moratorium on open-pit gold mining.[246] Also, in the pending – but confidential – case *Vattenfall AB and others v. Federal Republic of Germany*,[247] which concerns the phase-out of nuclear energy production in the host state, the termination of operating permits of the investor is likely to be relevant.

2. Introduction of Environmental Restrictions After Investment Was Placed

There is potential for conflicts between the protection against expropriation and environmental regulation that is introduced after the investment has been made. However, the criteria set forth above emphasise, that expropriation can only be found when the threshold of 'substantial' economic deprivation is reached. In practical terms, this means that the value of the prop-

245 Lone Pine Resources Inc. v. The Government of Canada, Notice of Arbitration of 6 September 2013, paras 35, 36, 46, 48 *et seq.*

246 Infinito Gold Ltd. v. Costa Rica, ICSID Case No. ARB/14/5, Request for Arbitration of 6 February 2014, paras 31, 80, 98.

247 See footnote 243 in 'Chapter 4 – Standards of Fair Treatment'.

erty or the investor's respective control is practically annihilated. General regulation adopted for environmental purposes will not interfere with the investor's control over its investment. Furthermore, such laws are very unlikely to have a sufficiently detrimental economic effect.

A possible example is the imposition of emission targets. In introducing emission controls or reducing allowances, the host state creates additional environmental obligations for the investor. While such restrictions are likely to increase the costs of production, they leave the property of the investor intact. Even if the investment activity were no longer economically viable, the environmental restriction would not constitute expropriation, because it would not reach the threshold of significance.

The environmental restriction could also take the form of a cap-and-trade system like the European Emissions Trading Scheme. This way, the process of phasing out of specific substances is coupled with an incentive model. Either way, it is obvious that the introduction of such a scheme constitutes a change of the economic conditions underlying the investment.[248] These changes, however, are unlikely to rise to a level that meets the required economic threshold. In a decision concerning the national allocation plan for the European Emissions Trading Scheme, the Belgian Arbitration Court found that the imposition of a quota regime did not prejudice the property right of the owner of the installation.[249] It is very likely that an investment tribunal charged with deciding on the expropriating effect of such a scheme would reach a similar conclusion. Like the protection of property, the protection against expropriation would not be breached: The substance of the installations as well as their functionality remains intact. Accordingly, climate protection policies are unlikely to deprive even the owners of carbon-intensive assets of a substantial part of their investment.[250]

---

248 *Boute*, Anatole, 'Combating Climate Change and Securing Electricity Supply: The Role of Investment Protection Law', 16 European Environmental Law Review 2007, 227 (231).

249 Cour d'Arbitrage Belge, Arrêt N° 92/2006, Decision of 7 June 2006, rejecting the request to annul the decree of the Walloon region of 10 November 2004, Moniteur Belge of 23 June 2006, p. 32159 (B.16). The Belgian Court further held that the Scheme pursued a double legitimate objective, namely the reduction of European greenhouse gas emissions in an economically efficient and cost-effective manner. Accordingly, the environmental objective contributed to a high public interest.

250 Similarly, *Boute*, Anatole, 'The Potential Contribution of International Investment Protection Law to Combat Climate Change', 27 Journal of Energy & Natural Resources Law 2009, 333 (368–369); *Johnson*, Lise, 'International Investment Agreements and Climate Change: The Potential for Investor-State Conflicts and Possible Strategies for Minimizing It', 39 Environmental Law Reporter News & Analysis 2009, 39 Envtl. L. Rep. News & Analysis 11147 (11152).

Another example that is relevant in the context of environmental restrictions relates to restrictions on the use of land owned by an investor. These could be restrictions on the building activity in a stretch of land, because endangered species use the area for nesting. Imposing severe restrictions can practically lead to the land becoming devoid of economic use. In such a situation, the restrictions substantially reduce the value of the property, so that the measure may reach the relevant economic threshold. In evaluating the measure, it would first be relevant to assess if the restrictions were adopted in a non-discriminatory way that respected the requirements of due process. If this was the case, a balancing exercise of the opposing interests, which should take account of the proportionality of the measure, should be applied. The environmental objective, especially its rooting in science and its determination through an environmental impact assessment would be important. If the restrictions were not sufficiently based on scientific considerations, it could be likely that they were intended to disguise a direct taking of the property. However, if the process of implementation and the environmental assessment of the measure were genuine, the restriction would be more likely to be non-compensable regulation. The entirety of the factors indicates whether the restrictions impose a special sacrifice on the investor, for which there should be compensation.

II. Scenario No 2: Introduction of Scheme Supporting Environmentally Friendly Investments as Potential Violation of Other Investments

In the light of the criteria established for an environmental measure constituting expropriation of investment, it is rather obvious that the granting of subsidies to some investors is no expropriation of other investors. Such subsidies do not significantly interfere with the investment of the other investors: The investors retain control over their investments and – consequently – are not deprived of the economic value. That the subsidy potentially makes the competitors more competitive, does not constitute expropriation. Accordingly, in my understanding, this scenario can never be considered expropriatory.

III. Scenario No 3: Alterations to a Scheme Supporting Environmentally Friendly Investments

The third scenario concerns alterations to schemes that have been implemented to induce investment in environmentally friendly technologies after these investments have been made. When the investor relies on a scheme to financially support its investment, the non-payment of the agreed assistance has implications for the value of the investment. As portrayed in prior chapters, guaranteed tariffs for energy produced in an environmental advantageous or renewable way are examples of such schemes. The non-payment of the guaranteed tariffs can result in the investment activity not being economically viable.

The issue whether unilateral changes to tariff structures constitute expropriation has been discussed in a multitude of investment decisions – in connection with changes to agreed tariff structures for public utilities in Argentina. Even though the changes in this specific context did not promote environmental objectives, the awards are telling. They indicate that the violation or denial of contractually agreed rights in itself does not equal expropriation under the protective standard of an investment treaty. The changes to a tariff structure are unlikely to reach the economic threshold for expropriation. In cases relating to Argentinean utility tariffs, investment tribunals found that changes or interference with tariff structures, even coupled with other measures that were unhelpful for the investment, did not reach the threshold of expropriation.[251] In such a situation, the economic impact is generally not sufficient, because the investor remains in control of its investment – even if the management of the investment is partly affected. Likewise, the tribunal in *Nykomb Synergetics Technology Holding AB v. Latvia* swiftly dismissed the claim of the investor that the non-payment of agreed tariffs for energy produced by way of co-generation constituted indirect expropriation. The tribunal focused on the investor's continued possession of the investor of its investment, since neither assets had been taken, nor shareholders' rights or the control of the management over the investment had been interfered with.[252]

---

[251] Azurix v. Argentine Republic, ICSID Case No. ARB/01/12, Award of 14 July 2006, para 322; CMS Gas Transmission Company v. The Argentine Republic, ICSID Case No. ARB/01/8, Award of 12 May 2005, paras 263–264; LG&E v. Argentina, ICSID Case No. ARB/02/1, Decision on Liability of 3 October 2006, paras 198–200; Enron Corporation and Ponderosa Assets, L.P. v. Argentine Republic, ICSID Case No. ARB/01/3, Award of 22 May 2007, para 236; Sempra Energy International v. The Argentine Republic, ICSID Case No. ARB/02/16, Award of 28 September 2007, paras 285–286; National Grid plc v. The Argentine Republic, Award of 3 November 2008, para 155.

In contrast, the decision in Compañiá de Aguas del Aconquija S.A. and Vivendi Universal v. Argentine Republic, ICSID Case No. ARB/97/3, Award of 20 August 2007, paras 7.5.28–7.5.34, which found expropriation, did not concern alterations to a tariff structure and the complete opposition of the province to the privatisation of water distribution and its implication were considered expropriatory.

[252] Nykomb Synergetics Technology Holding AB v. Latvia, Arbitration Institute of the Stockholm Chamber of Commerce (ECT), Award of 16 December 2003, para 4.3.1.

It follows from these cases that a change of tariff structures is unlikely to constitute expropriation, even if it goes hand in hand with other measures negatively affecting the investment. In the light of the parameters set forth above, it is my understanding that this would be the case even if the withdrawal of the support system affected the economic viability of the investment.[253] The economic threshold for finding expropriation is very high and is not reduced depending on the societal reason for which the tariff was promised. Furthermore, investors will generally not lose control over their investment, which also speaks against the finding of expropriation.

Another example is the creation of emission credits through schemes supporting environmentally advantageous investments. Alterations in the scheme that result in substantial changes to the amount of emission credits allocated, for example, to the Joint Implementation or Clean Development Mechanism projects can have a negative impact on the profitability of the respective investment. Even if the financial support that the emission credits represent constitutes an important pillar of the economic viability of the investment, such alteration is unlikely to meet the threshold of expropriation. The investor remains in control of its investment which is not annihilated, even if the generated amount of emission credits is reduced. Accordingly, such changes are unlikely to amount to an indirect expropriation; the control over, and the value of, the investment being most certainly not annulled.[254]

The assessment may lead to a different result, if the scheme to which the carbon credits owe their value is abandoned altogether. In such a scenario, the investment in credits has lost all economic value. In line with the approach set forth above, the abandonment of the scheme has to be scrutinised as to its non-discriminatory nature and its observance of due process. Furthermore, the interest of the investor has to be balanced against the reasons for the abandonment of the scheme. For investors that did not generate credits as part of their investment activity, but that purchased carbon credits as their investment activity, the complete abandonment of the trading scheme would completely devalue the investment and could therefore constitute expropriation.[255] Since carbon credits have no inherent value in the absence of a functioning system, an investor in the credits would be com-

---

253 Similarly, *Boute*, Anatole, 'The Potential Contribution of International Investment Protection Law to Combat Climate Change', 27 Journal of Energy & Natural Resources Law 2009, 333 (362).

254 Similarly, *Boute*, Anatole, 'The Potential Contribution of International Investment Protection Law to Combat Climate Change', 27 Journal of Energy & Natural Resources Law 2009, 333 (363).

255 Finding such an abandonment of a scheme to constitute expropriation, *Bennett*, Lisa, 'Are tradable Carbon Emissions Investments? Characterization and

pletely deprived of its investment. This fact strongly alludes to the expropriatory nature of the cancellation of such a scheme.

IV. Scenario No 4: Withdrawal of Support Scheme Because Investment Affects the Environmental Objective

Like the third scenario, the fourth scenario relates to changes made to a scheme adopted to support environmentally friendly investments. In this scenario, however, the alterations to the scheme are implemented, because the support system has a detrimental effect on the environment. As far as the portrayal in Scenario No 3 has not identified a potential expropriation, namely because the economic deprivation of the investor did not reach the relevant threshold, the current scenario comes to the same conclusion. The withdrawal of a tariff originally offered to energy produced in a purportedly environmentally friendly manner or the restriction of the generation of carbon credits do not substantially deprive the owner of its investment, irrespective of the reason for which the changes were implemented.

With regard to investment in carbon credits and the subsequent cancellation of the underlying trading scheme, the assessment requires balancing of the opposing interests. If the cancellation of the scheme were a non-discriminatory regulatory measure that was adopted in line with due process to further an environmental objective – namely not subsidising an increase in greenhouse gas emissions – the measure would only be considered expropriatory in rare circumstances. In determining if this was such a rare situation, a balancing exercise of the relevant factors would shed light on the question of whether the economic loss the investor had to sustain singled the investor out in a way that demanded it to make a special sacrifice. In such a situation, the specific environmental damage that the sustained scheme was causing would constitute a significant element of the overall assessment. Accordingly, the abandonment of the scheme could be found not to constitute expropriation, despite its significant impact on the investor.[256]

Ramifications under International Investment Law', 85 New York University Law Review 2010, 1581 (1602).

[256] *Contra*, *Bennett*, Lisa, 'Are tradable Carbon Emissions Investments? Characterization and Ramifications under International Investment Law', 85 New York University Law Review 2010, 1581 (1604). Bennett recognises the possible impact of the public purpose the cancellation of the scheme could further (1603), but believes that a tribunal employing a balancing approach would "probably" find expropriation.

F. Compensation

The fourth element of lawful expropriation is – as has been mentioned above – the payment of compensation. If the host state has foreseen the payment of compensation, the tribunal has to decide whether the amount is appropriate. In practice, it is likely that the amount of compensation granted by the host state is lower than the amount the investor considers satisfactory. In the practically more relevant case of indirect expropriation, the host state has generally not connected the measure to the payment of expropriation. In such cases, the investment tribunal has to determine the appropriate level of compensation. The identification of the appropriate amount of compensation is difficult in any real case. However, in this study the debate is restricted to discussing the basic features of the criterion of compensation in the context of environmental expropriation. To this end, this section will set forth the general parameters which guide the level of compensation and specifically discuss whether the environmental purpose for adopting the expropriatory measure influences the payable amount.

I. Compensation Standard for Lawful Expropriation

The debate as to the accurate level of compensation for expropriation in international law has been largely shaped by the formula of 'prompt, adequate and effective'[257] compensation. Irrespective of discussions about the legitimacy and the impact of expropriation and nationalisation in the decades following decolonisation within the international community,[258] the 'prompt, adequate and effective'-formula is contained in a multitude of bilateral investment treaties.[259] Even though the formula may not accurately reflect the standard of compensation in customary international law,[260] – an

---

[257] This exact wording of the obligation for payment of compensation stems from a note sent by U.S. Secretary of State Cordell Hull to Mexico in August 1938. See, for historical context, *Sornarajah*, M., The International Law on Foreign Investment (2010), p. 414 and *Lowenfeld*, Andreas F., International Economic Law (2008) pp. 475–481.

[258] *Lowenfeld*, Andreas F., International Economic Law (2008) pp. 481–493. See also *Sornarajah*, M., The International Law on Foreign Investment (2010) pp. 413 *et seq*.

[259] See, for example, Article 6 para 1 lit c, paras 2–4 2004 U.S. Model BIT; Article 13 paras 1–4 2004 Canada Model BIT; Article 10.7 para 1 lit c, paras 2–4 CAFTA-DR; Article 5 para 2 2006 France Model BIT.

[260] Shahin Shane Ebrahimi, Cecilia Radene Ebrahimi, Christina Tandis Ebrahimi v. Government of the Islamic Republic of Iran, Award of 12 October 1994, Award No. 560-44/46/47-3, 30 Iran-US CTR 170 para 88; see for an overview of international decisions and adopted resolutions promulgating a different view: *Levy*, Tali,

issue which is outside the scope of this study – its widespread use in investment treaties shows that the formula is accepted even by states that previously opposed it.[261] Few investment treaties require a different standard.[262] Apparently, and not surprisingly, states seeking to attract foreign investment are nowadays prepared to accept the threefold standard in the protective treaties they conclude.

Compensation is 'prompt', when it is paid without unnecessary delay and it is 'effective' when it is paid in an easily transferable currency.[263] Even though these elements may be disputed in a specific case, they have no inherent connection to environmental reasons for the expropriation. In contrast, the 'adequateness' of compensation, which relates to the amount of compensation to be paid, could arguably be influenced by considerations stemming from the reasoning behind the motivation for the expropriatory measure. Accordingly, the adequateness of compensation deserves further scrutiny.

II. Adequateness of Compensation

According to the general understanding, an adequate compensation results in payment of the fair market value of the investment immediately prior to the expropriating act.[264] The fair market value is an assessment of the value of the property from the independent perspective of a third party, objectively derived from comparable data on market transactions and profitability estimates.[265] It reflects the sum that an informed, not pressured third

---

'NAFTA's Provisions for Compensation in the Event of Expropriation: A Reassessment of the "Prompt, Adequate and Effective" Standard', 31 Stanford Journal of International Law 1995, 423 (433 *et seq*).

261 See for an evaluation of the altered position of Mexico: *Levy*, Tali, 'NAFTA's Provisions for Compensation in the Event of Expropriation: A Reassessment of the "Prompt, Adequate and Effective" Standard', 31 Stanford Journal of International Law 1995, 423 (424–429, 441 *et seq*).

262 See, for example, Article 5 para 1 UK-India BIT which refers to 'fair and equitable' compensation instead.

263 *Griebel*, Jörn, Internationales Investitionsrecht (2008) p. 77.

264 PCIJ Case Concerning the Factory at Chorzów (Germany/Poland) Judgment of 13 September 1928, (Series A, No 17, 3) (47); *Marboe*, Irmgard, Calculation of Compensation and Damages in International Investment Law (2009), paras 2.69, 2.98; *Merrill*, Thomas W., 'Incomplete Compensation for Takings', 11 New York University Environmental Law Journal 2002, 110 (113); *Wälde*, Thomas W./*Sabahi*, Borzu, 'Compensation, Damages, and Valuation' in: The Oxford Handbook of International Investment Law (Muchlinski, Peter et al. (Eds.) 2008) 1049 (1070, 1081). For a specific reference in treaties, see, for example, Article 6 paras 2–4 2004 U.S. Model BIT; Article 13 para 2 2004 Canada Model BIT.

265 *Marboe*, Irmgard, Calculation of Compensation and Damages in International Investment Law (2009) paras 2.97, 2.99.

party would be willing to pay for the property. When determining the 'adequateness' of compensation, tribunals thus intend to establish an objective valuation of the expropriated property.[266]

Even though the terms of 'compensation' and 'damages' are often used interchangeably, compensation – as one requirement for lawful expropriation – should be distinguished from damages that have to be paid for a violation of international law or a breach of contract. The function of compensation is "the replacement of the value of the expropriated property", whereas damages intend to constitute "full reparation of the damage incurred".[267] These differences can influence the methodology for determining the amount the state has to pay. Accordingly, 'adequate compensation' for lawful expropriation does not necessarily equal 'damages', which a host state would have to pay for unlawful expropriation or the breach of another obligation contained in the investment treaty.[268] In the context of determining compensation, the financial situation of the expropriated investor is not compared to the hypothetical situation in which the investor would have been in the absence of expropriation. Rather, the value of the expropriated property is compensated.

The valuation of the compensation derives from an objective and abstract assessment of data and estimates available, so that the subjective perspective of the investor is not decisive. There are different practical methods to determine the level of compensation. The data available in the specific case determines the extent to which speculative elements influence the process

---

266 See, for example, the tribunal in Marion Unglaube and Reinhard Unglaube v. Republic of Costa Rica, ICSID Case No. ARB/08/1, ICSID Case No. ARB/09/20, Award of 16 May 2012, para 309, which expresses the need to establish the "highest and best use subject to all pertinent legal, physical, and economic contraints". In that case, this meant not to rely on high density usage appropriate to a large city, but rather on "usage appropriate to the environmentally-sensitive surroundings".

267 *Marboe*, Irmgard, Calculation of Compensation and Damages in International Investment Law (2009) para 2.96. See also Article 31 of the Draft Articles on State Responsibility, which sets forth the state's obligation to make "full reparation" for any injury caused by an international wrongful act.

268 In footnote 15 above it is suggested that every indirect expropriation is an unlawful expropriation for failure to provide for the payment of compensation. While this is convincing with regard to acts which use a regulatory or creeping element to disguise their expropriatory nature, such a verdict appears less straightforward in light of the difficult process of determining the distinguishing line between regulation and expropriation. In the absence of a clear-cut distinction between regulation and expropriation, an act cannot be classified as intrinsically 'unlawful' if it fulfilled all the criteria of a lawful expropriation, except for the payment of compensation. In cases, in which the line is so difficult to draw, such understanding would place a significant burden onto the host state. For this discussion, such expropriatory acts will accordingly not be considered 'unlawful'.

of valuation. The method that is most widely used – to determine both compensation and damages – currently appears to be the discounted cash flow method ("DCF").[269] DCF is based on the idea that the value of an enterprise is determined by "forecasting and discounting the cash flows" it generates.[270] Other methods relied on by tribunals are the book value of the investment as a going concern and the amount invested.[271] In the context of compensation for lawful expropriation, a tribunal typically does not award *lucrum cessans* – lost profits.[272] This is a method for awarding damages which are to be differentiated from the commercial value of the property that is to be compensated as fair market value.[273]

The adjective 'adequate' arguably leaves room for interpretation. While it is not as wide as 'appropriate', adequateness describes a concept which –

---

269 *Simmons*, Joshua B., 'Valuation in Investor-State Arbitration: Toward a More Exact Science', 30 Berkley Journal of International Law 2012, 196 (224 *et seq*). Simmons, however, perceives inconsistency and hesitation in tribunals regarding the use of the DCF method (226–233). See also LG&E v. Argentina, ICSID Case No. ARB/02/1, Award of 25 July 2007, paras 34–35, which explicitly considers the DCF method to be the correct validation method in cases of expropriation. See, for a succinct overview of the issues considered in a DCF valuation, *Smutny*, Abby Cohen, 'Some Observations on the Principles Relating to Compensation in the Investment Treaty Context', 22 ICSID Review Foreign Investment Law Journal 2007, 1 (11–12).

270 *Simmons*, Joshua B., 'Valuation in Investor-State Arbitration: Toward a More Exact Science', 30 Berkley Journal of International Law 2012, 196 (222). See also *Wälde*, Thomas W./*Sabahi*, Borzu, 'Compensation, Damages, and Valuation' in: The Oxford Handbook of International Investment Law (Muchlinski, Peter et al. (Eds.) 2008) 1049 (1074).

271 *Simmons*, Joshua B., 'Valuation in Investor-State Arbitration: Toward a More Exact Science', 30 Berkley Journal of International Law 2012, 196 (223–224). Simmons emphasises that these two methods on their own do not lead to a determination of the fair market value. See also the overview of methods given by *Wälde*, Thomas W./*Sabahi*, Borzu, 'Compensation, Damages, and Valuation' in: The Oxford Handbook of International Investment Law (Muchlinski, Peter et al. (Eds.) 2008) 1049 (1062–1063) and the principles set forth in the World Bank Guildelines on the Treatment of Foreign Direct Investment (1992), IV para 6 (available at: http://italaw.com/documents/WorldBank.pdf).

272 Shahin Shane Ebrahimi, Cecilia Radene Ebrahimi, Christina Tandis Ebrahimi v. Government of the Islamic Republic of Iran, Award of 12 October 1994, Award No. 560-44/46/47-3, 30 Iran-US CTR 170, para 96.

273 *Wälde*, Thomas W./*Sabahi*, Borzu, 'Compensation, Damages, and Valuation' in: The Oxford Handbook of International Investment Law (Muchlinski, Peter et al. (Eds.) 2008) 1049 (1067). Similarly, *Simmons*, Joshua B., 'Valuation in Investor-State Arbitration: Toward a More Exact Science', 30 Berkley Journal of International Law 2012, 196 (222–223); *Ripinsky*, Sergey/*Williams*, Kevin, Damages in International Investment Law (2008) p. 279; *Smutny*, Abby Cohen, 'Some Observations on the Principles Relating to Compensation in the Investment Treaty Context', 22 ICSID Review Foreign Investment Law Journal 2007, 1 (15–16).

other than the adjectives 'full' or 'complete' – arguably contains an element of appraisal. The issue that will be more closely looked at is whether the concept leaves room for societal factors influencing the amount of compensation. Can an environmental justification for expropriation influence or annihilate the compensation to be paid by the host state?

III. Potential Influence of Societal Factors on Level of Compensation

All lawful expropriations are undertaken to further a public purpose. However, as has been seen above,[274] the standard against which the public purpose is assessed is not a very stringent one. Furthering an environmental objective is arguably more laudable than pursuing other motives, especially because the environmental benefit is very likely not to be restricted to the territory or interest of the host state.[275] Since the issue of whether a measure is considered a taking or not ultimately boils down to the question of who has to bear the cost of the government policy – society at large or the investor – one might ask whether the 'all-or-nothing'-solution that investment law seems to offer is appropriate.

The societal reasons for which the property has been expropriated, may influence the level of compensation that is considered 'adequate'. It has been suggested that in cases in which there is a preponderant public interest in the taking, especially if the expropriation is motivated by environmental treaty commitments, tribunals should consider waiving the obligation to compensate.[276] Legally, there could be a rebate for measures furthering internationally accepted environmental objectives. There could also be a reduction of the level of compensation deriving from the conflict between two opposing obligations. More practically, the environmental rules which prevent the continuation of the investment undertaking could influence the determination of the value of the expropriated enterprise. It will be tested in the following if these hypotheses are reflected in decisions in investment or other international law.

---

274 See above at pp. 304 *et seq.*

275 The interconnectedness of environmental matters and subject areas has been extensively portrayed in the 'Chapter 1 – Environmental Norms and Principles'.

276 *Sornarajah*, M., The International Law on Foreign Investment (2010) p. 389.

1. Investment Arbitration

The question of whether the public purpose underlying the expropriation of a certain asset can annihilate the obligation to pay compensation for the expropriating state was famously denied by the investment tribunal in *Compañía del Dessarollo de Santa Elena S.A. v. Republic of Costa Rica*. The tribunal, which had to determine the exact amount of compensation for an act of direct expropriation undertaken by the host state to protect wildlife,[277] stated the following:

> "While an expropriation or taking for environmental reasons may be classified as a taking for a public purpose, and thus may be legitimate, the fact that the Property was taken for this reason does not affect either the nature or the measure of the compensation to be paid for the taking. That is, the purpose of protecting the environment for which the Property was taken does not alter the legal character of the taking for which adequate compensation must be paid. The international source of the obligation to protect the environment makes no difference.
>
> Expropriatory environmental measures – no matter how laudable and beneficial to society as a whole – are, in this respect, similar to any other expropriatory measures that a state may take in order to implement its policies: where property is expropriated, even for environmental purposes, whether domestic or international, the state's obligation to pay compensation remains."[278]

The tribunal clearly expresses that it considers an expropriation for an environmental purpose not to be different from any other expropriation. It states that "the international source of the obligation to protect the environment" does not influence the obligation to compensate. The tribunal focuses on the determination of the measure as an expropriatory act – which is not in dispute – and sees no reason to distinguish it from any other expropriatory act.

The tribunal's approach has been criticised for demonstrating an alleged mind-set among arbitrators in investment cases which gives primacy to investment rules even if faced with significant environmental issues or host state obligations contained in environmental agreements.[279] Even though I doubt that the tribunal's finding should be understood in such a far-reaching manner, it leaves little interpretative scope for restricting the amount of

---

[277] The facts of the case have briefly been summarised above at pp. 303 *et seq.*

[278] Compañía del Dessarollo de Santa Elena S.A. v. Republic of Costa Rica, ICSID Case No. ARB/96/1, Award of 17 February 2000, paras 71–72.

[279] *Miles*, Kate, 'International Investment Law and Climate Change: Issues in the Transition to a Low-Carbon World', Society of International Economic Law, Working Paper No. 27/08, 2008, p. 19. The author further concludes that the approach taken by the tribunal suggests that "arbitral tribunals will give very little weight, if any, to global environmental objectives".

compensation because of the societal reasons for the expropriation of the property. It is clear that not every valid societal reason can lead to expropriation being non-compensable. Otherwise, the rights of the investor would be annihilated. However, the finding of the tribunal in *Compañía del Dessarollo de Santa Elena S.A. v. Republic of Costa Rica* that the international source of the obligation to protect the environment "makes no difference" appears overly simplistic. The importance of conciliating different obligations under international law with each other cannot be brushed aside all too easily. Since there is generally no hierarchy among several areas of international law, both sets of norms have to be consolidated in case of conflict. The award does not discuss whether any consolidation is due under the condition that both obligations do not exclude each other – as will always be the case if one is a payment obligation. The decision indicates that the payment obligation remains unaffected in any event.

Another investment tribunal similarly found that an international convention countering the investment did not exclude the expropriated investor's right to compensation. The tribunal in *Southern Pacific Properties (Middle East) Limited v. Arab Republic of Egypt* dealt with the cancellation of a contract between the state and the investor regarding the construction of hotel facilities in the plateau area of the Pyramids, which was found to amount to expropriation. Even though the tribunal held that the UNESCO Convention did not exclude the investor's right to compensation,[280] it found the international obligation to have a practical impact on the valuation of the property for the purpose of compensation. First, the tribunal refused to apply the DCF method for calculating the compensation owed to the investor for loss of the investment, because the project had not existed "for a sufficient period of time to generate the data necessary" for the calculation.[281] Second, the tribunal explicitly stated that the investor could not be awarded '*lucrum cessans*' – profits foregone – because the intended sale of lots would have been illegal in the future and the profits therefore illegitimate. The tribunal reasoned that

> "[... the] lot sales in the areas registered with the World Heritage Committee under the UNESCO Convention would have been illegal under both international law and Egyptian law after 1979, when the registration was made. Obviously, the allowance of lucrum cessans may only involve those profits which are legitimate. [...]
>
> Thus, [... the tribunal] could only award lucrum cessans until 1979, when the obligations resulting from the UNESCO Convention with respect to the Pyramids

---

280 Southern Pacific Properties (Middle East) Limited v. Arab Republic of Egypt, ICSID Case No. ARB/84/3, Award of 20 May 1992, para 154.

281 Southern Pacific Properties (Middle East) Limited v. Arab Republic of Egypt, ICSID Case No. ARB/84/3, Award of 20 May 1992, para 188.

> Plateau became binding on the Respondent. From that date forward, the Claimants' activities on the Pyramids Plateau would have been in conflict with the Convention and therefore in violation of international law, and any profits that might have resulted from such activities are consequently non-compensable.[282]

Accordingly, the tribunal found that profits which could only have been made in violation of international law could not be factored into the valuation of the expropriated property. Even though the specific calculation of *lucrum cessans* is not directly relevant for calculating compensation for lawful expropriation, the approach emphasises the relevance of other (international) obligations of the host state.

The findings of the tribunal, however, are only partly telling for the issue under discussion for the following two reasons: First, the tribunal awarded significant compensation to the investor, which encompassed all out-of-pocket expenses with interest and, further, compensation for the loss of opportunity to make a commercial success of the project.[283] The upcoming illegality of the project under international law did not meaningfully reduce the amount of compensation awarded to the investor. Second, it appears that few expropriations are based on obligations of international law which forbid an investment activity in such an explicit way. Environmental conventions rarely prohibit activities – specific actions or actions in specific locations – with the same precision as the UNESCO Convention does for designated sites.[284] Accordingly, such specific conflicts are rare. Nevertheless, the arbitral decision demonstrates that international obligations of the host state can constitute a relevant factor in the valuation of the expropriated property.

---

282 Southern Pacific Properties (Middle East) Limited v. Arab Republic of Egypt, ICSID Case No. ARB/84/3, Award of 20 May 1992, paras 190–191.

283 Southern Pacific Properties (Middle East) Limited v. Arab Republic of Egypt, ICSID Case No. ARB/84/3, Award of 20 May 1992, para 198 *et seq*. In total, the tribunal awarded over U.S. $ 27.6 million.

284 The tribunal in Santa Elena explicitly stated that it would not "analyse the detailed evidence submitted regarding what Respondent refers to as its international legal obligation to preserve the unique ecological site that is the Santa Elena Property". (Compañía del Dessarollo de Santa Elena S.A. v. Republic of Costa Rica, ICSID Case No. ARB/96/1, Award of 17 February 2000, footnote accompanying para 71). Presumably, irrespective of the actual environmental value of the property, there would not have been a prohibition as specific as the UNESCO Convention, since environmental law generally refers to certain habitat or types of landscape to be protected, but not to singular and precise sites for protection.

2. European Court of Human Rights

The ECtHR understands the obligation to compensate in the case of an expropriation of property in a more flexible manner. The Court has repeatedly found that the objective of the expropriation "may call for less than reimbursement of the market value".[285] The wide margin of discretion that the ECtHR grants to states, demands no more than a reasonable relationship between the value of the property and the compensation paid. However, the possible limitation of the compensation applies only to cases of lawful expropriation which are the result of measures implemented to achieve greater social justice.[286] In such cases, the ECtHR applies a lenient control of the adequacy of compensation, in which it only assesses whether the relationship between the value of the property taken and the compensation paid is manifestly disproportionate.[287] In cases, in which land is specifically taken, for example to construct something on it, the ECtHR does not accept a reduced level of payable compensation.[288]

It has been argued that the standard of 'adequate compensation' that the ECtHR applies does not result in less generous compensation than the standard required in international law.[289] However, for the context of investment arbitration, the approach of relying on a wide margin of appreciation concerning compensation does not appear helpful. From a legal perspective, it is clear that investment treaties do not give significant leeway to the host state with regard to the level of compensation. In contrast to the ECHR, which does not contain any reference to the compensation to be paid, investment treaties generally use specific language to define the level of the compensation. For this reason, the ECtHR may be more reluctant than investment tribunals to substitute the state's assessment of the 'adequacy' of

---

[285] ECtHR Case of Lithgow and Others v. United Kingdom (Application no. 9006/80; 9262/81; 9263/81; 9265/81; 9266/81; 9313/81; 9405/81) Judgment of 8 July 1986, para 121; ECtHR Case of James and Others v. United Kingdom (Application no. 8793/79) Judgment of 21 February 1986, para 56.

[286] *Ripinsky*, Sergey/ *Williams*, Kevin, Damages in International Investment Law (2008) p. 82.

[287] *Ruiz Fabri*, Hélène, 'The Approach Taken by the European Court of Human Rights to the Assessment of Compensation for "Regulatory Expropriations" of the Property of Foreign Investor', 11 New York University Environmental Law Journal 2002, 148 (166).

[288] *Ripinsky*, Sergey/ *Williams*, Kevin, Damages in International Investment Law (2008) p. 82.

[289] *Ruiz Fabri*, Hélène, 'The Approach Taken by the European Court of Human Rights to the Assessment of Compensation for "Regulatory Expropriations" of the Property of Foreign Investor', 11 New York University Environmental Law Journal 2002, 148 (173).

the payable compensation with its own assessment. From a practical perspective, the host state will frequently not have used its margin of appreciation: In the particularly relevant cases of indirect expropriation, the host state may not consider the measure to constitute expropriation so that it will not have proposed a validation – leaving the investment tribunal without a value to compare in terms of proportionality. Nevertheless, the understanding that expropriatory measures not aiming at the acquisition of property, but intended to further societal aims for the good of society may require a reduced level of compensation is a relevant proposition.

3. Decisions of the Iran-U.S. Claims Tribunal

The decisions of the Iran-U.S. claims tribunal did not have to take account of a specific societal motive guiding the expropriation or of international obligations inducing the decision to expropriate. The cases concerned the nationalisation or taking of property in the wake of the Iranian Revolution. However, the decisions emphasise the necessity to take account of the social and economic surroundings in which the expropriation took place for the evaluation of the compensation. Specifically, the "significant and negative impacts of the Iranian Revolution" are taken into account when assessing the market value of the property.[290] Similarly, one decision focuses on the need for the appropriate compensation to reflect the pertinent facts and circumstances of each case. It stresses that "changes in the general political, social, and economic conditions [...] might have affected the [...] business prospects" of the respective enterprise.[291]

The tribunal's approaches express the understanding that the value of an investment depends, inter alia, on the economic and political surroundings in which it is set.[292] If – for reasons unrelated to the expropriatory measure – the relevant market changes and the value of the property diminishes, the

---

290 Phelps Dodge International Corp. and Overseas Private Investment Corp. v. The Islamic Republic of Iran, Award of 19 March 1986, Award No. 217-99-2, 10 Iran-US CTR 121, para 30.

291 Shahin Shane Ebrahimi, Cecilia Radene Ebrahimi, Christina Tandis Ebrahimi v. Government of the Islamic Republic of Iran, Award of 12 October 1994, Award No. 560-44/46/47-3, 30 Iran-US CTR 170, paras 95, 107.

292 This understanding is also embraced by the investment tribunal in the decision American Manufacturing & Trading, Inc. v. Republic of Zaire, ICSID Case No. ARB/93/1, Award of 21 Februar 1997, para 7.15. The tribunal rejects the evaluation methods proposed by claimant, because that "would serve unjustly to enrich the investor who, rightly or wrongly, has chosen to invest in a country such as Zaire, believing that by so doing the investor is constructing a castle in Spain or a Swiss chalet in Germany without any risk, political or even economic or financial or any risk whatsoever".

adequate level of compensation shrinks as well. This understanding is also reflected in the idea of risk adjustment. Risk adjustment of the appropriate level of compensation should reflect, first, the probability of the occurrence of future events which constitute a risk for the investment and, second, the detrimental impact of the risk over an extended period, taking account of the probability that the risk materialises.[293] Accordingly, the adequate level of compensation is not static, but depends on the political, legal and economic conditions in the host state – and on the conditions that can be expected in the foreseeable future.

IV. Evaluation

The jurisprudence on the level of compensation to be paid for expropriatory acts in international law does not recognise an explicit reduction of the payable amount in cases of expropriation for reasons of environmental protection. This understanding is based on good arguments. First, every lawful expropriation is based on a public purpose. As has been shown above, this concept grants states significant leeway. However, if tribunals were meant to implicitly evaluate the societal character of the measure in the determination of the level of compensation, they would have the power to favour some public purposes over others. This would significantly reduce the clarity of the concept of expropriation. Second, taking account of societal factors in the valuation of the property would require a framework stipulating which and when societal factors had to be considered. Giving a tribunal unchecked leeway in that regard would lead to arbitrary decisions. Third, it has been shown above that the scope for finding – indirect – expropriation is rather limited in connection with environmental measures. Measures that genuinely and transparently pursue an environmental aim constitute indirect expropriation "only in rare circumstances". These rare circumstances are characterised by imposing a special sacrifice on the investor. Situations, which meet the threshold, require that the investor be compensated.

Nevertheless, the decisions emphasise that the valuation of the property for the purpose of compensation takes place in the market in the specific host state, which is bound to be influenced by surrounding legal, political and economic factors. By means of the valuation methods that are applied – such as DCF – foreseeable changes have to be taken into account which could lead to a reduction of the value of the property. Since future profitability is a factor in the assessment of the value, environmental restrictions

293 *Wälde*, Thomas W./*Sabahi*, Borzu, 'Compensation, Damages, and Valuation' in: The Oxford Handbook of International Investment Law (Muchlinski, Peter et al. (Eds.) 2008) 1049 (1077).

that prevent or will, in the foreseeable future, restrict the economic activity of the investment influence the determination and reduce the value of the investment. In this sense, there is no distinction between the surrounding factors and a restriction of the investment activity by an obligation of international law. In this context, the findings of the tribunal in *Southern Pacific Properties (Middle East) Limited v. Arab Republic of Egypt* are telling. If the intended investment activity would be illegal in the future, the value of the investment as a going concern is reduced.[294] Accordingly, the host state can indirectly influence the market within which the expropriated property is evaluated.

Regarding the level of compensation, one can finally ask whether environmental references in the investment treaty may reduce the level of payable compensation. The most interesting principle in that regard is the polluter-pays-principle.[295] This recognised principle of environmental law, which is explicitly mentioned in Article 19 paragraph 1 ECT, however, does not directly apply to a foreign investor. As Principle 16 of the 1992 Rio Declaration promulgates, the principle has to be incorporated into national law. If the host state has organised its national legal system in a way that it accords to the polluter-pays principle (or entails fines), obligations stemming from national environmental law can be made the subject of a counter-claim. Penalties that the investor would have to pay for breaches of national law can reduce the due compensation if they are demanded in a counter-claim.[296] This possibility, however, only exists on condition that the investor has incurred a penalty for polluting activity or breaching national environmental laws. The polluter-pays principle is not a broad concept that transcends concrete obligations.

V. Intermediate Summary

The hypothesis that the environmental justification for expropriating property directly reduces the payable compensation cannot be confirmed. A general rebate for promoting an environmental objective is not within the parameters of the valuation. Even if the expropriatory measure is adopted pursuant to an international environmental obligation of the state, no rule

[294] An example in the environmental sphere could concern measures which cancel licenses for the production of toxins. The effect has to be so substantial that they constitute expropriatory acts. In the valuation of the property, an upcoming international prohibition to use the toxin would have to be considered.

[295] See in 'Chapter 1 – Environmental Norms and Principles' at pp. 75 *et seq.*

[296] See generally for counter-claims, *Wälde*, Thomas W./*Sabahi*, Borzu, 'Compensation, Damages, and Valuation' in: The Oxford Handbook of International Investment Law (Muchlinski, Peter et al. (Eds.) 2008) 1049 (1098).

calling for a reduction of the payable compensation can be detected. The polluter-pays principle is a striking name, but has no impact unless it is incorporated into the national laws of the host state. If it is thoroughly implemented it can constitute the basis for a counter-claim by the host-state, thus reducing the payable compensation.

Still, the tribunal can indirectly take account of the environmental obligation as one surrounding element which influences the market value and consequently reduces the investment's future profitability. The investor bears the risk of such surrounding factor reducing the value of the investment. Political and legal changes, which reduce the profitability of an economic undertaking, are similarly relevant in the assessment of damages for a violation of other investment protection obligations.[297]

G. Conclusion

Out of all three major standards for the protection of foreign investors, which have been reviewed in this study – non-discrimination, fairness and expropriation – indirect expropriation for allegedly environmental reasons has received the greatest attention in scholarly writing and public opinion. However, the criteria for indirect expropriation as set forth in the relevant case law indicate that the potential for conflicts between the regulatory interest of the state and the property rights of the investor is rather limited.

Expropriation requires a substantial deprivation of the economic benefits or of control over the investment. Regulatory measures, not direct forms of taking, are the most likely means to further environmental objectives. In practice, regulatory measures which fulfil the requirements of lawful expropriation – namely the ones that are non-discriminatory and being enacted in line with due process — very rarely have such a significant economic impact on an investor. Nevertheless, in cases in which they do, there is no straightforward assessment of the dividing line between non-compensable regulation and compensable expropriation. The best starting point is to assume that environmental regulation, which is non-discriminatory and in line with

297 The calculation of damages for a violation of a standard of non-discrimination or the standard of fair and equitable treatment remains outside of the scope of this study. Nevertheless, the parameters determined in the context of compensation, according to which the surrounding factors determine the value of the investment and the possibility to make profits, also influence the assessment of damages in cases of a breach of the obligations. See for example American Manufacturing & Trading, Inc. v. Democratic Republic of the Congo, ICSID Case No. ARB/93/1, Award of 21 February 1997, 36 ILM (1997), 1534 where the general circumstances relating to the risk level in the host state were taken into consideration in the assessment (paras 7.15, 7.18).

due process, is expropriatory only in rare circumstances. To assess whether there is such a rare situation, all relevant factors, such as the regulating interest of the state and economic deprivation of the investor, have to be balanced against each other. If the balance of interest leans towards the side of the investor or if the analysis indicates a special sacrifice being imposed on the investor, an investment tribunal should find compensable expropriation.

The expropriation provisions of investment treaties are unlikely swords to strike down environmental regulation. The abstract question of whether the investor or the society at large has to pay the price for general environmental regulation is predominantly answered in favour of the state, if the regulation meets procedural standards. Even though the answer may be less straight forward regarding the withdrawal or denial of environmental permits, the protection against expropriation does not shield the investor that seeks economic opportunities in the host state from all risks associated with changing – environmental – laws.

Conclusion

Peace, development and environmental protection
are interdependent and indivisible.
Principle 25 Rio Declaration, 1992

This study indicates that measures adopted for environmental protection can generally be reconciled with the investment standards contained in bilateral and multilateral investment treaties. The scopes of the standards of investment protection do not constitute a barrier to the introduction of effective environmental measures and standards. Rather, when becoming a party to international investment treaties, the host state does retain a broad enough policy space. Investment tribunals – being the ultimate judges of the legitimacy of a measure in cases of conflict – respect the powers of the host state to adopt regulation intended to further environmental objectives. Accordingly, genuine environmental measures do not constitute a violation of the investment standards.

To reach this legal conclusion, the study has analysed how investment tribunals assess measures which were purportedly adopted by the host state to further environmental objectives, but were considered by investors to breach the standards of non-discrimination or fairness or to constitute expropriation. The findings that could be derived from the limited case law suggest that investment tribunals are determined to ascertain whether the respective measure has genuinely been adopted as a means to advance environmental protection. Tribunals thus focus on differentiating between *bona fide* regulation aimed at environmental protection and other measures which covertly further objectives contravening the treatment standards contained in applicable investment treaties. Whereas the exact elements of such determination differ with regard to each standard, the assessment is characterised by the same set of factors. This conclusion will summarise the legal findings derived from the standards under review, before turning to a more practical evaluation of the implications for host states. The chapter closes with an outlook on anticipated future procedural developments.

I. Legal Findings Derived from the Study

The evaluation of conflicts between environmental and investment protection, as found in investment awards indicates that the standards of investment protection are generally flexible enough to accept measures that a host state has adopted to genuinely further an environmental objective. The study has demonstrated that even though each standard requires different tests, the necessary assessment evolves around a common set of factors.

1. Relevant Findings for the Specific Standards

The assessment of standards prohibiting discrimination – i.e. the standards of national and most-favoured nation treatment as well as the prohibition against discriminatory measures – has demonstrated that these standards do not only protect the interests of foreign investors, but do also offer host states the necessary latitude to introduce measures legitimately furthering an environmental policy. The legitimacy of the environmental measure is primarily derived from the justification of the environmental measure, namely whether there is a legitimate environmental aim that the state intends to further and whether there is a sufficiently reasonable 'nexus' between the environmental objective and the measure.

Investment tribunals undertake a coherence review of the environmental aim. In practice, this means that the more closely the environmental objective which the host state purports to further mirrors internationally endorsed environmental objectives, the more likely an investment tribunal is to accept the measure as genuine. However, the requirements as to the strength of the 'nexus' between the environmental objective and the measure, are – in the light of the limited case law – not completely clear yet. In my opinion, an investment tribunal should exercise restraint when evaluating the strength of the nexus, as it will generally lack both the scientific knowledge and the information regarding the administrative processes in the host state to evaluate the merit of the respective measure. Similarly, it is not for a tribunal to evaluate whether the aopted measure constitutes the measure 'least disruptive' of international investment. Accordingly, the reasonableness of the nexus between the objective and the measure should only be subjected to a coherence review.

The investment decisions analysed in this study have demonstrated that tribunals can also perceive the standard of non-discrimination as offering an uncomplicated way around assessing environmental issues in detail. The choice of the elements that are compared can be used – depending on the facts of the case – to consider that the investors, which are allegedly treated differently, are not in a 'like situation'. In my opinion, such an easy approach should not be chosen, as it does not address the concern voiced by the investor. In contrast, a different approach is to be welcomed, which concludes that two similar investments are not in 'like circumstances' if they result in differing environmental impacts. Understood in this way, the comparison of the investments offers ample opportunity to factor in the environmental impact of investment projects. Whether an investment tribunal finds that the environmental consequences of one investment are so strikingly different from those of a similar investment that they are not in a like situation, will be influenced by a myriad of factors in each specific case.

The assessment of the standards of fairness – most notably the standard of fair and equitable treatment – has shown that four fundamental pillars are relevant to the tribunals' evaluation. On the substantive side, investment tribunals evaluate the investor's legitimate expectations and the relevant degree of stability of the regulatory framework. In this context, investment tribunals seek to balance the investor's interest in stability with the legitimate right of the host state to introduce regulation and measures aimed at furthering environmental protection. Fairness demands that the more specific the assurances given to the then putative investor have been in relation to the stability or other criteria of the legal framework, the more reduced is the policy space of the host state to adopt diverging regulation.

The two procedural cornerstones of the standard are the notions of transparency and due process. The respect for these principles has to be expressed in the way the host state has adopted the environmental measure under review. One relevant aspect is the procedure the host state has relied on in evaluating the scientific basis for the adopted measure. An investment tribunal assesses the plausibility of the chosen methods to gather and evaluate scientific evidence, but refrains from independently evaluating the scientific evidence or the environmental objective as such. Likewise, the procedural pillars require the host state to respect its own legislative and administrative processes leading to the implementation of the regulation. They also inform the assessment of the host state's dealing with the investor. However, investment tribunals do not hold the host state to procedural perfection.

The four pillars of the standard of fairness emphasise that the assessment of an environmental measure involves a balancing exercise of all relevant factors. Fairness is a fluid concept that cannot be achieved by relying on static approaches. Accordingly, it aims to find a compromise between those aspects of stringency and stability, on which the investor seeks to rely, and the policy space of the host state, which advocates flexibility of the legal framework. An investment tribunal which takes account of and balances these opposing factors is likely to find a fair solution to the dispute.

With regard to the protection against expropriation, it is the primary task of an investment tribunal to distinguish an environmental regulatory measure from an expropriatory act. The assessment has demonstrated that there is little space for a conflict between a genuine environmental measure and the protection against expropriation, as expropriation requires a substantial deprivation of the economic benefits or of control over the investment. Regulatory measures that fulfil the requirements of lawful expropriation – namely being non-discriminatory and being enacted in line with due process – do very rarely have such a significant economic impact on an investor.

The study has shown that the dividing line between non-compensable regulation and compensable expropriation cannot be assessed easily or abstractly. While it is clear that a regulatory measure which is non-discriminatory and has been adopted in line with due process only rarely meets the threshold of expropriation, it is not sufficiently clear in which circumstances investment tribunals will consider a dispute to constitute such a rare situation. In my opinion, a tribunal should balance all relevant factors against each other. This means that the regulatory interest of the host state has to be balanced against the economic deprivation of the investor, taking account of the process of adopting the measure. If the balancing exercise of these factors indicates that the regulation burdens the investor with a special sacrifice, an investment tribunal should find compensable expropriation.

2. Common Features

The study suggests that on an abstract level investment tribunals are primarily guided by two aspects when assessing a potential violation of the standards of investment protection. The first essential feature for the assessment is the differentiation between *bona fide* regulation aimed at environmental protection and measures that use an alleged environmental objective as a smokescreen to further objectives contrary to the standards. The second feature that can be detected is the relevance of the balancing approach: Investment tribunals aim to reconcile differing interests and objectives by weighing the respective elements against each other.

With regard to the determination of the first feature, three factors are important. One factor for assessing if a measure is a genuine vehicle to further an environmental objective is the finding – or absence – of protectionist intent on the part of the host state. If the reasons for the adoption of the regulatory measure are intermingled with other, non-legitimate reasons – such as the desire to favour a national competitor or industry – an investment tribunal is unlikely to accept the measure as genuine. Indices of protectionism, which are on record, will probably lead the investment tribunal to consider the measure to be a violation of the conflicting treatment standard. This approach can be problematic if the respective measure has been adopted with the participation of a multitude of government officials, as different people or entities can intend to further different agendas. In a democratic society, in which the advantages or disadvantages of a potential measure are openly debated, even one single voice praising the measure on protectionist grounds could be documented. The study has indicated that investment tribunals are likely to place considerable emphasis on such evidence. However, in my understanding, each measure has to be assessed on an objective basis, so that the expression of protectionist ideas cannot be the singular criterion for determining its legitimacy.

The second important factor for the assessment concerns the process through which the supposedly environmental measure has been adopted. The study has shown that investment tribunals place considerable emphasis on procedural propriety. The process through which the environmental measure has been adopted and implemented must have been non-discriminatory and transparent and must have respected the tenets of due process. The acting authority, the chosen procedure, the potential use of emergency measures, the participation of members of the public and the speed of administrative interaction can all be subject to review. While investment tribunals have indicated that the procedure is not to be evaluated against a standard of perfection, it is accurate to state that – depending on the measure under review – the threshold remains high. The predominant reason for the significance of the adopted procedure is probably that divergences from the norm are easily detectable and that they imply ulterior motives.

The third relevant factor is the review of the scientific evidence on which the state relied for adopting the environmental measure. The assessment of the decisions rendered by investment tribunals illustrates that the host state is granted deference in deciding whether it intends to adopt a measure – and if yes, which measure it intends to adopt. Tribunals require an assessment of the alleged scientific evidence that favours the implementation of the respective measure. In this sense, investment tribunals refrain from setting forth their own material assessment of the scientific facts and processes on which the host state has relied. The more in line with internationally recognised environmental objectives the measure is, the less likely it is that an investment tribunal considers the measure to breach standards of investment protection.

The study has demonstrated that investment tribunals do not intend to review the scientific evidence materially, but that they rather undertake a coherence review of the applied scientific methods and contributions. Accordingly, investment tribunals generally accept the environmental justification of the measure set forth by the host state, if it is based on evidence that has been scientifically generated. In cases in which the best method of undertaking scientific studies and evaluating evidence is subject to discussion, an investment tribunal is likely to accept the approach undertaken by the state as legitimate, as long as it reflects generally recognised scientific procedures. Investment tribunals have not considered it necessary that the route chosen by the host state is unequivocally convincing. There can be different opinions and scientific evaluations, as long as the measures applied give an unambiguous picture of one scientifically supportable approach.

The host state's assessment of the scientific evidence should be more intensely scrutinised if other, less legitimate concerns could have been reasons for the adoption of the respective measure by the host state. However, the decisions analysed above have not pointed to such an approach. It can be stated that the evaluation of a host state's assessment of the scientific evidence in such a case is not central to the tribunal's determination. So far, no investment tribunal has had to evaluate a measure adopted that is reliant on a proper application of the precautionary principle. The assessment of evidence through the precautionary principle requires less substantive evidence, the more significant the potential damage is, so that it places a greater emphasis on the potential risk of the occurrence of the damage. With the precautionary principle being an internationally recognised means of assessing scientific data, it is my understanding that investment tribunals will appreciate it as a proper tool of risk assessment in the light of the deference owed to the state.

Concerning the second feature – the balancing of the relevance of different interests – investment tribunals demonstrate that they recognise the importance of both the policy space of the host state to adopt regulation and the necessary protection of the economic interest of the foreign investor. The study has shown that the investment decisions seek to reconcile competing legitimate interests. While the factors that have to be balanced differ in every instance, environmental considerations – to the extent that they are verifiable – are never disregarded. Within a balancing exercise, the economic impact of the measure will play an important role. This is the element that matters most to the investor and can also be indicative of potential ulterior reasons of the host state to introduce the respective measure. Its relevance is most precisely discussed in the context of evaluating the expropriatory impact of a measure. However, the practice of investment tribunals does not indicate a common approach to balancing different factors. The exercise thus is likely to differ in each case.

II. Practical Evaluation

The study has demonstrated that the standards of investment protection are generally in line with environmental regulation introduced by the host state, insofar as the regulatory measure lives up to the procedural requirements determined for its adoption and implementation. The spectrum is very limited for investment tribunals to find genuine environmental measures fulfilling the procedural requirements to violate the standards of investment protection. This legal determination, however, is in danger of falling short of the realities abundant in many recipient countries of foreign investment. The thorough legal assessment in this study would be incomplete without a critical practical evaluation of the requirements applied by investment tribunals to the standards of investment protection. The realities of the legislative and administrative framework in the host state may differ substantively from those of the 'model host state' and the quasi ideal measures which investment tribunals appear to envisage in their assessment.

1. The Environmental Framework at the Moment of the Investment Decision

The portrayal of the criteria on which investment tribunals rely to determine whether a measure breaches treaty standards on investment protection indicates that the level of environmental regulation in place at the moment the investment decision is made is of crucial importance. Since foreign investors generally have to accept the laws in force in the host state when they start investing, there is one clear observation to be made: The more sophisticated the environmental framework in the host state is at the time of the investment decision, the less potential there is for conflicts between environmental measures and the investment activity.

In a host state that has embraced a high and precise level of environmental protection, an investor cannot be led to believe that certain environmental restrictions will not be relevant for its investment. There is little ambiguity for an investor to draw a perception differing from the accurate standard of environmental protection. The study has suggested that two significant possibilities for conflict between investment and environmental protection exist: One relates to legitimate expectations of the foreign investor and the other concerns subsequent alterations to the regulatory framework. The more strict and stringent environmental regulation is at the time of the investment decision, the less potential there is for government officials to make promises which lead the investor to perceive the regulation as less onerous than it is. Furthermore, a host state with a comprehensive environmental framework has a reduced need to introduce altering environmental regulation. With significant environmental issues having been addressed, there is less need to further strengthen the regulatory framework – irrespective of the continuous changes to the level of environmental protection. Furthermore, in an environment that is highly regulated an investor has to expect that the levels of regulation be continuously tightened further, as investment tribunals have stated.

This assessment points to a practical problem: Lots of countries do not have a balanced and adjusted environmental framework yet. Western developed countries usually have adopted concise environmental regulation, whereas this is not the case with most developing countries. Such countries generally also lack the resources to implement environmental regulation or feel hard-pressed to focus on other vital issues for the countries' development. Similarly, states that change their political and economic regime may require time and resources to adjust their environmental framework. Those developing countries that do not have a stringent set of strict environmental laws in place are potentially also most in need of foreign investment to boost their economic prospects.

Consequently, there is significantly more potential for a conflict between the investment provisions and environmental regulation in a developing country than in a developed country. If the mining law of the host state, for example, does not properly condition the granting of permits upon environmental criteria when the investor starts its investment activity, a conflict is imminent. If, for example, the conditions of the respective environmental impact assessment are not sufficiently stringent to account for the potential environmental dangers, conflict is imminent as well. For these reasons, conflicts between environmental considerations and the treaty protection of an investor are likely to be more frequent – and more fundamental – in countries which have not had the capacity or appreciation for the relevance of a stringent environmental framework beforehand.

2. The Legislative and Administrative Reality in the Host State

The study has also demonstrated that investment tribunals emphasise the relevance of procedural implications in defining the protective scope of investment standards. In this context, transparency and the notion of due process are particularly important. While investment tribunals refrain from materially assessing the alleged scientific justification of the respective environmental measure, they scrutinise the process through which the measure has been adopted and implemented in a detailed manner. The procedural standard which is expected of a host state is onerous, even though investment tribunals have stated that they do not apply a standard of administrative perfection.

In a host state that is still developing or lacking economic and institutional resources, the administrative processes may not have matured enough yet to reach the level of procedural propriety that investment tribunals rely on as guidance. Similar to the environmental framework, the overall procedural framework in many developing countries is unlikely to reflect the same level of administrative and procedural accuracy as that in developed countries in the first world.[1] As a consequence, the legal requirements for adopting environmental measures, for securing the participation of those that will be affected and for the accountability of government officials will lack precision in those developing countries. Therefore, the risk that even a well-intended measure does not live up to the procedural standard demanded by investment tribunals is significantly higher.

This observation leads to a juxtaposition of two opposing approaches. On the one hand, the concept of 'fairness' is objective, in the sense that a measure is either fair or unfair; there is little middle ground. Therefore, there is good reason to subject the procedural process that has led to the adoption of the measure to an objective review. On the other hand, however, demanding that developing countries live up to the rather onerous standard that investment tribunals have applied to the adoption process of environmental measures in developed countries means practically imposing higher hurdles for developing host states. In the light of structural deficiencies of the procedural framework, the introduction of a well-intended environmental measure is more likely to be considered a breach of the standards of investment protection in these states.

It could be argued that the administrative functioning of a state requires an economic set-up that not all developing countries are able to live up to at the moment. The strict application of the standard of fairness may lead to much-needed reform of political culture and transparency in a developing country.[2] Over time, it is possible that investment decisions set benchmarks for procedural propriety, which encourage host states to ameliorate

---

[1] See, as an overview, *Transparency International*, Corruption Perceptions Index 2013, available at: http://cpi.transparency.org/cpi2013/results/. The Report, which ranks countries according to their perceived levels of public sector corruption, demonstrates that levels of public sector corruption tend to be higher in less developed countries.

[2] See, for example, *Gaines*, Sanford E., 'Environmental Policy Implications of Investor-State Arbitration under NAFTA Chapter 11', 7 International Environmental Agreements: Politics, Law and Economics 2007, 171 (180), who finds that the subsequent developments in *Metalclad v. Mexico* indicate an amelioration of environmental legislation in Mexico, even if problems with enforcement remain.

administrative processes for foreign investors and nationals alike. However, the initial price for this alteration may be high. In a country which lacks resources to implement and to adhere to fair procedures at all administrative levels to ensure a transparent decision-making process based on thoroughly tested scientific evidence, the payment of significant compensation could constitute a further set-back.

From the analysis of case law, it is not clear whether investment tribunals adjust the level of procedural propriety required with regard to transparency and due process to the general level of the administrative framework in each host state. While it is not the mandate of an investment tribunal to assess the abstract level of procedural propriety within a host state, some investment tribunals have found that the circumstances prevailing in the host state are to be taken into account in adjudicating on a claim.[3] In my opinion, investment tribunals should not completely neglect the kind of decision making processes the respective host state can actually accomplish.[4] Otherwise, developing countries could be deterred from introducing environmental regulation.

3. Practical Implications of the Conflict

The practical issue whether the rules of foreign investment protection, in reality, prevent host states from addressing environmental problems and introducing measures, has remained largely outside of the scope of this legal study. Likewise, the study does not aim to evaluate the alleged 'chilling' impact of investment arbitration, which is said to have a prohibitive impact due to the financial threat that the award of compensation to the investor

---

[3] Investment tribunals have, for example, considered the fact that host states were in a state of political transition as relevant, Parkerings-Compagniet AS v. Lithuania, ICSID Case No. ARB/05/8, Award of 11 September 2007, para 335; Joseph Charles Lemire v. Ukraine, ICSID Case No. ARB/06/18, Decision on Jurisdiction and Liablity of 14 January 2010, para 317; Saluka Investments BV (The Netherlands) v. The Czech Republic, Award of 17 March 2006, paras 357–358; Genin and others v. Estonia, ICSID Case No. ARB/99/2, Award of 25 June 2001, para 370. See also for the relevance of an economic crisis, LG&E v. Argentina, ICSID Case No. ARB/02/1, Decision on Liability of 3 October 2006, paras 139, 237–239.

[4] Similarly, *Romson*, Åsa, 'International Investment Law and the Environment', in: Sustainable Development in World Investment Law (Cordonier Segger, Marie-Claire et al. (Eds.) 2011) 37 (42–43, 52) who convincingly points out that environmental statistic and and scientific evidence may be expensive to produce for a developing state and that, at the same time, an investor cannot legitimately expect such a state base its actions as coherently on such evidence, as a developed state could do.

constitutes. The debate over the effect that investment obligations and the possibility of investment awards have on the level of environmental regulation within a host state remains ongoing.

Some commentators argue that investment obligations have a detrimental effect on the environment in countries in which the legislative framework is weak or weakly enforced.[5] Others point out that, generally, the more developed and open to foreign investment a country is, the stronger is its environmental legislation.[6] The latter position appears to miss the difficulties that impoverished states face when introducing and – even more – when enforcing a stringent environmental framework. Although it may be true that the most prosperous countries and the most fervent advocates of foreign investment today are those with the strictest environmental regulation, this does in no way guarantees that a developing country opening up to foreign investment today would thereby acquire prosperity and stringent environmental regulation. Rather, it is my understanding that the process of adopting environmental restrictions is likely to take a considerable amount of time. Considerable amounts of biodiversity and natural habitat can be lost forever before such regulation has been set up and enforced. If the environmental regulation is not sufficiently strict before a foreign investment takes place, there can be a clash with the interests of the investor. Even though the host state is not prevented from introducing the environmental measures, it may have to pay for the privilege – if only in the form of fees for defending its position before an investment tribunal. Such a threat is reduced if the country has enacted stringent environmental regulation prior to the entry of the investor.

However, current investment disputes against developed states of the first world demonstrate that even those states can have their regulation challenged by a foreign investor. But those states will generally be in a better position: Their administrative framework is likely to be more established and their financial situation makes it easier for them to settle a claim with a payment or to buy sufficient expertise to defend the claim. Nevertheless, developed countries which have been strong advocates of strict investment

---

5 See, for the example of Costa Rica, *Lindo*, Victoria R., 'Hydroelectric Power Production in Costa Rica and the Threat of Environmental Disaster through CAFTA', 29 Boston College International and Comparative Law Review 2006, 297 (309, 315).

6 *Kolo*, Abba/*Wälde*, Thomas, 'Environmental Regulation, Investment Protection and "Regulatory Taking" in International Law', 50 International and Comparative Law Quarterly 2001, 811 (815) declaring that "[p]rosperous societies are those that maximise their integration into the global economy – while those that insulate themselves tend to be the most impoverished ones with the lowest environmental standards."

protection, appear to slightly alter their approach in the face of more and more disputes in which they take the position of the respondent.

The study has demonstrated that the influence of democratic processes on the treatment of the foreign investor has yet to be properly developed. One issue that has been repeatedly raised is that the voice of one protectionist in the discussion concerning the adoption of an environmental measure should not be considered to 'infect' the whole measure. Democracy has to be a competition of different voices, which crave to be heard. Another related issue concerns restrictions on the ability of governmental officials to criticise a foreign investor for its performance and to express their discontent with the privatisation of services. While it cannot be considered as fair treatment if an official calls upon the public not to pay their bills to the investor, a clear demarcation of what government officials can say in a democratic society is still missing.[7] A further related issue is connected to public opposition to an investment project. Surely, neighbours to an installation have to have the right to freely demonstrate against it and to aim to persuade officials to stop its operation. The host state has to give weight both to the right to demonstrate and to express an opinion as well as to the right of the investor to be treated fairly. Even in a mature democracy, this juxtaposition is likely to give rise to significant tension.

On a general note, it appears that investment arbitration has to come to terms with scenarios where the basis of the investment treaty is challenged by relevant factors, which were not foreseen when the treaty was concluded. An example is the difficulty which investment tribunals have had in adjudicating claims stemming from the severe economic crisis in Argentina. The diverging approaches towards the concept of 'necessity' clearly underline this.[8] It is likely that arbitrators are becoming more sympathetic of the argu-

[7] See the determination in Azurix v. Argentine Republic, ICSID Case No. ARB/01/12, Award of 14 July 2006, para 376 for the governor's call on customers not to pay their bills and the finding of procedural unfairness in Compañiá de Aguas del Aconquija S.A. and Vivendi Universal v. Argentine Republic, ICSID Case No. ARB/97/3, Award of 20 August 2007, paras 7.4.19–7.4.45. See for criticism of alleged misrepresentation of democratic legitimacy by investment tribunals, *Mayeda*, Graham, 'International Investment Agreements Between Developed and Developing Countries: Dancing With the Devil? Case Comment on the Vivendi, Sempra and Enron Awards', 4 Mc Gill International Journal of Sustainable Development Law and Policy 2008, 189–230 (206–207). See also the tribunal's findings in Biwater Gauff (Tanzania) Ltd. v. United Republic of Tanzania, ICSID Case No. ARB/05/22, Award of 24 July 2008, paras 624–627 which severely restrict the rights of government officials to criticise the performance of foreign investors.

[8] Suez, Sociedad General de Aguas de Barcelona S.A., and InterAguas Servicios Integrales del Agua S.A. v. The Argentine Republic, ICSID Case No. ARB/03/17, Decision on Liability of 30 July 2010, paras 229–243; CMS Gas

ments of the host state in the face of the global economic crisis, which is shattering the economic foundations of developed countries. The stability of the regulatory framework may also be called into question in a state which has liberated itself from a dictatorship that was in power for several decades – a process which currently takes place in the Middle East. Can such a state really be ordered to fulfil contracts and grant investment opportunities promised by the old regime – especially if they are exceedingly favourable to a foreign investor?[9]

III. Perspectives for the Future

One of the criticisms that investment treaties and investment arbitration face is that they are one-sided and have a bias for the position of the foreign investor. Even though the study has demonstrated that host states generally have ample leeway to introduce measures that protect the environment, it cannot be denied that the foreign investor has a significant procedural advantage over other stakeholders: Only the investor can initiate investment proceedings. In contrast, the position of those that fear a negative impact of the investment on the environment or on their livelihoods is marginalised. The following section will briefly portray the defects that result in the perception of an imbalance and invoke ideas for mitigation.

Transmission Company v. The Argentine Republic, ICSID Case No. ARB/01/8, Award of 12 May 2005 paras 315–331; Sempra Energy International v. The Argentine Republic, ICSID Case No. ARB/02/16, Award of 28 September 2007, paras 344–355; Enron Corporation and Ponderosa Assets, L.P. v. Argentine Republic, ICSID Case No. ARB/01/3, Award of 22 May 2007, paras 304–313; LG&E v. Argentina, ICSID Case No. ARB/02/1, Decision on Liability of 3 October 2006, paras 248–259; AWG Group Ltd. v. The Argentine Republic, Decision on Liability of 30 July 2010, paras 249–265; National Grid plc v. The Argentine Republic, Award of 3 November 2008, paras 256–262; CMS Gas Transmission Company v. The Argentine Republic, ICSID Case No. ARB/01/8, Annulment Proceeding, Decision of 25 September 2007, paras 130–134 and the subsequent annulment of the awards in Enron Corporation and Ponderosa Assets, L.P. v. Argentine Republic, ICSID Case No. ARB/01/3, Annulment Proceeding, Decision on the Application for Annulment of the Argentine Republic of 30 July 2010, para 405; Sempra Energy International v. The Argentine Republic, ICSID Case No. ARB/02/16, Annulment Proceeding, Decision of 29 June 2010, para 159.

[9] See, for example, the pending dispute in Ampal-American Israel Corporation and others v. Arab Republic of Egypt (ICSID Case No. ARB/12/11), which concerns the export of natural gas that has been agreed by the old regime prior to the revolution in Egypt.

1. The Need for Host States to Protect Their Citizens

There is a discrepancy between the protection of the investor's interests through the mechanisms of the investment regime and the inability of the citizens to successfully defend their interests with regard to the impact of the investment activity. The citizens of the host state are most directly affected by the impact of an investment activity that has negative consequences for the environment and for their health and livelihood. Accordingly, local communities may have an interest in demanding restrictions to or the prohibition of an investment activity. Several of the investment decisions portrayed in this study noted local opposition towards investment projects. Further, in a scenario in which the investment activity has destroyed the environment or human life, the inhabitants of the host state have a desire to seek compensation from the investor.

Depending on the legislative framework of the host state, local communities frequently face difficulties in demanding restrictions to the investment activity and in bringing compensation claims against foreign investors. Deficiencies of administrative processes, which constitute hurdles to due process and transparency in some less developed countries, can prevent local communities from successfully demanding regulation. There may be unwillingness on the part of the government to sufficiently regulate foreign investment activity, especially if multinational corporations are involved. Frequently, there is not one 'common interest' in the host state with regard to the foreign investment. Governments and influential elites that are often not directly affected by the negative consequences of the investment activity may have other interests than supporting their fellow citizens in their demand for restrictions on dangerous investment activity. Rather, those in power may aim to maintain the image of an investment-oriented state to induce further investment. Sometimes, personal profiteering of the elite could be a motive, too. However, it would be the task of the host state to put efficient regulation in place and see to it being enforced.[10]

---

[10] There are two important points to be taken into consideration: First, regulation and its enforcement are frequently insufficient in less developed states, which are largely depending on foreign investment. Second, the governments of many host states do not care enough about the well-being of certain groups of their inhabitants and thus do not side with them if environmental or societal problems occur in connection with an investment activity. The latter factor is very important in reality and marks a stark contrast to the alignment of interests that *Miles*, Kate, 'International Investment Law: Origins, Imperialism and Conceptualizing the Environment', 21 Colorado Journal of International Environmental Law and Policy 2010, 1 (38–40) describes between the investor and its home state.

See also *Smith*, David N., 'The Way We Think: Ethics, Health and the Environment in International Business', 5 Asian Journal of WTO & International Health

Being barred from the powerful mechanisms of investment arbitration, residents of the host state may face significant difficulties in bringing claims against foreign investors if the activity has destroyed the environment, indigenous forms of life or impacted on the life or health of people. Once again, the framework in the host state may be insufficient to protect the interests of the citizens of the host state. Deficiencies in the structure or in the impartiality of the judiciary constitute barriers to the adjudication of such compensation claims in the host state. While a forum outside the host state could offer procedural advantages, citizens of the host state frequently face admissibility issues in such situations as well as the material problem that the corporate structure of the investor makes it impossible to engage the parent company when claiming substantive amounts of compensation for major violations.[11]

These issues – briefly sketched – are not a consequence of the regime of foreign investment. Rather, they point to structural and societal issues within the host state. Investment treaties cannot address inadequacies within a host state as long as the nationals of the host state are concerned.

Law and Policy 2010, 25 (40–41) for a portrayal of how governmental failures in enforcement and inattention of foreign investors to the specific circumstances in the host state reinforce each other.

[11] See the portrayal of examples of local communities in the host state facing difficulties in bringing such claims, by *Miles*, Kate, 'International Investment Law: Origins, Imperialism and Conceptualizing the Environment', 21 Colorado Journal of International Environmental Law and Policy 2010, 1 (26–37). The author analyses the attempts by local Indonesian communities to acquire compensation for the pollution and consequent destruction of ecological life within a river from a foreign investor before Australian courts as well as the legal actions against Union Carbide Corporation following the lethal gas leakage in Bhopal, India in 1984. In cases involving multinational companies, the forum of the parent company would be of specific relevance, since the parent company is likely to remain solvent even if the entity investing abroad ceases its operation. Furthermore, a jurisdiction like the U.S. offers tools like broad rules on document discovery and the rule on punitive damages. However, in common law jurisdictions, the doctrine of '*forum non conveniens*' enables a national court to decline jurisdiction if it is an inappropriate or inconvenient forum.

Additionally, the legal separation from the parent company could lead to the claim being dismissed. The reliance on the separate corporate personality of the entity investing abroad in the proceedings against Union Carbide Corporation and the subsequent dismissal of the case, is in stark contrast to the openness of investment tribunals not to let a claim fail because of difficulties with the corporate structure of the investor. See, for example, the decision of the investment tribunal in *S.D. Myers Inc. v. Canada*, which did "not accept that an otherwise meritorious claim should fail solely by reason of the corporate structure adopted by a claimant in order to organise the way in which it conducts its business affairs" (Partial Award on the Merits, 13 November 2000, para 229).

International law emphasises that it is the duty of the host state to protect the interests of its own citizens. However, the existence of the strong material and procedural protection granted to the foreign investor in an investment treaty could amplify the willingness of government officials not to restrict the foreign investor. Furthermore, the international rules protecting the foreign investor emphasise potential procedural inadequacies in the host state.

In the light of the apparent inability or unwillingness especially of less developed host states to protect their country and inhabitants from dangers and negative impacts of a dangerous investment activity, it could be helpful to integrate elements of corporate social responsibility into the investment regime.[12] Investment treaties could foresee the possibility of counterclaims for the host state in cases in which the investor claims compensation. Furthermore, an investor that wants to rely on the protection of an investment treaty could be subjected to certain standards of conduct, such as enforceable social and environmental obligations. This could be understood as an orientation towards the concept of 'sustainable development'. Furthering the concept of sustainable development should result in high levels of protection for the foreign investor, coupled with obligations of corporate social and environmental responsibility for the investor.[13] Like this, the investor would have to take the interests of other stakeholders into account and would simultaneously profit from the protection of its investment.

2. Changes to the Content and Interpretation of Investment Treaties

The study has demonstrated that, so far, only a limited number of investment treaties establish an intention of the state parties for the concepts of environmental protection and sustainable development to constitute relevant factors in the interpretation of the respective treaty. Furthermore, the exist-

[12] See, for example, the United Nations-backed initiative on Principles for Responsible Investment (http://www.unpri.org/); the development of the ISO 14000 family on environmental management (http://www.iso.org/iso/theiso14000family_2009.pdf). See, generally, *Muchlinski*, Peter, 'Corporate Social Responsibility', in: The Oxford Handbook of International Investment Law (Muchlinski, Peter et al. (Eds.) 2008) 637–687. See also the analysis of *Hepburn*, Jarrod/*Kuuya*, Vuyelwa, 'Corporate Social Responsibility and Investment Treaties', in: Sustainable Development in World Investment Law (Cordonier Segger, Marie-Claire et al. (Eds.) 2011) 589 (601, 608) of indirect and soft-law approaches to corporate social responsibilities in recent free trade agreements.

[13] See the Model International Agreement on Investment for Sustainable Development by the International Institute for Sustainable Development as an attempt to further the notion of sustainable development.

ing references are often rather weak and not sufficiently precise. They allow investment tribunals to take account of environmental objectives in the interpretative exercise, but are in danger of not having a relevant influence due to their wording and position outside the realm of the provisions on investment protection. Accordingly, the analysis has shown that environmental references so far have not played a significant role in the evaluation of investment claims. While the references underline that investment agreements are not to be understood in isolation of other aspects of international law, there is no systematic approach through which investment tribunals assess the relevance of the references as part of the 'interpretative context' of the investment protection provisions.

The text of an investment treaty is agreed by the two or more states that are party to the agreement. Accordingly, the state parties have the sovereignty to adopt other and more adequate treaty provisions. It is for states to decide which objectives they consider relevant enough to be inserted into investment treaties in a meaningful way. If states wish to give weight to concepts like environmental protection in the context of investment protection, they have to give clear indications in the bilateral or multilateral investment agreements to which they become a party. It is in their power to be explicit about the importance they wish to accord to environmental concepts.[14] Even though the study has, inter alia, demonstrated the power of arbitral tribunals in shaping the law of foreign investment, it is important not to lose sight of the constitutive role of the content of investment treaties: Just like states, arbitral tribunals are bound by the treaties they are set up to apply.

In the light of the findings of this study and of the societal issues hinted at above, it is my understanding that a reconciliatory approach to environmental and social objectives, on the one hand, and to the economic interests of the foreign investor, on the other hand, is most likely to result in a satisfactory regime for all stakeholders. The concept that embodies this approach and supports the view that economic, environmental and societal considerations are mutually supportive, is the concept of sustainable devel-

---

14 *Stern*, Brigitte, 'The Future of International Investment Law: A Balance Between the Protection of Investors and the State's Capacity to Regulate' in: The Evolving International Investment Regime: Expectations, Realities, Opinions (Alvarez, José et al. (Eds.) 2011) 174 (175). The author expressly states that if states do not include provisions stating that investment is linked to sustainable development into their investment treaties, "arbitration can only play a very marginal, or even a nonexistent role, in making investments foster sustainable development". The investment arbitration system can only resolve problems which are addressed in the substantive rules that have to be applied by the arbitral tribunals, so that the responsibility for enacting the rules clearly falls on states.

opment. As the study has demonstrated, it is a concept which enjoys measurable support in the international arena. This understanding goes hand in hand with the evolving appreciation of the concept of 'development' as increasingly embracing notions of environmental and social relevance.

Even if investment tribunals are still "rather hesitant" to integrate rules of law as prescribed by the concept of sustainable development,[15] it has to be kept in mind that the interpretative power regarding investment treaties does not exclusively rest with the tribunals. The state parties to the investment treaty also have a legitimate role to play.[16] As far as it is the intention of state parties that considerations of sustainability be taken into account in the application of investment treaties, they can express this view – not only in the text of newly-adopted investment treaties, but also in interpretative notes and in pleadings in arbitral proceedings. The state parties can emphasise that they understand sustainable development as a 'metaprinciple' – as international dispute resolution bodies do –[17] to add a relevant interpretative background to terms stemming from older investment treaties that are devoid of significant environmental references.

It thus depends on the will of the states to enhance the relevance of environmental considerations in investment law. They can jointly modify existing agreements and emphasise relevant objectives when they conclude further agreements. Arguably, the circumstances for such an alteration of the regime of foreign investment have never been better. Commentators have detected a general "return of the state" – meaning a trend in which more and more states argue for nationalisation of industries or apply measures to protect their own economies.[18] This trend is noticeable even in those countries which have been the most fervent supporters of strengthening the

---

[15] *Kentin*, Esther, 'Sustainable Development in International Investment Dispute Settlement: The ICSID and NAFTA Experience', in: International Law and Sustainable Development: Principles and Practice (Schrijver, Nico et al. (Eds.) 2004) 309 (325). See also *Mayeda*, Graham, 'International Investment Agreements Between Developed and Developing Countries: Dancing With the Devil? Case Comment on the Vivendi, Sempra and Enron Awards', 4 Mc Gill International Journal of Sustainable Development Law and Policy 2008, 189 (204) arguing for the application of a 'sustainable development analysis' in investment arbitration in reliance on Article 31 para 3 lit c VCLT. This understanding is based on the consideration of sustainable development as constituting customary international law.

[16] See for a comprehensive assessment of the dual role of states in investment arbitrations and especially in relation to interpretation, *Roberts*, Anthea, 'Power and Persuasion in Investment Treaty Arbitration: The Dual Role of States', 104 American Journal of International Law 2010, 179–225.

[17] See 'Chapter 1 – Environmental Norms and Principles', pp. 68 *et seq.*

[18] *Alvarez*, José E., 'The Return of the State', 20 Minnesota Journal of International Law 2011, 223 (234–235).

rights of foreign investors in the past.[19] Ultimately, it is up to the states to decide how the regime should be shaped in the future.

3. Institutional Implications

Institutional aspects of the arbitral proceedings have remained outside of the scope of this study. Nevertheless, the institutional implications according to which the arbitral proceedings are conducted can shape the relationship of investment agreements with environmental standards.[20] Traditionally, investment arbitration has been closely connected to the core tenets of commercial arbitration, with the confidentiality of the proceedings being particularly important. However, with the recognition that investment cases can significantly impact on areas of public policy within the host state, the interest of the public to participate in the proceedings has to be accommodated.

Therefore, investment tribunals have accepted the input of *amici curiae*. The role of the *amicus curiae* is not restricted to a specific type of interested group and has been taken up by non-governmental organisations advocating environmental or social interests, business associations and the European Community.[21] While the specific role given to these interested third parties will be defined by the arbitral tribunal reliant on the procedural rules which are to guide the arbitration,[22] they are generally allowed

19 *Alvarez*, José E., 'The Return of the State', 20 Minnesota Journal of International Law 2011, 223 (235–236) emphasises the example of the U.S., portrays their current positions and model treaty language to conclude that "if the United States led the charge in favo[u]r of investor protections, it now appears to be leading the drive in the opposite direction".

20 Each party can introduce environmental evidence and experts as part of its submissions. The tribunal may decide to admit environmental experts in accordance with the rules on evidence. See, for example, Articles 34–36 of the ICSID Rules of Procedure for Arbitration Proceedings and Articles 27, 29 of the 2010 UNCITRAL Arbitration Rules. Some BITs contain specific rules on environmental experts, see Article 32 U.S.-Rwanda BIT and Article 32 U.S.-Nicaragua BIT.

21 *Levine*, Eugenia, '*Amicus Curiae* in International Investment Arbitration: The Implications of an Increase in Third-Party Participation', 29 Berkley Journal of International Law 2011, 200 (209–214).

22 See, Article 32 para 2 and Article 37 para 2 ICSID Rules of Procedure for Arbitration Proceedings and decision in Aguas Argentinas, S.A., Suez, Sociedad General de Aguas de Barcelona, S.A. and Vivendi Universal, S.A. v. Argentine Republic, ICSID Case No. ARB/03/19, Order in Response to a Petition for Transparency and Participation as Amicus Curiae, 19 May 2005. See for a discussion of the provisions, *Bernasconi-Osterwalder*, Nathalie, 'Transparency and Amicus Curiae in ICSID Arbitrations', in: Sustainable Development in World Investment Law (Cordonier Segger, Marie-Claire et al. (Eds.) 2011) 191–207.

to make written submissions with regard to the issues that are of interest to them. The extent to which the third party submissions of an environmental group can influence the outcome of the investment arbitration, cannot be assessed in this brief portrayal. The submissions may play a role in underlining the societal implications of a dispute, but it is unlikely that they address relevant points which have not been referred to by the parties to the dispute.

An arbitral tribunal has to find a balance between allowing interest groups to contribute and to facilitate the proceedings without unnecessary delay. An overuse of the mechanism could obstruct the proceedings and lead to its inefficiency.[23] Furthermore, the parties may still have a right to confidentiality.[24] It is the task of the arbitral tribunal to define the scope of third party participation. The role of the *amicus curiae* is to help the tribunal with relevant facts, so that an abstract discourse about environmental standards, for example, might not be helpful. However, when the parties' submissions are not disclosed to the third parties, it will be difficult for them to address the most relevant aspects of the dispute. Accordingly, the impact of this participation should not be over-estimated. It is an unlikely remedy for the fear of 'fragmentation' in international law.

IV. Conclusion

The discussion above leads to the conclusion that a 'model host state' is unlikely to violate investment protection provisions when it introduces a genuine environmental measure. While rich developed countries can comply with these standards, it is doubtful if the average developing country without comprehensive administrative structures can live up to these standards. This is even more the case since the potential for conflicts is most pronounced if the host state does not have a stringent environmental framework in place when the investor starts its investment activity. Developing countries are less likely to have a sophisticated permit system in place which takes account of all potential environmental implications prior to the start

---

23 See the examples given by *Stern*, Brigitte, 'The Future of International Investment Law: A Balance Between the Protection of Investors and the State's Capacity to Regulate' in: The Evolving International Investment Regime: Expectations, Realities, Opinions (Alvarez, José et al. (Eds.) 2011) 174 (188–189).

24 See discussion by *Bernasconi-Osterwalder*, Nathalie, 'Transparency and Amicus Curiae in ICSID Arbitrations', in: Sustainable Development in World Investment Law (Cordonier Segger, Marie-Claire et al. (Eds.) 2011) 191 (206), who criticises the restrictions imposed on the third submissions by the tribunal in *Biwater Gauff (Tanzania) Ltd. v. United Republic of Tanzania.* See, however, the 2014 UNCITRAL Rules on Transparency in Treaty-based Investor-State Arbitration.

of the investment activity. Accordingly, it is more likely that an investment dispute arises when there is a need for subsequent strengthening of the regulation.

Nevertheless, the investment regime constitutes an incentive for all host states to ameliorate their administrative framework – and increased stringency and transparency would additionally benefit the citizens of the host state. Embracing the concept of sustainable development would result in understanding development in a holistic manner: The respect for the property rights of foreign investors would be explicitly coupled with environmental and societal criteria – and the advance of fairness and good governance. This should reduce the potential for tensions between economic and environmental objectives and would slowly decrease the fear that legitimate environmental measures could constitute a violation of investment standards by the host state.

Bibliography

Aagaard, Todd S., 'Environmental Law as a Legal Field: An Inquiry in Legal Taxonomy', 95 Cornell Law Review 2009, 221–282

Aaken, Anne van, 'Fragmentation of International Law: The Case of International Investment Law', XVII Finnish Yearbook of International Law 2006, 91–130

Adam, Rachelle, 'Missing the 2010 Biodiversity Target: A Wake-Up Call for the Convention on Biodiversity?' 21 Colorado Journal of International Environmental Law and Policy 2010, 123–166

Aldrich, George H., 'What Constitutes a Compensable Taking of Property? The Decisions of the Iran-United States Claims Tribunal', 88 American Journal of International Law 1994, 585–610

– The Jurisprudence of the Iran-United States Claims Tribunal (Oxford: Clarendon Press, 1996)

Alvarez, José E., 'The Return of the State', 20 Minnesota Journal of International Law 2011, 223–264

Alvarez-Jiménez, Alberto, 'The *Methanex* Final Award, An Analysis from the Perspective of Environmental Regulatory Authorities and Foreign Investors', 23 Journal of International Arbitration 2006, 427–434

American Law Institute, 'Restatement of the Law (Third) of the Foreign Relations of the United States' Volume 1, 1987

Antal, Edit, 'Lessons From NAFTA: The Role of the North American Commission for Environmental Cooperation in Conciliating Trade and Environment', 14 Michigan State Journal of International Law 2006, 167–189

Baetens, Freya, 'The Kyoto Protocol in Investor-State Arbitration: Reconciling Climate Change and Investment Protection Objectives', in: Sustainable Development in World Investment Law (Cordonier Segger, Marie-Claire/Gehring, Markus W./Newcombe, Andrew (Eds.) Alphen aan den Rijn: Kluwer Law International, 2011) 683–715

Barstow Magraw, Daniel/*Hawke*, Lisa D., 'Sustainable Development', in: The Oxford Handbook of International Environmental Law (Bodansky, Daniel/Brunnée, Jutta/Hey, Ellen (Eds.) Oxford: Oxford University Press, 2007) 613–638

Baughen, Simon, 'Expropriation and Environmental Regulation: The Lessons and NAFTA Chapter 11', 18 Journal of Environmental Law 2006, 207–228

Been, Vicki/*Beauvais*, Joel C.,'The Global Fifth Amendment? NAFTA's Investment Protections and the Misguided Quest for an International "Regulatory Takings" Doctrine', 78 New York University Law Review 2003, 30–143

Ben Hamida, Walid, 'La prise en compte de l'intérêt général et des impératifs de développement dans le droit des investissements', 135 Journal du Droit International 2008, 999–1033

Bennett, Lisa, 'Are tradable Carbon Emissions Investments? Characterization and Ramifications under International Investment Law', 85 New York University Law Review 2010, 1581–1617

Bernasconi-Osterwalder, Nathalie, 'Transparency and Amicus Curiae in ICSID Arbitrations', in: Sustainable Development in World Investment Law (Cordonier Segger, Marie-Claire/Gehring, Markus W./Newcombe, Andrew (Eds.) Alphen aan den Rijn: Kluwer Law International, 2011) 191–207

Beyerlin, Ulrich, 'Different Types of Norms in International Environmental: Policies, Principles and Rules', in: The Oxford Handbook of International Environmental Law (Bodansky, Daniel/Brunnée, Jutta/Hey, Ellen (Eds.) Oxford: Oxford University Press, 2007) 425–448

Birnie, Patricia/*Boyle*, Alan/*Redgwell*, Catherine, International Law and the Environment (Oxford: 3rd Edition, Oxford University Press, 2009)

Bodansky, Daniel, Art and Craft of International Environmental Law (Cambridge (Massachusetts): Harvard University Press, 2010)

Boute, Anatole, 'Combating Climate Change and Securing Electricity Supply: The Role of Investment Protection Law', 16 European Environmental Law Review 2007, 227–248

– The Potential Contribution of International Investment Protection Law to Combat Climate Change', 27 Journal of Energy & Natural Resources Law 2009, 333–376

Brown, Chester, 'Bringing Sustainable Development Issues before Investment Tribunals', in: Sustainable Development in World Investment Law (Cordonier Segger, Marie-Claire/Gehring, Markus W./Newcombe, Andrew (Eds.) Alphen aan den Rijn: Kluwer Law International, 2011) 175–188

Brownlie, Ian, Principles of Public International Law (Oxford: 7th Edition, Oxford University Press, 2008)

Calliess, Christian, 'Vorsorgeprinzip und Beweislastverteilung im Verwaltungsrecht', Das Deutsche Verwaltungsblatt 2001, 1725–1733

Christie, G. C., 'What Constitutes A Taking of Property under International Law?', 38 British Yearbook of International Law 1962, 307–338

Clapp, Jennifer, 'What the Pollution Havens Debate Overlooks', 2 Global Environmental Politics 2002, 11–19

Clean Development Mechanism-Executive Board, Report of the 58th Meeting of 26 November 2010, CDM-EB-58

Clean Development Mechanism-Meth Panel, Note on AM0001: Incineration of HFC 23 Waste Streams, Report of 44th Meeting 2010, at: http://cdm.unfccc.int/Panels/meth/meeting/10/044/mp44_an02.pdf

Coe, Jack Jr./*Rubins*, Noah, 'Regulatory Expropriation and the *Tecmed* Case: Context and Contributions', in: International Investment Law and Arbitration: Leading Cases from the ICSID, NAFTA, Bilateral Treaties and Customary International Law (Weiler, Todd (Ed.) London: Cameron May, 2005) 597–667

Cole, Matthew A./*Elliott*, Robert J.R., 'FDI and the Capital Intensity of "Dirty" Sectors: A Missing Piece of the Pollution Haven Puzzle', 9 Review of Development Economics 2005, 530–548

Commission, Jeffrey P., 'Precedent in Investment Treaties, A Citation Analysis of Developing Jurisprudence', 24 Journal of International Arbitration 2007, 129–158

Congyan, Cai, 'China-US BIT Negotiations and the Future of Investment Treaty Regime: A Grand Bilateral Bargain with Multilateral Implications', 12 Journal of International Economic Law 2009, 457–506

Cordero Moss, Giuditta, 'Full Protection and Security', in: Standards of Investment Protection (Reinisch, August (Ed.) Oxford: Oxford University Press, 2008) 131–150

Corten, Olivier/*Klein*, Pierre (Eds.) Les conventions de Vienne sur le droit des traités : commentaire article par article (Brussels: Bruylant, 2006)

– (Eds.), The Vienna Convention on the Law of Treaties, A Commentary (Oxford: Oxford University Press, 2011)

Craik, Neil, The International Law of Environmental Impact Assessment (Cambridge: Cambridge University Press, 2008)

Dameris, Martin/*Peter*, Thomas/*Schmidt*, Ulrich/*Zellner*, Reinhard, 'Das Ozonloch und seine Ursachen', 41 Chemie in unserer Zeit 2007, 152–168

DiMascio, Nicholas/*Pauwelyn*, Joost, 'Nondiscrimination in Trade and Investment Treaties: Worlds Apart or Two Sides of the Same Coin?', 102 American Journal of International Law 2008, 48–89

Di Pietro, Domenico, 'Applicable Law Under Article 42 of the ICSID Convention and the Case of Amco v. Indonesia' in: International Investment Law and Arbitration: Leading Cases from the ICSID, NAFTA, Bilateral Treaties and Customary International Law (Weiler, Todd (Ed.) London: Cameron May, 2005) 223–279

Dolzer, Rudolf, Eigentum, Enteignung und Entschädigung im geltenden Völkerrecht (Berlin: Springer Verlag, Beiträge zum ausländischen öffentlichen Recht und Völkerrecht 88, 1985)

– 'Indirect Expropriation of Alien Property', 1 ICSID Review Foreign Investment Law Journal 1986, 41–65

– 'Indirect Expropriations: New Developments', 11 New York University Environmental Law Journal 2002, 64–93

– 'Fair and Equitable Treatment: A Key Standard in Investment Treaties', 39 International Lawyer 2005, 87–106

– 'National Treatment: New Developments', OECD Conference Paper, Paris 2005, at: http://www.oecd.org/investment/internationalinvestmentagreements/36055356.pdf

Dougherty, Kara, 'Methanex v. United States: The Realignment of NAFTA Chapter 11 with Environmental Regulation', 27 Northwestern Journal of International Law and Business 2007, 735–754

Ederington, Josh, 'NAFTA and the Pollution Haven Hypothesis', 35 Policy Studies Journal 2007, 239–244

Emroy Jr., Richard W., 'Probing the Protections in the Rotterdam Convention on Prior Informed Consent', 2000 Colorado Journal of International Environmental Law and Policy 2000, 47–69

Eskeland, Gunnar S./*Harrison*, Ann E., 'Moving to Greener Pastures? Multinationals and the Pollution Haven Hypothesis', 70 Journal of Development Economics 2003, 1–23

Esty, Daniel C./*Geradin*, Damien, 'Environmental Protection and International Competitiveness' 32 Journal of World Trade 1998, 5–46

European Commission, 'Communication on the Precautionary Principle', COM(2000) 1 final, 2 February 2000

– 'White Paper on Environmental Liability', COM(2000) 66 final, 9 February 2000

– 'Communication on the support of electricity from renewable energy sources', COM(2005) 627 final, 7 December 2005

– Press Release, IP/11/56, 21 January 2011

Falsafi, Alireza, 'Regional Trade and Investment Agreements: Liberalizing Investment in a Preferential Climate', 36 Syracuse Journal of International Law and Commerce 2008, 43–85

Fauchald, Ole Kristian, 'The Legal Reasoning of ICSID Tribunals: An Empirical Analysis', 19 European Journal of International Law 2008, 301–363

Fietta, Stephen, 'Expropriation and the "Fair and Equitable" Standard, The Developing Role of Investor's "Expectations" in International Investment Arbitration', 23 Journal of International Arbitration 2006, 375–399

Fortier, Yves L./*Drymer*, Stephen L., 'Indirect Expropriation in the Law of International Investment: I Know It When I See It, or Caveat Investor', 19 ICSID Review Foreign Investment Law Journal 2004, 293–327

Freestone, David, 'International Fisheries Law Since Rio: The Continued Rise of the Precautionary Principle', in: International Law and Sustainable Development: Past Achievements and Future Challenges (Boyle, Alan/Freestone, David (Eds.) Oxford: Oxford University Press, 1999) 135–164

Gaillard, Emmanuel/*Banifatemi*, Yas, 'The Meaning of 'and' in Article 42(1), Second Sentence, of the Washington Convention: The Role of International Law in the ICSID Choice of Law Process', 18 ICSID Review Foreign Investment Law Journal 2003, 375–411

Gaines, Sanford E., 'The Polluter-Pays Principle: From Economic Equity to Environmental Ethos', 26 Texas International Law Journal 1991, 463–496

– 'Environmental Policy Implications of Investor-State Arbitration under NAFTA Chapter 11', 7 International Environmental Agreements: Politics, Law and Economics 2007, 171–201

Gardiner, Richard, Treaty Interpretation (Oxford: Oxford University Press, 2008)

Giese, Alenka S./*Kahley*, William J./*Riefler*, Roger F., 'Foreign Direct Investment: Motivating Factors and Economic Impact', 20 Journal of Regional Analysis and Policy 1990, 105–127

Green, Andrew, 'Climate Change, Regulatory Policies and the WTO: How Constraining are Trade Rules?', 8 Journal of International Economic Law 2005, 143–189

Griebel, Jörn, Internationales Investitionsrecht (Munich: Verlag C.H. Beck, 2008)

Grierson-Weiler, Todd/*Laird*, Ian A., 'Standards of Treatment', in: The Oxford Handbook of International Investment Law (Muchlinski, Peter (Ed.) Oxford: Oxford University Press, 2008) 259–304

Hahn, Robert W., 'Ethanol: Law, Economics and Politics', 19 Stanford Law and Policy Review 2008, 434–469

Hardin, Garrett, 'The Tragedy of the Commons', 162 Science 1968, 1243–1248

Heathcote, Sarah, 'Circumstances Precluding Wrongfulness in the ILC Articles on State Responsibility: Necessity', in: The Law of International Responsibility (Crawford, James/Pellet, Alain/Olleson, Simon (Eds.) Oxford: Oxford University Press, 2010) 491–501

Hepburn, Jarrod/*Kuuya*, Vuyelwa, 'Corporate Social Responsibility and Investment Treaties', in: Sustainable Development in World Investment Law (Cordonier Segger, Marie-Claire/Gehring, Markus W./Newcombe, Andrew (Eds.) Alphen aan den Rijn: Kluwer Law International, 2011) 589–609

Higgins, Rosalyn, 'The Taking of Property by the State: Recent Developments in International Law', Recueil des Cours 1982-III, 259–391

– 'Some Observations on the Inter-Temporal Rule in International Law', in: Theory of International Law at the Threshold of the 21st Century. Essays in Honour of Krzysztof Skubiszewski (Markarczyk, Jerzy (Ed.) The Hague: Kluwer Law International, 1996) 173–182

– 'A Babel of Judicial Voices? Ruminations from the Bench', 55 International and Comparative Law Quarterly 2006, 791–804

Hillgenberg, Hartmut, 'A Fresh Look at Soft Law', 10 European Journal of International Law 1999, 499–515

Hirokawa, Keith H., 'Disasters and Ecosystem Services Deprivation: From Cuyahoga to the Deepwater Horizon', 74 Albany Law Review 2011, 543–556

Hoffmann, Anne K., 'Indirect Expropriation', in: Standards of Investment Protection (Reinisch, August (Ed.) Oxford: Oxford University Press, 2008) 151–170

Housman, Robert, 'The North American Free Trade Agreement's Lessons For Reconciling Trade and the Environment', 30 Stanford Journal of International Law 1994, 379–422

Howse, Robert/*Chalamish*, Efraim, 'The Use and Abuse of WTO Law in Investor-State Arbitration: A Reply to Jürgen Kurtz', 20 European Journal of International Law 2009, 1087–1094

Hughes, Sara/*Partzsch*, Lena/*Gaskell*, Joanne, 'The Development of Biofuels in the Context of the Global Water Crisis', 7 Sustainable Development Law & Policy 2007, 58–62

Hunt, Nathaniel Hemmerick, 'One Step Forward, Two Steps Back: The Central American Free Trade Agreement and the Environment', 35 Georgia Journal of International and Comparative Law 2007, 545–574

Intergovernmental Panel on Climate Change (IPCC), Working Group I Fourth Assessment Report: The Physical Science Basis (2007), at: http://www.ipcc.ch/publications_and_data/publications_ipcc_fourth_assessment_report_wg1_report_the_physical_science_basis.htm

International Law Association, 'New Delhi Declaration of Principles of International Law Relating to Sustainable Development', 2 April 2002, 2 International Environmental Agreements: Politics, Law and Economics 2002, 211–216

International Law Commission, Report of the International Law Commission on the Work of Its Forty-Third Session, 29 April to 19 July 1991 (A/46/10)

– Second Report on State Responsibility, Addendum of 30 April 1999 (A/CN.4/498/Add.2), by Special Rapporteur James Crawford

– Fragmentation of International Law: Difficulties arising from the Diversification and Expansion of International Law, Report of the Study Group of the International Law Commission of 13 April 2006 (A/CN.4/L.682), finalised by Martti Koskenniemi

– Fragmentation of International Law: Difficulties arising from the Diversification and Expansion of International Law, Report of the Study Group of the International Law Commission of 18 July 2006 (A/CN.4/L.702)

Ipsen, Knut, Völkerrecht (Munich: 5th Edition, Verlag C.H. Beck, 2004)

Jenkins, Benjamin W., 'The Next Generation of Chilling Uncertainty: Indirect Expropriation under CAFTA and Its Potential Impact on Environmental Protection', 12 Ocean and Coastal Law Journal 2007, 269–304

Johnson, Lise, 'International Investment Agreements and Climate Change: The Potential for Investor-State Conflicts and Possible Strategies for Minimizing It', 39 Environmental Law Reporter News & Analysis 2009, 11147–11160

Johnson, Pierre Marc/*Beaulieu*, André, The Environment and NAFTA: Understanding and Implementing the New Continental Law – Why a North American Agreement on Environmental Cooperation? (Washington D.C.: Island Press, 1996)

Joubin-Bret, Anna/*Rey*, Estelle-Marie/*Weber*, Jörg, 'International Investment Law and Development' in: Sustainable Development in World Investment Law (Cordonier Segger, Marie-Claire/Gehring, Markus W./Newcombe, Andrew (Eds.) Alphen aan den Rijn: Kluwer Law International, 2011) 15–31

Juhasz, Antonia, 'Democracy vs. Corporate Rule: How the Central American Free Trade Agreement (CAFTA) Allows Investor Rights to Trump the Public Interest', Statement of May 2004, at: http://www.ifg.org/news/CaftaPress.html

Kahn, Jordan C., 'Striking NAFTA Gold: Glamis Advances Investor-State Arbitration', 33 Fordham International Law Journal 2009, 101–155

Kammerhofer, Jörg, 'The Theory of Norm Conflict Solutions in International Law', in: Sustainable Development in World Investment Law (Cordonier Segger, Marie-Claire/Gehring, Markus W./Newcombe, Andrew (Eds.) Alphen aan den Rijn: Kluwer Law International, 2011) 83–98

Kentin, Esther, 'Sustainable Development in International Investment Dispute Settlement: The ICSID and NAFTA Experience', in: International Law and Sustainable Development: Principles and Practice (Schrijver, Nico/Weiss, Friedl (Eds.) Leiden: Martinus Nijhoff Publishers, 2004) 309–338

Kerr, Richard A., 'There Is More to "Acid Rain" Than Rain', 211 Science 1981, 692–693

Kill, Theodore, 'Don't Cross the Streams: Past and Present Overstatement of Customary International Law in Connection With Conventional Fair and Equitable Treatment Obligations', 106 Michigan Law Review 2008, 853–880

Kim, Hyung-Jin, 'Subsidy, Polluter Pays Principle and Financial Assistance among Countries', 34 Journal of World Trade 2000, 115–141

Kinnear, Meg N./*Björklund*, Andrea K./*Hannaford*, John F.G. (Eds.) Investment Disputes under NAFTA, An Annotated Guide to NAFTA Chapter 11 (Alphen aan den Rijn: Kluwer Law International, 2006)

Klabbers, Jan, 'Some Problems Regarding the Object and Purpose of Treaties', VIII Finnish Yearbook of International Law 1997, 138–160

– 'Reluctant Grundnormen: Articles 31 (3) (C) and 42 of the Vienna Convention on the Law of Treaties and the Fragmentation of International Law', in: Time, History and International Law (Craven, Matthew/Fitzmaurice, Malgosia/Vogiatzi, Maria (Eds.) Leiden: Martinus Nijhoff Publishers, 2007) 141–161

Kloepfer, Michael, Umweltschutzrecht (Munich: Verlag C.H. Beck, 2008)

Knox, John H., 'The Neglected Lessons of the NAFTA Environmental Regime', 45 Wake Forest Law Review 2010, 391–424

Kolo, Abba/*Wälde*, Thomas, 'Environmental Regulation, Investment Protection and "Regulatory Taking" in International Law', 50 International and Comparative Law Quarterly 2001, 811–848

Kossoy, Alexandre/*Ambrosi*, Philippe, State and Trends of the Carbon Market 2010 (Washington: Carbon Finance at the World Bank, 2010)

Kotera, Akira, 'Regulatory Transparancy', in: The Oxford Handbook of International Investment Law (Muchlinski, Peter/Ortino, Federico/Schreuer, Christoph (Eds.) Oxford: Oxford University Press, 2008) 617–636

Krajewski, Markus/*Ceyssens*, Jan, 'Internationaler Investitionsschutz und innerstaatliche Regulierung, Eine Untersuchung anhand der bilateralen Investitionsabkommen Deutschlands', 45 Archiv des Völkerrechts 2007, 180–216

Kreindler, Richard H., 'The Law Applicable to International Investment Disputes', in: Arbitrating Foreign Investment Disputes: Procedural and Substantive Legal

Aspects (Horn, Norbert (Ed.) The Hague: Kluwer Law International, 2004) 401–424

Kriebaum, Ursula, Eigentumsschutz im Völkerrecht (Berlin: Duncker & Humboldt, 2008)

Krumbiegel, Peter, Der Sonderopferbegriff in der Rechtsprechung des Bundesgerichtshofes (Berlin: Duncker & Humboldt 1975)

Kummer, Katharina, 'The International Regulation of Transboundary Traffic in Hazardous Wastes: The 1989 Basel Convention', 41 The International and Comparative Law Quarterly 1992, 530–562

Kunich, John Charles, 'Losing Nemo: The Mass Extinction Now Threatening the World's Ocean Hotspots', 30 Columbia Journal of Environmental Law 2005, 1–133

Kurtz, Jürgen, 'A General Investment Agreement in the WTO? Lessons from Chapter 11 of NAFTA and the OECD Multilateral Agreement on Investment', 23 University of Pennsylvania Journal of International Economic Law 2002, 713–789

– 'The Use and Abuse of WTO Law in Investor-State Arbitration: Competition and Its Discontents', 20 European Journal of International Law 2009, 749–771

– 'The Use and Abuse of WTO Law in Investor-State Arbitration: Competition and Its Discontents: A Rejoinder to Robert Howse and Efraim Chalamish', 20 European Journal of International Law 2009, 1095–1098

Kutas, Géraldine/*Lindberg*, Carina,/*Steenblik*, Ronald, Biofuels – At What Cost? Government Support for Ethanol and Biodiesel in the European Union (Geneva: International Institute for Sustainable Development, 2007)

Lallas, Peter L., 'The Stockholm Convention on Persistent Organic Pollutants', 95 American Journal of International Law 2001, 692–708

Langlet, David, 'Safe Return to the Underground? The Role of International Law in Subsurface Storage of Carbon Dioxide', 18 Review of European Community & International Environmental Law 2009, 286–303

Larson, Eric Thomas, 'Why Environmental Liability Regimes in the United States, the European Community, and Japan Have Grown Synonymous With the Polluter-Pays Principle', 38 Vanderbilt Journal of Transnational Law 2005, 541–574

Lawrence, Jessica C., 'Chicken Little Revisited: NAFTA Regulatory Expropriations after Methanex', 41 Georgia Law Review 2006, 261–309

Lee, S.G./*Kang*, S. G., 'The Effects of Sulphur Dioxide on Atmospheric Corrosion of Galvanized Steel', 16 Journal of Materials Science Letters 1997, 902–905

Leeks, Annie, 'The Relationship Between Bilateral Investment Treaty Arbitration and the Wider Corpus of International Law: The ICSID Approach', 65 University of Toronto Faculty of Law Review 2007, 1–40

Levine, Eugenia, '*Amicus Curiae* in International Investment Arbitration: The Implications of an Increase in Third-Party Participation', 29 Berkley Journal of International Law 2011, 200–224

Levy, Tali, 'NAFTA's Provisions for Compensation in the Event of Expropriation: A Reassessment of the "Prompt, Adequate and Effective" Standard', 31 Stanford Journal of International Law 1995, 423–453

Lindo, Victoria R., 'Hydroelectric Power Production in Costa Rica and the Threat of Environmental Disaster through CAFTA', 29 Boston College International and Comparative Law Review 2006, 297–322

Lipson, Charles, Standing Guard: Protecting Foreign Capital in the Nineteenth and Twentieth Centuries (Berkeley: University of California Press, 1985)

Lowe, Vaughan, 'Sustainable Development and Unsustainable Arguments', in: International Law and Sustainable Development: Past Achievements and Future Challenges (Boyle, Alan/Freestone, David (Eds.) Oxford: Oxford University Press, 1999) 19–37

Lowenfeld, Andreas F., International Economic Law (Oxford: 2nd Edition, Oxford University Press, 2008)

MacDonald, Gordon J., 'Environment: Evolution of a Concept', 12 Journal of Environment & Development 2003, 151–176

Madalena, Iganacio, 'Foreign Direct Investment and the Protection of the Environment: The Border Between National Environmental Regulation and Expropriation', 12 European Environmental Law Review 2003, 70–82

Marboe, Irmgard, Calculation of Compensation and Damages in International Investment Law (Oxford: Oxford University Press, 2009)

Martin, Marisa, 'Trade Law Implications of Restricting Participation in the European Union Emissions Trading Scheme', 19 Georgetown International Environmental Law Review 2007, 437–474

Matz-Lück, Nele, 'Harmonization, Systemic Integration, and 'Mutual Supportiveness' as Conflict-Solution Techniques: Different Modes of Interpretation as a Challenge to Negative Effects of Fragmentation?', XVII Finnish Yearbook of International Law 2006, 39–53

Mayeda, Graham, 'Playing Fair: The Meaning of Fair and Equitable Treatment in Bilateral Investment Treaties', 41 Journal of World Trade 2007, 273–291

– 'International Investment Agreements Between Developed and Developing Countries: Dancing With the Devil? Case Comment on the Vivendi, Sempra and Enron Awards', 4 Mc Gill International Journal of Sustainable Development Law and Policy 2008, 189–230

McLachlan, Campell, 'The Principle of Systematic Integration and Article 31 (3) (c) of the Vienna Convention', 54 International & Comparative Law Quarterly 2005, 279–319

Merrill, Thomas W., 'Incomplete Compensation for Takings', 11 New York University Environmental Law Journal 2002, 110–135

Meyerholt, Ulrich, Umweltrecht (Oldenburg: 3rd Edition, BIS Verlag, 2011)

Miles, Kate, 'International Investment Law and Climate Change: Issues in the Transition to a Low-Carbon World', Society of International Economic Law, Working

Paper No. 27/08, 2008, at: http://www.ssrn.com/link/SIEL-Inaugural-Conference.html

– 'International Investment Law: Origins, Imperialism and Conceptualizing the Environment', 21 Colorado Journal of International Environmental Law and Policy 2010, 1–47

– 'Sustainable Development, National Treatment and Like Circumstances in Investment Law', in: Sustainable Development in World Investment Law (Cordonier Segger, Marie-Claire/Gehring, Markus W./Newcombe, Andrew (Eds.) Alphen aan den Rijn: Kluwer Law International, 2011) 265–293

Millennium Ecosystem Assessment, Ecosystems and Human Well-Being, Biodiversity Synthesis (Washington D.C.: World Resources Institute, 2005)

Moloo, Rahim/*Jacinto*, Justin, 'Environmental and Health Regulation: Assessing Liability under Investment-Treaties', 29 Berkeley Journal of International Law 2011, 1–65

Muchlinski, Peter, 'Corporate Social Responsibility', in: The Oxford Handbook of International Investment Law (Muchlinski, Peter/Ortino, Federico/Schreuer, Christoph (Eds.) Oxford: Oxford University Press, 2008) 637–687

Nash, Jonathan Remy, 'Too Much Market? Conflict Between Tradable Pollution Allowances and the "Polluter Pays" Principle', 24 Harvard Environmental Law Review 2000, 465–535

Newcombe, Andrew, 'The Boundaries of Regulatory Expropriation in International Law', 20 ICSID Review Foreign Investment Law Journal 2005, 1–57

– 'General Exceptions in International Investment Agreements', in: Sustainable Development in World Investment Law (Cordonier Segger, Marie-Claire/Gehring, Markus W./Newcombe, Andrew (Eds.) Alphen aan den Rijn: Kluwer Law International, 2011) 355–370

Orakhelashvili, Alexander, 'Recent Practice on the Principles of Treaty Interpretation', in: 40 Years of the Vienna Convention on the Law of Treaties (Orakhelashvili, Alexander/Williams, Sarah (Eds.) London: British Institute of International and Comparative Law, 2010) 117–154

Organisation for Economic Co-operation and Development (OECD), 'Council Recommendations on Guiding Principles Concerning the International Economic Aspects of Environmental Policies', C(72)128, 26 May 1972

– '"Indirect Expropriation" and the "Right to Regulate" in International Investment Law', OECD Working Papers on International Investment (2004/4)

Ortino, Federico, 'Non-Discriminatory Treatment in Investment Disputes', in: Human Rights in International Investment Law and Arbitration (Dupuy, Pierre-Marie/Francioni, Francesco/Petersmann, Ernst-Ulrich (Eds.) Oxford: Oxford University Press, 2009) 344–366

Ottinger, Richard L., 'Biofuels: Potential, Problems & Solutions', 19 Fordham Environmental Law Review 2009, 253–263

Paparinskis, Martins, 'Regulatory Expropriation and Sustainable Development', in: Sustainable Development in World Investment Law (Cordonier Segger, Marie-

Claire/Gehring, Markus W./Newcombe, Andrew (Eds.) Alphen aan den Rijn: Kluwer Law International, 2011) 299–327

Pâques, Michel, 'L'*emission trading* à la Cour d'Arbitrage', Aménagement-Environnement 2006, 181–190

Parra, Antonio R., 'Applicable Law in Investor-State Arbitration', in: Contemporary Issues in International Arbitration and Mediation: The Fordham Papers 2007 (Rovine, Arthur W. (Ed.) Leiden: Martinus Nijhoff Publishers, 2007) 3–12

Paulsson, Jan, Denial of Justice in International Law (Cambridge: Cambridge University Press, 2005)

Paulsson, Jan/*Douglas*, Zachary, 'Indirect Expropriation in Investment Treaty Arbitrations, Indirect Expropriation in Investment Treaty Arbitrations', in: Arbitrating Foreign Investment Disputes, Procedural and Substantive Legal Aspects (Horn, Norbert/Kröll, Stefan (Eds.) The Hague: Kluwer Law International, 2004) 145–158

Pavoni, Riccardo, 'Mututal Supportiveness as a Principle of Interpretation and Law-Making: A Watershed for the "WTO-and-Competing-Regimes" Debate?', 21 European Journal of International Law 2010, 649–679

Percival, Robert V., 'China's "Green Leap Forward" Toward Global Environmental Leadership', 12 Vermont Journal of Environmental Law 2011, 633–657

Peretz, Neil, 'Carbon Leakage under the European Union Emissions Trading Scheme: Is It a Major Policy Concern?', 23 Tulane Environmental Law Journal 2009, 57–91

Pillai, Bharathi, 'Moving Forward to 2012: An Evaluation of the Clean Development Mechanism', 18 New York University Environmental Law Journal 2010, 357–411

Pimm, Stuart L., 'Biodiversity: Climate Change or Habitat Loss – Which Will Kill More Species?' 18 Current Biology 2008, R 117–R 119

Posser, Herbert/*Altenschmidt*, Stefan, 'European Union Emissions Trading Directive', 23 Journal of Energy & Natural Resources Law 2005, 60–72

Powers, Melissa, 'King Corn: Will the Renewable Fuel Standard Eventually End Corn Ethanol's Reign?', 11 Vermont Journal of Environmental Law 2010, 667–708

Radi, Yannick, 'The Application of the Most-Favoured Nation Clause to the Dispute Settlement Provisions of Bilateral Investment Treaties: Domesticating the "Trojan Horse"', 18 European Journal of International Law 2007, 757–774

Ratner, Steven R., 'Regulatory Takings in Institutional Context: Beyond the Fear of Fragmented International Law', 102 American Journal of International Law 2008, 475–528

Rayfuse, Rosemary, 'Biological Resources', in: The Oxford Handbook of International Environmental Law (Bodansky, Daniel/Brunnée, Jutta/Hey, Ellen (Eds.) Oxford: Oxford University Press, 2007) 362–393

Redgwell, Catherine, 'National Implementation', in: The Oxford Handbook of International Environmental Law (Bodansky, Daniel/Brunnée, Jutta/Hey, Ellen (Eds.) Oxford: Oxford University Press, 2007) 922–946

Reisman, W. Michael/*Sloane*, Robert D., 'Indirect Expropriation and Its Valuation in the BIT Generation', 74 British Yearbook of International Law 2003, 115–150

Riley, Sophie, 'A Weed by Any Other Name: Would the Rose Smell As Sweet if It Were a Threat to Biodiversity?', 22 Georgetown International Environmental Law Review 2009, 157–184

Ripinsky, Sergey/*Williams*, Kevin, Damages in International Investment Law (London: British Institute of International and Comparative Law, 2008)

Roberts, Anthea, 'Power and Persuasion in Investment Treaty Arbitration: The Dual Role of States', 104 American Journal of International Law 2010, 179–225

Roberts, Mark W./*Grabiel*, Peter M., 'A Window of Opportunity: Combating Climate Change by Amending the Montreal Protocol to Regulate the Production and the Consumption of HFCs and ODS Banks', 22 Georgetown International Environmental Law Review 2009, 99–155

Romson, Åsa, 'International Investment Law and the Environment', in: Sustainable Development in World Investment Law (Cordonier Segger, Marie-Claire/Gehring, Markus W./Newcombe, Andrew (Eds.) Alphen aan den Rijn: Kluwer Law International, 2011) 37–52

Ross, Jenifer, 'Legally Binding Prior Informed Consent', 10 Colorado Journal of International Environmental Law and Policy 1999, 499–529

Rotman, David, 'The Price of Biofuels', 111 Technology Review 2008, 42–51

Royalty, Kent W./*Ross*, Dianna, 'NAFTA Chapter 11: "Tantamount to Expropriation": Tantamount to Explosive', 21 The International Trade Journal 2007, 299–327

Ruiz Fabri, Hélène, 'The Approach Taken by the European Court of Human Rights to the Assessment of Compensation for "Regulatory Expropriations" of the Property of Foreign Investor', 11 New York University Environmental Law Journal 2002, 148–173

Sadeleer, Nicholas de, Environmental Principles: From Political Slogans to Legal Rules (Oxford: Oxford University Press, 2002)

– 'The Precautionary Principle in International Law', in: The Transformation of International Environmental Law (Kerbrat, Yann/Maljean-Dubois, Sandrine (Eds.) Oxford/Paris: Editions A. Pedone and Hart Publishing, 2011) 73–88

Sampliner, Gary H., 'Arbitration of Expropriation Cases under U.S. Investment Treaties – A Threat to Democracy or the Dog That Didn't Bark?', 18 ICSID Review Foreign Investment Law Journal 2003, 1–43

Sands, Philippe, 'International Law in the Field of Sustainable Development', 65 British Yearbook of International Law 1994, 303–381

– 'Treaty, Custom, and the Cross-Fertilization of International Law', 1 Yale Human Rights and Development Law Journal 1998, 85–105

– 'Sustainable Development: Treaty, Custom and the Cross-Fertilization of International Law', in: International Law and Sustainable Development: Past Achievements and Future Challenges (Boyle, Alan/Freestone, David (Eds.) Oxford: Oxford University Press, 1999) 39–60

Sands, Philippe/*Commission*, Jeffrey, 'Treaty, Custom and Time: Interpretation/Application?', in: Treaty Interpretation and the Vienna Convention on the Law of Treaties: 30 Years On (Fitzmaurice, Malgosia/Elias, Olufemi/Merkouris, Panos (Eds.) Leiden: Martinus Nijhoff Publishers, 2010) 39–58

Sands, Philippe/*Peel*, Jacequeline, Principles of International Environmental Law (2012) (Cambridge: 3rd Edition, Cambridge University Press, 2012)

Schatz, Andrew, 'Discounting the Clean Development Mechanism', 20 Georgetown International Environmental Law Review 2008, 703–742

Schill, Stephan W., 'Do Investment Treaties Chill Unilateral State Regulation to Mitigate Climate Change?', 24 Journal of International Arbitration 2007, 469–477

– 'Multilateralizing Investment Treaties through Most-Favored-Nation Clauses', 27 Berkley Journal of International Law 2009, 496–569

Schreuer, Christoph, The ICSID Convention: A Commentary (Cambridge: Cambridge University Press, 2001)

– 'The Concept of Expropriation under the ECT and Other Investment Protection Treaties', in: Investment Arbitration and the Energy Charter Treaty (Ribeiro, Clarisse (Ed.) New York: Huntington, 2006) 108–159

– 'Protection against Arbitrary and Discriminatory Measures', in: The Future of Investment Arbitration (Rogers, Catherine A./Alford, Roger P. (Eds.) New York: Oxford University Press, 2009) 183–198

– 'Diversity and Harmonization of Treaty Interpretation in Investment Arbitration', in: Treaty Interpretation and the Vienna Convention on the Law of Treaties: 30 Years On (Fitzmaurice, Malgosia/Elias, Olufemi/Merkouris, Panos (Eds.) Leiden: Martinus Nijhoff Publishers, 2010) 129–152

Schwarzenberger, Georg, International Law as Applied by International Courts and Tribunals (London: Volume 1, 3rd Edition, Stevens & Sons Limited, 1957)

Simmons, Joshua B., 'Valuation in Investor-State Arbitration: Toward a More Exact Science', 30 Berkley Journal of International Law 2012, 196–250

Smaling, Rudolf M., 'Environmental Barriers to Widespread Implementation of Biofuels', 2 Environmental & Energy Law & Policy Journal 2008, 287–308

Smith, David N., 'The Way We Think: Ethics, Health and the Environment in International Business', 5 Asian Journal of WTO & International Health Law and Policy 2010, 25–52

Smutny, Abby Cohen, 'Some Observations on the Principles Relating to Compensation in the Investment Treaty Context', 22 ICSID Review Foreign Investment Law Journal 2007, 1–23

Snodgrass, Elizabeth, 'Protecting Investors' Legitimate Expectations – Recognizing and Delimiting a General Principle', 21 ICSID Review Foreign Investment Law Journal 2006, 1–58

Soloway, Julie A., 'Environmental Regulation as Expropriation: The Case of NAFTA's Chapter 11', 33 Canadian Business Law Journal 2000, 92–127

Sornarajah, M., The International Law on Foreign Investment (Cambridge: 3rd Edition, Cambridge University Press, 2010)

Stern, Brigitte, 'The Future of International Investment Law: A Balance Between the Protection of Investors and the State's Capacity to Regulate' in: The Evolving International Investment Regime: Expectations, Realities, Opinions (Alvarez, José/Sauvant, Karl P. (Eds.) New York: Oxford University Press, 2011) 174–192

Subedi, Surya P., 'The Challenge of Reconciling the Competing Principles within the Law of Foreign Investment with Special Reference to the Recent Trend in the Interpretation of the Term "Expropriation"', 40 International Lawyer 2006, 121–141

– International Investment Law: Reconciling Policy and Principle (Oxford: Hart Publishing, 2008)

Sureda, Andrés Rigo, 'Precedent in Investment Treaty Arbitration', in: International Investment Law for the 21st Century: Essays in Honour of Christoph Schreuer (Binder, Christina/Kriebaum, Ursula/Reinisch, August/Wittich, Stephan (Eds.) Oxford: Oxford University Press, 2009) 830–842

Sussman, Edna, 'The Energy Charter Treaty's Investor Protection Provisions: Potential to Foster Solutions to Global Warming and Promote Sustainable Development, 14 ILSA Journal of International and Comparative Law 2008, 391–404

Suy, Eric, 'Le Préambule' in: Liber Amicorum Judge Mohammed Bedjaoui (Yakpo, Emile/Boumedra, Tahar (Eds.) The Hague: Kluwer Law International, 1999) 253–269

Swan, Alan C., 'NAFTA Chapter 11 – "Direct Effect" and Interpretative Method: Lessons From Methanex v. United States', 64 University of Miami Law Review 2009, 21–88

Swanson, Timothy, Global Action for Biodiversity (London: Earthscan Publications Ltd., 1997)

Tienhaara, Kyla, Expropriation of Environmental Governance: Protecting Foreign Investors at the Expense of Public Policy (Cambridge: Cambridge University Press, 2009)

Transparency International, Corruption Perceptions Index 2013 (2013) at: http://cpi.transparency.org/cpi2013/results/

Trouwborst, Arie, Precautionary Rights and Duties of States (Leiden: Martinus Nijhoff Publishers, 2006)

– 'The Precautionary Principle in General International Law: Combatting the Babylonian Confusion', 16 Review of European Community and International Environmental Law 2007, 185–195

Tudor, Ioana, The Fair and Equitable Treatment Standard in the International Law of Foreign Investment (Oxford: Oxford University Press, 2008)

United Nations Conference on the Law of Treaties, 'Official Records: Documents of the Conference' (1971), A/CONF.39/11/Add.2

United Nations Conference on Trade and Development (UNCTAD), 'Foreign Investment and Performance Requirements: New Evidence from Selected Countries' (2003), UNCTAD/ITE/IIA/2003/7

– 'Transparency' (2004), UNCTAD/ITE/IIT/2003/4

– 'World Investment Report 2007, Transnational Corporations, Extractive Industries and Development' (2007) at: http://unctad.org/en/docs/wir2007_en.pdf

– 'World Investment Report 2010, Investing in a Low Carbon Economy' (2010) at: http://unctad.org/en/docs/wir2010_en.pdf

United Nations Development Programme (UNDP), 'Clean Development Mechanism: A User's Guide' (2003) at http://content.undp.org/go/newsroom/publications/environment-energy/www-ee-library/climate-change/undp-cdm-manual.en

United Nations Environment Programme (UNEP) Governing Council Decision SS.VII/4 of February 2002, 'Compliance with and Enforcement of Multilateral Environmental Agreements', UNEP(DEPI)/MEAs/WBG.1/3, Annex 2

– 'Towards Sustainable Production and Use of Resources: Assessing Biofuels' (2009) at: http://www.unep.fr/scp/rpanel/pdf/assessing_biofuels_full_report.pdf

Van Damme, Isabelle, 'Some Observations about the ILC Study Group Report on the Fragmentation of International Law: WTO Treaty Interpretation against the Background of Other International Law', XVII Finnish Yearbook of International Law 2006, 21–38

Villiger, Mark E., Commentary on the 1969 Vienna Convention on the Law of Treaties (Leiden: Martinus Nijhoff Publishers, 2009)

Viñuales, Jorge E., 'Access to Water in Foreign Investment Disputes', 21 Georgetown International Law Review 2009, 733–760

Viñuales, Jorge E./*Jesko Langer*, Magnus, 'Managing Conflicts Between Environmental and Investment Norms in International Law', in: The Transformation of International Environmental Law (Kerbrat, Yann/Maljean-Dubois, Sandrine (Eds.) Oxford: A. Pedone & Hart, 2011) 171–191

Wagner, J. Martin, 'International Investment, Expropriation and Environmental Protection', 29 Golden Gate University Law Review 1999, 465–527

Wälde, Thomas, 'International Disciplines on National Environmental Regulation: With Particular Focus on Multilateral Investment Treaties', in: International Investments and Protection of the Environment: The Role of Dispute Resolution Mechanisms (International Bureau of the Permanent Court of Arbitration (Ed.) The Hague: Kluwer Law International, 2001) 29–71

Wälde, Thomas W./*Hobér*, Kaj, 'The First Energy Charter Treaty Arbitral Award', 22 Journal of International Arbitration 2005, 83–104

Wälde, Thomas W./*Sabahi*, Borzu, 'Compensation, Damages, and Valuation' in: The Oxford Handbook of International Investment Law (Muchlinski, Peter/Ortino, Federico/Schreuer, Christoph (Eds.) Oxford: Oxford University Press, 2008) 1049–1124

Walter, André von, 'The Investor's Expectations in International Investment Arbitration', in: International Investment Law in Context (Reinisch, August/Knahr, Christina (Eds.) Utrecht: Eleven International Publishing, 2008) 173–200

Wara, Michael, 'Measuring the Clean Development Mechanism's Performance and Potential', 55 UCLA Law Review 2008, 1759–1803

Weber, Rolf H./*Darbellay*, Aline, 'Regulation and Financial Intermediation in the Kyoto Protocol's Clean Development Mechanism', 22 Georgetown International Environmental Law Review 2010, 271–305

Weidemaier, W. Mark C., 'Toward a Theory of Precedent in Arbitration', 51 William and Mary Law Review 2010, 1895–1958

Weiler, Todd, 'Saving Oscar Chin: Non-Discrimination in International Investment Law', in: International Investment Law and Arbitration: Leading Cases from the ICSID, NAFTA, Bilateral Treaties and Customary International Law (Weiler, Todd (Ed.) London: Cameron May, 2005) 557–595

Werksman, Jacob/*Baumert*, Kevin A./*Dubash*, Navroz K., 'Will International Investment Rules Obstruct Climate Protection Policies? An Examination of the Clean Development Mechanism', 3 International Environmental Agreements: Politics, Law and Economics 2003, 59–86

Wiener, Jonathan B., 'Precaution', in: The Oxford Handbook of International Environmental Law (Bodansky, Daniel/Brunnée, Jutta/Hey, Ellen (Eds.) Oxford: Oxford University Press, 2007) 597–612

Wirth, David A., 'Hazardous Substances and Activities', in: The Oxford Handbook of International Environmental Law (Bodansky, Daniel/Brunnée, Jutta/Hey, Ellen (Eds.) Oxford: Oxford University Press, 2007) 394–422

World Bank, World Bank Guidelines on the Treatment of Foreign Direct Investment (1992), at: http://italaw.com/documents/WorldBank.pdf

World Commission on Environment and Development, 'Our Common Future – the Brundtland Report' (1987) Annex to UN Doc A/42/427

Wyllie, Candice A., 'A Comparative Analysis of Nondiscrimination in Multilateral Agreements: North American Free Trade Agreement (NAFTA), Energy Charter Treaty (ECT), and General Agreement on Tariffs and Trade (GATT)', 18 Willamette Journal of International Law and Dispute Resolution 2010, 64–108

Yannaca-Small, Katia, 'Fair and Equitable Treatment Standard: Recent Developments', in: Standards of Investment Protection (Reinisch, August (Ed.) Oxford: Oxford University Press, 2008) 111–130

Yoder, Andrew J., 'Lessons From Stockholm: Evaluating the Global Convention on Persistent Organic Pollutants', 10 Indiana Journal of Global Legal Studies 2003, 113–156

Zander, Joakim, The Application of the Precautionary Principle in Practice: Comparative Dimensions (Cambridge: Cambridge University Press, 2010)

Zhou, Jian, 'National Treatment in Foreign Investment Law: A Comparative Study from a Chinese Perspective', 10 Touro International Law Review 2000, 39–153

Ziegler, Andreas R., 'Most-Favoured-Nation (MFN) Treatment', in: Standards of Investment Protection (Reinisch, August (Ed.) Oxford: Oxford University Press, 2008) 59–86

Table of Decisions

Permanent Court of International Justice

Case Concerning the Factory at Chorzów (Germany/Poland) Judgment of 13 September 1928, (Series A, No 17, 3)

The Oscar Chinn Case (Britain/Belgium) Judgment of 12 December 1934 (Series A/B No 63, 65)

International Court of Justice

Asylum Case (Colombia/Peru) Judgment of 20 November 1950, ICJ Reports 1950, 266

Reservations to the Convention on the Prevention and Punishment of the Crime of Genocide, Advisory Opinion of 28 May 1951, ICJ Reports 1951, 15

Legal Consequences for States of the Continued Presence of South Africa in Namibia (South West Africa) notwithstanding Security Council Resolution 276 (1970), Advisory Opinion of 21 June 1971, ICJ Reports 1971, 16

Case Concerning Aegean Sea Continental Shelf (Greece/Turkey) Judgment of 19 December 1978, ICJ Reports 1978, 3

Case Concerning Military and Paramilitary Activity in and against Nicaragua, (Nicaragua/United States of America), Judgment on the Merits of 27 June 1986, ICJ Reports 1986, 14

Case Concerning Elettronica Sicula S.p.A. (ELSI) (United States of America/Italy), Judgment of 20 July 1989, ICJ Reports 1989, 15

Case Concerning the Gabčíkovo-Nagymaros Project (Hungary/Slovakia) Judgment of 25 September 1997, ICJ Reports 1997, 7

Case Concerning the Gabčíkovo-Nagymaros Project (Hungary/Slovakia) Separate Opinion of Judge Weeramantry, ICJ Reports 1997, 88

Case Concerning Oil Platforms (Islamic Republic of Iran/United States of America), Judgment of 6 November 2003, ICJ Reports 2003, 161

Legal Consequences of the Construction of a Wall in the Occupied Palestinian Territory, Advisory Opinion of 9 July 2004, ICJ Reports 2004, 136

Case Concerning Pulp Mills on the River Uruguay (Argentina/Uruguay) Provisional Measures Order of 13 July 2006, ICJ Reports 2006, 113

Case Concerning Pulp Mills on the River Uruguay (Argentina/Uruguay) Dissenting Opinion of Judge ad hoc Vinuesa to Order on Provisional Measures, ICJ Reports 2006, 147

Case Concerning Pulp Mills on the River Uruguay (Argentina/Uruguay) Judgment of 20 April 2010, ICJ Reports 2010, 14

Case Concerning Pulp Mills on the River Uruguay (Argentina/Uruguay) Separate Opinion of Judge Cançado Trindade to Judgment of 20 April 2010, ICJ Reports 2010, 135

World Trade Organisation Decisions

United States – Tax on Petroleum and Certain Imported Substances, L/6175 – 34S/136, GATT Panel Report adopted on 17 June 1987

United States – Restrictions on Imports of Tuna, DS29/R, GATT Panel Report adopted on 16 June 1994

United States – Standards for Reformulated and Conventional Gasoline, DS2/AB/R, WTO Appellate Body Report of 29 April 1996

European Communities – Measures Concerning Meat and Meat Products (Hormones), DS26/AB/R, WTO Appellate Body Report of 16 January 1998

United States – Import Prohibition of Certain Shrimp and Shrimp Products, DS58/AB/R, WTO Appellate Body Report of 12 October 1998

Korea – Measures Affecting Imports of Fresh, Chilled and Frozen Beef, DS161/AB/R, WTO Appellate Body Report of 11 December 2000

European Communities – Measures Affecting Asbestos and Asbestos Containing Products, DS135/AB/R, WTO Appellate Body Report of 12 March 2001

United States – Import Prohibition of Certain Shrimp and Shrimp Products (Malaysian Recourse to Article 21.5), DS58/RW, WTO Panel Report of 15 June 2001

United States – Measures Affecting the Cross-Border Supply of Gambling and Betting Services, DS285/AB/R, WTO Appellate Body Report of 7April 2005

European Communities – Measures Affecting the Approval and Marketing of Biotech Products, DS291-3/R, WTO Panel Report of 29 September 2006

Brazil – Measures Affecting Imports of Retreated Tyres, DS332/AB/R, WTO Appellate Body Report of 3 December 2007

International Tribunal of the Law of the Sea

MOX Plant Case, Case No 10 (Ireland v. United Kingdom) Order of 3 December 2001

MOX Plant Case, Case No 10 (Ireland v. United Kingdom) Order No 3 of 24 June 2003

Southern Bluefin Tuna Case, Cases No 3 and 4 (New Zealand, Australia v. Japan) Order of 27 August 1999

Southern Bluefin Tuna Case, Cases No 3 and 4 (New Zealand, Australia v. Japan) Order of 27 August 1999, Separate Opinion of Judge ad hoc Shearer

Southern Bluefin Tuna Case, Cases No 3 and 4 (New Zealand, Australia v. Japan) Order of 27 August 1999, Separate Opinion of Judge Treves

Southern Bluefin Tuna Case, Cases No 3 and 4 (New Zealand, Australia v. Japan) Order of 27 August 1999, Separate Opinion of Judge Laing

Decisions of Investment Tribunals

Antoine Abou Lahoud and Leila Bounafeh-Abou Lahoud v. Democratic Republic of the Congo, ICSID Case No. ARB/10/4, Award of 7 February 2014

ADC Affiliate Limited and ADC & ADMC Management Limited v. Republic of Hungary, ICSID Case No. ARB/03/16, Award of 2 October 2006

ADF Group Inc. v. United States, ICSID Case No. ARB (AF)/00/1, Award of 9 January 2003

AES Summit Generation Limited and AES-Tisza Erömü Kft v. The Republic of Hungary, ICSID Case No. ARB/07/22 (ECT), Award of 23 September 2010

Amco Asia Corporation and others v. Republic of Indonesia, ICSID Case No. ARB/81/1, Decision on the Application for Annulment of 16 May 1986

American Manufacturing & Trading, Inc. v. Republic of Zaire, ICSID Case No. ARB/93/1, Award of 21 Februar 1997

Archer Daniels Midland Company and Tate & Lyle Ingredients Americas, Inc. v. United Mexican States, ICSID Case No. ARB (AF)/04/5, Award of 21 November 2007

Franck Charles Arif v. Republic of Moldova, ICSID Case No. ARB/11/23, Award of 8 April 2013

Asian Agricultural Products Ltd. v. Republic of Sri Lanka, ICSID Case No. ARB/87/3, Award of 27 June 1990

AWG Group Ltd. v. The Argentine Republic, Decision on Liability of 30 July 2010

AWG Group Ltd. v. The Argentine Republic – Suez, Sociedad General de Aguas de Barcelona S.A., and InterAguas Servicios Integrales del Agua S.A. v. The Argentine Republic, ICSID Case No. ARB/03/17 – Suez, Sociedad General de Aguas de Barcelona, S.A. and Vivendi Universal, S.A. v. Argentine Republic, ICSID Case No. ARB/03/19, Common Separate Opinion of Arbitrator Pedro Nikken to Decision on Liability of 30 July 2010

Azinian, Davitian, & Baca v. Mexico, ICSID Case No. ARB (AF)/97/2, Award of 1 November 1999

Azurix v. Argentine Republic, ICSID Case No. ARB/01/12, Award of 14 July 2006

Walter Bau v. Thailand, Award of 1 July 2009

Bayindir Insaat Turizm Ticaret Ve Sanayi A.S. v. Islamic Republic of Pakistan, ICSID Case No. ARB/03/29, Award of 27 August 2009

BG Group Plc v. Argentina, Award of 24 December 2007

Biloune and Marine Drive Complex Ltd v. Ghana Investments Centre and the Government of Ghana, Award on Jurisdiction and Liability of 27 October 1989

Biwater Gauff (Tanzania) Ltd. v. United Republic of Tanzania, ICSID Case No. ARB/05/22, Award of 24 July 2008

Bosh International, Inc and B&P Ltd Foreign Investments Enterprise v. Ukraine, ICSID Case No. ARB/08/11, Award of 25 October 2012

Burlington Resources Inc. v. Republic of Ecuador, ICSID Case No. ARB/08/5, Decision on Liability of 14 December 2012

Canfor Corporation v. United States of America; Terminal Forest Products Ltd. v. United States of America, Decision on Preliminary Questions of 6 June 2006

Chemtura Corporation v. Government of Canada, Award of 2 August 2010

CME Czech Republic B.V. v. Czech Republic, Partial Award of 13 September 2001

CMS Gas Transmission Company v. The Argentine Republic, ICSID Case No. ARB/01/8, Award of 12 May 2005

CMS Gas Transmission Company v. The Argentine Republic, ICSID Case No. ARB/01/8, Annulment Proceeding, Decision of 25 September 2007

Compañiá de Aguas del Aconquija S.A. and Vivendi Universal v. Argentine Republic, ICSID Case No. ARB/97/3, Award of 20 August 2007

Compañía del Dessarollo de Santa Elena S.A. v. Republic of Costa Rica, ICSID Case No. ARB/96/1, Award of 17 February 2000

Consortium R.F.C.C. v. Kingdom of Morocco, ICSID Case No. ARB/00/6, Award of 22 December 2003

Continental Casualty Company v. Argentina, ICSID Case No. ARB/03/9, Award of 5 September 2008

Corn Products International, Inc. v. United Mexican States, ICSID Case No. ARB(AF)04/01, Partial Award of 15 January 2008

Deutsche Bank AG v. Democratic Socialist Republic of Sri Lanka, ICSID Case No. ARB/09/2, Award of 31 October 2012

Duke Energy Electroquil Partners & Electroquil S.A. v. Republic of Ecuador, ICSID Case No. ARB/04/19, Award of 18 August 2008

EDF International S.A., SAUR International S.A. and León Participaciones Argentinas S.A. v. Argentine Republic, ICSID Case No. ARB/03/23, Award of 11 June 2012

EDF (Services) Limited v. Romania, ICSID Case No. ARB/05/13, Award of 8 October 2009

El Paso Energy International Company v. The Argentine Republic, ICSID Case No. ARB/03/15, Decision on Jurisdiction of 27 April 2006

Enron Corporation and Ponderosa Assets, L.P. v. Argentine Republic, ICSID Case No. ARB/01/3, Award of 22 May 2007

Enron Corporation and Ponderosa Assets, L.P. v. Argentine Republic, ICSID Case No. ARB/01/3, Annulment Proceeding, Decision on the Application for Annulment of the Argentine Republic of 30 July 2010

Eureko B.V. v. Republic of Poland, Partial Award of 19 August 2005

Feldman v. Mexico, ICSID Case No. ARB(AF)/99/1, Award of 16 December 2002

Fireman's Fund Insurance Company v. United Mexican States, ICSID Case No. ARB(AF)/02/1, Award of 17 July 2006

Gami Investments, Inc. v. Mexico, Award of 15 November 2004

Vito G. Gallo v. Canada, Statement of Claim of 23 June 2008

Vito G. Gallo v. Canada, Statement of Defence of 15 September 2009

Vito G. Gallo v. Canada, Award of 15 September 2011

Generation Ukraine, Inc. v. Ukraine, ICSID Case No. ARB/00/9, Award of 16 September 2003

Genin and others v. Estonia, ICSID Case No. ARB/99/2, Award of 25 June 2001

Glamis Gold, Ltd. v. U.S.A., Award of 8 June 2009

Industria Nacional de Alimentos, S.A. and Indalsa Perú, S.A. (formerly Empresas Lucchetti, S.A. and Lucchetti Perú, S.A.) v. Republic of Peru, ICSID Case No. ARB/03/4, Award of 7 February 2005

International Thunderbird Gaming Corporation v. Mexico, Award of 26 January 2006

International Thunderbird Gaming Corporation v. Mexico, Separate Opinion by Arbitrator Thomas Wälde

Jan de Nul N.V. and Dredging International N.V. v. Arab Republic of Egypt, ICSID Case No. ARB/04/13, Award of 6 November 2008

Joy Mining Machinery Limited v. Arab Republic of Egypt, ICSID Case No. ARB/03/11, Decision on Jurisdiction of 6 August 2004

Klöckner Industrie-Anlagen GmbH v. United Republic of Cameroon, ICSID Case No. ARB/81/2, Annulment Decision of 3 May 1985

Lauder v. Czech Republic, Award of 3 September 2001

Joseph Charles Lemire v. Ukraine, ICSID Case No. ARB/06/18, Decision on Jurisdiction and Liablity of 14 January 2010

L.E.S.I. S.p.A. et ASTALDI S.p.A. v. Algeria, ICSID Case No. ARB/05/3, Award of 12 November 2008

LG&E v. Argentina, ICSID Case No. ARB/02/1, Decision on Liability of 3 October 2006

LG&E v. Argentina, ICSID Case No. ARB/02/1, Award of 25 July 2007

Loewen Group, Inc. and Raymond L. Loewen v. United States, ICSID Case No. ARB(AF)/98/3, Award of 26 June 2003

Maffezini v. Spain, ICSID Case No. ARB/97/7, Award on the Merits of 13 November 2000

M.C.I. Power Group L.C. and New Turbine, Inc. v. Ecuador, ICSID Case No. ARB/03/6, Award of 31 July 2007

Merrill & Ring Forestry L.P. v. Canada, Award of 31 March 2010

Methanex v. United States, Partial Award of 7 August 2002

Methanex v. United States, Award of 3 August 2005

Methanex v. United States, Claimant Methanex Corporation's Reply to the Amicus Curiae Submissions of Earthjustice and the International Institute for Sustainable Development of 23 April 2004

Metalclad Corporation v. United Mexican States, ICSID Case No. ARB(AF)/97/1, Award of 30 August 2000

Metalpar S.A. and Buen Aire S.A. v. Argentine Republic, ICSID Case No. ARB/03/5, Award of 6 June 2008

Ioan Micula, Viorel Micula, S.C. European Food S.A, S.C. Starmill S.R.L. and S.C. Multipack S.R.L. v. Romania, ICSID Case No. ARB/05/20, Award of 11 December 2013

Middle East Cement Shipping and Handling Co. S.A. v. Arab Republic of Egypt, ICSID Case No. ARB/99/6, Award of 12 April 2002

Mobil Investments Canada Inc. and Murphy Oil Corporation v. Canada, ICSID Case No. ARB(AF)/07/4, Decision on Liability and on Principles of Quantum of 22 May 2012

Mondev International Ltd. v. United States of America, ICSID Case No. ARB(AF)/99/2, Award of 11 October 2002

MTD Equity Sdn. Bhd. & MTD Chile S.A. v. Chile, ICSID Case No. ARB/01/7, Award of 25 May 2004

MTD Equity Sdn. Bhd. & MTD Chile S.A. v. Chile, ICSID Case No. ARB/01/7, Decision on Annulment of 21 March 2007

National Grid plc v. The Argentine Republic, Award of 3 November 2008

Noble Ventures, Inc. v. Romania, ICSID Case No. ARB/01/11, Award of 12 October 2005

Nykomb Synergetics Technology Holding AB v. Latvia, Arbitration Institute of the Stockholm Chamber of Commerce (ECT), Award of 16 December 2003

Occidental Exploration and Production Company v. The Republic of Ecuador, LCIA Case No. UN3467, Award of 1 July 2004

Olguín v. Paraguay, ICSID Case No. ARB/98/5, Award of 26 July 2001

Parkerings-Compagniet AS v. Lithuania, ICSID Case No. ARB/05/8, Award of 11 September 2007

Victor Pey Casado and President Allende Foundation v. Republic of Chile, ICSID Case No. ARB/98/2, Award of 8 May 2008

Pac Rim Cayman LLC v. Republic of El Salvador, ICSID Case No. ARB/09/12, Notice of Intent of 9 December 2008

Pac Rim Cayman LLC v. Republic of El Salvador, ICSID Case No. ARB/09/12, Notice of Arbitration of 30 April 2009

Pac Rim Cayman LLC v. Republic of El Salvador, ICSID Case No. ARB/09/12, Claimant's Response to Respondent's Preliminary Objections of 26 February 2010

Pac Rim Cayman LLC v. Republic of El Salvador, ICSID Case No. ARB/09/12, Decision on the Respondent's Jurisdictional Objections of 1 June 2012

Plama Consortium Limited v. Bulgaria, ICSID Case No. ARB/03/24, Decision on Jurisdiction of 8 February 2005

Plama Consortium Limited v. Bulgaria, ICSID Case No. ARB/03/24, Award of 27 August 2008

Pope & Talbot Inc. v. Canada, Interim Award of 26 June 2000

Pope & Talbot Inc. v. Canada, Award on the Merits of Phase 2 of 10 April 2001

Pope & Talbot Inc. v. Canada, Award in Respect of Damages, 31 May 2002

Pope & Talbot Inc. v. Canada, Counter Memorial of 29 March 2000

PSEG Global, Inc., The North American Coal Corporation, and Konya Ingin Elektrik Uretim ve Ticaret Limited Sirketi v. Turkey, ICSID Case No. ARB/02/5, Award of 19 January 2007

Railroad Development Corporation v. Republic of Guatemala, ICSID Case No. ARB/07/23, Award of 29 June 2012

Rumeli Telekom A.S. and Telsim Mobil Telekomunikasyon Hizmetleri A.S. v. Kazakhstan, ICSID Case No. ARB/05/16, Award of 29 July 2008

Saipem S.p.A. v. The People's Republic of Bangladesh, ICSID Case No. ARB/05/07, Award of 30 June 2009

Salini Costruttori S.p.A. and Italstrade S.p.A. v. Kingdom of Morocco, ICSID Case No. ARB/00/4, Decision on Jurisdiction of 31 July 2001

Salini Costruttori S.p.A. and Italstrade S.p.A. v. Jordan, ICSID Case No. ARB/02/13, Decision on Jurisdiction of 9 November 2004

Saluka Investments BV (The Netherlands) v. The Czech Republic, Award of 17 March 2006

SAUR International SA v. Republic of Argentina, ICSID Case No. ARB/04/4, Decisison on Jurisdiction and Liability of 6 June 2012

S.D. Myers Inc. v. Canada, Partial Award on the Merits, 13 November 2000

S.D. Myers Inc. v. Canada, Separate Opinion by Arbitrator Bryan Schwartz, 12 November 2000

Sempra Energy International v. The Argentine Republic, ICSID Case No. ARB/02/16, Award of 28 September 2007

Sempra Energy International v. The Argentine Republic, ICSID Case No. ARB/02/16, Annulment Proceeding, Decision of 29 June 2010

SGS Société Générale de Surveillance S.A. v. Republic of the Philippines, ICSID Case No. ARB/02/6, Decision on Objections to Jurisdiction of 29 January 2004

Waguih Elie George Siag and Clorinda Vecchi v. The Arab Republic of Egypt, ICSID Case No. ARB/05/15, Award of 1 June 2009

Siemens A.G. v. Argentine Republic, ICSID Case No. ARB/02/8, Decision on Jurisdiction, 3 August 2004

Siemens A.G. v. Argentine Republic, ICSID Case No. ARB/02/8, Award of 6 February 2007

Suez, Sociedad General de Aguas de Barcelona S.A., and InterAguas Servicios Integrales del Agua S.A. v. The Argentine Republic, ICSID Case No. ARB/03/17, Decision on Liability of 30 July 2010

Suez, Sociedad General de Aguas de Barcelona, S.A. and Vivendi Universal, S.A. v. Argentine Republic, ICSID Case No. ARB/03/19, Decision on Liability of 30 July 2010

Técnicas Medioambientales Tecmed, S.A. v. United Mexican States, ICSID Case No. ARB (AF)/00/2, Award of 29 May 2003

TECO Guatemala Holdings, LLC v. Republic of Guatemala, ICSID Case No. ARB/10/23, Award of 19 December 2013

Tokios Tokelés v. Ukraine, ICSID Case No. ARB/02/18, Award of 26 July 2007

Toto Costruzioni Generali S.p.A. v. Republic of Lebanon, ICSID Case No. ARB/07/12, Award of 7 June 2012

Tulip Real Estate and Development Netherlands B.V. v. Republic of Turkey, ICSID Case No. ARB/11/28, Award of 10 March 2014

Ulysseas, Inc. v. The Republic of Ecuador, Award of 12 June 2012

Marion Unglaube and Reinhard Unglaube v. Republic of Costa Rica, ICSID Case No. ARB/08/1, ICSID Case No. ARB/09/20, Award of 16 May 2012

United Parcel Service of America Inc. v. Government of Canada, Award of 24 May 2007

Vattenfall AB, Vattenfall Europe AG, Vattenfall Europe Generation AG v. Federal Republic of Germany, ICSID Case No. ARB/09/6, Request for Arbitration of 30 March 2009

Vattenfall AB, Vattenfall Europe AG, Vattenfall Europe Generation AG v. Federal Republic of Germany, ICSID Case No. ARB/09/6, Award of 11 March 2011

Waste Management II v. United Mexican States, ICSID Case No. ARB(AF)/00/3 (NAFTA), Award of 30 April 2004

Wena Hotels Ltd. v. Arab Republic of Egypt, ICSID Case No. ARB/98/4, Award of 8 December 2000

Wena Hotels Ltd. v. Arab Republic of Egypt, ICSID Case No. ARB/98/4, Decision of the Ad Hoc Committee on the Application for Annulment of 28 January 2002

Submissions in Other Investment Proceedings

William Ralph Clayton, William Richard Clayton, Douglas Clayton, Daniel Clayton and Bilcon of Delaware Inc. v. Government of Canada, Amended Statement of Claim of 3 December 2009

William Ralph Clayton, William Richard Clayton, Douglas Clayton, Daniel Clayton and Bilcon of Delaware Inc. v. Government of Canada, Amended Statement of Defence of 18 December 2009

Dow AgroSciences LLC v. Canada, Notice of Arbitration of 31 March 2009

Ethyl Corporation v. Canada, Statement of Claim of 2 October 1997

Ethyl Corporation. v. Canada, Statement of Defence of 27 November 1997

Infinito Gold Ltd. v. Costa Rica, ICSID Case No. ARB/14/5, Request for Arbitration of 6 February 2014

Lone Pine Resources Inc. v. The Government of Canada, Notice of Arbitration of 6 September 2013

Windstream Energy LLC v. Government of Canada, Notice of Arbitration of 5 November 2013

Windstream Energy LLC v. Government of Canada, Response to the Notice of Arbitration of 5 December 2013

Iran-U.S. Claims Tribunal

Starret Housing Corp. v. Iran, Interlocutary Award of 19 December 1983, Award No. ITL-32-24-1, 4 Iran-US CTR 122

Tippetts, Abbett, McCarthy, Stratton v. TAMS-AFFA Consulting Engineers of Iran, Award of 22 June 1984, Award No. 141-7-2, 6 Iran-US CTR 219

Sedco, Inc. v. National Iranian Oil Co, and the Islamic Republic of Iran, Interlocutory Award of 24 October 1984, Award No. ITL 55-129-3, 9 Iran-US CTR Rep 248

Phelps Dodge International Corp. and Overseas Private Investment Corp. v. The Islamic Republic of Iran, Award of 19 March 1986, Award No. 217-99-2, 10 Iran-US CTR 121

Starrett Housing Corp v. Iran, Award of 14 August 1987, Award No. 314-24-1, 4 Iran-USCTR 112

Emanuel Too v. United States of America et al., Award of 29 December 1989, Award No. 460-880-2, 23 Iran-US CTR 378

Shahin Shane Ebrahimi, Cecilia Radene Ebrahimi, Christina Tandis Ebrahimi v. Government of the Islamic Republic of Iran, Award of 12 October 1994, Award No. 560-44/46/47-3, 30 Iran-US CTR 170

Other International Arbitration Cases

L. F. H. Neer and Pauline Neer (U.S.A./United Mexican States) Arbitral Decision of 15 October 1926, 4 UN Reports of International Arbitral Awards 60

Island of Palmas (Netherlands/U.S.A.) Award of 24 April 1928, 2 UN Reports of International Arbitral Awards 829

Trail Smelter Arbitration (U.S.A./Canada) Award of 16 April 1938 and 11 March 1941, 3 UN Reports of International Arbitral Awards 1905

Mox Plant Case – Dispute Concerning Access to Information under Article 9 of the OSPAR Convention (Ireland/United Kingdom) Final Award of 2 July 2003, 23 UN Reports of International Arbitral Awards 59

Mox Plant Case – Dispute Concerning Access to Information under Article 9 of the OSPAR Convention (Ireland/United Kingdom) Dissenting Opinion of Gavan Griffith to Final Award of 2 July 2003, 23 UN Reports of International Arbitral Awards 119

Arbitration Regarding the Iron Rhine Railway (Ijzeren Rijn) (Belgium/Netherlands) Decision of 24 May 2005

Affaire concernant l'apurement des comptes entre le royaume des Pays-Bas et la république Française en application du protocole du 25 Septembre 1991 additionnel à la Convention relative à la protection du Rhin contre la pollution par les chlorures du 3 Décembre 1976 (Netherlands/France), Award of 12 March 2004

Courts of the European Communities

European Court of Justice, PreussenElektra AG v. Schleswag AG, C-379/98, Judgment of 13 March 2001

European Court of Justice, Commune de Mesquer v. Total France SA, C-188/07, Judgment of 24 June 2008

European Court of Justice, Société Arcelor Atlantique et Lorraine and Others v. Premier ministre, Ministre de l'Écologie et du Développement durable, Ministre de l'Économie, des Finances et de l'Industrie, C-127/07, Judgment of 16 December 2008

European General Court, Arcelor SA v. European Parliament and Council of the European Union, T-16/04, Judgment of 2 March 2010

European Court of Human Rights

Case of Golder v. United Kingdom (Application No. 4451/70) Judgment of 21 February 1975

Case of Tyrer v. United Kingdom (Application No. 5856/72) Judgment of 25 April 1978

Case of Sporrong and Lönnroth v. Sweden (Application No. 7151/75; 7152/75) Judgment of 23 September 1982

Case of James and Others v. United Kingdom (Application No. 8793/79) Judgment of 21 February 1986

Case of Lithgow and Others v. United Kingdom (Application No. 9006/80; 9262/81; 9263/81; 9265/81; 9266/81; 9313/81; 9405/81) Judgment of 8 July 1986

Case of Mellacher and Others v. Austria (Application No. 10522/83; 11011/84; 11070/84) Judgment of 19 December 1989

Case of Fredin v. Sweden (Application No. 12033/86) Judgment of 18 February 1991

Case of Pine Valley Developments Ltd and Others v. Ireland (Application No. 12742/87) Judgment of 29 November 1991

Case of Katte Klitsche de la Grange v. Italy (Application No. 12539/86) Judgment of 19 September 1994

Case of Loizidou v. Turkey (Application No. 15318/89) Grand Chamber Judgment of 18 December 1996

Case of Pinnacle Meat Processors v. United Kingdom (Application No. 33298/96) European Commission on Human Rights Decision of 21 October 1998

Case of Guerra v. Italy (Application No. 116/1996/735/932) Grand Chamber Judgment of 19 February 1998

Case of Matthews v. United Kingdom (Application No. 24833/94) Grand Chamber Judgment of 18 February 1999

Case of McElhinney v. Ireland (Application No. 31253/96) Grand Chamber Judgment of 21 November 2001

Case of Al-Adsani v. United Kingdom, (Application No. 35763/97), Grand Chamber Judgment of 21 November 2001

Case of Hatton and Others v. United Kingdom (Application No. 36022/97) Grand Chamber Judgment of 8 July 2003

Case of Taşkin and Others v. Turkey (Application No. 46117/99) Judgment of 10 November 2004

Case of Bosphorus Hava Yolları Turizm ve Ticaret Anonim Şirketi v. Ireland (Application No. 45036/98) Grand Chamber Judgment of 30 June 2005

Inter-American Court of Human Rights

Inter-American Court of Human Rights, Interpretation of the American Declaration of the Rights and Duties of Man Within the Framework of Article 64 of the American Convention on Human Rights, Advisory Opinion OC-10/89 of 14 July 1989

National Court Decisions

Belgium

Cour d'Arbitrage Belge, Arrêt N° 92/2006, Decision of 7 June 2006, Moniteur Belge of 23 June 2006, p. 32159

Canada

Supreme Court of British Columbia, United Mexican States v. Metalclad, Reasons for Judgment of the Honorable Mr. Justice Tysoe of 2 May 2001

France

Conseil d'État, Société Arcelor Atlantique et Lorraine, Société Sollac Méditerranée, Société Ugitech et al., Arrêt N° 287110, Decision of 8 February 2007

Germany

Bundesgerichtshof, KZR 19/95, Judgment of 22 October 1996

Bundesgerichtshof, VIII ZR 160/02, VIII ZR 161/02, VIII ZR 322/02, Judgment of 11 June 2003

India

Indian Supreme Court, Vellore Citizens' Welfare Forum v. Union of India (1996), AIR1996SC2715

Indian Supreme Court, Indian Council For Enviro-Legal-Action v. Union of India and Ors. Etc (1996), 1996 AIR 1446

Pakistan

Supreme Court of Pakistan, Shehla Zia v. WAPDA (1994), SC 693

United States of America

U.S. Supreme Court, Mononghahela Navigation v. U.S., Decision of 27 March 1893, 148 U.S. 312 (1893)

U.S. Supreme Court, Penn Central Transportation Corp. v. New York City, Decision of 26 June 1978, 438 U.S. 104 (1978)

U.S. Supreme Court, Lucas v. South Carolina Coastal Council, Decision of 29 June 1992, 505 U.S. 1003 (1993)

Table of Treaties and Other International Instruments

General Treaties

Statute of the International Court of Justice (signed 26 June 1945, entry into force 24 October 1945)

1947 General Agreement on Tariffs and Trade (signed 30 October 1947, entry into force 1 January 1948) (GATT)

1950 European Convention on Human Rights (signed 4 November 1950, entry into force 3 September 1953) (ECHR)

1952 Protocol 1 to the European Convention of Human Rights (signed 20 March 1952, entry into force 18 May 1954)

1969 Vienna Convention on the Law of Treaties (signed 23 May 1969, entry into force 27 January 1980) (VCLT)

1982 United Nations Convention on the Law of the Sea (signed 10 December 1982, entry into force 16 November 1994) (UNCLOS)

1994 Marrakech Agreement Establishing the World Trade Organisation (signed 15 April 1994, entry into force 1 January 1995) (WTO)

1994 WTO Agreement on the Application of Sanitary and Phytosanitary Measures (SPS Agreement) (signed 15 April 1994, entry into force 1 January 1995)

Treaty on the Functioning of the European Union (signed 13 December 2007, entry into force 1 December 2009)

Environmental Treaties

1900 Convention Destinée à Assurer la Conservation des Diverses Espèces Animales vivant à l'Etat Sauvage en Afrique qui sont Utiles à l'homme ou Inoffensive, London 19 May 1900, 4 IPE 1607

1902 Convention to Protect Birds Useful to Agriculture, Paris 19 March 1902 (entry into force 20 April 1908) 4 IPE 1615

1911 Convention between the United States of America, the United Kingdom of Great Britain and Northern Ireland, and Russia, for the Preservation and Protection of Fur Seals, Washington 7 July 1911 (entry into force 15 December 1911) 8 IPE 3682

1916 Convention between the United States and Great Britain for the Protection of Migratory Birds in the United States and Canada, Washington 7 December 1916, 4 IPE 1638

1940 Convention on Nature Protection and Wild Life Preservation in the Western Hemisphere (signed 12 October 1940, entry into force 1 May 1942)

1946 International Convention for the Regulation of Whaling (signed 2 December 1946, entry into force 10 November 1948)

1949 Washington Convention for the Establishment of an Inter-American Tropical Tuna Commission (signed 30 May 1949, entry into force 3 March 1950)

1971 Ramsar Convention on Wetlands of International Importance especially as Waterfowl Habitat (signed 2 February 1971, entry into force 21 December 1975)

1972 Convention for the Conservation of Antarctic Seals (signed 1 June 1972, entry into force 11 March 1978)

1972 Paris Convention Concerning the Protection of the World Cultural and Natural Heritage (signed 16 November 1972, entry into force 17 December 1975) (UNESCO Convention)

1972 London Convention on the Prevention of Marine Pollution by Dumping of Wastes and Other Matter (signed 29 December 1972, entry into force 30 August 1975)

1973 Washington Convention on International Trade in Endangered Species of Wild Fauna and Flora (signed 3 March 1973, entry into force 1 July 1975) (CITES Convention)

1973 Agreement on the Conservation of Polar Bears (signed 15 November 1973, entry into force 26 May 1976)

1979 Convenio para la Conservación y Manejo de la Vicuña (signed 20 December 1979, entry into force 19 March 1982)

1979 Bonn Convention on Conservation of Migratory Species of Wild Animals (signed 23 June 1979, entry into force 1 November 1983)

1979 Berne Convention on the Conservation of European Wildlife (signed 19 September 1979, entry into force 1 June 1982)

1979 Geneva Convention on Long-Range Transboundary Air Pollution (signed 13 November 1979, entry into force 16 March 1983)

1981 Abidjan Convention for Co-Operation in the Protection and Development of the Marine (signed 23 March 1981, entry into force 5 August 1984)

1982 Jeddah Convention for the Conservation of the Red Sea and Gulf of Aden Environment (signed 14 February 1982, entry into force 20 August 1985)

1983 Convention for the Protection and Development of the Marine Environment of the Wider Caribbean Region (signed 24 March 1983, entry into force 11 October 1986)

1985 ASEAN Agreement on the Conservation of Nature and Natural Resources (signed 9 July 1985, not in force)

1985 Agreement of Cooperation between the United States of America and the United Mexican States Regarding the Transboundary Shipments of Hazardous

Waste and Hazardous Substances (signed 19 July 1985, entry into force 29 November 1985) 26 ILM 25 (1987)

1986 Agreement Between the Government of Canada and the Government of the United States of America Concerning the Transboundary Movement of Hazardous Waste (signed 26 October 1986, entry into force 8 November 1986)

1987 Montreal Protocol on Substances that Deplete the Ozone Layer Relating to the Restrictions on Use and Production of CFCs, Halons, Hydrochlorofluorocarbons, and Other Substances (signed 16 September 1987, entry into force 1 January 1989)

1988 Convention on the Regulation of Antarctic Mineral Resource Activities (signed 2 June 1988, not in force)

1988 Protocol Concerning the Control of Emissions of Nitrogen Oxides or Their Transboundary Fluxes to the 1979 Geneva Convention on Long-Range Transboundary Air Pollution (signed 13 October 1988, entry into force 14 February 1991)

1989 Basel Convention on the Control of Transboundary Movements of Hazardous Wastes and Their Disposal (signed 22 March 1989, entry into force 5 May 1992)

1990 Protocol Concerning Specially Protected Areas and Wildlife to the Convention for the Protection and Development of the Marine Environment of the Wider Caribbean Region (signed 18 January 1990, entry into force 17 June 2000)

1990 London Adjustments and Amendments to the Montreal Protocol on Substances that Deplete the Ozone Layer (signed 29 June 1990, entry into force 10 August 1992)

1990 International Convention on Oil Pollution Preparedness, Response and Co-Operation (signed 30 November 1990, entry into force 13 May 1995)

1991 Bamako Convention on the Ban of the Import into African and the Control of Transboundary Movement and Management of Hazardous Wastes Within Africa (signed 30 January 1991, entry into force 10 March 1999)

1991 Alpine Convention (signed 7 November 1991, entry into force 6 March 1995)

1992 Convention on the Protection and Use of Transboundary Watercourses and International Lakes (signed 17 March 1992, entry into force 6 October 1996)

1992 UNECE Convention on the Transboundary Effects of Industrial Accidents (signed 17 March 1992, entry into force 19 April 2000)

1992 Helsinki Convention on the Protection of the Marine Environment of the Baltic Sea Area (signed 9 April 1992, entry into force 17 January 2000)

1992 Convention on the Protection of the Black Sea Against Pollution (signed 21 April 1992, entry into force 15 January 1994)

1992 United Nations Framework Convention on Climate Change (signed 9 May 1992, entry into force 24 March 1994) (UNFCCC)

1992 Convention on Biological Diversity (signed 5 June 1992, entry into force 29 December 1993)

1992 Convention for the Protection of the Marine Environment of the North-East Atlantic (signed 22 September 1992, entry into force 25 March 1998) (OSPAR Convention)

1993 Lugano Convention on Civil Liability for Damage Resulting from Activities Dangerous to the Environment (signed 21 June 1993, not in force)

1994 Agreement on the Protection of the River Meuse (signed 26 April 1994, entry into force 1 March 1995)

1994 Agreement on the Protection of the River Scheldt (signed 26 April 1994, entry into force 1 March 1995)

1994 Convention on Cooperation for the Protection and Sustainable Use of the River Danube (signed 29 June 1994, entry into force 1 March 1995)

1994 Oslo Protocol on Further Reduction of Sulphur Emissions to the 1979 Geneva Convention on Long-Range Transboundary Air Pollution (signed 29 June 1994, entry into force 22 October 1998)

1994 North American Agreement on Environmental Cooperation (signed 14 September 1993, entry into force 1 January 1994) (NAAEC)

1995 Barcelona Protocol for the Prevention and Elimination of Pollution of the Mediterranean Sea by Dumping from Ships and Aircraft or Incineration at Sea to the Barcelona Convention for the Protection of the Marine Environment and the Coastal Region of the Mediterranean (signed 10 June 1995, not yet in force)

1995 Agreement for the Implementation of the Provisions of the United Nations Convention on the Law of the Sea of 10 December 1982 Relating to the Conservation and Management of Straddling Fish Stocks and Highly Migratory Fish Stocks (signed 4 December 1995, entry into force 11 December 2001)

1996 Syracuse Protocol for the Protection of the Mediterranean Sea Against Pollution From Land-Based Sources and Activities (signed 7 March 1996, entry into force 11 May 2008)

1996 London Protocol to the London Convention (signed 7 November 1996, entry into force 24 March 2006)

1996 Inter-American Convention for the Protection and Conservation of Sea Turtles (signed 1 December 1996, entry into force 1 May 2001)

1997 Kyoto Protocol to the United Nations Framework Convention on Climate Change (signed 11 December 1997, entry into force 16 February 2005) (Kyoto Protocol)

1998 Aarhus Protocol on Heavy Metals to the 1979 UNECE Convention on Long-Range Transboundary Air Pollution on Persistent Organic Pollutants (signed 24 June 1998, entry into force 29 December 2003)

1998 UNECE Convention on Access to Information, Public Participation in Decision-Making and Access to Justice in Environmental Matters (signed 25 June 1998, entry into force 30 October 2001) (Aarhus Convention)

1998 Rotterdam Convention on the Prior Informed Consent Procedure for Certain Hazardous Chemicals and Pesticides in International Trade (signed 10 September 1998, entry into force 24 February 2004)

1999 Convention on the Protection of the Rhine (signed 12 April 1999, entry into force 1 January 2003)

2000 Cartagena Protocol on Biosafety to the Convention on Biological Diversity (signed 29 January 2000, entry into force 11 September 2003)

2000 Convention on the Conservation of Highly Migratory Fish Stocks in the Western and Central Pacific (signed 5 September 2000, entry into force 19 June 2004)

2001 Stockholm Convention on Persistent Organic Pollutants (signed 22 May 2001, entry into force 17 May 2004)

2001 International Convention on the Control of Harmful Anti-fouling Systems on Ships (signed 5 October 2001, entry into force 17 September 2008)

2003 Protocol on Civil Liability and Compensation for Damage Caused by the Transboundary Effects of Industrial Accidents on Transboundary Waters to the 1992 Convention on the Protection and Use of Transboundary Watercourses and International Lakes and to the 1992 Convention on the Transboundary Effects of Industrial Accidents (signed 21 May 2003, not in force)

2003 African Convention on the Conservation of Nature and Natural Resources (signed 11 July 2003, not in force)

2008 Agreement on the Environment between Canada and the Republic of Peru (signed 29 May 2008, entry into force 1 August 2009)

United Nations

General Assembly Resolution, 'Resolution on Permanent Sovereignty over Natural Resources', Resolution 1803 (XVII), UN Doc. A/5217 (1962), 14 December 1962

1972 Declaration of the United Nations Conference on the Human Environment, 16 June 1972

General Assembly Resolution, 'Declaration on the Establishment of a New International Economic Order', UN Doc. A/RES/S-6/3201, 1 May 1974

General Assembly Resolution, 'Protection of Global Climate for Present and Future Generations of Mankind', UN Doc. A/RES/43/53, 6 December 1988

1992 Rio Declaration on Environment and Development (Report of the United Nations Conference on Environment and Development, UN Doc. A/CONF.151/26 (Vol. I), Annex 1 (Rio Declaration)

Agenda 21 (UN Doc. A/CONF.151/26 (Vol. I), Annex 2)

General Assembly Resolution, 'United Nations Millennium Declaration', UN Doc. A/RES/55/2, 18 September 2000

World Summit on Sustainable Development, 'Plan of Implementation of the World Summit on Sustainable Development', UN Doc. A/CONF.199/20, 4 September 2002

General Assembly Resolution, 'World Summit Outcome', UN Doc. A/RES/60/1, 24 October 2005

Treaty Organisations

CITES

1994 Resolution Conf. 9.24 (Rev. CoP14), amended, 'Criteria for Amendment of Appendices I and II', June 2007, at: http://www.cites.org/eng/res/all/09/E09-24R14.pdf

Convention on Biological Diversity

Decision V/8 of the COP 5, 'Alien species that threaten ecosystems, habitats or species', May 2000, at: http://www.cbd.int/decision/cop/?id=7150

Kyoto Process

Decision 7/CP.4, FCCC/CP/1998/16/Add.1, 14 November 1998

Decision 14/CP.5, FCCC/CP/1999/6/Add.1, 4 November 1999

2001 Marrakech Accords, at: http://unfccc.int/cop7/documents/accords_draft.pdf

Report of the Conference of the Parties serving as the meeting of the Parties to the Kyoto Protocol on its sixth session, held in Cancun from 29 November to 10 December 2010, 'Action taken by the Conference of the Parties serving as the meeting of the Parties to the Kyoto Protocol at its sixth session', FCCC/KP/CMP/2010/12/Add.1, 15 March 2011

Montreal Protocol

Decision II/5 of the Second Meeting of the Parties to the Protocol, UNEP/OzL.Pro.2/3, 29 June 1990)

Decision IV/5 and Annexes IV, V of the Fourth Meeting of the Parties to the Protocol, UNEP/OzL.Pro.4/15, 25 November 1992

WTO

Doha Ministerial Declaration, WT/MIN(01)/DEC/1, 14 November 2001, at: http://www.wto.org/english/thewto_e/minist_e/min01_e/mindecl_e.htm

European Council

Directive 79/117/EEC of 21 December 1978

Directive 85/337/EEC of 27 June 1985

Directive 91/156/EC of 18 March 1991 (Waste Framework Directive)

Directive 96/61/EC of 24 September 1996

Directive 96/82/EC of 9 December 1996 (EC Seveso Directive)

Directive 2001/18/EC of 12 March 2001

Directive 2003/30/EC of 8 May 2003

Directive 2003/87/EC of 13 October 2003

Directive 2003/96/EC of 27 October 2003

Directive 2009/29/EC of 23 April 2009

Bilateral Investment Treaties

1959 Germany-Pakistan BIT (signed 25 November 1959, entry into force 28 November 1962)

1971 Germany-Mauritius BIT (signed 25 May 1971, entry into force 27 August 1973)

1981 Germany-Bangladesh BIT (signed 6 May 1981, entry into force 14 September 1986)

1991 Netherlands-Czech Republic BIT (signed 29 April 1991, entry into force 1 October 1992)

1991 Argentina-Chile BIT (signed 2 August 1991, entry into force 1 January 1995)

1991 Germany-Albania BIT (signed 31 October 1991, entry into force 18 August 1995)

1991 Canada-Argentina BIT (signed 5 November 1991, entry into force 29 April 1993)

1991 U.S.-Argentina BIT (signed 14 November 1991, entry into force 20 October 1994)

1993 United Kingdom-Ukraine BIT (signed 10 February 1993, entry into force 10 February 1993)

1993 U.S.-Ecuador BIT (signed 27 August 1993, entry into force 11 May 1997)

1994 U.S. Model BIT

1994 U.S.-Georgia BIT (signed 7 March 1994, entry into force 10 August 1999)

1994 Netherlands-Estonia BIT (signed 14 March 1994, entry into force 1 April 1995)

1994 U.S.-Trinidad and Tobago BIT (signed 26 September 1994, entry into force 26 December 1996)

1994 U.S.-Uzbekistan BIT (signed 16 December 1994)

1995 U.S.-Albania BIT (signed 11 January 1995, entry into force 4 January 1998)

1995 UK-India BIT (signed 14 March 1994, entry into force 6 January 1995)

1995 U.S.-Honduras BIT (signed 1 July 1995, entry into force 11 July 2001)

1995 U.S.-Nicaragua BIT (signed 1 July 1995, entry into force 23 August 1996)

1996 Canada-Barbados BIT (signed 29 May 1996, entry into force 17 January 1997)

1996 U.S.-Croatia BIT (signed 13 July 1996, entry into force 20 June 2001)

1997 Canada-Trinidad and Tobago BIT (signed 17 January 1997, entry into force 24 September 1998)

1997 Canada-Croatia BIT (signed 3 February 1997, entry into force 30 January 2001)

1997 U.S.-Jordan BIT (signed 2 July 1997, entry into force 12 June 2003)

1997 U.S.-Azerbaijan BIT (signed 1 August 1997, entry into force 2 August 2001)

1998 U.S.-Bolivia BIT (signed 17 April 1998, entry into force 6 January 2001)

1998 United Kingdom-Uganda BIT (signed 24 April 1998, entry into force 24 April 1998)

1998 U.S.-Mozambique BIT (signed 1 December 1998, entry into force 3 March 2005)

1999 U.S.-El Salvador BIT (signed 10 March 1999)

1999 Canada-El Salvador BIT (signed 31 May 1999)

1999 Spain-Trinidad and Tobago BIT (signed 3 July 1999, entry into force 17 September 2004)

1999 U.S.-Bahrain BIT (signed 29 September 1999, entry into force 30 May 2001)

2001 Finland-Tanzania BIT (signed 19 June 2001, entry into force 9 October 2002)

2001 Germany-Bosnia and Herzegovina BIT (signed 18 October 2001, entry into force 11 November 2007)

2001 Finland-Bosnia and Herzegovina BIT (signed 1 November 2001, entry into force 8 December 2001)

2002 China-Bosnia and Herzegovina BIT (signed 26 June 2002, entry into force 1 January 2005)

2002 China-Trinidad and Tobago BIT (signed 22 July 2002, entry into force 24 May 2004)

2003 India Model BIT

2003 Finland-Kyrgyzstan BIT (signed 23 April 2003, entry into force 8 December 2004)

2003 Finland-Nicaragua BIT (signed 17 September 2003)

2003 France-Bosnia and Herzegovina BIT (signed 12 December 2003, entry into force 18 December 2005)

2004 Canada Model BIT

2004 U.S. Model BIT

2004 Jordan-Singapore BIT (signed 29 April 2004, entry into force 22 August 2005)

2004 Finland-Armenia BIT (signed 5 October 2004, entry into force 20 March 2007)

2005 Belgium-Luxembourg-Sudan BIT (signed 7 November 2005)

2005 Belgium-Luxembourg-Madagascar BIT (signed 29 September 2005, entry into force 29 November 2008)

2005 Finland-Nigeria BIT (signed 22 June 2005, entry into force 20 March 2007)

2005 Finland-Guatemala BIT (signed 14 April 2005, entry into force 6 January 2007)

2005 Germany-Afghanistan BIT (signed 20 April 2005, entry into force 12 October 2007)

2005 Finland-Zambia BIT (signed 7 September 2005)

2005 U.S.-Uruguay BIT (signed 4 November 2005, entry into force 1 November 2006)

2006 Finland-Ethiopia BIT (signed 23 February 2006, entry into force 3 May 2007)

2006 Finland-Belarus BIT (signed 8 June 2006, entry into force 10 April 2008)

2006 Germany-Trinidad and Tobago BIT (signed 8 September 2006)

2006 Canada-Peru BIT (signed 14 November 2006, entry into force 20 June 2007)

2006 France Model BIT

2006 Model International Agreement on Investment for Sustainable Development (by the International Institute for Sustainable Development)

2007 Columbia Model BIT

2007 Draft Norway Model BIT

2008 German Model BIT

2008 U.S.-Rwanda BIT (signed 19 February 2008, entry into force 1 January 2012)

2009 Canada-Latvia BIT (signed 5 May 2009, entry into force 24 November 2011)

Belgium, Luxembourg-Guinea BIT (status unknown)

Multilateral Investment Treaties

1994 Energy Charter Treaty (signed 17 December 1994, entry into force 16 April 1998)

2007 COMESA Investment Agreement (signed 23 May 2007, not yet in force)

Free Trade Agreements

1992 North American Free Trade Agreement (NAFTA) (signed 17 December 1992, entry into force 1 January 1994)

1994 Mexico-Costa Rica FTA (signed 5 April 1994, entry into force 1 January 1995)

1996 Canada-Chile FTA (signed 5 December 1996, entry into force 5 July 1997)

1997 Mexico-Nicaragua FTA (signed 18 December 1997, entry into force 1 July 1998)

1998 Central America-Dominica FTA (signed 16 April 1998, entry into force 3 October 2001 and later, respectively)

1998 Chile-Mexico FTA (signed 17 April 1998, entry into force 1 August 1999)

2000 Mexico-El Salvador, Guatemala, Honduras FTA (signed 29 June 2000, entry into force 15 March 2001 and later, respectively)

2000 New Zealand-Singapore FTA (signed 18 August 2000, entry into force 1 January 2001)

2002 Japan-Singapore FTA (signed 13 January 2002, entry into force 30 November 2006)

2002 Centralamerica-Panama FTA (signed 6 March 2002, entry into force 11 April 2003 and later, respectively)

2002 EFTA-Singapore FTA (signed 26 June 2002, entry into force 1 January 2003)

2003 Chile-Korea FTA (signed 15 February 2003, entry into force 1 April 2004)

2003 Australia-Singapore FTA (signed 17 February 2003, entry into force 28 July 2003)

2003 U.S.-Singapore FTA (signed 6 May 2003, entry into force 1 January 2004)

2003 U.S.-Chile FTA (signed 6 June 2003, entry into force 1 January 2004)

2003 Panama-Taiwan FTA (signed 21 August 2003, entry into force 1 January 2004)

2003 Panama-Singapore FTA (signed 21 August 2003, entry into force 1 January 2004)

2004 U.S.-Australia FTA (signed 18 May 2004, entry into force 1 January 2005)

2004 U.S.-Morocco FTA (signed 15 June 2004, entry into force 1 January 2006)

2004 Thailand-Australia FTA (signed 5 July 2004, entry into force 1 January 2005)

2004 Central American-Dominican Republic-United States FTA (signed 5 August 2004, entry into force 1 March 2006 and later, respectively) (CAFTA-DR)

2004 Japan-Mexico FTA (signed 17 September 2004, entry into force 1 April 2005)

2005 Thailand-New Zealand FTA (signed 19 April 2005, entry into force 1 July 2005)

2005 India-Singapore FTA (signed 29 June 2005, entry into force 1 August 2005)

2005 Korea-Singapore FTA (signed 4 August 2005, entry into force 2 March 2006)

2005 Japan-Malaysia (signed 13 December 2005, entry into force 13 July 2006)

2006 U.S.-Oman FTA (signed 19 January 2006, entry into force 1 January 2009)

2006 U.S.-Peru FTA (signed 12 April 2006, entry into force 1 February 2009)

2006 Taiwan-Nicaragua FTA (signed 16 June 2006, entry into force 1 January 2008)

2006 Chile-Peru FTA (signed 22 August 2006, entry into force 1 March 2009)

2006 Japan-Philippines FTA (signed 9 September 2006, entry into force 11 December 2008)

2006 U.S.-Colombia FTA (signed 22 November 2006, entry into force 15 May 2012)

2006 China-Pakistan FTA (signed 24 November 2006, entry into force 1 July 2007)

2006 Chile-Colombia FTA (signed 27 November 2006, entry into force 8 May 2009)

2007 Chile-Japan FTA (signed 27 March 2007, entry into force 3 September 2007)

2007 Japan-Thailand FTA (signed 3 April 2007, entry into force 1 November 2007)

2007 Taiwan-El Salvador and Honduras FTA (signed 7 May 2007, entry into force 1 January 2008 and later, respectively)

2007 Japan-Brunei Darussalam FTA (signed 18 June 2007, entry into force 31 July 2008)

2007 U.S.-Panama FTA (signed 28 June 2007, entry into force 21 October 2011)

2007 U.S.-Korea FTA (signed 30 June 2007, entry into force 15 March 2012)

2007 Colombia-El Salvador, Honduras, Guatemala FTA (signed 9 August 2007, entry into force 13 November 2009 and later, respectively)

2007 Japan-Indonesia FTA (signed 20 August 2007, entry into force 1 July 2008)

2007 Pakistan-Malaysia FTA (signed 8 November 2007, entry into force 1 January 2008)

2008 China-New Zealand FTA (signed 7 April 2008, entry into force 1 October 2008)

2008 Canada-Peru FTA (signed 29 May 2008, entry into force 1 August 2009)

2008 Peru-Singapore FTA (signed 29 May 2008, entry into force 1 August 2009)

2008 Chile-Australia FTA (signed 30 July 2008, entry into force 6 March 2009)

2008 Canada-Colombia FTA (signed 21 November 2008, entry into force 15 Augusto 2011)

2009 ASEAN, Australia and New Zealand FTA (signed 27 February 2009, entry into force 1 January 2010)

2009 Peru-China FTA (signed 28 April 2009, entry into force 1 March 2010)

2009 Malaysia-New Zealand FTA (signed 26 October 2009, entry into force 1 August 2010)

2010 Bolivia-Mexico FTA (signed 17 May 2010, entry into force 7 June 2010)

Other Investment-Related Instruments

1965 Washington Convention on the Settlement of Investment Disputes Between States and Nationals of Other States International Centre for Settlement of Investment Disputes (signed 18 March 1965, entry into force 14 October 1966)

Interpretation of the NAFTA Free Trade Commission of 31 July 2001

2006 ICSID Rules of Procedure for Arbitration Proceedings

2010 UNCITRAL Arbitration Rules

2014 UNCITRAL Rules on Transparency in Treaty-based Investor-State Arbitration

National Material

Germany

1949 German Basic Law (*Grundgesetz*)

Richtlinien zur Förderung von Maßnahmen zur Nutzung erneuerbarer Energien im Wärmemarkt (20 July 2012)

United States

Note sent by U.S. Secretary of State Cordell Hull to Mexico in August 1938

2005 National Energy Policy Act

Subject Index